The Hove
Blue

14th Edition

HOVE
COLLECTORS
BOOKS

The Blue Book
14th Edition
Published June 2003
Hove Collectors Books
30, The Industrial Estate, Small Dole
West Sussex, BN5 9XR, UK
Fax: +44(0)1273-494992
Email: info@hovebooks.com
web: www.hovebooks.com

British Library Cataloguing-in-Publication Data
A catalogue record for this book is available
from the British Library

ISBN 1-874707-36-7

14th Edition edited by John Wade
Design and layout GDC Ltd

Printed by Biddles Ltd,
Guildford and Kings Lynn.

Additional photographs courtesy of
Canon Camera Company, Inc., Tokyo, Christie's,
South Kensington, Philip Condax, KEH Camera
Brokers, Mamiya Camera Company, Jack Naylor,
Auction House, Germany, Geoff Wilkinson,
John Wade and many users who have
contributed photographs

Contents

Introduction

Welcome to the 14th edition of the Hove International Blue Book. It is three years since the last edition was published and, in that time, a lot has happened in the world of camera collecting – and, as always, the Blue Book is here to keep you up to date on those changes and how they affect you as a collector.

If this is the first time you have bought the Blue Book, then you are going to find it a mine of often unexpected information. If you have bought editions in the past, you'll find a lot new in this edition to intrigue and interest you.

The fact is that, for more than a quarter of a century, the Blue Book has been recognised as a major player in the field of camera collecting, not only as a guide to the prices of collectable cameras, but also in the information it supplies with each entry and its general advice to the collector. It can do this because it has a unique pedigree. Where other camera guides might be compiled by one or two people, the Blue Book has been put together, added to and amended over the years by a series of editors, each of whom is an expert in his own field.

The first Blue Book was produced in America, hence its name, a 'blue book' in American jargon referring to a catalogue or list of items, not necessarily cameras. It was compiled by an American author who had been publishing less ambitious catalogues of collectable cameras from as far back as the early 1970s, when camera collecting began to take a hold.

In 1989, the rights to the book were acquired by another American author who stayed at the editing helm, but sold the publishing rights to an English photographic dealership, who used it as the cornerstone of a small book publishing sector. After two editions under this publisher, the rights were again sold, this time to the present publisher, Hove Photo Books, Britain's foremost publisher of books for the photographic collector. This is the 5th edition published by Hove and the 2nd to be edited by the present editor, John Wade, an avid collector who has been writing books and articles on collectable cameras in the British photo press for more than twenty-five years.

What's new?

Under the present editor, the Blue Book has begun to look in new directions. The main thrust is, and always has been, the directory, an A to Z of collectable cameras with descriptions, price guides and rarity values. But alongside this, the Blue Book is now offering much more general information to collectors. It is becoming more of a camera collector's handbook, containing information unavailable in more conventional price guides.

So in this new edition, you will find a lot of new information. Not just new cameras and pictures in the directory section, but also useful tips on market trends, camera restoration, ways to date your collectable cameras, the importance of certain landmark cameras and – for the first time – a new section on the growing trend in cine camera collecting, with its own mini-directory.

There's a slightly new look to the

valuations too. This was something which was instigated with the previous edition, in reference to the way prices and value can fluctuate. Unlike some other price guides, we have come to accept that prices not only go up and down in accordance with the current market and the condition of the equipment, but that they can also vary according to how the item is being sold: by a dealer, by a fellow collector or at auction.

For all those reasons, the last edition of the Blue Book introduced a new system that replaced specific prices with a price code from 'A' to 'L'. These codes can then be interpreted by the collector as a working guide to the value. It is a

system that proved popular with readers last time, and so we have retained it for this issue. It should always be acknowledged, however, that currency rates do fluctuate, and readers are advised to check rates against the pound – the currency in which the values are originally estimated – for the most accurate valuation of a camera in the directory. You will find a key to the price codes printed on cards throughout the book, and you can remove these to use as bookmarks.

At the top end of this scale, where the range of values vary by greater increments, we have also added '+' or '–' signs to give a more accurate valuation.

Here's how those price codes line up:-

		£	euros	$
A	Up to	10	15	15
B	Between	10-24	15-40	15-40
C	Between	25-45	45-75	45-75
D	Between	50-90	80-150	80-150
E	Between	100-125	160-350	160-350
F	Between	250-400	375-750	375-750
G	Between	500-950	800-1,600	800-1,600
H	Between	1,000-2,250	1,700-3,500	1,700-3,500
I	Between	2,500-4,500	4,000-7,500	4,000-7,500
J	Between	5,000-9,000	8,500-15,000	8,500-15,000
K	Between	10,000-24,000	17,000-40,000	17,000-40,000
L	Above	25,000	45,000	45,000

Prices changes

How have prices and values of collectable cameras changed since the last edition of the Blue Book? The answer, with certain exceptions, is not a lot.

Generally speaking, at the time of going to press with this edition, the market in collectable cameras is rather flat, although there are still a few places where prices are rising. Leicas, which

have always held their price, are still strong and even rising a little, even if the sudden surges of price jumps seen in the past are no longer the norm. Specialist cameras from the late 1800s are also performing well, as is equipment from the early days of film making. This includes not only early cine cameras, but also associated movie paraphernalia, such as whole, or even just short strips, from early cine films.

This interest in movie cameras,

however, has been showing significant price rises only really in the very early equipment from the late 1890s and early 1900s, and that mostly made for 35mm film. Equipment for 16mm and 9.5mm film, from 1923 onwards has also been enjoying small but steady rises in value, but those increases do not apply quite as much to the 8mm equipment that was available from 1932 onwards. Despite which, it can still be said that all movie equipment, with the possible exception of the plethora of very ordinary 8mm cameras from the 1960s, is at least holding on to the increase in interest and prices which began a few years back.

Shortly before the last edition of the Blue Book was published, the Japanese Stock Market collapsed. Such was the importance and proliferation of Japanese collectors, this inevitably had an effect on prices around the world. Before that Stock Market collapse, the Japanese were prolific collectors, and seemed to have more money to spend than their western counterparts. Without even leaving their own country, many of them bought by mail order from dealers elsewhere in the world, and they bought by postal bids at auctions, also from places outside Japan. For dealers, the prices that Japanese collectors were prepared to pay became the official prices for certain cameras, however inflated they might have seemed. And, as those Japanese collectors fought to outbid each other, buying from dealers who were quick to see a way of making more profit, so the prices went up and up.

The same was true of auctions, both in international sales, such as those at Christie's, and in smaller postal auctions such as those organised by the Photographic Collectors Club of Great Britain. Once again, the price that the Japanese were prepared to pay forced up the prices for other collectors.

When the Japanese Stock Market collapsed, Japanese collectors stopped buying, almost overnight and in a short time at least one major London dealer, who had, until then, relied on Japanese custom for a major area of sales, went into voluntary liquidation, citing the collapse of the Japanese economy as a major reason for the failure of his business. Other dealers who had not relied quite so exclusively on the Japanese

Early cine cameras like this Ertel will always command high prices.

market, readjusted their sights and carried on.

Some prices dropped, but most simply stabilised, and although prices in certain areas have increased slightly over the last three years, the rate of increase is certainly nothing like it once was.

The collecting market and the prices collectors are prepared to pay can be affected by the economy in general, and the world economy took a major hit on 11th September 2001, when the World Trade Centre in New York came under the most serious terrorist attack in America's history. Repercussions of the effect this attack had on the American stock market echoed around the world. Dealers in the UK reported an immediate dip in the prices collectors were prepared to pay at that time, a situation which has now corrected itself, but which has still prevented prices overall seeing major increases.

Today, the signs are that the Japanese collecting market is beginning to come back, although dealers in England report that their sales are not so much to individuals, as to other Japanese dealers who then sell the items onto to their customers. Japanese collectors, then, might well be paying higher prices to dealers in their own country, but the overall effect on prices outside Japan, once again, remains the same.

Another factor that has affected prices since the last edition of the Blue Book, has been the rise in popularity of internet auction sites, Ebay in particular. These mean more dealers are reaching a wider audience (At the time of writing, Ebay boasts 46,000,000 registered users, and that figure will undoubtedly be even higher by the time you read this.) It also means that collectors who would not consider themselves to be dealers as such, can offer just one or two cameras on the auction site.

Just as with any auction, this can affect prices. If not too many people are interested in a particular item, then a camera might go for a ridiculously low price. Likewise, two collectors after the same thing and prepared to pay top prices to get it means that another item might sell for a wildly inflated price.

This has always been the case with any auction, but with the auction in question being on the internet, and therefore available to anyone with an internet-configured computer, the prices realised are more likely to affect – not to say confuse – what we might call the 'true' price.

Collecting trends

One factor which has affected both prices and collecting trends is the state of the British economy. Since the last Blue Book was published, UK interest rates have fallen to a low, not seen for more than 30 years. It means people have more money to spend, but it also means that traditional forms of investment are yielding much lower returns than was the case only a few years ago. Many UK investors, therefore, have begun looking at new ways to grow their money. One result of that has been seen in the way more and more people have been investing in property. Another faction has moved into buying antiques – and that includes classic cameras.

So many collectors who previously only looked upon their cameras as collector's items, have begun to see them much more as investments. And since any antique needs to be in the best possible condition in order to grow in value, that means it is the pristine equipment that is being snapped up more than that which shows signs of wear.

So good condition equipment is getting harder to find, which is pushing up the prices, but on the other hand, the weakness of the market, compared to a few years back, means that fewer collectors can actually afford to buy. As a result, people aren't buying particular brands in the way they once did, but instead, they are bargain hunting for anything of top quality at the right price.

All this leads to a rather confusing state of affairs. Average to good condition middle-of-the-road stalwarts like the Retina IIIC and Voigtlander Bessa that used to sell regularly are now selling far less if they are found on their own. But find these and similar cameras in good condition in their original boxes – the kind of thing that makes an investor's eyes gleam – and they immediately demand higher prices than used to be the case.

Meanwhile, the reported growing interest in later models, reported in the last issue of the Blue Book, has continued, and these days cameras from the 1960s and even as late as the 1970s are attracting collectors. The line drawn by many, however, is the point in the 1970s when electronics began to take over. Whilst most collectors today acknowledge that the presence of a battery in a camera might be necessary to power an exposure meter, most draw the line at cameras that use batteries to power shutters or even – whisper it quietly – autofocus!

This change in emphasis to later models can be attributed to two basic reasons: the fact that many of the early cameras are becoming increasingly difficult to find, and can be prohibitively expensive when they are discovered; and the fact that new and younger collectors see, as collectors items, the kind of cameras that older collectors still think of as 'modern'.

Pristine condition, rare cameras in original boxes, like these Reid Leica copies, are rising in value and are appealing to investors as much as collectors.

As mentioned above, cine camera collecting continues to grow, though more slowly, in the UK at least, than might have been anticipated a few years back. The interest in movie equipment, however, is decidedly stronger in mainland Europe.

Russian cameras continue to be seen in greater numbers and hence at lower prices than when the country was closed to outsiders, which in turn has led to an increased interest in equipment from that part the world.

With the exception of very early equipment, mentioned above, wood and brass is no longer quite as popular as it once was, apart from in America, where such cameras tend to be bought more and more for use.

Even the 1970s are now becoming of interest to collectors. This Olympus XA from 1979 is typical of the new breed of collectable.

For much the same reason, old lenses – for both still and cine cameras – that once did not sell too well have begun to be in demand, not so much by collectors, but by photographers who are buying them and adapting them for use on still cameras.

All of which makes it difficult to spot any real trends in collecting at the moment. Perhaps the best way to describe the market as this latest edition of the Blue Book goes to press, is to say, for the moment at least, that it is trendless.

Russian cameras like this Hapyucc (also branded as the Narciss), first made in the 1950s as the only 16mm single lens reflex, no longer demand the prices they once did.

Camera Collecting as a Hobby

If you are new to camera collecting, you probably find yourself regretting not having started years ago, when prices were cheaper. If so, you have just stumbled on the first rule of collecting: The best time to start was ten years before you did.

In fact, if you want to start collecting, there is no time like the present. Forget what might seem to have been the now unattainable bargains of the past, and concentrate on what you can find today. Yes, prices were cheaper some years ago, mainly because there wasn't the demand. But the demand has, in itself, opened up the market, so that today it is far easier to buy collectable cameras — a fact that actually keeps prices stable. Also, if you compare the price of an average (as opposed to a super-rare) collectable camera of today with what it cost ten or twenty years ago, taking its value against national wage averages, you might be surprised to learn that a great many collectable cameras haven't soared in price in real terms, only kept pace with inflation.

So how and when did camera collecting begin? Well, it began to take off as a major hobby during the early to middle 1970s. Up until then, there were camera collectors, but they were few and far between, rarely meeting with one another or even knowing of each other's existence.

These people were often amateur, and sometimes professional photographers who had originally bought an older camera to use, only to become fascinated by its operation and craftsmanship, and one thing inevitably led to another. Independent of each other, they began looking for old cameras. Photographic dealers, where customers traded in old equipment for new, were prime targets and collectors would leave their names and phone numbers with such dealers in the hope of a call. Junk shops were a source of collectable equipment, although very few cameras had yet to attain the respect of real antique dealers.

Gradually, over the course of a few brief years, the hobby took off in a big way. Collectors' clubs were formed. Fairs began to be organised. Major auction houses like Christie's started to feature camera auctions. Photographic dealers gave over some of their shelf space to older, more collectable equipment. And eventually, specialised dealers, selling nothing but collectable cameras, opened their doors.

Where to buy

The first thing a new collector should do — if you haven't done so already — is join a club. The Photographic Collectors Club of Great Britain (PCCGB) is one of the best world-wide, holding not only an annual national meeting and fair, but any number of regional meetings at regular intervals throughout the year. Here collectors meet, listen to talks, gather new information and sell or swap cameras between themselves. The club also has many sub-divisions for members interested in specific camera manufacturers. Many other clubs for camera collectors exist elsewhere around the world. Check the club listings later in this book to find the one nearest to you.

Camera fairs make the ideal starting point for a new collector.

Where else can the newcomer find cameras to collect and what is the best way of buying?

Camera fairs make an ideal starting point. Members of the PCCGB get a listing of fairs all over the country, published on a regular basis, otherwise watch out for them advertised in the classified sections of photographic magazines. Camera fairs attract recognised dealers, but also private collectors. These are the best people to buy from, because they are not there to make huge profits, only to charge a fair price, and because they have been collecting for so many years, they often have some fascinating cameras to sell on.

Prices at specialised dealers are usually higher than at camera fairs, but on the other hand, the equipment might be in better condition, and if there is anything wrong with it, they'll tell you, reducing the price accordingly. That's something you won't always get at a camera fair! It's also worth remembering the sheer range of equipment that they have available. Dealers can get their hands on equipment that ordinary collectors can only dream about finding elsewhere. Also because they have contacts among

Specialist dealers can usually offer top quality and rarity, but at a price.

a great many collectors, they know who wants what and are consequently in a good position to offer you a decent price if you are selling or part exchanging.

Auctions come in two types: national and local. Nationally, auction houses like Christie's have regular sales entirely of collectable camera gear every few months. Locally, look out for auctions of house clearance items. These are the places to pick up bargains. If you are a newcomer to collecting, you might not fully understand how an auction works, so let's pause for a moment to look at how you buy at one.

It starts with the viewing, which is usually held the day before or sometimes right up to just before the sale starts. This is where you go to look at what's on offer. Before the start of the sale, go to the registration desk, where someone will take your name, address, possibly your telephone number and maybe proof of identity. Then they will give you a number. In the sale room, the auctioneer calls up each lot, and he (not you) starts the bidding by suggesting a price. If you are interested, raise your hand. The auctioneer will then increase the price and someone else will bid, and he raises the price again. You keep bidding until you are the last one in, at which point the item is knocked down to you. You then hold up your number. Afterwards, you go to the collection point, quote your number, pay your money and collect your goods. But beware, because the price you bid might be less than the price you are asked to pay. That's because a buyer's premium — usually around ten per cent — is added to the price and, at the larger auction houses, if the camera you are buying is subject to VAT or other sales taxes, that too could be added.

Antique markets rarely include specialist camera dealers, but you might find cameras on more general stalls, among the china and glassware. Although not a major source for collectable cameras, they can be fruitful at times and are often good places to look for accessories like exposure meters as opposed to actual cameras.

Flea markets and junk fairs are much the same as antique markets, except that the items on sale are a lot less prestigious. Although you do hear stories of unbelievable bargains, it is actually quite rare to find anything really valuable at a junk fair or flea market. For the camera collector, they make better places for building up a collection of simple snapshot cameras.

What to buy

So if you know where to buy, the next question is what to buy.

When you start out, you'll probably buy everything and anything. But as you get more into the hobby, you might decide you would prefer to specialise.

Some collectors specialise in cameras made by a specific manufacturer, and perhaps the most popular of all is Leitz, the makers of Leica equipment. There are collectors who buy nothing but Leica cameras, lenses and accessories, and there are whole books devoted to nothing but the many different variations of this marque. Leica cameras are perhaps the most expensive of collectable cameras, but other manufacturers are of interest to other collectors, who might specialise in Zeiss Ikon, Voigtlander, Kodak, Nikon, Canon, etc. If you want to know more about that approach it's a good idea to join one of the specialist groups of enthusiasts. (See club listings pages).

Collectors often concentrate on certain types of equipment, such as stereo, subminiature or even novelty cameras.

Another alternative is to collect certain types of camera: single lens reflexes, twin lens reflexes, small format plate cameras, larger wood and brass types, box cameras, stereo, 35mm models. One especially popular category is subminiatures. Here you can find just about all the other types, each reduced in size to take small format film. Subminiatures are attractive and also have the advantage of taking up less display space than others.

Actual styles can also form a collection, with the art deco period perhaps being the most popular. Art Deco was a decorative arts style that was popular between 1910 and 1940. Its themes were based on classical motifs, reduced to simple, geometric shapes, often seen in architecture and sculpture, but equally seen in cameras, notably those produced in and around the 1930s.

Landmarks provide another interesting route to take, looking at specific models which introduced the earliest model of a popular camera style: the first 35mm single lens reflex, the first

Art Deco cameras like this Beau Brownie can be particularly attractive, and make another area in which collectors might specialise.

rollfilm twin lens reflex, the first camera to take 127 or 120 film, the first camera with auto exposure, the first with a coupled rangefinder, or perhaps the first model made by each of several well-known manufacturers.

Or how about looking for cameras from certain countries? Japan is an obvious one and perhaps just a little too prolific to form the basis for a single collection. But English camera makers provide an interesting focal point, covering a wide span in both time and styles. The same goes for French manufacturers. Russian cameras are particularly interesting because many of them are copies of well-known makes from the West, whilst others show real innovation in design not seen before or since. At one time, Russian cameras, with the exception of makes like Zenit, Zorki and Fed, were difficult to buy in the West. But since the opening up of the country, many more Russian cameras have come on to the market and prices of what were once

considered exceptionally rare models have consequently fallen.

Even Chinese cameras have their devotees, and for much the same reason as Russian cameras.

Dates are worth keeping in mind, and it's not a bad idea to draw certain boundaries in your collecting. Camera manufacture really began in 1839 with the launch of the daguerreotype process, and cameras from this early era are both rare and expensive. For these reasons, most general collectors will have few cameras made before 1900.

Some collectors draw the line at 1939, the year the Second World War broke out. It makes a convenient stopping point, since the post-war years saw so many changes in camera styles. By the same token 1945, the year the war ended, makes an interesting starting point, and one that is currently growing in popularity among collectors. In fact, if you are new to collecting, the period between mid-1940s, into the 1970s and even into the early 1980s is one that is certainly worth considering. It was a time when many new designs came on to the market and many of the older ones died. The 1960s saw the real start of the SLR revolution, the 1970s refined the SLR and the 1980s started the autofocus boom.

Cameras from this era are certainly easier to find than the earlier models, and for the newcomer, the prices are more attractive than what might be paid for a super-rare camera from the really early days of photography.

Collecting tips

However you organise your collection, there are a few general points that the beginner should keep in mind. Perhaps the most important aspect is cosmetic appearance. For a camera to be truly collectable, it needs to be in the best possible condition. Some minor examples of use do no harm, but whenever possible, avoid really tatty examples with torn leatherwork, brass showing through enamelling, fungused or misty lenses, jammed aperture blades and sticky shutters. They look ugly when displayed and they invariably fail to sell on when you want to replace them.

That said, there is no harm in buying a camera in bad condition, if the price is right and if you are sufficiently skilled to renovate it (see a later chapter of this book for hints and tips on renovation). It is also permissible to buy a rough version of a model that you really want, providing you have the strength of will to replace it with a better version when the opportunity arises. The big mistake is to ignore the opportunity of upgrading your collection and to use any spare cash to buy further tatty cameras.

Remember that camera collecting is an investment as much as a hobby and it's the camera in the best condition that increases in value.

Watch out for fakes, and don't confuse them with replicas. A replica is a modern-day version of a truly historic camera, made and genuinely sold as a replica rather than the real thing. Two examples that come to mind are the Ur Leica and the first Kodak. Also, since the last Blue Book was published, Leitz has produced a replica of the Leica '0' Series — a small series of Leicas that were originally produced to test the market before the actual Leica I was launched. There's not much chance that you might be fooled by something like the Ur Leica, because although there are a fair

number of replicas on sale, only two (or some claim, three) of the real thing were ever made. So it's a certainty that the one you see at a camera fair will be identified as, and sold as, a replica. The same goes for one of those '0' series Leicas, even though the real cameras were originally made in slightly higher numbers. The Kodak might be a little more difficult to identify. This was made in a limited edition in 1988 to celebrate the centenary of the first model. When

It's not the original, it's not a fake, it's a quite legitimate replica of a Leica landmark – one of the '0' series, first made to test the market before the Leica I was launched.

it is sold, it is still usually identified as a replica, but would be a little easier to pass off as one of the originals if some clever faker managed to age it convincingly.

Which brings us to true fakes. At one time, fakery was confined to the Victorian era of cameras, where it was relatively easy to make what was essentially little more than a wooden box with a contemporary lens on it. But today, fakers are getting more ambitious and there are rumours of factories in places like Poland set up for the sole purpose of faking collectable cameras. You should be particularly wary of what appears to be a super-rare camera such as the Leica Luxus — a gold-plated Leica I with lizard skin covering — turning up at a camera fair.

Even certain collectors are guilty of faking, albeit in a perfectly innocent way. Those who are especially good at repairs and restoration will often make one good camera out of the parts of several others, ending up with a camera that is different in its specification from any true model, and which could get mistaken for a one-off rarity. There is one English collector who has developed the knack of making stereo cameras out of Prakticas. He has no intention of passing them off as originals, but imagine the scene some 50 years hence when one of his cameras turns up at some future camera fair on in an auction and gets mistaken for a rare prototype from the Praktica factory.

The problem is that the better the fake, the more difficult it is for the lay person to identify it as such and the truth of the matter is that you could easily buy a faked version of one of the more common collectables without ever knowing it. But if you see, or are offered, what you know to be a very rare camera at a surprisingly good price, then beware, and if in any doubt walk away from it. You owe it, not only to yourself, but also to future generations of collectors, to do everything you can to prevent fakes getting into the open market.

Storing and displaying your collection

Different collectors have different ideas of how to store and display their collections. For some, it becomes almost an obsession to be able to see and hold every camera they own. For them, nothing short of a room full of glass-fronted cabinets will suffice.

Others keep their cameras stored away in cupboards and even filing cabinets. If this is your way, remember to have a good 'filing system' — something that will enable you to find any camera easily. Small tags attached by thin twine to camera strap eyelets on camera bodies make an ideal way of numbering your collection, and these numbers can then be cross-referenced to written records or a computer database. Such records might refer simply to the name of the camera, or you might use them to list details of the year of manufacture, something of its history etc. This is particularly easy if you are listing your collection on a computerised database, where you can add details as and when you have time or new facts come to light.

The loft or attic of a house is a one place that many collectors store their collection, but if you use that space, take care. First, never forget just how heavy most collectable cameras are and remember just how much strain you are putting on joists. Advice from a friendly builder or surveyor wouldn't come amiss. Also remember that lofts and attics rarely have heating or insulation in them. So the area will be extra cold in winter and super hot in summer — not ideal conditions for your collection.

If you are storing rather than displaying, always make sure that your cameras are well protected. Bubble wrapping is ideal for the job.

Finally, don't leave your cameras to stand or be stored for years without occasionally operating them. Firing shutters on all speeds, especially the slow ones, turning focusing rings and aperture controls will help make sure they continue to work and stay in the condition you originally found them in.

What's the Date?

You've bought a collectable camera. You know it's old but you have no real idea of *how* old. So how do you go about accurately putting a date to it? For some makes and types of camera, it's easy, but for others you have to do a bit of detective work, weighing up two, three or even more factors, which all together add up to at least placing your camera firmly between certain sets of dates, or ideally on a specific year.

Some companies kept records of serial numbers that are still available today. These can pinpoint not merely when a certain camera was made, but exactly when your specific model came off the production line. But for the majority of camera companies, it must be said that such detailed records have been lost in the mists of time. Leica excepted, this is particularly true of German companies such as Zeiss whose records were lost during the Second World War.

Nevertheless, if you follow the clues, it is still possible to hit the year of a camera's manufacture fairly accurately. Here are some of those clues to point you in the right direction.

Patent dates

One thing you should not do is confuse patent dates with actual launch dates. Some manufacturers stamped these dates inside bodies. You'll find them, for example, on the inside of the detachable backs of many early Kodak folding cameras. But remember that patents always preceded actual launch dates, sometimes by a few years, often by much longer. The patent date can make

a starting point because it gives you a time before which the camera could *not* have been made, but it won't give you the date the camera was actually manufactured.

For Zeiss collectors, here is a list of American patent numbers and their dates of issue.

Camera directories

The Blue Book that you are reading gives dates for as many of its entries as possible, and these are as accurate as it has been possible to get them. But if you think we are wrong and can prove it, we want to hear from you, so that we can correct later editions.

Also in this issue, you will find for the first time, a section on landmark cameras. This gives a breakdown of when certain makes of camera were first seen and when certain styles or types first arrived on the market. In each case, it gives details of the specific camera that launched one of the new styles, but even if you don't have that actual named camera, this can still give you a starting point for your investigations. For example...

Cameras that took 16 pictures on 120 or 127 size film were made by many, many different manufacturers, but whoever made yours couldn't have made it before 1923, because that's when Ensign did it for the first time with a camera called the Cupid.

Small rollfilm twin lens reflexes were built by an abundance of makers all over the world, but none before 1928 when Franke and Heidecke introduced the original Rolleiflex.

Zeiss United States Patent numbers

Year	Number	Year	Number	Year	Number
1850	6891	1882	251,685	1914	1,083,267
1851	7865	1883	269,820	1915	1,123,212
1852	8622	1884	291,016	1916	1,166,419
1853	9512	1885	310,163	1917	1,210,389
1854	10,358	1886	333,494	1918	1,251,458
1855	12,117	1887	355,291	1919	1,290,027
1856	14,009	1888	375,720	1920	1,326,899
1857	16,324	1889	395,305	1921	1,364,063
1858	19,010	1890	418,665	1922	1,401,948
1859	22,477	1891	443,987	1923	1,440,362
1860	26,642	1892	466,315	1924	1,478,996
1861	31,005	1893	488,976	1925	1,521,590
1862	34,045	1894	511,744	1926	1,568,040
1863	37,266	1895	531,619	1927	1,612,790
1864	41,047	1896	552,501	1928	1,654,521
1865	45,085	1897	574,369	1929	1,696,897
1866	51,784	1898	596,467	1930	1,742,818
1867	60,658	1899	616,871	1931	1,787,424
1868	72,959	1900	640,167	1932	1,839,190
1869	85,503	1901	664,827	1933	1,892,66
1870	98,460	1902	690,385	1934	?,941,449
1871	110,617	1903	717,521	1935	1,985,878
1872	122,304	1904	748,567	1936	2,026,516
1873	134,504	1905	778,834	1937	2,066,319
1874	146,010	1906	808,618	1938	2,014,004
1875	158,350	1907	839,799	1940	2,185,170
1876	171,641	1908	875,679	1941	2,227,418
1877	158,813	1909	908,436	1942	2,268,540
1878	198,733	1910	945,010	1943	2,307,007
1879	211,078	1911	980,178	1944	2,338,081
1880	223,211	1912	1,013,095	1945	2,366,154
1881	236,137	1913	1,049,326	1946	2,391,856

Other modern books also date cameras as accurately as possible, but beware of accepting what the author says as gospel truth. Where possible, check other sources and try to get at least two that agree. Don't forget also that authors often take information from each other, and mistakes can get passed on from book to book.

Old books and magazines

Whenever you visit a camera fair, antique market or secondhand bookshop, look out for old books and magazines that carry reviews of the latest equipment and advertisements for cameras. Used carefully, and providing you understand some of the pitfalls, these can give you accurate estimates of camera dates.

Going back to source with original books and magazines can usually give you the most accurate information about dates of launch.

Two of the most useful magazines for this purpose are Amateur Photographer, which was first published in 1894, and the British Journal of Photography, which was first published in 1854. Being weekly rather than monthly publications, these can be relied on more than most. So if one of them mentions in their editorial sections that a new piece of equipment has just been launched, then the date of the magazine is a pretty safe bet. But do bear in mind that the date the news of the item arrived in the UK (or any other country whose magazines you are using) might be a year or so after the camera was officially launched in its home country.

Also bear in mind that just because you see a camera advertised as "new" in one of the magazines' advertisements, it doesn't mean that it was actually launched current with the issue you are looking at. The same advert might have been running for several weeks, months, or even years! If you have previous issues, check back.

Another good source is the British Journal Photographic Almanac, which was first published in 1860 and thereafter at yearly intervals. By comparing issues year by year and checking the first appearance of a particular camera in the advertisements, you can get a pretty good idea of its launch date. In early issues, the BJ, as it is known among collectors, listed equipment in a regular section called *Epitome of Progress,* but in 1924, the equipment news was separated out in a section called *Recent Introductions in Apparatus and Materials,* which speaks for itself. From 1925 on, this became a section simply called *New Goods.*

One point to be aware of, though. Being an annual publication, the BJ was up to a year in production, so publication dates of issues in which equipment appears for the first time, are very often one year later than the date of the actual launch.

The BJ was published in this form until 1962, when it changed its style and content. From being a small format almanac, full of editorial and advertisements that are genuinely useful to the collector, it turned into a larger format book that majored more on its pictorial content. These later issues are not as useful as the earlier ones.

There's one other point to keep in mind when looking at advertisements in publications of this type. Making printing blocks so that cameras could be illustrated in advertisements was an expensive business in those days. So, very often, if a manufacturer launched a new camera that was very similar in appearance to the previous model, they simply wouldn't bother with a new illustration. For that reason, some pictures in advertisements do not actually show the precise camera being described in the text.

American film numbers by date of introduction

101:	1895	111:	1898	121:	1902	620:	1932
102:	1895	112:	1898	122:	1903	135:	1935
103:	1896	113:	1898	123:	1904	828:	1935*
104:	1897	114:	1898	124:	1905	126:	
105:	1898	115:	1898	126:	1906	1963**	
106:	1898	116:	1899	127:	1912	110:	
107:	1898	117:	1900	128:	1912	1972***	
108:	1898	118:	1900	129:	1912	Disc:	1981
109:	1898	119:	1900	130:	1912	APS:	1996
110:	1898	120:	1901	616:	1932		

 *   also known as Bantam
 **   also known as Instamatic, not the same as 126 of 1906
 ***   also known as Pocket Instamatic, not the same as 110 of 1898

Film sizes

Today, cameras have, by and large, been standardised to use two sizes of film: 35mm or 120. But in times past, there was a proliferation of different sizes, with manufacturers often launching a new camera with a new size of film, that then went on to become a standard size for other makers. The most notable examples are 120, first seen in the Kodak Brownie in 1900; 127, first seen in he Vest Pocket Kodak of 1912; and 35mm, first seen in the Leica of 1925. So you can use the film size as indication of the first date that a camera might have been produced.

Here are some examples of film size numbers and the years of their launch.

Company names

Over the years, new companies were launched, old ones ceased to trade, while others merged to form new companies. Knowing the precise dates when these things happened give you another clue to the earliest date that a particular manufacturer might have built a camera. Here are some examples...

Kodak

During a period of a little over 30 years, Eastman Kodak bought or absorbed the following companies.

1895: the Boston Camera Manufacturing Company.
1898: the American Camera Company
1899: the Blair Camera Company
1903: Rochester Optical Company
1907: Folmer and Schwing
1932: Nagel.

Houghton and Ensign

1904: G. Houghton and Son became Houghtons Ltd
1925: Houghtons merged with Butchers to form Houghton-Butcher
1930: Houghton-Butcher sold cameras under the name of Ensign

APM

1921: Amalgamated Photographic Manufacturers Ltd, otherwise known as APM, was formed from the amalgamation of a number of well-known British manufacturers that included Marion, Paget and Rajar.

1929: the company split, and camera making continuing under the name of Soho Ltd.

Zeiss Ikon
1926: Zeiss Ikon was formed from the amalgamation of Goerz, Ica, Ernemann and Contessa-Nettel.

Camera names

The first appearance of a well-known name gives a cut-off point before which those names would not have been seen. Here's a list of when certain household names first appeared on a camera (as opposed to the dates the various companies were actually founded).

The Minolta name appeared long before it was first seen in the West. This is a Semi-Minolta I and a Minolta Best, both from 1934.

1935: Canon
1936: Olympus
1937: Minox
1948: Hasselblad (SLRs)
1948: Nikon
1948: Polaroid
1948: Zorki
1951: Ilford
1957: Pentax

1840: Voigtländer
1888: Kodak
1895: Sanderson
1900: Brownie
1900: Ernemann
1902: Graflex
1925: Leica
1926: Zeiss Ikon
1928: Agfa
1928: Rolleiflex
1930: Ensign
1931: Minolta
1933: Exakta
1934: Fed

Shutters and lenses

Camera manufacturers of the past didn't always make their own shutters or lenses, but preferred to add other well-known names to their bodies. So knowing when certain shutters or lenses first appeared also gives you an earliest date from which to work.

A camera's shutter can help point you towards its age. Left to right here are Compur dial set, Compur rim set and Unicum shutters.

Here are the dates when certain shutters first appeared.

1897: Unicum
1901: Automat
1904: Goerz Sector
1904: Compound,
1912: Compur dial set
1928: Compur rim set

The following lens names first made their appearance on these dates.

1893: Cooke
1895: Protar
1901: Aldis Anastigmat
1902: Helia
1902: Tessar
1904: Dagor
1914: Xpres
1918: Aviar

Lens coating appeared mostly after 1945, although beware of earlier lenses that were coated several years after their original manufacture.

Zeiss lenses (often coupled with Compur shutters) were used on a great many different camera bodies, even in Japan before the Japanese began their own lens production, so knowing the dates and serial numbers of lenses from this particular company can be a strong clue to the date of the camera. Here's a list of Zeiss serial numbers with their appropriate dates.

The Tessar lens was introduced in 1902, and was used on cameras for many years to come.

Zeiss serial numbers

1912	173400-200500		1928	903100-908150
1913	208500-249350		1929	919800-1016900
1914	249900-252700		1930	1020500-1239700
1915	282800-284500		1931	1239701-1365600
1916	285200-288100		1932	1365601-1389300
1917	289000-298150		1933	1436650-1456000
1918	298200-322750		1934	1500450-1590000
1919	322800-351600		1935	1615750-1752300
1920	375200-419800		1936	1774800-1942800
1921	433250-438350		1937	1950100-2220000
1922	438900-498000		1938	2268000-2528000
1923	561250-578300		1939	2528001-2651200
1924	631850-648500		1940	2652000-2678000
1925	652200-681751		1941	2678001-2790350
1926	686800-703200		1942	2799600-?
1927	722200-798250			

It is worth noting that many cameras originally sold with one lens and shutter combination, might have been changed later as owners updated their equipment. Also remember that many camera models were originally sold with a choice of shutter and lens combinations, according to the price and the taste of the customer. These combinations might also be affected by the country in which a camera was sold, as importers and distributors often changed the specifications. A French lens on a German camera, for example, could indicate that a particular item, though manufactured in Germany, was originally sold in France.

Camera features

Certain features that are common to different manufacturers can also help identify a date. Here are the dates that certain well-known features first made their appearance.

1890s: Use of Nickel plating (shiny and looking a little yellow) dates.

1892: First appearance of red windows for film winding, then fairly regularly from 1895.

1900: First of traditional folding design with drop-down bed and lens panel pulled out along rails.

1900: Square corners on bellows began to change to chamfered corners.

1910: Bellows, mostly red until this time, began to appear in black.

The Autographic feature on Kodak cameras first appeared in 1914.

1914: The Autographic Back, identified as a small flap on the back of mostly Kodak cameras, launched, lasting until 1933.

1916: First camera with coupled rangefinder.

1920: Self-erecting folding mechanisms began to appear.

1923: First use of twin red windows for film winding.

1925: First truly practical use of 35mm in a still camera, using the now traditional 24 x 36mm format.

1928: First rollfilm twin lens reflex.

The Rajar No.6, launched in 1929, was probably the first camera with a Bakelite body.

1929: First use of Bakelite in camera body design

1930s: Chrome plating appeared around the middle of he decade.

1933: First small format rollfilm SLR.

1935: Introduction of built-in meters.

1936: First 35mm SLR.

1938: First automatic exposure control.

1948: First instant picture camera.

1954: First popular use of instant return mirror in an SLR.

1960: First use of through the lens metering in a non-SLR.

1963: First use of through the lens metering in a 35mm SLR.

1963: First camera with electronic shutter.

1963: First Instamatic for 126 film.

1968: First automatic single lens reflex.

1972: First 110 camera

1978: First autofocus compact camera.

1980: First autofocus lenses for manual SLRs.

1981: First disc camera.

1985: First body-integral autofocus SLR.

1988: First of the modern style of disposable cameras.

1989: First commercial use of digital imaging in a camera.

Hidden codes

In the 1940s and 1950s, Kodak used a hidden code in the serial numbers of some of their lenses to indicate when they were built. The code consists of a series of letters that translate into numbers, like this:-

C A M E R O S I T Y
1 2 3 4 5 6 7 8 9 0

To date the lens, look for the letters and compare them to the appropriate numbers below them in the table. For example, a serial number beginning with the letters 'ER' denotes the lens was made in 1945.

At one time, Hasselblad used a similar system on bodies and film magazines that ran like this:-

V H P I C T U R E S
1 2 3 4 5 6 7 8 9 0

You will also find a hidden code on some Chinese cameras, that uses the first two figures of the serial number to denote the number of years after liberation that the camera was made. Liberation was in 1949, so a camera whose serial number begins, for example, with the figures '21', was made in 1970 (1949 + 21 = 1970).

Many Russian cameras and lenses made between 1950 and 1980, show the year of manufacture in the first two digits of the serial number. So if, for

FED serial numbers

Year	Serial numbers
1934	31-4000
1935	4000-16000
1936	16000-31000
1937	31000-53000
1938	53000-82000
1939	82000-116000
1940	116000-148000
1941	148000-175000
1942-45	No Camera Production
1946	175000-176000
1947	176000-186000
1948	186000-203000
1949	203000-221000
1950	221000-248000
1951	248000-289000
1952	289000-341000
1953	341000-424000
1954	424000-560000
1955	560000-700000

example, the serial number is quoted as 56083307, the camera was most likely made in 1956. This offers an ideal way of comparing bodies and lenses to see if a later lens has been added to an earlier body.

Serial numbers

Undoubtedly, the most accurate way of identifying the date a camera was launched is to check its serial number against an authentic list. For Leica collectors, that's relatively easy, because Leica has kept extensive records since Day One (see next chapter). For collectors of other marques, finding lists of serial numbers is not so easy, but here are some that will help collectors of Fed and Foca.

Foca models and dates

Foca "PF1", one star

1946	16,001-20,300
1947	20,301-21,200
1948	60,001-61,300
1949	61,301-65,200
1950	65,201-67,700
	68,201-68,700
1951	67,701-68,200
	68,701-69,200
	69,701-69,999
	100,001-101,150
1952	69,201-69,700
	101,151-101,550
	160,001-161,000
1953	101,551-101,999

Foca "Standard" one star

1953	500,001-502,050
1954	502,051-503,150
1955	503,151-504,100
1956	504,101-505,300
1957	505,301- ?

Foca "PF2" two stars

1946	10,001-15,999

Foca "PF2b" two stars

1947	25,001-37,000
1948	37,001-46,600
1949	56,601-53,000
	54,401-55,350
1950	53,001-54,401
	55,351-56,000
1951	56,001-59,500
	125,000-150,000
1952	59,501-60,000
	90,001-92,700

1953	300,000-300,550
	92,701-94,999
1954	300,551-302,100
1955	302,101-303,700
1956	303,701-306,000
1957	306,001- ?

Foca "PF3" three stars

1952	90,001-92,700

(taken from the PF2b list of the same year)

1953	92,701-89,999

(taken from the PF2b list of the same year)

	400,001-400,650
1954	400,651-402,400
1955	402,401-404,100
1956	404,101-406,400
1957	406,401-?

Foca Universal no stars

1949	70,001-74,800
1950	74,801-80,400
1951	80,401-84,650
1952	170,000-174,000
1953	84,651-86,900
1954	86,901-87,999
1955	200,501-201,250

Foca Universal "R" no stars

1955	200,001R-
1956	200,901R-
1957	203,301R ?

FOCASPORT

1955	10,001S-23,600S
1956	23,601S-48,500S
1957	48,501S- ?

*From 1947 until 1951, about 1200 PF3 cameras were made. These cameras used serial numbers taken from the "PF2b" list. They fall between two ranges. 25,000-59,999 and 125,000-150,000.

Identifying Leica cameras

Compared to collectors of other marques, Leica collectors have it easy when identifying the dates of manufacture – though not so easy when it comes to identifying individual models.

The apparent problem for the newcomer looking at the early models comes from the fact that the camera names were not actually named on the body. The Leica I series of cameras which began in 1925, is readily identifiable because, without a built-in rangefinder, the body was significantly different from the models that followed. But from the first model of the Leica II in 1932 up to the IIIG, last of the screw-lens models in 1956, only minor cosmetic and mechanical changes marked the difference between the models.

Not so with the M-series of cameras which began in 1954 (two years before he last screw lens camera). M-series cameras do have their models marked on the body and are more easily identifiable.

However, none of this matters too much to the collector setting out to identify the precise year or model of the Leica camera they have bought, because every camera has its own serial number and Leica makes its list of serial numbers, with camera models and year of manufacture, readily available to collectors.

The list of Leica camera and lens serial numbers are reproduced here by kind permission of Leica Camera GmbH. This listing is essentially for use as a quick reference guide for the dating of a Leica camera or lens. The lists are in manufacturing batches. In a number of cases, particularly in the more recent post-war period, not all allocated numbers were used.

In the Leica screw period the individual batches were often much smaller than would be indicated by this quick reference list. You will often find individual cameras that are of a different model than that indicated in the list. For example, you might come across a Leica Standard with a serial number that indicates it should be one of a batch of 1000 Leica IIIa cameras. This is because, before the war, the Leitz company were willing to supply a special order camera to an individual customer: it would then be allotted a number from the current production batch. Leica Historica, the German Leica historical society, once published a screw camera listing that analysed production almost down to individual cameras by model and date and ran to 190 A4 pages of detail. This listing was compiled from the hand-written ledgers, which still exist in the factory, where every single camera produced was recorded, with its model type, date and destination.

Another anomaly that can arise with screw, and some M cameras, is caused by the Leitz policy, up to at least the end of the 1960s, of offering an upgrading service. Examples might be from Leica I to Leica II, or Leica II to Leica III or IIIa. After the war, flash synchronisation was also offered for earlier models. For these reasons you can see that an original Leica I could have been converted several times during its life, but it always retained its original serial number. This can be disappointing for the collector who comes into possession of a camera with the serial number of what should have been a valuable collector's item, but which has been converted into something much more up-to-date but far less valuable now!

Leitz also upgraded lenses for customers by changing the front ring on, say, an Elmax to a standard Elmar ring. Later they offered to change the aperture scale to the later type. They also coated earlier lenses. So it is quite possible to find an early unnumbered lens, that was not originally rangefinder coupled, that has been converted to a later, coated specification.For all the above reasons, use these serial number lists with caution. They are only a quick reference guide. The more detailed Leica publications from HOVE BOOKS will give further help in identifying Leica cameras, lenses and accessories and act as guides into the fascinating Leica world.

Leica serial numbers up to 2000

This information reproduced by the kind permission of Leica Camera AG

See end of table for key to abbreviations

Leica No	Model	Year	Leica No.	Model	Year	Leica No.	Model	Year	Leica No.	Model	Year
100–130	I	1923	141851–141900	II	1934	157251–157400	II	1935	165101–165300	II	1935
131–1000	I	1925	141901–142250	III Chrom	1934	157401–158300	IIIa	1935	165301–165500	Standard	1935
1001–2445	I	1926	142251–142350	II	1934	158301–158350	Standard	1935	165501–165975	III	1935
2446–5433	I	1926-27	142351–142500	III	1934	158351–158400	II	1935	165976–166075	IIIa	1935
5434–5700	I	1928	142501–142700	I Standard	1934	158401–158650	IIIa	1935	166076–166600	III	1935
5701–6300	Compur	1926-29	142701–143425	III	1934	158651–159000	III	1935	166601–166750	IIIa	1935
6301–13100	I	1928	143426–143750	II Chrom	1934	159001–159200	IIIa	1935	166751–166900	III	1935
13101–13300	Compur	1929	143751–143900	Standard	1934	159201–159350	Standard	1935	166901–167050	IIIa	1935
13301–21478	I	1929	143901–144200	III	1934	159351–159550	III	1935	167051–167175	III	1935
21479–21810	Compur	1930	144201–144400	II	1934	159551–159625	IIIa	1935	167176–167200	IIIa	1935
21811–34450	I	1930	144401–144500	Standard	1934	159626–159675	III	1935	167201–167225	III	1935
34451–34802	Compur	1930	144501–145600	III	1934	159676–160325	IIIa	1935	167226–167700	IIIa	1935
34803–34817	I (Luxus)	1930	145601–145800	Standard	1934	160326–160375	III	1935	167701–167705	III	1935
34818–60000	I	1930	145801–146200	III	1934	160376–160450	I	1935	167751–168000	Standard	1935
60001–71199	I	1931	146201–146375	II	1934	160451–160700	II	1935	168001–168200	II	1935
71200–101000	II	1932	146376–146675	III	1934	160701–161150	I	1935	168201–168250	III	1935
101001–106000	Standard	1932	146676–146775	II	1934	161151–161450	Standard	1935	168251–168325	IIIa	1935
106601–107600	II	1933	146776–147000	III	1934	161451–161550	IIa	1935	168326–168400	III	1935
107601–107757	III	1934	147001–147075	Standard	1934	161551–161600	II	1935	168401–168500	IIIa	1935
107758–108650	I	1934	147076–147175	II	1934	161601–161800	IIIa	1935	168501–168600	IIIa	1935
108651–108700	III	1933	147176–147875	St Chrom	1934	161801–161950	III Chrom	1935	168601–168725	IIIa	1935
108701–109000	III	1933	147876–148025	II Chrom	1934	161951–162100	IIIa	1935	168726–168750	III	1935
109001–111550	III	1933	148026–148850	III Chrom	1934	162101–162175	III	1935	168751–168850	IIIa	1935
111551–111580	II Chrom	1933	148851–148950	II Chrom	1934	162176–162350	IIIa	1935	168851–169000	Standard	1935
111581–112000	III	1933	148951–149350	III Chrom	1935	162351–162400	III	1935	169001–169200	III	1935
112001–112500	II Chrom	1933	149351–149450	St Chrom 1934-35		162401–162500	III	1935	169201–169350	Standard	1935
112501–114000	III	1933	149451–149550	II Chrom 1934-35		162501–162625	III	1935	169351–169450	II	1935
114401–114050	III	1933	149551–150000	III Chrom	1935	162626–162675	IIIa	1935	169451–169550	III	1935
114053–114400	III	1934	150001–150124	Reporter 1934-36		162676–162750	III	1935	169551–169650	II	1935
114401–115300	II Chrom	1933	150125–150200	Second with 1/1000	1936	162751–162800	IIIa	1935	169651–170150	IIIa	1935
115301–115650	III	1934	150201–150850	III Chrom 1934-35		162801–162825	III	1935	170151–170500	III	1935
115651–115900	II Chrom	1934	150851–151100	Standard	1935	162826–162925	IIIa	1935	170501–171300	IIIa	1935
115901–116000	St Chrom	1934	151101–151225	III	1935	162926–162975	III	1935	171301–171550	II	1935
116001–123000	III Chrom	1934	151226–151300	II	1935	162976–163050	IIIa	1935	171551–171900	Standard	1935
123001–123580	Standard	1934	151301–152500	III	1935	163051–163100	III	1935	171901–172250	IIIa	1935
123581–124800	III Chrom	1933	152501–152600	St Chrom	1935	163101–163225	IIIa	1935	172251–172300	III	1935
124801–126200	III Chrom	1933	152601–153175	III Chrom	1935	163226–163250	III	1935	172301–172350	IIIa	1935
126201–126800	III	1934	153176–153225	II	1935	163251–163400	IIIa	1935	172351–172600	III	1935
126801–137400	III	1934	153226–153550	III	1935	163401–163450	Standard	1935	172601–172800	Standard	1935
137401–137625	Standard	1934	153551–153700	II	1935	163451–163550	IIIa	1935	172801–173000	Standard	1935
137626–138700	III Chrom	1934	153701–154150	III	1935	163551–163775	III	1935	173001–173125	IIIa	1935
138701–138950	St Chrom	1934	154151–154200	II	1935	163776–163950	IIIa	1935	173126–173176	IIIa	1935
138951–139900	III Chrom	1934	154201–154800	III	1935	163951–164150	Standard	1935	173177–173425	IIIa	1935
139901–139950	Standard	1934	154801–154900	St Chrom	1935	164151–164275	IIIa	1935	173426–173475	III	1935
139951–140000	II	1934	154901–156200	III	1935	164276–164675	III	1935	173476–173500	IIIa	1935
140001–141500	III Chrom	1934	156201–156850	IIIa 1/1000	1935	164676–164900	IIIa	1935	173501–173650	Standard	1935
141501–141850	Standard	1934	156851–157250	III	1935	164901–165000	II	1935	173651–173675	IIIa	1935
						165001–165100	III	1935	173676–173725	III	1935

Leica No	Model	Year	Leica No.	Model	Year	Leica No.	Model	Year	Leica No.	Model	Year
173726–173825	IIIa	1935	184801–184950	III	1936	198901–199200	IIIa	1936	216501–216800	IIIa	1936
173826–173900	III	1935	184951–185200	IIIa	1936	199201–199300	III	1936	216801–217000	III	1936
173901–174025	IIIa	1935	185201–185350	III	1936	199301–199500	IIIa	1936	217001–217200	IIIa	1936
174026–174075	III	1935	185351–185500	II	1936	199501–199600	III	1936	217201–217300	III	1936
174076–174100	IIIa	1935	185501–185650	Standard	1936	199601–199800	II	1936	217301–217500	Standard	1936
174101–174125	III	1935	185651–185700	III	1936	199801–200100	IIIa	1936	217501–217700	III	1936
174126–174150	IIIa	1935	185701–185800	Standard	1936	200101–200200	III	1936	217701–217900	II	1936-37
174151–174400	III	1935	185801–186100	IIIa	1936	200201–200500	IIIa	1936	217901–218300	IIIa	1936-37
174401–174650	II	1935	186101–186200	III	1936	200501–200650	II	1936	218301–218700	II	1936
174651–174675	IIIa	1935	186201–186500	IIIa	1936	200651–200750	Standard	1936	218701–218800	III	1936
174676–174750	III	1935	186501–186550	III	1936	200751–201200	III	1936	218801–219600	IIIa	1936
174751–174950	IIIa	1935	186551–186800	IIIa	1936	201201–201300	IIIa	1936	219601–219800	II	1936
174951–175125	III	1935	186801–186900	III	1936	201301–201400	III	1936	219801–219900	IIIa	1936
175126–175200	IIIa	1935	186901–186950	IIIa	1936	201401–201600	IIIa	1936	219101–220000	III	1936
175201–175350	III	1935	186951–187000	III	1936	201601–201700	Standard	1936	220001–220300	IIIa	1936
175351–175450	IIIa	1935	187001–187100	IIIa	1936	201701–202300	IIIa	1936	220301–220500	II	1936
175451–175500	III	1935	187101–187200	III	1936	202301–202450	II	1936	220501–220600	III	1936
175501–175700	Standard	1935	187201–187400	IIIa	1936	202451–202600	IIIa	1936	220601–220700	III	1936
175701–175750	III	1935	187401–187500	III	1936	202601–202700	III	1936	220701–220900	IIIa	1936
175751–175850	IIIa	1935	187501–187650	II	1936	202701–202800	IIIa	1936	220901–221000	III	1936
175851–175900	III	1935	187651–187775	III	1936	202801–202900	II	1936	221001–221300	IIIa	1936
175901–176100	IIIa	1935	187776–187785	IIIa	1936	202901–203100	IIIa	1936	221301–221400	III	1936
176101–176150	III	1935	187786–187850	III	1936	203101–203300	III	1936	221401–222150	III	1936
176151–176250	IIIa	1935	187851–188100	IIIa	1936	203301–203400	Standard	1936	222151–222200	III	1936
176251–176300	III	1935	188101–188300	III	1936	203401–204100	IIIa	1936	222201–222300	IIIa	1936
176301–176600	IIIa	1935	188301–188600	Standard	1936	204101–204200	III	1936	222301–222700	Standard	1937
176601–177000	III	1935	188601–188750	II	1936	204201–204300	IIIa	1936	222701–223000	II	1937
177001–177400	IIIa	1935	188751–189300	IIIa	1936	204301–204500	II	1936	223001–223300	III	1937
177401–177550	III	1935	189301–189475	III	1936	204501–204600	III	1936	223301–223600	IIIa	1936
177551–177600	IIIa	1935	189476–189800	IIIa	1936	204601–204800	IIIa	1936	223601–223700	III	1936
177601–177700	III	1935	189801–189900	III	1936	204801–205000	III	1936	233701–224600	IIIa	1936-37
177701–177800	Standard	1935	189901–190200	III	1936	205001–205100	III	1936	224601–224800	Standard	1936-37
177801–177900	IIIa	1935	190201–190500	III	1936	205101–205300	III	1936	224801–224900	IIIa	1936-37
177901–178000	III	1935	190501–190700	IIIa	1936	205301–205400	IIIa	1936	224901–225000	III	1936-37
178001–178100	IIIa	1935	190701–190900	III	1936	205401–205500	II	1936	225001–225200	III	1936-37
178101–178250	III	1935	190901–191100	IIIa	1936	205501–205700	Standard	1936	225201–225300	III	1936-37
178251–178550	IIIa	1935	191101–191200	III	1936	205701–207300	IIIa	1936	225301–225400	IIIa	1936-37
178551–178600	III	1935	191201–191300	II	1936	207301–207400	II	1936	225401–225600	III	1936-37
178601–179200	IIIa	1935	191301–191350	IIIa	1936	207401–207600	Standard	1936	225601–226300	IIIa	1936-37
179201–179250	III	1935	191351–191500	III	1936	207601–207800	III	1936	226301–226400	III	1936-37
179251–179500	IIIa	1935	191501–191650	II	1936	207801–208000	III	1936	226401–227000	IIIa	1936-37
179501–179575	II	1935	191651–191750	Standard	1936	208001–208300	III	1936	227001–227050	III	1936-37
179576–179800	Standard	1935	191751–191850	III	1936	208301–208600	IIIa	1936	227051–227600	III	1936-37
179801–179900	II	1935	191851–192100	IIIa	1936	208601–208800	III	1936	227601–227650	III	1936-37
179901–180100	IIIa	1935	192101–192400	III	1936	208801–209000	IIIa	1936	227651–231500	III	1936-37
180101–180400	III	1935	192401–192500	IIIa	1936	209001–209600	III	1936	231501–231600	III	1936-37
180401–180475	IIIa	1935	192501–192800	III	1936	209601–209900	II	1936	231601–231800	IIIa	1936-37
180476–180700	III	1935	192801–192950	II	1936	209901–210100	IIIa	1936	231801–231900	III	1936-37
180701–180800	Standard	1935	192951–193200	IIIa	1936	210101–210200	III	1936	231901–232200	III	1936-37
180801–181000	II	1935	193201–193450	Standard	1936	210201–210400	IIIa	1936	232201–232500	III	1936-37
181001–181450	IIIa	1935	193451–193500	IIIa	1936	210401–210900	Standard	1936	232501–232800	III	1936-37
181451–181550	III	1935	193501–193600	III	1936	210901–211000	III	1936	232801–232900	III	1936-37
181551–181600	IIIa	1935	193601–194300	IIIa	1936	211001–211600	IIIa	1936	232901–233400	IIIa	1936-37
181601–181700	III	1935	194301–194650	III	1936	211601–211700	III	1936	233401–233500	III	1936-37
181701–182000	IIIa	1935	194651–194851	II	1936	211701–211801	IIIa	1936	233501–233700	Standard	1936-37
182001–182050	III	1935	194851–194950	Standard	1936	211801–211900	II	1936	233701–233800	III	1936-37
182051–182300	IIIa	1935	194951–196200	IIIa	1936	211901–212400	IIIa	1936	233801–234000	IIIa	1936-37
182301–182350	III	1935	196201–196300	III	1936	212401–212700	Standard	1936	234001–234100	II	1936-37
182351–182500	IIIa	1935	196301–196400	IIIa	1936	212701–212800	IIIa	1936	234101–234200	III	1936-37
182501–182700	Standard	1935	196401–196550	II	1936	212801–213200	III	1936	234201–234500	III	1936-37
182701–182850	II	1935	196551–196750	Standard	1936	213201–213300	IIIa	1936	234501–234600	III	1936-37
182851–183500	IIIa	1935	196751–197400	III	1936	213301–213500	Standard	1936	234601–235100	IIIa	1937
183501–183600	II	1935	197401–197500	Standard	1936	213601–213700	II	1936	235101–235200	III	1937
183601–183750	Standard	1935-36	197501–197550	IIIa	1936	213701–214400	IIIa	1936	235201–235800	IIIa	1937
183751–184400	IIIa	1936	197551–197800	III	1936	214401–214800	Standard	1936	235801–235875	III	1937
184401–184450	III	1936	197801–198200	IIIa	1936	214801–215300	IIIa	1936	235876–236200	IIIa	1937
184451–184700	IIIa	1936	198201–198400	III	1936	215301–216000	III	1936	236201–236300	III	1937
184701–184750	III	1936	198401–198800	IIIa	1936	216001–216300	IIIa	1936	236301–236500	IIIa	1937
184751–184800	IIIa	1936	198801–198900	III	1936	216301–216500	III	1936	236501–236700	II	1937

Leica No	Model	Year	Leica No.	Model	Year	Leica No.	Model	Year	Leica No.	Model	Year
236701–236800	IIIa	1937	253001–253200	IIIa	1937	271101–271600	Standard	1938	196901–297100	II	1938
236801–236900	III	1937	253201–253400	III	1937	271601–271700	II	1938	297101–297200	IIIa	1938
236901–237000	IIIa	1937	253401–253500	IIIa	1937	271701–271800	III	1938	297201–297400	III	1938
237001–237200	III	1937	253501–253600	III	1937	271801–272300	IIIa	1938	297401–297900	IIIa	1938
237201–237500	IIIa	1937	253601–253800	Standard	1937	272301–272400	II	1938	297901–298000	III	1938
237501–237600	III	1937	253801–254000	IIIa	1937	272401–274800	IIIa	1938	298001–299000	IIIa	1938
237601–238000	III	1937	254001–254200	III	1937	274801–275200	III	1938	299001–299200	III	1938
238001–238100	III	1937	254201–254600	IIIa	1937	275201–275350	IIIa	1938	299201–299500	IIIa	1938
238101–238500	IIIa	1937	254601–254800	II	1937	275351–275650	II	1938	299501–299600	III	1938
238501–238600	III	1937	254801–254900	III	1937	275651–275675	IIIa	1938	299601–299800	IIIa	1938
238601–238800	IIIa	1937	254901–256400	IIIa	1937	275676–275700	II	1938	299801–299900	III	1938
238801–238825	III	1937	256401–256600	Standard	1937	275701–275800	IIIa	1938	299901–300000	Standard	1938
238826–238900	IIIa	1937	256601–256800	III	1937	275801–276400	III	1938	300001–300100	Reporter	1938
238901–239000	III	1937	256801–256900	III	1937	276401–277000	IIIa	1938	300101–300200	Standard	1938
239001–239100	IIIa	1937	256901–257400	IIIa	1937	277001–277100	III	1938	300201–300300	II	1938
239101–239300	III	1937	257401–257525	III	1937	277101–277500	IIIa	1938	300301–300400	Standard	1938
239301–239400	IIIa	1937	257526–257600	IIIa	1937	277505–277900	Standard	1938	300401–300700	IIIa	1938
239401–239600	III	1937	257601–257800	Standard	1937	277901–278100	II	1938	300701–300800	III	1938
239601–239700	IIIa	1937	257801–258200	III	1937	278101–278200	III	1938	300801–301000	III	1938
239701–239800	III	1937	258201–259500	IIIa	1937	278201–278500	IIIa	1938	301001–301100	IIIa	1938
239801–240000	Standard	1937	259501–259800	II	1937	278501–278525	III	1938	301101–301400	IIIa	1938
240001–241000	IIIb	1937-38	259801–259900	Standard	1937	278526–278550	II	1938	301401–301500	III	1938
241001–241100	IIIa	1937-38	259901–260000	IIIa	1937	278551–278600	III	1938	301501–301600	II	1938
241101–241300	III	1937-38	260001–260100	Reporter	1937	278601–278800	Standard	1938	301601–301700	Standard	1938
241301–241500	IIIa	1937-38	260101–260200	IIIa	1937	278801–279000	IIIa	1938	301701–301800	III	1938
241501–241700	II	1937-38	260201–260600	III	1937	279001–279200	III	1938	301801–301900	III	1938
241701–241900	Standard	1937-38	260601–260800	IIIa	1937	279201–279400	II	1938	301901–302000	III	1938
241901–242000	II	1937-38	260801–260900	III	1937	279401–280000	IIIa	1938	302001–302500	IIIa	1938
242001–243000	IIIb	1937-38	260901–261200	IIIa	1937	280001–286500	IIIb	1938	302501–302800	II	1938
243001–243400	IIIa	1937-38	261201–261300	III	1937	286501–286800	Standard	1938	302801–302900	III	1938
243401–243500	III	1937-38	261301–261500	IIIa	1937	286801–287000	III	1938	302901–303200	IIIa	1938
243501–243800	II	1937-38	261501–261600	III	1937	287001–287200	III	1938	303201–303300	III	1938
243801–244100	IIIa	1937-38	261601–261800	IIIa	1937	287201–287300	III	1938	303301–303700	IIIa	1938
244101–244200	III	1937-38	261801–262000	Standard	1937	287301–287400	IIIa	1938	303701–303800	III	1938
244201–244400	Standard	1937-38	262001–262800	IIIa	1937	287401–287600	II	1938	303801–303900	Standard	1938
244401–244600	III	1937-38	262801–263000	III	1937	287601–288000	IIIa	1938	303901–304400	IIIa	1938
244601–244800	IIIa	1937-38	263001–263600	IIIa	1937	288001–290200	IIIb	1938-39	304401–304500	III	1938
244801–245000	Standard	1937-38	263601–263900	II	1937	290201–290500	III	1938	304501–304700	III	1938
245001–245100	IIIa	1937-38	263901–264000	III	1937	290501–290800	III	1938	304701–304800	III	1938
245101–245300	III	1937-38	264001–264800	IIIa	1937	290801–291000	IIIa	1938	304801–304900	IIIa	1938
245301–246200	IIIa	1937-38	264801–265000	Standard	1937	291001–291200	Standard	1938	304901–305000	III	1938
246201–246300	III	1937-38	265001–266000	IIIb	1937	291201–291500	IIIa	1938	305001–305600	IIIa	1938
246301–246400	IIIa	1937-38	266001–266100	IIIa	1937	291501–291600	III	1938	305601–305700	III	1938
246401–246500	III	1937-38	266101–266200	III	1937	291601–291800	IIIa	1938	305701–305800	Standard	1938
246501–246700	II	1937-38	266201–266400	IIIa	1937	291801–292000	Standard	1938	305801–306200	IIIa	1938
246701–247500	IIIa	1937-38	266401–266500	III	1937	292001–292200	II	1938	306201–306300	III	1938
247501–247600	II	1937-38	266501–266800	II	1937	292201–292400	Standard	1938	306301–306500	II	1938
247601–248300	IIIa	1937-38	266801–266900	IIIa	1937	292401–292600	IIIa	1938	306501–306600	III	1938
248301–248400	III	1937-38	266901–267000	III	1937	292601–292700	III	1938	306601–306800	IIIa	1938
248401–248600	Standard	1937-38	267001–267700	IIIa	1937	292701–293000	IIIa	1938	306801–307000	IIIa	1938
248601–248900	IIIa	1937	267701–267800	III	1937	293001–293100	III	1938	307001–307500	IIIa	1938
248901–249000	III	1937	267801–267900	IIIa	1937	293101–293200	IIIa	1938	307501–308000	Standard	1938
249001–249200	III	1937	267901–268000	Standard	1937	293201–293400	III	1938	308001–308100	IIIa	1938
249201–249400	II	1937	268001–268100	IIIa	1937-38	293401–293500	II	1938	308101–308200	IIIa	1938
249401–249500	III	1937	268101–268200	III	1938	293501–293900	IIIa	1938	308201–308300	II	1938
249501–249700	Standard	1937	268201–268400	IIIa	1937	293901–294000	Standard	1938	308301–308500	Standard	1938
249701–249800	III	1937	268401–268500	III	1938	294001–294600	IIIb	1938	308501–308600	III	1938
249801–249900	III	1937	268501–268700	IIIa	1938	294601–294800	II	1938	308601–308700	IIIa	1938
249901–250300	IIIa	1937	268701–268800	III	1938	294801–294900	III	1938	308701–308800	IIIa	1938
250301–250400	III	1937	268801–269300	IIIa	1938	294901–295100	IIIa	1938	308801–309000	IIIa	1938
250401–251200	IIIa	1937	269301–269400	III	1938	295101–295200	III	1938	309001–309200	Standard	1938
251201–251300	III	1937	269401–269600	IIIa	1938	295201–295300	IIIa	1938	309201–309300	IIIa	1938
251301–251500	Standard	1937	269601–269700	III	1938	295301–295400	Standard	1938	309301–309400	IIIa	1938
251501–251600	IIIa	1937	269701–270100	IIIa	1938	295401–295500	III	1938	309401–309500	IIIa	1938
251601–251800	II	1937	270101–270200	III	1938	295501–296000	IIIa	1938	309501–309700	III	1938
251801–252000	III	1937	270201–270300	II	1938	296001–296200	II	1938	309701–310000	IIIa	1938-39
252001–252200	II	1937	270301–270400	IIIa	1938	296201–296500	IIIa	1938	310001–310200	III	1938-39
252201–252900	IIIa	1937	270401–271000	IIIa	1938	296501–296600	III	1938	310201–310400	IIIa	1938-39
252901–253000	III	1937	271001–271100	II	1938	296601–296900	Standard	1938	310401–310500	III	1938-39

Leica No	Model	Year	Leica No.	Model	Year	Leica No.	Model	Year	Leica No.	Model	Year
310501–310600	IIIa	1939	326001–327000	IIIb	1939	352501–352900	II	1940-42	700001–710000	M3	1954
310601–311000	III	1938-39	327001–327200	II	1939	352901–353600	Standard	1940-42	710001–711000	IIIf Vorl ELC	1954
311001–311200	II	1939	327201–327400	III	1939	353601–353800	Reporter	1942-43	711001–713000	IIIf Vorl	1954
311201–311400	IIIa	1939	327401–327500	IIIa	1939	353801–354000	Standard	1942-47	713001–729000	IIIf Vorl	1954
311401–311700	III	1939	327501–327600	III	1939	354001–354050	IIIa	1941-47	729001–730000	IIIf Vorl ELC	1954
311701–311800	IIIa	1939	327601–327800	IIIa	1939	354051–354075	IIIa	1941-46	730001–746450	M3	1955
311801–311900	III	1939	327801–328000	Standard	1939	354076–354100	II	1947	746451–746500	M3 ELC	1955
311901–312000	IIIa	1939	328001–329000	IIIb	1939	354101–354200	IIIa	1947	746501–750000	M3	1955
312001–312200	Standard	1939	329001–329400	Standard	1939	354201–354400	II	1942-44	750001–759700	M3	1955
312201–312400	IIIa	1939	329401–329600	II	1939	354401–355000	IIIb	1946	759701–760000	M3 ELC	1955
312401–312500	III	1939	329601–329800	IIIa	1939	355001–355650	Standard	1947-48	760001–762000	If	1955
312501–312800	Standard	1939	329801–329900	III	1939	355651–356500	III	1939	762001–765000	If	1955
312801–313000	IIIa	1939	329901–330000	IIIa	1939	356501–356550	IIIa	1947-48	765001–773000	IIIf Vorl	1955
313001–313100	III	1939	330001–330200	III	1939	356651–356700	II	1947-48	773001–774000	IIIf ELC	1955
313101–313200	IIIa	1939	330201–330300	II	1939	356701–357200	IIIa	1948-50	774001–775000	IIIf	1955
313201–313300	III	1939	330301–330500	Standard	1939	357201–358500			775001–780000	M3	1955
313301–313400	IIIa	1939	330501–330700	III	1939	358501–358650	II	1948	780001–780090	M3 ELC	1955
313401–313500	Standard	1939	330701–330800	IIIa	1939	358651–360000			780091–780100	If	1957
313501–313600	III	1939	330801–331000	Standard	1939	360001–360100	IIIa	1940-42	780101–787000	M3	1955
313601–314000	III	1939	331001–332000	IIIb	1939	360101–367000	IIIc	1940	787001–789000	IIf	1955
314001–314100	III	1939	332001–332500	IIIa	1939	367001–367325	IIIc	1941-44	789001–790000	If	1955
314101–314300	I	1939	332501–332600	III	1939	367326–367500	IIIc	1945	790001–799000	IIIf	1955
314301–314500	Standard	1939	332601–333000	IIIa	1939	367501–368800	IIIc	1940-41	799001–799999	IIf	1956
314501–314600	II	1939	333001–333100	II	1939	368801–368950	IIIc	1941	800000–805000	M3	1955
314601–314700	III	1939	333101–333300	III	1939	368951–369000	IIIc	1941	805001–805100	M3 ELC	1955
314701–314800	IIIa	1939	333301–333600	Standard	1939	369001–369050	IIIc	1941	805101–807500	M3	1955
314801–314900	III	1939	333601–334000	IIIb	1939	369051–369450	IIIc	1941	807501–808500	If	1956
314901–315000	IIIa	1939	334001–334200	III	1939	369451–390000	IIIc	1941-42	808501–810000	IIf	1956
315001–315100	II	1939	334201–334400	IIIa	1939	390001–397650	IIIc	1943-46	810001–815000	IIIf	1956
315101–315400	IIIa	1939	334401–334600	II	1939	397651–399999			815001–816000	If	1956
315401–315500	II	1939	334601–335000	IIIa	1939	400000–440000	IIIc	1946-47	816001–816900	M3	1956
315501–315700	IIIa	1939	335001–337000	IIIb	1939-40	440001–449999	IIc	1948-51	816901–817000	M3 ELC	1956
315701–315800	III	1939	337001–337200	II	1939	450000	IIIc	1949	817001–820500	M3	1956
315801–316100	IIIa	1939	337201–337400	IIIa	1939	450001–451000	IIc	1951	820501–821500	IIf	1956
316101–316400	III	1939	337401–337500	III	1939	451001–455000	IIf	1951	821501–822000	IIf	1956
316401–316700	IIIa	1939	337501–337900	IIIa	1939	455001–460000	Ic	1949-50	822001–822900	IIf	1956
316701–316900	Standard	1939	337901–338100	II	1939	460001–465000	IIIc	1948-49	822901–823000	IIIf Kältef	1956
316901–317000	II	1939	338101–338200	IIIa	1939	465001–480000	IIIc	1949	823001–823500	IIIf	1956
317001–318000	IIIb	1939	338201–338600	III	1939	480001–495000	IIIc	1949-50	823501–823867	IIIf ELC	1956
318001–318200	IIIa	1939	338601–338900	IIIa	1939	495001–520000	IIIc	1950	823868–825000	IIIf	1956
318201–318300	II	1939	338901–339000	III	1939	520001–524000	Ic	1950-51	825001–826000	IIIg	1956
318301–318500	Standard	1939	339001–340000	IIIb	1939-40	524001–525000	IIIc	1950-51	826001–829750	IIIg	1956
318501–318800	II	1939	340001–340200	IIIa	1939	525001–540000	IIIf	1950-51	829751–829850	IIIf ELC	1956
318801–318900	IIIa	1939	340201–340400	III	1939	540001–560000	IIIf	1951	829851–830000	M3 ELC	1956
318901–319000	III	1939	340401–340600	IIIa	1939	560001–562800	Ic	1951	830001–837500	M3	1956
319001–320000	IIIb	1939	340601–340700	III	1939	562801–565000	If	1951	837501–837620	M3 ELC	1956
320001–320200	II	1939	340701–341000	IIIa	1939	565001–570000	IIIf	1951	837621–837720	IIIf ELC	1956
320201–320400	III	1939	341001–341300	II	1939-40	570001–575000	IIf	1951-52	837721–839620	M3	1956
320401–320600	IIIa	1939	341301–341500	Standard	1939	575001–580000	If*	1952-53	839621–839700	M3 ELC	1956
320601–320700	II	1939	341501–341700	III	1939	580001–610000	IIIf	1951-52	839701–840500	M3	1956
320701–321000	Standard	1939	341701–341900	IIIa	1939	610001–611000	IIIf ELC	1952	840501–840820	M3 ELC	1956
321001–322000	IIIb	1939	341901–342000	III	1939	611001–615000	IIf*	1952-53	840821–844780	M3	1956
322001–322200	II	1939	342001–342200	Standard	1939	Leica with light weight shutter			844781–845000	M3 ELC	1956
322201–322700	Standard	1939	342201–342300	III	1939	615001–650000	IIIf	1952-53	845001–845380	IIIg ELC	1956
322701–322800	IIIa	1939	342301–342900	IIIa	1939	650001–655000	IIf	1953	845381–850900	IIIg	1956
322801–323000	III	1939	342901–343100	III	1939	655001–673000	IIIf	1953	850901–851000	If	1956
323001–324000	IIIb	1939	343101–344000	IIIb	1939	673001–674999	If	1953-54	851001–854000	M3	1957
324001–324100	Reporter	1939	344001–348500	IIIb	1939-40	675000	IIf	1953	854001–858000	M3	1957
324101–324700	IIIa	1939	348501–348600	Standard	1939-40	675001–680000	IIf	1953-54	858001–861600	IIIg	1957
324701–324800	III	1939	348601–349000	IIIb	1940	680001–682000	If	1955	861601–862000	IIIg ELC	1957
324801–325000	II	1939	349001–349050	Reporter	1940	682001–684000	If	1955	MP-1-MP11	MP Chrom	1956
325001–325200	IIIa	1939	349051–349300	Standard	1940	684001–685000	IIIf ELC	1953	862001–866620	M3	1957
325201–325275	III	1939	349301–351100	IIIb	1940	685001–699999	IIIf Vorl	1954	866621–867000	M3 ELC	1957
325276–325300	IIIa	1939	351101–351150	II	1940	700000	M3	1954	867001–871200	IIIg	1957
325301–325400	I	1939	351151–352000	IIIb	1940				871201–872000	IIIg ELC	1957
325401–325600	IIIa	1939	352001–352100	III	1940				872001–877000	M3	1957
325601–325800	III	1939	352101–352150	II	1940				877001–882000	IIIg	1957
325801–325900	IIIa	1939	352151–352300	II	1940				882001–886700	M3	1957
325901–326000	II	1939	352301–352500	Reporter	1940-42				MP-13-MP150	MP Schw L.	1957
									MP-151-MP-450	MP Chrom	1957
									886701–887000	M3 ELC	1957
									887001–888000	Ig	1957
									888001–893000	IIIg	1957
									893001–894000	M3	1957

Leica No	Model	Year	Leica No.	Model	Year	Leica No.	Model	Year	Leica No.	Model	Year
894001-894570	M3 ELC	1957	971501-972000	IIIg	1959	1039001-1040000	M3	1961	1128001-1128400	MD	1965
894571-898000	M3	1957	972001-974700	M3	1959	1040001-1040066	M1	1962	1128401-1130000	M3	1965
898001-903000	M3	1957	974701-975000	M3 ELC	1959	1040067-1040068	M3	1962	1130001-1130300	M2 Lack	1965
903001-903300	M3 ELC	1957	975001-975800	M2	1959	1040069-1040070	M1	1961	1130301-1132900	M2	1965
903301-907000	IIIg	1957	975801-976100	M2 Vorl	1960	1040071	M3	1961	1132901-1133000	M2 ELC	1965
907001-910000	Ig	1957	976101-976500	M2	1959	1040072-1040094	M1	1961	1133001-1134000	M3	1965
910001-910500	M3	1957	976501-979500	M3	1959	1040095-1040096	M3	1962	1134001-1134150	M3 Lack	1965
910501-910600	M3 Olive L.	1957	979501-980450	M1	1959	1040097-1040600	M1	1961	1134151-1135000	M3	1965
910601-915000	M3	1957	980451-980500	M1 Olive L.	1960	1040601-1043000	M3	1961	1135001-1135100	M3 ELC	1965
915001-915200	M3	1957	980501-982000	IIIg	1959	1043001-1043800	M3	1961	1135101-1136000	MD	1965
915201-916000	M3	1957	982001-982150	M2 Vorl	1960	1043801-1044000	M2 Schw L.	1962	1136001-1136500	MD	1965
916001-919250	M3	1958	982151-982900	M2	1959	1044001-1046000	M3 Schw L.	1962	1136501-1137000	MD	1966
919251-920500	M3	1958	982901-983500	M2 Vorl	1959	1046001-1046500	M1	1962	1137001-1138900	M2 ELC	1966
920501-920520	M3	1958	983501-984000	M2	1959	1046501-1047800	M3	1962	1138901-1139000	M3	1966
920521-924400	M3	1958	984001-984200	M3 ELC	1959	1047801-1048000	M3 ELC	1962	1139001-1140900	M3	1966
924401-924500	M3 ELC	1958	984201-987000	M3	1960	1048001-1050000	M2	1962	1140901-1141000	M3 ELC	1966
924501-924568	Ig	1958	987001-987200	M3 ELC	1960	1050001-1050500	M1	1962	1141001-1141896	MD	1966
924569-924588	Ig	1958	987201-987300	M2 ELC	1960	1050501-1053100	M2	1962	1141897-1141968	Postk	1966
924589-926000	Ig	1958	987301-987600	Ig	1960	1053101-1053250	M2 Lack	1962	1141969-1142000	Postk 24x27	1966
926001-926200	M2	1957	987601-987900	IIIg	1960	1053251-1054900	M2	1962	1142001-1145000	M2	1966
926201-926700	Ig	1958	987901-988025	IIIg Schw L.	1960	1054901-1055000	M2 ELC	1962	1145001-1155000	L'flex	1966
926701-928922	M3	1959	988026-988350	IIIg	1960	1055001-1059849	M3	1962	1155001-1157590	M3	1966
928923-929000	Postk	1958	988351-988650	M2	1960	1059850-1059999	M3 Lack	1962	1157591-1157600	M3 Lack	1966
929001-931000	M2	1958	988651-989250	M2 Vorl	1960	1060000	M3	1962	1157601-1158995	M3	1966
931001-933000	M2	1958	989251-989650	M2 Vorl	1960	1060001-1060500	M1	1962	1159001-1160200	MDa	1966
933001-934000	IIIg	1958	989651-989800	M2	1960	1060501-1061700	M2	1962	1160201-1160820	MD	1966
934001-934200	IIIg ELC	1958	989801-990500	M2 Vorl	1960	1061701-1061800	M2 ELC	1962	1160821-1161420	MDa	1966
934201-935000	IIIg	1958	990501-990750	M2 Schw L.	1960	1061801-1063000	M2	1962	1161421-1163770	M2	1966
935001-935512	MP2	1958	990751-993500	M3	1960	1063001-1065000	M3	1962	1163771-1164046	M4 mot	1966
935513-937500	M2	1958	993501-993750	M3 Schw L.	1960	1065001-1065200	M3 ELC	1962	1164047-1164845	M2	1966
937501-937620	M2	1958	993751-995000	M2	1960	1065201-1067500	M3	1962	1164846-1164865	M3	1966
937621-937650	M2 ELC	1958	995001-995100	M2 ELC	1960	1067501-1067870	M1	1963	1164866-1164940	Postk 24x36	1967
937651-940000	M2	1958	995101-995400	M2 Vorl	1960	1067871-1068000	Postk	1963	1164941-1165000	M2	1967
940001-942900	M2	1958	995401-996000	M2	1960	1068001-1070000	M2	1963	1165001-1173000	L'flex	1967
942901-943000	M2 ELC	1958	996001-998000	M3	1960	1070001-1074000	M3	1963	1173001-1173250	L'flex SL	1968
943001-944000	IIIg	1958	998001-998300	M3 ELC	1960	1074001-1074500	M1	1963	1173251-1174700	L'flex	1968
944001-946000	M2	1958	998301-1000000	M3	1960	1074501-1077000	M2	1963	1174701-1175000	L'flex SL	1968
946001-946300	M2	1958	1000001-1003700	M3	1960	1077001-1080000	M3	1963	1175001-1178000	M4	1967
946301-946400	M2 ELC	1958	1003701-1004000	M3 ELC	1960	1080001-1085000	L'flex	1964-5	1178001-1178100	M4 ELC	1967
946401-946900	M2	1958	1004001-1005100	M2 VW	1960	1085001-1085450	M1	1963	1178101-1185000	M4	1967
946901-947000	M2 ELC	1958	1005101-1005350	M2 VW	1960	1085451-1085500	M1	1963	1185001-1185150	M4 mot	1968
947001-948000	M2	1958	1005351-1005450	M2 ELC	1960	1085501-1088000	M2	1963	1185151-1185290	M4 Lack	1968
948001-948500	IIIg	1958	1005451-1005750	M2	1960	1088001-1091000	M3	1963	1185291-1185300	Postk 24x27	1968
948501-948600	M2 ELC	1958	1005771-1007000	M2	1960	1091001-1091300	M1	1964	1185301-1195000	M4	1968-69
948601-949100	M2 Schw L.	1958	1007001-1011000	M3	1960	1093501-1093750	M2 Lack	1964	1195001-1205000	L'flex SL	1968
949101-949400	M2 Vorl	1958	1011001-1014000	M2	1960	1093751-1093800	M2 ELC	1964	1205001-1206736	MDa	1968-69
949401-950000	M2	1959	1014001-1014300	M3 ELC	1960	1093801-1097700	M3	1964	1206737-1206891	M4 mot	1969
950001-950300	M1	1959	1014301-1017000	M3	1960	1097701-1097850	M3 Lack	1964	1206892-1206941	Postk 24x36	1969
950301-951900	M3	1959	1017001-1017500	M1	1961	1097851-1098000	M3 ELC	1964	1206942-1206961	Postk 24x27	1969
951901-952000	M3 ELC	1959	1017501-1017900	M2	1961	1098001-1098100	M1	1964	1207000	M2 Lack	1968
952001-952015	MP2	1959	1017901-1018000	M2 ELC	1961	1098184-1098300	M1	1964	1207001-1207480	M4 Lack	1968-69
952016-952500	M1	1959	1018001-1020100	M2	1961	1098301-1099800	M2	1964	1207481-1215000	M4	1968-69
952501-954800	M3	1959	1020101-1020200	M2 ELC	1961	1099801-1099900	M2 ELC	1964	1215001-1225000	L'flex SL	1969
954801-954900	M3 ELC	1959	1020201-1022000	M2	1961	1099901-1100000	M3	1964	1225001-1225800	M4 Lack	1969
954901-955000	M3 ELC	1959	1022001-1022700	M3	1961	1100001-1102000	M3	1964	1225801-1235000	M4	1969
955001-956500	IIIg	1959	1022701-1023000	M3 ELC	1961	1102001-1102500	M1	1964	1235001-1245000	L'flex SL	1969-70
956501-957000	M1	1959	1023001-1027800	M3	1961	1102501-1102800	MD	1964	1245001-1246200	MDa	1969
957001-959400	M3	1959	1027801-1028000	M3 ELC	1961	1102801-1102900	M1	1964	1246201-1248100	M4 Lack	1969-70
959401-959500	M3 Schw L.	1959	1028001-1028600	M1	1961	1102901-1103000	M3	1965	1248101-1248200	M4 mot	1969
959501-960200	M2 Vorl	1959	1028601-1031800	M2	1961	1103001-1104900	M2	1965	1248201-1250200	M2R	1969-70
960201-960500	M2	1960	1031801-1032000	M2 Schw L.	1961	1104901-1105000	M2 ELC	1965	1250201-1254650	M4	1970
960501-961500	M2	1959	1032001-1035400	M3	1961	1105001-1106900	M3	1965	1254651-1255000	MDa	1970
961501-961700	M3 ELC	1959	1035401-1035925	M1	1961	1106901-1107000	M3 ELC	1965	1255001-1265000	L'flex SL	1970
961701-966500	M3	1959	1036001-1036050	M2 ELC	1961	1107001-1109000	M3	1965	1265001-1266000	MDa	1970
966501-967500	M1	1959	1036051-1036350	M3 ELC	1961	1109001-1110500	M3	1965	1266001-1266100	M4 Lack	1970-71
967501-968350	M2	1959	1036351-1037950	M2	1961	1110501-1112000	M3	1965	1266101-1266131	M4 Olive	1970
968351-968500	M3 ELC	1959	1037951-1038000	M2 ELC	1962	1112001-1114975	M2	1965	1266132-1267100	M4 Lack	1970
968501-970000	IIIg	1959	1038001-1038800	M3	1961	1114976-1115000	Postk	1965	1267101-1267500	M4 mot	1970
970001-971500	M2	1959	1038801-1039000	M3 Schw L.	1961	1115001-1128000	L'flex	1965	1267501-1273921	M4	1970-71
									1273922-1273925	Postk 24x27	1971

Leica No	Model	Year
1273926-1274000	Postk 24x36	1971
1274001-1274100	M4 mot	1971
1274101-1275000	MDa	1971
1275001-1285000	L'flex SL	1971
1285001-1286200	MDa	1971
1286201-1286700	M4 Lack	1971
1286701-1286760	Postk 24x27	1972
1286761-1287000	Unbel't	
1287001-1287050	M5 Null Series	1971
1287051-1287250	M5 Hell	1971
1287251-1288000	M5 Schwz	1971
1288001-1289000	M5 Hell	1971
1289001-1291400	M5 Schwz	1971-72
1291401-1293000	M5 Hell	1971-72
1293001-1293672	MDa	1971-72
1293673-1293770	MDa Blitzsp	1972
1293771-1293775	M4-KE7	1972
1293776-1293877	MDa Blitzsp	1972
1293878-1294000	Postk 24x27	1972
1294001-1294500	M5 Hell	1972
1294501-1295000	M4-KE7	1972
1295001-1296500	L'flex SL	1972
1296501-1300000	M5 Schwz	1972
1300001-1335000	CL	1973-74
1335001-1336990	L'flex SL	1972
1336991-1337110	L'flex SL mot	1972
1337111-1338220	L'flex SL	1972
1338221-1338300	L'flex SL	1972
1338301-1339870	L'flex SL	1972
1339871-1339900	L'flex SL mot	1972
1339901-1341450	L'flex SL	1972
1341451-1341470	L'flex SL mot	1972
1341471-1342020	L'flex SL	1973
1342021-1342050	L'flex SL mot	1973
1342051-1342900	L'flex SL	1973
1342901-1343000	L'flex SL mot	1973
1343001-1344400	L'flex SL	
1344401-1344500	L'flex SL	1972
1344501-1345000	L'flex SL	1973
1345001-1347000	M5 Hell	1972
1347001-1354000	M5 Schwz	1972
1354001-1355000	M5 Hell	1972
1355001-1356500	M5 Hell	1973
1356501-1360000	M5 Schwz	1973
1360001-1361500	MDa	1973-74
1361501-1363000	M5 Hell	1973-74
1363001-1365000	M5 Schwz	1973
1365001-1365380	L'flex SL	1973
1365381-1365470	L'flex SL mot	1973
1365471-1366990	L'flex SL	1973
1366991-1367090	L'flex SL mot	1973
1367091-1367950	L'flex SL	1973
1367951-1368020	L'flex SL mot	1973
1368021-1368850	L'flex SL	1973
1368851-1368900	L'flex SL mot	1973
1368901-1369800	L'flex SL	1973
1369801-1369875	L'flex SL2 Null Series	1974
1369876-1370700	L'flex SL	1973
1370701-1372440	L'flex SL	1974
1372441-1372630	L'flex SL mot	1974
1372631-1374000	L'flex SL	1974
1374001-1375000	L'flex SL	1974
1375001-1378000	M5 Schwz	1973-74
1378001-1379000	M5 Hell	1973-74
1379001-1380000	MDa	1974
1380001-1381650	M4 Schwz	1974
1381651-1382600	M4 Schwz ELC-Gravur	1974

Leica No.	Model	Year
1382601-1383000	M5 Hell	1974-75
1383001-1384000	M5 Schwz	1974-75
1384001-1384600	M4 Schwz	1974
1384601-1385000	MDa	1974-75
1385001-1386000	L'flex SL2	1974-75
1386001-1386100	L'flex SL2	1975
1386101-1386600	L'flex SL2	1974-75
1386601-1386700	L'flex SL2 mot	1975
1386701-1387450	L'flex SL2	1974-75
1387451-1387500	L'flex SL2	1975
1387501-1391760	L'flex SL2	1974-75
1391761-1392000	L'flex SL2 mot	1975
1392001-1393420	L'flex SL2	1975
1393421-1393510	L'flex SL2 mot	1975
1393511-1394300	L'flex SL2	1975
1394301-1394600	L'flex SL2 mot	1975
1394601-1395000	L'flex SL2	1975
1395001-1410000	CL	1974-75
1410001-1412550	MDa	1975-76
1412551-1413350	M4 Schwz ELC-Gravur	1975
1413351-1415000	M4 Schwz	1975
1415001-1415140	L'flex SL2	1975
1415141-1415230	L'flex SL2 mot	1975
1415231-1421000	L'flex SL2	1975
1421001-1421150	L'flex SL2 mot	1975
1421151-1425000	L'flex SL2	1975
1425001-1440000	CL	1975-76
1440001-1443000	L'flex SL2	1975-76
1443001-1443170	M4 Schwz	1975
1443501-1446000	L'flex SL2	1976
1446001-1446100	R3 Hell LW	1976
1446101-1447100	R3 Hell LP	1976
1447101-1449000	R3 Schwz LP	1976-77
1449001-1450500	R3 Schwz LW	1976
1450501-1450900	R3 Hell LW	1977
1450901-1468000	R3 Schwz	1977-78
1468001-1468100	M4-2 LP	1977-78
1468101-1470000	R3 Olive LP	1977-78
1470001-1479000	R3 Schwz LP	1977-78
1479001-1480000	R3 Hell LP	1978
1480001-1482000	M4-2	1978
1482001-1485000	R3 Olive LP	1978
1485001-1491000	R3 Schwz LP	1978
1491001-1492250	R3 Hell LP	1978
1492251-1502000	R3 MOT LP	1978
1502001-1508000	M4-2	1978-79
1508001-1523750	R3 MOT LP	1979
1523751-1523850	R3 Schwz LP	1979
1523851-1524850	R3 Gold LP	1979
1524851-1525350	R3 Hell LP	1979
1525351-1527200	M4-2	1979
1527201-1527700	M4-2 Gold	1979-80
1527701-1528150	M4-2	1980
1528151-1528650	M4-2 Gold	1980
1528651-1533350	M4-2	1980
1533351-1543350	R4 Schwz	1980-81
1543351-1545350	R4 Hell	1980-81
1545351-1546350	MD-2	1980-81
1546351-1552350	M4-P	1981
1552351-1562350	R4 Schwz	1981
1562351-1564350	M4-P	1982
1564351-1574350	R4 Schwz	1981-82
1574351-1576350	R4 Hell	1982
1576351-1586350	R4 Schwz	1982
1586351-1590350	M4-P	1982
1590351-1590550	R4 Schwz	1982

Leica No.	Model	Year
1590551-1592550	R4 Hell	1982
1592551-1602550	R4 Schwz	1982
1602551-1604550	R4 Hell	1982
1604551-1606550	M4-P	1982-83
1606551-1616550	R4 Schwz	1983
1616551-1618550	R4 Hell	1983
1618551-1620550	M4-P Hell	1983
1620551-1622550	M4-P	1983-84
1622551-1632550	R4 Schwz	1983
1632551-1636550	R4s	1983
1636551-1637550	M4-P Hell	1983
1637551-1642550	R4s	1983
1642551-1643750	M4-P	1984
1643751-1648750	R4s	1984
1648751-1649250	MD-2	1985
1649251-1651250	M4-P	1984-85
1651251-1652250	R4 Gold	1984-85
1652251-1657250	R4s	1984-85
1657251-1659250	M6	1984-85
1659251-1664250	R4 Schwz	1984-85
1664251-1664350	MD-2	1984-85
1664351-1665350	R4 Hell	1984-85
1665351-1669350	M6	1985
1669351-1674350	R4	1985-86
1674351-1678350	M6	1985
1678351-1682350	M6	1985
1682351-1682950	M6 Hell	1986
1682951-1687950	R4s-2	1985-86
1687951-1691950	M6	1986
1691951-1692950	M4-P LW inc. 270 M6	1986
1692951-1694950	R4s	1986
1694951-1696450	R4 Schwz	1986
1696451-1701450	R5 Schwz	1986
1701451-1704600	M6	1986
1704601-1704800	MD-2	1986
1704801-1705450	M6	1986
1705451-1707450	M6 Hell	1986
1707451-1711450	M6 Schwz	1986
1711451-1714450	M6 Hell	1987
1714451-1719450	M6 Schwz	1987
1719451-1720450	R5 Hell	1987
1720451-1724450	R5 Schwz	1987
1724451-1728450	M6 Schwz	1987
1728451-1732450	R5 Hell	1987
1732451-1733450	R5 Hell	1987
1733451-1738450	M6 Schwz	1988
1738451-1741450	M6 Hell	1988
1741451-1745450	M6 Schwz	1988
1745451-1755450	R6 Schwz	1988
1755451-1758450	M6 Hell	1988
1758451-1762450	M6 Schwz	1988
1762451-1765750	R5 Schwz	1988
1765751-176800	R6 Hell	1988
1768001-1770220	R5 Schwz	1989
1770221-1770485	R5 Schwz	1989
1770486-1772500	R5 & R6 Hell	1989
1772501-1775000	M6 Hell	1989
1775001-1777000	R5 & R6 Hell	1990
1777001-1777500	M6 Hell	1990
1777501-1779000	R6 & R-E Schwz	1990
1779001-1782000	M6 Schwz	1990
1782001-1783000	R5, R6, R-E	1990
1783001-1786000	M6 Schwz	1990
1786001-1788000	R5, R-E Schwz	1990
1788001-1790000	R5, R-E Schwz	1991

Leica No.	Model	Year
1790001-1790500	M6 Hell	1991
1790501-1791000	M6 Hell	1991
1791001-1793000	R5, R-E Schwz	1991
1793001-1794500	M6 Hell	1991
1794501-1797000	M6 Schwz	1991
1797001-1799000	R5, R-E Schwz	1991
1799001-1800000	R5, R-E Schwz	1991
1800001-1850000	Leica Mini	1991
1850001-1900000	Leica Mini II	1993
1900001-1903500	R-E, R6.2 Schwz	1991
1903501-1904500	M6 Hell	1991
1904501-1906500	M6 SW	1991
1906501-1907500	M6 Hell	1991
1907501-1908500	R-E, R6.2 Schwz	1991
1908501-1912000	R7 SW	1991
1912001-1914000	R6.2 Schwz	1991
1914001-1915000	M6 Hell	1992
1915001-1918000	M6 SW	1992
1918001-1918020	M5 Hell	1992
1918021-1919020	M6 Hell	1992
1919021-1920000	R7 Hell	1992
1920001-1923000	R7 SW	1992
1923001-1924000	R6.2 Hell	1992
1924001-1926000	R7 Hell	1992
1926001-1928000	M6 Hell	1992
1928001-1931000	M6 Hell	1992
1931001-1932000	M6 Hell	1992
1932001-1932002	M4.2 Gold	1993
1932003-1933000	R6.2 Hell	1993
1933001-1934000	R7 SW	1993
1934001-1935000	R7 SW	1993
1935001-1936000	M6 Hell	1993
1936001-1937000	M6 Hell	1993
1937001-1937999	R6.2 SW	1993
1938000-1938750	M6	1993
1938151-1940000	R7 SW	1993
1940001-1941000	R7 SW	1993
1941001-1991000	Mini Zoom	1993
1991001-1993000	M6 Hell	1993
1993001-1995000	R6.2 SW	1993
1995001-1997000	M6 SW	1993
1997001-1998000	R6.2 Hell	1993
1998001-1999000	R7 SW	1993
1999001-1999998	R7 Hell	1994
2000000	R7 for WWF	1994
2000011-2000999	M6 Hell	1994
2001000-2001353	M6	
2001354-2001999	M6 Hell	1994
2002000-2002100	M6	
2002101-2003000	M6 Hell	1994
2003001-2004000	M6 SW	1994
2004001-2005000	M6 Hell	1994
2005001-2005941	M6 Hell	1994
2005942-2007000	M6 SW	1994
2007001-2008000	M6.2 Hell	1994
2008001-2009000	R7 Hell	1994
2009001-2011000	M6 Hell	1994
2011001-2013000	R7 SW	1994
2013001-2063000	Mini Zoom	1994
2063001-2065000	M6 SW	1995
2065001-2066000	R7 Hell	1995
2066001-2166000	Minilux	1995
2166001-2167000	R7 SW	1995
2167001-2168000	R6.2 Hell	1995

Leica camera serial numbers

Leica No.	Model	Year
2168001–2170000	M6 Hell	1995
2170001–2170500	R6.2 SW	1995
2170501–2171000	R6.2 Hell	1995
2171001–2171200	R7	1995
2171201–2173000	M6 SW	1995
2173001–2174000	R7 SW	1995
2174001–2176000	M6 Hell	1995
2176001–2176700	M6	1995
2176701–2177000	R6.2 SW	1995
2177001–2177250	M6	1995
2177251–2177750	R7 SW	1995
2177757–2178000	R6.2 SW	1995
2178001–2179000	R6.2 Hell	1995
2179001–2181000	M6 SW	1995
2181001–2181575	R7 SW	1995
2181576–2182000	R7 SW	1995
2182001–2183000	R7 SW	1995
2183001–2184000	R7 SW	1995
2184001–2185000	M6 Hell	1995
2185001–2235000	Mini Zoom	1995
2235001–2236000	M6 Hell	1995
2236001–2236500	R6.2 SW	1996
2236501–2237500	R7 Hell	1996
2237501–2238500	R6.2 SW	1996
2238501–2239000	R7 SW	1996
2239001–2240000	M6 SW	1996
2240001–2241000	R7 SW	1996
2241001–2265000	Mini 3	1996
2265001–2277000	Mini 3 DB	1996
2277001–2278000	R6.2 SW	1996
2278001–2278211	M6	1996
2278301–2278588	M6	1996
2279001–2280500	M6 SW	1996
2280501–2281000	R6.2 SW	1996
2281001–2281400	M6	1996
2281401–2282400	R7 SW	1996
2283001–2283125	M6	1996
2283201–2283325	M6	1996
2283401–2283525	M6	1996
2283601–2283625	M6	1996
2283626–2284125	R6.2 SW	1996
2284126–2284999	M6 SW	1996
2285000	R8	1996
2285001–2286000	R8	1996
2286001–2287500	S1 (Scanners)	1996
2287501–2288500	M6 Hell	1996
2288501–2289500	M6 SW	1996
2289501–2290500	M6 Hell	1996
2290501–2291500	R8	1996
2291501–2293500	R8	1996
2293501–2295000	R8	1997
2295001–2297000	M6 SW	1997
2297001–2299000	R8	1997
2300000	M6 for Museum	1997
2300001–2300996	M6	1997
2301001–2321000	Mini 3	1997
2321001–2331000	Mini 3 DB	1997
2331001–2332000	M6 Hell	1997
2332001–2382000	Z2X	1997
2382001–2412000	Z2X Data Back	1997
2412001–2414000	R8	1997
2414001–2416000	M6 SW	1997
2416001–2418000	R8	1997
2418001–2419000	M6 Hell	1997
2419001–2420000	M6 Hell	1997
2420001–2422000	R8	1997
2422001–2423000	M6 Hell	1997
2423001–2425000	M6 SW	1997
2425001–2427000	M6 Hell	1997
2427001–2429000	R8	1997
2429001–2429500	R6.2 Hell	1997
2429501–2431500	R8	1997
2431501–2431600	M6 Hell	1998
2431601–2431800	M6 SW	1998
2431801–2433800	M6 SW	1998
2433801–2435800	R8	1998
2435801–2455800	Minilux Zoom	1998
2455801–2457800	M6 SW	1998
2457801–2463800	Digilux	1998
2463801–2463850	M6 SW	1998
2463851–2464100	M6 SW	1998
2464101–2466100	R8	1998
2466101–2470100	M6 TTL	1998
2470101–2470300	M6 SW	1998
2470301–2475300	M6 TTL	1998
2475301–2477300	R8	1998
2477301–2482300	M6 TTL	1999
2482301–2482800	R6.2 Hell	1999
2482801–2487800	Z2X DB	1999
2490000–2490150	M6 150j Optik	1999
2490157–2495150	Z2X DB	1999
2495151–2499999	M6 TTL	1999
2500000	M6 TTL	
	Vaclav Havel	1999
2500001–2502000	M6 Schwz L.	1999
2502001–2517000	Z2X DB	1999
2517001–2527000	Z2X	1999
2527001–2547000	Digilux Zoom	1999
2547001–2552000	M6 TTL	1999
2552001–2552500	R6.2 Hell	1999
2552501–2554500	R8	1999
2554501–2554650	M6 TTL 0.85	2000
2555001–2555200	M6 TTL	1999
2555201–2555300	M6 TTL	2000
2556001–2571000	C1	1999
2571001–2581000	Z2X DB	1999
2581001–2591000	Z2X	1999
2591001–2591500	R6.2 Hell	1999
2591501–2596500	M6 TTL	1999
2596501–2626500	Digilux 4.3	2000
2626501–2676500	C11	2000
2676501–2680500	O Series	2000
2680501–2680900	NSH	2000
2681201–2681400	M6 TTL	2000
2681401–2683400	M6 TTL	2000
2688001–2688500	M6 TTL 0.85	2000
2688501–2688500	M6 TTL 0.85	2000
2688501–2688500	M6 TTL 0.85	2000
2688501–2703800	Z2X	2000
2703501–2704300	R6.2 Hell	2000
2704301–2705300	Digilux 4.3	2000

Key

Abbreviation	Meaning
Blitzsp	Motorised MDa
ELC	E. Leitz, Canada
Hell	Silver-chrome
Kältef	Winterised
Lack	Paint
LP	Leitz Portugal
LW	Leitz Wetzlar
Null Series	Pre-Production Model
Post	Post Camera
Schwz	Black-chrome
Schw L.	Black Paint
St	Standard
Unbel't	Not Issued
Vorl or VW	Delayed Action

Spaces in 'M' Camera list relate to Military Camera Production

Note: It is not possible in a summary list such as this to list all the variations within batches. For example, cases are known where one or two cameras of a particular model may bear a serial number allocated to a batch of cameras of a different model. These are not later conversions, but probably represent a special order. For fuller information on screw cameras readers are referred to the Leica Historica publication listed in the Bibliography. Readers will also note that batches of numbers, sometimes just a few, sometimes a lot, are missing from the later lists. These are not transcribing errors, they are missing from the lists supplied by the Leica company.

Leica lens serial numbers up to 2000

This information reproduced by the kind permission of Leica Camera AG

Year	Leica No.
1933	156001–195000
1934	195001–236000
1935	236001–284600
1936	284601–345000
1937	345001–416500
1938	416501–490000
1939	490001–538500
1940	538501–565000
1941	565001–582250
1942	582295–593000
1943	593001–594880
1944	594881–595000
1945	595001–601000
1946	601001–633000
1947	633001–647000
1948	647001–682000
1949	682001–756000
1950	756001–840000
1951	840001–950000
1952	950001–1051000
1953	1051001–1124000
1954	1124001–1236000
1955	1236001–1333000
1956	1333001–1459000
1957	1459001–1548000
1958	1548001–1645300
1959	1645301–1717000
1960	1717001–1827000
1961	1827001–1913000
1962	1913001–1967100
1963	1967101–2015700
1964	2015701–2077500
1965	2077501–2156300
1966	2156301–2236500
1967	2236501–2254400
1968	2254401–2312750
1969	2312751–2384700
1970	2384701–2468500
1971	2468501–2503100
1972	2503101–2556500
1973	2556501–2663400
1974	2663401–2731900
1975	2731901–2761100
1976	2761101–2809400
1977	2809401–2880600
1978	2880601–2967200
1979	2967201–3013600
1980	3013601–3087000
1981	3087001–3160500
1982	3160501–3249100
1983	3249101–3249900
1984	3294901–3346200
1985	3346201–3383200
1986	3383201–3422890
1987	3422891–3455870
1988	3455871–3481900
1989	3481901–3503150
1990	3503151–3540467
1991	3540468–3583830
1992	3583831–3610679
1993	3610680–3644475
1994	3644476–3677030
1995	3677031–3730290
1996	3730291–3770920
1997	3770930–3818624
1998	3818625–3857849
1999	3857850–3882996
2000	3882997

Repair and Restoration

A working example of a classic camera in good cosmetic condition is always going to be more valuable than a tatty, non-working model. That much is obvious. Equally obvious is the fact that if you are content to own a poor-class example of a camera, you will be able to pick it up at a lower cost than you would have to pay for a better example. Some collectors are happy to do this just to own a particular model that they couldn't readily afford in the normal way.

But what if you could buy the camera in poor condition and renovate it to its former glory, making it more appealing to the eye whilst adding to its value at the same time? That's the reason why many collectors learn the art of repair and restoration.

Restoring an old camera is not a job to be taken lightly. You need a certain dexterity if you are not going to make its condition worse than when you started.

Also, it's worth considering the fact that it is possible to over-restore a camera, so that its condition looks totally false for its age. That could degrade its value as much as under restoring might. Sometimes, the appeal of an older camera lies in the fact that it has seen some use. This is especially true of older wood and brass cameras which, over the years, have developed a patina, in the way of old furniture, that is a major part of their appeal. Restore them to the way they were when new and they will no longer look authentic.

Having accepted that, here are a few pointers towards carrying out your own repair and restoration projects.

Restoring leather

Rather than using standard cleaning materials, you need one specially designed for old leatherwork, and

Renovation of a camera, if handled well, can add to its value and appeal.

although no such cleaner is made specifically for cameras, it is possible to use one designed for the restoration of old book bindings. One such is a product called Fortificuir, which is ideal for reviving old leather. At the time of writing, it can be obtained from Alfred Maltby & Sons, 28-30 St. Michael's Street, Oxford OX1 2EB. Call them first on 01865 213113.

Failing that, shoe polish can be used, providing you use the right type and apply it correctly. The leather on old cameras very often loses its sheen, and if you apply standard shoe polish, it simply seeps into the pores of the leather, which will remain dull. A better bet is to use the kind of shoe polish designed, not so much to clean shoes as to restore scuff marks, particularly on children's shoes. Ask your local shoe shop for a restoring or an anti-scuff polish. Then use it sparingly. Dab it on lightly a little at a time, and polish it off with a cloth or tissue almost immediately.

Removing old leather

Leather on older cameras was usually attached to the metal beneath with shellac. To remove it without damage, carefully lift an edge and run a small brush loaded with methylated spirits across the line where the leather is attached to the metal. As the methylated spirit softens the shellac, gently peel the leather back and apply more methylated spirits as fresh shellac is revealed. Continue until all the leather has been removed.

Replacing leather

The first task is to find a source for suitable leather, and you can often find that at flea markets and in secondhand shops. Look for old leather handbags, gloves, diaries and the like that are made of, or covered in, leather that has a similar grain to that on the camera you are restoring. Or, if you are starting from scratch, choose a grain that won't look out of place on the camera.

Start by cutting the leather to the required shape. If you have managed to take the old leather off in one piece, you can use this as a template. Otherwise, try making a template out of paper first, get that to fit correctly, then use it to cut out your pattern. Leather can be cut with a sharp scalpel, obtainable from a modelling shop. Use a steel ruler to cut straight edges and work on a cutting board, obtainable from good artists' supply shops. And take care – one slice of a sharp scalpel and you could loose a finger!

Sometimes the leatherwork on a camera body has an embossed line that matches a groove in the metal or wood beneath. To match that, start by cutting the leather a little oversize, then soak it in water. When it is completely limp, place it over the bare area of the camera body and run a tool over the leather, digging it gently into the groove beneath. When the line has been clearly marked, allow the leather to dry naturally at room temperature before gluing into position.

To attach the leather to the body, use a glue such as Evostick, coating it on the leather side only and applying whilst the glue is still wet. You will find this should hold firmly, but will still peel back if necessary.

Stiffening bellows

Old and sagging bellows can be given a new lease of life by first of all opening them and propping them up with pieces of cardboard to keep them in their correct position. Next, using a paintbrush, apply a five per cent solution of Unibond in water to the inside surface of the bellows and, when complete, use a hair dryer to dry it. Make sure that the folds do not touch each other while the bellows are still wet.

Cleaning shutters

With a little care, shutters such as those made by Compur and Prontor can be cleaned and slow speed mechanisms persuaded to work again if you go about things in the right way. Most importantly, never be tempted to oil them with household lubricants. Instead, start by removing the shutter from the camera and carefully dismantling it to strip out any glass elements associated with lenses that are often embedded into the shutter housing. A set of jewellers screwdrivers will be found useful for the purpose.

With the glass removed, place the shutter in a de-greasing solvent, which you can buy in a motoring accessories shop. This will remove grease without leaving any residue. Remove it and allow to dry naturally.

When the mechanism is completely dry, place it in a capped jar containing a small amount of finely powdered graphite, which you can make yourself by shaving off the lead from a hard pencil. Shake the jar carefully then remove the shutter and blow off the loose graphite powder.

Then reassemble the shutter, putting back the glass elements and re-attach it to the camera. Keep the jar of graphite powder for future use.

Cleaning old brass

If old brasswork on a camera has developed a patina with age, then it should be left as it is. This is a good example of the way a camera can be 'over restored' to a point where it no longer looks natural.

Black marks on the brass can be lightly buffed with very fine emery paper, making sure to move it in one direction only, then the brass polished with metal or brass cleaner.

Removing the lacquer from brass is not particularly recommended, because it is not easy to replace. Some collectors have been known to use model maker's varnish for the purpose, but the final effect isn't to everyone's taste. If you want to try it, experimentation on an unimportant piece of brass is advised. If you do decide to take this route, old lacquer can be removed by soaking the fittings overnight in a solution of washing soda. Verdigris can be removed with vinegar.

Renovating wooden cameras

The body of wooden camera can be carefully sponged with water containing a few drops of liquid ammonia to remove dirt. Holes and cracks can be filled with plastic wood, which should be left for a few days to harden. Once dry and hard, any surplus can be removed with fine glasspaper, then stained with water-colour paints to match the rest of the body. Finish the job by polishing the repaired area with red shoe polish.

Making ground-glass

Valve grinding paste from motoring accessory shops or engineering companies is useful for grinding plain glass and turning it into ground-glass to replace missing or broken focusing screens. Apply it with fine wire wool, rubbing lightly to get the best effect, continually washing and checking until the opacity of the glass is right.

The problem of finding the right kind of glass to begin with is easily solved by using photographic plates, very often found in junk boxes at camera fairs. Not only is the glass used in photographic plates thin and perfectly flat, it is also cut to precisely the right size, depending on the format of the plate and the camera it is made for. The emulsion can be removed from the plate by dissolving it in hypo or any standard black and white darkroom fixer, before washing and allowing it to dry naturally. When you have finished, you will have a matt or slightly rough side to the glass where you have been grinding it, backed by the untouched glossy side. The screen goes into the camera with the rough side towards the lens.

Black enamelling

Where the black enamel wears away from the base metal of a camera body, it can be replaced with care, using enamel paint from a model shop. The overall effect, however, can sometimes look too glossy, so it's worth experimenting with mixing matt and glossy paints together in various ratios to get exactly the right look. Practising on an old piece of metal is important before committing yourself to the actual camera.

To apply the enamel to small areas, use a suitably-sized paintbrush and allow the enamel to flow from its tip onto the surface. It is possible to develop a technique in which the enamel is allowed to flow off the end of the brush without its hairs actually making physical contact with the camera itself. The important thing is to apply the enamel in one direction only. Never return to the same area and paint over it as this will lead to brush marks.

If it's possible to remove a top plate, base plate or any other part of as body completely from the camera, then paint can be sprayed onto the surface, using a car paint spray can. Several coats might be needed, allowing each to dry before the next is applied.

Internet Collecting

In the three years since the last edition of the Hove International Blue Book was published, the Internet has become part of everyday life for many people. And with the rise of the internet, camera collecting has, for many, become a high-tech business, whether the web is used for general information, for buying or selling equipment.

The website for Hove Books, publishers of the Hove International Blue Book, is a good example of what you can see and find on the internet. Go to www.hovebooks.com and you find a list of the vast range of books published by Hove for camera collectors, together with details about the company and how to find them, plus an order form that can be printed out, filled in and posted to receive any book in the range.

For those not yet online, the mere thought of using the Internet seems like magic, not to mention expensive and just a little daunting. But the truth is that once you have even the least expensive computer hooked up to the world wide web, you can find your way around with comparative ease, and you'll soon be using your computer for buying, selling and researching much of what you need to know about your collection.

E-bay is probably the most famous auction site world-wide, and can always be relied on to have has a good selection of collectable cameras on offer.

Data gathering

For many, the internet has become indispensable for research purposes. Collectors who once had to seek out books on their chosen subject (often unsuccessfully), buy or borrow them and then work their way laboriously through pages of text just to find one small piece of elusive information, can now find almost any data they require with little more than a few clicks of their computer mouse.

If you know the address of the website you require, it's simply a matter of keying that address into the appropriate box in your chosen web browser – of which Microsoft's Internet Explorer is the most commonly used – then sitting back and waiting for the information to appear on your computer screen.

If you don't have the address, then that presents no problem, because you will actually get more information by using a search engine. There are many of these to choose from. Logging onto any of them, allows you to enter a subject in the appropriate box and to then ask the software to search for any website that contains reference to your chosen subject.

Examples of search engines used for this purpose include:

Yahoo (**www.yahoo.co.uk**),
Lycos (**www.lycos.co.uk**),
Google (**www.google.com**)
Ask Jeeves (**www.ask.co.uk**).

At the time of writing, going to the Google site and specifying 'camera collecting' as the subject to search for,

Internet dealers like MW Classic Cameras, based in the UK, offer a wide range of collectable cameras at realistic prices.

provided no less than 86 pages, each of which contained an average of 12 suggested sites. When you also consider that many of those sites also had links to several other sites, you soon see just how much potential there is in this way of working. By the time you read this, there will undoubtedly be even more sites up and running.

One thing to beware of, however, is just how accurate the information being dispensed really is. Many sites to which you turn are official ones, set up by recognised companies and corporations. Information obtained from such areas should be reliable.

Then there are sites put together by people who are true experts in their own fields and, once again, you should be able to rely to a great extent on what they say.

But there are also sites that have been launched by people who are pure amateurs, wanting little more than to see their names on the web with a few details of their collections. Their intentions are honourable enough, but you should be wary of information from such sites that is stated blandly without any real back-up. At the end of the day, the best bet is to try to get two or more independent and different sources that agree on the data they are putting out.

Buying and selling

In the past few years, the Internet has become the in place for buying and selling all kinds of goods – and collectable cameras are no exception.
Call up the website of a recognised camera dealer and you will see lists of current stocks, with descriptions and prices. On certain types of equipment, some dealers even operate a service whereby you can request a picture of the piece of equipment you wish to buy and this will be e-mailed to you as a digital image.

Once you have chosen what you want, you can either call the dealer by telephone and buy by mail order in the traditional way, or you can buy on-line by keying in your credit card number, along with the address for delivery directly onto the site.

Some sites are also run by independent collectors offering goods for sale, but it goes without saying that you need to check things out thoroughly before you start sending cheques or quoting credit card numbers to total strangers who don't have the security of a recognised company or organisation behind them.

Auctions

The internet auction has lately become one of the most popular ways of buying and selling collectable cameras. The best site is probably ebay (**www.ebay.co.uk** for UK sales and **www.ebay.com** for American sales).
Selling is simple. You first have to register, by following simple online instructions. You can then place equipment on the site, together with a digital picture if you wish. You can also fix a reserve price, below which the equipment will not be sold should the bids not reach that amount.

Buying is equally simple. Once registered, you simply look through the lists and, if there is something you wish to buy, you place your bid on screen, along with a security id and password, previously agreed when you registered.

Each item is placed on the site for a specified number of days and, as it gets close to the finishing time, bidding is usually seen to get brisk. The winner is the person who has placed the highest bid at the time the auction finishes, the final price being ascertained as a small percentage above the next highest bid below yours, rather than the actual amount you have entered as your highest bid.

Once the auction has finished, ebay takes a percentage of the sale from the seller, but unlike traditional auctions where a buyer's premium is usually levied, the buyer is charged nothing extra. The buyer and seller are then automatically put in touch with each other by e-mail and it is up them to decide how the cash will be paid and how the goods will be transported.

Useful web pages

The list which follows can in no way be considered a definitive one for all the websites of interest to camera collectors. But it will provide a good starting point for discovering information on many types of cameras, their specifications, values and where you might be able to buy them.

This is the first time such a list has been published in the Hove International Blue Book, and it is a list that will grow with future editions. Readers who have come across useful websites not mentioned here are welcome to send details for consideration in the next edition.

www.xs4all.nl/~wichm/cinemat.html: A lot of very useful information, lists, reviews and pictures for collectors of vintage movie cameras and projectors.

www.acecam.com/britain1.html: Index of UK camera shops where collectable cameras can be purchased.

www.alpareflex.com/Links.htm: A directory of various interesting cameras.

www.amazon.com: The renowned internet bookseller with a major section on collectable cameras.

www.andrewscameras.co.uk: English photo dealer that has specialised in collectable cameras for over 30 years.

www.atozee.com/web/antiques/cameras.shtml: Official website of the Nikon Historical Society.

www.canon.com/camera-museum: detailing a lot of information about early Canon cameras.

www.christies.com: Details of the auctions of vintage and collectable cameras held regularly by the world's leading auction house for this subject.

www.classic-cameras.com: The place to find the best books on camera collecting.

www.cookeoptics.com: A history of Cooke lenses.

www.cosmonet.org/camera/index_e.html: Information on more than 100 classic cameras, including Voigtländer Prominent, Bessa and Perkeo, as well as many less well known models.

www.craigcamera.com/lit_coll.htm: A guide to late 19th and early 20th Century box, plate and folding cameras.

www.ebay.co.uk: Auction site where you can sell and bid for collectable cameras.

www.exakta.org/internet.html: Interesting information for Exakta collectors.

www.hovebooks.com: Details of all books published by Britain's biggest publisher of books on collectable cameras, including the Hove International Blue Book.

www.kjsl.com/mailman/listinfo/idcc: A site where you can ask questions and post your own information about collecting.

www.krphoto.com: General inform- ation for classic camera collectors.

www.krphoto.com: General information on camera collecting, but with emphasis on Polaroid.

www.mclassic.com: Dealers in collectable cameras, specialists in mail order and internet sales.

www.members.optusnet.com.au/~msafier/cameraholics: The website of the Brisbane Cameraholics, an Australian based group of collectors.

www.members.tripod.com/Nigel_Richards: Personal look at Victorian images, tintypes, ambrotypes and daguerreotypes as well as subminiature cameras and Kodaks.

www.mirandacamera.com: History and descriptions of this camera company's products.

www.movie-camera.com: History, pictures and descriptions of antique movie cameras.

www.netcontax.com/progress.asp: The place to ask questions about equipment made by Zeiss Ikon.

www.oldtimercameras.co.uk: The place to purchase back copies of articles, news items and instructions books on just about any collectable camera you can think of.

www.pccgb.org: The official website of the Photographic Collectors Club of Great Britain.

www.people.clarityconnect.com/webpages/wilensky/camera.html: A personal look at 35mm camera collecting with links to other sites.

www.peterlanczak.de/ihagee.htm: Detailing the history, patents, and products of the Ihagee company.

www.photobooksonline.com/books/camcoll.html: One place to order collectors' books.

www.r-cube.co.uk/fox-talbot: The official website of the Fox Talbot museum at Laycock in Wiltshire.

www.rit.edu/~andpph/text-ansco.html: Rare look at the laboratory of Ansco, the film maker from the viewpoint of an ex-employee.

www.sedelmeier.com/camera.htm: Details of books on repair and maintenance of collectable cameras.

www.theclassiccamera.com: London-based dealer that specialises in Leica, new and collectable.

www.trenholm.org/hmmerk/HMbook15.html: Photographs and brief descriptions of some unusual cameras.

www.usinternet.com/users/rniederman/cameras.htm: Pictures, descriptions and histories of a vast range of wood and brass cameras made before 1900.

www.usinternet.com/users/rniederman/links.htm: A very useful site that gives direct links to numerous other sites whose subjects include:

- American dry-plate field cameras
- Cameras in the George Eastman House Collection – rare and beautiful cameras photographed and on display
- Rarely seen coloured Kodak cameras
- A history of Ensign cameras
- The history of Deardorff cameras
- Historical background and adverts for rare box cameras
- A history of Kodak cameras
- Photographic clubs and societies around the world
- Photographic museums

www.wctatel.net/web/crye/res-ref.htm: A useful list of camera directories, including the Hove International Blue Book.

www.well.com/user/silver/idccinfo.html: A site where you are invited to join the Internet Directory of Camera Collectors, with your name, contact details and particular interests.

www.well.com/user/silver: Details of the evolution of the camera.

www.westval.com/brownie: The website of the President of the Southern California Brownie Camera Collectors club.

Landmark Cameras

Down through the ages, there have been certain cameras that set trends, landmark cameras that represented the first of a new breed whose design concept would last and influence other cameras for sometimes as much as half a century. Being landmarks, such cameras are eminently collectable and worth seeking out. Here's a guide to what to look for.

1839: The Daguerreotype camera

This was the world's first commercially successful camera, invented and designed by Louis Jacque Mandé Daguerre. It was built by Alphonse Giroux, and measured around 20" x 15" x 12", taking $8^{1}/_{2}$" x $6^{1}/_{2}$" plates, the size which later became known as whole plate.

The lens had an aperture of approximately f/15, a focal length of eight inches and exposure was controlled by a metal cap that slid aside for the appropriate length of time, before being slid back again. The image was focused on a ground glass screen at the back of the body, to which a mirror was attached at 45° to correct the upside down view as the photographer looked down into it.

Images produced by this and other daguerreotype cameras were first generation positives, with no intermediary negatives, exposed on silver-plated copper, and the process was complicated, not to say lethal if not handled correctly.

That original camera is obviously unavailable for collecting (rumour has it that it's in Sweden at the moment), but for those with deep pockets, other daguerreotype cameras can very occasionally be found, albeit at high prices.

1888: The Kodak

This was the camera that took photography out of the hands of experts and brought it to the man in the street. It was a box-type camera designed by a New York bank clerk called George Eastman, and was the first commercial camera to use celluloid rollfilm.

The camera came ready-loaded with enough film for 100 pictures and had to be returned to the factory for processing, after which it was returned, ready-loaded, with another film.

Very few find their way onto the collector's market, although you might find one of a small range of replicas that were made by Kodak for promotional purposes in the 1980s.

1895: The Sanderson

Frederick Sanderson was a cabinet maker as well as a wood and stone carver, who wasn't content with the basic rising and crossing front movements found on cameras of his time. So he used his skills as a cabinet maker, with his knowledge of photography, to come up with a new design of camera, which he named after himself.

The secret of the Sanderson's success lay in the way the front panel was slotted into twin arms pivoted to the front of the body, with a threaded stud passing through slots in each arm, topped by a knurled knob to clamp the panel into any position. With all four arms independently hinged, the front panel could be locked totally out of square. Rise and fall, tilt and swing of the lens were all controlled by that one pair of knurled knobs.

His cameras were originally built by a company called Holmes Brothers and

marketed by Houghtons, but in 1904, the two companies merged and Houghton's became the manufacturers. Sanderson cameras in different sizes, together with their derivatives made by other manufacturers, are readily available on the collector's market.

1900: The Brownie

The Brownie was the camera that really popularised snapshot photography. It was designed by Frank Brownell, a former cabinet maker turned camera manufacturer, and the camera name is sometimes assumed to have come as a derivation of his own name. In fact, the camera was named because the Brownie was aimed at introducing children to the delights of photography. A Brownie, at that time in America, was another name for a mischievous imp, popularised by Canadian children's writer Palmer Cox. To that end, the box for the camera was decorated with the little fellows.

The first Brownie was made of jute board and wood with a fixed focus, fixed aperture lens and a rotary shutter for instantaneous or time exposures. A 'V' pattern of lines on top of the body served as the only viewfinder on the original model, but within a few months of its launch, a clip-on viewfinder was available as an extra. The camera took six pictures, 6cm square on No. 117 film.

The original model is not uncommon, whereas the No.2 Brownie, launched in 1901 and whose main claim to fame is that it introduced 120 size film, can be found by the thousand.

1900: No. 3 Folding Pocket Kodak

One of the most popular styles of camera right through until as late as the 1960s was the rollfilm folder, in which a bed dropped down at right angles to the body to reveal rails along which the lens panel was drawn out.

It was a style seen on countless cameras during the first half of the 20th Century, but the camera that launched the idea was the No. 3 Folding Pocket Kodak, with early models featuring a leather-covered lens panel, not seen on subsequent copies of this design. The camera took 118 size film and produces images 10 x 8 cm.

Although derivatives of this design can be found in abundance at every camera fir, this very first model is a little harder to come by.

1912: Vest pocket Kodak

In the early days of rollfilm cameras, there were many different size of film available. Apart from 120, however, the only other size that survived significantly down through the years was 127, and that came with the launch of the Vest Pocket Kodak.

This was a small camera with a lens panel that pulled forward on bellows, supported by criss-cross struts, known as lazy tongs. The first model sold between 1912 and 1914, then in 1915, Kodak introduced their Autographic back to the camera.

The life of the Vest Pocket Kodak in that form ended in 1925, when Kodak launched the Model B. Still taking 127 film and with a fairly simple specification, this one followed the style of larger folding cameras with a bed that dropped down from the body and a lens panel that pulled out on rails.

Both models are fairly easy to find at collectors' fairs.

1916: Kodak No. 3A Autographic Special

Rangefinders became popular in 35mm cameras during the 1930s, but the first camera to feature a built-in, coupled rangefinder was the Kodak No. 3A Autographic Special, distinguished from other folding cameras of the period by the two, small rectangular rangefinder windows beneath the lens.

In use, the photographer stood at right angles to the subject, looking into the side of one of the windows and seeing the scene as a split image. Turning a knurled wheel on the opposite side of the baseboard focused the lens and lined up the image, at which point the lens was in focus. The camera took pictures 14 x 8 cm on 122 size film.

Early models in good condition are quite rare today.

1922: Debrie Sept

This was a 35mm camera which predated the Leica. But the feature that makes it a landmark is the built-in motor drive, driven by clockwork. Loading 17 ft of 35mm film in special cassettes provided a 15 second burst of movie action which, being a hand-held camera, made it popular with newsreel photographers of the day.

But the Sept was a still camera too, taking around 250 pictures, 18 x 24 mm half frame size, either in a continuous sequence or one at a time, the clockwork motor winding the film automatically after each exposure.

The single speed shutter provided instantaneous or time exposures and it was possible to combine several still exposures with perhaps a 10-second burst of movie action, all on the same length of film.

The Sept is relatively rare today.

1923: Ensign Cupid

One way manufacturers found to economise on film was to double the number of exposures that could be obtained from a single loading. This was done by reducing the format and adding two red windows. The film was wound until the figure '1' appeared in the first window, the exposure was made, then the film was wound again until '1' appeared in the second window. After that exposure, the film was wound again until '2' appeared in the first window... and so on until 16 exposures had been made.

The Ensign Cupid was the first 16-on camera and used 120 film. Other than that innovation, it was a fairly basic, although unusually-shaped, camera with a fixed focus, aperture and shutter speed.

The 16-on style didn't really catch on until the 1930s, when Ensign's patent on the idea ran out. It was then popularised by the Kolibri, made by Zeiss Ikon, to take 16 exposures on 127 film.

The Ensign Cupid is not common, but can still sometimes be found on the collectable market at a reasonable price.

1925: The Leica I

The first Leica was designed by Oskar Barnack, who was Director of Research at Leitz from 1911. Inspiration for a completely new kind of camera struck while he was working on a prototype cine camera and he designed the Leica to use cine film – 35mm being the standard gauge at that time.

The name was derived from LEItz CAmera, and the first model was launched at the Leipzig Spring Fair in 1925, with a 50mm f/3.5 Anastigmat lens. The viewfinder was mounted separately on top of the body, rather than built in and there was no rangefinder. Less than 150 were made. Soon after, another model was released with a 50mm f/3.5 Elmax. These are two rarest models of the first cameras. The one you most often see is the third variant, launched in 1926, with a 50mm f/3.5 Elmar lens.

Today, those first two models are difficult to find. But for the collector who can afford it, Leica I cameras with Elmar lenses are easy to come by.

1928: The Rolleiflex

The original Rolleiflex was the first truly compact, rollfilm twin lens reflex. Its genesis lay in a stereo camera called the Heidoscop, the first product to be produced by the German company of Franke and Heidecke when it was formed in 1920.

Whilst most stereo cameras contented themselves with two lenses, the Heidoscop had three. The two outside lenses were for producing stereo pairs of pictures, the one in the middle reflected its image, via a 45° mirror, up to a ground-glass screen under a hood on the top of the body.

The Heidoscop, which took glass plates, led to the similarly-designed Rolleidoscop, made for rollfilm in 1926, and that in turn led to the original Rolleiflex, when the makers simply turned the camera on its side, so that the body was vertically, rather than horizontally styled and removed one of the taking lenses.

That first model took six square exposures on 117 film, advanced by a knob, rather than the crank handle that later became a Rollei trademark. The lens was a 75mm f/4.5 or f/3.8 Zeiss Tessar, set in a Compur shutter with speeds from 1 second to 1/300 second, plus 'B' and 'T'.

Original models can be found comparatively easily today at fairly reasonable prices.

1933: The Exakta

The Exakta, made by Ihagee in Dresden, was the first truly compact rollfilm single lens reflex, designed to take eight exposures, 4 x 6.5 cm, on a roll of 127 film. A year after its launch, a second model was introduced, similar to the first but with the addition of slow shutter speeds. The new version was called the Exakta B and only then did the first version take on the name Exakta A.

These early Exakta were unusual in shape, triangular with the sides of the camera sloping away from the lens. The shutter release was on the front of the

body, not the top, and it was released with the left hand. Focusing was by a helical screw around the lens barrel. The viewfinder was a waist-level type and there was a sports finder too.

Today, the Exakta B is easier to find than that first Model A.

1935: Twin Lens Contaflex

As well as being unusual (though not unique) in being a twin lens reflex that took 35mm film, the Twin Lens Contaflex has also gone down in history as the first camera with a built-in photo electric exposure meter. It was made by Zeiss Ikon.

The meter's cell was situated under a flap above the viewing lens, comprising a series of prisms that concentrate the cell on the same angle of view as the standard lens. Three scales were engraved beneath the cell, with the lower showing the film speed and the next showing apertures. An arrow on this second scale was set against the appropriate speed setting below. Beside the focusing hood, a meter needle floated in a window and a lever on the right of the camera was turned to bring the needle to a central mark. At that point, shutter speeds were read off against apertures on the two scales above the lens and transferred manually to the camera.

This is a rare camera today that demands high prices.

1936: The Kine Exakta

Here's the camera that has gone down in history as the world's first 35mm single lens reflex, although some claim that honour for a Russian camera called the Sport, made around the same time.

Whatever the facts, there is no doubt that the Kine Exakta, derived from its 127 film forerunner, was the one that defined the future of SLRs with a design that wasn't a million miles away from what we know and love today.

The problem of focusing on a smaller than usual waist-level viewfinder screen were solved by a magnifier built into the viewfinder hood. Early models had round magnifiers, later models had square ones. Other features included a film cutter that allowed the film to be sliced inside the body so part could be removed in the dark for processing, a twin cassette system that removed the need for rewinding, focal plane shutter with speeds from 1/1000 second out to a full 12 seconds, delayed action and flash synchronisation for bulbs at all speeds.

Today, the round magnifier versions are rarer than the square and consequently command higher prices.

1938: Super Kodak Six-20

Automatic exposure came, for the first time, from Kodak in 1938 with the introduction of this camera, a large folding model with a meter cell above the lens.

The output from the cell moved a meter needle and, once it had reached its appropriate setting, the shutter release was lightly pressed to move a comb-like mechanism that trapped the needle where it stood. A spring-loaded connection on the aperture control then moved until it came up against the locked needle, adjusting the aperture as it moved. Further pressure on the shutter release then exposed the film.

Masks adjusted the light reaching the cell as the shutter speeds were changed and the camera was automatic between 1/25 second and 1/200 second. For longer exposures, settings had to be adjusted by hand. The meter was calibrated only for the speed of Kodak Verichrome film.

This is a very rare camera today.

film magazines and viewfinders became a major aspect of the design. In an age when press cameras and view cameras prevailed, it was also a brave step to make it a single lens reflex with a format still considered by some at the time to be on the small side.

Equally innovative was the use of a fresnel lens in place of a ground-glass focusing screen, leading to a brighter and easier-to-focus image.

Despite their age, many older Hasselblads are still in use by professional photographers and so are as likely to be sold as working cameras as they are collector's items.

1948: The Hasselblad

The Swedish-made Hasselblad is often quoted as being the first 6 x 6cm single lens reflex, but the Primarflex, Reflex Korelle and Exakta 66 all predated it by more than a decade. The Hasselblad, however, was the world's first 6 x 6cm SLR with an interchangeable film back, and so the Hasselblad became the role model for rollfilm SLRs of the future.

What set the Hasselblad apart from other cameras of its type was the way it was designed on a modular basis. So quick-change interchangeable lenses,

1948: Polaroid Model 95

This was the first truly viable instant picture camera. It took the shape and the form of an old-fashioned folding design with the lens panel pulled out along rails on a drop-down bed, but was much larger than conventional cameras of the type.

Film came on two rolls that were dropped into the body either side of he lens. The larger one consisted of specially treated paper, the smaller one held a negative paper, and the two were connected by a paper leader. After exposure, the leader was pulled from a slot to pull the exposed paper negative from one spool and the sensitised printing paper from the other into contact, sandwiching them together through a set of rollers. Pods of chemical, consisting of a special developer and fixer in one solution and situated on the film strip, burst under pressure from the rollers, spreading the solution evenly between the two layers of paper.

The negative image developed first. Then the unused silver salts were converted to a soluble solution by the chemistry from the pods and diffused through to the print paper, where they were reduced to silver. The result was a positive image, produced in around one minute.

Polaroid cameras, in general, can be found in abundance, and this one, though rarer than most, can still be found at reasonable prices.

1948: Contax S

The claim to be the world's first 35mm camera with an eye-level pentaprism viewfinder has been attributed to two cameras – the Contax S and the Rectaflex. Each lays claim to being the

first, but the Contax has the earlier patent date and was probably launched just ahead of its rival, if only by a few weeks.

It was made by the VEB Zeiss Ikon company in East Germany, after a split which had taken Zeiss Ikon proper to West Germany after the Second World War. It was also the first camera with the 49mm screw thread that became extremely popular among later Japanese SLRs, particularly Pentax.

The Rectaflex was made in Italy and there were two models, one with a top shutter speed of 1/1000 second, the other with 1/1300 second. The camera also had two small cross prisms cemented into the focusing screen to produce a split image rangefinder.

Today, the Contax is moderately easy to find, the Rectaflex a little rarer.

1959: Nikon F

Nippon Kogaku was formed in 1917, principally to make optical goods and Scientific instruments. It went on to produce 35mm rangefinder cameras, starting with the Nikon I in 1948 with a design that owed a lot to the Contax II, all of which were highly successful, leading the company to turn their sights to an SLR in the late 1950s.

The Nikon F was the first real system 35mm SLR, designed for use with a vast range of interchangeable lenses, viewfinders and other accessories that even included a motor wind. And, at a time when other manufacturers were still using screw-fit lenses, the Nikon F, influenced by the old rangefinder cameras they had previously produced, went for the easier-to-use bayonet fit.

The camera was a tough, reliable, easy-to-use workhorse and it is little wonder that it became the camera that every professional photographer aspired to owning for the next decade or more.

They can be found fairly easily today, but are often well used because of their reputation among professional photographers.

1963: Topcon RE Super

This was the first single lens reflex to use through the lens metering. It wasn't the first camera with the feature, because that honour goes to the Mec

16SB, made in 1960. However, that was a 16mm subminiature camera and the Topcon, being an SLR, was the one that set the style for the future.

The Topcon, which used a CdS metering system, also featured a removable pentaprism viewfinder, shutter speeds from 1 – 1/1000 second and was usually sold with a 58mm f/1.4 lens.

1978: Konica C35AF

Today's proliferation of autofocus compacts have their genesis in this camera which used a special module produced by Honeywell and made available to camera manufacturers of the time.

The camera had two small windows beside the viewfinder and either side of the lens. One contained a fixed mirror, the other a pivoting mirror, rather like an old-fashioned manual rangefinder. Between them, was a prism that reflected light down to an electronic focus detector which, in turn, controlled a tiny sliding lever that interacted with the movement of the lens.

As the lens moved through its focusing range, the camera's electronics recognised when the two images coincided as a point when the image contrast was suddenly increased. At that point, a solenoid was activated which shot out a tiny sliding lever that stopped the lens in its tracks. Only then did the shutter release to take the picture — all in the space of about 80 milliseconds.

Few consider this to b a collector's item these days and so it can be found relatively cheaply.

1985: Minolta 7000

The first autofocus mechanisms on 35mm came from the likes of Canon, Ricoh, Nikon and Olympus, with the autofocus mechanism built into the lenses, making them unwieldy and ugly.

Minolta's camera, however, built the mechanism in the camera body for the first time, making it slightly bulkier than other current SLR bodies, but with the appropriate lenses scaled down to the size of normal manual focus lenses.

Autofocus aside, the Minolta 7000 also offered exposure modes that included standard programme, wide programme and tele programme, together with the world's first automatic multi-program selection.

By today's standards the autofocus function of this camera would be considered sluggish, so not many are being used for normal photography. They can, however, still be found fairly easily on the collector's market.

Modern Collectables

Not every collectable camera has to be old. Some modern cameras become collector's items the moment they are launched, the prime example being almost anything made by Leica. When the M6 was launched in 1984, it was made as a usable camera, never intended to be a collector's item as such. But there were collectors, people who cherish all things Leica, who bought the camera, new in its box, never removed the outer wrapping, never even opened the box itself and who have kept the complete package in this condition ever since. Undoubtedly the same thing is happening right now with the Leica M7 that was introduced towards the end of 2002.

Minox is another company that, in the past few years, has also introduced a very unusual range of modern collectables with a series of subminiature classics, designed and produced as copies of true classic cameras, made to a scale if 1:2.5. They all accept Minox film, easily bought from specialist dealers, and are fully functioning.

The range, at the time of writing, includes a Leica If, Leica IIIf, Leica M3, Contax I, Hasselblad SWC and Rolleiflex. By the time you read this, there might be even more. Those with Internet access can check out the situation by logging onto www.minox.com and clicking on 'Classic cameras'.

But not all modern collectables have to be as expensive as these Leica and Minox models...

Low budget collectables

For some collectors, the latest disposable cameras make an interesting and colourful collection, and the fact that they are made to be disposable means that the vast majority of them won't survive. As the different types are superseded, the old ones are already beginning to be sort after by specialist collectors. Look out especially for those produced to celebrate certain events, such as the Millennium, or World Cup soccer matches.

The Minox miniature Leica with a full size M3.

Disposable cameras are worth collecting if they are connected with an event. This one was launched in 2000 to celebrate the new Millennium.

Then there are cameras which the manufacturers obviously thought to be a good idea at the time, but which never really caught on. The Sirius Action Tracker is a prime example. A fairly basic, plastic snapshot camera, it has the unusual feature of taking four pictures, in sequence, on a single frame of 35mm film. It was aimed at snapshotters who wanted to record sporting action, but it never found its market and, within a short while of being launched, it was being discounted. Today, it can be regularly found at camera fairs.

Polaroid is another manufacturer worth keeping an eye on. Since publication of the last Blue Book, the company has moved in a big way into a series of unusually-shaped instant picture cameras aimed straight at the party market, most of which are extremely attractive to the modern collector. Alternatively, look out for slightly older Polaroid cameras that were launched in connection with events or people no longer in the news. The company's Spicecam is a perfect example. It relates to the Spice Girls, a British girl band that was extremely popular when the last Blue Book was published, but whose members

no longer perform together as they once did.

Or how about cameras that are given away for promotional purposes? The inclusion of a trade name on a camera of the past, made for a specific company or exhibition, usually ups its value today. So watch out for the modern equivalents on 35mm compacts and other snapshot models.

Kodak Instamatic cameras are still very cheap and can often be picked up at flea markets. But these, again, were definite landmark cameras, especially if you find some of the unusual types, such as the Instamatic 400 with its built-in clockwork motordrive. Some of the more sophisticated cameras made for 110 film are also commanding new respect these days.

The Spicecam, launched by Polaroid to tie in with the Spice Girls, a very popular girl band of the time.

Then there are the fun cameras and special one-offs that usually arrive in the shops around Christmas, produced principally as presents for children. They often take the same basic design, but add to it with special mouldings of subjects like animals, or children's fictional characters. The Wallace and Gromit characters, for example, were immortalised on one such camera, which sold in a special pack that included film in its own specially designed box, a photo album and instructions for getting the best pictures from the camera. Likewise the children's TV characters known as the Telly Tubbies. Imagine the current value of an equivalent complete box set made, say, back in the 1930s and you can understand why it's no bad idea to buy this kind of equipment today and keep it for the future.

A Wallace and Gromit camera, tied in with a popular stop-motion film at the time of its launch and now no longer available.

Cameras like these are, in their own way, limited editions, because once a current fad or phase ends, they cease to remain popular and production stops. The manufacturers know that and produce only enough to satisfy current trends, before moving on to the next craze.

Medium budget collectables

Since the 1970s is an era in which many of today's established collectors began collecting, it's a decade that is still considered by many to be too modern for consideration. A new generation of collectors, however, is beginning to think differently, and as more interest

develops, so prices are starting to climb.

We're talking here about cameras such as the Olympus OM-1, first of the compact 35mm single lens reflexes; the Nikon EM, that company's first real foray into cameras for the amateur; or perhaps the Konica FS-1, first 35mm single lens reflex with a built-in electric motor drive.

Look out too for examples of early autofocus cameras. The Konica C35AF, which was the first automatically focusing 35mm compact, can still be bought for next to nothing. But as the 1970s become more acceptable to the collector, this is a 1978 collectable that could begin to grow in value. Likewise, early autofocus single lens reflexes like the Canon T80, or the special autofocus lenses made by Canon and Ricoh to convert manual focus cameras for automatic focusing are beginning to attract the interest of collectors.

The Canon T80 – not vintage, but still a landmark as one of the earliest autofocus 35mm single lens reflexes.

Older Polaroid cameras are also starting to appeal to the serious collector. Although this type of collector might ignore the very latest instant picture cameras mentioned above, show him an SX-70 from the 1970s or an SLR680 from the 1980s and it might be a different matter

The Polaroid SX-70 Sonar Autofocus was actually the world's first autofocus single lens reflex.

Another medium budget market is the APS camera. Alongside conventional and, frankly, uninteresting cameras, many APS models are currently being produced in all kinds of weird and wonderful colours and designs, destined to be collectable in the future. In much the same vein, even some novelty digital cameras are now beginning to appeal to collectors for the first time.

High budget collectables

Of course there are still a large amount of modern collectables that command high prices that make them prohibitive to the average collector, and the company that still tops that list is Leica, with its fairly regular introduction of limited editions, launched for special occasions. They include cameras like the following:

A special edition of the Leica M6, commissioned by Jaguar to mark the 50th anniversary of the Jaguar XK120 sports car in 1948, and made in a limited run of 50 cameras, numbered XK1 to XK50.

The Ein Stück Leica, an M6 produced

in a limited edition of 996 and covered in calf skin embossed with the Leica logo, to mark the listing of Leica AG on the stock exchange.

The Anton Bruckner Leica, an M6 covered in grey-blue embossed iguana leather to commemorate the 100th anniversary of the death of the famous Austrian composer, produced in a limited edition of 200, representing 20 cameras for each of his 10 symphonies.

A Leica M6 with the Danish Royal Crest, made in a limited edition in 1995.

The Leica M6 Royal Wedding, engraved with the Danish Royal Crest and the wedding date, 18th November 1995, produced in a limited edition of 200.

The Leica M6J, a camera that is basically an M6 with strong design influences from the original M3, made in a limited edition of 1,640, to mark 40 years of Leica M cameras.

The Royal Photographic Society M6, made in a limited edition of 100 to mark the centenary of the Royal Photographic Society in England, the top plate engraved with the RPS coat of arms.

Minox too has introduced its fair share of limited editions. Apart from those miniature classics mentioned at the start of this chapter, the company has also launched, in recent years, a series of special occasion cameras. They include:

The Minox AX subminiature, produced in black in a limited edition of 222.

The Walter Zapp Minox AX, a 24-carat gold-plated subminiature, made in a limited edition of 250 to celebrate 50 years of Minox manufacture in Germany and engraved with the signature of Walter Zapp, the camera's inventor.

The Minox MDC Gold, a 24-carat gold-plated version of the traditional MDC 35mm camera, made in a limited edition of 555, for no particular reason other than to appeal to the collector's market.

Although Hasselblad isn't always considered to be collectable in the way that, say, Leitz or Zeiss cameras are, the marque is attracting a growing band of enthusiasts, and it's a manufacturer that has also introduced limited editions in recent years. Since Hasselblad was the camera used for the moon landings, they include a special EL/M, made in a limited run of 1,500 in 1979 to celebrate ten years on the moon; and a chrome EL/M with a light grey vinyl body, made in a limited run of 1,500 in 1981 to mark the 20th anniversary of Hasselblad's participation in the US space programme. The company has also produced a number of special editions to celebrate anniversaries of landmark models.

Some other manufacturers too have occasional excursions into the special, one-off camera, aimed at collectors: Olympus with its 'O' product, a few specials from Minolta, Rollei with special editions of its 35mm range and TLRs dedicated to famous users of the marque.

Cameras like these are made purely to entice rich collectors to add to their growing collection, something which Leica fanatics in particular can rarely resist — assuming they have the cash to afford them. Such cameras are nearly always sold in special commemorative boxes, usually made of quality wood, with silk linings.

Some modern cameras, whilst not specifically made as collectors' items, still command the attention of the collector, because of their unusual or unique design concepts. The Contax G1, now superseded by the G2, is a prime example. Although a modern camera in every sense of the word, with its electronic systems, automated exposure modes and autofocus options, it was, at the time of its launch, the first real interchangeable lens, non-reflex camera made in years. Unlike other cameras mentioned above, it was never intended to be produced as a special or limited edition, but is nevertheless becoming a collector's item.

All of these cameras were expensive when they were launched, but they have each grown even more in value in only a few years since they were first seen. They are not everyone's idea of what constitutes a collectable camera, but if you are in collecting for the investment, and can afford them, they can only rise in value in the years ahead.

The Helmut Newton Rolleiflex 2.8 GX, made in association with one of the camera's most famous professional users.

Collecting Cine Cameras

Since publication of the last edition of the Hove International Blue Book three years ago, there has been a steadily growing interest in cine camera collecting. Where once these cameras were relegated to the rubbish boxes found under tables at collectors' fairs, they are now beginning to find their way to the table top, to stand side by side with the best collectable still cameras.

Several reasons have been put forward for the emergence of this trend. For many, it's a new challenge, a new direction to take in collecting, and one that, for the moment at least, is still wonderfully inexpensive. In the world of still camera collecting, the most sought after equipment is likewise the most technically interesting, and conse-quently the most expensive. Some collectors of still cameras have come to the point where they already have everything they want and can afford, but can't afford to move up to the next level of collecting. For others, who were on a tight budget right from the start, collecting still cameras has always meant concentrating on the less expensive folders, box cameras and simple snapshot models, with little chance of being able to afford some of the more sophisticated cameras of the past. Not so with cine, where 8mm cameras that cost small fortunes at the time of their launch are now well within the reach of the kind of collector who could never hope to buy their still camera counterparts.

But it isn't just the price of this equipment that is attracting collectors. Cine cameras, for those who appreciate ingenious mechanics, are certainly attractive propositions in their own terms. And, interestingly, there were times when cine cameras were ahead of their still camera counterparts when it came to innovation. Right from the earliest days, interchangeable lenses were available on even the cheapest cine cameras. Features such as built-in meters, through the lens metering and zoom lenses were to be found on cine cameras before they became the norm on their still counterparts. A turret with two or three different focal lengths of lenses mounted on the same camera body was commonplace on cine cameras, whereas a similar feature is found on no more than just a handful of still cameras — and then in a way that was aesthetically ugly compared to the way they were integrated into cine design.

So cine cameras can be a fascinating subject for both the new collector and the established one who is looking for a new direction. Either way, the question is, where do you begin?

A good starting point is 1923, the year that Eastman launched the first 16mm camera in America and Pathé launched the first 9.5mm model in France. There had been cine cameras before this date of course, the earliest truly practical examples of equipment capable of shooting and projecting a moving image dating back to the 1890s. But this early equipment is rare, expensive and, to be fair, was of interest to specialist collectors long before the present interest began to emerge.

Before those two cameras from America and France were launched, cinematography was an expensive business, with most cameras being made for film studios and other professional uses. But the launch of the 16mm and 9.5mm gauges put moving pictures firmly in the hands of amateur cinematographers, and before long other companies were jumping on the bandwagon to produce their own versions.

Then in 1932, just nine years after the launch of the 16mm gauge, Kodak again revolutionised amateur cinematography with the launch of 8mm film and the cameras to match. Known initially as Double-Eight, later to be referred to as Standard-8, these cameras actually took short lengths of 16mm film, double-sprocketed and designed to be run through the camera first one way, then removed, the spools transposed and the film run through again in the opposite direction. The result was 25ft of film with two images side by side across its width. After processing, the film was split down the middle and the two ends joined to form one 50ft length for projecting.

These Double-Right cameras were by far the most popular among amateur cinematographers and cameras for this gauge can be found in abundance on the collector's market. In seeking them out, however, care should be taken to avoid the less sophisticated models, of which there were many, and go for cameras with the more interesting or unusual specifications, as well as those that, for one reason or another, were landmarks of their time.

Included in this are several variations of the 8mm gauge that came and went in the years from 1932 until the demise of amateur cinematography. They included Single-8, which used a different type of film that really was 8mm wide, run through the camera only once; cameras that took Double-Eight film pre-loaded by the user into cartridges; others that took special factory-loaded cartridges in place of film spools; and of course Super-8, Kodak's all new and most sophisticated

version of 8mm ever, launched in 1965.

Then there were cine cameras that doubled as projectors and others that were designed to take both moving and still images on the same film, features that make them just that little bit more interesting and worthwhile as collectables.

Perhaps, for the established still camera collector who has doubts about making the change, seeking out these still/cine models could make a good starting point and at least give some justification for taking a look at the collectable merits of cine cameras. But beware. Once you've crossed that line, you might find it difficult to turn back.

CINE CAMERA DIRECTORY

This year for the first time, the Hove International Blue Book is publishing a brief guide to collectable cine cameras. The following, however, is not meant to be definitive. To make it so would be to double the size of the book, whose main content continues to be dedicated to still cameras, their specifications and values.

The cameras selected for this small cine directory, then, have been chosen because they are landmarks that began a new trend in camera design, or because they might have some unusual or interesting specification that makes them of extra interest to the collector. Unlike the main still camera directory in this book, they have been listed chronologically, in the order they were launched, irrespective of manufacturer. The list has been restricted to 8mm, 9.5mm and 16mm cameras.

The price and rarity codes quoted here are similar to those used in the book's main directory for still cameras. Note, however, that in the world of cine collecting, unlike still camera collecting, extra rare does not always mean extra expensive, simply because there isn't as high a demand among collectors for cine cameras as there is for still cameras.

Cine-Kodak Model A: R4* F

1923. First 16mm camera. Box shaped, hand cranked. Took enough film for 4 minutes shooting without reloading. Sold as an outfit with the Kodascope projector. Short focus f/3.5 Kodak Anastigmat lens. Clockwork motor drive later launched to replace hand crank. Became known as the Model A when the Model B was launched.

Pathé Baby: R4* C

1923. First 9.5mm camera. Hand cranked with 20mm f/3.5 Berthiot or f/1.9 Dallmeyer Kine lenses. Camo and Motrix clockwork motor drives launched for it in 1926.

Cine-Kodak Model B: R3* C

1926. 16mm for 50ft or 100ft spools. Complete restyle of the original model to more compact size. Clockwork motor ran 20ft of film to one wind. Fixed focus 20mm f/6.5 Anastigmat or f/3.5 lenses. First model with waist-level viewfinder. New model with eye-level viewfinder and focusing f/1.9 lens in 1927.

Zeiss Ikon Kinamo S10: R3* C

1929. 16mm, cartridge load for 32ft of film. At 4.5 x 3.5 x 2.5 ins, one of the smallest 16mm cameras ever made. Clockwork drive with indicator to show spring tension. Unusual claw mechanism that worked from the back of the film, away from the shutter.

Cine-Kodak Eight-20:   R2* C

1932. Double-8. The first 8mm cine camera. Fixed focus f/3.5 Kodak Anastigmat lens, 16 fps. Fold up viewfinder in carrying handle.

Cine-Kodak Special: R4* F

1933. 16mm. Very sophisticated for a 16mm camera, incorporating many of the features hitherto seen only in 35mm models, including double exposure, lap dissolves, fades, slow motion, etc. Variable slit shutter, speeds 8-64 fps. Eye-level and reflex viewfinders. Interchangeable film chambers. Two-lens turret incorporated a range of lenses from 15mm wideangle to 6-inch telephoto.

Midas: R3* D

1933. 9.5mm. Camera and projector combined. Battery driven as a camera, hand cranked with the same batteries powering the bulb as a projector. f/2.5 Taylor Hobson lens was fixed focus for shooting but could be focused for projection.

Dekko Cameras Dekko: R3* C

1934. 9.5mm. Bakelite body with chrome fittings. Art Deco design, although the name Dekko referred to the Hindi world for 'look'. Interchangeable lenses. Originally supplied with choice of three lenses.

Bell & Howell Filmo 121:   R3* C

1934. 16mm. Unusual in its time for taking cartridge, holding 50ft of film, that slotted into the camera's rectangular body. Waist-level and direct vision viewfinders. Interchangeable lenses.

Home Cine Cameras Campro   R3* C

1935. 9.5mm. Combined camera and projector. Clockwork motor for both shooting and projecting, with internal torch bulb powered by external battery or transformer. Esdar f/3.5 fixed focus lens with adaptor for projection. Three apertures on sliding metal strip for 'bright', 'dull' and 'project'.

Univex A-8:   R3* C

1936. Single-8. The first single-8 camera. Spool loaded, as opposed to cartridge used in most other Single-8 systems. Black, die-cast art deco style body with exposure calculator engraved on side. Ilex Univar f/5.6 lens. Wire frame fold-down viewfinder.

Ditmar: R4* D

1936. 9.5mm in black and chrome bodies or rare special models sold in tortoiseshell finish (pictured). Aperture scale visible in viewfinder for changes whilst filming. Film speeds could be changed while filming. Took 30ft chargers. Two release buttons for 16 and 32 fps film speeds. Interchangeable lenses.

Bolex H16:   R2* F

1936. 16mm. First of range of models that continued into the 1970s. Semi-automatic loading, movie speeds 8-64 fps. Single frames with shutter speeds of 1/10-1/1000s and Time. Forward and reverse action for whole 100ft of film. Three-lens turret on half-circle plate. Viewfinder parallax adjustment down to 20 inches. Motor could be disengaged from mechanism to allow rewinding of complete film with counter working backwards. Wide range of C-mount lenses. Pictured camera is Series IV from 1947.

Williamson Cine Camera Gun   R4* D

1937. 16mm in special cassettes. Made to train RAF observers and pilots in aerial gunnery. Electrically driven for shooting speeds of 16 or 20 fps. Sometimes found separate from gun mounting and with Extension lens.

Agfa Movex 8:   R2* B

1938. First Single-8 camera to use film in a cartridge. Made of aluminium in black enamel. Fixed focus 12mm f/2.8 anastigmat lens with built-in lens hood.

Ditmar Photocell Camera: R4* D

1938. Double-8. One of the earliest cameras to have a built-in meter coupled to the aperture control. Metal-bodied camera with twin buttons for normal and slow motion. Inter-changeable lenses.

Eumig Electric C4:   R2* B

1938. Double-8. The first electric motor in an amateur cine camera. Fixed focus f/2.5 Berthiot Anastigmat lens, single speed shutter. Interchangeable lens.

Bolex H8:   R3* F

1938. Double-8. An 8mm version of the H16 which, broadly speaking, followed a similar development pattern to the H16 models. Made to take 25ft, 50ft or 100ft reels. Advertised as 'the most advanced 8mm cine camera in the world'.

Emel Model C93 De Luxe: R4* E

1940. Double-8. Circular-shaped turret head for three lenses. Five shooting speeds. Adjustable viewfinder worked on a telescopic system for focal lengths 6.5mm to 50mm and incorporated parallax correction. Exposure guide, backwind, single picture device and picture frame counter. A wideangle converter and corresponding viewfinder tube was also available.

Universal Cinemaster G-8:   R2* C

1941. Single-8 or Double-8. Last in a range of cameras from this company designed to take both types of 8mm film.

Bell & Howell 605B: R2* B

1951. Double-8. Unusual twin-lens turret that places the spare lens above the actual camera body. Lenses supplied were Serital 0.5 inch f/1.9 and Kinotel 1.5 inch f/3.2, which rotated around central pivot. Auxiliary lenses on same turret to adapt viewfinder's field of view.

Nizo Heliomat S2R: R3* C

1952. Double-8. Claimed as the first 8mm camera with built-in photo electric exposure meter. Unusually styled turret with two lenses plus a lens-shaped meter situated vertically, one above the other. Lenses and meter coupled for semi-auto match-needle exposure setting. Interchangeable lenses.

Leveque LD8: R5* E

1953. Double-8. Zoom-type viewfinder gave angles of view for focal lengths between 23mm and 100mm. Parallax corrected by control which tipped the unit up and out in a diagonal movement for distances between 0.75 metres and infinity. Three lens turret. Film footage counter plus separate individual frame counter for use in conjunction with built-in rewind crank.

Movikon 8: R2* C

1953. Double-8. Unusually styled camera held horizontally with feed and take-up spools arranged side by side parallel to the lens axis. Film was twisted as it left the first spool, passed through the gate and twisted again before being taken up on the second spool. First model finished in brown-red colour. Following models in grey. First of a series that included the Movikon 8B with built-in meter. Similar body style also found in the Movinette 8 and 8B.

Bauer 88:   **R2* B**

1954. Double-8. Die-cast metal body, unusual and attractive for blue-green hammered lacquer finish. Interchangeable lenses.

Bolsey 8:   **R3* E**

1956. Single-8 in special Bolsey cartridges. Probably the smallest cine camera ever made, measuring a mere 8 x 6 x 2.5 cm. Navitar 10mm f/1.8 focusing lens. Single shooting speed of 16 fps, plus facility for shooting single frames at still camera shutter speeds of 1/50, 1/100, 1/200, 1/300 and 1/600 second. Telephoto converter lens available.

Gevaert Carena: **R4 D**

1954. Double-8. Stylish slimline body in light maroon enamel. Speeds of 8, 16, 24 and 32 fps, 12.5mm f/1.8 Som Berthiot lens with Waterhouse stops. Built-in orange and pale yellow filters.

Camex Reflex: **R3* E**

1956. Double-8. First 8mm single lens reflex. Built-in meter behind lens. Signals in viewfinder to show when correct exposure is set, plus start and finish of usable film. Click signal to indicate every 20ft of film shot.

Wittnauer Cine-Twin: R5* E

1957. Double-8. Unusual camera and projector combined. 400-watt bulb contained in body, film reel arms folded up from inside when side was removed. Camera was battery driven, but attached to a mains-operated base containing fan and motor for projection. 6.5mm f/1.9 Elitar Soligor, 13mm f/2.3 Wittnauer Chronostar and 38mm f/1.9 Elitar Soligor on turret for filming, plus 1-inch f/1.6 Wittnauer Chronostar for projection.

Pathé Webo Super 16: R4* E

1958. 16mm in 50 ft and 100 ft spools. Starting knob with four positions for lock, continuous filming, single picture and time exposure via cable release socket. Totally closing variable shutter

with shooting speeds of 8, 16, 24, 32, 64 and 80 fps. Rewind handle. Frame counter that counted individual frames exactly. Warning bell for over winding. Reflex viewfinder plus optical viewfinder. Three-lens turret for all C-mount lenses. 9.5mm version (pictured) also produced with similar specification but different range of lenses.

Pathé Prince: R3* C

1959. 9.5mm. Single speed of 16 fps, marked 'cine' on the body, plus single frame, marked as 'snapshot', an indication of the way the camera was designed to be used with the Princess projector to project still or cine pictures on the same film.

Beaulieu MR8: R3* D

c1960. Double-8. Stylish design in green crackle finish. Reflex viewing through 9-35mm f/1.8 Angenieux zoom lens. Speeds of 12, 18, 24, 48 and 64 fps

Leica Leicina 8S: R2* D

1960. Double-8. Reflex viewing. Standard lens plus converters for wideangle and telephoto. Electric motor for driving film and electric rewind. Auto exposure through lens with manual override, single speed at 16 fps. Dygon 15mm f/2 lens.

Carena Zoomex: R3* D

1961. Double-8. Unusually styled slim bodied camera with Angenieux K2 7.5-35mm zoom lens. Reflex viewfinder. Auto and manual exposure.

Agfa Movex Reflex: R4* C

1963. Double-8. Auto exposure with manual override. Variogon 7.5-37.5mm f/1.8 zoom lens, microscreen coupled rangefinder in reflex viewfinder. Front element of lens interchangeable with converter to make 13mm f/1.8 macro lens. Spool loaded or by pre-loaded cassettes.

Ricomite 88E: R2* C

1963. Double-8. Slimline pocket camera with semi-auto exposure. Fully auto exposure, electrically driven, single shooting speed of 16 fps. Standard lens in body was Rikenon 13mm f/1.8, which could be adapted with wideangle and telephoto Rikenon accessory lenses.

Sekonic Dualmatic Zoom: R2* C

1963. Double-8. Unusual flip-over feature that allowed film to be reversed half way through run without removing and reloading. S-Resonar 11.5-25mm f.1.8 zoom lens.

Kodak Instamatic M4:   R1* B

1965. One of the first Super-8 cameras. The M2 featured manual exposure control, fixed focus f/1.8 lens, optical viewfinder, fixed shooting speeds of 18 fps and exposure guide on side of body. The M4, launched at the same time, added CdS exposure control and low light warning.

Chinon Concorde: R3* C

1964. Double-8. Unusually shaped body with built-in handgrip. Automatic exposure with manual override. 9.5-30mm f/1.8 zoom lens. Reflex viewfinder. Battery operated. Single shooting speed of 16 fps plus single exposure.

Minolta Minoltina 8:   R2* C

1965. Double-8 in pre-loaded cartridges. Slim body with built-in grip that folded up to make a lens protector. Reflex viewfinder. Rokkor 8-25mm f/1.8 manually operated zoom lens. Auto exposure with indication of aperture in body window and warning light in viewfinder.

Fujica P1: R2* C

1966. Single-8. Launched as Fuji's answer to Kodak's Super-8 system. Fully auto CdS exposure with apertures shown in viewfinder. Fujinon 11.5mm f/1.8 fixed focus lens. Fixed shooting speed of 18 fps.

Ilford Elmo C-200 Power Zoom Reflex: R4* E

1966. Double-8 and Super-8 options via interchangeable backs. Fully auto exposure with manual override, 9-36mm f/1.8 zoom lens.

Kodak XL33: R1* B

1971. Super-8. Fully auto exposure in unusually shaped body made to be held horizontally. Kodak Ektar 9mm f/1.2 lens. Single shooting speed of 18 fps. A-D filter switched in manually.

Polaroid Polavision: R2* B

1977. Instant movie system that shot film in its own camera, then instantly processed it in a special projector / player, ready for showing within 90 seconds. Could only be used with Polaroid's special Phototape – the company's name for the instant cine film.

Agfa Family: **R2* B**

1980. Super-8 cine camera that doubled as still camera. Film shown on special viewer adaptable to make instant prints from cine frames, using Kodak instant photography system.

More information about cine camera collecting and a much more comprehensive directory of collectable equipment can be found in The Collector's Guide to Cine Cameras, published by Hove Books.

Museums for Collectors

AUSTRALIA

Michaels Classic and Antique Camera & Video Museum

Over seven thousand collectable photographic items displayed. Contact Curator John Tracey; Michaels Buildings, Cnr. Elizabeth & Lonsdale streets, Melbourne, Australia. PO Box 2047S GPO Melbourne Phone: + 61 3 670 2259 Fax: + 61 3 670 0074.

BELGIUM

Museum Voor Fotografie

Waalse Kaai 47 Antwerpen, Belgium, B-2000 A wide view on the world of photography, yesterday, today and tomorrow. Open 10:00-5:00pm, except Mondays. Contact Roger Coenen at (03) 2162211.

THE CZECH REPUBLIC

National Museum of Technology

Holesovice, Kostelni 42, Prague-7, The Czech Republic. Tel: (2) 373651. Excellent display of still and motion picture cameras, the finest in central Europe and ranks right up with the best.

FRANCE

Musée Français de la Photographie

78 rue de Paris, PO Box 03-Bievres, France 91570. Cameras, photographs, accessories, and documentation. Open everyday from 10:00-12:00 and 2:00-6:00, holidays included. Contact Andrè Fage, Conservateur en Chef at (6941) 1060.

Musée National des Techniques

Conservatoire National des Arts et Mètiers, 270 Rue Saint-Martin, Paris, France, 75003. Cameras from 1850 to present day. Microphotography by Dagron for carrier pigeons, stereo cameras and spy cameras, motion study photography by Marey and Muybridge. Open 10:00-5:30 Tuesday-Saturday. Contact Mr. Jaques Foiret at (1) 402-72220 or 402-72371. The camera section has been closed for renovation for several years, but may be open by now. It is suggested you contact them before visiting.

GERMANY

Agfa-Gevaert Foto Historama

Bischofsgartenstrasse-1. D-50667 Köln, West Germany. Contact Dr. Bodo von Dewitz, Director, at (0221) 2212411.

Berlin Museum fur Verhehr und Technic

Trebbiner Strasse 9 DW-1000 Berlin 61. (030) 254-840.

Deutsches Museum

Museuminsel, D-80536 Munich, West Germany.

Essen, Abring Foto Museum

Burg-Horst,Haus Horst 1, DW-4300, Essen14. (0201) 53 86 90. Large camera display plus private museum; by appointment.

Leica Museum

Leica Camera GmbH, Oskar Barnack Strasse 11, Postfach 11 80, D-6336 Solms, Germany. Leica Cameras and accessories. Open 9:00-5:00pm by arrangement. Tel: (6442) 2080.

Münchner Stadt Museum
St Jakobsplatz, D-80334 Munich, West Germany.

Optisches Museum Oberkochen
Am ülweiher 15, D-73447. Oberkochen, Baden-Würtemberg, West Germany, Historical and modern eyeglasses, telescopes, binoculars, surveying instruments, cameras and microscopes. Open 10:00-1:00pm and 2:00-4:00pm Monday-Friday, 9:00-12:00 Sunday. Closed Saturdays and holidays.
Tel: (07364) 202878.

ITALY

Museo Nationale del Cinema
Palazzo Chiablese, piazza San Giovanni, 2, Turin, Italy, 10122. Photograph and camera collections, Cinema Massimo magazine, vintage film and magic lantern shows. Contact for Camera collections, Ms. Donata Pesenti; Photograph collections, Ms. Marica Marcellino, at (011) 5661148 or 5661387.

JAPAN

JCII Museum
23 Ichiban-cho, Chiyoda-ku, Tokyo, 102, Japan. Although small, this museum has a truly extraordinary collection with frequently changing exhibits. The only example of a Giroux Daguerrotype Camera in Asia is in the collection of this museum. A 'must see' for anybody visiting Japan with an interest in cameras.

City of Yokahama Camera Museum
Cultural Officer, Yokahama, Japan. Recently the city of Yokahama acquired the very large Naylor Collection and expects to build a museum to house it

which will open next year. This is all the information we have at this time. A visitor to Japan later next year is advised to contact the above address for up-to-date information.

REPUBLIC OF SLOVAKIA

Petzval Museum
Spisska Bela, Republic of Slovakia. Located in the home which was his birthplace, the museum is dedicated to Josef Max Petzval, who designed the first high-speed lens. The museum contains an excellent exhibit of early Petzval lenses and the cameras that used them.

SOUTH AFRICA

Bensusan Musuem of Photography
17 Empire Rd., Parktown, South Africa.

THAILAND

Department of Photographic Science
Faculty of Science, Chulalongkorn University, Phyathai Road, Bangkok, Thailand. The Photographic Science Department of this university administers a recently opened museum of photographic technology that occupies a new building on the campus. It is the first and only photographic museum in SE Asia. An excellent collection includes cameras used by more than a century of Thai royalty. Contact above address for opening times.

UK

Barnes Museum of Cinematography
44 Fore Street, St. Ives, Cornwall, England.

Buckingham Movie Museum
Printers Mews, Market Hill, Buckingham, England.

Fenton Photography Museum
Port Erin, Isle of Wight, England.

Fox Talbot Museum of Photography
Lacock, Near Chippenham, Wiltshire, England, SN15 2LG. Fox Talbot collection. Open 11:00-6:00 pm everyday except Good Friday, March 1st to November 5th. Tel: 0124 973459.

Medina Camera Museum
Golden Hill Fort, Freshwater, Isle of Man, England.

Museum of the History of Science
Broad Street, Oxford, England, OX1 3AZ. Cameras and photographic accessories, early and experimental photographs, Specimens of scientific interest, (early Colour). Open 10:30-1:00pm and 2:00-4:00pm, Monday-Friday, except bank holidays, and Easter and Christmas weeks. Tel: (01865) 277280.

National Museum of Photography, Film, and Television
Princes View, Bradford, West Yorkshire, England, BD5 0TR, Kodak Museum, Interactive and Theatrical reconstruction in museum displays on the past, present and future of photography and television. Changing special exhibitions. Open 11:00-6:00 Tuesday-Sunday, Contact Roger Taylor at (01274) 727488.

Science Museum
Exhibition Road, South Kensington, London, England, SW7 2DD. Photographic and Cinematographic equipment and photographs from 1835 to present day. Open 10:00-6:00 Monday-Saturday, 11:00-6:00 Sundays.

The Royal Photographic Society
The Octagon, Milsom Street, Bath, England BA1 1DN. Comprehensive collection of cameras photographs from the very beginning of photography. Open 9:30-5:15pm, Contact Mrs. P. Roberts, or Miss K. Rouse at (01225) 62841 ext. 212.

Woodspring Museum
Burlington Street, Weston-super-Mare, Avon, England BS23 1PR. A good cross section of the progress of photography since the 1890s. Of special interest is a Bertsh "Chambre Automatique" from about 1861. Photo accessories are also on display. Free admission. Open 10:00-5:00, Monday-Saturday, open Bank holidays except Good Friday, Christmas and New Year. Tel: (01934) 621028.

Woolstaplers Hall Museum
High Street, Chipping Campden, Gloucestershire, England, GL55 6HB. Projectors, plate cameras, Kodak cameras, Contax cameras and other photographic paraphenalia. Open 11:00-6:00 daily from April 1st to October 31st. Contact Mrs. J. Griffiths, Curator at (01386) 840289.

The British Photographic Museum
Bowden House, Totnes, South Devon, England, TQ9 7PW. Camera collection on display, gift shop and Tea Room available. Contact Christopher or Belinda Petersen at (01803) 863664.

Royal Museum of Scotland
Chambers Street, Edinburgh, Scotland.

USA

California Academy of Science
Golden Gate Park, San Francisco, California, USA, 94118. 400 items late 19th and 20th century cameras and equipment. Open 9:00-5:00 pm

Monday-Friday Display partially up. Contact Dr. Robert Sayers, Anthrology Dept. at 415-750-7163.

Florida State Museum

Gainesville, FL, USA Gallery of Photographic History, 10010 Lanehart Road, Little Rock, Arkansas, USA, 72204. Major photographic library, prints, but very little equipment. Open by appointment only. Contact Greer H. Lile at (501) 666-7409 or 455-0179.

George Eastman House, The International Museum of Photography

900 East Avenue, Rochester, New York 14622. Tel: 716/271-3361. Certainly the finest museum of photography in North America, possibly the world.
A must for anyone interested in photographic technology. Open Tuesday-Sunday 10-5. Archives may be visited by appointment. Contact Todd Gustavson, Technology Archivist.

Henry Ford Museum and Greenfield Village

PO Box 1970, 20900 Oakwood Blvd, Dearborn, MI, USA, 48121. Small collection of cameras from 1890-1980. Open 9:00-5:00pm daily except Christmas and Thanksgiving. Contact the Curator of Communications at (313) 271-1620

Jacksonville Museum

Courthouse Sq., Jacksonville, FL, USA. Housed in a large old Courthouse and maintained by the Southern Orega Historical Society. The Peter Britt Gallery is a display of the life and times of photographer Britt. Daguerrean images; studio artifacts but very limited camera diplay, makes this a fascinating display.

Los Angeles County Museum of Natural History

900 Exposition Blvd, Los Angeles, California USA, 90007. Historical photographs concerning the growth and development of Los Angeles, and southern California. Includes Southwest Indians. Open 1:00-4:00 pm Monday-Friday at the Seaver Center. Tel: (213) 744-3359.

The Magic Lantern Castle Museum

The only purely Magic Lantern Museum in the World; Research and library facilities. Contact; Jack Judson, Jr. Castellen/Curator. 1419 Austin Highway, San Antonio, Texas 78209 at (210)-805-0011. Fax: 210-822-1226.

National Museum of American History

Smithsonian Inst, Washington, DC, USA, 20560 Part of the vast Smithsonian collection. Often called "America's attic". Camera and photography display in general has been taken down. No indication as to when it will be restored in any form. Open 10:00-5:30 pm, every day but Christmas Day. Contact Eugene Ostroff, Curator at 202-357-2059.

Stonefield Village

Nelson Dewey State Park, Cassville, Wisconsin,USA, 53806. Replica of 1890s Photographer's Shop. Open 9:00-5:00 pm. Tel: (608) 725-5210.

University of Texas

Harry Ransom Humanities Research Center, Box 7219, University of Texas at Austin, Austin, TX, USA, 78713-7219. Excellent collection based on the former Helmut Gernsheim Collection (which contained the world's earliest photograph by Niepce). It relates to the entire history of photography, its growth and impact on world culture. Open 9.00-5.00 p.m. Monday-Friday. Appointments and reservations requested. Contact Roy Flukinger, Curator, at 512-471-9124.

Clubs for Collectors

AUSTRALIA

Photographic Collectors Society
14 Warne Street, Eaglemont, Victoria, 3084, Australia. Newsletter, published quarterly. Tel: (03) 457-1050.

Sydney Stereo Camera Club
PO Box 465, Pymble, NS, 2073, Australia. For Stereo photographists. Bi-monthly newsletter, monthly membership meetings. Contact Judy Archer, Secretary.

BELGIUM

Photographica
Chausee de la Hulpe 382, Brussels, 1170, Belgium, Tel: (2) 673-8490.

CANADA

Photographic Historical Society of Metropolitan Toronto
PO Box 115, Postal Station "S", Toronto, Ontario, M5M 4L6, Canada. Tel: (416) 483-4185.

Western Canada Photographic Historical Association
PO Box 33742, Vancouver, British Columbia, V6J 4L6, Canada. Tel: (614)-873-2128.

The Photographic Historical Society of Canada
10 Northolt Court, Islington, Ontario, M9A 3B1, Canada.

FRANCE

Club Niepce Lumiere
35 Rue de la Mare a l'Ane, Montreuil, 93100, France.

GERMANY

Club Daguerre
Mohlenstrasse 5, Leverkusen, Hitdorf, D-5090, West Germany. (02173)-40080. Two news letters published four times a year. Annual membership meeting, more frequent regional meetings. About 450 members. Membership fees 100 Dm/year. Contact Klaus Storsberg.

Ihagee Historiker Gesellschaft
Charlottenburger Strasse 22A, Leverkusen, D-5090, West Germany.

Leica Historica
C/O Klaus Grothe, Bahnhof Str.53, D3252, Bad Münder 1, Germany, Membership DM50/year, includes 3-4 newsletters (Vidom) published each year, two annual meetings per year, usually at a location near Wetzlar, about 470 members.

HOLLAND

Dutch Society of Photographica Collectors
PO Box 4262, Haarlem, 2003EG, Netherlands. Illustrated magazine published four times a year. International camera shows twice a year, with more than 200 dealers, and 2,300 visitors. Regional meetings two or three

times a year with 60 dealers. Postal auction four times a year. Museum outings several times each year. More than 1,100 members including 1,000 Dutch members, and more than 100 world wide members. Hfl 40 for Dutch membership, Hfl 47 for foreign membership, US$25.00 foreign. Contact Harry van Kohl, secretary.

Ihagee Historiker Gesellschaft
Tesselschadelaan 20, Hilversum, 1217LH, Netherlands.

UK

Hasselblad Forum Magazine
The 'Hasselblad Forum' magazine is published in Sweden by Victor Hasselblad AB and is normally only available on annual subscription. Four issues, containing many excellent contributions from expert photographers from all over the World, are printed each year and these will be sent to members free of charge. Hasselblad (UK), York House, Empire Way, Wembley, Middlesex, HA90 QQ. Tel: 0181 903 3435. Fax: 0181 902 2565.

Ihagee Historical Association
c/o Teamwork, 11 Shelton St, London, WC2H 9JN, England, Fax: (1) 379-0981.

Leica Historical Society
Greystoke, 8 Driffold, Sutton Coldfield, West Midlands, B73 6HE, England.

MPP Club
The Club aims to foster the use and application of MPP cameras and products by the free exchange of information between members through the postal circulation of notebooks with members hints and tips and the issue of periodic Gazettes. By that means members can seek solutions to some of the problems they may encounter in using or collecting MPP cameras. Meetings will mostly be at the Photo-collectors fairs, such as Dartford or others in the London region. Locations which are idea opportunities to meet and discuss matters of mutual interest. The repair of members cameras may well depend upon sourcing of spare parts. The Club can already assist to some degree in this, and provide flat lens panels which can be supplied to order as well as bellows ex-stock for some models at modest prices. Membership is open to professional and amateur users and to collectors, and to those who may seriously be considering the purchase of an MPP camera to further their photographic interests. To all those who thereby qualify, the Club has a lot to offer and they should become members. The annual subscription is only £6. Further information and additional application forms are available from: Mr Mike Meurisse, Hon. Secretary MPP Users' Club. Tel: 01932 863769.

Magic Lantern Society of Great Britain
"Prospect", High Street, Nutley, East Sussex TN22 3NH. UK subs, £15 for Journal and newsletter.

Pentax Club and Magazine
Tel: 01483 418473. Fax: 01483 419270. E-mail: Pentax.magazine@ski.co.uk. Please call for more information.

Photographic Collectors Club of Great Britain
Membership Secretary, 5 Buntigford Road, Puckeridge, Ware, Hertfordshire, SG11 1RT, England. Photographica World and Tailboard newsletter

published quarterly. Meetings regularly, all over Great Britain. Annual fair in May.

The Historical Group of the Royal Photographic Society
The Octagon, Milsom Street, Bath, Avon, BA1 1DN, England.

The Pen F Register
c/o 1 Sylvan Close, Hemel Hempstead, Hertfordshire, HP3 8DN, England.

The Stereoscopic Society
Hon. Secretary Sue Makinson, 36 Silverthorn Drive, Hemel Hempstead, Herts HP3 8BX, UK. Quarterly magazine, monthly meetings from September to May in London and Coventry. Also annual convention. Current membership fee £13/year. Website http://www.stereoscopy.com/stereosociety. Write or fax 01442 250266 for colour leaflet and application form.

The Voigtländer Verein
Hon. Secretary, Chris Haupt, 33 Woodhayes Road, Frome, Somerset BA11 2DG. The group was formed in 1994 by a small group of enthusiasts. We now have around 100 members worldwide. The word 'Verein' in German means 'fellowship.' We are not dealers but amateur collectors and historians. Our quarterly magazine 'Voigtländer Matters' comprises of members' articles on, and the gathering of detailed information about, all Voigtländer products and history, but mainly about their cameras and lenses. We always encourage active participation from our members and their responses to questionnaires on various cameras and accessories has added considerably to our detailed knowledge of Voigtländer camera development. We are currently updating and revising Dr Neil Wright's definitive 'Checklist of Voigtländer Cameras', the copyright of which he has most generously given to us.

Third Dimension Society
2, Davison Road, Darlington, Co. Durham, DL1 3DR, England. Telephone (0325) 59272, quarterly magazine. Membership fee £7/year, contact D.C. Wardle, Membership Secretary.

USA

American Photographical Historical Society
520 West 44th Street, New York, NY,10036,USA, Tel: (212)-594-5056. Photographica magazine published four times a year. Eight membership meetings a year, and two camera shows annually. Over 400 members worldwide. Annual dues in the United States US$ 22.50. Foreign membership is available. Contact George Gilbert.

American Society of Camera Collectors
4918 Alcove Avenue, North Hollywood, CA, 91670, USA, Telephone (213)-769-6160.

Atlanta Photographic Collectors Club
PO Box 98291, Atlanta, GA, 30345, USA.

Bay Area Photographic Association
2538 34th Avenue, San Francisco, CA, 94116, USA, Tel: (415)-664-6498.

Chicago Photographic Collectors Society
PO Box 375, Winnetka, Ill, 60093, USA.

Club Daguerre-Darrah
2562 Victoria, Witchita, KA, 67216, USA, Tel: (316)-265-0393.

Delaware Valley Photographic

Association
PO Box 74, Delanco, NJ, 08075, USA.

International Kodak Historical Society
PO Box 21, Flourtown, PA, 19031, USA.

International Photographic Historical Organization
PO Box 16074, San Francisco, CA, 94116, USA, Tel: (415)-681-4356.

Leica Historical Society of America
7611 Dornoch Lane, Dallas, TX, 75248, USA, (214) 387-5708. Viewfinder magazine and Leica Catalogue published four times a year. Annual membership meeting. More than 1,000 members. US$ 28.00 membership fee for the USA, Canada and Mexico, all other countries, US$ 28.00 by surface mail, US$ 37.00 by airmail.

Michigan Photographic Historical Society
PO Box 202, Wayne, MI, 48184, USA, Tel: (313)-721-5126.

Midwest Photographic Historical Society
19 Hazelnut Court, Florissant, MO, 63033, USA.

Miranda Club
PO Box 2001, Hammond, Indiana, 46323, USA, Contact Thomas Surovek.

The Magic Lantern Society
Contact the President Jack Judson, Jr. 445 Burr Road, San Antonio Texas 78209. Phone (210) 824-9995. Fax: (210) 822-1226). The Magic Lantern Castle museum is associated with the club.

National Stereoscopic Association
PO Box 14801, Columbus, OH, 43214, USA. Magazine published six times a year. Regional meetings and annual convention held in the US. More than 2200 members, worldwide. US$22 in the United States, US$32 foreign surface mail, and US$46 by airmail.

Nikon Historical Society
PO Box 3213, Munster, IN, 46321, USA. Tel: (708)-895-5319. The Nikon Journal is published four times a year. The Nikon Historical Society held its second convention in March of 1990. More than 150 members worldwide. Annual dues is US$ 25/year for the United States and Canada, Foreign membership is US$ 35/year. Contact Robert Rotoloni.

Pennsylvania Photographic Historical Society
PO Box 862, Beaver Falls, PA, 15010, USA. Flash Pan newsletter five times a year. Five meetings are held annually. 40 regional members, US$10 annual dues, US$15 for family membership. No foreign membership is available at the present time. Membership fees are US$10/year, US$15 for family. Contact B.J. Tarr.

Photographic Collectors of Houston
1201 McDuffie, #104, Houston, TX, 77019, USA.

Photographic Collectors of Tucson
PO Box 18646, Tucson, AR, 85731, USA. Tel: (602) 721-0478.

Photographic Historical Society of New England
PO Box 189, West Newton Branch, Boston, MA, 02165, USA. Tel: (617)-277-0207. Magazine, New England Journal of Photographic History, published four times a year. Monthly meetings held, except July and August. Over 450 members worldwide. Dues are US$18 for US and Canada, US$35 for

foreign each year. Contact Jack Naylor.

Puget Sound Photographic Collectors Society
10421 Delwood Dr. SW, Tacoma, WA, 98498, USA. Tel: (206)-582-4878, Membership fee US$10.

Rochester Photo Historical Society
PO Box 9563, Rochester, New York 14604. This was the first club for camera collectors in the United States.

The Movie Machine Society
50 Old Country Road, Hudsen, MA, 01749, USA. Quarterly Bulletin Sixteen Frames.

The Ohio Camera Collectors
PO Box 282, Columbus, OH, 43216, USA, Annual show Memorial Day weekend. Membership meeting on the first Saturday of each month, more than 100 members. Contact John Durand (614) 885-3224.

The Photographic Historical Society
PO Box 9563, Rochester, NY, 14604, USA.

The Photographic Historical Society of the Western Reserve
PO Box 25663, Cleveland, OH, 44125, USA. Tel: (216)-382-6727. Membership meetings on the third Wednesday of each month, except August. 100 members. Contact William S. Nehez.

Tri-State Photographic Collectors Society
8910 Cherry, Blue Ash, OH, 45242, USA. Tel: (513)-891-5266.

Western Photographic Collectors Association
PO Box 4294, Whittier, CA, 90607, USA. (213) 693-8421. Quarterly, 24 page Journal on coated stock. Membership meetings held monthly, plus two trade shows a year. 450 Members. Regular membership fee (receiving meeting notices) US$25, Corresponding US$20, Foreign US$30. Contact William P. Carroll.

Zeiss Historical Society
PO Box 631, Clifton, NJ, 07012, USA. (201)-472-1318.

How to read the directory

Throughout the following directory of collectable cameras, various shortforms and abbreviations have been used for functions and features as well as rarity and value.

Something which often confuses newcomers is the fact that rarity and value do not always go hand in hand. For example, the majority of Leica cameras, even the earliest models, are far from rare, even though they are valuable. Some other cameras might not be seen very often and can therefore be classified as raré, even though when they are found, they tend not to be expensive. Condition also plays its part in these two factors. A camera which is rare and expensive in mint condition might be fairly common and less expensive when well worn.

So before you look up any camera in the directory, take a few moments to consider the following points about rarity, condition and value, as well as understanding the various abbreviations which are used throughout the directory.

Condition

Guide prices are for cameras in generally excellent condition. That means 80% to 100% original finish and no evidence of restoration. There are a number of instruments that rarely ever will be found in good working condition. For example, the Contaflex TLR and a number of Zeiss 35mm cameras made in the 1930s fitted with focal plane shutters will rarely be functional. Furthermore they are extremely difficult to have serviced and the older they get

the problem only gets worse as the service people, who once did the work, and the parts become increasingly scarce. The same is true of the Super Kodak 620, a very rare camera with an equally delicate shutter and automatic exposure control system. In this instance, the cosmetic condition of the camera will be the most important consideration.

The presence of the original packaging is particularly important if it is very old and or a special type such as the first Brownies, or the art-deco cameras of Eastman Kodak in the 1930s.

For cameras in other states of condition, add or subtract from the Guide price as follows:

Mint Condition

100% original finish,everything perfect, in new condition in every respect, add 50% to the list prices. If the camera is over 50 years old, this number may go higher. Very rare cameras R4 to R5, this figure raises to 100% or more.

Very Good Condition

60% original finish, item complete but wood, or leather slightly scratched; scuffed or marred metal work, but no corrosion or pitmarks. Lens and viewfinder clean, shutter and other mechanical parts in working order (with exceptions noted above), restorable with minimum effort and expense. Deduct 15-25% from listed prices.

Good Condition

50% original finish, minor wear on exposed surfaces, no major parts broken or missing but may need some minor replacements, metal rusted or pitted in places but can be cleaned, leather scuffed and/or aged, wood scratched, marred and may have minor cracks, but restorable. The lens will show use and the shutter may be in questionable mechanical condition, but repairable. Collectors are less and less interested in these cameras, and you might find you have a difficult time trading them off or selling them.

The other side of this coin is that they are easier to find and if you are skilled in restoration techniques and prepared to invest the time they can be a bargain. Deduct about 40% to 60% from listed price.

Fair Condition

25% original condition, well used and worn, in need of parts replacement and refinishing, leather cracked or missing, lens clouded or damaged, metal parts pitted and gears rounded, shutter inoperable, wood finish almost gone and in need of complete restoration. These cameras are usually sold for parts, to someone who has the same camera in better condition, but maybe needs a screw or spring which can be salvaged from the fair camera. Even worse than the "fair" camera is a strictly parts-only camera. Deduct 60% to 90% from listed price.

Exceptions

Very rare cameras, those with a four to five star or considered unavailable are frequently exceptions to the preceding rules. The older and rarer a camera becomes the more difficult it is to find in truly mint condition. If one does turn up, it may be worth triple the listed price. At the same time a camera that is considered in good condition, but very rare, may still command a very high price. Collectors are cautioned to be very careful of evidence of extensive restoration with valuable instruments. Restored cameras are usually less interesting to collectors than cameras in original condition; it can depend very much on the country and particular collecting speciality. They are usually an attempt by a shrewd dealer to make a poor camera into something it is not. Few serious collectors will be willing to pay the money asked for such mutilations.

For usable cameras, such as the Leica M3 (EL134), or the Bessa II (V0105), needing repair, deduct the cost of repair from the listed price. Be warned, though, that the repair of complex rangefinder or SLR cameras can prove expensive. Competent repair people are becoming increasingly harder to find (and more costly), a trend that can easily depress the prices of cameras needing work, that you may wish to use.

Rarity

Rarity indicates a camera's accessibility for purchase to the collector. The harder it is to find, the higher the rarity factor. Rarity factors are indicated by a star rating system, ranging from 1* to 5*, as in previous editions. We have added an additional category in this issue:

Unavailable

A camera in this category exists in such limited quantities that they are either all in museums or a very few private collections.

When they do come on the market, the price can be staggering. Very few cameras in this category are in the Guide, however several are listed mainly for reasons of historical interest.

Rare cameras are usually in that category regardless of the country they are found in. They are recognised as being in limited supply by collectors internationally. At the lower end of the scale in categories 1, 2 or even 3, there is a strong geographic factor working. For example, a Kodak collector will find their task considerably easier for US products at home, likewise, a collector in Europe or Japan will find it easier to locate the more common domestically made cameras in their own countries. As is the case with prices, it is important to think of Rarity ratings as guides, adjusting them for location. The ratings are defined as follows:

1* Cameras with a one-star rating can be found easily. They are frequently found in box lots at lower level auctions or market stalls. Since they are so easily obtained, a collector has large choice. They were mass-produced and widely distributed for a number of years. Most simple box and folding cameras fall into this category. A good example is a 3A Folding Kodak made for nearly a quarter-of-a-century with minor changes.

2* Cameras with a two-star rarity are slightly more difficult to find. They were usually more costly to purchase new. Rather than finding them at virtually all jumble sales, a collector will need to work a bit harder to find a good sample. Folding plate cameras such as the Zeiss Contina II are in this grouping.

Before World War II folding plate cameras and the better grade folding roll film instruments were offered with a large variety of lens and shutter combinations, sometimes the available choice being determined by the country it was sold in. At the lowest end of the scale it may be fitted with a simple achromat in a three speed shutter. The same basic camera was also being sold with a Zeiss Tessar lens in a Compur shutter. Although the first cost was much higher for the expensive models, this difference is not necessarily reflected in the collectors' market.

3* Three-star cameras will take more searching out. Camera fairs with itinerant dealers, many with excellent inventory, will generally be a good source of three-star cameras, but they do turn up in flea markets from time-to-time. The Kodak Chevron and the Foth-Flex are examples of three-star cameras.

4* A camera may be of four-star rarity for a number of reasons. If it is very old, say early Victorian, time and the changing needs of evolving technology may have combined to destroy most of them. The surviving instruments are in very short supply, or the original production run may have been very small.

5* Five-star level of rarity instruments exist mostly in museums or very large private collections. As recently as a decade ago instruments at this level still turned up occasionally in antique shops etc., but an increasing number of collectors and a greater amount of knowledge about cameras makes such "lightning strikes" increasingly unlikely. The Ben Akiba Cane Camera, and a number of daguerrotype cameras fall into this area.

U   Unavailable. Instruments in this category are sometimes difficult to define. To a large extent you can use the definition of five-star cameras with an important difference. The original production run was very low and the surviving instruments have all been accounted for. The O-Series Leica is a good example of such a camera.

Leica Cameras and Accessories

Leica collecting is the most highly developed and specialised field of camera collecting. There are three main reasons for this. The Leica, although not the first to use 35mm cine film, was the first serious 35mm camera and it revolutionised photography. Leica users pioneered the real-life style of photography we are familiar with today. So it has immense historic significance. Secondly, its makers, Ernst Leitz, from the beginning saw it as a system camera. They developed interchangeable lenses and a myriad of accessories to expand its use into all types of photographic applications, so there are literally thousands of individual items, all beautifully engineered. Thirdly, and most significantly, there is more information available about the Leica than any other camera. This is because the archives of Ernst Leitz at Wetzlar survived the war, being neither destroyed nor looted.

A tremendous amount of research on the Leica has been carried out and published. Complete serial number lists are available, pinpointing the year of manufacture of each individual camera and lens. The history of many individual cameras is known, giving them a special value.

For the camera collector wanting to add some Leica examples to a general collection the Blue Book will provide adequate guidance, and furthermore place the Leica cameras in the context of cameras generally. The Leica specialist collector, however, needs much more detailed information and should turn to the Hove specialist Leica publications listed in the advertisement section of the book. In particular, the Hove Leica International Price Guide gives a finer division of rarity on a scale of 1 to 10 for cameras, lenses and accessories, necessary because of the many variations within individual models and the very limited production of some.

Abbreviations

Certain abbreviations are used throughout the listings in the Blue Book. Here's how to read them...

(?): approximate.

*: one lens and shutter combination of several variations.

+: the "+" sign after a price indicates that the camera would probably sell for considerably more on today's market than it sold for when the price was originally figured.

BIM: built-in light meter.

C: Year of manufacture. The dates in the Zeiss section are precise; elsewhere the dates are approximate. A single date usually indicates the year the camera model first appeared.

CFPS: cloth focal-plane shutter.

Counterfeit: a camera, represented by the seller to the buyer as being historically accurate, but appearing to be of a make or model different from that which it really is. Counterfeit Leica cameras are usually Russian.

CRF: coupled rangefinder.

exp: exposure.

Fake: a camera which has been made to seem that which it is not, and which is represented by the seller to the buyer as original. A Leica "Luxus"which is really a re-worked Leica I(A) but found on a dealer's table at a show as a true "Luxus"would be called a fake. Beware of fakes, before making an expensive purchase, know all the facts about the camera and the seller. More and more"Fakes" are being made in Eastern Europe, and shipped into the West for the chance to turn a fast mark or pound.

FPS: focal plane shutter.

mfg: manufactured.

MFPS: metal focal-plane shutter.

NSR: no sales recorded.

Qty: quantity.

Replica: a camera, represented to the buyer by the seller as being not historically accurate. Replica cameras are not sold to fool anybody. Leica "Luxus" cameras are sometimes made from Leica I(A) cameras, "Ur" Leica cameras are indeed made by Leitz, and are faithful to the original, but alas...

RFR: rangefinder.

s: seconds.

Slr: single lens reflex.

Snr: serial number range.

VFR: viewfinder.

On cameras where more than one price is quoted for variations of the same type (e.g. chrome/black/military markings, etc) the value and rarity ratings apply to that of the basic camera in the section.

Leica 250GG with Motor, c1942 Courtesy to 1996 Auction Team Breker, Köln.

Glossary

Definitions of camera types, accessories and terms used in still and cine camera collecting.

(S) = still cameras only
(C) = cine cameras only
(S&C) = still and cine cameras

Accessory shoe: (S&C) Clip usually found on the top plate of a still camera and occasionally on the top or side of a cine camera to accommodate accessories such as flashguns, exposure meters and rangefinders.

A-D filter: (S&C) Pink-coloured filter used to correct the blue cast that results from shooting, in daylight, film balanced for artificial light. Usually seen as a separate accessory for still cameras. Some cine cameras (especially Super-8 models) had them built in so the same film could be used for either light source.

Amateur Photographer: (S&C) Weekly British photographic magazine, originally known as The Amateur Photographer, first published in 1884 and still published today. Known to most photographers as AP.

Angle of view: (S&C) Extent of the view taken in by the lens or viewfinder. A wideangle lens gives a wide angle of view; a standard lens gives the view most associated with that of the human eye; a telephoto lens gives a narrow angle of view.

AP: (S&C) See Amateur Photographer

Aperture priority: (S) An automatic metering system in which the aperture is chosen first and a corresponding shutter speed or shooting speed is automatically set.

Aperture: (S&C) Variable opening to control the amount of light that is allowed through the lens and onto the film. Measured in f-stops

Artificial light film: (S&C) Film that is made to give correct rendition of tones when shot under artificial light. For cine film, this usually means Photoflood lighting, rather than tungsten.

ASA: (S&C) American Standards Association, a measure of film emulsion speeds.

Auto exposure: (S&C) A method of setting shutter speeds and/or apertures in a still camera to automatically give the correct exposure for different levels of light. In a cine camera, auto exposure controls only apertures against shooting speeds.

Autofocus: (S&C) Automatic lens focusing system.

'B' setting: (S) Standing for brief time or bulb (from the days when camera shutters could be tripped by a pneumatic bulb on the end of a length of rubber tube). A camera setting in which the shutter remains open whilst the control is pressed and closes again when it is released.

Bed: (S) Part of a folding camera that folds down from the main body to support the lens panel.

Between lens shutter: (S) A leaf type shutter that is situated between the elements of a lens.

BJ: (S&C) See British Journal Photographic Almanac.

Box Brownie: (S) Generic term that has come to be accepted for any box-shaped camera, principally inspired by the

Brownie series of cameras made by Kodak.

Box form: (S) Description of camera that is basically box shaped.

Brief time: (S) see 'B' setting.

British Journal Photographic Almanac: (S&C) Established in 1860 and published annually thereafter with articles about photography, plus details of the latest advances and reviews of new equipment for the year. Collected for its value in the research of cameras and photographic equipment. Usually known to collectors as the BJ.

Cable release: (S&C) Device screwed into a shutter release or other socket in the camera body that allows the shutter to be released without accidentally jogging the actual camera.

Capacitor: (S) Part of a flashgun that stores electricity so that the flash is always fired by the same maximum voltage even when a battery is low.

Cartridge: (C) Enclosed case containing pre-loaded cine film for slotting directly into the camera, obviating the necessity for manual loading from spool to spool.

Cassette: (S&C) Container for film. Placed in a still camera, the film is wound out of the cassette and back again at the end of the roll. Some early cameras featured cassette to cassette loading so that rewinding was unnecessary. Usually applied to 35mm film, but occasionally used in other sizes too. In cine cameras, usually associated with a cartridge that can be hand-loaded with conventional film spools prior to placing in the camera.

CdS: (S&C) Form of metering that relies on light falling on a cell and changing its resistance when a current is supplied from a battery.

Celluloid: (S&C) The base on which early films were coated.

Cement: (C) Glue used to stick to pieces of film together during editing.

Central processing unit: (S) Computer chip in electronic cameras that correlates and controls functions.

Cine camera: (C) Device for shooting frames of film sequentially at a set speed which, when projected in a similar way, give the impression of a moving image.

Cine Projector: (C) Device for projecting film shot in a cine camera.

Claw: (S&C) The mechanism that pulls cine film through the camera's gate, working in synchronisation with the shutter to allow each frame to stop momentarily for exposure. Occasionally used as a form of film advance in a still camera.

C-mount: (C) Universal lens mount adopted by many manufacturers of 16mm cine cameras.

Coincident image rangefinder: (S) Mechanism in a camera's viewfinder, or sometimes a separate unit, used for measuring distance. Its view shows two views of the same scene. When the two are brought together and coincide by turning the focus control, or a thumbwheel on a separate unit, the image is in focus.

Colour temperature: (S&C) Measured on the Kelvin scale to denote if the film is balanced – or suitable for use in – daylight (5,000°K), Photofloods (3,400°K), or tungsten (3,200°K).

Compound lens: (S&C) Lens made up of individual elements in groups.

Concave: (S&C) A lens that is thinner in its centre than at its edges.

Convex: (S&C) A lens that is thicker at

its centre than at its edges.

Crank: (S&C) Used to wind cine camera's clockwork motor. Sometimes a separate small handle that is inserted into the body to backwind the film. Also used to advance the film one frame at a time on some still cameras.

Cut: (C) The point where a cameraman stops filming before moving onto the next shot.

Cutaway: (C) A shot of a different but related subject used to link two sequences of film.

Daylight film: (S&C) Film that is made to give correct rendition of tones when shot in normal daylight conditions.

Depth of field: (S&C) The amount of an image that is acceptably sharp on either side of the point at which the lens is actually focused. Varies with the use of apertures, focal length and camera-to-subject distances.

DIN: (S&C) Deutsche Industrie Norm — German standards organisation, a method of calibrating film speeds.

Direct vision viewfinder: (S&C) Eye level viewfinder that looks directly at the subject.

Disc: (S) Film frames arranged around a rotating disc, used in place of the usual rollfilm in disc cameras.

D-mount: (C) Universal lens mount adopted by many manufacturers of Double-8 or Standard-8 cameras.

Double stroke: (S) Type of lever wind on a camera that takes two strokes to advance the film one frame.

Double-8: (C) The most prolific of all 8mm gauges. Actually 16mm film with extra sprocket holes that was run through a camera twice, then slit and joined after processing. Also known as Standard-8.

DX coding: (S) Method of automatically setting film speeds in electronic cameras, controlled by coded information on the cassette.

Editing: (C) Method of cutting and joining film to remove unwanted material or to build up a particular sequence.

Electronic flash: (S) Method of flash photography that incorporates a reusable flash tube in place of the older flashbulbs that could be used only once.

Elements: (C) Individual lenses that go to make up a compound lens.

Emulsion: (S&C) The light-sensitive layer on a film that records the image.

Enlarger: (S) Darkroom apparatus for projecting a negative onto a sheet of printing paper and so controlling the size of the print.

EV: (S&C) See Exposure Values.

Exposure calculator: (S&C) A mechanical device built into many cine cameras that allows the calculation of the correct exposure based on such factors as subject, time of day, time of year and brightness of the sun. Also occasionally found on still cameras.

Exposure meter: (S&C) Apparatus that measures the amount of light falling on a subject and expresses it in terms apertures against shutter speeds or shooting speeds, according to a set film speed.

Exposure Values: (S&C) Method of measuring exposure and expressing it as a series of numbers that refer to specific light levels irrespective of which shutter speed and aperture combination is used. For example, 1/30 second at f/11 on a still camera is actually the same exposure as 1/60 second at f/8 or 1/125 second at f/5.6, but they all have an EV of 12. Used more for still photography than cine.

Exposure: (S&C) The amount of light that is allowed to reach the film, based on prevailing lighting conditions to give a correct rendition of the subject.

Fade: (C) Progressively darkening the image on film until the film is black, or lightening it from black until it is correctly exposed. Usually effected by use of a fade control or variable shutter.

Filter factor: (S&C) The amount by which exposure has to be increased to allow for the density or colour of a filter. A 2x filter factor requires exposure to be increased by one stop, a 3x factor by two stops, etc.

Filter: (S&C) Device placed in front of the lens to change the tones of a picture. In black and white photography, coloured filters are used to separate colours that would otherwise record as a similar tone of grey. In colour photography they are more often used to correct colour casts such as when using tungsten balanced film in daylight (A-D filter), or to filter out haze in distance landscapes (UV filter).

Flashbulb: (S) Small bulb for use in pre-electronic flashguns, made for once only use.

Flashcube: (S) Sealed cube with four flashbulbs embedded in it.

Focal length: (S&C) The distance between the centre of a lens and its sharply focused image when the subject is at infinity. Used to calibrate and identify different types of lens. Long focal lengths indicate telephoto lenses, short focal lengths indicate wideangle lenses.

Focal plane shutter: (S) A shutter consisting of two blinds that run in the focal plane. As the shutter is released, the first blind begins its travel followed by the second. Shutter speeds are controlled by the speed of the travel in combination with the width of the slit between the blinds.

Focal plane: (S&C) The place where the film is positioned in a camera.

Focusing screen: (S) Screen, particularly one made of ground glass, onto which an image is thrown for focusing, usually from the camera's lens, sometimes from an auxiliary lens.

Focusing: (S&C) Method of moving the lens in relation to the film to attain a sharp image when the subject is at different distances.

Folder: (S) Term used to describe a folding camera.

Fps: (C) Acronym, used in cine terms, for frames per second.

Frame line: (C) The division between two frames of cine film.

Frames: (C) Individual frames that record a series of still images that combine to give the impression of movement.

Frames per second: (C) The number of individual cine frames exposed by the camera each second. Most amateur cine cameras adopted a standard of 16fps, although some (notably Bolex) pushed for 18fps. When Super-8 was launched, 18fps became the norm.

Fresnel lens: (S) Lens that consists of concentric rings each with a convex surface. Used in the form of a plastic sheet behind focusing screens to enhance illumination.

F-stop: (S&C) Another name for the aperture setting.

Galvanometer: (S&C) A device that deflects a needle according to minute charges of electrical current. Used in exposure meters to move a needle across a set scale.

Gate: (S&C) The place where individual frames of a cine film are exposed. Incorporates a mechanism to draw the film into position, allowing it to remain still for the exposure before pulling the next frame into position.

Gauge: (C) The width of a cine film – i.e. 8mm, 9.5mm, 16mm, 35mm.

Ground glass screen: (S) Screen on which a camera's image is projected. Sometimes on the back of a camera, but also incorporated into the viewfinders of single and twin lens reflexes.

Head: (C) The device that records and plays back sound onto and from magnetic recording tape.

Hot shoe: (S) Special form of accessory shoe which incorporates electrical connections that mate with a flashgun.

'I' setting: (S) See instantaneous.

Infinity: (S&C) Distance setting on a lens, basically any distance after about 10 metres from the camera when using a standard lens.

Instamatic: (S&C) Trade name of Kodak which should only be applied to that company's 126 cartridge film cameras made from 1963. Often wrongly used as the generic term for any snapshot camera.

Instamatic: (S&C) Trade name of Kodak which should only be applied to that company's cameras. Used initially for still photography cartridge-load cameras made from 1963, then used again for the first Super-8 cameras in 1965.

Instant return mirror: (S) Front surfaced mirror incorporated in a single lens reflex to reflect the image from the lens into the viewfinder. The mirror flips up a fraction of second before the exposure is made. If it returns to its original position automatically straight away after exposure, rather than having to be wound into position as the film is advanced, then it is known as 'instant return'.

Instantaneous: (S) Any shutter speed on a camera other than the 'B' or 'T' settings, but usually used to refer to a single speed of around 1/50 second on snapshot cameras.

Iris: (S&C) Adjustable aperture opening that controls the amount of light reaching the film.

ISO: (S&C) International Standards Organisation, a method of calibrating film speeds.

Jump cut: (C) A change between two shots in which the subject changes, but the camera position remains the same.

Kelvin: (S&C) The scale against which colour temperature is measured.

Lantern slides: (S) Glass plates of positive images made by a still camera for projection purposes in a magic lantern.

Lantern: (S) See magic lantern.

Leader: (C) Spare film at the start of a cine film spool, used to prevent light reaching the emulsion during loading, and which then has to be run off before actual shooting begins.

Leaf shutter: (S) Shutter that relies on iris blades opening and closing to control speeds, usually found between the lens elements or in the body behind the lens.

LED: (S&C) See Light Emitting Diode.

Lens converter: (S&C) Add-on device which changes the focal length of a lens. Usually seen as a separate accessory for still cameras, but more often as part of a three-lens turret on cine cameras. The camera has a standard lens which is converted to wideangle or telephoto by use of separate converters mounted on the turret.

Light emitting diode: (S&C) Small device that glows brightly when a low current is applied to it, used to indicate information in a camera's viewfinder or on the body.

Lip synch: (C) Term used in cine to indicate that the synchronisation between the picture and the soundtrack is perfectly matched.

M synchronisation: (S) Type of flash synchronisation in which the contact is made slightly before the shutter reaches its maximum opening. Used mostly for photography with flashbulbs which need time to build to their maximum power.

Magazine: (C) Another word for a film cartridge

Magic lantern: (S) Early still projector for projecting lantern slides.

Maltese cross: (C) Type of cine camera shutter that cuts off light as the film advances through the gate, then allows light through when the film has stopped for its exposure. Takes its name from its shape. Also seen in some projectors.

Manual exposure: (S&C) Exposure mode in which shutter speeds or shooting speeds and apertures are set by hand, rather than automatically. Also used in still photography to describe cameras in which the correct exposure is suggested by an in-built meter by means of matching needles or LEDs, though not set automatically.

Match needle metering: (S&C) Method of measuring exposure in a still camera by adjusting apertures and/or shutter speeds until two needles coincide or one meets a predetermined mark. On a cine camera, more often only the aperture is adjusted against a standard shooting speed.

Meniscus lens: (S) Simple lens consisting of a single piece of glass with one convex and one concave surface.

Monochromatic: (S&C) Usually used to refer to black and white pictures, although it actually means any image which is composed of a range of different tones of the same colour.

Monochrome: (S&C) One colour, usually black, plus white that makes up a photographic image.

Negative: (S&C) Film that runs through the camera which, when processed, shows all tones reversed and from which the final print – either paper based in still photography or film for projection in cine – is made.

Neutral density filter: (S&C) A filter of darkened glass that reduces light transmission without affecting the colours of the scene.

NiCad: (S) A type of rechargeable battery.

Open aperture metering: (S&C) Method of metering in which the reading can be taken at the lens's widest aperture, rather than at its taking aperture.

Open frame viewfinder: (S&C) Simple viewfinder usually made of two metal or wire frames.

Optical viewfinder: (S&C) Viewfinder that uses lenses to approximate the scene that will appear on film.

Pan: (S&C) Movement of camera from side to side whilst shooting or filming. Applied more to cine techniques than to still.

Parallax: (S&C) The difference between the view seen by the lens and that seen by the viewfinder in non-reflex cameras.

Pentaprism: (S) Device used in a single lens reflex to bounce the light around the viewfinder after it has been reflected from the reflex mirror and onto the focusing screen. The resulting image is the correct way round and right side up.

Perforations: (S&C) See sprocket holes

Persistence of vision: (C) The ability for the human eye to retain an image momentarily after it has been removed from the line of sight.

Photoflood: (S&C) Extra high wattage of bulb, typically up to 500 watts, used for shooting stills or cine filming indoors.

Photokina: (S&C) Major German photographic exhibition.

Polarising filter: (S&C) Filter which causes light to vibrate in a single plane only. Used to reduce reflections, darken blue skies and increase colour saturation. Also, two such filters can be used with their planes at right angles to each other to shoot stereo pairs of pictures. (See next entry)

Polarising spectacles: (S&C) Spectacles made up of two polarising filters placed at right angles to each other. Worn whilst looking at a film shot with polarising filters and orientated appropriately on the two images, the effect is for each filter to cut out the light from one of the images. In this way, each eye sees a different image and the brain combines them to give an illusion of three dimensions.

Positive image: (S&C) Image on film in which all tones are rendered correctly.

Program exposure: (S) Form of automation which sets both shutter speeds and apertures automatically.

Rangefinder: (S&C) Device, either built into a camera or made to be fitted as a separate accessory. Compares the subject from two different angles and so assesses its distance.

Red eye: (S) The effect that results from a flashgun's light being reflected off the retina at the back of a human eye and giving the impression of red pupils. Caused when the flashgun is set too close to the camera lens.

Red window: (S) Small circular window in the back of a camera body through which numbers, printed on the film's backing paper, can be read.

Reflex viewfinder: (S&C) Viewfinder that uses a mirror system to look directly through the camera lens.

Reflex: (S) A method of reflecting an image via a mirror onto the screen of a camera's viewfinder. Found in both single lens and twin lens reflexes.

Rotary shutter: (S) Circular disc with an aperture cut in it, which revolves behind the lens to control shutter speeds.

Selenium cell: (S&C) Used in exposure meters. As light strikes selenium, it generates minute amounts of electricity which are used deflect a needle and so indicate exposures.

Self erecting: (S) System in a folding camera that causes the lens to automatically spring into the taking position as the camera is unfolded.

Semi-auto exposure: (S&C) System in which exposure is adjusted manually, but in reference to indications made by a camera's built-in meter, most often the alignment of two needles, or one needle against a predetermined mark.

Shooting speeds: (C) Range of speeds at which a cine camera's shutter opens and closes in synchronisation with film travelling through the gate. On most amateur cameras, 16 fps (or sometimes 18 fps) was the norm. Slower speeds (8 or 12 fps) made the image appear to run faster when projected. Faster speeds

(24, 32, 64 fps) gave the impression of slow motion when projected.

Shot: (C) A sequence in a film.

Shutter blind: (S) One blind of a focal plane shutter.

Shutter priority: (S) Form of automatic exposure in which the user sets the shutter speed and the camera automatically selects and sets the correct aperture.

Shutter speeds: (S) The times for which a camera shutter is actually open. Usually expressed in fractions of a second, but can run to whole seconds.

Shutter: (S&C) Device in a camera to control the amount of time light is actually falling onto the film.

Single lens reflex: (S&C) Camera in which the image from the lens is reflected directly into the viewfinder so that the image seen in the viewfinder is exactly the same as that which will appear on the film.

Single stroke: (S) Type of lever wind on a camera that takes only one stroke to advance the film one frame.

Single-8: (C) Film gauge, 8mm wide, differentiated from Double-8 by being run through the camera only once.

SLR: (S&C) See single lens reflex.

Snapshot camera: (S) Any form of simple camera with the bare minimum of controls.

Split-image rangefinder: (S&C) Mechanism in a camera's viewfinder, used for measuring distance. Its view shows the scene split horizontally across the centre. When the two halves of the image are brought together by turning the focus control, the image is in focus.

Sprocket holes: (S&C) Perforations at the side of a film. Most often applied to 35mm in still photography film, but also 8mm, 9.5mm, 16mm and 35mm cine film. In still photography, the sprocket holes are used to advance the film one frame at a time between pictures. In cine, used by the claw mechanism to drag the film through the gate in a continuous run.

Sprocket: (S&C) Cogged wheel around which film is led to advance still film in the camera, or to lead it to and from the gate in some cameras and most projectors.

Standard lens: (S&C) Lens of average focal length which provides a view similar to that scene by the human eye.

Standard-8: (C) Name variant for Double-8.

Stereo: (S&C) The effect of shooting two pictures from two slightly different viewpoints similar to the spacing between the human eye so that, when each image is viewed independently, one with each eye, an impression of three dimensions is produced.

Stop down metering: (S) Method of metering in which the lens has to be stopped down to its taking aperture before an accurate exposure reading can be obtained.

Stop: (S&C) See F-stop.

Synchronisation: (C) The match between sound and picture when a film is projected.

'T' setting: (S) Standing for time. A camera setting in which the shutter opens when the release is pressed and remains open until it is pressed again.

Telephoto lens: (S&C) Any lens that has a focal length longer than a standard lens. Used to magnify the image and bring far subjects closer on film.

Three-dimensional: (S&C) The appearance of depth in a projected film. See polarising filter, polarising spectacles and stereo.

Through the lens metering: (S&C) Method of metering which measures light actually through the lens of the camera.

Through the lens metering: (S&C) Method of metering which measures light actually through the lens of the camera.

Tilt: (C) Movement of a camera up and down during filming.

Time exposure: (S) Exposure in which the shutter is held open for longer than the normal fraction of a second. Very often manually timed and used with the camera's 'B' or 'T' settings.

TLR: (S) See twin lens reflex.

Top plate: (S) The top of the camera that houses controls such as shutter release, film wind, frame counter, etc.

Track: (C) Movement of a camera backwards and forwards during filming.

Trailer: (C) Spare film at the end of a spool after exposed film is finished, used to keep light from the emulsion when the film is removed from the camera.

Transparency: (S) Film that shows a positive image.

Tripod: (S&C) Adjustable three-legged support to keep a camera firm whilst shooting. One designed for cine use should include a pan and tilt head that allows the camera to be panned left and right or tilted up and down independently.

TTL: (S&C) See through the lens metering

Tungsten: (S&C) Normal room lighting.

Turret: (S&C) A panel that holds two or more lenses and which can be rotated into position for filming. Also seen on a very few and rare still cameras.

Twin lens reflex: (S) Type of camera with two lenses, one to take the picture, the other to reflect a similar, though not exactly the same, image to a screen in the viewfinder.

Viewfinder: (S&C) Device for estimating what the image on the film will look like. Built into nearly all cameras, though missing from some specialist models. Rangefinder cameras without reflex viewing will often use separate viewfinders that fit into the accessory shoe when certain specialist lenses are in use.

Waterhouse stops: (S) Series of apertures cut into a metal sheet, used as inexpensive alternative to iris aperture control.

Wideangle lens: (S&C) Any lens that has a focal length shorter than the standard lens. Increases the field of view, allowing the picture to contain more at the sides, top and bottom.

X synchronisation: (S) Type of flash synchronisation in which the contact is made exactly as the shutter reaches its maximum opening. Used mostly for photography with electronic flash which reaches its maximum power almost instantaneously.

Zoom lens: (S&C) Lens of variable focal length.

Zoom: (C) The apparent movement backwards and forwards during cine filming, caused by adjustment of a zoom lens on a static camera.

Camera Directory
A-Z

COLLECTABLE CAMERAS, SPECIFICATIONS, PRICES, VALUES, RARITY RATINGS AND YEARS OF MANUFACTURE

A

Acro Scientific Products Co
Chicago, USA

Acro R: R3* C+
c1938, Bakelite RFR camera for 3 x 4cm frames on 127 roll film, f3.5 lens, Alphax shutter, built-in extinction meter, un-coupled RFR.

Acro IV: R3* B
Without extinction meter or RFR.

Adams & Co
London, England

The firm of A. Adams was founded in 1886 by Arthur L. Adams in London. By the 1890's they were general photographic suppliers, offering studio furniture, painted backgrounds and all the other requirements of the photographers of the day. Eventually they began making cameras for sections of the market, at prices from £1 to £20. In the early 1900's Adams dropped their cheaper range of cameras to concentrate on high quality, exquisitely made cameras for the professional and advanced amateur. Two of these were the square bellows "Challenge" and the tapered bellows "Club", both in production until the late 1930's. Arthur Adams designed most of the cameras himself, concentrating on reliable plate and film changing systems and accurate, vibrationless shutters.

Adams Deluxe Hand Camera: R4* F

Box magazine camera; pneumatic shutter to 1/1000s; dark focusing red Russian leather bellows; could be used with Eastman-Walker roll holder; polished wood magazine holder. Same camera covered in red leather with 18 karat gold fittings, shutter and handle was made for Queen Victoria. C 1890's. 3 models made; No.1. Single ext; Quarter and Half-plate, 4" x 5" Dallmeyer Stigmatic Series 1 F6 lens: No. 2 Double ext. 4" x 5" Quarter-plate; Zeiss Satz Convertible F6.3 lens: No. 3 Triple ext; 4" x 5" Quarter-plate; Zeiss Satz Convertible F7 lens: No. 4: c1902; As No. 3 with addition of Adams FP shutter 1/150-1/1000s.

Radex Reflex: R3* F
1927. More cost effective version of the company's Minex range, made only in 3½" x 2½" and quarter plate formats. Rise and fall on front. Special feature was a blind that automatically operated to form a light-tight closure when the mirror was in its up position, allowing the use of extra wideangle lenses. Supplied with extra wide aperture f3.5 or f2.7 lenses.

No. 1 Yale Photographic Outfit:
                               R3* C+
c1890's. Black paper covered cardboard box camera; 2" x 2" exp on plates.

No. 5 Yale Stereo Detective: R4* G
c1890's. Leather covered camera; 7½"
Zeiss lenses; rack focusing; concealed
bellows. Leather changing bag back.

Minex Reflex: R4* E+
1929. New features added in this year
to range of cameras available since
c1910. Self-capping focal plane shutter
with a new movement to guarantee
accuracy of speeds. Greater triple
extension added, four-way swing front
retained from previous models. Made in
3½" x 2½", quarter plate, half plate,
postcard and 10 x 15 cm sizes. Up to
10" x 8" could also be made to order.

Minex Tropical: R4* I

c1930. 3¼" x 4¼" tropical SLR camera;
CFPS ⅛-1/1000s. Teak wood
construction with polished brass
fittings.

Idento: R3* E
c1908 3¼" x 4¼" folding camera; Ross
Homocentric 5" f5.3 lens.

Vaido: R4* G
c1920. Quarter plate and 5" x 4" plate
cameras with swing front and rising

front, revolving back. Model A with
front shutter, Model B with focal plane
shutter.

Vesta: R4* E
c1920. Roll film and plate models,
featuring the lazy tongs design. Rollfilm
models utilised larger negative area on
the film than most other cameras of the
type. Featured Adams' Identoscope
viewfinder, claimed to more accurate
and brighter than rivals. Made in sizes
from 6 x 4.5 cm up to 5½" x 3½".
Stereo version also available.

Videx: R3* E
c1904. 3¼" x 4¼" SLR camera; Tessar
21cm f4.5 lens.

Adox Kamerawerk
Wiesbaden, Germany

*(Also Dr. C. Schleußner Fotowerk,
Frankfort a/M, Germany)*

Adox Adrette: R2* C–
c1939, 35mm camera with telescoping
front; Schneider Radionar 50mm f2.9
lens; Compur Rapid shutter, 1-1/500 s,
36 exp, 24 x 36mm. This camera is
identical to the Wirgin Edinex, and may
be made by Wirgin.

Adox Sport: R2* B
c1935-51, folding VFR camera for 6 x 9
or 6 x 4.5cm frames on 120 rollfilm,
Anastigmat f6.3 or f4.5/105mm lens.

Adox Sport O: R2* B
c1949, folding VFR camera for 6 x 9 or
6 x 4.5cm frames on 120 roll film,
Radionar f4.5/10.5cm lens, Vario
shutter, 1/25-1/100s, synch. Postwar
version Sport.

Adox Sport I: R2* B
c1950, Pronto shutter.

Adox Sport II: R2* B
c1950, Prontor shutter.

Adox Sport Ia: R2* B
c1952, folding VFR camera for 6 x 9cm
or 6 x 6cm frames on 120 roll film,
Cassar f4.5/105mm lens, Pronto
shutter, synch. Addition of new chromed
top plate, double exposure prevention,
and accessory shoe. Both formats
visible in optical VFR.

Adox Sport IIa: R2* B
c1952, Prontor S shutter.

Adox Sport IIIa: R2* B
c1952, Prontor SV shutter.

Adox Sport Rouge: R4* D
c1952. With special red leatherette body
covering, and red leather bellows.

Adox Tempo: R3* C–
c1935, folding vrf camera for 6 x 4.5cm
frames on 120 roll film, many
lens/shutter combinations including the
top of the line Xenar f2.8/75mm lens in
Compur Rapid shutter.

Adox Trumpf: R3* B
c1932, folding VFR camera for 6 x 9 or
6 x 4.5 frames on rollfilm, Anastigmat
f4.5/105mm lens, Vario shutter.

Adox Trumpf II: R3* B
c1934, folding VFR camera for 6 x 9 or
6 x 4.5 frames on rollfilm, many
lens/shutter combinations, typically
Xenar f4.5/105mm lens, Compur Rapid
shutter. Addition of body release, new

film pressure plate, and better lens
availability.

Junka: R3* B
c1949, metal VFR camera for 3 x 4cm
frames on special Schleussner/Junka
film, f8/45mm lens, simple shutter.

Adox 66:   R1* B
c1950, black Bakelite TLR type box
camera for 6 x 6cm frames on rollfilm,
f8 lens, simple shutter, choice of three
lenses with focusing from 1m to inf.

Adox Blitz: R2* A
c1950, black Bakelite TLR type box
camera for 6 x 6cm frames on roll film,
f8 lens, simple shutter, basically the 66
camera with provision for flash.

Adox Golf: R2* B
c1952, folding VFR camera for 6 x 6
frames on roll film, Cassaren f4.5/75mm
lens, Pronto shutter, accessory shoe,
body release, knob wind.

Adox Golf II: R2* B
c1952, folding VFR camera for 6 x 6
frames on roll film. Prontor S shutter.

Adox Golf IV: R2* B
c1952, folding VFR camera for 6 x 6
frames on roll film, Cassar f3.5/75mm
lens. No model III is known to exist.

Adox Golf 63:   R2* A
c1954, folding VFR camera for 6 x 6
frames on roll film, Adoxar f6.3/75mm
lens,Vario shutter, accessory shoe, body
release, knob wind. The cheapest
version of the Adox Golf family.

Adox Golf 63 S: R2* B

c1956, folding VFR camera for 6 x 6 frames on roll film. Addition of a selftimer.

Adox Me-Golf: R3* C

c1955, folding RFR camera for 6 x 6cm frames on roll film, CRF, Cassar f3.45 or 4.5/75mm lens, Pronto or Prontor S shutter, self timer, synch. Advertised as the "cheapest 6 x 6 RFR of the day!".

Adox 300:   R4* E

c1956, 35mm RFR camera with interchangeable film magazine backs, each back having its own film counter and film reminder system, built-in light meter, Cassar f2.8/45mm lens and Synchro Compur MXV shutter with EV scale, or Xenar f2.8/45mm lens and Compur Rapid XV shutter with EV scale. Original price included one magazine, not three as is sometimes mentioned. Additional magazines were available for 56DM each.

Adox Golf IA: R2* A

c1963, 35mm VFR camera, (not to be confused with the folding roll film Golf series), Adoxon f2.8/45mm lens, Prontor 125 shutter.

Adox Golf IA: R2* A

c1964, 35mm VFR camera, (not to be confused with the folding roll film Golf series), Adoxon f2.8/45mm lens, Prontor-matic shutter, built-in light meter, red green diode light metering.

Adox Golf IIIA: R3* B

c1954. 35mm VFR camera, (not to be confused with the folding roll film Golf series), Radionar L f2.8/45mm lens, Prontor 500 shutter, built-in light meter. The most expensive of the 35mm Golf

series, using a rare earth glass lens.

Adox Polo: R2* A

c1959. metal 35mm VFR camera, Adoxar f3.5/45mm lens, Pronto shutter.

Adox Polo IS: R2* A

c1959, metal and plastic 35mm VFR camera, Radionar L f2.8/45mm lens, Pronto shutter.

Adox Polo IB: R2* A

c1964, metal and plastic 35mm VFR camera, Adoxar f3.5/45mm lens, Prontor shutter.

Adox Polomat: R2* A

c1959, 35mm VFR camera with built-in coupled light meter, Radionar L f2.8/45mm lens, Prontor LK shutter.

Adox Polomat 1:   R2* B

c1959, 35mm VFR camera with built-in coupled light meter, Radionar L f2.8/45mm lens, Prontor 500LK shutter, bright line parallax marking in the VFR.

Adox Polomat 2:   R2* A

c1959, 35mm VFR camera with built-in coupled light meter visible in the VFR and on the top plate, Radionar L f2.8/45mm lens, Prontormat shutter.

Adox Polomatic 2:   R2* A

c1961, 35mm VFR camera with built-in coupled light meter, Radionar L f2.8/45mm lens, Prontor Lux shutter.

Adox Polomatic 3:   R2* A

c1961, 35mm VFR camera with built-in coupled light meter, Radionar L f2.8/45mm lens, Prontormat-S shutter.

Adox Polomatic 3S: R2* A
c1961, 35mm VFR camera with built-in coupled light meter, Radionar L f2.8/45mm lens, Prontor-Matic shutter, lens opening visible in the VFR.

L'Aiglon: R3* E–
c1934. Meniscus lens; single speed shutter; 8 exp, 12 x 14mm on special roll film. Mfd in France.

Agilux Ltd
Croydon, England

Agiflash: R1* A+
c1954. Bakelite covered in leatherette. 8 exp. on 127. Built-in socket for flashbulbs. Detachable flash reflector.

Agiflex: R2* C+
c1947. Rigid body SLR for 8 exp. on 120. Leather-covered metal body, based on the Reflex Korelle. Waist-level finder. 80mm f/3.5 Agilux with helical focusing. Shutter 1/25-1/500s. Slight redesign of bayonet to take extra lenses with the Model II in 1949, which also added shutter speeds to 2s. Restyled in 1854 for Model III.

Agiflex II: R2* C+
1949; 6 x 6cm SLR camera; FPS 1/25-1/500s. 12 exp on 120 roll film; several versions; Models- I £50, II £100, III £150.

Agifold: R2* C
c1956. Rollfilm camera for 12 pictures on 120 film. Uncoupled rangefinder and extinction meter built in. 75mm f4.5 Agilux anastigmat lens, shutter speeded 1-1/350s. Removable back, unusual in a rollfilm camera of this type, to allow addition of now rare cut film back.

Agimatic: R2* C

c1956. 35mm with uncoupled rangefinder. 45mm f/2.8 Agilux. Shutter 1-1/300s.

Aires Camera Industries Co
Tokyo, Japan

Aires 35-IIIL: R2* C–
c1955, 35mm RFR camera, Coral f1.9/45mm coated lens, Seikosha MXL 1-1/500s, CRF.

Aires 35 IIIA: **R2* C–**
c1957, 35mm RFR camera.

Aires 35-V: **R3* D–**
c1960, 35mm RFR camera,
interchangeable Coral f1.5/4.5cm lens,
Seikosha MX shutter 1-1/400s, built-in
light meter, CRF, bright line fields of
view for 50mm and 100mm in VFR.

Accessory lenses for Aires 35-V

W/A Coral f3.2/35mm lens: **B+**
Tele Coral f3.5/100mm lens: **C**

A.F.I.O.M.
Pordenone, Italy

Wega: **R3* F–**

1950. Cfps, 1/20-1/1000s, Vfr only, no
Rfr, flash synch. Screw mount Trixar
f3.5/50mm lens. Only about 1000
cameras are thought to have been made.

Wega IIa: **R3* F**

1950-51. Cfps, 1/20-1/1000s, separate
Rfr/Vfr windows, flash synch. Screw
mount Trixar F3.5/50mm lens.

Air King Products Companies Inc
New York, USA

Air King Camera Radio: **R3* E–**
c1948. Combination tube-type radio and
plastic 828 roll film camera; finished in
brown "lizard-skin".

Aivas and Chauvet
France

Le Fin de Siecle: **R4* F+**
c1892. Aplanat f8 lens; 9 x 12cm plates;
magazine back.

Charles Alibert
Paris, France

Photo-Sac a Main: **R4* I**

c1895. Lady's handbag detective
camera; Rapid Rectilinear 150mm f12
lens; non-capping rotary shutter; single
exp. 9 x 12cm on dry plates.

Alpa –refer to Pignons, S.A.

Alsaphot

Alsaphot
(Société Alsacienne d'Optique et de la Photographie), France

Dauphin: **R3* B**
c1950, simple TLR camera for 6 x 6cm frames on roll film.

Ajax: **R3* B**
c1950, metal bodied VFR camera for 6 x 6cm frames on roll film, collapsible Alsar f3.5/75mm lens, Alsaphot shutter, 1-1/300s, accessory shoe.

Cady: **R3* B**
c1950, metal bodied VFR camera for 6 x 6cm frames on roll film, collapsible Alsaphot Anastigmat f6.3/75mm lens, simple shutter, accessory shoe.

D'Assas: **R3* B**
c1950, metal bodied VFR camera for 6 x 6cm frames on roll film, collapsible Boyer Topaz f4.5/75mm lens in Alsaphot shutter, 1/25-1/200s, tubular VFR, accessory shoe.

Maine: **R2* A**
c1957, simple metal bodied 35mm VFR camera, knob advance, Berthiot f2.8/45mm lens in Alsaphot shutter, 1/25-1/200s, accessory shoe.

Maine II: **R2* B**
c1960, Lever advance instead of wind knob.

Maine IIIa: **R2* B**
c1962, with built-in light meter.

Memox: **R3* D**
c1930s. Small size, but full frame 35mm camera with direct vision optical viewfinder, f3.5 lens and shutter speeded 1/25-1/150s.

Cyclope: **R3* F**

1950-52, aluminium bodied VFR camera for 6 x 9cm frames on roll film, unique rigid construction using internal mirrors to lengthen the light path, eliminating the need for bellows, making a solid, compact camera. coated Boyer Saphir f4.5/ 105mm lens, Prontor II shutter to 1/175s, lens placement makes this camera hard to miss. Designed by Lucien Dodin, father of the split-image RFR, about 1800 made. Though very rare, one or two of these cameras show up at the annual camera fair at Bievre, France.

Cyclope II: **R4* G+**
1953. Boyer Saphir f3.5/105mm lens, Prontor II shutter to 1/200s, and "Deluxe" finish, only 200 made, and these were made against the advice of Mr. Dodin, whose calculations showed that there was too much light fall-off with the lens wide opened at f3.5 for the mirror system to work well.

Altissa Kamerwerk
Dresden, former East Germany

(Post war continuation of Eho-Kamera-Fabrik GmbH, Emil Hofert, Dresden, Germany, see Eho listing for pre-war cameras)

Altuca: **R3* B**
c1949, metal roll film camera for 6 x 6 frames, collapsible f3.5/75mm lens, simple three speed shutter.

Altix II: **R4* C–**
c1947 35mm VFR camera for 24 x 24mm frames, f3.5 35mm lens in simple bti shutter. Name written on the camera front. Interesting as a continuation of the pre-war Altissa, pleasing body style, quite rare.

Altix III: **R3* C–**
1950, 35mm VFR camera for 24 x 36mm frames, Meritar f2.9/50mm lens in simple bti shutter. The first full-frame Altix.

Altix IV: **R3* C–**
c1951, 35mm VFR camera, now with accessory shoe and flash synch outlet, Trioplan f2.9/50mm lens in Cludor 1-1/200s or Vebur 1-1/250s shutter, with and without film reminder dial.

Altix V: **R4* C–**
c1957, 35mm VFR camera with interchangeable Trioplan f2.9 or CZ Jena f2.8/50mm lens in Tempor shutter, 1-1/250s. The first Altix with interchangeable lens, quite rare.

Altix V, c1957.

Altix N: **R2* C–**
c1958, 35mm VFR camera, with interchangeable CZ Jena f2.8 or Trioplan f2.9/50mm lens in Tempor shutter 1-1/250, new body style, The first Altix to be identified on the camera itself, "Altix-n" on the front or top of the camera.

Altix-NB: **R2* C–**
c1958, 35mm VFR camera, inter-changeable CZ Jena f2.8 or Trioplan f2.9/50mm lens in Tempor shutter, with the addition of uncoupled built-in light meter.

Altissa: **R2* C+**
c1957, all metal box camera for 6 x 6 frames on roll film, top mounted optical finder, simple shutter, Altissar Periscope f8 lens, not to be confused with the pre-war Altissa. This camera was copied by the Chinese and called the Xing Fu.

Accessories for Altix Cameras	
Primagon f4.5/35mm lens:	**B**
Telefogar f3.5/90mm lens:	**B+**

American Advertising & Research Corp
Chicago, Illinois, USA

Cub: **R2* A**
c1950's. Plastic roll film box camera; meniscus lens and sector shutter; 828 roll film; side comes off to load. Later known as Scenex. Original cost was $15 – less than the cost of a roll of film; also given away as toothpaste premium.

American Camera Mfg Co
Northboro, Massachusetts, USA

Founded in 1895 by Thomas Blair, the American Camera Mfg. Co. marketed Buckeye Brand cameras, and also supplied them to E. & H.T. Anthony and Co. In 1896 the company was sold to George Eastman, who wanted control of a number of important patents.

No. 2 Buckeye: **R2* C+**
c1899. Box roll film camera; 4" x 5" exp on plates. Method of shutter tensioning and arrow in lens opening similar to Blair box cameras.

No. 1 Tourist Buckeye: **R3* D+**
c1895. Folding roll film camera; $3\frac{1}{2}$" x $3\frac{1}{2}$" exp on roll film.

***American Optical Co. –
refer to Scovill Mfg. Co.***

American Safety Razor Corp
Camera Division, New York, USA

ASR Fotodisc: **R4* F**
c1960. Two part camera consisting of film disc and lens mount; 32mm Rapodis-ASR lens; single speed shutter. 8 exp, 22x24mm on circular film, 10cm in diameter in special holder.

Ansco Inc (Agfa G.A.F.)
Binghamton, New York, USA

In 1902, E. & H.T. Anthony and Company merged with the Scovill and Adams Company, forming the Anthony and Scovill Company; in 1907, the company name was shortened to Ansco. In 1928 the company was merged with Agfa Products Inc. and Agfa Rawfilm Corp. of New York under the name of Agfa Ansco Corp. In 1939 the company name was changed to General Aniline & Film Corp., commonly referred to by its initials, G.A.F. Corp. For simplicity, German Agfa cameras are included in the following listing.

**Anthony & Scovill Solograph
Plate Camera:**   **R3* E–**
c1901. 4" x 5" plate view camera; Scovill & Adams Co. lens and shutter; red bellows.

Anthony & Scovill Stereo Solograph:
                                       R3* F
c1901. 4" x 6" folding stereo camera; 4" x 6" exp on dry plates.

Anthony & Scovill Roll Film Camera:
R3* D+

c1901. Wollensak lens; wood interior with detailed engraving. Separate roll film back. In 1907 this became the No. 8 Ansco.

Anthony & Scovill 4"x 5" Box Camera:
R3* C–

c1902. No variable aperture control; red window; 6 or 12 exp, 4" x 5" on roll film. In 1907 this became the No. 3 Ansco.

Anthony & Sovill 3¼" x 4¼"
Box Camera: R2* C

c1903; side variable aperture setting; dual vf; side shutter release; dual pushbutton rear opening; wood interior; 6 or 12 exp, 3¼" x 4¼". In 1907 this became the No. 2 Ansco.

Anthony & Scovill 3¼" x 4¼"
Box Camera: R2* C

c1900; key wind top shutter release; single top vf; rear slide back opening; wood interior; 6 or 12 exp on roll film. In 1902 this became the No. 1 Ansco.

No. 4 Ansco Model D: R3* C–

c1905; Wollensak lens; 3¼" x 4¼" exp on 118 roll film.

Dollar Box Camera: R2* A

c1910; 3½" x 2½" box camera.

No. 0 Buster Brown Camera: R3* B

c1921. The Buster Brown box camera was available in six basic models plus several special versions covered in coloured leather with polished brass fittings. The #0, 2, 2A, 2C, 3, 3A are worth about the same.

No. 3A Folding Buster Brown Camera:
R2* C+

c1915; Actuf shutter; 6 or 10 exposure, 3¼" x 5½".

No. 5 Ansco, Model C: R2* C–

roll film camera; horizontal format; red bellows.

Ansco Jr. Model A: R2* C+

c1912, 6 or 12 exp, 2¼" x 4¼".

Ansco Jr. Model B: R2* C

c1912, 6 or 12 exp, 2¼" x 4¼"

No. 4 Ansco: R2* C
c1912, 6 or 12 exp, 3¼" x 3¼".

No. 6 Ansco Model D: R2* C
c1912, 6 or 12 exp, 3¼" x 4¼"

No. 0 Ansco: R2* C
c1914, vest pocket camera; Ansco Anastigmat f6.3 or Modico Anastigmat f7.5 lens; 1⅝" x 2½" exp; front pulls straight out.

Vest Pocket Ansco No. 2: R2* B+
c1914, 6x9cm roll film camera; Ansco Anastigmat lens; Bionic shutter; 8 exp, 6x9cm on 120 roll film.

No.1A Automatic Camera: R3* E

c1925, clockwork motor drive roll film camera; Ilex Anastigmat f6.3 lens; Ilex Semi-Automatic shutter 1/25-1/100s; 2¾" x 4⅛" exp on D6 or D12 roll film. Spring wound motor automatically advances film after each exp at rate of approx 1 exp per sec.

Ansco Readyset Camera: R2* C
c1926, 120 roll film folding camera; maroon leather, brass hardware.

No.1A Readyset Royal: R2* C+
c1926, 116 roll film folding camera;
116 Antar lens; Readyset shutter I, T;
brown ostrich covering, matching brown
bellows.

No.1A Readyset Special: R2* C–
c1926, 116 roll film folding camera;
Antar lens; Readyset shutter I, T and B;
dark reddish brown covering, brown
bellows.

No.1 Readyset Royal: R2* C+
c1926, 120 roll film folding camera;
120 Antar lens and shutter; dark tone
coloured sealskin covering, grey
bellows.

No.1A Readyset Royal: R3* C+
c1926, 116 roll film folding camera;
Wollensak Velostigmat f6.3 lens; shutter
1/10-1/100s, I, T; brown ostrich
covering, brown bellows.

Photo-Vanity: R4* G+
c1926, vanity-case type detective
camera; containers for rouge, powder
and lipstick; small Ansco box camera
fitted; operates through exterior of
case. 8 exp, 4 x 6.5cm on 127 roll film.

Memo (1927): R2* D

c1927, half-frame
35mm box camera;
Ilex-Ansco Cinemat
40mm f6.3 lens; Ilex
shutter 1/25-1/100s.
Rapid film shift
mechanism. The
Memo used special
cassettes, originally
wood and later
metal.

Official Boy Scout Memo Camera:
R3* E+
c1927, wooden bodied, olive drab
finish, with boy Scout insignia, miniature
camera; 50 exp, 18 x 23mm on 35mm
film.

Billy I: R3* A
c1928, folding VFR camera for 6 x 9cm
frames on roll film, Igestar 105mm f8.8
lens; Agfa shutter 1/25-1/100s, squarish
body ends make this camera easy to
identify.

Billy II: R2* A

c1930s, folding VFR camera for 6x9cm
frames on roll film, Agfa Anastigmat
f7.7 lens; Agfa shutter 1/25- 1/100s.

Billette F4.5: R3* A
c1930s, folding VFR camera for 6x9cm
frames on roll film, either Oppar or
Solinar Anastigmat f4.5 lens, Compur
shutter, the top of the line "Billy".

Billy Record 8.8:   R2* A
c1930s, folding VFR camera for 6 x 9cm frames on roll film, Igestar f8.8/10cm lens, Automat shutter.

Billy Record 7.7:   R2* A
c1930s, folding VFR camera for 6 x 9cm frames on roll film, Igestar f7.7/10cm lens, Automat or Automat S shutter.

Billy Record 6.3:   R2* A
c1930s, folding VFR camera for 6 x 9cm frames on roll film, Igestar f6.3/10cm lens, Vario or Pronto S shutter.

Billy Record 4.5:   R2* B
c1930s, folding VFR camera for 6 x 9cm frames on roll film, Apolar f4.5/10.5cm lens, Prontor II-S shutter.

Billy Compur: R2* B
c1935, folding VFR camera for 6 x 9cm frames on roll film, Apotar or Solinar f4.5/10.5cm lens, Compur or Compur Rapid shutter.

Agfa Record I: R3* B
c1950s, folding VFR camera for 6 x 9cm frames on roll film, Agnar f6.3 or f4.5/105mm lens, Vario or Pronto shutter, with and without accessory shoe or body mounted shutter release.

Agfa Record III: R3* D
c1950s folding RFR camera for 6 x 9cm frames on roll film, Solinar f4.5/105mm lens, Synchro Compur shutter, accessory shoe, built-in un-coupled RFR, body mounted shutter release

Trolita: R3* C–
c1938, plastic folding VFR camera for 6 x 9cm or 6 x 4.5cm frames on roll film, Apotar f4.5/10.5cm lens, Compur or Prontor II shutter. Produced at the same time as the Trolix box camera (AS156) from "Trolit", a kind of thermo plastic.

Standard 6 x 9:   R3* A
c1930s, metal folding VFR camera for 6 x 9cm frames on roll film, marked "Standard" on the lens stand, Anastigmat f4.5 or 6.3/105mm lens, Automat shutter.
Standard De Luxe: R2* C+
c1930, 6 x 9cm folding camera; Agfa Anastigmat f6.3/105mm lens; 6 x 9cm plates.

Ansco Memory Kit: R3* E+
c1930, consists of No. 1 Readyset Royal camera in ostrich covering, instruction book, room for 4 rolls of film in walnut wood gift box.

Agfa Ansco Readyset
Moroccan Camera: R3* D+

c1930's, 120 roll film folding camera; Antar lens; blue bellows, embossed blue Moroccan leather.

Agfa Ansco Readyset Traveler: R2* C–
c1930's. Antar lenses; cloth covered in combination stripes, grey bellows; two models for 120 and 115 roll film.

**Ansco Vest Pocket Readyset
127 Camera: R2* C+**
c1930s. Wollensak lens; 5 colours available; orange, blue, green, red and turquoise.

Agfa Ansco View: R3* E

c1939. 5" x 7" view camera; Wollensak Verito Portrait lens.

Agfa Flexilette: R2* D

1960. 35mm twin lens reflex with waist-level finder. 45mm f2.8 Color Apotar lenses in Prontor shutter. 1-1/500s.

Memo (1940):   R2* C+

c1940. 35mm folding camera; Agfa Memar 50mm f3.5 lens; Ansco shutter ¹/₂-1/200s. Rapid shift film mechanism.

Speedex: R2* B–
c1940, 120 roll film folding camera; 85mm f4.5 lens; 12 exp, 2¹/₄" x 2¹/₄" on 120 roll film.

Automatic Reflex: R3* D+

c1947, 2¼" x 2¼" TLR; Ansco Anastigmat 83mm f3.5 coated lens; Ansco shutter 1-1/400s; 12 exp, 2¼" x 2¼" on 120 roll film. Eye-level focusing, built-in magnifying lens for critical focus. The Automatic Reflex was originally introduced in 1947 without flash synch. The 1949 version had factory installed flash synch for class F bulbs.

Isolar: R2* B

c1930s, Agfa Solinar 135mm f4.5 lens; Compur shutter; double extension bellows; ground glass back; 9 x 12cm plates.

Karat 3.5:   R3* C–

c1937, 35mm folding VFR camera, Solinar f3.5/5cm lens, Compur Rapid shutter, 12 exposures on special Agfa cartridges, also available post-war as the "Agfa 12/3.5".

Karat 4.5:   R2* B+

c1935, 35mm folding VFR camera, Agfa Oppar 5.5cm f4.5 lens, Vario shutter 1/25-1/125s, 12 exposures on special Agfa cartridges.

Karat 6.3:   R2* C–

c1934, 35mm folding VFR camera, Anastigmat-Igestar f6.3/5cm lens,Vario shutter, 1/25-1/100s,12 exposures on special Agfa cartridges.

Karat 12/2.8:   R3* C

c1946, folding RFR camera for 12 exposures on special Agfa cartridges, Xenar f2.8/50mm lens, Compur Rapid shutter, this camera became the Karat 36 of 1949.

Karat 36:   R2* D

c1949, 35mm folding RFR camera, Soligon, Heligon or Xenar f2.8/50mm coated lens; Synchro-Compur shutter 1-1/500s, CRF. Used orthodox 35mm in normal cassettes.

Karat 36, c1949.

Karat IV;   R2* D

c1959, 35mm folding RFR camera; Agfa Solinar f2 or f2.8/50mm coated lens; prontor SVS shutter, 1-1/300s redesigned top plate, with centred accessory shoe.

Agfa Optima I: R2* C

c1961. 35mm camera. Auto exposure by red/green indicators in viewfinder. Metal body, leatherette covered. 45mm f2.8 Color Agnar and Prontorlux shutter, 1/30-1/500s.

Agfa Optima II: R2* C

c1961. Similar to first model with 45mm f2.8 Color Apotar and Prontormator shutter. First pressure of release automatically selects between 1/30s and 1/250s with the appropriate aperture.

Agfa Optima III: R2* C

c1961. Similar to second model with 45mm f2.8 Color Apotar and Compur shutter 1/30-1/500s. Apertures and speeds selected automatically.

Agfa Optima IIIS: R2* C

c1961. Similar to Optima III with rangefinder and parallax compensation in the viewfinder.

Agfa Optima Reflex: R2* D+

1961. 35mm twin lens reflex with eye-level viewfinder. Twin 45mm f2.8 Color Apotar coated lenses in Prontor Special shutter, 1/30-1/250s. Auto-exposure with low light indicator in viewfinder.

Agfa Silette: R2* C+

c1957, metal 35mm VFR camera, Colour Apotar f2.8/45mm lens, Prontor SVS shutter, lever advance, top plate mounted shutter release, centred VFR and accessory shoe, also exists with off centre bright line finder.

Agfa Ambi Silette: R3* D

c1950s, metal 35mm RFR camera with interchangeable Colour Solinar f2.8/50mm lens, Synchro Compur shutter, VFR with fields of view for 35mm, 50mm, and 90mm.

Lenses for Ambi Silette

Colour Ambion f4/35mm lens: C–
Colour Telinear f4/90mm lens: C–

Agfa Silette I: R2* B–

c1962, metal 35mm VFR camera, Colour Agnar f2.8/45mm lens, Prontor 125 shutter, off-centre VFR and accessory shoe, front mounted shutter release, new square cornered design.

Agfa Silette L: R2* B+

c1957, metal 35mm VFR camera, Colour Solinar f2.8/50mm lens, Compur Rapid shutter, built-in light meter, lever advance, top plate mounted shutter release, off centre VFR and accessory shoe.

Agfa Silette L: R2* B–

c1962, metal 35mm VFR camera, Colour Apotar f2.8/45mm lens, Prontor 125 shutter, built-in coupled light meter, off-centre VFR, centred accessory shoe, front mounted shutter release, new square cornered design.

Agfa Silette SL: R2* C–

c1957, metal 35mm VFR camera, Colour Solinar f2.8/50mm lens, Compur Rapid shutter, built-in light meter for match needle metering, lever advance, top plate mounted shutter release, off centre VFR and accessory shoe.

Agfa Silette LK: R2* C–

c1958, metal 35mm VFR camera, Colour Apotar f2.8/50mm lens, Prontor LK shutter, built-in coupled light meter, lever advance, top plate mounted shutter release, off centre VFR and accessory shoe.

Agfa Super Silette: R3* C–

c1959, metal 35mm RFR camera, Colour-Solinar f2.8/50mm or Soligon f2/50mm lens, Synchro Compur shutter, built-in light meter, CRF, off-centre VFR, centred accessory shoe, front mounted shutter release, new square cornered design.

Agfa Super Silette LK: R2* C–
c1960s, metal 35mm RFR camera, Colour Apotar f2.8/45mm lens, Prontor 125 shutter, built-in coupled light meter controls aperture, CRF, off-centre VFR, centred accessory shoe, front mounted shutter release, new square cornered design.

Agfa Silette Automatic: R3* C–
metal 35mm RFR camera, Colour-Solinar f2.8/50mm lens, Prontor SLV shutter, built-in light meter for match needle metering, CRF, off-centre VFR and accessory shoe, top plate mounted shutter release.

Agfa Silette F: R2* B–
c1963, metal 35mm VFR camera, Colour Agnar f2.8/45mm lens, Prontor 125 shutter, flash for AG-1 bulbs, off-centre VFR , front mounted shutter release, square cornered design.

Agfa Silette Rapid I: R2* B–
c1965, metal 35mm VFR camera using special Agfa Rapid cassettes, Colour Agnar f2.8/45mm lens, Parator shutter, like (AS190).

Agfa Silette F: R2* B–
c1965, metal 35mm VFR camera using special Agfa Rapid cassettes, Colour Agnar f2.8/45mm lens, Parator shutter, built-in flash for AG-1 bulbs.

Agfa Silette Rapid L: R2* B–
c1962, metal 35mm VFR camera using

special Agfa Rapid cassettes, Colour Apotar f2.8/45mm lens, Prontor 250 shutter, built-in coupled light meter.

Agfa Solinette II: R2* C+
1954. 35mm folding camera. Light alloy die casting covered with grained plastic. 50mm f3.5 Apotar in Prontor SV shutter, 1-1/300s + B. Button on the back doubles as exp counter reset and to free sprockets for rewinding.

Agfa Isola: R2* B–
c1950s, horizontally styled metal VFR camera for 6 x 6cm frames on 120 roll film,collapsible Agnar f6.3/75mm lens, Singlo-2 shutter, body mounted shutter release.

Agfa Isola I: R2* B–
c1950s, horizontally styled metal VFR camera for 6 x 6cm frames on 120 roll film, collapsible meniscus lens and simple shutter, body mounted shutter release.

Agfa Isoly I: R2* B–
c1960s, metal VFR camera for 4 x 4cm frames on 120 roll film, Achromat lens, simple shutter.

Agfa Isoly II: R2* B–
c1960s, metal VFR camera for 4 x 4cm frames on 120 roll film, Agnar f6.3/55mm lens, Single shutter.

Agfa Isoly III: R2* B–
c1960s, metal VFR camera for 4 x 4cm frames on 120 roll film, Colour Apotar f3.9/60mm lens, Pronto shutter.

Agfa-Box: R1* B–
c1930s, metal box camera for 6 x 9cm frames on roll film, three position indicator for focusing.

Agfa Trolix-Box: R3* C
c1938, plastic box camera for 6 x 9cm frames on roll film, meniscus lens, simple shutter, metal carrying handle, Produced at the same time as the Trolita folding camera, from "Trolit", a kind of thermo plastic.

Agfa Metalbox-45:   R1* B–
c1938, metal box camera for 6 x 9cm frames on roll film, meniscus lens, simple shutter.

Agfa Cadet-A8:   R2* B–
c1937, metal box camera for 6 x 4.5cm frames on roll film, meniscus lens, simple shutter.

Agfa Synchro-Box: R1* B–
c1949, metal box camera for 6 x 9cm frames on 120 roll film, built-in yellow filter.

Agfa Clack: R2* B–
c1950s, horizontally styled metal VFR camera, 6 x 9cm frames on roll film, simple lens and shutter.

Agfa Heli-Clack 9 x 12:   R3* C+
c1930s, folding plate camera for 9 x 12cm plates, Heliar f4.5/10.5cm lens, Compur shutter.

Agfa Heli-Clack 6.5 x 9:   R3* B–
c1930s, horizontally styled folding plate camera for 6.5 x 9cm plates, Agfa Anastigmat f4.5/105mm lens, Agfa shutter.

Agfa Isorette: R3* C
c1935, folding VFR camera for 6 x 6cm or 6 x 4.5cm frames on roll film, many lens/shutter combinations, among which are Igestar f6.3/70mm lens, Vario shutter and Apotar f4.5/70mm lens, Compur shutter. Not to be confused with the post-war "Isolette".

Agfa Isolette 6x6:   R3* B–
c1949, folding VFR camera for 6 x 6cm frames on roll film, Apotar f4.5/85mm lens, Prontor shutter, centre mounted accessory shoe, body mounted shutter release.

Agfa Isolette 4.5x6:   R3* C+
c1949, folding VFR camera for 6 x 4.5cm frames on roll film, Solinar f4.5/80mm lens, Compur Rapid shutter, body mounted shutter release.

Agfa Isolette II: R2* B–
c1950s, folding VFR camera for 6 x 6cm on roll film, Apotar f4.5/85mm lens, Prontor shutter, new designed top plate, body mounted release.

Agfa Isolette III: R3* C+
c1950s, folding RFR camera for 6 x 6cm frames on roll film, un-coupled RFR, Apotar or Solinar f4.5/85mm lens, Prontor or Synchro Compur shutter, body mounted shutter release.

Agfa Isolette V: R3* B–
c1950s, folding VFR camera for 6 x 6cm frames on roll film. Agnar f4.5/80mm lens, Vario shutter, no body mounted shutter release, off-centre mounted accessory shoe.

Agfa Super Isolette: R3* C–
c1950s, folding RFR camera for 6 x 6cm frames on roll film, CRFR, Solinar f3.5/85mm lens, Synchro Compur shutter, body mounted shutter release, no more ruby window, automatic frame counting.

Isolette L: R2* C+
c1950s, folding VFR camera for 6 x 6cm frames on roll film, or 24 x 36mm frames on special paperbacked Agfa film, Colour Apotar f4.5/85mm lens; Pronto shutter; built-in light meter.

Agfa Solinette: R2* B–
c1952, folding 35mm VFR camera, Apotar f3.5/5cm lens, Prontor SV shutter, accessory shoe.

Agfa Solinette II: R2* C+
35mm folding camera. Light alloy die casting covered with grained plastic. 50mm f/3.5 Apotar in Prontor SV shutter, 1-1/300s+B. Button on the back doubles as exposure counter reset and to free sprockets for rewinding.

Agfa Super Solinette: R3* C+
c1953, folding 35mm RFR camera, CRF, Solinar f3.5/50mm lens, Synchro Compur shutter, accessory shoe.

Agfa Click-I: R1* B–
c1959, plastic bodied horizontally styled box type camera, 6 x 6cm frames on 120 roll film, meniscus lens, simple shutter.

Agfa Click-II: R1* B–
c1959, plastic bodied horizontally styled box type camera, 6 x 6cm frames on 120 roll film, meniscus lens, simple shutter, built-in close-up lens.

Memo Automatic (1964):   R2* C+

c1964. Half-frame 35mm motor drive camera; Memar f2.8 coated lens; fixed shutter speed. Selenium photo-electric exp meter controls diaphragm for correct exp. Spring wound motor cycles 10-15 exp per wind at a rate of about 1 exp per sec. Mfd. by Ricoh, Japan for G.A.F., New York.

Agfa Flexilette: R2* C+
35mm twin lens reflex with waist-level finder. 45mm f/2.8 Color Apotar lenses in Prontor shutter. 1-1/500s.

E. & H.T. Anthony & Company
New York, USA

Edward Anthony opened his first daguerreotype studio in 1841, in New York City. In 1842, he and J. M. Edwards established a daguerreotype portrait studio in Washington D.C., where they photographed all the members of Congress, as well as many other prominent citizens. In 1843 Anthony established the National Miniature Gallery in New York City, where he operated a studio and sold photographic equipment and supplies. The company name changed many times: it was known as Edward Anthony and Howard Chilton from 1842 to 1843; as Anthony, Edwards & Chilton in 1843; as Anthony, Edwards & Co. from 1844 to 1845; Anthony, Edwards & Clark from 1844 to 1845; as Anthony Clark & Co. from 1845 to 1847; and as Edward Anthony from 1847 to 1862.

From 1849 to 1851, Edward Anthony operated his studio and manufactured equipment and supplies in New York City. During this time, Mathew Brady's studio was located in the same building. Anthony moved uptown in 1851, and opened his new offices and a warehouse at 308 Broadway. At the same time he also opened a factory in the city. The Anthony firm, at this time was one of the largest importers and manufacturers of photographic equipment and supplies in the United States.

Anthony's brother joined the company in 1853. In 1862, the name of the company was changed to Edward & Henry T. Anthony and Company, and later to E. & H.T. Anthony and Company. In 1869, the firm moved to 591 Broadway. In 1880, E. & H.T. Anthony and Company became agents to sell dry plates for George Eastman; in 1888, they began marketing the world's first flexible base film. The management of the company changed at this time, both Anthony brothers having died by 1888.

In 1902, E. & H.T. Anthony and Company merged with the Scovill and Adams Company, forming the Anthony and Scovill Company; the manufacturing facilities were transferred to Binghamton, New York. In 1907, the company name was shortened to Ansco.

Anthony 4 Gem Tube Carte de Visite Camera: R4* I–

c1860, wet plate outfit with cherry wood stand; single early track. With plate holder with glass corners, dipper, dipping tank and box of early colouring dyes.

Anthony Victoria Ferrotype Camera: R4* H

c1879, four tube 5" x 7" multiple ferrotype camera; four Darlot lenses, 1, 2, 4 or 8 exp on a 5" x 7" plate. Patent perfection stand invented by L.H. Stoddard.

Anthony 8"x10" Universal Portrait and Ferrotype Camera: R4* E

c1872; 4 Darlot Petzval 6½" f4 lenses; rubber bellows. 8" x 10" wet plate holder with glass corners specially fitted with 7" x 10" and 5" x 7" inserts: takes 1 or 4 exp on an 8" x 10" plate; 8 exp on a 7" x 10" plate; 4 or 8 exp on a 5" x 7" plate.

Anthony Climax 8"x10" View and Portrait Camera: R4* G+

c1872; Darlot stereo lenses in adjustable lens board; lever focusing screw; double swing back; revolving 5" x 7" back. Ivory label, multiple attachments, separate ground glass frame. Early elevating stand.

Anthony Equipment No. 2: R4* F

c1881; 5" x 7" view camera; Prosh triplex lens and shutter; double dry plate holder. Early model was finished in black ebony. Rare.

Anthony Equipment No. 3: R4* F+

c1881; 5" x 8" dry plate camera for single or stereo exp; pair of E & A single achromatic lenses; 5" x 8" double dry plate holder; black ebony construction. Original price $15 with tripod and case.

Anthony 11"x14" Novel View Plate Camera: R3* G

c1885; (preceded Patent Novellette); E. & A. Universal finder; 10 sizes: 4" x 5" to 18" x 22". Anthony unjointed wood tripod. The bellows could rotate from a horizontal to vertical format. Patent February 20, 1883.

Anthony 11"x14" Novel View Plate Camera c1885.

Anthony 5"x8" Novel View: R3* E+

c1885; 5" x 8" view camera; Prosh Duplex lens and shutter; double swing. Early version of revolving back. 10 sizes: 4" x 5" to 18" x 22".

Anthony 4"x5" Patent Novellette View Camera: R4* F

c1887. 4" x 5" view camera; E.A. Rapid No. 1 lens; waterhouse stops; Anthony's drop shutter; solid wood bed.

Anthony Patent Bijou 3¼" x 4¼" Camera: R4* F–

c1884; 3¼" x 4¼" view camera; E. A. No.1 Hemispherical lens; waterhouse stops. Available with or without swing back; polished mahogany with brass fittings. Camera in photograph is fitted with an optional guillotine shutter. Smallest Anthony camera: dimensions, 5" x 5" x 3½"; weight, 14½ ounces.

Anthony English Style Compact Camera: R3* F–

c1888, 5" x 8" compact view camera; reversible back; 16" bellows extension; telescopic bed for long focus lenses; folded size, 9⅛" x 9⅛" x 3⅛". 4 sizes: 5" x 7" to 8" x 10".

Anthony Cooper Universal Enlarging Lantern: R4* F–

c1887, used as an 8" x 10" enlarging camera, copying camera, portrait camera or magic lantern. The kerosene burner lamp and condensers were removed for daylight enlarging. Patent by Cooper & Lewis.

Anthony's Phantom Camera: R4* E+

8" x 10" view camera; revolving back using key hole slots. 5 sizes: 4¼" x 6½" to 8" x 10". c1888.

Anthony Vincent 8"x10": R3* F–

c1890, cone shaped Anthony single combination lens; reversible back; telescoping bed. 4 sizes: 5" x 7" to 8" x 10".

Schmid's Patent Detective Camera, Original Model: R5* I–

c1883, box-type detective camera. 6 sizes: 8 x 10.5cm; 10.5 x 12.5cm; 11.5 x 16.5cm; 12.5 x 20cm; 16.5 x 21.5cm; 20 x 25cm on plates. c1882 non folding handle. First American camera designed to be hand held.

Schmid's Patent Detective Camera, Second Model: R5* I–

c1885, 3¼" x 4¼" detective camera; E. Anthony Rapid Rectilinear 6½" f8 lens; interchangeable waterhouse stops; variable speed rotary shutter; brass handle that folds down. 6 sizes, 3¼" x 4¼" to 8" x 10". Patent 1883.

Schmid's Patent Detective Camera – Third Camera: R5* I–
c1886, 4" x 5" camera; removable back; side focusing lever; takes Eastman-Walker roll holder.

Anthony Climax Detective Camera: R4* G+

c1885-89. wood finish detective camera; lenses of varying focal length used without removing shutter. Camera could be fitted in patent satchel handbag. 4" x 5" exp (larger sizes made to order).

Anthony's Climax Detective Camera: R4* G–
c1888. Leather covered detective camera; lenses of varying focal length; separate rear compartment was available with 5 double holders; 4" x 5" exp (larger sizes made to order).

Anthony's Satchel Detective Camera: R5* J+
c1887. Satchel-type detective camera; Dallmeyer Rapid Rectilinear lens; guillotine shutter. A satchel covered in alligator skin contained a Climax Detective Camera. 4" x 5" exp on plates.

Anthony's Satchel Detective Camera, c1887.

Anthony PDQ (Photography Done Quickly): R4* F+
c1890, 4" x 5" detective camera; E & A single achromatic No. 1 lens, rotating stops; variable speed shutter and focusing; removable ground glass; reversible finder.

Anthony Lilliput Detective Camera: R4* H
c1886. Detective camera in small leather handbag; 65mm f8 lens; covers a 60 degree angle; variable speed sector shutter; 6 exp, 2½" x 2½" on glass plates or film; camera measures 4" x 4" x 6".

Anthony Model Manhattan: R3* E
c1886, 5" x 8" mahogany view camera; single achromatic EA nickel plated lens; Anthony nonpareil shutter. Inexpensive model: lacks rising front; does not fold, has swings. 3 sizes: 4" x 5" to 5" x 8" and stereo.

Anthony Model Manhattan, c1886.

patent lamp hooks. The Anthony Champion could also be used as a non-stereo camera by changing to a single centre mounted lens and removing the internal separation. Non stereo models are about 40%-50% less expensive.

Anthony Model 2B: **R4* E**

c1888, 5" x 8" view camera; Garland shutter; rising front; swing back; dark mahogany construction with brass fittings. 6 sizes: 4" x 5" to 8" x 10".

Anthony Champion 8B: **R4* E**
c1888. 8" x 10" view camera; E & A cone shaped single achromatic No. 4 lens; swing back; back bed lock, folding bed with patent clamps (pat. February 20, 1888); mahogany finish with brass fitting; holder, case.

Anthony Champion Model 5"x8"
Stereo Camera: **R4* F+**
c1885. 5" x 8" stereo view camera; swing back; bed locks from rear; stereo

---

Anthony Champion Model 5"x7"
View Camera: **R3* F+**

c1888. 5" x 7" view camera; Darlot lens; rotating stops; swing back; patent clamp hooks; rear bed locks. 6 sizes and stereo format.

Anthony Model NPA: R4* F–

c1888. 5" x 8" stereo camera; EA wide angle nickel plated lens; rising front; patent swing back; patent clamp hooks; Anthony Climax tripod; Anthony Universal finder. Complete outfit:

Anthony Patent Novelette
View Camera   R3* F–

c1890. The Novelette used the same rotating bellows system as the Novel to change from horizontal to vertical format. Normally fitted with an achromatic lens. Cherry or walnut natural wood finish. Available in sizes from 4 x 5 to 11 x 14 inches. There were various models fitted with minimum to elaborate tilts and swings.

Anthony Patent Novellette
View Camera: R4* E+

8" x 10" view camera; J. Dallmeyer R.R. lens; revolving bellows; E & A Universal finder; double swing back; patent clamp hooks; polished mahogany construction. 7 sizes: 4" x 5" to 11" x 14". Original price, $33. Patent February 20, 1888.

Anthony Patent Novelette
Stereo Camera: R4* G

c1890. This camera has been fitted with optional stereo lenses, and an internal separator. When removed and a single lens installed, it was a regular view camera.

Anthony Victor Camera: R4* E+

c1888. Anthony single combination wide angle lens; rising front; single swing; double rack and pinion movement; patent swing back. Eclipse double plate holder. 6 sizes: 4" x 5" to 8" x 10".

Anthony Fairy Camera: R4* E+

c1890. 5" x 8" view camera; EA nickel lens; rack, cog wheel and pinion focusing; Anthony Universal wood finder; reversible back; key hole slots for revolving back; polished Circassian walnut wood. 6 sizes: 4" x 5" to 8" x 10". Early wood stand.

Anthony Knickerbocker Camera:
R3* E+

c1891. 5" x 7" view camera; EA single achromatic nickel plate lens; reversible back single swing; back focus; nickel plated fittings. 4 sizes: 5" x 7" to 8" x 10".

Anthony Normandie Camera: R4* E+

c1890. $6\frac{1}{2}$" x $8\frac{1}{2}$" view camera; Darlot lens; back focus; revolving stops; single swing; reversible back. 9 sizes: 4" x 5" to 14" x 17".

The Klondike Camera: R4* D+

c1898, box plate camera; adjustable shutter speeds; adjustable diaphragm; dry plates, $3\frac{1}{4}$" x $4\frac{1}{4}$".

Climax Multiplying Camera: R4* F–

c1901. 5" x 7" camera; single Darlot portrait tube; multiple exp on 5" x 7" plate.

Anthony Climax Portrait Camera:
R2* F–
c1888, brass lens; double swing back; bed extends to 49". Anthony Automatic Cabinet Attachment: sliding ground glass replaced by plate holder. c1888. Complete with No.1 New York Camera and stand.

Anthony 4"x5"Climax
Enlarging Camera: R3* E
c1890, reducing or copying camera; reversible back; lens can be used inside or outside camera. 9 sizes: 4" x 5" to 20" x 24".

Anthony Clifton View Camera: R4* E

c1901. Anthony drop shutter; double swing back and front; front and back focus; reversible back; red bellows. 6 sizes: 5" x 7" to 14" x 17".

Anthony Lantern Slide Camera: R4* E

c1888, for copying negatives 4" x 5" or smaller on $3\frac{1}{4}$" x $4\frac{1}{4}$" plates. Revolving ground glass frame; folding extension bed.

Anthony View Camera: R3* E–

c1900, $6\frac{1}{2}$" x $8\frac{1}{2}$" view camera; homocentric lens; Kolios shutter; nickel plated fittings. Ivory label marked: E. & H.T. Anthony, New York, Chicago.

Anthony Accessories

Anthony CDV Albums: C

2 versions, c1860s.

Fuming box for albumen paper: R4* H+

c1875, mahogany construction with lead lined drawers. Used ammonia to increase the speed of albumen paper (first suggested by H.T. Anthony in 1862).

Anthony Graphoscope: R3* E
c1870s, viewer for photographs and stereo cards.

Dry Plates: R4* B
c1888, distributed by E. & H.T. Anthony for the Eastman Dry Plate Co.

Anthony's Climax Kerosene Dark Room Lantern: R3* C+
c1888, has three large illuminating surfaces with reflector.

Anthony's Retouching Frame: R2* D

c1885, for retouching negatives; has drawer for brushes, stippling pencils and reflecting mirror.

Karl Arnold
Marienberg, Germany

Karma Flex 4x4 model II: R3* F–
c1932, SLR type for 4cm x 4cm frames on roll film.Vidar or Victor or Regulyt f4.5/60mm lens, guillotine shutter 1/25 -1/100s.

Karma Flex 4x4 model I: R3* F
c1932, TLR type box camera (fixed focus) for 4cm x 4cm frames on roll film "Spezial" f9 lens, simple shutter .

Karma Flex 6x6 model II: **R4* E–**
c1932, TLR for 6cm x 6cm frames on roll film, Victar or Pololyt f3.5/75mm lens, CPFS to 1/500s.

Karma Flex 6x6 model I: **R4* E**
c1932, TLR type box camera (fixed focus) for 6cm x 6cm frames on roll film, "Spezial" f7.7 lens, simple shutter, waist level VFR convertible to eye level VFR.

Karma: **R4* E**
c1932, RFR camera for 6cm x 6cm frames on roll film, Victar or Pololyt f3.5/75mm lens, CPFS to 1/500s, basically the bottom half of a Karma Flex 6 x 6 model II, with tubular VFR and uncoupled RFR.

APM
London, England

Altrex: **R2* C**
c1920s. Drop-bed folding camera for $2^1/_4$" x $3^1/_4$" pictures. Shutter speeds 1/10-1/100s. Focusing lens, swing spool holders. Choice of f7.7 or f6.3 lenses

Beltrex: **R2* C**
c1920s. Similar to Altrex, but with shutter speeds 1s to 1/300s.

Focal Plane Camera Model A: **R3* D**
c1920s. Strut folding camera for $2^1/_4$" x $3^1/_4$" plates. f4.5 lens. Sold with three single metal slides.

Focal Plane Camera Model B: **R3* D**
c1920s. Similar to Model A, but sold with three double book form backs.

Focal Plane Camera Model de Luxe: **R3* D**
c1920s. Similar to the Models A and B, but with wider body for use with rollfilms. Sold with choice of APM f4.5 anastigmat, f4.5 Cooke Aviar, f4.5 Dallmeyer or f 4.5 Ross Xpress lenses.

Vest Pocket de Luxe: **R2* C**
c1920s. Drop-bed folding camera for $2^1/_2$" x $1^5/_8$" pictures on rollfilm. Shutter speeds 1/10-1/100s. Choice of f7.7 or f6.3 lenses

Apparate & Kamerabau
Friedrichshafen, Germany

Akarex I: **R3* C**

c1954, 35mm RFR camera, non-interchangeable Isco Westar f3.5/45mm lens in either Prontor, 1/25-1/200s or Prontor SVS 1-1/300s shutters, lever wind.

Akarex III: **R3* C**
c1955 35mm RFR camera with interchangeable lens/VFR assemblies, Isco Westar f3.5/35mm or Schneider Xenon f2/50mm lens, Synchro Compur 1-500s shutter. Schnieider 35mm and 90mm accessory lenses with attached finders were available.

Akarette model "O":   R3* C+

1949-50, black metal bodied 35mm VFR camera with interchangeable lens, Schneider Xenar f3.5/50mm, Schneider Xenar f2.8/45mm or Schneider Xenon f2/50mm normal lens, behind the lens leaf shutter 1/25-1/200s, two viewfinders for fields of view corresponding to 35mm, 50mm, and 75mm, f4.5/35mm lens and f3.5/75mm lenses available, see (AP003) and (AP004).

Akarette model II: R3* C+

1950-54, metal bodied 35mm VFR camera with interchangeable lens, Schneider Xenar f3.5/50mm, Schneider Xenar f2.8/45mm or Schneider Xenon f2/50mm normal lens, behind the lens leaf shutter 1/25-1/200s, two viewfinders for fields of view corresponding to 35mm, 50mm, and 75mm, selector lever on the front of the camera marked "50mm" and "75mm" allows blocking one of the VFR windows. f4.5/35mm lens, and f3.5/75mm lenses available. Much like the model "O", with the addition of chrome trim, vrf selector lever and self timer.

Akarelle: R3* C+

1954-55, metal bodied 35mm VFR camera with interchangeable lens, Schneider Xenar f3.5/50mm, Schneider Xenar f2.8/45mm or Schneider Xenon f2/50mm normal lens, Prontor S shutter 1/25-1/200s, two viewfinders for fields of view corresponding to 35mm, 50mm, and 90mm, selector lever on the front of the camera marked "50mm" and "90mm". f4.5/35mm lens, and f3.5/90mm lenses available. Much like the Akarette model II, with the addition of lever wind, front mounted strap lugs and 90mm field of view VFR. Late cameras have no selection lever, but rather fields marked in the VFR.

Akarelle Automatic S: R2* C–

c1960, 35mm VFR camera, non-interchangeable Isco Westanar f2.8/45mm lens, built-in lightmeter coupled to shutter, providing automatic exposure, speed selected indicated in the VFR.

Akarelle V: R2* B

c1961, simple 35mm VFR camera, Arretar f2.8/45mm lens, Vario Shutter, 1/25-1/200s

Akarelle W: R3* C

c1963, 35mm VFR camera with interchangeable Colour-Wilon f2.8/50mm lens, Prontor SVS shutter, 1-1/300s, Lineogon f3.5/35mm WA accessory lens w/shoe mount wide angle viewer available. (price is for camera with two lenses and WA VFR.)

Arette 1A: R3* C

1956. 35mm VFR camera. 45mm f2.8 Westar Prontor-SVS shutter 1-1/300s + B. Synch for bulb and electronic flash.

Arette-IB: R3* C–
c1956, 35mm VFR camera with non interchangeable Westar or Xenar f2.8/45mm lens, Prontor SVS shutter, 1-1/300s, lever advance built-in light meter.

Arette IC: R3* C–
c1957, 35mm camera with coupled RFR and non interchangeable Westar or Xenar f2.8/45mm lens, Prontor SVS shutter, 1-1/300s, lever advance like the Arette IB, but with CRF, new body style, and without built-in light meter.

Arette ID: R3* C–
c1957, 35mm camera with coupled RFR and non interchangeable Westar or Xenar f2.8/45mm lens, Prontor SVS shutter, 1-1/300s, lever advance like the Arette IC, but with built-in EV scale light meter.

Arette-A: R3* C–
c1957, 35mm VFR camera with non-interchangeable Arettar 2.8/45mm, Isconar f2.8/45mm lenses, Vario shutter, 1/25-1/200s or Prontor SVS shutter, 1-300s, 1:1 optical VFR so both eyes could be open when using the camera.

Arette BN: R3* B+
1958. Replacement for the IB. Similar specification but with lever wind transferred to baseplate and a redesigned top plate, incorporating the exp meter. Rewind knob is flush with body and springs up at a touch.

Arette-BW: R3* C–
c1959, 35mm VFR camera with interchangeable Schneider Xenon f2/50mm lens, Prontor SVS, 1-1/300s, field of view for 50mm and 90mm marked in VFR, built-in light meter. Late models (c1960), have the meter mounted in the front centre of the top plate, and Wilon f2.8/50mm lens. 90mm accessory lens available.

Arette DN: R3* C–
c1958, 35mm camera with coupled RFR and non-interchangeable Westar or Xenar f2.8/45mm lens, Prontor SVS shutter, 1-1/300s, built-in EV scale light meter, lever advance like the Arette ID, but lightmeter reading visible in the VFR.

Schneider Xenagon f3.5/35mm lens and finder assembly: C–
Schneider Tele-Xenar f3.5/90mm lens and finder assembly: C+
Schneider Xenar f4.5/35mm lens: C–
Schneider Tele-Xenar f3.5/75mm lens: D–
Schneider Tele-Xenar f3.5/90mm lens: D
Telexon f5.6/90mm lens: C

Industria Argentina
(SIAF)

Bislent: R4* D+

c1950, Bakelite stereo VFR camera for 2.5 x 3.5cm single frames or stereo pairs vertically on 120 roll film, simple lens and shutters, each lens has its own release.

Rex-Junior: R4* C–

c1950, Bakelite VFR camera for 6 x 6cm frames on 120 or 620 film, Lujo f10/8.5cm lens, simple shutter, made under license from Gevaert.

Rex: R4* C

c1950, Bakelite VFR camera for 6 x 9cm or 6 x 4.5cm on 120 or 620 film, Lujo f10/9.1cm lens, simple shutter.

Gradosol.   R3* B+

Argus Inc
Ann Arbor, Michigan, USA

Argus K: R3* D–

c1939, 35mm camera; Argus Anastigmat 50mm f4.5 lens; Ilex shutter 1/25-1/200s. Extinction meter coupled to lens diaphragm. This camera represents the only attempt to couple an extinction meter to the diaphragm of a 35mm camera.

Argus K, c1939.

Argus A   R3* D–

Argus A (gold coloured version).

c1937. At the time of its introduction, the Argus A was the least expensive 35mm camera available. It was made in a number of colours these included black (most common), grey, brown, ivory, and gold. Coloured models, particularly the gold version, are considerably more valuable.

Argus A2B: R2* B

c1939-1950. 35mm camera; Argus Anastigmat 50mm f4.5 lens; Argus shutter 1/25-1/50s.

Argus C-3   R1* B

c1940. 35mm RFR camera; Cintar Anastigmat 50mm f3.5 lens; five rivets on the back hinge indicates pre-war production. The Argus C-3 was arguably the most popular 35mm camera on the market from c1940-1955. It was rugged, inexpensive, and produced good results.

Argus C3 Matchmatic: R1* B

35mm RFR camera, add-on non-coupled Selenium meter. Two tone colour design.

Argus Golden Shield: R2* C–

Chrome metal front plate, and "Golden Shield" emblem.

Argus A3:   R1* B

c1942, 35mm camera; Argus Anastigmatic 50mm f4 lens; Argus shutter 1/25-1/50s. Built-in extinction exp meter.

Argus C4:   R1* B

c1951, 35mm RFR camera; Cintar 50mm f2.8 coated lens; Argus shutter 1/10-1/300s, CRF.

Argus C4

Argus C44:   R2* C–

c1951, 35mm RFR camera, with interchangeable Cintagon 50mm f2.8 coated lens, Argus shutter 1/25-1/300s, CRF.

Accessories and lenses for C44	
35mm f4 wide angle lens:	B
100mm f3.5 telephoto lens:	B
VFR for 50mm, 35mm, and 100mm:	B
light meter for C44:	A

Argus Autronic 35:   R1* C–

Cintar 50mm f3.5 lens; synch shutter 1/30-1/500s. Selenium photo-electric cell controlled exp. c1960-1962.

Arsenal Zavod

(Arsenal works), Kiev, Ukraine, (formerly USSR.)

Originally made with machinery removed from the Zeiss factory at the end of WWII, Kiev 35mm RFR cameras have been in production ever since. Like their Contax look-a-like relatives, they tend to have shutter problems which are very difficult to repair. For these cameras, at least, the first two digits of the serial number give the year of production. As the Arsenal factory grew, other camera models came into production. Some cameras, especially the Kiev 88 are still available.They are included because of their origins and design, their relatively low price is the reason they are in many collections.

Kiev 2:   **R3* D+**
1948-57; Vertical mfps, 1-1/1250s, combined RFR/VFR windows, interchangeable Contax bayonet type mount, earliest cameras have lenses marked "3K" (maybe meaning Sonnar/ Krasnogorsk) later cameras have f2.0/50mm Jupiter 8 lens.

Kiev 2A: **R3* D+**
1957-59; PC synch added, name written in Cyrilic and Latin letters.

Kiev 3:   **R3* D**
1951-57; Vertical mfps, 1-1/1250s, combined RFR/VFR windows, interchangeable Contax bayonet type mount, f2.0/50mm Jupiter 8 lens uncoupled built-in meter located on the top of the camera body.

Kiev 3A: **R2* D–**
1957-59; Vertical mfps, 1-1/1250s, combined RFR/VFR windows,
interchangeable Contax bayonet type mount, f2.0/50mm Jupiter 8 lens as the Kiev 3, but with PC synch added to the front of the camera body.

Kiev 4:   **R2* D–**
1959-79, Vertical mfps, 1-1/1250s, combined RFR/VFR windows, interchangeable Contax bayonet type mount, f2.0/50mm Jupiter 8M lens uncoupled built-in meter located on the top of the camera body as the Kiev 3 (but smaller and more sensitive), PC synch added to the front of the camera body. Redesigned camera back like post-war Contax, film memo.

Kiev 4A: **R2* D–**

1959-79; Vertical mfps, 1-1/1250s, combined RFR/VFR windows, interchangeable Contax bayonet type mount, black f1.8/53mm Helios 103 lens as the Kiev 4, but with reduced top shutter speed and hot shoe in addition to the PC synch on the front of the camera body, no meter, black rewind and film advance knobs.

Kiev 4AM: **R2* D–**
1979-81; Vertical mfps, 1-1/1000s, combined RFR/VFR windows, interchangeable Contax bayonet type mount, black f1.8/53mm Helios-103 lens as the Kiev 2A, but with reduced

top shutter speed and hot shoe in addition to the PC synch on the front of the camera body, self timer, no meter, black rewind crank and film advance knob.

Kiev 4M: **R2* D–**
as Kiev4 AM, but for built-in uncoupled light meter

"No Name" Kiev: **R4* F**
c1963, Vertical mfps, 1-1/1250s, combined RFR/VFR windows, Contax bayonet type mount. Often thought of as having been made at the post war Zeiss plant in East Germany, these cameras were really produced in the Soviet Union, concurrently with the Kiev 4A, for export to the West.

Kiev 5:   **R4* E-**
c1968, 35mm RFR camera, built-in lightmeter, interchangeable Jupitor-8M f2/50mm lens using Kiev/Contax mount, side mounted rewind crank, MFPS $^1/_2$-1/1000s, made in limited numbers.

Kiev 35A: **R2* C**
c1985, black plastic 35mm VFR camera, copy of Minox 35GT.

Accessories and lenses for Kiev 35mm RFR cameras	
Jupiter-12 35mm f2.8: in chrome	**D–**
Jupiter-12 35mm f2.8: in black	**D–**
Jupiter-9 85mm f2.0: in chrome	**D–**
Jupiter-9 85mm f2.0: in black	**C+**
Jupiter-11 135mm f4 lens (copy of Zeiss Sonnar):	**C+**
Jupiter-11 135mm f4 lens (fat barrel):	**D**
Kiev Stereo (copy of Zeiss Stereotar):	**G–**
3.5cm accessory VFR:	**C**
8.5cm accessory VFR:	**C**

(Note: no 13.5cm finder was produced, and the only turret type finder made in the USSR was made by and for Zorki.)

Kiev-Vega: **R3* C**
c1965, subminiature camera for use with Minolta 16 cassettes, focusing f3.5/23mm Industar lens, shutter speeds 1/30, 1/60, & 1/200s. Grey or Brown.

Kiev-30:   **R3* C–**
c1975, subminiature camera, as (KV111), but in black, often found in a complete set, including developing tank adaptor and unused film. (for outfit add 50%).

Kiev-30M: **R3* C–**
c1989, subminiature camera. Stencilled name on the front.

Kiev 30M 1949-89:   **R4* D+**
1989, as Kiev 30M, but no name, engraved "Kiev 1949-1989" on back, Red star with hammer and sickle engraved on front.

Kiev 10 Automat: **R4* E–**
c1965, 35mm SLR with interchangeable bayonet mount Helios f2/50mm lens, unique metal rotary focal plane shutter, $^1/_2$-1/1000s, built-in non-TTL light meter, shutter speed preferred automatic to total manual operation, lever advance, bottom mounted rewind crank.

Lenses for Kiev 10	
20mm f4 lens:	**D–**
37mm f2.8 lens:	**C**
85mm f2.8 lens:	**D**

Kiev 6C: R2* E–

c1970, SLR for 6 x 6cm frames on 120 or 220 film, horizontally styled much like a large 35mm SLR, interchangeable Volna f2.8/80mm lens in Pentacon Six breech mount. CFPS 1-1/1000s, removable waist level finder.

Kiev 60:   R2* E–

c1980, SLR for 6 x 6cm frames on 120 or 220 film. Improved film transport and "more convenient shutter release button position", often found with the TTL metering prism, sometimes found in hard leather outfit case with lens hood, and accessory shoe.

Lenses for Kiev 6, 6C or 60

Zodiak-8b 30mm f3,5 wide angle lens:	E
Mir-26b 45mm f3.5 wide angle lens:	D+
Mir-38b 65mm f3.5 wide angle lens:	D
MC Vega-28b 120mm f2.8 telephoto lens:	D
Kaleinar-3b 150mm f2.8 telephoto lens:	D+
MC Telear-5b 250mm f5.6 telephoto lens:	D+

Salyut: R3* D+

c1965, 120 SLR for 6 x 6cm frames, copy of 1000F Hasselblad, f2.8/80mm lens in interchangeable mount, MFPS 1/2-1000s, interchangeable film backs, removable waistlevel finder, non-automatic lens aperture, usually found not working.

(Note: because of patent infringement problems, Salyut cameras were made for domestic consumption only.)

Salyut S (C):   R3* D+

c1967, as (KV120) but for semi-automatic aperture – à la Exakta.

Kiev 80:   R2* D

c1975, 120 SLR for 6cm x 6cm frames, interchangeable f2.8/80mm lens in bayonet mount, interchangeable backs, removable waist level finder, automatic lens aperture, MFPS 1/2-1/1000s, these cameras are famous for being unreliable, and not up to hard use.

Zenith 80:   R3* D

c1975, export version of the Kiev 80, but not very successful.

Kiev 88:   R2* E–

c1984. Now with hot shoe synch, often found with the TTL metering prism, lens shade, extra film back in a hard leather case as a "Kiev 88TTL" outfit, MFPS 1/2-1/1000s, as with the preceding Kiev 120 SLRs, these cameras are famous for being unreliable, easily broken, hard to repair. (complete "TTL" outfit adds 100%).

Current Lenses for Zenith 80, Kiev 80 and 88

Zodiak-8B 30mm f3,5 wide angle lens:	E
Mir-26B 45mm f3.5 wide angle lens:	D
Mir-38B 65mm f3.5 wide angle lens:	D
MC Vega-28B 120mm f2.8 telephoto lens:	D–
Kaleinar-3B 150mm f2.8 telephoto lens:	D+
MC Telear-5B 250mm f5.6 telephoto lens:	E–

Asahi Optical Co
Tokyo, Japan

For further information see Pentax and Pentax SLR 35mm Cameras 1952-1989, by Danilo Cecchi, Hove Collectors Books, 1990.

Asahi Kogaku Goshi Kaisha Asahi was founded in 1919 to produce lenses for spectacles, telescopes, etc. In 1929 it started to produce photographic lenses for many other manufacturers. In 1952 they introduced their first camera, the SLR Asahiflex. In 1957 the Asahi Pentax was the first Japanese 35mm SLR camera with a pentaprism.

Asahiflex I: **R3* F+**

c1952, 35mm SLR camera; Takumar 50mm f3.5 lens with interchangeable screw mount; CFPS 1/20-1/500s. First Japanese 35mm SLR.

Asahiflex Ia: **R3* F–**
35mm SLR camera; as model I FPS 1/25-1/500s; Second x terminal for flash; c1953; called Ia by collectors.

Asahiflex IIB: **R3* E+**

35mm SLR camera; Takumar 58mm f2.8 preset lens with interchangeable screw mount; FPS 1/20-1/500s. Waist-level vf

and eye-level optical vf. c1954. First 35mm SLR with combined focusing and viewing to use instant-return mirror.

Asahiflex IIa: **R3* E+**
c1955 35mm SLR Camera; As IIb with slow speeds of 1/2 1/5 1/10 added by knob on the front.

Pentax Auto 110:   **R2* C+**

c1979. SLR for 110 film, interchangeable f2.8/24mm normal lens, behind the lens automatic shutter, lever wind. The Pentax Auto 110 was the only 110 format camera to be designed as a complete system with a variety of interchangeable lenses. When first marketed it came in a fitted box with lenses, filters, strobe, and auto winder. A completely intact boxed system increases value by 30-50%.

Pentax Auto 110 Super: R2* D
c1982; as 110 with brighter viewing screen; self-timer; single stroke advance; slow speed indicator on screen; price with 24mm F2.8 lens.

Accessories for the Pentax Auto 110

f2.8/18mm Wide angle lens: **C+**
f2.8/50mm Telephoto lens: **C+**
F2.8/70mm Telephoto lens: **D**
F2.8/40-70mm Zoom lens: (scarce)   **E**
1.7x Vivitar Converter: **C+**
Auto winder: **B+**

Asahi Pentax S3

Asahi Pentax: R2* E+
c1958; 35mm SLR; FPS; slow speed knob on front 1-1/10s fast speeds 1/25-1/500s; 42 x 1mm Lens mount; lens 55mm f2.2 Takumar manual setting lens; Lever film advance.

Asahi Pentax S1:   R1* D

c1961; 35mm SLR; FPS; 1-1/500; f/2 Auto Takumar lens; shutter coupled to separate exp meter at T setting.

Asahi Pentax S2:   R1* D

c1959; 35mm SLR; FPS;1-1/500s. B.T. All speeds on one knob on top plate; 55mm f/2 Auto Takumar lens; U.S.A. models "H2" logo replaced the "AO" on the pentaprism.

Asahi Pentax SV: R1* D

c1963-1967; 35mm SLR; FPS 1-1/1000s T B: 55mm f/1.8 Fully automatic Super Takumar lens; Delayed action self-timer under rewind knob; "H3v" logo in U.S.A.

Asahi Pentax S3:   R1* D
c1960; 35mm SLR; FPS;1-1/500s.or 1-1000s; f/1.8 Auto Takumar lens; few S3's had clip on exp meter facility; many variations of this camera; Sold in U.S. as Asahi Honeywell.

Asahi Pentax Sla: R1* D

c1963; 35mm SLR; FPS 1-1/500s. As SV model without self-timer; "HIa" logo in U.S.A.

Asahi Pentax S2 Super: R1* C+

c1959, 35mm SLR; Same as the SV model, mainly sold in Japan; The word SUPER was not engraved on any part of the camera.

Asahi Pentax Spotmatic: R1* D

c1965; 35mm SLR; FPS 1-1/1000s & B; Self-timer; First Pentax with TTL metering,with Cds cells, needle visible in finder, Powered by 1.5v batt in base; multi stroke film advance lever; ASA settings under speed dial; Exp. meter switch above FP and X flash contacts;

Asahi Pentax SL: R1* C+

c1968; 35mm camera as the Spotmatic without the exp meter.

Asahi Pentax Spotmatic Motor Drive: R2* F+

c1966; Standard Spotmatic with modified base to take 12volt motor drive; Exp. 3 frames per sec. price camera and motor.

Asahi Pentax Spotmatic II or SPII: R1* D

c1971; Reintroduced Standard Spotmatic; Hot-shoe added; Exp meter increased to ASA3200; New range of lenses Super Multi Coated Takumar (SMR) for metering at all apertures; Sold as Asahi Honeywell Pentax in USA.

Asahi Pentax Spotmatic SPF: R1* D

c1973; As the SPII with shutter release lock; SMC Takumar lenses switch on exp meter when fitted; "F" on front "SPF" on top plate.

Asahi Pentax Spotmatic 1000: R1* D

c1973; 35mm SLR; FPS 1-1/1000s.;full metering; no self-timer; no hot shoe; 50mm f/2 Lens;

Asahi Pentax Electro Spotmatic: R1* D

c1971; sold in Japan; the first electronic Pentax; Aperture priority; Electronic FPS 1/1000 to slowest speed, set by light meter; some manual shutter speeds; 1/60s. max flash synch.

Asahi Pentax ES: R1* D

c1972; As the Electro Spotmatic; With 5 manual speeds 1/60 to 1/1000 & B; Switch for Automatic shutter 8s to 1/1000s.and film speed ring under rewind button; 6volt batt; no self-timer; Takumar 50mm f/1.4 lens.

Asahi Pentax ES.

Asahi Pentax K1000:   **R1* D+**

c1976; 35mm SLR; K mount version of SP 1000; no self-timer;no view button; no film speed disc;no FP flash contact; 55mm f/2 SMC lens.

Asahi Pentax ESII: **R1* D**
c1947; As the ES with shutter on eyepiece for use with self-timer; battery in base; safety lock on release; 55mm f/1.8 Lens; exp meter range ASA 3200; *(Chrome Price plus 50%)*

Asahi Pentax K2 DMD: **R1* E+**
(Data Motor Drive) c1976-1980; 35mm SLR; same as K2 with modified base to take motor drive and data back.

Asahi Pentax K2:   **R1* C+**
c1975; 35mm Electronic SLR; vertical MFPS 8s-1/1000s B; K2 on front; self-timer;preview button; mirror lock; FP & X flash contacts next to rewind knob; full exp and shutter info on Screen;

Pentax LX: **R4* E**
1980. Pentax's first professional SLR. Auto exp for aperture priority, shutter priority and program modes. Spot metering. Electronic and mechanical shutter 125s-1/2000s. Accepts all K-mount lenses. Part of a complete system that includes data backs motor drives and autowinders. Limited edition in gold also available.

Asahi Pentax KX: **R1* D+**
c1975; 35mm SLR; mechanical CFPS 1-1/1000s.; Window in base of pentaprism; self-timer; preview button; mirror lock; FP & X contacts on front; Silicon cell metering; K lens mount.

Pentax ME: **R1* D**

Asahi Pentax KM: **R1* D+**
c1975; 35mm SLR; mechanical CFPS 1-1/1000s.; Cds metering; as KX except; no shutter release lock; no mirror lock; no batt check; no aperture window;no film label slot; no motor drive.

1977. Aperture priority automation only. Shutter speeds 8s-1/1000s. Also available as the ME SE, a special edition with brown leather covering.

Pentax ME Super: **R1 A**
1980. Aperture priority and manual metering. Shutter 4s-1/2000s. Speeds set by dual push-button controls. Also available as the ME Super SE, a special edition with brown leather covering.

Pentax ME-F: **R1* D+**
1981. Similar to the ME but with autofocus capability with the AF35-70mm f2.8 zoom, incorporating a focusing motor.

Note: Pentax made many more SLRs in the 1970s and 1980s, some with only minor variations in specification. They included models such as the MG, MV, MV1 and MX, before moving onto the P range of cameras in 1985. Full details and specifications can be found in the book Japanese 35mm SLR Cameras by Bill Hansen and Michael Dierdorff, published by Hove Books.

Australian Camera Manufacturers, Australia
A.C.M.A., Australia

Sportshot: **R3* C–**
c1938, VFR bakelite camera for 6 x 9cm on 120 or 620 film, curved film plane, Lentar f13.5 lens, simple shutter, base of camera marked "British made", but this was common practice for Australian-made products before WWII. Available in black, brown, red, and green.

Sportshot, c1938.

Automatic Radio Co
Boston, Massachusetts, USA

Tom Thumb Camera Radio: **R3* E**

c1938, combination AM radio and detective camera; Maestar 57.5mm lens; reflex finder; 3 x 4cm exp on 127 film.

B

A.H. Baird
Edinburgh, Scotland

Baird Single Lens Stereo Camera:

R4* F

c1910. Tessar 18cm f4.5 lens; rollerblind shutter; single or stereoscopic exposure by displacing the lensboard right, centre, or left. Mahogany tailboard with brass fittings.

Max Balbreck
J. Joux, Paris, France

L'Alethoscope: **R4* E–**

c1925, stereo camera; Rapid Rectilinear lenses or Balbreck, Steinheil, Goerz, Zeiss Anastigmat; 5 speed guillotine shutter; changing magazine for 12 plates. 2 sizes: 6 x 13cm, 45 x 107mm.

B. & W. Manufacturing Co
Toronto, Canada

Press King: **R4* E–**

c1950. 4" x 5" press camera; Kodak Ektar 127mm f4.5 coated lens; Graphic MX shutter 1-1/400s 4" x 5" exp on cut film.

W. Bayer
Freital, Germany

Bayerflex: **R3* E–**

c1936. Anastigmat 75mm f3.5 lens, Pololyt Laak, Rathenow; FPS 1/25-1/500s.

Ch. Bazin et L. Leroy
Paris, France

Le Stereocycle: **R4* E+**

c1898. 6 x 13cm stereo camera; Koch Anastigmat 85mm f9 lens; guillotine shutter; 6 x 13cm plates; turning camera upside down activates plate changing mechanism.

Balda Werke.
Max Baldweg
Dresden, Germany (pre 1945)

then:

Balda-Kamerewerk-Bünde
Westfalen, West Germany

Balda Roll-Box: **R2* A**

c1934, metal box camera for 6 x 9cm frames on roll film, simple lens and shutter.

Balda Stahlbox: **R2* A**

c1936, metal box camera for 6 x 9cm frames on roll film, simple lens and I and B shutter. The name means "Steelbox".

Balda Dreibild-Box: **R2* A**

c1935, box camera for 6 x 9cm, 6 x 6cm or 6 x 4.5cm frames on roll film, simple lens and shutter. The name means "Three picture box".

Balda-Box: **R3* A**

c1935, metal box camera for 6 x 9cm frames on roll film.

Balda Poka-Duplex: **R3* A**

c1934, box camera for 6 x 9cm or 6 x 4.5cm frames on roll film, simple "close" and "distant" focusing.

Balda Poka II: **R3* A**

metal box camera for 6 x 9cm frames on roll film, built-in close-up lens. Later cameras offered in red, blue, grey, green and beige, and with 6 x 6cm capacity (coloured camera adds 200% to the price).

Balda Mickey Roll-Box: **R3* C–**
c1936, simple box camera using 127 film for 6.5 x 4cm frames, advertised as the "camera for everyone", available in three models, Model "O" with meniscus lens, Model I with "better" lens and provision for cable release, and Model II, with simple focusing.

Balda Frontbox: **R2* A**
c1934, metal box camera for 6 x 9cm frames on roll film, marked "Balda Frontbox" on the camera front, in different styles.

Baldi: **R2* C–**
c1930, folding camera for 3 x 4cm frames on 127 film, many 50mm lenses were available, including f2.9 Xenar, f3.5 Vidanar, and f4.5 Tessar, in various Compur shutters.

Super Baldina (pre-war):   **R2* C**
c1934 folding camera with coupled RFR for 24 x 36mm film, many 50mm lens were offered including f2.8 Tessar and f2 Xenon, in various Compur shutters with either front element focusing or helicoid focusing mount. Early cameras have black top housings and shutter mounted shutter releases, while later cameras have chromed top housings and body mounted releases.

Baldina (pre-war):   **R2* B**
c1933, folding camera, but without built-in RFR, late cameras have body mounted shutter release.

Baldinette: **R2* B**
c1951, folding 35mm camera; Baldanar or radionar f2.8 or Baltar or Radionar f2.9 50mm lens; Prontor S, SV or Synchro Compur shutter.

Super-Baldinette: **R3* C+**
c1951, folding 35mm camera with CRF, Ennit f2.8/50mm lens in Prontor SV shutter,or Heligon f2/50mm lens in Compur shutter. (add 50% for Heligon lens).

Mess-Baldinette: **R3* C**

c1951, folding 35mm camera with uncoupled RFR, Baltar f2.9/5cm lens in Prontor shutter. This camera was intended as a less expensive alternative to the Super-Baldinette, but was priced only slightly higher than the Baldinette. Not sold in great quantities.

Baldafix: **R2* B**
c1953, folding camera for 6 x 9, 6 x 6, or 6 x 4.5cm frames on rollfilm, non automatic frame counting, no double exposure prevention, Ennar f4.5/10.5cm lens in Pronto shutter.

Baldalux: **R3* C**
c1953, folding camera for 6 x 9, 6 x 6,

or 6 x 4.5cm frames on rollfilm, automatic frame counting, double exposure prevention, Radionar f4.5 or Trinar f3.5 10.5cm lenses in Synchro Compur or Prontor SV shutter. The higher priced alternative to the Baldifix.

Baldamatic 1:   **2* C–**
Based on the Baldessa 1B, but with a new Prontormat shutter and a depth of field scale added to the 45mm f2.8 Color-Baldanar. Camera is automatic with two bands for daylight or flash on the aperture ring. Match needle metering. No shutter speeds or aperture settings are shown on the shutter control or the daylight section of aperture control. If turning the ring for exposure control takes it into the flash band, it means there is not enough natural light. The flash band then has f-numbers inscribed.

Baldax: **R2* C–**
c1954, folding camera for 6 x 6cm frames on rollfilm, automatic frame counting, Ennagon f3.5/7.5cm lens or Radionar f2.9/8cm lens in Prontor Sv shutter.

Super-Baldax: **R2* C+**
c1959, folding camera for 6 x 6cm frames on rollfilm, automatic frame counting, CRF, Baldar f2.9/8cm in Prontor SVS shutter or Ennit f2.8/8cm lens in Synchro Compur shutter.

Baldalette: **R3* C–**
c1949, folding 35mm camera with coated or uncoated Radionar f2.9/5cm lens in Pronto, Prontor or Compur Rapid shutter.

Rigona (post war):   **R3* C–**
c1954, folding 35mm camera, Rigonar f3.5/50mm lens in Pronto shutter.

Super Baldax, c1959.

Rigona (pre-war):   **R3* B+**
c1936, folding camera for 3 x 4cm frames on 127 rollfilm, Radionar f2.9/5cm or Vidanar f4.5/5cm lens in Prontor II or Vario shutter. Chrome top plate and body release were offered as options. Found with film wind on the top, or on the bottom!

Mess-Rigona: **R3* C**
c1954, folding 35mm camera with uncoupled RFR, Rigonar f3.5/5cm lens in Pronto shutter.

Baldix: **R2* B**
c1953, folding camera for 6 x 6 frames on 120 rollfilm, Ennagon f3.5 or Baltar f2.9 7.5cm lens in Prontor SVS shutter.

Mess-Baldix: **R3* C**
c1954, folding camera for 6 x 6cm frames on 120 rollfilm, uncoupled RFR, many lens and shutter combinations

were listed in catalogues, but the Ennagon f3.5/7.5cm lens in Prontor SV shutter is most often seen.

Jubilette: R3* C–
c1934, folding 35mm camera with Baltar f3.5/5cm lens in Compur shutter.

Venus: R2* C–
c1935, aluminium bodied folding 6.5 x 9 sheet film with Zeiss Tessar or other lens in Compur shutter.

Nizza: R2* C–
c1935, aluminium bodied folding 9 x 12cm sheet film camera with Zeiss Tessar or other lens in Compur shutter. Like so many other cameras of the same kind and era.

Juwella: R2* C–
c1938, folding camera for 6 x 9 frames on rollfilm, Juwella Anastigmat f6.3 or f4.5/10.5cm lens in Balda or other shutter.

Juwella II: R2* C–
c1938, folding camera for 6 x 9 or 6 x 4.5 frames on rollfilm, Juwella Anastigmat f6.3 or f4.5/10.5cm lens in Balda, Pronto or other shutter, for 6 x 4.5 format capability.

Pontina: R3* F–
c1936, folding camera for 6 x 9cm or 6 x 4.5cm frames on rollfilm, as with so many Balda cameras, the customer had a choice of several lens and shutter combinations, including Trioplan, Trinar, or Rarionar f4.5/10.5cm lens in Prontor I, Prontor II or Compur shutter.

Baldaxette: R3* D–
c1935, black folding camera for 6 x 4.5cm frames on rollfilm, CRF, automatic parallax correction, Trioplan, Radionar, Tessar, or Xenar 7.5cm lens in Compur shutter. Chrome model brings 20% less.

Baldaxette model-II: R3* C+

c1935, chrome folding camera for 6 x 6cm frames on rollfilm, CRF, automatic parallax correction, Trioplan, Radionar, Tessar, or Xenar 7.5cm lens in Compur shutter.

Super-Pontura: R4* F
c1939, folding camera for 6 x 9cm or 6 x 4.5cm frames on rollfilm, CRF, Trioplan f4.5 or f3.8/10.5cm lens or Tessar f4.5/10.5cm lens in Compur or Compur Rapid shutter. The lens assembly automatically returns to infinity when the camera is closed. The outbreak of war brought production to a standstill, and after 1945 no attempt was made to bring this camera back, few produced.

Piccochic: R2* C

Vest pocket camera; Vidanar 50mm f2.9 lens; Compur shutter; 16 exp, 3 x 4cm on 127 roll film.

Baldina (post war): R2* C–
c1954, 35mm VFR camera with interchangeable Baldinar, Xenon, Xenar, or Radionar 50mm lens in Pronto, Prontor, Compur-Rapid or Synchro-Compur shutter, Schneider 70mm Longar accessory lens available.

Super-Baldina (post war): R2* C+
c1954, 35mm camera with CRF and interchangeable Baldinar, Xenon, Xenar, or Radionar 50mm lens in Pronto, Prontor, Compur-Rapid or Synchro-Compur shutter, Schneider 70mm Longar accessory lens available.

Super Baldamatic: R3* D
1961. 35mm automatic camera with manual override. 45mm f2.8 Xenar. Compur shutter 1/30-1/500s. Shutter release on the front of the body and a left-handed lever wind that requires only half a turn to advance the film and cock the shutter led the manufacturers to claim that shooting was possible at one frame per second or even more.

Baldixette: R3* A

c1960, metal VFR camera for 6 x 6cm frames in 120 roll film, front element focusing Baldar f9/7.2cm lens in collapsible tube mount, simple shutter.

Baldessa: R2* A

c1957, 35mm VFR camera with Westanar f2.8/50mm lens in Prontor SVS shutter, top mounted shutter release, after 1964 the body style changed, and the shutter release was mounted on the front of the camera body.

Baldessa I: R2* A
c1957, 35mm VFR camera with brightline finder, Isconar f2.8/45mm lens in Pronto or Prontor SVS shutter.

Baldessa Ia: R2* B
c1957, 35mm camera with CRF, Baldanar f2.8/45mm lens in Priontor SVS shutter.

Baldessa Ib: R2* B

c1957, 35mm camera with CRF, and built-in light meter, Baldanar f2.8/45mm lens in Priontor SVS shutter.

Baldessa F: R2* A
c1964, Built-in AG-1 flash lamp holder.

Baldessa LF: R2* A

c1964, with built-in light meter.

Baldessa RF/LK: R2* B
c1964, 35mm RFR camera, Westanar f2.8/45mm lens, Prontor shutter, CRF, but for built-in AG-1 flash lamp holder, built-in light meter with automatic aperture control.

Baldessa RF/LK, c1964.

Baldessa F/LK: R2* A
c1964, without CRF.

Baldessa RF: R2* D+
c1964, without light meter.

R. & J. Beck Ltd
London, England

Frena: R2* E

c1897, box-type detective camera; Beck Achromatic single 4" f11 lens; rotating shutter $\frac{1}{5}$-1/80s; 50 exp, 6.5 x 9cm on sheet film in magazine.

Frena Deluxe: R3* F–
c1897, box-type detective camera; 40 exp, 6.5 x 9cm on special sheet film. Covered with brown calveshide, gold metal-plated fittings.

Kamera-Fabrik Woldemar Beier
Freital, Germany

Beier-Box model "O":   R3* B
c1929, metal box camera for 6 x 9 frames on rollfilm

Beier-Box model "I":   R3* C
c1930, metal box camera for 6 x 9 frames on rollfilm, with the addition of a wire frame finder and better lens.

Beier-Box model "II":   R3* B
c1930, metal box camera for 6 x 9 frames on rollfilm, with the addition of a built-in close-up lens.

Beira: R4* D

c1931, folding strut type camera for 36 exp, 24 x 36mm on 1.6m of "normal movie film". Early cameras were without RFR, later cameras added a coupled RFR. Many lens and shutter combinations were offered, among them Meyer Trioplan f2.9/50mm lens in Compur shutter 1-1/300s and Leitz Elmar f3.5/50mm in Compur Rapid shutter, 1-1/500s, a Meyer Makro Plasmat f2.7/50mm lens was also offered in catalogues of the day. Coupled RFR adds 100%, Elmar lens adds 100%, EST Makro Plasmat adds 100%.

Beirette (pre-war):   R3* C–
c1938, folding 35mm VFR camera, Steinheil Cassar f2.9/5cm lens in Compur shutter, 1-1/200s.

Beirette (post war):   R2* A
c1965, simple metal 35mm camera from the East German firm of VEB Beier.

Belca Werke
Dresden, Germany

Belplasca: R3* E

c1955. 35mm stereo camera; Tessar 37.5mm f3.5 lens; shutter 1-1/200s.

Bell & Howell Inc
Chicago, Illinois, USA

Foton: R4* F+

c1948, 35mm spring-wind motor drive camera; Taylor & Hobson-Cooke Amotal 50mm f2.2 coated lens with interchangeable screw mount;

additional three lug bayonet mount for accessory telephoto lens. Mfps 1-1/1000s; spring-wind motor drive advances film and cocks shutter at a maximum rate of 6 frames per sec. and cycles 9-15 exp per winding. Cook Telephoto 216mm f5.6 coated lens, F+. Cook Telephoto 4" coated lens, E. Prices higher in Japan.

Stereo Vivid: R2* E–
c1951, 35mm stereo camera; Steinheil Cassar or Rodenstock Tridar f3.5 lens; guillotine shutter 1/10-1/100s, CRF. Taking the film under a roller reduced the inter-lens separation to 65mm. Originally by Three Dimension Co.

Stereo Colourist: R2* D+
c1952, 35mm stereo camera; Rodenstock Trinar f3.5 lens; Velio shutter 1/10-1/200s, bulb, flash. Originally by Three Dimension Co, and manufactured in Germany by Bodenseewerk Apparate und Maschinenbau GmbH, Uberlingen, Germany, and offered by them as the "Boden-Stereo."

Bell Camera Co
Grinnell, Iowa, USA

Bell's Straight Working Panoram Camera: R4* F–
Horizontal format, folding bellows camera; 5 panoramic exp, 11½" x 3¼" on roll film. C 1908.

Bell 14: R3* B
c1960. Subminiature camera; 12 x 14mm exp on 16mm roll film. Manufactured in Japan.

H. Belleni & Fils
Nancy, France

Jumelle Bellieni: R3* E
c1899, 9 x 14cm stereo camera; Zeiss Protar 135mm f8 lenses; pneumatic, circular 5 speed shutter. Magazine for 12 plates.

Jumelle Bellieni: R3* E–
c1896, 12.9 x 18cm stereo camera; Zeiss Protar 110mm f8 lenses; 6 speed rotating shutter; changing mechanism for 12.9 x 18cm plates. Panoramic setting; rising and sliding lens panel.

Curt Bentzin
Görlitz, Germany

After 1945 the factory was "nationalised" and became the Optik-Primar-Kamera-Werke VEB . Cameras from this factory are located at the end of this listing, and are considered a continuation of the pre-war production.

Primar Reflex 6.5 x 9: R3* F–
"Spiegel Camera Reflex" c1920s, SLR for 6.5cm x 9cm plates, several lenses offered including Biotessar f4.5/13.5cm lens, self capping CFPS ⅕-1/1000s.

Primar Reflex 9 x 12: R3* F–
c1920. "Spiegel Camera Reflex", SLR for 9cm x 12cm plates, several lenses offered including Tessar f4.5/18cm lens, self capping CFPS ⅓-1/1000s.

Primar Reflex 10 x 15: R3*
F–"Spiegel Camera Reflex" c1920s, SLR for 10cm x 15cm plates, Tessar f4.5/21cm lens, self capping CFPS ⅓-1/1000s.

Primar Reflex 13 x 18: R3* F–
"Spiegel Camera Reflex" c1920s, SLR for 13cm x 18cm plates, Tessar f4.5/25cm lens, self capping CFPS $\frac{1}{4}$-1/1000s.

Primar Reflex 3$\frac{1}{4}$ x 4$\frac{1}{4}$: R3* F–
c1920s "Spiegel Camera Reflex", SLR for 31/4inch x 41/4 inch plates, Tessar f4.5/25cm lens, self capping CFPS $\frac{1}{3}$-1/1000s.

Primarette: R4* F+
1933. Twin lens camera that is not a twin lens reflex. 8 exp on 127. Viewing lens and taking lens each linked to the body by its own bellows. Top lens moves up and down during focusing for parallax correction. 75mm f3.5 Meyer Trioplan, Primotar or Tessa lenses. Rimset Compur shutter 1-1/250s + T & B. Rare.

Primar Folding Reflex 6.5 x 9: R3* D–
c1920s, "Klapp Reflex Primar" folding SLR camera for 6.5 x 9cm plates several lenses offered including Biotessar f2.8/13.5cm lens, CFPS $\frac{1}{5}$-1/1000s.

Primar Folding Reflex 9 x 12: R3* D+
c1920s, "Klapp Reflex Primar" folding SLR camera for 9cm x 12cm plates several lenses offered including Tessar f4.5/18cm lens, CFPS $\frac{1}{4}$-1/1000s.

Primar Folding Reflex 10 x 15: R3* D+
c1920s, "Klapp Reflex Primar" folding SLR camera for 10 x 15cm plates, Tessar f2.8/13.5cm lens, CFPS $\frac{1}{3}$-1/1000s.

Primar Folding Reflex 3$\frac{1}{4}$ x 4$\frac{1}{4}$: R3* D–
c1920s, Klapp Reflex Primar folding SLR camera for 3$\frac{1}{4}$" x 4$\frac{1}{4}$" plates, Boitessar f2.8/16.5cm lens, CFPS $\frac{1}{3}$-1/1000s.

Primar 6.5 x 9: R3* D
c1920s, "Fokal Primar" c1920s, folding VFR camera for 6.5 x 9cm plates, several lenses offered including Doppel Plasmat f4/12cm, CFPS $\frac{1}{8}$-1/1000s.

Primar 9 x 12: R3* D
c1920s, "Fokal Primar" folding VFR camera for 9cm x 12cm plates several lenses offered including Makro Plasmat f2.9/15cm lens, CFPS $\frac{1}{5}$-1/1000s.

Primar 10 x 15: R3* D
c1920s, "Fokal Primar" c1920s, folding VFR camera for 10 x 15cm plates, several lenses offered including Doppel Plasmat f4/18cm lens, CFPS $\frac{1}{5}$-1/1000s.

Primar 13 x 18: R3* D+
c1920s, "Fokal Primar" folding VFR camera for 13 x 18cm plates, several lenses offered including Doppel Plasmat f4/21cm lens, CFPS $\frac{1}{4}$-1/1000s.

Night Primar: R4* G
c1929, "Nacht Primar" VFR camera for 6.5cm x 9cm plates, Plasmat f1.9/9cm lens, CFPS 8-1/1000s.

Stereo Primar: R3* E
c1910, strut folding stereo VFR camera for 4.5cm x 10.7cm plates, Tessar f4.5/12cm lenses, CFPS 1-1/1000s.

Stereo reflex Primar: R4* F+
c1915, strut folding stereo reflex camera for 4.5cm x 10.7cm plates, Anastigmat f6.8/9cm lenses, both lenses used for reflex viewing.

Plan Primar: R3* C–
c1930s, folding VFR camera for 6.5cm x 9cm plates, several lens and shutters offered including front element focusing Trioplan f6.3/10.5 lens, Vario shutter.

Horizontal Primar: R3* D–
c1920s, "Quer Primar", horizontal format folding VFR camera, available with and without CFPS, triple extension bellows, Tessar f3.5/13.5cm lens, Compur shutter, (CFPS adds 50%).

Horizontal Primar Stereo: R3* E
c1920s, "Quer Primar", horizontal format folding stereo VFR camera, available with and without CFPS, triple extension bellows, Tessar f4.5/9cm lenses, Compur shutters, with stereo lenses, (CFPS adds 50%).

Universal Square Primar 9 x 12:
                    R3* C+
c1920s, Universal Quadrat Primar folding drop bed VFR camera for 9cm x 12cm plates, available with and without CFPS, Plasmat f4/15cm lens, Compur shutter, (CFPS adds 25%).

Universal Square Primar 10 x 15:
                    R3* D
c1920s. Universal Quadrat Primar folding drop bed VFR camera for 10cm x 15cm plates, available with and without CFPS, Satz Plasmat f4.5/17.3cm lens, Compur shutter, (CFPS adds 25%).

Universal Square Primar 13 x 18:
                    R3* D
c1920s. Universal Quadrat Primar folding drop bed VFR camera for 13cm x 18cm plates, available with and without CFPS, Plasmat f4/21cm lens, Compur shutter, (CFPS adds 25%).

Primarflex 6x6:   R3* E+

c1930's, SLR for 6x6cm frames on 120 roll film, glass plates in small holders could be used. Interchangeable Trioplan f2.8/10cm lens, CFPS 1-1/1000s. Rarely found with a properly functioning shutter. The Primarflex was a very advanced camera for its time with a complete set of interchangeable lenses and a quick-change loading system. Its basic design in advanced form became the first Hasselblad in 1948. The late Dr. Victor Hasselblad once commented that the 6x6 Primarflex had strongly influenced him when he was designing the Hasselblad camera.

Bermpohl & Co
Berlin, Germany

Bermpohl Single Exposure
Colour Camera: **R4* H–**
(BN100)c1920 ; Meyer Plasmat 215mm
f/4 lens; Compound shutter 1-1/75s, 9 x
12cm plate holders. The incoming light
was split into three components by 2
internal semi-transparent mirrors. Three
plates one each for red, green, and blue
light were exposed.

Berning- (see Robot listing)

Bertram
Munich, Germany

Bertram-Kamera: **R4* F**
1954. Professional camera for press and
sports photographers. Metal body,
bellows, CRF for all lenses. Viewfinder
automatically changes as lens is fitted.
Focusing scale in viewfinder. Parallax
corrected. Compur shutter 1-1/400s +
T & B. Self timer. Swing back. Rollfilm
and cut film holders. Image size: $2^1/_4$ x
$3^1/_4$ inch. Xenar 105mm, Angulon 65mm
and Tele Xenar 180mm.

Adolphe Bertsch
Paris, France

Chambre Automatique de Bertsch:
R5* I–
Brass wet plate camera; Achromatic
meniscus lens; lens cap controls exp.
Single exp, $2^1/_2$" x $2^1/_2$" on wet collodion
plate. C 1861. One of the first camera
outfits to include materials necessary
for the sensitising and developing of
wet plates.

**Stereo Chambre Automatique
de Bertsch:**   **R5* J**
c1865 brass stereo version of Bertsch's
Chambre Automatique; paired Petzval
stereoscopic objectives, lens cap
controls exp. Measures $3^3/_4$" x $4^1/_2$" x
$6^3/_8$". Takes 2 exp, $2^3/_8$" on wet collodion
plates. This was one of the first camera
outfits which included materials
necessary for the sensitizing and
developing of wet plates.

Biflex 35:   **R4* H**

35mm camera; Tritar 2cm f2.5 lens; 200
exp on 35mm roll film. Mfg. in
Switzerland. c1945. Possibly made for
British intelligence.

Binoca: White: R4* G
Red/Black: R4* G

c1950, subminiature binocular camera; camera is included in a 2.5x power binocular. Bicon 40mm f4.5 lens; variable speed shutter and bulb. 16mm film in cassette. Mfd in Japan.

Blair Camera Co
Boston, Massachusetts, USA

In 1879, Thomas H. Blair founded the Blair Tourograph Co. in Connecticut. In 1881, he moved to Boston, Massachusetts, where he incorporated as the Blair Tourograph and Dry Plate Company; on March 5, 1886 the company name was changed to the Blair Camera Company. The firm was purchased in 1899 by the Eastman Kodak Co; in 1907 the company assets were moved to Rochester, New York, where for a few years some cameras were inscribed "Blair, Division of the Eastman Kodak Co." George Eastman needed one of Blair's important patents – paper backed roll film. Without question this convenient daylight loading system was critical to the expansion of snapshot photography.

Baby Hawkeye: R4* B–
roll film box camera; 2" x 2" exp on roll film. c1897.

Blair 4" x 5" View Camera: R4* E

c1880, brass Dallmeyer No. 1 R.R. lens; front focus; tilting and reversible back; sliding bottom lock; mahogany with brass fittings.

**Blair's Improved Reversible
Back Camera:**   R4* E
c1890, 5" x 7" view camera; rack and pinion front focusing; bed mfg. in 3 sections. Sizes: 4" x 5" to 8" x 10".

**Detective and Combination Camera
(first model):**   R4* E
c1888, 4" x 5" detective camera; glass focusing; front shutter cocking; side shutter adjustments; oak finish, brass fittings. First model had removable knob for ground glass focusing.

**Detective and Combination Camera
(second model):**   R4* Wood: E
Leather: E+
c1890, 4" x 5" detective camera; removable rear panel for group glass focusing; counter on side for film or plates; oak finish, brass fittings; used with Eastman-Walker roll film holder.

Detective and Combination Camera
(third model):   **R4* Wood: E**
                                      Leather: E
c1890, 4" x 5" detective camera;
focusing and shutter release on top with
Eastman-Walker roll holder; separate
ground glass for critical focusing by
removing rear panel; nickel or brass
plated fittings, dark mahogany finish.

English Compact View Camera: R3* E
c1890, $6\frac{1}{2}$" x $8\frac{1}{2}$" view camera;
reversible back; double extension
bellows; mahogany finish, brass fittings.
7 sizes: $3\frac{1}{4}$" x $4\frac{1}{4}$" to 10" x 12".

Folding Hawkeye: R4* 4x5" size: D+
                         5x7" size: E+
c1890, 5" x 7" folding camera; Bausch &
Lomb Rapid Rectilinear lens; Blair
shutter. 4" x 5"

Hawkeye Detective Camera: R3*
                           Wood: E
                         Leather: E

c1890, box-type detective camera.

Kamaret: **R4* F**
c1891. Rapid Rectilinear lens; double
exp prevention; 2 speed guillotine
shutter; for 100 exp, 4" x 5" without
reloading. First camera to place film
spools in front instead of to rear of
camera, thus shortening the camera,

making it more compact. Original price
$40. Distributed by E. & H.T. Anthony.

Lucidograph: **R4* F+**

c1885, 4" x 5" view camera; Pantagraph
R.R. $5\frac{3}{4}$" lens.

No. 3 Combination Hawkeye: R4* E+
c1905, $3\frac{1}{4}$" x $4\frac{1}{4}$" roll film and plate
camera; roll holder lifts up for focusing,
similar to No. 4 Screen Focus Kodak.

No. 4 Weno Hawkeye: R2* B
c1900, $3\frac{1}{2}$" x $4\frac{1}{2}$" box camera.

No. 4 Combination Hawkeye: R4* E+
c1904, 4" x 5" roll film and plate camera; roll holder lifts up for focusing, similar to No. 4 Screen Focus Kodak.

Petite Kamarette: R3* F
c1892, miniature box roll film camera. Round exp, 3½" diameter on roll film.

Stereo Hawkeye Model No. 4: R4* F–

c1890's, roll film stereo camera; Bausch & Lomb Optical Co. Rapid Rectilinear lenses U.S. 4; shutter 1-1/100s. Red bellows; leather covered body.

Tourist Hawkeye: R4* D+

c1900, wooden folding roll film camera; 2 speed shutter; 3½" x 3½" exp on roll film or plates; exp counter at back.

Tourist Hawkeye Special Camera:
**   R3* E**

c1897, 4" x 5" camera; Rapid Rectilinear Unicum shutter. Sliding and rising front; fine focus; red bellows.

Weno: R3* E–
c1903. Rapid Rectilinear lens; Bausch & Lomb shutter; 9 x 18cm exp on roll film.

Weno Stereo Hawkeye: R4* E+
folding roll film stereo camera; 3½" x 6" exp on roll film.

Bland & Co
England

Bland & Co. Wet Plate: R4* H
c1850, brass lens L.F. Colas; wet plate holder; ground glass screen

Edmund Bloch
Paris, France

Photo-Cravate (Bloch's Detective
Photo Scarf):   R5* I+
c1890, magazine camera concealed in

cravate; periscopic lens, 25mm f16; single speed pneu-matic shutter; 6 exp, 23mm diameter on dry plates. The buyer had a choice of colours, styles, and patterns. Original cost of the complete outfit was 60 francs.

Le Physiographe: R5* G

c1910, monocular detective camera; Krauss Tessar 51mm f6.3 lens; 4.5 x 5cm exp on plates.

Stereo Physiographe: R5* H–
c1896, stereo binocular-type detective camera; Krauss Tessar 51mm f6.3 lenses; single speed rotating shutter; 45 x 107mm exp on plates.

Leon Bloch
Paris, France

Photo Bouquin: R5* I–
c1904, stereo book-type detective camera; achromatic lenses; rotary shutter; central vf concealed in binding. 45 x 107mm exp on plates. The Photo Bouquin was the only stereoscopic book camera.

Physio Pocket: R4* H–
The Physio Pocket is identical to the Physiographe, the latter name was used after about 1909-10. Several different lenses were used including the Cooke Anastigmat to the Krauss Tessar.

Bodenseewerk Aparate und Maschinenbau GmbH
Uberlingen, Germany

Boden-Stereo: R3* D+
c1953, 35mm stereo camera; Rodenstock Trinar f3.5 lens; Gauthier Velio shutter 1/10-1/200s, bulb, flash.The same camera as the Stereo-Colourist, offered by Bell and Howell, but under the manufacturer's own name.

Bolsey Corp of America
New York, USA

Jacques Bolsey was a Swiss designer who was responsible for the Bolex movie camera amongst several others. His American 35mm cameras were innovative, sturdy and inexpensive.

La Belle Pal: R3* D
35mm rf camera; Wollensak Anastigmat 44mm f4.5 coated lens.

La Belle Pal.

Bolsey B: R2* B

c1949 35mm RFR camera, Wollensak f3.2/44mm lens, shutter 1/25-1/200s, CRF.

Bolsey B2: R2* B

c1949. 35mm RFR camera, with double exposure prevention, and flash synch, Wollensak shutter 1/10-1/200.

Bolsey B2 (U.S. Army): R3* E–

c1949. similar to Model B2, except special plate on top with U.S. Army engraving, and olive drab paint.

Bolsey B2 (U.S. Air Force): R3* E–

c1949, similar to Model B2, except special plate on top with U.S.A.F. engraving.

Bolsey C: R3* D–

c1950, 35mm TLR; Wollensak Anastigmat f3.2/44mm lens, Wollensak Alphax shutter 1/10-1/200s, CRF. (prices much lower in the USA).

Bolsey C22 "Set-O-Matic": R2* D–
c1953, 35mm TLR, with "Set-O-Matic" flash calculator. (prices much lower in the USA).

Bolsey 8: R4* E

c1956, 8mm still and motion picture camera; Bolsey-Elgeet 10mm f1.8 Navitar lens; rotary shutter 1/50-1/600s. Special cassette holds 25 ft of 8mm film. Single exp stop mechanism, variable shutter speeds, automatic footage counter.

Bolsey Jubilee: R3* C+
c1955, 35mm rf camera; Bolsey-Steinheil Anastigmat 45mm f2.8 lens; Bolsey Gauthier Auto-Synchro shutter 1/10-1/200s, CRF.

Boltavit: R3* C–
Boltar 40mm f7.7 lens; shutter 1/25-1/50-1/100s; 12 exp, 25 x 25mm on 35mm roll film. Metal cast body. c1936.

Boniforti & Balleno
Milano, Italy

Perseo: R4* G+

c1948, 35mm RFR camera with coupled interchangeable f3.5 or Heligon f2/50mm lens, CFPS 1/20-1/1000s. front mounted shutter release, several variations exist with different shutter speed dials, film counters, and logo placements, in all around 200 units were produced.

A. Boreaux
Basle, Switzerland.

Nana: R4* E
c1913, 45 x 107mm stereo camera; Suter 62mm f6.8 lenses; 6-speed guillotine shutter. Metal body covered with Morrocan leather.

Boston Camera Co
Boston, Massachusetts, USA

Hawkeye Detective Camera: R3* E

c1889, box-type detective camera.

Boumsel
Paris, France

Longchamp: R2* B

c1935. Bakelite TLR for 3 x 4cm format on 127 film. Simple lens and single speed shutter. Probably made at the Norca factory for Boumsel. Also found in brown bakelite, from after the war.

Auteuil: R4* C+

c1948. Brown bakelite, based on the Longchamp body, but with 50mm/f3.5 Topaz lens in a Gitzo shutter, or a 50mm/f3.5 FAP Anastigmat in a Rapid-Synchro shutter. A real sales flop, left-over bodies were made into Longchamp cameras.

Azur: R3* B

c1948. Folding roll film cameras for 6 x 9cm format. Available in several combinations of lens and shutters.

Carl Bralin Camerawerk
Nurnberg, Germany

Paxette I: R2* B

c1950,35mm VFR camera, Pointar, Kataplast or Cassar f2.8/45mm lens, Prontor S shutter; built-in extinction meter, lever wind on early cameras.

Paxette 1A: R2 C

1957. 35mm VFR camera, similar to the Paxette 1M with small modifications. Film speed indicator extended to 200ASA. Lens and shutter entirely new: four-element 50mm f2.8 Plastigon in a Prontor-SVS exposure value shutter.

Paxette IM: R2* C–

c1951, 35mm camera with uncoupled RFR, Cassar or Kataplast f2.8/45mm lens; Pronto or Prontor S shutter.

Paxette II: R3* C

c1953, 35mm VFR cameras with interchangeable lenses, Cassar or Kata f2.8/45mm lens in Prontor S shutter, built-in extinction meter.

Paxette IIM: R2* D–

c1953, 35mm camera with uncoupled RFR, interchangeable Cassar or Kata f2.8/45mm lens; Pronto or Prontor S shutter.

Super Paxette Ib: R2* D

c1958, 35mm camera with CFR; Kata f2.8/45mm lens; Pronto shutter.

Super Paxette I: R2* D

c1958, 35mm camera with CFR, Prontor SVS shutter, Kata f2.8/45mm lens.

Super Paxette IL: R3* D

c1958, 35mm camera with CRF and brightline finder, fixed f2.8/50mm Katagon lens in Pronto or Prontor SVS shutter.

Super Paxette IIL: R3* D

c1958, 35mm camera with brightline finder and interchangeable Tessar, Cassarit, or Xenar f2.8/50mm lens or Quinon f2/50mm lens in Prontor SVS shutter. All Super Paxette II cameras have in common accessory lenses from 35mm to 200mm coupled with the RFR, and built-in fields of view for 35mm-135mm.

Super Paxette II: R3* D
c1956, 35mm camera with coupled RFR; interchangeable Cassarit, Tessar, or Xenar f2.8/45mm lens in Prontor SVS shutter.

Super Paxette IIB: R3* C+
c1957, 35mm camera with coupled RFR; interchangeable Cassarit, Tessar, or Xenar f2.8/45mm lens in Prontor SVS shutter.

Super Paxette IIBL: R3* D–
c1958, 35mm camera with coupled RFR; interchangeable Cassarit, Tessar, or Xenar f2.8/45mm or Katagon f2.8/50mm lens in Prontor SVS shutter, built-in light meter.

Paxette Automatic Reflex: R3* D–
c1958, 35mm SLR with body mounted light meter coupled to interchangeable Ultralit f2.8/50mm lens, Synchro-Compur shutter 1-1/500s, several top styles and meter positions.

Paxette Automatic Reflex IB: R3* D–
c1958, 35mm SLR with body mounted light meter not coupled to fix mounted Cassarit f2.8/50mm lens, Synchro-Compur shutter 1-1/500s, lightmeter reading visible in the VFR.

Paxette Automatic: R3* C+
c1959, 35mm camera with CRF, VFR with fields of view for 35mm, 50mm, 85mm and 135mm, built-in light meter coupled to aperture and shutter speeds, interchangeable f2.8/50mm Colour-Ennit lens in Prontor-SLK shutter.

Paxette Automatic, c1959.

Paxette Electromatic: R2* B
c1960, simple 35mm VFR camera with single speed shutter, and automatic aperture control, f5.6/45mm fixed focus lens.

Paxette Electromatic IA: R2* C
c1961, 35mm VFR camera, automatic aperture control, interchangeable Trinar f2.8/40mm lens, field of view for accessory 75mm lens marked in VFR, special electronic flash offered as accessory.

Paxette Electromatic III: R2* C–
c1963, 35mm VFR camera with full automatic or manual control, Ultralit f2.8/40mm lens in Prontormatic shutter, 1-1/500s.

Accessories for Paxette cameras

Optical VFR for 35mm and 85mm fields of view:	**B+**
Optical VFR for 90mm field of view:	**B+**
Optical VFR for 135mm field of view:	**B+**
Optical VFR for 200mm field of view:	**B**
Choroplast f4.5/35mm lens:	**B**
Choroplast f3.5/38mm lens:	**B**
Tele-Rotelar f4/75mm lens:	**C–**
Neoplast f5.6 85mm lens:	**C**
Telexon f5.6/85mm lens:	**C–**

Telenar f3.8/90mm lens: **C**
Telexon f3.8/135mm lens: **C+**
Telenar f5.6/135mm lens: **C–**
Tele Ennalyt f4.5/200mm lens: **D–**

Imperial Box 6 x6:   **R2* A**
c1950, box camera for 6 x 6 frames on roll film, with and without synchro.

Imperial Box 6 x 9:   **R2* A**
c1950, box camera for 6 x 9 frames on roll film, with and without synchro.

Nimco: **R3* A**
c1952, 6 x 6 box camera produced by Braun for other retail sellers.

Norca I: **R2* B**
c1952, folding VFR camera for 6 x 9 frames on rollfilm, f8/105mm lens, Pronto shutter.

Norca II: **R2* B**
c1952, folding VFR camera for 6 x 9 frames on rollfilm, F6.3 Gotar lens in Prontor-s shutter.

Norca III: **R2* B**
c1952, folding VFR camera for 6 x 9 or 6 x 6 frames on rollfilm, f4.5 Gotar lens, Pronto shutter.

Norca II Super: **R3* C**
c1953, folding RFR camera for 6 x 9 or 6 x 6 frames on roll film, f6.3/105mm Cassar lens, Prontor-s shutter.

Norca IV Super: **R3* C**
c1953, folding RFR camera for 6 x 9 or 6 x 6 on roll film, f4.5/105mm Cassar lens, Prontor-S shutter.

Paxina I: **R3* B**
c1952, metal VFR camera for 6 x 6 frames on roll film, simple f7.7 lens in two speed shutter, square telescoping front.

Paxina II: **R2* B**
c1952, metal VFR camera for 6 x 6 frames on roll film, telescoping tube mounted Kata f3.5 or Steiner f3.5/75mm lens Vario shutter.

Paxina 29:   **R2* B**
c1953, metal VFR camera for 6 x 6 frames on roll film, telescoping tube mounted Steiner f2.9/75mm lens, Vario shutter.

Gloriette: **R2* C–**
c1954-57, 35mm VFR camera, lever advance,Cassar f2.8/45mm lens, Vario, Pronto or Prontor shutter, different top plate styles.

Gloriette B: **R3* C–**
c1955, 35mm VFR camera, lever advance, Cassar f2.8/45mm lens, Prontor-SVS shutter, built-in uncoupled light meter.

Gloria: **R3* C**
c1958, metal RFR camera for 6 x 6 frames on rollfilm, uncoupled RFR, telescoping front, Praxar f2.9/75mm lens, Pronto or Prontor-SVS shutter.

Colourette Super I: **R2* B**
c1958, 35mm camera CRF, lever advance, Cassar f2.8/45mm lens, Compur-Rapid shutter.

Colourette Super IB: **R3* C–**
c1958, 35mm camera CRF, lever advance, fixed mount Plastagon f2.8/45mm lens, Compur-Rapid shutter, Built-in light meter.

Colourette Super IBL: **R3* C–**
c1958, 35mm RFR camera, lever advance, fix mount Cassar, Culminar, Ysarex or Xenar f2.8/50mm lens, Synchro Compur shutter, built-in light meter.

Colourette Super II: **R3* C+**
c1958, 35mm camera CRF, lever advance, interchangeable Cassar, Culminar, Ysarex or Xenar f2.8/50mm lens, automatic depth of field indicator,Compur-Rapid shutter with EV values.

Colourette Super IIB: **R3* E–**
c1958, 35mm camera CRF, lever advance, interchangeable Cassar, Culminar, Ysarex or Xenar f2.8/50mm lens, automatic depth of field indicator,Compur-Rapid shutter with EV values, built-in light meter.

Brins Patent Camera,
London, England: **R4* H+**
c1891, 30mm f3.5 lens; simple shutter. Circular exp, 25mm diameter; lens at rear permits use as monocular. Mfd in London, England. This camera, if authentic reaches an R5 rarity level, almost unavailable. Beware of cleverly made fakes which are worth about 25% of an original.

A. Briois
Paris, France

Le Revolver Thompson: **R5* K–**
c1862 revolver-type detective camera; Petzval-type 40mm f2 lens; rotary shutter. 4 exp, 23mm diameter on circular wet collodion plates, 75mm diameter.

British Camera Manufacturing Company
England

Duoflex: **R5* F**
1930. Not to be confused with Kodak's Duaflex, this is a box-form single lens reflex whose focusing screen is upright and parallel to the lens, the image formed by two mirrors at 45° and viewed via an eyepiece in the back of the body. Could also be used at waist level via a further mirror that reflected the image to the top of the camera under a hood. Unusual shutter formed from two metal flaps to provide $1/5$-1/800s. Dallemeyer f4.5 $4^3/_4$" lens. Also available with Ross Xpress or Zeiss Tessar lenses.

Andre Brizet
Paris, France

Le Physioscope: **R4* E**
c1922, 6 x 13cm stereo camera; Tessar Krauss 74mm f6.3 lenses; Stereo Compur shutter 1-1/150s. Rising lens panel; changing magazine for 12 plates.

Brooklyn Camera Co
Brooklyn, New York, USA

The Brooklyn Camera: **R3* E–**
c1885, 1/4 plate view camera; non-folding bed; collapsible bellows.

Christian Bruns
Munich, Germany

Bruns Detective Camera: R5* I–

c1893, 3¼" x 4¼" detective camera; 144mm f6.3 lens. Magazine holds 12 exp, 3¼" x 4¼". The camera has two Vfr: the first is a waist-level reflex viewer; the second consists of a separate bellows with ground glass, which is assembled on top of the camera—the camera lens slides upward and is positioned on the Vrf.

Bullard Camera Co
Springfield, Massachusetts, USA

Bullard Magazine Camera: R4* D
c1898, plate-loading magazine folding camera; eighteen 4" x 5" plates.

Burleigh Brooks Optics
Hackensack, New Jersey, USA

Brooks Veriwide: R2* F+
wide-angle panoram camera; Super-Angulon 47mm f8 coated lens; Synchro-

Compur shutter 1-1/500s; 8 exp, 6 x 9cm on 120 roll film. Users pay more than collectors for this.

Busch Camera Co
Chicago, Illinois, USA

Busch Verascope F40:   R4* F

c1950, 35mm stereo camera; Berthiot 40mm f3.5 coated lenses; CRF. Version of French made Richard Verascope F40 for U.S. market.

W. Butcher & Co
London, England

William Butcher joined his father's pharmacy business in Blackheath in what is now south London in 1889. He had an obsessive interest in photography, and developing and printing rapidly became a major part of the business. In 1896 he leased a workshop nearby to make cheap cameras, d & p kits, etc., under the brand name "Primus". The photographic business developed so fast that in 1902 Butcher moved to a large building, in the centre of London. It was now a separate business under the name of W. Butcher & Sons, Ltd. The majority of cameras were now imported, or made from imported parts, mainly from Hüttig. The outbreak of war in 1914 cut off Butcher's supplies, so a joint manufacturing company was formed with Houghton's, the Houghton Butcher Manufacturing Company, to make cameras for both companies. They continued to be marketed separately until complete amalgamation came in 1926 as Houghton-Butcher (Great Britain) Ltd. Ensign Ltd. was formed in 1930 to market the products. Some Butcher models continued into the Ensign era, which is covered in the Houghton section.

Cameo: R2* C

c1900. Small, folding plate cameras, made in $3^1/_2$" x $2^1/_2$" inch, quarter plate and post card sizes. Various lenses and shutters.

Carbine: R3 C

c1910. Folding drop bed cameras for quarter-plate and post card sizes. Lukos sector shutter, Choice of Aldis, Cooke, Dallmeyer and Ross lenses.

Clincher; R1* B

c1913-1919. Magazine box camera; wood body; Leatherette covered; T&I shutter; No1, 6 plates $2^1/_4$ x $3^1/_4$; No2 6 plates $3^1/_4$ x $4^1/_4$; No3 12 plates $3^1/_4$ x $4^1/_4$; No4 6 plates 9 x 12cm.

Coronet; R2* E

c1913-1919. Folding field camera; Mahogany and brass fittings; Turntable in baseboard; No1.Single Achromatic lens; revolving shutter; No2.Primus RR-Beck Symmetrical or Aldis Uno lenses; in front of roller blind shutter; both models made in quarter,half and whole plate.

The Little Nipper: R2* D

c1900. Made by Hüttig; $2^1/_2$" x $3^1/_2$" exp on plates of film; reversing finder; lens cap.

Midg; R1* B

c1902-1920. Drop plate magazine box cameras; (Imported) quarter plate and postcard sizes; No 0 Built in shutter and lens; Nos. 1, 2, 3, and 4. Have better lens shutter combinations; protected by front cover.

National; R2* F–

c1900-1905. Half plate folding field camera; Mahogany finish; Tapered bellows;Reversing back; 7" Ross f/6.3 Homocentric lens; Thornton-Pickard roller blind shutter.

Pilot; R1* B

c1904-1906. Falling plate magazine box camera;$3^1/_2$ x $2^1/_2$ plates.

Popular Pressman: R3* E+

c1910. One of the earliest plate reflexes to sell at a popular price. Made in quarter-plate and post card sizes. Focal plane shutter 1/10-1/1000s. Found with Aldis, Cooke, Dallmeyer and Ross lenses, generally f4.5.

Primus So-Li-To: R3* F+

c1897-1899. Collapsible box camera; morocco leather covered; Truncated pyramid; intended for cyclists and tourists.

Royal Mail Postage Stamp Camera:
R4* H

c1907. 15 postage stamp size photographs on a single plate.

The Stereolette: R4* E+

c1910. Made by Hüttig; 45 x 107mm stereo; meniscus lens; guillotine shutter; reflex viewer; spirit level; mahogany. 5 x 107mm exp on plates.

Watch Pocket Carbine, Tropical Model:
R3* D

120 roll film camera, Tessar 9cm/f4.5 lens, Dial-set Compur shutter, copper toned metal body, brown bellows.

Royal Mail Postage Stamp Camera.

C

A. Cadot
Paris, France

Scenographe Cadot: R4* E+
c1900. 9 x 18cm stereo camera; Aplanatic 150mm f11 lenses; guillotine shutter. Rising front panel. The lens on one side can be shifted to the centre to make a panoramic picture.

E. Caillon
Paris, France

Le Bioscope: R4* E–
c1915. 45 x 107mm stereo camera; Berthiot Saphir f6.3 or f4.5 lenses; shutter $\frac{1}{2}$-1/200s. Leather covered; rising and falling front; panoramic movement.

Le Megascope: R3* D+
c1915, 6 x 13cm stereo camera; Hermagis 85mm f6.3 lenses; guillotine shutter with variable speeds. Rising and falling front. Changing mechanism for 12 plates, 6 x 13cm.

Scopea: R4* D+
c1915. 45 x 107mm stereo camera; Balbreck Rectilinear 54mm lenses; 5 speed guillotine shutter.

Calypso: R4* F+
1960, 35mm underwater camera; Berthiot 35mm f2.5 coated lens, interchangeable bayonet mount with watertight O rings. mfps 1/30-1/500s. This was the first underwater camera that did not require a separate waterproof pressure housing. Jacques Cousteau, co-inventor of the Aqualung

was involved in its design. It is highly collectable. Nikon purchased the rights to the design and re-introduced it as the Nikonos Underwater Camera.

The Cameo: R3* D
c1950, 8 x 17cm folding stereo camera; Beck Symmetrical lenses. Ground glass back. 8 x 17cm exp on plates. Mfd in Britain.

Camera-Lite: R4* F+
Cigarette lighter-type detective camera; achromatic f8 lens. Similar to Echo 8, except has frame vfr instead of reflex vfr. c1956.

Camojet Ltd
Brentwood, Essex, England

Camojet: **R3* A**

1955. Subminiature for 14 x 14mm images on 16mm rollfilm. Made from molded plastic. Supplied with a spare rollfilm back. Plastic projector also available.

The Canadian Camera and Optical Co
Toronto, Canada

Gem Glenco: **R4* D**
c1910, 4" x 5" folding plate camera; red bellows with brass fittings.

Candid Camera Corp of America

Perfex 44:   **R2* C+**

c1939-1940. 35mm RFR camera; Anastigmat 50mm f3.5 or f2.8 lens, interchangeable screw mount; CFPS 1-1/250s, B, synch.

Perfex Speed Candid: **R2* C**
c1938-1939. 35mm camera; Anastigmat 50mm f3.5 or f2.8 lens; CFPS 1/25-1/500s; non-coupled RFR.

Canon Camera Company Inc
Tokyo, Japan

For further information see Canon Rangefinder Cameras 1933-1968 by Peter Dechert, Hove Collectors Books, 1985, and Canon Compendium, Handbook of the Canon System (for rangefinder and SLR cameras) by Bob Shell, Hove Books, 1994.

Most of the cameras manufactured in Japan between 1947 and (late) 1951 were marked "Made in Occupied Japan", usually on the baseplate, rear door, or top cover. Many cameras made after 1952 were marked with variations of the E-P symbol (usually within a diamond) which meant that the specific camera (or lens) was allocated for sale in the military post-exchange system. E-P markings are common – they do not designate any specific model of camera. An earlier variation of the diamond marking encloses a series of Japanese characters that translate to "CPO" in English. This practice dates to 1947 (approximately). A slightly later version encloses the English letters "CPO" within a diamond. Both of these markings are uncommon today; originally they designated cameras made for testing purposes. These cameras were supplied to the army of occupation and for early sale to military personnel.

Group 1

*All cameras in this group have serial
numbers below 45,000. The slowest
instantaneous speed on the fast-speed
dial is 1/20s. All use 35mm film.*

Canon/NK Hansa: R5* J–

c1935, Nikkor f3.5 lens in bayonet
mount; CFPS 1/20-1/500s. Pop-up vf;
exp counter on front of body; top plate
usually marked "Hansa" but sometimes
not (if not the camera has sometimes
been called "Canon Original"). This
version was contemporaneously known
simply as "the Canon Camera" and is
distinguished by the engraved logo
"Nippon Kogaku Tokyo" next to the
serial number on its focusing mount,
signifying that it was made under the
supervision of Nippon Kogaku at Seiki
Kogaku Kenkyujo. It therefore can be
considered the earliest of both Canon
and Nikon lines. Mfd 10/1935-8/1937,
qty est 400-500. Price depending on the
presence of parts designed for earlier
unmarked Kwanons which are usually
found on only a few cameras among the
range under approximately serial 300.

Canon Hansa: R4* I+

Mfd 9/1937-6/1940, no "Nippon Kogaku
Tokyo" engraving next to focusing mount
serial number, signifying manufacture
under Seiki Kogaku K. K. K. control
allowing reorganisation and expansion of
the company. Qty est 600-700.

Canon S: **with these lenses: H+**
             with Regno-Nikkor: I–

c1938-1944. Nikkor f4.5, f3.5, f2.8 or
f2 lens in bayonet mount; CFPS 1-
1/500s. Pop-up vf, CRF; lever operated
slow-speed dial on front of body; exp
counter under wind knob; serial no. on
top plate. Qty 1600. This model shows
several variations: in the slow-speed dial
orientation, in the knob shape and
markings and in the construction and
markings of lens mounts. Some lenses
may not fit all mounts. The earliest f2
lens with interior front diaphragm scale
is the scarcest model; the f3.5 lens is
the most common. With f3.5 lens, with
f2.8 lens, with earliest interior-set f2
lens, with rimset f2.

Canon NS: R5* I–

c1939-1944. Similar to Canon S, except
does not have slow-speed dial. Nikkor
f4.5 or f3.5 lens. Qty est 100.

Canon J: R5* I+

c.1939-1944. Nikkor f4.5 or f3.5 lens in threaded mount similar to, but not identical to Leica mount; CFPS 1/20-1/500s. No RFR. No body plate patch over slow-speed dial area; vf in Leica-type top plate with straight edge near rewind knob. Qty est 200. c1/1939-1944.

Canon JS: R4* I–

c1941-1945, similar to Canon S except has front mounted slow-speed dial. (1-1/20s). Qty est 50.

Seiki X-Ray Camera: R4* F

c1939-1947. 35mm X-Ray recording camera; Nikkor f2 or Serenar f1.5 lens in massive bayonet mount; exp by darkslide. Wind knob has spring loaded chain. Qty unknown, possibly several thousand.

Canon X-Ray Camera: R4* G+

c1947-1951, similar to previous model, except marked "X-Ray Canon 35" on top. Qty unknown.

Canon S-I: R5* H–

c12/1945-11/1946. Nikkor f3.5 lens, post-war continuation of Canon S, and essentially identical to late wartime production; most serials should be later than 12386 but are mixed. Qty 97.

Canon J-II: R5* I–

c1945-1946. Top cover resembles its Leica counterpart, curving around small rewind knob. Some have a metal patch over the slow-speed dial area. Nikkor or Serenar f3.5 lens in non-Leica type thread mount. Qty 525. With Nikkor lens, or Serenar lens.

Seiki Canon S-II: R4* F+

c1946. Nikkor f3.5 or Seiki Kogaku Serenar f3.5 or f2 lenses. Inter-changeable lens mount, almost all with semi-Leica screw thread but a few early ones with Canon J-thread or in-between mounts. CFPS 1-1/500 s. Combined vf-RFR without variable magnification. "Seiki Kogaku Tokyo" maker's name on top. Qty 2000, more with J-thread mount; With F3,5 Nikkor; $1.1k £800 DM2k.

Canon S-II: R3* F–

c8/1947-1952. Similar to previous model, except all have "Canon Camera Co." logo and Nikkor or Canon Serenar lenses. Qty 5550.

Canon CX-35:   R4* F

c1951-1957. Late version of Canon X-Ray Camera. Canon f1.5 lens in bayonet mount. Marked "CX-35" on top cover. Qty unknown, probably several thousand.

Canon IIB: R3* E+

c1/1949-7/1952. Serenar f3.5 or f1.9 lens, CFPS 1-1/500s. Combined vf-RFR with three-stage magnification. A few later had flash synch rails. Qty 14,400. Without flash synch rail, $100-$175; more with synch rail.

Group 2

All models in this group have serial numbers between 45,000 and 169,990. The slowest instantaneous speed on the fast-speed dial is 1/25s. All have combined vf-RFR with three-stage magnification. Synched cameras all have side flash rail; they have no other flash outlet.

Canon 1950:   R5* H

Manufactured 7/1950-10/1950. Serenar f1.9 lens, CFPS 1-1/1000s; flashbulb rail

synch. Can quickly be distinguished by "Canon Camera Co. Ltd." maker's logo and serial between 50000 and 50199, and there are other differences. This version was briefly designated IIC by Canon, and most surviving examples have baseplates with "San Francisco" markings indicating sale (as model IIC or IVM) by C. R. Skinner in USA. Qty 50.

Canon IV: R3* E+

c4/1951-4/1952. Serenar f1.9 lens; CFPS 1-1/1000s, flashbulb synch. Two-piece vf magnification lever. Qty 1380. "Canon Camera Co. Inc." maker's logo.

Canon IIC: R4* F

c3/1951-8/1951. Serenar f3.5 or f1.9 lens; CFPS 1-1/500s, no synch. Two piece magnification vf lever. Qty 800.

Canon III: R3* E

c2/1951-12/1952. Serenar f3.5 or f1.9 lens; CFPS 1-1/100s, no synch. Two piece magnification lever. Qty 10,175.

Canon IIIA: R3* E

c12/1951-9/1953. Serenar f1.8 lens; CFPS 1-1/1000s, no synch. One piece magnification lever. Film reminder in wind knob. There were several variations in the interior construction, the manufacturer's logo, and the engraving. Qty 9025.

Canon IIA: R5* G+

c3/1952-9/1952. CFPS 1/25-1/500s, no synch. Slow-speed dial area covered by patch. Qty 99. Verify authenticity before paying premium price.

Canon IVF: R3* E

c12/1951-1952. CFPS 1-1/1000s, flash bulb synch. One piece magnification lever; film reminder; built-up interior wall next to film supply chamber. Qty 6880 includes Canon IVS**.

Canon IVS: R3* E+

c1952-5/1953. Has die-cast wall next to film supply chamber. Qty 6880 including Canon IVF.

Canon IVSB: R3* E+

Canon IVSB with 135mm f3.5 lens and 135mm finder.

c12/1952-3/1955. Canon f1.8 lens was standard (rather than Serenar); CFPS 1-1/1000s, flashbulb synch, X synch at C 1/15s setting on slow-speed dial. Slow-speed dial lock. Some other bodies were updated by Canon agencies to synch standards; these bodies show many variations. This model was often known overseas as IVS2, but IVSB is the factory designation. Qty 35,000.

Canon IID: R3* E–

c8/1952-2/1955. CFPS 1-1/500s, no synch. No film reminder; one piece magnification lever. Qty 21,700.

Canon IID1:   R3* E

Canon IID1 with later f1.2/50mm lens.

c10/1952-6/1954. Has film reminder in wind knob. Qty 2400.

Canon IIAF: R5* I–
c6/1953-8/1953. CFPS 1/25-1/500s, flashbulb synch. Slow-speed dial area covered by patch. This is the scarcest Canon camera; buyers should authenticate any camera. This camera was never marketed in U.S. Qty 15.

Canon IIF: R3* E

c7/1953-3/1955. CFPS 1-1/500s, flashbulb synch only. Some bodies are identified on the loading diagram inside the baseplate. Qty 12,000.

Canon IIS: R3* E+
c2/1954-3/1955. CFPS 1-1/500s, flashbulb synch and X synch at 1/15s position on slow-speed dial. Qty 1850.

Group 3
All models in this group have serial numbers between 170,000 and 235,000 (bottom loading) or between 500,001 and 599,900 (back loading), except as noted. All have combined vf-RFR with three-stage magnification. The slowest instantaneous speed on the fast speed dial is 1/30s and all have front mounted slow-speed dials. The fast speed index is on top of the shaft in the centre of the dial and it rotates with the dial during winding and exp.

Canon IVSB2:   R3* C+
c7/1957/1956, 4-CFPS 1-1/1000s, flashbulb synch, X synch on slow-speed dial at 1/15s and on fast-speed dial at 1/45s. Bottom loading. Qty 17,000. serial numbers between 120,000 and 230,000.

Canon IIS2:   R3* E
c2/1955-7/1956. CFPS 1-1/500s. Qty 16,600.

Canon IID2:   R3* E
c1955-7/1956. No synch. Qty 16,200.

Canon IIF2: R3* E+

c6/1955-4/1956. Only has flashbulb synch, no X synch. Qty 2420.

Canon VT: R3* E+

c4/1956-2/1957. Canon 50mm f1.2 lens and 35mm f1.8 lens were standard equipment on this camera, however the Canon 50mm f1.8 (black focusing ring) and 50mm f1.5 were also available. Identified on front of baseplate; back loading; baseplate trigger-wind film advance. Prototype models were often marked "Model V" (instead of "Model VT") and early advertising used that designation; at least four other minor variations exist. Qty 15,600.

Canon L2: R3* E+

c11/1956-12/1957. Identified on bottom of baseplate. Back loading; thumb-lever film advance. Qty 7,350.

Canon L1: R3* Black: G
  Chrome: E

c2/1957-12/1957. Identified on bottom of baseplate. No self-timer. Qty 8,000.

Canon VT-DeLuxe: R3* Black: G+
  Chrome: E

c2/1957-9/1957. Identified on front of baseplate. Cloth shutter curtains; no baseplate magazine opening key. Qty 3500.

Canon VT-DeLuxe-Z: R3* Black: G+
  Chrome: F−

c4/1957-6/1958. Has baseplate magazine opening key. Qty 4875.

Canon VT-DeLuxe-M: R4* Black: G+
  Chrome: F

c1/1958-8/1958. Identified "VT-DeLuxe" on front of baseplate and has original factory-installed metal shutter curtains; designated from the beginning as VT-DeLuxe-M in factory records. Qty 2550.

Canon L3: R3* E+

c10/1957-12/1958. Identified on bottom of baseplate. Qty 12,975.

Canon VL: R3* E+

c12/1957-12/1958. Metal FPS 1-1/1000s, flashbulb and X synch. Back-loading; thumb-lever film advance, self-timer. No identification on body, although a few prototypes made to test the metal shutter design were probably marked "Model L1" on the baseplate. Qty 5450.

Canon VL2:   **R3* E+**
c1/1958-12/1958. Lacks 1/1000s. speed. Qty 8450.

Group 4

All models in this group have shutter speeds 1-1/1000s. on a single non-spinning top-mounted dial, metal shutter curtains, full synch, back-loading, and combined vf-RFR with projected frame lines.

Canon VI-T: **R3* Black: H–**
                         Chrome: E+
c6/1958-7/1960. Identified on front of baseplate. Baseplate trigger wind;

three-stage vf magnification; shutter speed dial notched for accessory exp meter. Qty 8175.

Canon VI-L: **R3* Black: G**
                         Chrome: E+

c6/1958-3/1961. Thumb-lever film advance instead of baseplate trigger. This was the last Canon to lack model identification on body. Qty 10,350. Very few were imported to the U.S.

Canon P: **R3* Black: G+**
                      Chrome: E

c12/1958-5/1961. Identified on top cover. Qty 88,000.

Canon 7:   **R3* Black: H–**
                      Chrome: F

Canon 7 with f0.95 lens.

c1961. Identified on top cover. Qty 138,000. c6/1961-11/1964. The Canon 50mm f0.95 lens was introduced with this model which had a Leica-type thread mount with an outer bayonet flange. The Mirror Box 2 accessory housing was also introduced at this time; it accepted long focal length telephoto lenses. ($375 £250 DM650 With 50mm f0.95 lens).

Canon 7S: **R3* F**

c2/1965-8/1967. Identified on top cover. Several variations with minor cosmetic differences exist; Canon 7 vf optics. Qty est 16,000. No black bodies known to date; Body only £275; Chrome with f0.95 lens.

Canon 7sZ: **R3* F**
                                 Body F+

c8/1967-9/1968. Has revised finder optics differentiated by adjustment port above second "n" in topside "Canon" logo. Qty est 4000.

Group 5
Early Canon SLR cameras. All are identified on the camera body.

Canonflex: **R3* D**
c1/1959-7/1960, the first Canon SLR to be sold, with baseplate trigger wind, shutter to 1/1000s, removable finder. Uses Canonmatic lenses. Qty 17,000.

Canonflex RP: **R3* D**

c6/1960-1/1962.   Fixed   finder, Canomatic lenses. Qty 31,000.

Canonflex R2000:   **R3* D+**

c6/1960-1/1962. Top speed 1/2000s, Canomatic lenses. Qty 8800.

Canonflex RM: **R3* D+**

c2/1961-3/1964.   built-in   selenium meter, Canomatic lenses. Qty 72,000.

Canonex: **R2* D–**
c10/1963-5/1964. SLR camera, leaf shutter, fixed lens.

Canonex c1963-1964.

Canon FX: R2* D–

c4/1964-1966. CdS meter built-in FL lenses. This model did not have QL feature.

Canon FP: R2* D–

c10/1964-3/1966. No meter, FL lenses, no QL.

Canon Pellix: R3* D+

1964; 35mm SLR camera;Canon FL 50mm f1.8 lens, interchangeable breech-lock mount; mfps 1-1/1000s, FP, M, X synch. Cds through-the-lens meter. Stationary pellicle mirror splits incoming light between the film plane and viewfinder. Approximately $1/3$ of a f stop less light falls on the film and the finder is $1/3$ less brilliant. The word Pellix is derived from pellicle, the thin semi-transparent membrane used in beam-splitting cameras. The advantage of a stationary mirror was the lack of vibration when the mirror flipped up and the silent operation.

Canon Pellix-QL: R2* E–
c1966-1970; The "Quick Load" version of the Pellix.

Canon TL-QL: R2* C+
c1967-1972; Same as FT-QL except CFPS 1/500; no self-timer;

Canon TLB: R2* C+

c1972; 35mm SLR camera; FPS 1-1/500s budget version of the FTb ; no hot shoe;no mirror lock up; new style Cds meter.

Canon

Canon EX-EE: **R2* C+**

c1968-1973; SLR camera; TTL Cds meter; fixed lens with interchangeable front elements; shutter priority – manual; CFPS 1-1/500s, B; 1/60s. X flash exp.

Canon EX-Auto: **R2* C+**

c1972-1976; Name variant of the EX-EE.

Canon F-1:   **R2* E+**

c1970-1976; 35mm SLR camera; Canon's first professional camera; MFPS 1-1/2000s B; 1/60s B. X. Flash exp;

factory fitted motor drive to serial numbers under 200,001; interchangeable finders, screens & pentaprism; TTL Cds meter; Meter needle display.

Canon F-1 "Original":   **R2* E+**
c1972-1976; As F-1 with ability to accept add on motor drive MF.

Canon F-1n: **R2* F**
c1976; Slightly modified version of F-1; Identified by the plastic tipped film advance lever; film reminder frame on back.

Canon FT-QL: **R2* C**
c1966-1972; 35mm SLR camera;CFPS 1-1/1000s, B; FP1/30s, X1/60s. flash exp.; Cds Meter Needle display; mirror lock; battery check; self timer.

Canon FTb: **R2* Black E–**

c1970-1973; 35mm SLR camera; CFPS 1-1/1000s, B; FD lens mount; Hot shoe; 1/30s. FP. X1/60s. Flash exp.

Canon FTbn: **R2* Black E–**
c1973-1977; 35mm SLR camera; FD lens mount;CDS meter needle display; CFPS 1-1/1000s. B; FP 1/30s, X 1/60s. Flash exp; QL-system; mirror lock.

Canon EF: **R2* D+**

c1973-1977; 35mm SLR camera;FD mount; SPC meter, needle display; Exp warning; MFPS 30-1/1000s; X 1/125s. flash exp; mirror lock.

Canon TX: **R2* C**

c1974-1978; 35mm SLR camera;Cds meter; Exp warning; CFPS 1-1/500s. B; FP1/30s, X1/60 flash exp; Also marketed by Bell & Howell as FD35.

Canon AE-1:   **R2* D–**

c1976-1984; 35mm SLR camera; FD-N lens mount; SPC meter needle display; Exp. warning; CFPS 2-1/1000s B; X1/60s flash exp. self-timer; batt check.

Canon AT-1:   **R2* C+**

c1976-1982; 35mm SLR camera; FD-N lens mount; SPC meter needle display Exp warning; CFPS 2-1/1000s; 1/60s. X flash exp.

Canon A-1:   **R2* E–**
c1978-1986, 35mm SLR camera, FD-N mount; SPC meter; digital displays; interchangeable screens; CFPS 30s, 1/1000s. The Canon A-1 was the first to have a built-in computer chip that programmed the exposure functions of shutter speed and aperture setting. The A-1 is of interest to collectors who specialise in technical "firsts."

Canon AV-1: R2* D–

c1979-1983; 35mm SLR camera.SPC meter needle display; analog speed display; CFPS 2-1/1000s B; 1/60s. X Flash exp.

Canon AE-1 Program: R2* D

c1981-1986; 35mm SLR camera; SPC meter; shutter or aperture priority band manual; digital display; CFPS 2-1/1000s; 1/60s, X flash exp.

Canon AL-1: R2* C+

c1983-1985; 35mm SLR camera; SPC meter; needle display; camera shake warning; CFPS 2-1/1000s B; 1/60s X flash exp; FD-N mount.

Canon AL-1.

(unless otherwise indicated)
lenses for cameras:

NB, lenses marked "Seiki Kogaku"
should be for camera bodies also
marked "Seiki Kogaku"

Serenar 28mm f3.5:	D+
Serenar 35mm f3.5:	D
Serenar 35mm f3.2:	in Chrome, D–
Serenar 35mm f2.8:	E–
Serenar 5cm f3.5:	E
Serenar 50mm f3.5:	in Chrome C+
Serenar 5cm f2.0:	E+
Serenar 5cm f1.5:	E+
Serenar 50mm f1.8:	in Chrome C
Serenar 85mm f2.0:	in Chrome D
Serenar 85mm f1.9:	in Chrome D+
Serenar 100mm f4.0:	in Chrome D–
Serenar in S-bayonet mount, 13.5cm f4.0:	E
Serenar 13.5cm f4.0:	E+
Serenar 135mm f4.0:	in Chrome C+
Serenar 20cm f4.0:	very rare, H–
Canon Lens 25mm f3.5:	in Chrome, w/finder, F–
Canon Lens 28mm f2.8:	in Chrome D+
Canon Lens 28mm f3.5:	D
Canon Lens 35mm f1.8:	in Black D+
Canon Lens 35mm f1.5:	in Chrome E

Canon Lens 35mm f2.0:   in Black   D+
Canon Lens 35mm f3.5: in Chrome   C+
Canon Lens 50mm f0.95: in Black   E+
Canon Lens 50mm f1.2:   in Black   C+
Canon Lens 50mm f1.4:   in Black   D+
Canon Lens 50mm f1.5: in Chrome   C–
Canon Lens 50mm f1.8:   in Black   C–
Canon Lens 50mm f2.8:   in Black   C–
Canon Lens (some marked Serenar)
   85mm f1.5: in Chrome,   F
Canon Lens 85mm f1.8: in Black   D+
Canon Lens 85mm f2.0: in Chrome   D
Canon Lens 100mm f3.5: in Black   D–
Canon Lens 100mm f2.0 in Black   E–
Canon Lens 135mm f3.5:
                        in Chrome, C
                        in Black D–
Canon Lens: (for use with Mirror Box 2)
   135mm f2.5:   C+
Canon Lens (for use with Mirror Box)
   200mm f3.5:   D+
Canon Lens (for use with Mirror Box),
   400mm f4.0);   w/finder G–

Canon Rangefinder accessories

Mirror Box 1 reflex housing: E–

Canon accessory Viewfinders

35mm:	B+
85mm:	C
100mm:	C
135mm:	B+

Canonet: R2* B
1961. 35mm camera with large
Selenium cell surrounding lens. Auto
exposure controlled by Canon's 'Electric
Eye' system, so called because the
swing of the meter needle controls the
opening and closing of the aperture –
like the pupil of the eye. Exposure
automatically adjusted between f1.9
and f16 with speeds from 1-1/500s.
45mm Canon lens. Film travel right to
left. M & X synch. Lens hood reversible
to form a lens protector.

Mamiya Reflex with Canon lens: R4* E–

(about 1960). Special SLR combination
sold briefly by Olden Camera, New York.
Body mfd by Mamiya with an Exakta
lens mount – the standard lens was a
Canon 50mm f1.9 (auto Exakta mount).
This combination was unique in the U.S.
(original price, $118.50); a curiosity
item for Canon or Mamiya collectors.

Canon Dial 35:   R3* C

c1963. Unusually designed half-frame
35mm camera. Produces 72 pictures on
36 exposure cassette. Clockwork
mechanism advances film. f2.8, 28mm
lens. Shutter 1/30-1/250s. The exposure
meter which is wrapped around the lens
looks rather like a telephone dial, the
name of the camera.

Canon

Ion: **R2* B+**

1989. The first commercially available electronic camera. The initials stand for Image Online Network. Up to 50 full-colour pictures on 54 x 60mm disc. Fixed focus lens, all other functions automatic. Built-in flash. Capable of three shots per second.

Carl Zeiss
Jena, Germany

Werra: **R3* C**
1954-55, 35mm VFR camera with olive green body covering, f2.8/50mm coated Tessar in Compur Rapid shutter, 1-1/500s, knurled and knobbed aluminium film advance / shutter cocking ring, knob film rewind. (-75% without lens shade and/or screw in lens cap).

Werra IA: **R2* C**
1956-60, 35mm VFR camera with black body covering, f2.8/50mm coated Tessar in Synchro Compur Rapid shutter, 1-1/500s, knurled and knobbed aluminium film advance/shutter cocking ring, knob film rewind. (-75% without lens shade and/or screw in lens cap).

Werra IB: **R3* C-**
1960-62, 35mm VFR camera with black body covering, f2.8/50mm coated Tessar in Synchro Compur Rapid shutter,

1-1/500s or Vebur 250 or Prestor RVS 500 shutters, after 1961 the RVS shutter indicated a top shutter speed of 1/750s (putting this camera on the short list of cameras having leaf shutters with indicated speeds faster than 1/500s) smooth covered film advance/shutter cocking ring, knob film rewind, late cameras have a bright-line finder and round eye-piece. (-75% without lens shade and/or screw in lens cap, +50% for 1/750s shutter).

Werra IC: **R3* C-**
1962-64, 35mm VFR camera with black body covering, f2.8/50mm coated Tessar in Prestor RVS shutter 1-1/750s or Prestor RVS 500 shutter, smooth covered film advance/shutter cocking ring, crank film rewind. (-75% without lens shade and/or screw in lens cap).

Werra IE: **R2* C-**
1964-66, 35mm VFR camera with embossed black body covering, f2.8/50mm coated Tessar in Prestor RVS shutter 1-1/750s or Prestor RVS 500 shutter, with EV scale, smooth covered film advance/shutter cocking ring, crank film rewind, re-designed rounder top plate, (-75% without lens shade and/or screw in lens cap).

Carl Zeiss

Werra II: R3* C

1960-64, 35mm VFR camera with black body covering, f2.8/50mm coated Tessar in Prestor RVS 500 shutter, 1-1/500s smooth covered film advance/ shutter cocking ring, knob film rewind. built-in selenium meter with hinged cover and an exposure calculator on the camera back. (-75% without lens shade and/or screw in lens cap).

Werra IIE: R2* C–

1964, 35mm VFR camera with embossed black body covering, f2.8/50mm coated Tessar in Prestor RVS 750 shutter, 1-1/750s smooth covered film advance/ shutter cocking ring, crank film rewind. built-in selenium meter, but no exposure calculator on the camera back, accessory shoe, re-designed rounder top plate, (-75% without lens shade and/or screw in lens cap).

Werramat: R3* C

1961-64, 35mm VFR camera with embossed black body covering, f2.8/50mm coated Tessar in RVS 500 shutter, 1-1/500s smooth covered film advance/shutter cocking ring, knob film rewind. built-in selenium meter without hinged cover indicator needle visible in the VFR, without accessory shoe, streamlined lens housing (-75% without lens shade and/or screw in lens cap.)

Werramat E: R3* C

1961-64, 35mm VFR camera with embossed black body covering, f2.8/50mm coated Tessar in RVS 500 shutter, 1-1/500s smooth covered film advance/shutter cocking ring, knob film rewind. built-in selenium meter without hinged cover indicator needle visible in the VFR, with accessory shoe, streamlined lens housing (-75% without lens shade and/or screw in lens cap.)

Werra III: R3* D

1959-64, 35mm camera with coupled RFR and interchangeable lenses, black body covering, bayonet mount f2.8/50mm Tessar in front of Prestor RVS shutter, 1-1/750s, crank rewind, field of view indicated for 35mm,50mm, and 100mm in the VFR.(-75% without lens shade and/or screw in lens cap.)

Werra IIIE: R3* D

1964-66, 35mm camera with coupled RFR and interchangeable lenses, rounder body style with striated black body covering, bayonet mount f2.8/50mm Tessar in front of Prestor RVS shutter with EV scale, 1-1/750s, crank rewind, field of view indicated for 35mm,50mm, and 100mm in the VFR, (-75% without lens shade and/or screw in lens cap.)

Werra IV: R3* D

1959-62, 35mm camera with coupled RFR and interchangeable lenses, black body covering, bayonet mount f2.8/50mm Tessar in front of Prestor 500 shutter, 1-1/500s, crank rewind, field of view indicated for 35mm,50mm, and 100mm in the VFR, built-in selenium meter with hinged cover. (-75% without lens shade and/or screw in lens cap.)

Werra V: R3* D

1959, 35mm camera with coupled RFR and interchangeable lenses, rounded body with black covering, bayonet mount f2.8/50mm Tessar with Prestor 500 shutter, 1-1/500s, crank rewind, field of view indicated for 35mm, 50mm, and 100mm in the VFR, built-in selenium meter with hinged cover. (-75% without lens shade and/or screw in lens cap.)

Werramatic: **R3* D**
1961-64, 35mm camera with coupled RFR and interchangeable lenses, rounded body with black covering, bayonet mount f2.8/50mm Tessar in front of Prestor 500 shutter, 1-1/500s (after 1962, Prestor RVS 750 shutter, 1-1/750s), crank rewind, field of view indicated for 35mm,50mm, and 100mm in the VFR, built-in selenium meter without hinged cover. (-75% without lens shade and/or screw in lens cap, +50% for Prestor 750 shutter.)

Werramatic E: **R3* D**
1964-66, 35mm camera with coupled RFR and interchangeable lenses, rounded body with black covering, bayonet mount f2.8/50mm Tessar in front of Prestor RVS 750 shutter with EV scale, 1-1/750s, crank rewind, field of view indicated for 35mm,50mm, and 100mm in the VFR, built-in selenium meter without hinged cover, accessory shoe, re-designed rounder top plate with new decoration, (-75% without lens shade and/or screw in lens cap.)

Accessory Lenses for Werra cameras

Flektogon f 2.8/35mm lens:	**C+**
Cardinar f4/100mm lens:	**C+**
Stereo attachment:	**EST D**

Jules Carpentier
Paris, France

Jumelle Carpentier (4.5 x 6cm model):
                   R2* D
c1892, binocular-type detective camera; Rectilinear lens or Zeiss Anastigmat lens. 12 exp, 4.5 x 6cm on plates.

Jumelle Carpentier (4.5 x 6cm model).

Jumelle Carpentier (6.5 x 9cm model):
                   R2* D
c1892, binocular-type detective camera; Zeiss Krauss Anastigmat lenses; 18 or 24 exp, 6.5 x 9cm on plates.

Chiyoda Optical Co
Osaka, Japan

Minolta Autocord: **R3* C**
c1955. Twin-Lens Reflex for 6x6cm images on 120 rollfilm. Rokkor f3.5, 75mm lens. Shutter 1-1/400s. Self cocking and auto-stop winding. This was the first in a series of very popular TLR's for about 10 years.

C.D. Chinaglia Domenico
Belluno, Italy

Kristall: **R3* E+**

1952. Cfps, 1/20-1/1000, Vfr only, no Rfr. flash synch, "E" for electronic flash, "V" for bulbs. Screw mount Krinar F3.5/50mm, SOM Berthiot f2.8/50mm, or Schneider-Xenon f2.0/ 50mm lens. Less than 1000 cameras are thought to have been made.

Kristal 2:   **R4* F–**
c1949, 35mm RFR camera with interchangeable Trixor, Trigon, Vistor, or Steiner f3.5/50mm lens, among others, CFPS 1/20-1/1000s, copy of Leica II.

Kristall 2a: **R4* F–**

c1950, as Model 2s, but for internal synchro selector, (Identical to that of the Wega IIa).

Kristall 2s: **R4* F–**
c1950, Cfps, 1/20-1/1000s, separate Rfr/Vfr windows. Screw mount Steinar f3.5/50mm, SOM Berthiot f2.8/50mm, Schneider-Xenon f2.0/50mm, or Anastigmat Trixar f3.5/50mm lens. Both the top plate and the base plate are of polished steel, and are not chrome plated.

Kristall 3:   **R4* F**
1951. Cfps, 1-1/1000s, separate Rfr/Vfr windows. Screw mount Steinar f3.5/50mm, SOM Berthiot f2.8/50mm, Schneider-Xenon f2.0/ 50mm, or Anastigmat Trixar f3.5/50mm lens. This model is the same as the 2, with slow speeds added.

Kristall 3s: **R4* F–**
Added PC synch on the front of the body.

Kristal 3s, type 2:   **R4* F**
Redesigned top plate, looking more like the Kristall 53.

Kristall 53:   **R3* F**

Kristall 53 showing VFR selection lever.

1953. Cpfs, 1-1/1000s, separate Rfr/Vfr windows, Vfr with fields of view for 28mm, 35mm, 50mm, 75mm, 90mm, and 105mm lenses. Screw mount Krinar f3.5/50mm, SOM Berthiot f2.8/50mm, or Schneider-Xenon f2.0/ 50mm lens. Less than 1000 cameras are thought to have been made.

Kristall R: R4* F

1954. Cfps, 1/20-1/1000s, combined Rfr/Vfr window with built-in orange filter to improve Rfr contrast, flash synch. Screw mount Krinar f3.5/50mm, SOM Berthiot f2.8/50mm, or Schneider-Xenon f2.0/50mm lens.

Century Camera Co
Rochester, New York, USA

The Century Camera Co. was founded in 1900 by five former employees of the Rochester Optical Co.; the company was located in Rochester, N.Y. In 1903 Eastman Kodak Co. bought controlling interest in the firm. In 1907 the name was changed to Century Camera Div., Eastman Kodak Co.; in 1917 it became part of the Folmer-Century Div., of Eastman Kodak Co.

Century Enlarging & Reducing Camera: R3* D+

c1890s. 5" x 7" enlarging and reducing camera; extension bellows; lantern slide attachment. Polished wood finish, brass fittings.

Century Grand Sr: R3* E–

5" x 7" c1902. Folding plate camera (top-of-the-line); Planatic Series III triple convertible lens. Red triple extension (24") bellows; front double sliding rack and pinion; back swings; dovetailed construction; covered with black cowhide. Sizes: 4" x 5" or 6½" x 8½" Original price, $45.

Century Plate Camera: R3* D+

c1910. 4" x 5" plate camera; Wollensak lens; Century shutter. Red bellows; brass fittings.

Century Stereo Camera: R4* F

c1900s. 5" x 7" folding plate stereo camera; stereo shutter 1-1/100s. 5" x 7" exp on dry plates.

Century View Camera: R3* E+

c1900. 5" x 7" view camera; rear focus; double extension bellows. Polished mahogany finish with brass fitting. Brass label: Century Camera Co., Rochester, N.Y. Several sizes from 4" x 5" to 11" x 14".

Certo Kamerawerk
Dresden, Germany

Many models were around for years without great changes, note that dial set Compur shutters are found on cameras before 1928, afterwards, rimset Compur shutters were used. Sometimes this is the only difference between identical camera models made ten years apart.

Dolly Model A: **R2* C–**
c1930, 3 x 4cm strut folding camera, front focusing Radionar f4.5/50mm lens, Compur shutter 1-1/300s.

Dolly Model B: **R2* C–**
c1930, 3 x 4cm strut folding camera, lever focusing Radionar f2.9/50mm lens, Compur shutter 1-1/300s.

Dolly Model B, c1930.

Dolly 4 x 6.5:   **R2* B**
c1935, 4 x 6.5cm bed folding camera, Tessar f3.5/70mm lens, Compur shutter.

SS Dolly Model A: **R3* C–**
c1937, folding bed camera for 4.5 x 6cm or 6 x 6cm on 120 roll film, interchangeable Trioplan f2/75mm lens among others, Compur shutter.

SS Dolly Model C: **R3* C**
c1937, folding bed camera, but for use with either rollfilm or plates, interchangeable Xenar f2.8/75mm lens among others, Compur shutter.

Super Sport Dolly Model A: **R2* D–**
c1936, folding bed camera for 6 x 4.5cm or 6 x 6cm frames on 120 roll film, coupled RFR, after 1939 with built-in extinction meter, interchangeable Tessar f2.8/75mm lens among others, Compur shutter, early cameras are all black, later ones have a chromed top plate.

Super Sport Dolly Model C: R3* D–

c1936. For plates or rollfilm.

Dollina: R2* B+

c1932, 35mm VFR strut bed folding camera for 24 x 36mm frames, many variations during production, early cameras lack body release and are more black than later versions, Cassar f2.9/50mm lens among others, Compur shutter.

Dollina II: R3* C+

c1933, 35mm RFR strut folding camera for 24 x 36mm frames, CRF, Xenar f2/45mm lens among others, Compur shutter, available in either chrome or black.

Dollina III: R3* D+

c1936, 35mm folding RFR camera, CRF, new body style, Xenon f2.50mm lens among others, Compur or Compur Rapid shutter.

Super Dollina: R2* D+

c1937, 35mm RFR camera, Cassar f2.9/50mm lens among others, Compur or Compur Rapid shutter 1-1/500s.

Super Dollina II: R3* D+

c1950, 35mm RFR camera, CRF, coated Jena Tessar f2.8/50mm lens, Compur Rapid shutter 1-1/500s, PC synch connection.

Certo Super Six: R3* D+

c1951, folding RFR camera for 6 x 6cm on 120 roll film, or 24 x 36mm on 35mm film with special adaptor, CRF, coated Jena Tessar f2.8/80mm lens, Synchro Compur shutter.

Certo-phot: R2* A

c1955, all metal rollfilm camera for 6 x 6cm frames, simple focusing f8 lens, simple shutter 1/50s.

Certo-matic: R3* B–

c1960, Now with built-in uncoupled light meter.

Certolob O: R2* B+

c1925, leather bellows folding bed camera for 6.5 x 9cm film packs or plates, leather covered wooden body, Trioplan f4.5/105mm lens among others, Vario shutter.

Certolob: R2* B+

c1925, Xenar f2.9/105mm lens among others, Compur shutter, like (ER104) but with lens adjustments, and better finish.

Certoruf 9 x 12:   R2* B+

c1925, leather bellows folding bed camera for 9 x 12cm film packs or plates, geared bed focusing Unofocal f4.5/135mm lens among others, Compur shutter, leather covered wooden body, waist lever finder mounted centrally on the front standard, double extension bellows.

Certoruf 10 x 15cm: R2* B+

c1925, 10 x 15cm plates or film packs. Xenar f4.5/165mm lens among others.

Certorex: R2* B+

c1925, leather bellows folding bed camera for 9 x 12cm film packs or plates, lever focusing Unofocal f4.5/135mm lens among others, Vario shutter, leather covered wooden body, waist lever finder mounted centrally on the front standard.

Certotrop 6.5 x 9:   R2* B+

c1925, leather bellows folding bed camera for 6.5 x 9cm film packs or plates, metal body, geared bed focusing Trioplan f2.9/105mm lens, Compur shutter, after 1930 with quick change lens/shutter mount.

Certotrop 9 x 12:   R2* B+

c1925, 9 x 12cm film packs or plates, Xenar f4.5/135mm lens among others, Compur shutter.

Certotrop 10 x 15:   R2* B+
c1925, 10 x 15cm film packs or plates, Xenar f4.5/165mm lens among others, Compur shutter.

Certoruhm: R3* B+
c1925, "Quer" format, simply put, the camera has a square body with removable back allowing horizontal or vertical framing without turning the whole camera, wooden body, drop bed for perspective control, Xenar f4.5/135mm lens among others, Compur shutter.

Certochrom 9 x 12:   R2* B+
c1925, leather bellows folding bed camera for 9 x 12cm plates or film packs, drop bed, metal body, interchangeable Xenar f4.5/135mm lens among others, Compur shutter.

Certochrom 10 x 15:   R2* B+
c1925, as previous model but for 10 x 15cm plates or film packs.

Certoplat: R3* C
c1925, leather bellows folding bed camera for 9 x 12cm plates or film packs, specially made for use with Plasmat f4/15cm lens, Compur shutter, double extension bellows, otherwise as Certoruf 9 x 12.

Certokunst: R3* C−
c1925, leather bellows folding bed camera for 9 x 12cm plates or film packs, interchangeable Xenar f4.5/135mm lens among others, drop bed, tilting lens standard, intended for architectural or studio use.

Certosport 9 x 12:   R2* B+
c1925, leather bellows folding bed camera for 9 x 12cm plates or film packs, Xenar f4.5/135mm lens among others, Compur shutter, like Certoruf 9 x 12 but with wire frame finder.

Certosport 6.5 x 9:   R3* C−
c1930, leather folding bed camera for 6.5 x 9cm film packs or plates, interchangeable Eurynar f4.5/105mm lens among others, Compur shutter, metal body, wire frame finder.

Certonet O: R2* B
c1925, folding VFR camera for 6 x 9cm frames on roll film, Radionar f4.5/120mm lens, Vario shutter.

Certonet XIV: R2* B−
c1928, folding VFR camera for 6 x 9cm frames on roll film, Radionar f4.5/120mm lens, Vario shutter, wire frame finder, bubble level next to waist lever finder.

Certonet XV: R2* B−
c1927, folding VFR camera for 6 x 9cm frames on roll film, Radionar f4.5/120mm lens, Compur shutter, wire frame finder.

Damen Kamera: R5* I
c1905, folding bed camera for 6 x 9cm plates, in the form of an ornate ladies handbag. Beware of Eastern European forgeries!

Doppel-Box: R3* C
c1935, Certomat lens; single speed shutter. 8 exp, 6 x 9cm or 16 exp, 4.5 x 6cm on 120 film. Format changed by turning dial.

Certo-Box A: R2* B–
c1930, metal box camera with fixed focus f11 lens, 6 x 9cm on roll film.

W.I. Chadwick
Manchester, England

Chadwick Detective Camera: R4* E
c1890, box-type.

Chadwick Patent Stereoscopic Camera: R4* F–

c1892, ¼ plate stereoscopic camera; single or stereo achromat lenses. Folding rectangular bellows; rotating waterhouse stops. Stereo exp on two ¼ plates.

J.T. Chapman
Manchester, England

The British Detective Camera: R3* E–
c1890, box-type detective camera; Wray lens (brass barrel) with waterhouse stops; Thornton Pickard string-set shutter. 2¼" x 3¼" exp on dry plates.

Chase Magazine Camera
Newburyport, Massachusetts, USA

Chase Magazine Camera: R3* D
c1899, box-type magazine camera. 12 exp, 4" x 5" loaded in a magazine.

Chevillon Drop-Plate Magazine Camera: R3* C–
c1905. Rapid Rectilinear lens; rotating shutter.

Chicago Camera Co
Chicago, Illinois, USA

Photake Camera: R4* G–
c1896, achromat 120mm f14 lens; guillotine shutter; 5 exp, 2" x 2" on dry plates.

Chicago Ferrotype Co
Chicago, Illinois, USA

Mandelette Postcard Camera: R3* D
c1915, direct positive ferrotype camera. 2¼" x 3¼" direct positive exp on paper.

Mandel Photo Postcard Camera:
                                 R3* D+
c1915, street camera. Direct positives, rectangular (2" x 3") or small circular images.

Wonder Automatic Cannon Photo Button Machine: R4* F+
c1913, cannon-shaped street detective camera; round exp, 25mm diameter on ferrotype plates. Produced button-size tintypes to insert in breast pins. The camera came complete with tripod, 300 plates, pins, and developing chemicals.

Child Guidance Products Inc
Los Angeles, California, USA

Mick-A-Matic: Model I	R4* D+
Model II	R3* C+

c1969; Toy camera in the shape of Mickey's head. Meniscus lens in nose; simple sector shutter; flash synch using flash cubes; 126 Instamatic film. There were two models. On the first model, the shutter was tripped by pulling down Mickey's right ear. This caused a problem with camera movement so a more conventional shutter release was used on the second version.

Model I is worth TWICE the amount. On occasion the camera is found unused complete in its original bubble-wrapped box adding substantially to its value.

Chiyotax Camera Company
Japan

All cameras listed here were made under contract by the Reise Camera Company.

Chiyoca 35:   R4* G–
c1951, 35mm VFR camera with interchangeable rigid Hexar f3.5/50mm lens, CFPS 1/20-1/500s, Leica Standard copy.

Chiyoca 35-1F: R4* G–
c1952, Added synch, collapsible Lena QC f3.5/50mm lens.

Chiyoca IIF: R3* F+
c1953, 35mm RFR camera with interchangeable screw mount Reise or Lena QC f3.5/50mm lens, CFPS 1/20-1/500s, copy of Leica II.

Chiyotax IIIF: R3* F+
1954, 35mm RFR camera with screw mount Lena QC F3.5/5cm lens, 1-1/500s CFPS, separate RFR/VFR windows, diopter adjustment, double male pin type flash synch. Later cameras marked "Reise Camera Company", are identical to this earlier version, and are valued the same. Prices are higher in Japan.

La Cinescopie S.A.
Brussels, Belgium

Le Photoscopique: R3* G–
c1930; OIP Gand Labor 45mm, f3.5 lenses; Ibsor shutter 1-150s. 50exp, 24 x 24mm with special cassettes.

Cincinatti Clock and Man. Co
Cincinnati, Ohio, USA

Cinclox Camera 16mm Model 3-S:
                     R2* B
1930, oval shaped 16mm movie camera; Cine Wollensak Velostigmat 1" f2.5 lens. Optical finder; footage indicator; variable speed mechanism; key wind operation.

Cine 8 Emel: R3* D–
c1935-1936. 8mm movie camera; 3 lens turret for Berthiot 12.5, 116mm and 35mm lenses; 5 speeds from 8 to 64

frames per second. First 8mm camera with back-wind capability.

Ciro Cameras Inc
Delaware, Ohio, USA

Ciro 35R: R2* B–
c1950. 35m RFR camera; Wollensak Anastigmat 50mm f4.5 coated lens; Alphax shutter 1/10-1/200s, CRF.

Ciro 35S: R2* B–
c1950. 35mm RFR camera; Wollensak Anastigmat 50mm f3.5 coated lens.

Ciro 35T: R2* B+
c1950. 35mm RFR camera; Wollensak Anastigmat 50mm f2.8 coated lens; Rapax shutter 1-1/400s.

Ciroflex A: R2* A

c1942. 2¼" x 2¼" TLR camera; Wollensak Velostigmat 85mm f3.5 lens; Alphax shutter 1/10-1/200s. 12 exp, on 120 roll film.

Ciroflex B: R2* A
c1948. 2¼" x 2¼" TLR camera.

Ciroflex C: R2* A
c1948. 2¼" x 2¼" TLR camera.

Ciroflex D: R2* B–
c1950. 2¼" x 2¼" TLR camera.

Ciroflex E: R2* B+
c1950. 2¼" x 2¼" TLR camera.

Ciroflex F: R2* B+
c1950. 2¼" x 2¼" TLR camera; Raptar f3.2 lens; Rapax shutter 1-1/400s. 12 exp on 120 roll film.

City Sale and Exchange
London, England

City sale and Exchange was not a camera manufacturer, but a leading camera dealer that sold many different makes of camera, many of which they badged with their own name – Salex – which was abbreviated from the full name of the company.

Salex Focal Plane Camera: R3* D
c1920. Unusually designed strut folding camera, made in vest pocket, 3½" x 2½" and quarter plate sizes. Salex Anastigmat f5.5 lens. Sliding viewfinder that doubled as a lens protector. Salex Anastigmat f4.5 lens.

Salex Studio Camera: R4* E
c1920. Mahogany plate camera with full range of movements, Made in post card, half plate and full plate sizes. Sold as a body only, lenses extra.

Salex Reflex: **R4* E**
c1915. Sold only in the $3^1/_2$" x $2^1/_2$" size. Made of wood, covered in leather. Shutter speeds from 1/15-1/1000s. Salex f4.5 anastigmat lens.

Salex Reflex De Luxe: **R4* E+**
c1915. Similar to Salex Reflex, but sold with six dark slides stored in the base of the camera body, from which only one slide at a time could be removed, in an effort to prevent double exposures. Rising front. Sold with a choice of lenses that included Koristka-Salex f4.5, Cooke f4.5, Cooke f3.5 and Ross Xpress f4.5.

Latimer Clarke

Latimer Clarke: **R5* H**
c1857. pantograph movement for sequential exp with single lens camera.

Clarus Camera Co
Minneapolis, Minnesota, USA

Clarus MS-35:   **R2* D–**
c1950, 35mm RFR camera, Wollensak Velostigmat f2.8/50mm coated lens, CFPS 1/25-1/1000s, CRF, first version with flash synch, and accessory shoe built-into the top plate. These cameras sell for 50% more in Europe.

Clarus MS-35:   **R2* C+**
c1954. Without flash synch, and with simple added on accessory shoe. This was an attempt to cut the cost of manufacturing the camera. Eventually, the Clarus Company went out of business, and the remaining camera parts were probably bought by the Wescon Company.

Clement and Gilmer: **R3* F–**
c1908, tailboard stereo camera. Mahogany finish with red bellows. Mfd in Paris, France.

Le Clopic: **R3* E**
c1903, Zeiss Krauss 136mm f8 lens; shutter 2-1/2000s. 6.5 x 9cm exp on plates. Mfd in Paris, France.

Le Clopic Reporter: **R3* E–**
c1903. 9 x 12cm camera; Berthiot Flor 135mm f4.5 lens; FPS 1/2-1/2000s. Mfd in Paris, France.

Close & Cone
New York, USA

Quad Camera: **R3* C+**
c1896. leather covered box camera; rotary wind shutter. 4 exp, $3^1/_2$" x $3^1/_2$" on plates.

Cluny: **R4* E**
c1910, box-type stereo camera; Protar 75mm f9 lenses; 3 speed guillotine shutter. Leather covered wooden body. Two models: 45 x 107mm and 6 x 13cm.

Company Francaise de Photographie
Paris, France

Photosphere: **R4* H**
1988. This is an unusual all-metal dry plate camera. A push-pull magazine contained 12 dry plates each 8x9cm. Early models were first available with individual double plate holders. Later, a variety of sizes were available. The lens was mounted in front of a half-sphere, and the shutter was mounted within the sphere. Lens periscope f13, focal length

95mm. Varying tension on a coil spring allowed approximate changes in shutter speed. Rarity R4 – the very unusual stereo model R5

Compco
USA

Compco Reflex II: **R2* A**
c1950, metal and plastic TLR type box camera for 6 x 6cm frames on roll film, simple lens and shutter. (prices higher in Europe).

Concava S.A.
Switzerland

Tessina: **R4* F**

c1960. Horizontal twin lens sub-miniature reflex camera. Exp. 14 x 21mm on 35mm film in special cassettes; f2.8 – 25mm lens, shutter 1/2-1/500s. The Tessina uses a clockworks mechanism to automatically advance the film. A silenced version which used a manual film advance was also available. The Tessina received some notoriety in the US as the spy camera used by the Watergate break-in group.

Accessories	
Watch strap	**D+**
Exp meter	**D+**
Watch	**F**
Prism finder	**D+**
Magnifier	**D**
Neck chain	**C+**
Daylight loader	**C+**

C.O.M.I.
Construzioni Ottico Meccaniche Italia Rome, Italy

Luxia: **R4* G**
1949. 35mm half frame camera, available in silver or gold-plate with reptile or pigskin covering. Models in black, red, green, blue and beige. 27mm f2.9 Delmak lens. Shutter 1/25-1/250s. Similar to, but rival with the Ducati, made by Societa Scientifica Radio Brevitti in Milan.

Conley Camera Co
Rochester, Minnesota, USA

Conley 4" x 5" Folding Plate Camera: R3* D+

c1900. R.R. lens; Conley Safety shutter. Polished wood interior with nickel plated fittings; red bellows.

Conley 5" x 7" Folding Plate Camera: R3* E–

c1890. Gundlach Triple Convertible lens; double extension bellows; rear swings and tilts; shifting, rising and falling front. Polished mahogany with nickel plated fittings; red bellows.

Conley Magazine Camera: R3* C+
c1904. Simple lens; rotary shutter. Twelve 4" x 5" exp on dry plates – drop plate changing mechanism.

Conley Postcard Camera: R3* C+
c1905. 3½" x 5" folding plate camera; Rapid Rectilinear lens; Klito shutter; vertical format; black bellows. Polished wood interior with nickel fittings.

Conley Stereoscopic Box Camera: R4* E+
c1906. Meniscus lenses; single speed shutter. Stereo exp on 5" x 7" dry plates.

Kewpie No. 2: R3* B–
side loading box camera; rotating waterhouse stops.

Contessa Nettel
Stuttgart, Germany

Adoro Tropical Camera: R4* F
c1925, 9 x 12cm tropical plate camera; Zeiss Tessar 15cm f4.5 lens; Compur shutter 1-1/150s.

Clarissa Tropical: R4* G+

c1919, 4.5 x 6cm tropical plate camera; Hugo Meyer Trioplan 7.5mm f3.5 lens; CFPS 1/20-1/300s.

Citoskop: R4* E

c1924, 45 x 107mm stereo camera; Tessar 65mm f4.5 lenses; Stereo Compur shutter, 1-1/300s.

Cocarette I: R2* C

c1922. Drop-bed folding camera. Single extension, but fitted with rising front. Choice of lenses and shutters including Anasigmat f6.3 in Derval shutter, Anastigmat f4.5 in Compur shutter and Tessar f4.5 in Compur shutter. Made for $3^1/_4$" x $2^1/_4$" pictures on rollfilm.

Cocarette II: R2* C

c1922. Similar to first model, but for $4^1/_4$" x $2^1/_2$" pictures on rollfilm.

Cocarette III: R2* C

c1922. Similar to first model, but for $4^1/_4$" x $3^1/_4$" pictures on rollfilm.

Cocarette IV: R2* C

c1922. Similar to first model, but for $5^1/_2$" x $3^1/_4$" pictures on rollfilm.

Cocarette De Luxe: R4* F

c1922. Four models, similar specifications to those above, but with f.5 Sonnar of f4.5 Tessar lenses. Brown leather and bellows

Contessa Nettel Sonnet: R4* G–

c1921, 4.5 x 6cm tropical camera; Tessar 7.5cm f4.5 lens; Compound shutter, 1-1/300s.

Baby Super Speed Deckrollo: R4* E+

1925. Vest pocket size camera for plates or film packs. Lens extends from the body on lazy tongs. Supplied with f2.7 Tessar lens. Focal plane shutter with slow speeds down to $^1/_2$s.

Deckrullo Tropical: R4* G–

c1925, 9 x 12cm tropical plate camera; Tessar 120mm f4.5 lens; teak construction, partially covered with brown leather, light brown leather bellows.

Deckrullo Tropical.

Piccolette, c1920.

Duchessa: **R4* F–**
c1926, 45 x 107mm folding stereo camera; Teronar f5.4 or Tessar f6.3 or f4.5 lenses; Compur shutter 1-1/250s. 45 x 107mm exp on plates.

Durol: **R2* C**
c1925. Folding camera with inter-changeable back for film or plate use, taking $3^1/_2$" x $2^1/_4$" pictures on either. Compur shutter, brilliant and eye-level viewfinders. Citona f4.5 lens.

Ergo: **R4* G**
c1924, monocular-type detective camera; Tessar 55mm f4.5 lens; Compur 1/25-1/100s. 4.5 x 6cm exp on plates. Sold originally as the Argus by Contessa Nettel (see Nettel Kamerawerk listing); later sold as the Ergo by Zeiss Ikon.

Piccolette: **R3* C+**
c1920, 127 roll film folding camera; Carl Zeiss Series IIb 7.5cm f6.3 lens; Compur shutter 1-1/300s. 8 exp, 4 x 6.5cm on 127 roll film.

Westca: **R3* D+**
c1914, all metal strut folding camera for 4.5 x 6cm plates, Aplanat f6.8/75mm lens.

Atlanta: **R5* G–**
c1915, plate camera for extra long (500mm or 800mm lens) for use as an aerial camera.CFPS, with either Aeroplast f6.8/500mm or f9/800mm lens.

Pixie: **R3* D+**
c1910, strut folding camera for 4 x 6cm frames on roll film, Tessar f6.3/70mm lens among others, various shutters.

Recto: **R3* D+**
c1925, strut folding camera for 4.5 x 6cm plates or film packs, various lenses and shutters, waist level reflex finder.

Nettix: R3* D
c1920, strut folding camera for 4.5 x 6cm plates or film packs, various lenses and shutters, wire frame finder.

Fiduca 6.5 x 9: R3* C–
c1920, metal bodied bed folding camera for 6.5 x 9cm plates or film packs, various lenses, Compur or Vario shutter.

Fiduca 9 x 12: R3* C–
c1920, metal bodied bed folding camera for 9 x 12cm plates or film packs, various lenses, Compur or Vario shutter.

Alino: R3* C
c1920, metal bodied bed folding camera for 6.5 x 9cm plates or film packs, double extension bellows, various lenses and shutters.

Suevia: R3* B+
c1920, metal bodied bed-folding camera for 6.5 x 9cm plates or film packs, various lenses and shutters, economy version.

Taxo: R2* B+
c1920, metal bodied bed-folding camera for 9 x 12cm plates or film packs, various lenses and shutters, economy version.

Donata: R2* B+
c1920, bed folding camera for 9 x 12cm plates or film packs, various lenses and shutters, double extension bellows.

Adoro 9 x 12: R2* B+
c1920, metal bodied folding bed camera for 9 x 12cm plates or film packs, various lenses and shutters, double extension bellows.

Adoro 10 x 15: R2* B+
c1920, metal bodied folding bed camera for 10 x 15cm plates or film packs, various lenses and shutters, double extension bellows.

Onito 9 x 12: R2* B
c1920, folding bed camera for 9 x 12cm plates or film packs, various lenses and shutters, economy version.

Onito 10 x 15: R2* B
c1920, folding bed camera for 10 x 15cm plates or film packs, various lenses and shutters, economy version.

Altura 9 x 12: R2* B+
c1920, folding bed camera for 9 x 12cm plates or film packs, various lenses and shutters.

Altura 10 x 15: R2* B+
c1920, folding bed camera for 10 x 15cm plates or film packs, various lenses and shutters.

Sonto: R3* C–
c1920, folding bed camera for 13 x 18cm plates or film packs, various lenses and shutters, double extension bellows.

Tessco: R2* C
c1925. Folding camera made for film packs, taking $3^1/_2$" x $2^1/_4$" pictures on either. Compur shutter, brilliant and eye-level viewfinders. Citona f4.5 lens.

Volupa: R3* B+
c1920, folding bed camera for 10 x 15cm plates or film packs, double extension bellows, various lenses and shutters.

Miroflex 6.5 x 9:   **R4* F**
c1919, strut folding SLR for 6.5 x 9cm plates or film packs, Tessar f4.5/120mm lens among others, CFPS, later cameras are from Zeiss-Ikon are more often found.

Miroflex 9 x 12:   **R4* F**
c1919, strut folding SLR for 6.5 x 9cm plates or film packs, Tessar f4.5/135mm lens among others, CFPS, later cameras are from Zeiss-Ikon are more often found.

Corfield
England

Periflex 1 (Black):   **R2* E**
1953-1958. Cfps, 1/30-1/1000s. The Corfield 35mm cameras used an unusual and unique focussing system. A small mirror could be inserted into the optical path manually on some models, automatically on others enabling the user to focus. Standard lenses were either f1.9/50mm, f3.5/45mm, or f2.8/50mm. Black top and bottom plates replaced by silver satin anodised finish in 1955.

Periflex 1 (Silver):   **R2* E**
1955. Similar to black version of the Model 1, but with top and bottom plates in anodised silver. Lens mount has addition of leatherette grip

Corfield 66:   **R4* F**

1961. Cfps, 1/10-1/500s. Interchangeable ground glass focusing, 6 X 6cm on 120 roll film using film back, or sheet film holders, interchangeable finders, 4 element Lumax f3.5/95mm lens. About three hundred cameras were made before production was halted.

Periflex Original: **R4* F+**
1953. Cfps, 1/30-1/1000s, reflex focusing using a small periscope which intercepts the aerial image before it reaches the film plane, interchangeable viewfinders, screw mount f3.5/50mm Lumar, front cell focusing, coated from 1954. Aluminium body, covered with light brown pigskin, black top and bottom plates. Glass pressure plate, sprocketless film advance.

Periflex 3, 1957.

Periflex 2:   **R2* F−**

1958. Cfps, 1/30-1/500s, reflex focusing using a small periscope which intercepts the aerial image before it reaches the film plane, interchangeable viewfinders, screw mount Lumax f1.9/50mm, f3.5/45mm or f2.8/50mm lens. Simplified version of Periflex 3 with the EV scale and film reminder omitted. Introduced after the more expensive Periflex 3.

Periflex 3:   **R3* E**

1957. Cfps, 1-1/1000s, reflex focusing using a small periscope which descends automatically when the film is advanced, to intercept the aerial image from the centre of the frame before it reaches the film plane. Interchangeable viewfinders, screw mount f3.5, 2.8, or 1.9/50mm Lumax lenses, focusing to 9 inches.

Periflex 3A: **R3* F**

1959. Cfps, 1-1/1000s, lever wind, reflex focusing using a small periscope which descends automatically when the film is advanced, to intercept the aerial image from the centre of the frame before it reaches the film plane. Interchangeable viewfinders, screw mount f3.5, 2.8, or 1.9/50mm Lumax lenses, focusing to 9 inches. Frame counter counts backward during rewind, showing number of frames rewound into the film cassette.

Periflex 3B: **R3* E+**

1960. Cfps, 1-1/1000s, lever wind, reflex focusing using a small periscope which descends automatically when the film is advanced, to intercept the aerial image from the centre of the frame before it reaches the film plane. Interchangeable viewfinders, screw mount f2.8 (four element), f2.4 (six element), f1.9 (six element) Lumax lenses. Distinguished by its three flash synch sockets, this camera represents the peak of the periflex range in features and complexity.

Periflex Gold Star: **R2* D+**

1961. Cfps, 1-1/300s using the same mechanism as the Prontor leaf shutter in order to give consistent and accurate exposure, lever wind, reflex focusing using a small periscope which descends automatically when the film is advanced, to intercept the aerial image from the centre of the frame before it reaches the film plane. Interchangeable viewfinders, screw mount f2.8 (four element), f2.4 (six element), f1.9 (six element) Lumax lenses. Usually found in quite good working order, quite usable even today.

Interplan: **R3* E−**

1960s. Cfps, 1-1/300s using the same mechanism as the Prontor leaf shutter in order to give consistent and accurate exposure, lever wind. Sold without lens, for use with Leica screw mount lenses (Interplan A), or Edixa/Pentax screw mount lenses (Interplan B), or Exakta bayonet (Interplan C). Based on the Periflex Gold Star, but simpler, without reflex focusing.

Interplan C.

Lenses made for the Periflex system 1950-60s

28mm, f3.5, Retro-Lumax, 1959   D−
35mm, f3.5, Retro-Lumax, 1957   C−
85mm, f1.5, Super Lumax, 1960,
                                 rare E
90mm, f2.8, Tele Lumax, 1961, rare D
95mm, f2.8, Lumax, 1960   D−
100mm, f4.0, Lumar, 1956   C+
135mm, f3.5, Tele Lumax, 1958
   (leather banded mount)   C+
135mm, f3.5, Tele Lumax, 1961
   (diamond turned mount) rare.   D
150mm, f3.5, Lumar,1954,
   only one known to exist
240mm, f4.5, Tele Lumax, 1960,
   special viewfinder, rare.   E+
400mm, f4.5, Tele Lumax, 1960, same
Vfr as 240mm lens, rare.   E+

Cornu
Paris, France

Ontoflex: **R4* E+**
c1939. TLR camera; Tessar 90mm f3.5 lens; Compur Rapid shutter 1-1/400s. 6 x 9cm exp, horizontal or vertical format.

Ontoscope: **R4* E**
c1925, 35mm stereo camera; Berthiot 40mm f3.5 lenses; shutter 1-1/400s. Pair of stereo exp, 24 x 30mm on 35mm film.

Ontoscope: **R3* D+**
c1925. 45 x 107mm stereo camera; Tessar 55mm f4.5 lenses; guillotine shutter $^1/_5$-1/400s. Changing magazine for 12 plates, 45 x 107mm.

Ontoscope: **R3* D+**
c1925, 6 x 13cm stereo camera; Berthiot 85mm f4.5 lenses; guillotine shutter $^1/_5$-1/300s. Panoramic settings; rising and falling front.

Reyna: **R4* D–**
1941, 35mm camera with cast aluminium body, 50mm/f3.5 Flor Berthiot or Saphir Boyer lens, Gitzo shutter 1/25-1/200s, no automatic stop when winding the film.

Reyna II: **R3* D–**
1942, 35mm camera with cast aluminium body, 50mm/f3.5 Flor Berthiot lens, Vario Reyna shutter, 1/25-1/100s, In Black or shiny Brown. With addition of automatic film stop.

Ontobloc I: **R3* C+**
c1947, 35mm camera with cast aluminium body, 50mm/f3.5 Saphir Boyer lens, Coronto shutter, 1-1/300s, owners of Reyna II cameras could have them fitted with the Coronto shutter by sending them back to the factory.

Ontobloc II: **R3* C+**
c1948, 35mm camera with cast aluminium body, 50mm/f3.5 Saphir Boyer lens, Coronto shutter, 1-1/300s, with chrome top plate.

Ontobloc III: **R3* C+**
c1948, 35mm camera with cast aluminium body, 50mm/f2.8 Flor Berthiot lens, Coronto-Rapid shutter, 1-1/400s, like previous model, but with faster shutter and lens.

Week-End Bob: **R3* C+**
c1946, 35mm camera with cast aluminium body, the same style as the Reyna cameras previously listed, but with simple shutter and lens. Grey body with gold coloured metal work.

Fama-Flor: **R3* D**
c1940, 35mm camera with cast aluminium body, distributed by the Maillard company, Fama shutter 1-1/300s, 50mm/f2.8 lens in inter-changeable mount. Built-in blind which protects the film from light when the lens/shutter are changed.

Fama-Flor II: **R3* D**
c1940, 35mm camera with cast aluminium body, with built-in vrf adjustable for 35mm, 50mm, and 90mm fields of view. A 35mm/f3.5 wide angle lens and a 90mm/f4.5 Telephoto lens were available for this, and the Fama-Flor camera. A complete set, including both accessory lenses adds 200% to the price.

Ontoscope: R2* D–

c1920. 6x13cm stereo camera with matched Tessar 8.5cm f4.5 lenses. Entire body nickel plated. Shutter 1/5 to 1/300s. Lens board may be shifted to centre for panoramic picture. Interchangeable magazines for glass plates or roll film.

Coronet
Birmingham, England

Cadet: R1 A
1957. Similar to Flashmaster (see below), with modifications to the film wind mechanism. Shutter release also shifted to front right of lens moulding. Camera not synchronised for flash.

Coronet Cameo: R2* D–

c1935, plastic sub-miniature camera; 13 x 17cm exp on 16mm roll film.

Cub: R1* B
1947. Light-weight Bakelite camera for 40x27mm images on Kodak's 828 film (also sold by Coronet as 888 and Ilford as 88). Fixed focus lens, instantaneous shutter. Lens extends from the body on metal tube. Folding eye-level viewfinder.

Cub Flash: R1* B
Similar to the cub but synchronised for flash. 'T' setting added to shutter, f11 and f16 apertures. Non folding viewfinder.

Coronet Midget: Black: R2* D
Brown/red: R2* D+
Green: R2* D+
Blue: R3* C+

c1934-35. During the 1930's this firm manufactured a large variety of simple cameras, the most famous of which was the Coronet Midget. Molded out of bakelite, the midget was available in a variety of colours (black, red, brown, blue, & green). The price varies greatly between colours.

Coronet "3D" Stereo Camera: R2* C+

c1954, plastic stereo camera, available in different colours; meniscus lens; single speed shutter. 4 stereo pairs or 8 single exp, 4.5cm on 127 film.

Coronet "Vogue": R3* D+

Streamlined plastic; front opening camera; 6 exp 50x30mm on special film; f10 meniscus lens. Instantaneous or B shutter.

Coronet "Cameo": R3* D+

c1948; Moulded Bakelite camera 2" x 1" x $1^{1}/_{4}$" Dim.; Fixed focus f11 Lens; 1/25 shutter; front of Vfr. slides into camera, rear of Vfr. folds over back.

Flashmaster: R1* A

1955. Beginners' camera for 12 exp on 120. Black plastic with chrome trim. Meniscus lens, everset shutter in an extension from the main body, direct vision viewfinder. Takes its name from being unusual in a camera of its type and price being flash synchronised.

Cosina Company Ltd
Nagano, Japan

Exacta Twin TL: R4* NSR

1970. Eye-level 35mm SLR. Made under contract for Ihagee, in West Germany. It used all existing Exacta lenses which were in generous supply. Schneider-Kreuznach Xenon lens f1.9, 50mm lens. Many of the features of the original Exacta appeared on the Exacta Twin TL in sophisticated form.

Jean Cros
St. Etienne, France

Reyna-Cross II: R4* D–

1942, 35mm camera with cast aluminium body, 50mm/f3.5 Flor Berthiot lens, Reyna/Cross shutter, 1/25-1/200s. Made in the "free" zone of France.

Reyna Cross III: R4* D–

35mm camera with cast aluminium body, now equipped with a 45mm/f2.9 lens, and Micromanic shutter, 1/25-1/200s.

Crown Camera Co
New York, USA

Crown Camera: R3* D+

c1910, cardboard box camera; meniscus lens; simple shutter. $1^{1}/_{4}$" x $1^{1}/_{2}$" exp on dry plates.

Curtis Colour Lab

Curtis Colour Scout: **R5* F–**
c1942, 2$\frac{1}{4}$" x 3$\frac{1}{4}$" colour camera;
Goerz Dogmar 7$\frac{1}{2}$" f4.5 lens; Compur
shutter.

Cyclops: **R4* F+**
c1950, binocular-type detective camera;
Telesigmar f4.5 lens; shutter 1/25-
1/100s. 16mm film in special cassettes.
Similar to Teleca Camera. Mfd in Japan.

D

The Daguerreotype Process

Daguerreotypes are highly prized by collectors. Ordinary portraits sell for up to £50 depending on the size, quality and beauty of the image.

Daguerreotypes of famous people by an identified portraitist can sell for several thousand pounds. An occupational — that is a daguerreotype of a worker with his tools — is especially valued. A $^1/_6$th-plate or a $^1/_4$-plate occupational will usually bring between £300 and £1,000. Outdoor scenes are rare and very desirable; they usually sell for between £500 and £1,500.

Daguerrian Sensitising Box: R5* H

c1845. American-style of sensitising box using either iodine or bromine for preparing quarter, sixth or ninth daguerreotype plates.

Daguerreotype Posing Stand: R5* H
c1845, cast-iron fluted stand; original paint.

Daguerreotype Camera: R5*
Complete: J+
Stand alone: G–
c1848. $^1/_4$ plate chamfered-box type daguerreotype camera. Manufacturer unknown; American construction.

Posing Stand (above), camera (below).

Dai-Ichi Optical Works
Japan

Chicon 35:   **R5* H–**
1954. Cfps, 1-1/500s, separate Rfr/Vfr windows, diopter adjustment. Screw mount Hexanon f3.5/50mm lens. Made in very small quantities, this camera was the forerunner of the Honor cameras from Mejiro Optical Works. Very Rare.

Zenobia: **R3* B**
1949-53. 16 exposures on 120 film, folding camera with between the lens shutter 1-1/500s, 75mm f3.5 Hesper Anastigmat lens.

Zenobiaflex: **R3* D**

c1953; 6 X 6cm TLR; Neo-Hespar 75mm f3.5 lens in Daiichi Rapid shutter 1-1/500s. B.

Dalka Industries Pty Ltd
Australia

Candid: **R4* C–**
c1939, plastic VFR camera for 6 x 6cm on 120 or 620 film, simple lens and shutter, believed to be a very early example of rigid polystyrene injection molding. very rare.

J.H. Dallmeyer
London, England

Dallmeyer Baby Speed Reflex: R3* E
1926. Small SLR for 4.5 x 6 cm format, specially made for the Dallmeyer Pentac 4" f2.9 lens. Self capping focal plane shutter speeded 1/10-1/800s. Focusing down to 12 inches.

Dallmeyer Dual: **R4* E**
c1932. Unusual in its time for taking 16 exposures on 120 film. Lens and shutter extend from behind twin flaps that open from camera body, supported on crossed struts. Focusing by radial lever. Dalmac f3.5 lens, wire frame viewfinder

Dallmeyer Press Reflex: **R3* E+**
c1925. Quarter-plate size reflex camera, leather covered, with reversing back, detachable focusing hood, lens cap and sky shade plus long extension for close focusing down to 18 inches. Ten speeds shutter from 1/15-1/1000s, 6" f3.5 Dallmeyer lens, extra wide aperture for this picture format at the time.

Dallmeyer Stereoscopic Wet-Plate Camera: R4* I+

c1861. Petzval lens rarer than later Rapid Rectilinear; flap shutter; rack and pinion focusing; mahogany wood with brass fittings.

Dallmeyer Speed Camera: R3* F–

c1923-1930s; Dropped baseboard formed side panel when in use; N&G FPS $1/8$-1/1000s; F 2.9 Pentac lens; Price given for 4.5 x 6cm, larger sizes quarter-plate, $3^1/2$ x $2^1/2$ less 40%

Dallmeyer Snapshot Camera: R3* C+

c1928. Simple folding camera using struts. 12 exposures in filmpack each 6.5x9cm. f6 Dallmeyer Anastigmat triplet. Simple single-speed shutter, T&B. Three position focusing.

Pentac: R4* E

c1920s. Rollfilm camera, taking 6 x 9 cm pictures, specially introduced to take the extra-wide aperture f2.9 Pentac lens, mounted in a Compur shutter. Rise and fall, plus cross movement. Detachable back suitable for plates or film packs. Interchangeable f6.5 Dallon lens also available.

J. Damoizeau
Paris, France

Le Cyclographe a Foyer Fixe: R5* I–

panoramic camera which can cover a full 360 degrees. Clockworks motor drives film past a slit. This model Cyclographe has a fixed focus lens and is rigid.

Variable focus Cyclographe (DA500):
R5 to unavailable NSR

Panoramic camera covering 360 degrees driven by a clockworks motor. Unlike the fixed focus model, the focusing Cyclographe is considerably larger and uses a bellows. There were two models, one for 7" film (178mm) and one for 9" (229mm) film.

Dan Camera Works
Tokyo, Japan

Dan 35 Model I:
R2* E

1946. 15 24 x 24mm exposures on 35mm size rollfilm. 50mm f4 Dan Anastigmat. Shutter speeds 1/25-1/100 + B.

Dan 35 Model II:
R2* E

1948. Similar to Model I but with auto frame counter.

Dan 35 Model III:
R2* E

1949. Similar to Models I and II, but with image size changed to 24x32mm and 40mm f3.5 Dan Anastigmat.

Dan Super 35:
R2 F

c1950. Similar to previous models with built-in rangefinder. 40mm f3.5 Eria Anastigmat lens. Shutter 1/25-1/200s + B. Flash synchronised.

J.B. Dancer
Manchester, England

J. B. Dancer's Stereo Wet-Plate Camera:
R5 to unavailable J

c1856. This camera was probably the first commercially produced stereo wet-plate camera.

Dangelmaier & Co
Reutlingen, Germany

This company changed names and address more than a few times in the 1950s and 60s, ending up in the mid 1970s as the Dacora/Weber company in Nürnberg. For simplicity all cameras are listed here, whether made in Reutlingen, Munich or Nürnberg.

Daco:
R3* B+

c1949, bakelite box camera for 6 x 6 frames on roll film, simple lens, two position focusing, three lens openings, f11, f16, and f 22, single speed shutter, no built-in handle!

Daci Royal:
R2* A

c1950, metal box camera for 6 x 6 frames on roll film, simple f9 lens, single speed shutter, synch connection.

Daci Royal I:
R2* A

c1950, metal box camera for 6 x 6 frames on roll film, simple f9 lens, single speed shutter, no synch connection.

Subita:
R2* B–

c1953, folding VFR camera for 6 x 6 frames on roll film, Astigmat f6.3/75mm lens, simple Singlo two speed shutter, without double exposure prevention or body release. A cheap version of the Dacora camera .

Dacora: R2* B+
c1953, folding VFR camera for 6 x 6 frames on roll film, Dacora f5.6/75mm lens, Vario shutter without double exposure prevention, or coated Dacora F3.5/75mm lens in Pronto or Prontor shutter with double exposure prevention!

Dacora-Record: R3* C−
c1954, folding camera for 6 x 6 frames on roll film, uncoupled RFR, lever film advance, Dignar f4.5/75mm lens or Ennar or Westar f3.5/75mm lens in Prontor-s or Prontor SVS shutter.

Dacora-Record-Royal: R3* C+
c1954, folding camera for 6 x 6 frames on roll film, coupled RFR, lever film advance, Dignar f4.5/75mm lens or Ennar or Westar f3.5/75mm lens in Prontor-S or Prontor SVS shutter.

Dignette: R2* B−
c1954-60, 35mm VFR camera, several body styles, several lens and shutter combinations, typically, Dignar f2.8/45mm lens in Vario shutter.

Super Dignette: R2* B−
c1955-60, 35mm VFR camera with built-in light meter, several body styles, several lens available, typically, Dignar f2.8/45mm lens in Vario or Pronto shutter.

Digna 6 x 6: R2* B−
c1954, metal VFR camera for 6 x 6 frames on roll film, several lens and shutter combinations available, typically Westar f2.9/75mm, Prontor shutter

Digna I: R2* B−
c1954, metal VFR camera for 6 x 6 frames on roll film, Achromat lens in single speed shutter, cheap version of the Digna 6 x 6.

Colour Digna 6 x 6: R2* B−
c1956, metal VFR camera for 6 x 6 frames on roll film, several lens and shutter combinations available, typically Achromat f4.5/75mm, Vario shutter, built-in extinction light meter.

Dacora CC: R2* B−
c1960, full automatic 35mm VFR camera, with manual possible, Ysarex f2.8/45mm lens, Prontormatic shutter.

Dakora 66: R2* B−
c1964, simple metal VFR camera for 6 x 6 frames on 120 roll film.

Dakora 44: R3* B−
c1964, simple metal VFR camera for 4 x 4 frames on 127 roll film.

Albert Darier
Geneva, Switzerland

L'Escopette de Darier: R5* J

Gun-type detective camera; Steinheil Antiplanet 90mm f6 lens; spherical shutter 1/25-1/100s. One of the first cameras to use Eastman roll film for 100 exp. 6.8 x 7.2cm. c1888.

nickel plated fittings. 4" x 5", 8" x 10". Users are willing to pay more than collectors.

Andre Debrie
Paris, France

Sept: R2* E

Darling: R4* F–

Sub-miniature camera; 16mm film in special cassette.

A. Darlot
Paris, France

Le Rapide: R4* I
c1887. Darlot rectilinear 135mm f8 lens; rotary between-the-lens shutter; 12 plates, 9 x 12cm in gravity-fed magazine.

L.F. Deardorff & Sons
Chicago, Illinois, USA

L.F. Deardorff & Sons View Camera:
R4* G
c1960. 5" x 7" view camera; front and rear swings and tilts; double extension bellows. Seasoned mahogany wood with

Sept, first model.
c1923, half-frame 35mm still camera, movie camera, projector, contact printer. Berthiot Stylor 50mm f3.5 lens. 250 exp on perforated 35mm film, 18 x 24mm images. Special cartridges held 17 feet of film. Sold by Societe Francais Sept. Two basic models. Flat front on first. Second model with a larger spring has rounded front. The Sept was frequently used by Hollywood cameramen during the silent film era for tricky shots requiring a very compact instrument.

Sept, second model.

Delaye
Paris, France

Le Prismac: **R5* H–**
c1906, stereo camera; Kenngott anastigmatic 54mm lenses; variable speed guillotine shutter. Le Prismac is fitted with internal prisms which eliminated the need to transpose stereo views when printing to positive.

Demarie-Lapierre-Mollier
Paris, France

Dehel: **R2* B–**
1940, 6 x 9cm folding roll film camera with various lenses and shutters, among which the Manar 90mm/f3.5 and f4.5 use a slightly curved film plane and pressure plate.

Dehel Primar: **R2* B+**
1940, 6 x 4.5cm roll film camera, with various lens and shutter combinations. Called "The Soldier's Camera" when first introduced in the Spring of 1940.

Telka-III (Dehel Super):   **R2* B+**
1948, 6 x 9cm folding roll film camera with CRF, 95mm/f3.5 Sagittar in Prontor shutter, speeds of 1-1/200s, early cameras have a black face plate on the shutter, while later ones have a chrome plate. Delivered with a test film taken with the camera at the factory to show the quality of the lens!

Telka-IIIA: **R3* C+**
1951, 6 x 9cm folding roll film camera with CRF, 95mm/f3.5 Sagittar in Prontor SV shutter, speeds of 1-1/200s, bright yellow VFR window to increase the contrast of the rangefinder image.

Telka-IIIB: **R2* D–**
1952, 6 x 9cm folding roll film camera with CRF, 95mm/f3.5 Sagittar in Prontor SV shutter with "EV" markings, speeds of 1-1/300s, special adaptor for using Bantam 828 colour film.

Telka-III "Professional":   **R4* E–**
1953, 6 x 9cm folding roll film camera with CRF, 95mm/f3.5 Sagittar in Prontor SV shutter, speeds of 1-1/300s, entirely black for that "professional look".

Telka-X: **R2* B+**
1950, 6 x 9cm folding roll film camera with simple lens and shutter, folding VFR, name marked on the shutter.

Telka-XX: **R2* B+**
1951, 6 x 9cm folding roll film camera with 110mm/f4.5 Manar lens in Gitzo shutter. Early cameras have a folding VFR, while later ones have a top plate similar to the Telka-III without CRF.

Telka-I: **R3* B+**
1954, 6 x 9cm folding roll film camera without CRF, 95mm/f3.5 Sagittar in Prontor shutter, speeds of 1-1/200s, essentially the same camera as the Telka-III, but without CRF.

Summa: **R3* C–**
1953, 6 x 9cm folding roll film camera with simple lens and shutter, or 110mm/f4.5 Manar lens in Gitzo shutter, folding VFR, name marked on the shutter. The same camera as the Telka-X, and Telka-XX, but delivered for a company in Monte Carlo. The name was quickly dropped, as an Italian camera already had the registered rights to the name.

Telka-II: **R3* C**
1955, 6 x 4.5cm roll film camera, front focusing 75mm/f3.5 Manar lens, Prontor S shutter, speeds of 1-1/200s, folding VFR.

Telka-Sport: **R4* E–**
1960, 6 x 4.5cm roll film camera, CRF 70mm/f3.5 Sagittar lens in an Atos shutter, speeds of 1-1/300s. Provided with adaptors for using Bantam 828 film. About 1000 cameras are said to have been made. The last camera made by Demarie-Lapierre-Mollier, a house which was originally founded in 1848.

Detrola Corp
Detroit, Michigan, USA

Detrola 400:   **R3* F**

c1938, 35mm rf camera; Wollensak Velostigmat 50mm f3.5 lens, interchangeable screw mount; CFPS 1-1/500s, CRF.

Detrola A: **R2* B–**
c1938, Bakelite VFR camera for 3 x 4cm frames on 127 film, fixed focus lens and shutter in collapsible tube mount. (prices less in the USA).

Detrola B: **R2* B+**
c1938, with built-in extinction meter. (prices less in the USA).

Detrola D: **R3* B–**
c1938, with f4.5 lens. (prices less in the USA).

Detrola E: **R3* B–**
c1938, with f3.5 lens. (prices less in the USA).

Detrola G :   **R2* B–**
c1938, Bakelite VFR camera for 3 x 4cm frames on 127 film, Detrola f4.5/2" lens, shutter 1/25-1/200s, collapsible tube mount, helociod focusing. (prices less in the USA).

Devin Colorgraph Co
New York, USA

Devin One-Shot Colour Camera: R5* F+

c1940. 6.5 x 9cm sheet film one-shot colour camera; Goerz Dogmar 5½" f4.5 lens; Compur dial-set shutter 1-1/250s, CRF.

QRS Kamra: **R3* D**
c1928, 35mm bakelite camera; Graf Anastigmat f7.7 lens; single shutter speed. 40 exp on 35mm film in special cassette.

QRS Kamra, c1928.

E. Deyrolle Fils
Paris, France

Le Scenographe of Dr. Candeze:
R5* H

c1874, landscape lens mounted on sliding panel – stereo pictures in two exp. 10 x 15cm on dry plates. Le Scenographe was an extremely early example of a compact and inexpensive dry-plate camera.

Dick Tracy Camera: R2* C
toy plastic camera; 127 roll film.

Diax Kamerawerk
Walter Voss, Ulm, Germany

Diax: R3* B+
c1948-52, metal 35mm VFR camera, Xenar f2.8/4.5cm lens, Compur Rapid shutter.

Diax Ia: R2* C

c1950, metal 35mm VFR camera with three finders, one each for 35mm, 50mm, and 90mm fields of view, interchangeable Xenar f2.8/45mm, Xenon f2/50mm, Westar, or Isconar f3.5/50mm lens, Synchro Compur shutter.

Diax II: R2* C
c1950, metal 35mm camera with coupled RFR, non-changeable Xenar f2.8, Xenon f2, or Heligon f2/45mm lens, Synchro Compur shutter.

Diax IIa: R2* C+
c1955, metal 35mm camera with coupled RFR, interchangeable Xenar f2.8/45mm, Xenon f2/50mm, Westar f3.5/50mm, or Isconar f3.5/50mm lens, Synchro Compur shutter. Built-in finder for 90mm lens located next to 50mm combined RFR/VFR.

Diax Ib: **R3* C**

c1956, metal 35mm VFR camera with three finders, one each for 35mm, 50mm, and 90mm fields of view, Westar f3.5, Isconar f3.5, Xenar f2.8 or Xenon f2/50mm lens, Synchro Compur shutter, lever advance, new body style compared with Diax Ia.

Diax IIb: **R2* D**

c1956, 35mm camera with coupled RFR for all lenses from 35mm to 135mm, separate VFR for 90mm lens located next to combined RFR/VFR, Isconar f3.5, Xenar f2.8 or Xenon f2/50mm lens, Synchro Compur shutter, lever advance, new body style compared with Diax IIa.

Diaxette: **R3* B–**

c1953, simple metal 35mm VFR camera, Cassar f2.8/45mm lens, Prontor shutter.

Accessories for Diax cameras

Xenagon f3.5/35mm lens:	**C–**
Isconar f4.5/85mm lens:	**C+**
Tele-Xenar f3.5/90mm lens:	**C+**
Tele-Xenar f4/135mm lens:	**C+**

Dan 35:   **R3* C+**

Dan 40mm f4.5 lens; single speed shutter; 12 exp on special cassettes, 24 x 24mm exp. c1950.

Ditmar
Vienna, Austria

Ditmar: **R3* C–**

c1939, 9.5mm movie camera; Cinor Berthiot 25mm f1.8 lens; 2 speeds: 16 and 32 frames per s; non-coupled photo-electric cell; 15mm cassettes. Manufactured in Austria.

Dom-Martin
Paris, France

Dom-Martin: **R4* F+**

c1903, press-type stereo camera; aluminium body. 2 sizes: 6 x 13cm, 8 x 16cm.

Doryu Camera Co
Japan

Doryu-2:   **R5* J+**

c1890, pistol-type detective camera; Dorimar 17mm f2.5 lens; 3 speed shutter. 10 x 10mm exp on special 16mm film. bullet shaped flash cartridges. In 1955, an improved model was produced with a 15mm f2.2 lens and a faster shutter.

Doryu flash cartridges: **R3* D+**

Packages of six bullet shaped flash cartridges have recently made their way into the market. They would be of more value to a Doryu owner, who might be willing to pay above the going price for a package to try out in his camera!

Dossert Detective Camera Co
New York, New York, USA

Dossert Detective Camera: **R4* F+**

c1890, 4" x 5" leather covered, box-type detective camera; 4" x 5" exp on dry plates; sliding panels to mask lens openings and ground glass opening.

---

007 Attache Case Camera: **R4* E+**
c1970, toy camera; radio, coding device, and telescope in attache case.

Dr. Doyer, M. Gillon
France

La Diplide: **R4* F–**
c1904, eye-level reflex camera; helicoid focusing to 0.5m. 6 x 13cm exp on roll film.

Dubroni
Paris, France

Dubroni Apparatus No. 1:   **R5* H+**

c1865. Rigid bodied camera for in-camera processing of single wet collodion plate. Lens cap controls exposure. Invented by Bourdin, Paris, France. (Dubroni is an anagram of Bourdin). Mfd. by Maison Dubroni, Paris, France. The first model shows the exposed bottle in which all the processing takes place.

**Dubroni Apparatus No. 1
(second version):**   **R5* G+**
c1866. Sides are enclosed and the internal bottle is ceramic. Both cameras were sold with a complete case containing all necessary chemicals for sensitising and processing the plate. They are very rarely found with the complete system.

Le Photo Sport: **R5* J–**
c1889, Darlot Planigraphe 210mm f9 lens; simple rotary shutter. 9 x 12cm plates.

Ducati
Milan, Italy

Ducati Simplex: **R3* F–**

c1938, half-frame 35mm camera; Ducati Etar f3.5/35mm lens; CFPS 1/25-1/250s.

Ducati (with rangefinder):   **R3* F**

c1938, half-frame 35mm camera, Vitor f3.5/35mm lens; CFPS 1/20-1/500s, CRF.

Durst S.A.
Switzerland

Automatica: R2* A

1961. Automatic 35mm camera. Setting the film speed also sets the aperture and the built-in meter selects the shutter speed, indicated by a needle in a top plate window. Override allows both shutter speeds and apertures to be set manually. 45mm f2.8 Schneider Durst Radionar and Prontor-SVS shutter 1-1/300s + B.

Duca: R3* D–

c1946, 35mm camera; Ducar 50mm f11 lens; shutter, T and I. 12 exp, 24 x 36mm on Agfa Rapid cassettes.

E

Earth KK
Japan

Guzzi: **R4 A**

c1938. Subminiature, cast metal camera for 20x20mm images on miniature rollfilm. Unmarked fixed focus lens, everset shutter for I & B. Similar to the post-war Top from the Top Camera Works.

Eastern Speciality Mfg Co
Boston, Massachusetts, USA

Springfield Union Camera: **R4* F–**

c1899, plate brought into plane of focus by rotating block inside camera; 4 exp, $3\frac{1}{2}$" x $3\frac{1}{2}$" on dry plates.

Albert Ebner & Co
Stuttgart, Germany

Ebner: **R3* D+**

c1938, plastic folding camera; Rodenstock-Trinar-Anastigmat 10.5cm f4.5 lens; Compur shutter 1-1/250s; 8 exp, $2\frac{1}{4}$" x $3\frac{1}{4}$" on 120 roll film.

Eder Patent Camera: **R4* F**

c1930. German folding plate camera; viewing lens and bellows paired horizontally with taking lens; 6 x 6cm exp on plate or film.

Eho Kamerafabrik
Dresden, Germany

After July 1939, known as the Amca Kamerawerk, Berthold Altman prop, Altmann lent the first three letters of his family name to Altissa, Altix, Altiflex and Altiscope line of cameras. See Altissa Kamerawerk for post-war cameras.

Altissa: **R2* D+**

c1939. Simple fixed focus box camera design with I and B speed shutter. Large optical finder in top with some models having reflex viewing adds 100% to the price. Not to be confused with the post-war Altissa, though looking very similar!

Eho Box: R2* A

1932-39, line of inexpensive box cameras in 6 x 6cm, 6 x 9cm, 6 x 4.5cm and 3 x 4cm formats with meniscus or better lenses, some with wire frame finders in addition to the typical waistlevel reflex finders. All are about the same price, though the smaller format cameras are rarer and go for 100% more.

Eho Stereo Box: R2* D–

c1936, simple box camera for stereo pairs 6 x 13cm on roll film, wire frame finder and reflex finder.

Altiflex: R3* C–

c1936-39, TLR for 6 x 6 frames on roll film with Victar or Trinar 75mm lens in Automat, Prontor II or Compur shutter, side mounted focusing handle.

Altiscope: R4* D

c1936, stereo camera for 6 x 13cm stereo pairs, or 6 x 6 single non-stereo frames, Victor f4.5/75mm lenses, simple three speed shutter, the same optical finder as used on the Altissa box camera.

Altix: R3* B+

c1937, 35mm VFR camera for 24 x 24mm frames on regular 35mm film, Laack f3.5/3.5cm lens, simple shutter. The first of the Altix cameras. (See ALTISSA listing for post-war cameras).

Eichapel
Germany

Noviflex: R4* F

1934. First single lens reflex made for the 12 on 120 film size. Focal plane shutter speeded 1/20-1/1000s, with special release for time exposures. Fixed lens on first model, interchangeable on second, with choice of three lenses – f3.5 or f2.9 Ludwig Victar, Meyer Trioplan or Schneider Xenar. Second model also incorporated a red window cover and added a direct vision finder to the reflex viewfinder.

Eiho Company
Taiwan

Drinks cans cameras: R1* A

c1977. All of the same basic design, but with different trade names on them. 110 cameras with fixed focus, aperture and shutter speeds. Designs include Coca Cola, Pepsi Cola, Miller Lite, 7-Up, Budweiser, Crown Paint and more.

L'Electra Plastica Industria S.A.
(L.E.P.I.S.A.) Barcelona, Spain

Fotex: R4* C

c1960, bakelite VFR camera for 6 x 9cm on roll film, simple lens and shutter, delivered with a bakelite lens/shutter cover just like the Photax by MIOM.

Elop Kamerawerk Flansburg
Germany

Elca: R4* E

1947. Small 35mm camera for 50 exposures, 24 x 24 mm. Took standard cassette, but had no rewind knob. Lens is f4.5 Elocar, but aperture control has only f9 and f6.3 settings. Fixed single speed shutter

Elca II: R4* D

1949. Better specified update of first model with Vario or Prontor-S shutter, speeded 1/25-1/200 or 1-1/300s respectively. Choice of 35mm f4.5 or 40mm f2.5 lenses.

c1950; 35mm camera; 50 exp 24 x 24mm; 3.5cm f4.5 Elocn lens; Prontor shutter;

E. Enjalbert
Paris, France

L'Alpiniste: R5* G−

c1886. Aplanatic lens; guillotine shutter. Magazine held 9 x 12cm plates which were changed manually through a leather pouch.

Photo Revolver (de Poche):   R5* J+

c1883, revolver-type detective camera; achromatised periscopic 70mm f10 lens; between the lens rotary sector shutter. 10 exp, 2 x 2cm on dry plates. Rotation of barrel (magazine) simultaneously changed the plate and cocked the shutter. The trigger acted as the shutter release.

Le Tourist d'Enjalbert: R5* F+

Steinheil lens with waterhouse stops; 8 exp on 13 x 18cm plates. c1880.

Erac Selling Co
London, England

Erac: R4* F+

c1931, pistol-type detective camera; fixed focus meniscus lens; 18 x 18mm exp on 20mm roll film. Film advance coupled to trigger and shutter. Invented by H. Covill and H. Steward.

Erica S.R.L.
Argentina

Atlas: R4* B+
c1950, metal box camera for 6 x 9cm frames on roll film, simple lens and shutter.

Heinrich Ernemann Werke A.G.
Dresden, Germany

Bob 0:   R2* B
c1924. Ernemann Double Erid 5" f8 lens; $4^1/_4$" x $3^1/_4$" exp on roll film.

Bob I: R2* B
c1924. Ernemann Ernastigmat $5^1/_4$" f 6.8* lens; Cronos shutter; $4^1/_4$" x $3^1/_4$" exp on roll film.

Bob II: R2* B
c1924. Ernemann Ernastigmat $5^1/_4$" f6.8* lens; Cronos shutter; $4^1/_4$" x $3^1/_4$" exp on roll film.

Bob III: R2* B+
Ernemann Ernastigmat $4^1/_8$" f6.8* lens; Cronos shutter; $3^1/_4$" x $2^1/_4$" exp on roll film. c1924.

Bob IV: R2* C
c1924. Ernemann Ernastigmat $4^1/_8$" f6.8* lens; Cronos shutter; $3^1/_4$" x $2^1/_4$" exp on roll film.

Bob V: R2* C
c1910-1913. Ernemann Ernastigmat 3" f6.8* lens; Cronos shutter; $2^1/_2$" x $1^5/_8$" exp on roll film.

Bob X: R4* F–
c1922, roll film stereo camera; Ernon 65mm f6.8 lenses; 45 x 107mm exp on roll film.

Bob XV: R4* F

c1924, roll film stereo camera; Ernemann Doppel-Anastigmat (Ernon) 65mm f6.8 lenses; interleaf shutter 1-1/1900s, optical vf, reflecting waist level vf. 45 x 107mm exp on roll film. c1924.

Bobette I: R3* D
c1923-1925. Ernoplast 50mm f4.5 lens; Automatic central shutter 1/25-1/100s; 22 x 33cm exp on special 40mm wide roll film.

Ermanox F2:   R5* I

1924. One of the first available light cameras. Vest pocket plate size with an enormous f2 lens that dominated the all metal body. Focusing down to 5ft, direct vision viewfinder, focal plane shutter speeded 1/20-1/1000 second.

Ermanox f1.8: R4* G+
c1926. 4.5 x 6cm miniature plate camera; Ernostar 85mm f1.8 lens; CFPS 1/20-1/1000s.

Ermanox (6.5 x 9cm): R4* G+
c1925, 6.5 x 9cm plate camera; Ernostar 125mm f1.8 lens; CFPS 1/20-1/1000s.

Erni: R3* E

c1920. Achromatic f12.5 lens; 2⁵/₁₆" x 1³/₅" exp on plates.

Ernoflex: R3* G

c1920. 4.5 x 6cm SLR camera; Ernon 75mm f3.5 lens; CFPS 1/20-1/1000s.

Ernoflex, Model II with Triple Extension: R4* F

c1925. 3¹/₄" x 4" folding SLR camera; Ernemann Ernon 7¹/₈" f3.5 lens; CFPS to

1/1000s. Probably the first SLR to couple the revolving back to movable masks in the vf area.

Ernemann Folding Reflex: **R4* F**
1925. Smaller version of the Ernemann reflex models, made for $3^1/_2$" x $2^1/_2$" pictures. Ernemann f3 lens of $5^1/_4$" focal length.

Ernoflex Miniature: **R3* G**
1925. Vest pocket size plate camera with focal plane shutter and f2.7 Ernostar lens. Folding design that uses metal struts for rigidity.

Film K Box Camera: **R3* C+**

c1914-1927; taking 4 x 6.5cm, 6 x 6cm, 5 x 7.5cm, 6 x 9cm, 6.5 x 11cm exp on roll film; lens f12.5; shutter 'T'& 'I'.

Globus Field View Camera: **R4* F–**

c1900, 13" x 18" view camera; Any number of brass lenses can be found mounted on this camera; FPS; double extension bellows; polished wood with brass fittings; black cloth-covered holders. Brass importer's label: Allison & Hadaway Corp., N.Y.

Stereo Ernoflex: **R5* H–**

c1925, 45 x 107mm stereo camera; Ernostar 75mm f4.5 lenses; CFPS 1/25-1/1200s.

Heag I: **R2* B+**
c1924. Ernemann Erid $3^{15}/_{16}$" f8 lens; $3^1/_2$" x $2^1/_2$" exp on plates.

Heag II: **R2* B+**
c1924. Ernemann Ernoplast $5^1/_4$" f4.5* lens; Cronos shutter; $4^1/_4$" x $3^1/_4$" exp on plates.

Heag III: **R2* B+**
c1924. Ernemann Erid $4^1/_8$" f8 lens; Cronos shutter $3^1/_2$" x $2^1/_2$" exp on plates.

Heag IV: R2* B+
c1924. Ernemann Ernastigmat 5¼" f6.8 lens; Cronos shutter; 4¼" x 3¼" exp on plates.

Heag V: R2* F–
(EW124): c1924. Zeiss Tessar 5¼" f6.3* lens; Cronos shutter; 4¼" x 3¼" exp on plates.

Heag VII: R2* B+
c1924. Zeiss Tessar ¼" f6.3* lens; Cronos shutter; 4¼" x 3¼" exp on plates.

Heag XI: R2* C–
c1924. Zeiss Tessar 7⅛" f6.3* lens; Cronos shutter; 6½" x 4¾" exposures on plates.

Tropical Heag XI: R4* G+

c1920. 9 x 12cm tropical plate camera; Tessar 13.5cm f6.3 lens; Compur 1-1/250s. Mahogany finish, brown bellows and brass fittings. 9 x 12cm exp on plates.

Heag XII: R3* C
c1911. 10 x 15cm camera; Ernon 150mm f6.8 lens; Ernemann central shutter.

Heag XII: R4* E+
c1907, model 3; 9 x 14cm stereo camera; Ernemann Double Anastigmat 15cm lens; shutter 1-1/300s.

Heag XI: R4* E
c1914. 45 x 107mm folding stereo camera; Ernemann Aplanat 65mm f6.8 lens; between lens shutter to 1/300s.

Heag XV: R4* C+

c1913-14. Folding camera; 4.5 X 6cm size; 80mm f6.8 Detective Aplomat lens; dial-set shutter; 1s, ½, ⅕, 1/25, 1/50, 1/100s; Two fixed brilliant Vfr on baseboard. Stereo version, quadruple prices.

Klapp:　　　　　　　　R3*　E–

c1920. Folding press camera (strut type); CFPS; various lenses from Bush Aplanat to Tessars and f2.7 Ernostar. Early models (illustrated) had single fold bellows; open viewfinder; later models had conventional bellows; protected viewfinder; Made in 6.5 x 9cm, 9 x 12cm, 10 x 15cm, 13 x 18cm.

Klapp Stereo:　　　　　R4*　G
c1911. Tessar 55mm f4.5 lenses; FPS; changing mechanism for 12 plates.

Tropical Klapp:　　　　　R4*　G+

c1914. 10 x 15cm plate camera; Tessar 165cm f4.5 lens; CFPS. Teak construction with brown leather bellows and brass fittings.

Miniature Klapp:　　　　R4*　F+

c1914-1925. 4.5 x 6cm folding camera; Anastigmat 75mm f4.5 lens; FPS to 1/1000s. 4.5 x 6cm exp on plates.

Liliput:　　　　　　　　R4*　F

c1913. Simple folding camera with achromatic lens, the least expensive camera made by Ernemann. 4.5 x 6cm images on glass plates.

Stereo Liliput:　　　　　R4*　F
c1914. Simple stereo camera, with achromatic lens which made 45x107mm stereo pairs on single glass plates.

Stereo Liliput, c1914.

Simplex: **R2* C+**
c1924. Double Erid 5 1/2" f11 lens; 3 1/2"
x 2 1/2" exp on plates.

Stereo-Simplex: **R3* D**
c1924. Ernemann Erid 2$^{3}/_{8}$" f8 lenses; 45
x 107mm exp on plates.

Rolf I: **R2* B+**
Ernemann Ernastigmat 3" f6.8* lens;
Cronos shutter to 1/100s; 2 1/2" x 1$^{5}/_{8}$" 8
exp on roll film. c1924.

Unette: **R4* D**
c1924, leather covered wooden bodied
box camera for 22 x 33mm exp on
special 40mm roll film, meniscus lens;
guillotine shutter.

Edward Eves Ltd
Leamingtom Spa, England

Edward Eves One Shot Color Camera:
    R4* G
1949. Beam-splitting colour camera
made for 5" x 4" plates in standard
Speed Graphic or MPP holders. Pellicle
reflectors split the image through tri-

colour set of filters mounted in glass.
Body of Elektron casting. Lens panel
with swing and tilt. 10$^{1}/_{2}$" f6 Taylor
Taylor & Hobson Aviar lens as standard,
10" f8 Aldis lens offered as a cheaper
alternative. Rack and pinion focusing.
Took the Kodak P 1200 plate.

Edward Eves Color Camera: **R4* G**
1951. Similar to the One Shot Color
Camera, but made for 3$^{1}/_{2}$" x 2$^{1}/_{2}$"
negative size. 13.5cm f4.8 Wray Lustrar
lens in Epsilon shutter.

Expo Camera Co
New York, New York, USA

Expo: **R3* E+**

*Expo (also manufactured in England
using the name Ticka).*

(1905-1939) Watch style detective
camera. Meniscus lens; 16 x 22mm
images on roll film in daylight loading
cassette. The Expo was also
manufactured in England using the
name Ticka.

Expo Police Camera: **R4* F**
c1911. Miniature detective camera;
meniscus f16 lens, adjustable
diaphragm; CFPS; 12 exp, 12 x 26mm
on roll film in special cassette.

F

Fabrik Fotografsches Apparats
Lübeck, Germany

Fotal: R4* A

c1950-54. Unusual cylindrical shape body with fixed focus 20mm f2.8 Optar lens. Prontor shutter. Made for 9.5mm size and 16mm rollfilm. Made in green, black, blue and reptile skin body covering.

FAP. Fabrique d'Appareils Photographique
Suresnes, France

Norca "A":   R3* E–

c1938, Bakelite 35mm VFR camera, with leather covering, 50mm/f3.5 Saphir or Flor lens in spring loaded collapsible tube, Gitzo btl shutter, speeds 1/25-1/300s, very like the Argus "A" camera.

Norca "B":   R3* C+

c1946, Bakelite bodied 35mm VFR camera, 50mm/f3.5 Saphir or Flor lens in collapsible tube, not spring loaded as the Norca "A", "Rapid-Synchro" copy of Compur Rapid shutter or simpler Norca shutter, speeds 1/25-1/300s. The story goes that the director of FAB was held in a German prisoner of war camp for 5 long years. Upon his release, he quickly picked up where he left off back in 1939. As a result, the Norca "B" was one of the first French cameras on the market in quantity after WWII.

Norca "Cmt":   R3* C+

c1948. Metal bodied 35mm VFR camera, keeping the same design as the Norca "A" and "B" cameras, black leather covering, top mounted accessory shoe, 50mm/f3.5 FAP Anistigmat lens in Rapid-Synchro Shutter, speeds 1-1/500s. Some dark brown cameras were made (worth 50% more).

Le Rower: R3* B+

c1948. Black bakelite VFR camera for 3 x 4cm format on special Gevaert film. Very like the Univex model A camera.

Norca Pin Up: R4* D
                                             R2* D–

based on the bakelite bodied Rower camera, 24 x 36mm format on 35mm film in special cassettes, 50mm/f3.5 FAP Anistigmat lens in Atos shutter, 1/10-1/300s, Optical VFR. Announced as the Norca PM (for petite module) then Norca Atomic, the name Pin Up was finally chosen. Only a few hundred made.

Gilles Faller
Paris, France

Chapeau Photographique: R5* J

c1884, hat-type detective camera; aplanatic lens covered by button at top of hat; 9 x 12cm plates loaded in double frame. Tripod folds into cane; camera could also be mounted in a hat provided by the buyer. Original price was 90 francs.

Gilfa (7 x 9cm):   R4* D+

c1920. Anastigmat 105mm f4.5 Virlot lens; Gitzo central shutter. Mahogany finish.

J. Fallowfield Ltd
London, England

Fallowfield Facile: R4* F+

c1890, box-type detective camera; 12 exposures, $3\frac{1}{4}$" x $4\frac{1}{4}$" on plates, Miall's patent.

Fallowfield Hand Camera: R4* F–
c1892, valise-type detective camera; similar to Hand Camera – a small valise covered in Moroccan crocodile skin.

Miall Hand Camera: R4* H+
c1891, valise-type detective camera; 8 x 10cm exp on plates (daylight loading). Size: 15 x 18 x 25cm; weight 2.3kg.

Fauvel
Paris, France

Fauvel: R4* E+
c1889, 8 x 16cm stereo camera; rising front.

Fauvel: R3* F–
c1912, 45 x 107mm stereo camera; Rapid Rectilinear lens; iris diaphragm; FPS.

Fauvel Post Card: R4* F–
c1899, 9 x 14cm stereo camera; cpfs; covered with Moroccan leather.

FED Machine Works
Kharkov, Ukraine (formerly USSR)

FED: R2* D+

Early FED and fake Leica.

1934-55. Cfps, 1/20 – 1/500s, no slow speeds, no synch, CRF. Inter-changeable Leica-type screw mount lens. The original FED camera was a copy of the Leica II camera. The history of the factory is quite interesting. About 700,000 FED cameras were made with no technical changes. At least six different engraving styles are known to exist. A table showing serial number information is located in the ID section, and will help you in establishing the year of manufacture of a FED camera. Early cameras, first 1000=G, serial numbered 31-4000 bring F, numbers 4000-20,000, E. Numbers above 10,000 are quite common.

FED-2 (First version):   R2* D+

1955-57. Cfps, 1/20 to 1/500s, no slow speeds, no synch, CRF. Interchangeable Leica-type screw mount lens. Not a true Leica copy, the first version FED-2 uses a combined rangefinder/ viewfinder window, removable back, and long base rangefinder. It kept, however the collapsible FED f3.5/50mm lens of its predecessor. US prices 50% higher.

FED-2 (Second version):   R2* D

1957-64. Like the first version FED-2, except with flash synch and self timer. Cfps, 1/20 to 1/500s, no slow speeds, no synch, CRF. Interchangeable Leica-type screw mount lens. Rigid FED/Industar 26M f2.8/52mm lens. Like the first version FED-2, except with flash synch and self timer. US prices 50% higher. (Red Blue and Green covered versions have been found, but they seem to have been recovered outside the factory, probably in Poland.)

FED-2L: R2* D

1964-70s. Cfps, 1/20 to 1/500s, no slow speeds, synch, CRF. Interchangeable Leica-type screw mount lens, Like the second version FED-2, but now with an improved f2.8, 52mm Industar-61 lens, made with rare earth glass containing Lanthanum, and self timer. US prices 50% higher.

FED-3 (First version):   R3* D

1962-64. Cfps, 1 to 1/500s, slow speeds, synch, CRF. Interchangeable Leica-type screw mount lens, self timer and f2.8/52mm Industar lens. Slow speeds, different diopter adjustment system, and a changed top plate came with this model. Very few were made before the introduction of the improved second version, though prices for each are the same. US prices 50% higher.

FED-3 (Second version):   R2* D

1964-80s. Cfps, 1 to 1/500s, slow speeds, synch, CRF. Interchangeable Leica-type screw mount lens, self timer. Using the f2.8, 52mm Industar-61 lens, and having a single-level top plate, the second version FED-3 also incorporated a rapid advance lever instead of the round knob used on all earlier FED cameras. Also sold as the Revue-3, this camera was made in quite large quantities. The "Olympic" model adds about 30% to the value of the camera. US prices 50% higher.

FED-4:   R2* D

c1964. Cfps, 1 to 1/500s, slow speeds, synch, CRF. Interchangeable Leica-type screw mount lens, self timer. Like the FED-3, with Industar-61 f2.8, 52mm lens, but with the addition of a built-in light meter. Also sold as the Revue-4. More common in Europe. US prices 50% higher.

FED-5A: R2* D

after 1978. Cfps, 1 to 1/500s, slow speeds, synch, CRF. Interchangeable Leica-type screw mount lens, self timer. An improved version of the FED-4, with the same features. US prices about 50% higher.

FED-5B: R2* D

after 1978. Cfps, 1 to 1/500s, slow speeds, synch, CRF. Interchangeable Leica-type screw mount lens, self timer. The same as the FED-5A, but without the built-in light meter. Not made for the export market. "Olympic" model adds 30% to the price. US prices about 50% higher.

FED-5C: R2* D

after 1978. Cfps, 1 to 1/500s, slow speeds, synch, CRF. Interchangeable Leica-type screw mount lens, self timer. The same as the FED-5A with the addition of a bright line viewfinder frame. US prices about 50% higher.

Zarya: R3* D

1958-59. Cfps, 1/20 to 1/500s, no slow speeds, synch. Interchangeable Leica-type screw mount lens. f3.5/52mm rigid mount Industar lens. Not a true Leica copy, and the only Russian Leica-type camera without a rangefinder. Very few were made, and since its original price was not much lower than the FED-2, it was not very successful on the market place. The current price does not reflect its rarity.

FED V (B): R5* NSR

1938. The same camera as other early FEDs, but with the addition of slow speeds and 1/1000s. It is said only 40 cameras were made.

FED S(C): R4* E+

1938. The same as other early FEDs, except with the addition of 1/1000s.

Counterfeit Leica: R3* F–

Some FED cameras are found with top plates engraved with Leitz markings. These cameras show very poor quality plating, and generally inferior work-manship when compared to the Leica's which they were attempting to mimic. On many cameras the top plate remains un-drilled where the accessory shoe would normally be placed.

FED Stereo: R3* F

c1989, 35mm stereo camera with Industar-81 f2.8.38mm lenses, simple shutter 1/30-1/650s, automatic exposure control. Though a new product, this camera has become an "instant" collectable.

Feinwerktechnik GmbH
Lahr, Germany

MEC 16: R2* C

c1956, subminiature camera, f2.8/20mm lens, shutter 1/25-1/1000s. 24 exp, 10 x 14mm on 16mm film, in brown, black or gold. (complete presentation case adds 200%).

MEC 16SB: R2* D–

c1957. Coupled TTL light meter and Heligon f2/22mm lens, shutter 1/30-1/1000s. "SB" stands for Simultan-Belichtungsmesser. This was the first non-SLR to offer TTL metering. (complete presentation case adds 200%).

Ferannia
Milan, Italy

Eura 66: R2* B+

1959. 12 exp on 120. Black plastic body with metal lens panel and chrome trim. Coated meniscus f8 lens. Everset shutter at 1/50s. Flash synch.

Astor: R2* B+

1953. 12 exp on 120. Alloy die cast. Double telescopic metal tube links lens to body. 75mm f4.5 lens made by Officine Galileo. Prontor-SV shutter 1-1/300s + B. X & M synch. Viewfinder indicator appears after exposure to act as film wind reminder.

Elioflex: R2 B+

1951. TLR for 12 exp on 120. Apertures f8-f22. Speeds 1/25-1/200s + B. Finished in black imitation leather and chrome.

Joseph Fetter

Photo Eclair: R5* H

c1886, concealed vest detective camera; rectilinear 40mm f8 lens; rotary sector shutter; 5 exp on 4 x 4cm plates. Plate changed by rotating camera back. Shutter differentiates this from the Gray and Stirn models. Later model had lens at base of camera, to allow addition of a 45 degree angle viewfinder.

FEX
Lyon, France

Compa Fex: **R5* E**
c1942; simple black wooden box camera
with frame finder made during the
German occupation of France. Very few
have survived.

Fex: c1944;   **R4* B+**
simple bakelite camera for 4.5 x 6cm
pictures on roll film. Replaced by Super
Fex in 1945. Fexar lens, single speed
shutter. The company made a large
number of simple plastic cameras
frequently found in French flee markets.
Curiously a nearly identical camera was
made in Czechoslovakia for several years
after the war. Both are clearly identified
as Made in France or Made in
Czechoslovakia.

Super-Fex: **R2* B–**
Simple black bakelite camera for 6 x 4.5
format on roll film. Metal wind knob.
Made in large quantities.

Ultra-Fex: **R1* A**

Simple black bakelite camera for 6 x 9
format on roll film. Made in many, many
versions, among which are the Sport-
Fex, the Uni-Fex, and the Delta, all
having the lens in a rectangular
collapsible mount. One of the most
commonly found French cameras.

Elite: **R2* B–**
One of the Ultra-Fex versions, but with
built-in extinction meter, and through
the use of a metal mask both 6 x 9cm
and 6 x 6cm formats were possible.
Often found with Colour-Fexar lens in
Atos shutter.

Finetta Werk, P. Saraber
Goslar, Germany

Finette: **R3* B+**
c1947, 35mm VFR camera, Fenar
f6.3/43mm lens, simple shutter.

Finetta: **R2* B+**
c1950, 35mm VFR camera, Finetar
f2.8/45mm lens, interchangeable
mount, FPS 1/25-1/1000s.

Finetta Super: **R2* B+**
c1951, 35mm VFR camera, interchangeable Finetar f2.8/45mm lens,
simple shutter, 1/25-1/100s, flat top
plate.

Finetta 88:   **R2* C–**
c1954, with 1/25-1/200s shutter.

Finetta 99:   **R3* E–**
c1955, 35mm VFR camera, Finetar
f2.8/45mm or Staeble-Finon f2.8/45mm
lens, interchangeable mount; FPS
1-1/1000s. Built-in spring motor drive –
20 exp in 10 seconds possible when
fully wound; Earlier version had no
slow speeds.

Finetta

Finetta 99, c1955.

Accessory lenses for Finetta cameras

Finettare f4.5/35mm wide angle lens: **C**
Finettare f4.5/70mm telephoto lens: **C**
Finettare f6.3/105mm telephoto lens: **C**

Dr. Foi
Geneva, Switzerland

Dr. Foi's Photographic Rifle: **R5* J**
c1984, rifle-type detective camera; Steinheil Antiplanet lens; Thury & Amey shutter. 11 plates, 9 x 10cm in magazine.

Foster Instruments Pty Ltd
Sydney, Australia

Swiftshot: **R2* B–**

c1951, metal box camera for 6 x 9 frames on 120 or 620 roll film, simple lens and shutter, built-in yellow filter, marked either "Model A" or "made in Australia" on the camera front, in red, black, blue, beige, grey, green or crocodile!

Foth & Co
Berlin, Germany (also see Gallus)

Foth Derby I: **R2* B+**

c1930, 127 roll film folding camera; Foth Anastigmat 50mm f3.5 lens; CFPS 1/25-1/500s; The first model made 1" x 1½" negatives; later 16 exp, 1¼" x 1¼" on 127 roll film.

Foth Derby II: **R2* D–**

c1934, 127 roll film folding camera; Foth Anastigmat 50mm f3.5 lens; CFPS 1/25-1/500 s, CRF. 16 exp, 1¼" x 1½" on 127 roll film.

Foth-Flex: R3* D

c1935, 2¼" x 2¼" TLR; Foth Anastigmat 75mm f3.5 lens; CFPS 1-1/500s; 12 exposures, 2¼" x 2¼" on 120 roll film. The Foth-Flex was the only medium format twin-lens reflex fitted with a focal plane shutter.

Foth Folding Camera: R4* D

c1930, 120 roll film folding camera; Foth Doppel Anastigmat 105mm f4.5 lens; Compound 1/25-1/100s. Some covered in alligator skin valued 50% higher.

Fotobras S.A. Ind. & Com.
Curtiba-Parana, Brazil

Brasilmatic Camera: R3* B

c1950, metal box camera for 6 x 9cm frames on roll film, simple lens and shutter.

Foto-Fex Kamerawerk
Fritz Kraftanski Berlin, Germany

Mini-Fex: R4* F

c1930, subminiature VFR camera for 13mm x 18mm frames on 16mm perforated film, various lens and shutters offered including Astrar f2.7 or "ultra fast" Pan-Tachar f1.8/25mm lens, Compur or Pronto shutter; Earliest cheapest model.

Mini-Fex MG: R4* G

c1939, sub-miniature VFR camera for 13mm x 18mm frames on 16mm perforated film, Trioplan f3.5 or "ultra fast" Pan-Tachar f1.8/25mm lens, Pronto shutter. The "MG" in the name refers to the German "Maschinen Gewahr", meaning machine gun. One sliding movement of a button located on the camera side armed the shutter, released the shutter, and transported the film.

Schoolboy-Box: R3* A

c1929, metal box camera for 4cm x 6cm plates, meniscus lens, two speed shutter.

FRAMA – Franz Matthias
Dresden, Germany

This photo retailer sold cameras under its house brand names. They were actually made by companies like Balda and Agfa.

Framax: R2* A

c1930, metal folding camera for 6 x 9cm frames on roll film, f4.5 or 6.3 lens, Prontor shutter among others.

Framafix: R2* A

c1930, metal folding camera for 6 x 9cm or 6 x 4.5 on roll film, Xenar f4.5/105mm lens among others.

Knipsy: R2* A

c1930, metal folding camera for 6 x 9cm frames on roll film, front lens focusing Trioplan f6.3 or f4.5/105mm lens, Vario or other shutter.

Plana: R3* B+

c1930, folding bed camera for 6 x 9cm plates or film packs, Xenar f4.5/105mm lens among others, Vario, Prontor or Compur shutter, wire frame finder.

Rolly: R2* A

c1930, metal folding camera for 6 x 9cm on roll film, Anastigmat f4.5/105mm lens among others, Vario or Pronto shutter, wire frame finder.

Francais
Paris, France

Le Cosmopolite: R4* E+

c1887. 2 Francais Rectilinear lenses (bayonet mounts) with waterhouse stops; behind the lens shutter. 9 x 12cm exp on plates.

Franka Camera Werke
Bayreuth, Germany

Bubi: R3* C+

c1915, strut folding camera for 6 x 4.5cm plates or film packs, simple shutter and lens, wire frame finder.

Bubi Velo: R3* D

c1915, strut folding camera for 6 x 4.5cm plates of film packs, Velonar f6.8/75mm lens, Compound shutter, wire frame finder.

Bubi 3 x 4: R2* A

c1930, metal folding camera for 3 x 4cm frames on 127 film, Victar f4.5/75mm lens among others, Prontor shutter.

Vest Pocket Model 50:   **R3* D**
c1921, strut folding camera for 6 x 4.5cm plates or filmpacks, with waist level finder and dialset Compur.

Bonafix: **R2* A**
c1930-1955, metal folding camera for 6 x 9cm or 6 x 4.5cm frames on roll film, f6.3/105mm lens, Vario shutter, most cameras after 1950 have chrome top plate, and allow 6 x 6cm instead of the 6 x 4.5cm format.

Idafix: **R3* A**
c1930, metal folding camera for 6.5 x 11cm frames on 130 roll film, Velostigmat f6.3/135mm lens, Pronto shutter.

Rolfix: **R2* A**
c1936-56, metal folding camera for 6 x 9cm or 6 x 6cm on 120 roll film, Trioplan f4.5/105mm lens among others, Compur shutter, several different variations.

Solida: **R2* B**
c1934-56, metal folding camera for 6 x 4.5cm frames on roll film, optical VFR, Victar f2.9/70mm lens among others, Compur shutter, several different variations.

Solida I: **R2* B–**
c1955, folding camera for 6 x 6cm or 4 x 4cm frames on 120 roll film, f4.5/75mm lens among others, Vario shutter.

Solida II: **R3* B+**
c1955, folding camera for 6 x 6cm or 4 x 4cm frames on 120 roll film, duel VFR

for 4 x 4 and 4 x 6, Ennagon f4.5/75mm lens among others, Pronto or Prontor shutter, variations made with lever advance and automatic frame counting.

Solida IIL: **R3* E–**
c1955, with built-in uncoupled EV light meter, 6 x 6cm only.

Solida III: **R2* B**
c1955, with faster Radionar f2.9/80mm lens, 6 x 6cm only.

Solida IIIL: **R3* C**
c1955. Now with uncoupled rangefinder.

Solida Junior: **R2* A**
1953. Folding rollfilm camera. 12 exp on 120. 75mm f3.5 Frankar. Vario shutter, synch for bulbs. Retractable spool chamber for easy loading.

Solida Record B: **R2* A**
c1960. Available with or without lever advance or automatic frame counting. f8/80mm lens, simple shutter.

Solida Record T: **R2* A**
c1963, all metal VFR camera for 6 x 6cm or 4 x 4cm on 120 roll film, f8/70mm lens with front lens focusing, simple shutter, available with lever advance and automatic frame counting for 6 x 6cm frames only.

Franka: **R3* B+**
c1950, 35mm VFR camera, Radonar f2.9/50mm lens, Compur shutter, lever wind, exposure table on top plate.

Frankanette: **R2* A**
c1958, 35mm VFR camera, Isconar f2.8/45mm lens among others, Pronto shutter.

Frankanette L: **R2* A**
c1958, 35mm VFR, Ennagon f2.8/45mm lens among others, Pronto shutter, built-in meter.

Super Frankanette: **R B**
c1958, 35mm VFR camera, Xenar f2.8/45mm lens among others, Prontor-SVS shutter.

Super Frankanette L: **R2* B+**
c1958, 35mm VFR camera with built-in light meter, Westanar f2.8/45mm lens among others, Prontor shutter, lever wind.

Super Frankanette E: **R2* B+**
c1958, 35mm RFR camera, Xenar f2.8/45mm lens, Printor-SVS shutter, CRF.

Super Frankanette EL: **R2* C–**
c1958, 35mm VFR with built-in meter and CRF, Xenar f2.8/45mm I Prontor-SVS shutter.

Super Frankanette SLK: **R2* B**
c1958, 35mm VFR camera with built-in coupled light meter, Xenar f2.8/45mm lens, Prontor-SLK shutter.

Francolour: **R2* A**
c1960, 35mm VFR camera with Frankar f2.8/45mm lens, Pronto or Vario shutter, lever wind.

G. Frank & Pearsall
Brooklyn, New York, USA

The Compact Camera: **R5* G+**
c1883, $6^{1}/_{2}$" x $8^{1}/_{2}$" view camera; $6^{1}/_{2}$" x $8^{1}/_{2}$" exp on dry plates.

Franke & Heidecke
Braunschweig, Germany

Heidoscop: **R3* F–**

c1921. 45 x 107mm reflex stereo camera; Zeiss Tessar 55mm f4.5 lens; Compound 1-1/300s; 45 x 107mm exp on plates.

Heidoscop: **R3* F–**
c1921. 6 x 13cm plate and cut-film reflex stereo camera; Zeiss Tessar 75mm f4.5 lenses; Compound shutter 1-1/300s; 6 x 13cm exp on plates or cut-film.

Rolleidoscop: **R3* G+**
c1925. 45 x 107mm reflex stereo camera; Zeiss Tessar 75mm f4.5 lenses; Compur 1-1/300s; 45 x 107mm exp on roll film.

Rollei 35: R2* E+
R3* F–

Rolleidoscop, c1925.

c1970, 35mm camera; Tessar 40mm f3.5 coated lens; shutter ½-1/500s. Black German model add 75% c1970.

Rolleidoscop: R3* G+

c1926. 6 x 13cm reflex stereo camera; Zeiss Tessar 75mm f4.5 lenses; Compur 1-1/300s; 6 x 13cm exp on roll film.

Rollei 35: R4* F+

Rollei 16S: R3* Black: D–
Red/green: D+

With Schneider lens, (gold-plated model): c1970, 35mm camera; Carl Zeiss Tessar 40mm f3.5 coated lens; shutter ½-1/500s.

1966, subminiature camera; Tessar 25mm f2.8 lens; 12 x 17mm exp on 16mm film.

Rollei A110: R3* C+

35B: R1* D+

1974. 110 film. Metal bodied camera with open-shut film wind. 23mm f2.8 Tessar. Automatic programmed exposure. Usually found in black. Rarer in brushed chrome and gold.

c1979-1978, 35mm camera;40mm Triotar F3.5 lens;Prontor shutter 1/30-

1/500s. B; uncoupled Selenium meter; ident. "B35" or "35B" on camera face.

35C: R4* (Rare) F–
c1969-1971. 35mm camera; Triotar f3.5/40mm lens; Prontor 1/30-1/500s. B shutter; no light meter.

35S: R2* F–
c1947-1980. 35mm camera; 40mm f2.8 Rollei HFT Sonnar lens; Rollei Compur $\frac{1}{2}$-1/500s. B. shutter; Serial No. under take up spool;Inscribed "Rollei 35S" on camera face.

35S Silver: R4* G
c1978. 35mm camera;40mm f2.8 Rolli Sonnar lens; Rollei Compur $\frac{1}{2}$-1/500s. B. Ident. "Rollei 35 S" followed by a wreath; Silver plate and Silver coloured leather.

35S Gold: R4* G
c1974-1976. 35mm camera; 40mm f2.8 Rollei Sonnar lens; Rollei Compur $\frac{1}{2}$-1/500s. B. shutter; Serial No. on back plate, also ident's Gold content; covered in Lizard or Alligator skin.

35T: R2* E+

c1974-1980. 35mm camera; 40mm f3.5 Tessar lens; Rollei Compur $\frac{1}{2}$-1/500s. B. shutter; "Rollei 35 T" on face; Serial No's under take up spool. Features other than the name, same as Rollei 35.

35 LED: R1* D
c1978-1982. 35mm camera; 40mm f3.5 Rolli Triotar lens; Rollei prontar 1/30-1/500s. shutter; Silicon photo diode cell light meter; coupled exp indicated in finder with red and green LED's; Hot shoe; "Rollei 35 LED" on face.

35SE: R2* F–

c1980-1982. 35mm camera; 40mm f2.8 Rolli HFT Sonnar lens; Rollei Compur $\frac{1}{2}$-1/500s. B. Shutter; Serial no's under feed spool; "35 SE" on face.

35TE: R2* E+

c1980-1982. 35mm camera;40mm f3.5 Tessar lens; Compur $\frac{1}{2}$-1/500s. B. Shutter; Serial No's under feed spool; Cds meter with LED indicators coupled to aperture, shutter, film speed; Hot shoe; "35 TE" on camera face.

35 Platin: R4* G+
Special Edition 1986; (FH150) 35mm Camera; 40mm F2.8 Rollei Sonnar lens.

35 Classic: R1* F+

c1990. 35mm camera; 40mm F2.8 Zeiss Sonnar HFT lens; Coupled Cds exp meter.

NOTE: Several Rollie 35mm Cameras have Tan Leather covering, these would be classed as R4 rarity.*

Rolleicord I: R3* E–

c1933-1935. Zeiss Triotar 75mm f4.5 lens; Compur shutter 1-1/300s. Original camera body, nickel plated art-deco design. Later version (after 1934) was covered with leather. Difficult to find in excellent condition.

Rolleicord IA: R3* C+

c1935-1941. Zeiss Triotar 75mm f4.5 or f3.8 lens; Compur shutter 1-1/300s.

Rolleicord II: R3* C+

1950. Zeiss Triotar 75mm f3.5 lens – equipped with factory coated 75mm f3.5 Triotar or Xenar lens after 1950. Compur shutter 1-1/300s (1938-1945); Compur-Rapid shutter 1-1/500s (1945-1951) – flash synch (1950-1951). Snr 612,000-1,135,999.

Rolleicord IIA: R3* C

1937. Twin lens reflex similar to the Rolleicord II, but with bayonet mounts added to taking and viewing lenses.

Rolleicord III: R3* C+

c1950-1953. Zeiss Triotar or Xenar 75mm f3.5 lens; Compur-Rapid shutter 1-1/500s. Snr 1,137,000-1,344,050. c1950-1953.

Rolleicord IV: R3* D–

c1953-1955. Xenar 75mm f3.5 lens; Synchro-Compur shutter 1-1/500s. Snr 1,344,051-1,390,999.

Rolleicord V: **R3* D–**
c1955-1957. Xenar 75mm f3.5 lens;
Synchro-Compur shutter IVS 1-1/500s.
Snr 1,500,000-(?).

Rolleicord Va: **R3* D   Vb= E–**
c1957-1960. Xenar 75mm f3.5 lens;
Synchro-Compur MXV shutter 1-1/500s.
Snr 1,584,000-1,940,999.

Rolleiflex (Original):   **R4* E–**
c1929-1932. Zeiss Tessar 75mm f4.5
lens until 1929; Zeiss Tessar 75mm f3.8
lens after 1929; Compur shutter 1-
1/300s. Snr up to 200,000.

Rolleiflex Standard 1932:   **R4* D**
c1932-1937. Zeiss Tessar 75mm f4.5,
f3.8 or f3.5 lens; Compur shutter 1-
1/300s. Snr 200,000-567,550.

Rolleiflex 1937:   **R3* D–**
c1937-1949. Zeiss Tessar 75mm f3.5
lens until 1945; Zeiss Tessar or Xenar
75mm f3.5 after 1945. Snr 280,000-
1,000,000.

Rolleiflex New Standard 1939: **R3* D–**
c1939-1941. Zeiss Tessar 75mm f3.5
lens; Synchro-Compur shutter 1-1/500s.
Snr 805,000-928,999.

Rolleiflex 1950:   **R2* D**
c1949-1951. Zeiss Tessar 75mm f3.5
(coated lenses marked "T" or Schneider
Xenar 75mm f3.5 (coated lenses marked
with red triangle) lens; Compur shutter
1-1/500s. Snr 1,100,000-1,168,000.

Rolleiflex Automat: **R2 D**
1951. One of the first Rolleiflexes to
reach the UK after WWII. TLR for 12 exp
on 120. Red window replaced by auto
film wind. Made to take Rolleikin 35mm
back and panoramic head. f3.5 Xenar
lens. Synchro-Compur shutter.

Rolleiflex "MX":   **R2* D**

c1951-1954. Zeiss Tessar or Xenar
75mm f3.5 lens; Synchro-Compur
shutter 1-1/500s. Snr 11,000-
1,427,999.

Rolleiflex 2.8A: **R2* E–**
2.8B with Biotar lens   **G+**
c1950-1953. Zeiss Tessar 80mm f2.8
lens; (a few cameras were mfd with
Biometar 80mm f2.8 lens, and are much
sought after, worth 150% or more);
Compur-Rapid shutter 1-1/500s. Snr
1,101,000-(?).

Rolleiflex 2.8C: **R3* E**
c1953-1956. Xenotar 80mm f2.8 lens;
Synchro-Compur shutter 1-1/500s. Snr
1,260,250-1,475,278.

Rolleiflex "MX" (EVS):   **R2* E–**
c1954-1956. Zeiss Tessar or Xenar
75mm f3.5 lens; Synchro-Compur

shutter LVS 1-1/500s. Snr 1,428,000-1,729,999.

Rolleiflex 2.8D: R3* E

c1955-1956. Zeiss Tessar or Xenotar 80mm f2.8 lens; Synchro-Compur EVS shutter 1-1/500s. Snr 1,600,000-1,620,999.

Rolleiflex 2.8E: R3* F

c1962-1965. Zeiss Planar or Xenotar 80mm f2.8 lens; Synchro-Compur MXV shutter 1-1/500s. Snr 1,621,000-1,665,999. c1958-1959. Rolleiflex 2.8E-2; Snr 2,350,000-2,357,999. c1959-1962. Rolleiflex 2.8E-3; Snr 2,360,000-(?).

Rolleiflex 3.5E: R3* F–

c1962-1965. Zeiss Planar or Xenotar 75mm f3.5 lens; Synchro-Compur LVS shutter 1-1/500s. Snr 1,740,000-1,869,000. c1957-1959. Rolleiflex 3.5E-2; Snr 2,480,000-2,482,099. c1960-1962. Rolleiflex 35.E-3; Snr 2,380,000-(?).

Rolleiflex 3.5 F: R3* F

1958. Zeiss Planar 75mm f3.5 coated lens; Synchro-Compur LVS shutter 1-1/500s.

Rolleiflex 2.8F: R4* F+

1960. Zeiss Planar 75mm f2.8 coated lens; Synchro-Compur LVS shutter 1-1/500s.

Rolleiflex T: R3* D+

1959. TLR for 12 exp on 120. Can be adapted to take 16 exp. 4x4cm or 16 exp 4 x 6.5cm. Aperture and speed settings can be linked and set by exposure values. 77mm f3.5 Tessar lens. Synchro-Compur shutter 1-1/500s.

Rolleiflex 4 x 4cm: R3* E–

1931. c1931-1939. Zeiss Tessar 60mm f3.5 or f2.8 lens; Compur shutter 1-1/300s; Compur-Rapid shutter 1-1/500s, after 1935. Snr 200,000-600,000.

Rolleiflex 4 x 4cm Sports (1938): R3* F–

c1938-1941. Zeiss Tessar 60mm f2.8 lens; Compur-Rapid shutter 1-1/500 s. Snr 622,000-733,000.

Rolleimagic: R3* D

1961. The first fully auto TLR. 12 or 16 exp on 120. Photo cell mounted behind plastic window about viewing lens. Meter needle appears between two red

markers when light is sufficient. Manual override of automation for flash or time exposures. 75mm f/3.5 Xenar lens. Prontormat-S shutter. Unpopular when launched due to ugly styling to incorporate auto exposure functions.

Rolleiflex 4 x 4cm (1957): R2* E–
Black F+

c1957. Zeiss Tessar 60mm f2.8 lens; Synchro-Compur shutter 1-1/500s.

SL26:   R3* D+

c1970. SLR Instamatic camera; Tessar 40mm f2.8 lens, interchangeable front element; behind-the-lens shutter $1/2$-1/500s. Instamatic film cartridge.

Tele Rolleiflex: R3* G

1959. Made mostly for portraiture. TLR, based on the Rolleiflex 2.8E, but using 135mm f4 Sonnar taking lens and

Heidosmat viewing lens of same focal length and aperture. Synchro-Compur shutter 1-1/500s. Apertures and shutter exposure value coupled. Removable optical flat in the film gate ensures perfect flatness of film for critical focusing.

Wideangle Rollei: R4* H–

1961. Wideangle lens version of the Rolleiflex. 55mm f4 Distagon lens, focusing down to 24 in. Synchro-Compur shutter 1-1/500s.

Franklin

Franklin Photographic Industries Inc
Chicago, Illinois, USA

Franklin Magazine 8: **R2* B–**
c1942. 8mm movie camera; mfd under Kodak license; Cine Raptar Wollensak 2" f2.5 lens.

French Detective Camera: **R5* G+**
c1895. H. Duplovich 120mm f6.8 lens; 6 x 9cm exp; plates changed by chain mechanism. Mfd in France.

French Dry Plate Camera: **R3* E+**
c1880. 7 x 9cm format rigid wooden camera; insertable disc stops. Mfd in France.

French Sliding Box daguerreotype Camera: **R5* I+**
c1845. Photographe a verres combines, 190mm f6 lens; pivoting plate shutter. Interchangeable front lens elements for various focal lengths; 6.5 x 7.5cm image. Mfd in France.

French Espionage Camera: **R5* F+**

c1940, pre-war subminiature detective camera; mfps 1/20-1/250s; 45 exp. Mfd in France. Invariably found without lens.

French Tailboard Camera: **R3* E+**
c1890s. 13" x 18" tailboard camera; wide angle lens; removable ground glass back; shifting front lens standard

(stereo); brass handle; red bellows. Mfd in France.

Fuji Photo Film Industry
Tokyo, Japan

Fuji Instant Camera – Models F50-S & F10: **R3* B**
c1981. Two instant cameras made in Japan under license from Eastman Kodak using the Kodak Instant system. After a famous lawsuit, Kodak was forced to discontinue making instant products in the U.S. although Fuji reached a separate agreement with Polaroid and continued to market the products in Japan. The F10 is a simple rigid camera with auto exposure – an electronic flash was optional. The F50-S was folding, had a built-in flash and had programmed exposure control. R1 in Japan, R3 elsewhere. The camera was not officially exported.

Fuji Photo Film Ltd
Tokyo, Japan

Fujicaflex: **R3* E**
c1954. Marketed as a premium TLR. Fujinar f2.8 83mm lens. Seikosha-Rapid shutter 1-1/400s. 6 x 6cm images on 120 film. Camera incorporated a number of innovations including a single knob for both film advance and focusing. Taking lens had a special close focusing position (2.3feet), without need of accessory lens.

Fujica GW690 Professional: **R3* NSR**
c1978. Eye-level medium format rf camera. 120/220 rollfilm, producing 6x9cm images. Fujinon f3.5, 90mm interchangeable lens.

242 **THE HOVE INTERNATIONAL BLUE BOOK**

G

Galileo Optical
Milan, Italy

Condor I: **R3* E–**

c1954. 35mm RFR camera; Galileo Eliog 560mm f3.5 lens; Galileo Iscus Rapid shutter 1-1/500s, CRF.

Gami 16:   **R4* F**

c1955, subminiature camera; Esanitar 25mm f1.9 lens; shutter ½-1/1000s; 12 x 17mm exposures on 17mm film in special cassettes; CRF.

Gallus
Corbevoie, France

Derlux: **R2* E**
c1948. Folding camera for 16 exposures on 127. Unusual all-metal highly aluminium polished body. Focal plane shutter from 1/25-1/500 sec, Gallix f3.5 lens. Design based on the pre-war Foth-Derby camera and known first as the Derby-Lux.

No.00 Stereoscopic Camera: **R3* D**
c1922. Stereo camera for beginners. Anastigmat 47mm lenses, time/instantaneous shutter, three apertures.

No.0 Stereoscopic Camera: **R3* D**
c1922. Similar to No.00 with lower quality lenses.

No.100 Stereoscopic Camera: **R4* E**
c1922. Better quality version of No.0, with 70mm lenses from Goerz, Krauss or Zeiss. Plate changing box, holding 6 plates also available.

No.150 Stereoscopic Camera: **R4* F**
c1922. Deluxe version of No.150 with shutter speeded from 2-1/250s. Very unusual viewfinder mounted on top to resemble a second, miniature camera, complete with ground glass screen and focusing hood.

Gamma Precision Machine
Rome, Italy

Gamma-I: **R4* F+**
1947. Cpfs, 1/20-1000s, CRF, special bayonet mount Koristka Victor

f3.5/55mm lens. Internal film cutter, allowed exposed 35mm roll film in special cassettes to be removed from the camera for processing in mid roll. Odd shaped camera body. Quite rare.

Gamma (Special): R5* G+

1948. The same body style as the Gamma-I, but without RFR or VFR.Cpfs, 1/20-1000s, special bayonet mount Koristka Victor f3.5/55mm lens. Internal film cutter allowed exposed 35mm roll film in special cassettes removed from the camera for processing in mid-roll. Odd shaped camera body. Extremely rare.

Gamma-III: R4* F+

1950-51. The same body style as the Gamma-I, but with slow speeds.Cpfs, 1-1000s, interchangeable Leica-type screw mount Koristka Victor f3.5/55mm lens or Beta f3.5/50mm lens. Internal film cutter allowed exposed 35mm roll film in special casettes to be removed from the camera for processing in mid roll. Shares the same odd shaped camera body as the other Gamma cameras, but has a different frame counter than Gamma-II.

Gamma-II: R4* F+

1950. The same body style as the Gamma-I, but with slow speeds. Cpfs, 1-1000s, interchangeable Leica-type

screw mount Koristka Victor f3.5/55mm lens or Beta f3.5/50mm lens. Internal film cutter allowed exposed 35mm roll film in special casettes removed from the camera for processing in mid roll. Quite rare. Even rarer Airforce version with f2.0/50mm Epitamitar lens valued at about 300% higher.

Gamma Works
Budapest, Hungary

Duflex: R5* H-

c1947, 35mm SLR which incorporated a number of advanced features for its time. Framing of different focal length lenses (although none were available), instant return mirror etc. As few as 500 were made and the Duflex is rarely found.

Gandolfi Ltd
Hampshire, England

Louis Gandolfi, later Louis Gandolfi & Sons, was founded in 1885, and is still in production. The earliest Gandolfi cameras were named The Compactum, The Collapsible, and The Special, all dating from 1895. The Compactum was

*made in sizes from half plate to 12"
x10". The Premier and the Simplex
followed and all were predecessors of
the Imperial. which became the
mainstay of the tapered bellows field
camera designs from Gandolfi. These
cameras are rare and no price
indications are available. At times from
1902 Gandolfi offered magazine box
type cameras and a range of tripods,
stands, shutters and lenses. Mostly, sold
over relatively short periods but the
hand and stand cameras remained until
the late thirties.*

**Universal square bellows camera: F to H
(depending on size and condition)**

1899. The first regular production
model made in six sizes: Half-plate, to
18" x 16"; later 5" x 4" and 5" x 7" models
were added. Made from mahogany with
solid brass fittings, this was a tailboard
camera with fixed front and rear
focusing. It had double swing reversible
back, rise and cross front parallel
bellows. Approximately 1,000 of these
cameras were produced.

Imperial camera: R4* G
A tapered bellows camera having
focusing front and rear standards with
swing and tilt movements making it the
predecessor of the present day Precision
camera. The Imperial was made in half-
plate, whole plate, 10" x 8" and 12" x 10"
sizes and continued with minor changes
until World War 2.

**Universal folding hand and stand
camera: R4* G**
This was a de luxe camera covered with
Morocco leather, bearing some
similarities to the Sanderson design.
First introduced about 1907 in $\frac{1}{4}$ plate
and 5" x 4" sizes and in postcard, half-
plate and 7" x 5" by 1910.

Precision tapered bellows camera:
Prices for 4" x 5" to 8" x 10" models
                                       G to H
Older models depending on size
and condition   **F to H**

Introduced in 1945 and continued in
manufacture to the present time, this is
a truly universal camera with a wide
range of movements. Convenient in the
studio and on location, where weight
and bulk are important. Usually
constructed in mahogany or teak,
occasionally rosewood examples are
found. The woodwork is deeply French
polished and the solid heavy gauge brass
fittings are hard lacquered. Black
polished wood and satin chrome plated
examples are occasionally found. Early
models have hinged focusing screens
and use double book form plateholders
in wood and brass to match the camera.

Gandolfi

Since the early 1960s, international standard spring backs have been available. Cameras individually made to such high standards of craftsmanship are expensive, whether old or new, and constitute a sound investment as well as a universal tool.

Prison camera:

Gandolfi produced a number of specialised cameras for Government departments. The prison service used Gandolfi equipment for identification records.

Professional Camera:　　　**R5* G+**
c1930s. Tailboard design, made from mahogany with leather bellows. Rise, fall and cross movements on front, double swing on back. Originally sold with double plate holders, but could be supplied with spring back for Kodak cut film holders.

Wide angle cameras:　　　**G to H-**
Box type wide-angle cameras fitted with the Goerz Hypergon lens. With extreme angles of view, the 75mm lens covering 8" x 10", at small apertures, no focusing was required and no bellows provided. These cameras are much sought after and complete with lens in good condition trade at G to H– depending on size.

Antonio Gatto
Pordenone, Italy

Sonne-IV:　　　**R4* F**
1948. Cfps, 1/20 to 1/1000s, CRF, interchangeable Leica-type screw mount Adlenar f3.5/50mm lens. On the earliest versions a rising sun is engraved next to the rangefinder window. No models I, II, or III seem to have been made. Quite rare.

Sonne-V:　　　**R4* F**
1950. Cfps, 1-1/1000s, flash synch, interchangeable Leica-type screw mount Schneider Xenar f3.5/50mm lens, or f2.8/50mm lens. Also found with "T" Elionar f3.5/50mm lens. Quite rare.

Sonne-C:　　　**R4* F**
1951. Cfps, 1-1/1000s, flash synch, interchangeable Leica-type screw mount Schneider Xenar f3.5/50mm lens, or f2.8/50mm lens. Also found with "T" Elionar f3.5/50mm lens. Similar to the Sonne-V, but with changed top cover.

Sonne-C4:　　　**R4* F**
1953. Cfps, 1-1/1000s, flash synch, interchangeable Leica-type screw mount Schneider Xenar f3.5/50mm lens, or f2.8/50mm lens. Also found with "T" Elionar f3.5/50mm lens. Separate slow speed control, and combines RFR/VFR window. Also known as the Sonne-Colour camera. Quite rare. It is difficult to find any Sonne cameras in condition "C" or better.

L. Gaumont & Cie
Paris, France

Block-Notes: **R3* E–**

c1903. 4.5 x 6cm vest pocket camera; Tessar f6.8 lens. 4.5 x 6cm model, $90-$175. 6 x 9cm model.

Stereo Block-Notes: **R3* E+**
c1903. 45 x 107mm stereo camera; Tessar f6.3 lenses.

Stereo Block-Notes: **R3* E**

1904. Compact folding stereo camera for 6 x 13cm glass plates in individual holders. Fixed focus anastigmat lenses

f5.5, 60mm. Six speed guillotine shutter.

"Reporter" Tropical Camera: **R5* G–**
c1924. 135mm f4.5 lens; FPS; 9 x 12cm exp on cut film.

Spido: **R3* E–**
c1899. 9 x 12cm; Zeiss Krauss Protar 136mm f8 lens; Decaux pneumatic shutter; 12 plates.

Spido Stereo: **R3* E+**

c1922, 6 x 13cm stereo camera; Hermagis Anastigmatic 85mm f6.3 lenses; variable speed guillotine shutter.

Spido Stereo (9 x 18cm model): R3* E+
c1900, black leather covered jumelle style camera; Goerz Dagor 110mm f6.8 lenses; Decaux 6 speed shutter. Changing mechanism for 12 plates, 9 x 18cm. Panoramic setting; rising and sliding lens panel.

G.B. Multiplying Camera: **R4* F–**
c1900. F.L. Chevalier lens; 12 exp, 25 x 25mm on 6 x 13cm plates by sliding and turning the plate holder. Manufactured in France.

Genie Camera Co
Philadelphia, Pennsylvania, USA

Genie: R4* F

c1890, box-type detective camera; push-pull movement changes plates and advances exp counter on brass magazine. $3\frac{1}{4}$" x $4\frac{1}{4}$" exp on plates in magazine.

G. Gennert
New York, New York, USA

Long Focus Montauk: R4* E–

c1890, brass shutter; red bellows; polished wood interior. Front and rear bellows extension for long focus (close-up photography).

Montauk: R4* D+

c1890. 4" x 5" box-type detective camera.

Montauk Multiplying Camera: R4* F–

c1890, shifting lens standard; sliding back. 32 exp on 5" x 7" plate. C.

Montauk Stereo: R4* F–

c1889, hand/stand-type stereo camera; Beck Symmetrical Rapid Rectilinear 5" lens or Bausch & Lomb; Bausch & Lomb iris diaphragm-type between lens shutter; short baseboard; rising front; reflecting finder. 3 sizes: $4\frac{3}{4}$" x $6\frac{1}{2}$, 5" x 7" and 5" x 8".

Kamerawerk Adolf Gerlach
Wuppertal, Germany

Ideal: R3* A

c1952-56, metal camera for 6 x 6 frames on roll film, simple f7.7 lens mounted in a collapsible tube, simple one speed shutter, cheap construction.

Trixette: R3* B+

c1954, metal camera for 6 x 6 frames on roll film, coated f5.6/75mm Supra-Anastigmat lens in "Spezial" shutter, 1/25-1/200s.

Trixette I: R3* B+

c1956, metal camera for 6 x 6 frames on roll film, coated f5.6/75mm Supra-Anastigmat lens in "Spezial" shutter, 1/25-1/200s, basically the same camera as Triyelte but with improved spring system for folding the lens, still interesting.

Ideal Box: R2* A

c1955, metal box camera for 6 x 9 frames on roll film, simple lens and shutter.

Ideal Colour 35: R3* B–

35mm VFR camera with coated Nixon or Nixonar f3.5/4.5cm lens "Spezial" shutter 1/25-1/200s. collected more for the "Nixon" name on the lens than for any other reason!

Geyer Maschinen
Berlin, Germany

Geyer Camera: R4* D–

c1929, 16mm movie camera; Carl Zeiss Triotar 25mm f2.9 lens. Hand crank or spring motor drive.

Geymet and Alker
Paris, France

Jumelle Photographique
(Jumelle de Nicour): **R5* I+**
c1867, binocular-type detective camera;
50 exp, 4 x 4cm in removable magazine.
Patented by Octave Nicour. The first
camera to use this disguise.

G.G.S.
Milan, Italy

Lucky: **R5* E**

1948. Small 35mm VFR camera. 50mm
f/3.2 Solar Anastigmat lens. Carica
shutter 1/20-1/200s. Some models also
have 1/25s added. Only around
3,000 made.

Luckyflex: **R3* F+**
c1948, metal TLR for 35mm film,
focusing Solar f3.2/50mm lens, GGS
shutter, 1/20-1/300s, very small
production, maybe 2000 units.

Globus Brothers
New York, New York, USA

Globuscope: **R3* NSR**

c1981, 35mm panoramic camera
capable of 360 degree images using
standard 35mm film cassettes. f3,
22mm lens. Effective shutter speed
1/400s. Camera rotational action is very
smooth via a viscous damped spring
motor.

A. & B. Glock

Glock: R4* F–
c1890, field-type stereo camera; single lens on sliding panel for sequential exp; rising front; 18 x 24cm.

Gnome Photographic Products
England

Baby Pixie: R1* B

c1950. Metal box camera. 16 exp on 620. Unmarked lens. Shutter for B & I only. Large metal viewfinder folds up from top. Leatherette covered. Chrome trim.

C.P. Goerz
Berlin, Germany

Stereo Ango: R4* E–
c1906. Goerz Dagor 120mm f6.8 lens; FPS 1/10-1/1000s. Paired exp on 9 x 18cm dry plates; film pack adapter; rising and sliding lens panel.

Anschutz Camera: R4* G+

c1890. Clement & Gilmer Wide Angle 25cm f15 lens, but usually found with original Goerz lens; eye level finder; CFPS. Introduced by Ottomar Anschutz, Prussia. The Anschutz Camera is of great historical interest because of its cloth focal plane shutter. Anschutz used this camera for early high-speed photography.

Anschutz: R3* D+
c1895, 9 x 12cm folding camera; Goerz Double Anastigmatic Series III No. 0, 120mm ;lens, CFPS. It utilised the dry collodion process.

Anschutz: R3* D+
c1912. 9 x 12cm folding camera; Dagor 135mm f6.8 lens; CFPS.

Anschutz De Luxe: R3* F–
c1910. 9 x 12cm folding camera; Goerz Doppel Anastigmat 180mm f6.8 lens; covered in dark green leather; CFPS.

Anschutz Stereo: R4* E+
c1912. 9 x 18 stereo camera; Goerz Doppel-Anastigmat 130mm lenses; Anschutz CFPS; 9 x 18cm exp on plates. CFPS.

Box Tengor: **R2* C**

1925. Smaller than most box cameras, fitted with a Hahn Goerz Frontar lens, with fixed aperture at f11. Portrait attachment also available. Made in two sizes for $3^1/_4$" x $2^1/_4$" or $4^1/_4$" x $2^1/_2$".

Coat Pocket Tenax: **R3* C+**

c1912; Strut type folding camera; exp 6.5 x 9cm on film packs or plates; 90mm f4.5 Dogmar lens.

Folding Reflex: **R4* F−**

c1912, 4" x 5" SLR camera; Goerz Doppel-Anastigmat f4.8 lens; Goerz Anschutz CFPS. 4" x 5" exp on plates.

Hypergon-Doppel-Anastigmat Wide Angle lens: **R5* G+**

c1900. Series X, 75mm f22 lens. Rotating fan blade in centre to permit uniform exp. The Hypergon was available in various focal lengths, covering 4 x 5 to 11 x 14". On rare occasions they are found with the original tube and bulb used to spin the propeller (usually dried out).

Manufoc Tenax: **R3* C**

c1925. Plate camera made in two sizes for $3^1/_2$" x $2^1/_2$" or $4^1/_4$" x $3^1/_4$". Equipped with double extension, rise and cross movements. Lens variations included f4.5 Dogmar, f6.8 Dagor, f6.3 Dogmar or f6.3 Tenastigmat in a Compur shutter. Film pack adapter also available.

Manufoc Tenax teak model: **R4* E+**

c1925. Made for tropical use, with teak wood, brass fittings and Russia leather bellows. Choice of f4.5 Dogmar or f6.8 Dagor lenses in Compur shutter.

Reporter: **R5* H+**

c1889, book-type detective camera; Goerz Aplanat 60 degree angle coverage lens; gravity shutter; 4 x 5.5cm exp on roll film.

Stereo Photo Binocle: **R5* H**

c1899, binocular-type detective camera; Dagor 75mm f6.8 lens; guillotine shutter; 45 x 107mm exp on plates. Could function as a mono or a stereo camera.

Rollfilm Tengor: **R2* C**

1925. Standard folding camera style in five sizes from vest pocket to post card. Made from aluminium covered in leather with nickel fittings. Each model was offered in a range of lenses and shutters, including f9 Frontar or f6.8 Tenaxiar in a speed shutter, or f6.8 Kalostigmat in a Compur shutter. A plate back with focusing screen was also available.

Tenax: R2* C+

c1922, 6 x 9cm roll film and plate camera; Goerz Anastigmat 12.5mm f6.3 lens; Goerz dial-set shutter 1-1/200s. 6 x 9cm exp on roll film and cut film.

Roll Tenax: R2* C+

c1921; Folding roll film camera; exp 4 x 6.5cm; Compur shutter; 7.5cm Dogmar f4.5 lens.

Vest Pocket Tenax: R3* D+

c1909. 4.5 x 6cm camera; Dogmar 75mm f4.5 lens; shutter 1-1/250s.

Stereo Vest Pocket Tenax: R3* E+

c1920. 45 x 107mm stereo plate camera; Dopp-Anastigmat Celor 60mm f4.5 lens; shutter ½-1/250s.

C.P. Goerz
Vienna, Austria

Minicord: R4* F–

c1951. 16mm subminiature TLR camera; Helgor 25mm f2.0 lens; mfps 1/10-1/400s; 10 x 10mm exp on 16mm film in special cassettes; eye level viewing through roof prism. Standard model black and chrome. Red leather and gold trim rare and much more valuable.

Goldeck 16:   R3* D
c.1960. Subminiature for 16mm film. 10x14mm images. Lever film wind. Bright frame finder. 20mm f2.8 Color Ennit. Interchangeable 50mm and 75mm advertised. 'C'-mount also allowed 16mm cine lenses to be fitted. Early model with fixed focus lens, later models offered focusing mount. Super model has 9-speed shutter.

Gugo II: R4* D+
1952. Metal bodied camera with lens extended on metal tube. 12 exp on 120. 3 inch f4.5 Kesar. Three-speed shutter, synch for flash.

R.R. Goldmann
Vienna, Austria

Universal Detective Camera: R5* E
c1890. Early hand-held dry plate camera for plates 13x18cm. Lens, anastigmat f6.3 by E. Francais of Paris. Unusual front mounted shutter for exposures $1/2$-1/1000s. Several sizes and a stereo model were available. It was finished in black lacquer.

Goldschmid
Switzerland

Binocle: R5* H+
c1890, binocular-type detective camera; Steinheil 15cm f6.3 lens; guillotine shutter; frame loaded plates, 5 x 6cm. One eye-piece was attached to the lens; the other to the plate loader.

Goltz & Breutmann
Dresden, Germany

Mentor-Compur-Reflex: R3* E–

c1928. 6 x 9cm SLR; Tessar 105mm f4.5 lens; Compur 1-1/250 s; 6 x 9cm exp on plates.

Mentor Folding Reflex: R3* E–
c1914. $3^{1}/_{4}$" x $4^{1}/_{4}$" folding reflex camera; Tessar 150mm f4.5 lens; CFPS 1/20-1/1000s.

Mentor Sport Reflex Camera: R3* E–
c1927. $3^{1}/_{4}$" x $4^{1}/_{4}$" reflex camera; Tessar 150mm f4.5 lens; FPS $1/_{8}$-1/300s.

Mentor Stereo Reflex: R4* F
c1914. 45 x 107mm stereo SLR camera; Zeiss Tessar 105mm f4.5 lenses; CFPS 1/15-1/1000s. 45 x 107mm exposures on plates.

Mentorett: R4* D

c1936. 6 x 6cm TLR; Mentor 75mm f3.5 lens; CFPS 1/15-1/600s; 12 exp, 2¹/₄" x 2¹/₄" on 120 roll film.

Le Gousset: R4* D+

c1910, achromatic lens; one speed shutter; 4.5 x 6cm film pack. Mfd in Paris, France.

Graph-Check Sequential Camera:
                                  R3* F–

c1975, 8 lens camera takes eight sequential photos on one sheet of 4" x 5" Polaroid film; each image is delayed incrementally from 1/10-4s. For analysing physical and mechanical motion. Still in frequent use.

Gomz

(State Optical Mechanical Works),

After WWII. known as LOMO (Leningrad Optical Mechanical Works) Leningrad, USSR. (now St Petersburg, Russia).

Leningrad: R3* E+

(In Cyrillic or Roman letters): 1953-59. Cfps, 1-1/1000s, adjustable flash synch, combined RFR/VFR, with frame lines for 35mm, 50mm, 85mm, and 135mm fields of view. Built-in spring drive for film transport. 10 exposures at 2-3 per second are possible when the spring is fully wound. Jupitor-8 f2.0/50mm lens. This camera was not made especially for the secret police as is sometimes mentioned. At 900 Rubels, it was the most expensive domestic 35mm camera offered in the USSR. Prices are 25-50% higher for this camera in Japan.

Sport (Cnopm):   R4* F+

1936? CFPS, 50mm f3.5 lens. This may be the first 35mm single lens reflex ever placed on the market. There is some question as to its date of introduction. 24 x 36mm images on regular 35mm film in special cassettes. Certain similarities suggest that its overall design may have been influenced by expatriate Zeiss engineers, but there is no hard evidence.

Sputnik: **R3* F+**

c1957, Bakelite stereo camera, for 6 x 13cm frames on 120 roll film f4.5/75mm lenses, ground glass focusing on reflex waistlevel VFR, between-the-lens shutter 1/10-1/100s, later cameras have 1/15-1-150s. (complete outfit with viewer adds 40%).

Smena: **R3* Black; C–**
                              Red; C+
c1953, Bakelite 35mm VFR camera, f4.5/40mm lens, shutter 1/10-1/100s.

Smena 2:   **R3* C–**
c1956, Bakelite 35mm VFR camera, f4.5/40mm lens, shutter 1/10-1/200s, accessory shoe. This camera was copied by the Chinese in their "Yangtze River" and "Hua Mountain" cameras.

Lubitel: **R2* B–**
c1954, bakelite TLR for 6 x 6cm on roll film, focusing f4.5/75mm lens, shutter 1/10-1/200s, copy of Voigtländer Brilliant.

Lubitel 2:   **R2* B–**

c1956, with flash synch.

Gerhard Goldammer
Frankfurt, Germany

Goldeck 16:   **R3* C+**

c1960. Subminiature for 16mm film. 10x14mm images. Lever film wind. Bright frame finder. 20mm f/2.8 Color Ennit. Interchangeable 50mm and 75mm advertised. 'C'-mount also allowed 16mm cine lenses to be fitted. Early model with fixed focus lens, later models offered focusing mount. Super model has 9-speed shutter.

Golda: R3* C–
c1950, 35mm RFR camera, uncoupled RFR, Trinar f3.5/45mm lens and Prontor shutter in collapsible tube mount.

Gugo-Knips: R2* B–
c1950, VFR camera for 6 x 6cm frames on 120 roll film, f8, f4.5, f3.5, or f2.9 lens and Vario or Pronto shutter in collapsible tube mount.

Gugo II: R4* B
c1952. Metal bodied camera with lens extended on metal tube. 12 exp. on 120. 3 inch. f/4.5 Kesar. Three-speed shutter, synch for flash.

Goldix: R2* B–
c1960, VFR camera for 4 x 4cm frames on 127 film, Goldeck f7.7/60mm lens, simple shutter.

(Graflex) The Folmer & Schwing Mfg Co
New York, USA

Deceptive Angle Graphic: R5* H+
c1901-04, rapid rectilinear 12.5cm, f6.3 lens. 3$^1/_4$" x 4$^1/_4$" plates. Right-angle detective type finder. False lenses on apparent front of camera made it look like a stereo camera, whilst the taking lens was on the side. When George Eastman purchased the company several

years later the inventory showed only a few in stock.

The Folding Pocket Graphic: R3* D+
Graphic R.R. lens; Automatic shutter; 3$^1/_4$" x 4$^1/_4$" exp. c1904.

The Graflex Camera: R4* F+
c1904. Zeiss Series VIIA f6.3* lens; CFPS 1/10-1/1200s. 4 models: 4" x 5", 5" x 5", 6$^1/_2$" x 8$^1/_4$", 10" x 8" $500.

The Graphic Camera: E-F
c1904. Goerz Series III* lens; sector shutter; leather covered mahogany. 3 models: 4" x 5", 5" x 7", 8" x 10".

The Graphic Sr: R4* E–
c1904. Bausch & Lomb Zeiss Convertible Series VIIa* lens; Diaphragm shutter. 2 models: 4" x 5", 5" x 7".

The Graphic Twin Lens Special: R5* G+

c1904. Zeiss Convertible No. 7 Series VIIa* lens; diaphragm shutter; 4" x 5" exp.

Reversible Back Cycle Graphic Special: R3* E–
c1904. Goerz Series III* lens; sector shutter; optional CFPS. 4 models: 4" x 5", 5" x 7", 6$^1/_4$" x 8$^1/_2$", 8" x 10".

The Reversible Back Graflex Camera:
R3* F–

c1904. Zeiss Series VIIA f6.3* lens; CFPS 1/10-1/1200s. 2 models: 4" x 5", 5" x 7".

Reversible Back Graphic:
R3* E–

c1904. Bausch & Lomb Zeiss Convertible Series VIIA* lens; diaphragm shutter. 4 models were sold: 4" x 5", 5" x 7", 6½" x 8½", 8" x 10".

Reversible Back Graphic Special:
R3* E–

c1904. Plastigmat* lens; diaphragm shutter. 3 models: 4" x 5", 5" x 7", 6½" x 8½".

The Sky Scraper Camera – Reversible Back – Double Swing:
R4* F–

c1904. Century Rapid Convertible lens; Wollensak shutter; maroon leather bellows, brass fittings. Walnut construction; rising front panel; extreme tilting back. 3 models: 8" x 10", 11" x 14", 14" x 17".

The Sky Scraper Special Camera:
R4* F+

c1904. Hypergon-Doppel-Anastigmat 75mm f22 lens; special recessed lens board permits use of extremely short focus lenses. 2 models: 8" x 10", 11" x 14".

Stereoscopic Graphic:
R4* G–

c1904. Graphic R.R. lens; CFPS 1/10-1/1200s, 5" x 7" exp.

The Telescopic Graphic Camera: R4* F
c1904. Graphic R.R.* lens; Automatic* shutter; 5" x 7" exp.

The Telescopic Stereo Graphic: R5* G+
c1904, matched Graphic R.R. lenses; CFPS 1/10-1/1200s.

The Tourist Graflex:
R3* F–

c1904. Cooke Series III f6.5* lens; CFPS. 2 models: 4" x 5", 5" x 7".

The Triple Lens Stereo Graphic: R5* G+
c1904. Matched pair of No. 7 Series VIIa Bausch & Lomb Zeiss Convertible lenses; CFPS 1/10-1/1200s. 5" x 7" exp.

(Graflex) Folmer & Schwing Div
Eastman Kodak Co, New York, USA

The Eastman Kodak Company acquired the Folmer and Schwing manufacturing company in 1905. It was operated as a division of Eastman Kodak making a premium line of cameras until it became an independent company in 1926. A number of instruments were made both before and after the ownership change with only minor design differences.

The Auto Graflex: R3* D
c1907-1923. Bausch & Lomb Zeiss Tessar Series IIb f6.3* lens; CFPS 1/10-1/1000s. 3 models: 3¼" x 4¼", 4" x 5", 5" x 7".

Banquet Panoramic View Camera:
R4* F+

c1920. 7 x 17; tilting front; front and rear rack and pinion focusing. Mahogany finish, brass fittings.

Cirkut Camera: R4* G–
Turner-Reich Convertible Anastigmat Series II* lens; Century No. 4 shutter. No. 5 Cirkut Camera, $1500 No. 6 Cirkut Camera , $2000.

No 10 Cirkut Camera: R4* H–

c1900; The early models, those made by the firm before it was purchased by Eastman Kodak used a small fan and air friction to control rotational speed. Later they used a mechanical governor. The #10 (meaning 10 inch wide film) is still used by panoramic enthusiasts today and was actually in production until just before the Second World War. The entire system consisted of a special geared tripod head, and a selection of gears to control speed. The absence of any of these critical components will lower the price.

No. 16 Cirkut Camera: R4* H

The Cirkut Outfit: R4* H–
c1908, panoramic camera; consists of R.B. Cycle Graphic with Cirkut Panorama attachment. Prices include a complete set of gears. No. 6 Cirkut Outfit. No. 8 Cirkut Outfit.

Graphic No. 0:   **R3* E–**

c1909-1920. Zeiss Kodak Anastigmat f6.3 lens; CFPS $\frac{1}{4}$-1/500s; 6 or 12 exp, 4.5 x 6cm on roll film.

The Naturalist's Graflex: **R5* H+**
c1907-1921. Bausch & Lomb Zeiss Protar lens, Series VIIa, No. 19 f6.3* lens; CFPS 1/10-1/1000s; 4" x 5" exp.

The 1A Graflex: **R3* E–**

c1909-1925. Kodak Anastigmat f4.5* lens; CFPS 1/10-1/1000s; $2\frac{1}{2}$" x $5\frac{1}{4}$" exp on 116 roll film.

The Press Graflex: **R4* E+**

c1908. Bausch & Lomb Zeiss Tessar Series Ic No. 16 f4.5* lens; CFPS $\frac{1}{5}$-1/1500s; 5" x 7" exp.

R.B. Tele Graflex: **R4* E–**
c1912-1923. CFPS 1/10-1/1000s. $3\frac{1}{4}$" x $4\frac{1}{4}$", c1915-1923, C. 4" x 5".

The Revolving Back Auto Graflex:
     R3* D+
c1909-1940. Bausch & Lomb Zeiss Tessar Series IIb No. 6 f6.3* lens; CFPS 1/10-1/1000s. 2 models: $3\frac{1}{4}$" x $4\frac{1}{4}$", 4" x 5".

The Revolving Back Cycle Graphic:
     R3* D+
c1908. Bausch & Lomb Plastigmat* lens; Volute shutter. (Graflex Focal Plane Shutter available as an accessory). 4 models: 4" x 5", 5" x 7", $6\frac{1}{2}$" x $8\frac{1}{2}$", 8" x 10".

Speed Graphic (Original): **R3* D+**

c1912-1940. Kodak Anastigmat f4.5* lens; cpfs 1/10-1/1000s. $3\frac{1}{4}$" x $4\frac{1}{4}$", c1913, 4" x 5", c1912-1927, $3\frac{1}{4}$" x $5\frac{1}{2}$", c1912, 5" x 7", c1913-1940.

Stereo Graflex: **R4* G–**
c1904. Zeiss Series VIIa No. 7* lens; CFPS 1/10-1/1000s; 5" x 7" exp.

The Stereo Auto Graflex: **R4* G–**
c1907-28. Bausch & Lomb Zeiss Tessar f6.3* lenses; CFPS 1/10-1/1000s; 5" x 7" exp.

The Stereoscopic Graphic: **R5* G**

c1908. Bausch & Lomb Protar VIIa No. 7 f6.3* lenses; CFPS 1/10-1/1000s; 5" x 7" exp.

The 3A Graflex: **R3* D–**

c1907-1926. Bausch & Lomb Zeiss Tessar Series IIb No. 5A f6.3* lens; CFPS 1/10-1/1000s; $3\frac{1}{4}$" x $5\frac{1}{2}$" exp on 122 roll film.

(Graflex) Folmer Graflex Corp
Rochester, New York

Anniversary Speed Graphic: **R2* E–**
c1940-1947. Kodak Anastigmat $5\frac{1}{2}$" f4.5 lens; Compur 1-1/250s; CFPS 1/10-1/1000s. $3\frac{1}{4}$" x $4\frac{1}{4}$", c1940-1947, 4" x 5".

Graflex Fingerprint Camera: **R3* D+**

c1930, pre-focused lens for making 1:1 photos of fingerprints or small objects; built-in illumination.

National Graflex – Series I: R3* D+
c1933-1935. Bausch & Lomb Tessar 75mm f3.5 lens, non-interchangeable mount; CFPS 1/30-1/500s. Ten exp, $2\frac{1}{4}$" x $3\frac{1}{4}$" on 120 roll film.

National Graflex – Series II: R3* E–

R.B. Graflex, Series B, c1925-1942.

c1934-41. Bausch & Lomb Tessar 75mm f3.5 lens, interchangeable mount; CFPS 1/30-1/500s. 10 exposures, $2\frac{1}{4}$" x $3\frac{1}{4}$" on 120 roll film.

Bausch & Lomb 140mm f6.3
Telephoto lens: R3* D

R.B. Graflex, Series B: R2* D
c1925-1942. Kodak Anastigmat f4.5 lens, screw thread interchangeable mount; CFPS 1/10-1/1000s. $2\frac{1}{4}$" x $3\frac{1}{4}$", c1925-1951, $3\frac{1}{4}$" x $4\frac{1}{4}$", c1925-1942, 4" x 5".

R.B. Graflex, Series C: R2* D
c1926-1935. Cooke $6\frac{1}{2}$" f2.5 lens; CFPS 1/10-1/1000s; $3\frac{1}{4}$" x $4\frac{1}{4}$" exp.

R.B. Graflex, Series D: R2* D
c1928-1945. CFPS 1/10-1/1000s; $3\frac{1}{4}$" x $4\frac{1}{4}$", c1928-1941, 4" x 5".

R.B. Home Portrait Graflex: R4* E

c1912-1942. Zeiss Tessar 10"* lens; CFPS 1-1/500s; 5" x 7" exp.

R.B. Super D Graflex: R3* E+

c1948-1958. Kodak Ektar 152mm f4.5* lens with semi-auto diaphragm; CFPS ⅕-1/1000s. 3¼" x 4¼", c1941-1963, 4" x 5".

Speed Graphic – 4" x 5": R3* D+

c1928-1939. Zeiss Tessar f4.5* lens; Dial-set Compur 1-1/300s; CFPS 1/10-1/1000s; 4" x 5" exp.

Graflex Inc
Rochester, New York, USA

Combat Graphic (70mm): R4* F+

1947-48. 70mm perforated film in cassettes; Kodak Ektar 100mm f2.8 coated lens; CFPS 1-1/500s; 2¼" x 3¼" inch images. Interchangeable lenses. Spring-wound film advance. Manufactured by Graflex for the US Army and was supplied in a fitted case with 3 lenses, flashgun, and filters. Price is doubled if complete . The 70mm Combat Graphic was designed by Hubert Nerwin Snr. who had designed the Contax II for Zeiss. It shows a startling resemblance to the Contax, although much much larger. Mr. Nerwin had gone to the US in 1946 as a part of "Operation Paperclip." This was a US Army project that transferred to the United States a large number of German scientists and engineers. Werner von Braun of rocket fame was part of this group.A civilian version of the 70mm Combat Graphic was marketed briefly with little success. Not more than 50 of them were made. The retail price of $1800.00 in 1950 was very high.

Combat Graphic: R3* F–

4" x 5" sheet film combat camera; Kodak Anastigmat Special 127mm f4.7 lens; Graphic shutter 1-1/400s, CFPS 1/30-1/1000s; 4" x 5" exp on cut film and film pack. Water and dust resistant wooden construction with olive drab paint. c1942. Standard camera used by the U.S. Armed Forces in WWII.

Graphic Jet: R4* E

c1961. 35mm motor drive camera; Graflex Optar 50mm f2 coated lens; Copal SVK, 1-1/500s, CRF. "Jet-O-Matic" motor consists of CO2 charger – drive motor automatically advances film and cocks shutter after each exp. Each CO_2 charger cycles 6 to 8 rolls of 20 exp 35mm film, at a maximum rate of 2 exp per s. Rapid wind film advance and shutter cocking may also be operated manually. Push button focusing moves film plane while lens remains stationary. Selenium photo-electric exp meter coupled to shutter. Mfd. in Japan, for Graflex Inc., Rochester. The CO_2 powered drive system of the Graphic Jet was not a design success and most of the cameras were used with the manual film advance. On rare occasions they are found with the original box and several CO_2 cartridges. The camera was made by Kowa Co. in Japan.

Graphic 35: R2* C–

c1956. 35mm rf camera; Graflex 50mm f3.5 coated lens; Prontor 1-1/300s.

Stereo Graphic: R2* D

c1955. 35mm stereo camera, optical VFR, fixed focus Graflar 35mm/f4 lenses, single shutter speed, 1/50s, each lens was set for a slightly different point of focus, thereby ensuring at least one of the stereo pair to have the major subject in sharp focus. This was known as the "Depthmaster" system. The same camera was sold as the "Wray Stereo Camera" in England.

Graphic View Camera: R3* E–
c1941-1950. 4" x 5" metal view camera.

Miniature Speed Graphic: R3* E
c1938-1947. Kodak Anastigmat Ektar 107mm f3.7 lens; Compur shutter 1-1/250s, CFPS 1/10-1/1000s; $2^1/_4$" x $3^1/_4$" exposure.

Pacemaker Crown Graphic:
R3* 2¹/₄" x 3¹/₄" E+
5" x 4" E+

c1947-65. Kodak Ektar 101mm f4.5* coated lens; Kodak Flash Supermatic shutter 1-1/400s. No FPS. 2¹/₄" x 3¹/₄", D+; 3¹/₄" x 4¹/₄", D+; 4" x 5", E. Still used by enthusiasts.

Pacemaker Speed Graphic: R3* E+
c1947-1970. Kodak Ektar 101mm f4.5* coated lens; Kodak Flash Supermatic shutter 1-1/400s, CFPS 1/30-1/1000s. The Pacemaker is the only Graphic model with a single body release for both front and FPS. 2¹/₄" x 3¹/₄", c1947-1958, 3¹/₄" x 4¹/₄", c1947-1962. 4" x 5".

Super Speed Graphic: R2* F–

1950-1970. 4" x 5" press camera; Graflex Optar 135mm f4.7 coated lens; special high speed between the lens Graflex shutter 1-1/1000s, without FPS , CRF.

Great Wall Camera Factory
Bejing, China

Great Wall DF-2:   R3* C+

1970s. 120 roll film Slr, metal behind the lens shutter, 1/30-1/200s, ruby windows for frame counting, removable metal mask for 6 x 4.5 size negatives. Waist level VFR, coated 90mm screw mount lens. Later models incorporated self timer, and flash synch. This copy of the 1930s "Super Pilot" is no longer in production.

Great Wall SZ-1:   R3* C+
1970s. Between the lens leaf shutter, 1-1/300s, combined RFR/VFR, fixed f2.8/45mm lens, built-in spring motor film advance. A copy of a Ricoh camera, early cameras sometimes had the political slogan "Serve the People" in Mao's handwriting on the top plate, and are quite rare, even in China. This adds 200% to the value.

Great Wall SZ-1, 1970s.

Great Wall SZ-2: R3* C+

1970s. Between the lens leaf shutter, 1-1/300s, combined RFR/VFR, fixed f2.8/45mm lens, built-in spring motor film advance. As the Great Wall SZ-1, but with internal changes.

J.J. Griffin and Son
London, England

Cyko No. 1: R4* F
c1902. 6.5 x 9cm all aluminium camera; Aplanatic 12cm lens; guillotine shutter.

Pocket Cyko: R4* F
c1902, all aluminium folding camera; 6.5 x 9cm exp.

W. Griffiths & Co
Birmingham, England

The Guinea Detective or Hand Camera: R5* E+
c1891. Valise type detective camera; single achromatic f9 lens; T and I settings. Original cost was one guinea.

Grundmann
Leipzig

Detective camera: R4* F+
wooden box detective camera; focusing lens tube; string set shutter; 9 x 12cm plates.

Guangdong Camera Factory
Guangdong, China

Pearl River: R3* C+

c1965. 2¼" x 2¼" TLR; Pearl River 75mm f3.5 coated lens; Pearl River shutter 1/25-1/250s. 12 exp, 2¼" x 2¼" on 20 roll film. Mfd in China.

Ets. E. Guerin & Co
Paris, France

Le Furet (The Ferret):   **R4* G+**
c1923-1929. 35mm camera; Hermagis Anastigmatic 40mm f4.5 lens; 3 speed rotary shutter; 25 exp on 35mm film. Designed in 1913; marketed. Smallest pre-Leica 35mm camera. Invented by M. Maroniez.

The Guilford: **R3* D+**

View camera; Ross Extra Rapid brass lens; Walnut finish, brass fittings and black bellows. Mfd in England.

Guilleminot Roux & Cie
Paris, France

Guilleminot Detective Camera: **R4* F+**
c1900, detective camera; Aplanat 150mm f9 lens; rotary sector shutter with 8 speeds. Ground glass viewing. Walnut finish, brass fittings.

Le Sphinx: **R5* G−**
c1891. Aplanat lens; rotary sector shutter. 9 x 12cm glass plates. This camera was fitted with a clockwork powered plate changing mechanism. The beginning of this type of camera automation.

Gundlach-Manhattan Optical Co
New York, USA

Bo Peep Camera: **R3* E−**

c1898. 4" x 5" folding plate camera; reversible finder; red bellows; solid wood front; wood interior.

Korona I: **R4* E−**

c1900. 4" x 5" folding camera; Gundlach Optical Triple Convertible lens and shutter; long focus bed; side, rear, top and front open for red double extension bellows.

Korona IV: R3* D

4" x 5" folding camera; Rapid Convertible lens; Gundlach Manhattan shutter 1-1/100s; 4" x 5" exposures on dry plates.

Korona Panoramic View: R4* G–

4" x 12" panoramic view camera; Triple Convertible Turner Reich lens. 4 sizes: 5" x 12", 7" x 17", 8" x 20", 12" x 20".

Korona Royal Stereo: R4* F

c1920s, 5" x 7" stereo camera; rear tilts; front shift. Polished wood interior with nickel plated fittings.

Korona Wide-Angle Camera: R5* F

c1920s. Special wooden plate camera for ultra wide-angle photography. Although taking a 10 x 8-inch plate, the maximum extension is only 6.5 inches from lens board to plate. Suitable for wide-angle lenses such as Goerz Hypergon. Rise, fall and swing movements, with plumbing device to ensure vertical position of plate.

Night-Hawk Detective Camera: R4* E+

c1905, box type detective camera; string set shutter; 4" x 5" exp on plates. Leather and wood finished versions.

Wizard Duplex No. 1:   R4* E+

c1904, folding 3¼" x 4¼" combination plate and roll film camera; roll holder for No. 3 Folding Pocket Kodak Film made by Eastman Kodak is removable for plate use.

Wizard Duplex No. 2:   R4* E+
c1904, combination roll film and plate folding camera. Hinged back is removable to permit accurate ground glass focusing.

Guthe & Thorsch
Dresden, Germany

Later Kamera Wertstütten and in 1959 VEB Kamera und Kinowerke Dresden, finally becoming part of the giant VEB Pentacon. For simplicity cameras are grouped by name with no regard as to which named company produced them.

Jolly: R3* C

1950. Subminiature for 10 x 15mm images from the KW works and made from stamped sheet metal. Fixed focus lens. I & B shutter.

KW Patent Etui 6.5 x 9:   R3* C+

c1930, 6.5 x 9cm folding plate camera, Tessar 120mm f4.5 lens among others, (earliest cameras have dial set, later ones have rim set) Compur shutter 1-1/250s among others, double or single extension bellows, known for its ultra slim design.

KW Patent Etui 9 x 12:   R3* C+
c1930, 9 x 12cm folding plate camera, Trioplan f3.8/135mm lens among others, (earliest cameras have dial set, later ones have rim set) Compur shutter 1-1/250s among others, known for its ultra slim design.

KW Patent Etui Deluxe: R4* E+
c1932, 6.5 x 9cm or 9 x 12cm folding plate camera, Tessar lens among others, Compur shutter 1-1/250s. Brown or blue or red leather covering with matching bellows.

Pilot Twin Lens Reflex: R4* F–

c1931, 127 roll film TLR camera, Schneider Xenar 5cm f3.5 lens among others, Compur, shutter 1-1/300s; 3 x 4cm exp on 127 roll film, early cameras have the "Pilot" name in script, after 1935 "Pilot" is in all upper case printing.

Pilot 6:   **R2* C+**

c1934, roll film SLR for 6 x 6cm frames on 120 film, KW Anastigmat f2.9, f3.5, f4.5 or f6.3/75mm lens, FPS, early models 1/25-1/100s, later models 1/15-1/150s.

Pilot Super: **R3* D**

c1936, roll film SLR for 6 x 6cm or 6 x 4.5cm frames on roll film, screw mount Laack f2.9/75mm lens among others, FPS 1/20-1/200s, built-in extinction meter.

KW Reflex Box: **R3* D**

c1936, roll film SLR for 6 x 9cm frames on 120 film, f6.3 or 4.5/105mm lens, FPS 1/25-1/100s.

Pocket Dalco: **R3* C+**

c1932. Name variation for Patent Etui Deluxe.

Praktiflex: **R3* C+**

c1937, 35mm SLR interchangeable Xenar f3.5/50mm lens among others, CFPS 1/20-1/500s, top mounted shutter release, fixed waist level finder.

Praktiflex II: **R3* C+**

c1940, 35mm SLR interchangeable Xenar f3.5/50mm lens among others, CFPS 1/20-1/500s, front mounted shutter release, fixed waist level finder.

Praktica: **R2* B+**

c1948, 35mm SLR, post-war version of the Praktiflex, different in name and shutter speeds (1-1/500s) only.

Praktica FX: **R2* C–**

c1954, with F and X synch connections on the camera front.

Praktica FX 2:   **R2* C–**

c1956, with new finder hood and PC type synch.

Praktica FX 3:   R2* C–
c1958, with automatic aperture.

Praktina FX: R2* C
c1954, 35mm SLR with interchangeable Biotar f2/50mm lens among others, CFPS 1-1/1000s, built-in direct vision VFR, often found with spring motor and 250 exposure back (motor and back each add 100%).

Praktisix: R3* D+
c1955, roll film SLR for 6 x 6cm frames on 120 film, interchangeable Tessar or Biometer f2.8/80mm lens, CFPS 1-1/1000s, interchangeable waistlevel VFR, often found with shutter problems.

Praktisix II: R2* D+
c1969, as (GT114) but with brighter finder and the same shutter problems.

Pentacon six: R3* E–
c1970, as (GT115) but now made by VEB Pentacon, and capable of 120 (twelve exposures 6 x 6cm) or 220 (twenty four exposures 6 x 6cm) film operation.

Pentacon six TL: R2* E–
c1975-90, the last in the line of 120 SLRs from Dresden, finally the shutter is more reliable, and the film advance is redesigned. This camera is often bought by someone who wants to start on medium format with a small budget, or by a collector looking for an interesting usable piece at a bargain price.

Lenses and accessories for Praktisix/Pentacon six

Flektagon 50mm f4.0 w/angle lens:	**E–**
Flektagon 65mm f2.8 w/angle lens:	**D**
Biometer 120mm f2.8 telephoto lens:	**D**
Sonnar 180mm f2.8 telephoto lens:	**E–**
Sonnar 300mm f4.0 telephoto lens:	**E–**
Orestegor 300mm f4.0 telephoto lens:	**D**
Orestegor 500mm f4.0 telephoto lens:	**E+**
TTL prism meter:	**C**
Magnifying finder:	**B+**
Prism finder:	**B+**

Praktiflex in black/chrome with Tessar 3.5/5cm; Praktiflex in black/grey with Tessar 3.5/5cm; Praktiflex in red/chrome with Biotar 2.0/5.8cm and an unopened Isopan F 1.6m refill.

H

Haake et Albert
Frankfurt a/M, Germany

Badecker: R5* H+
c1892, book type detective camera; Voigtlander Euryscop 80mm lens; 24 exp on 4.5 x 6cm plates.

Haglund
Germany

L'Album Camera: R5* H+
c1889, book type detective camera; guillotine shutter. 2 plates, 10 x 12.5cm in pivoting magazine.

W. Haking
Hong Kong

Halina 35x: R1* B

1959. 35mm camera resembling a scaled down Leica screw model. Metal body with black grained leathercloth. 45mm f3.5 Halina Anastigmat lens. Shutter 1/25-1/200 + B.

Halina 6-4: R1* B
1961. Dual format camera for 12 or 16 exp on 120. Twin viewfinders to cover each format. f8 Halina Achromat, apertures punched out of metal plate. Shutter 1/50s + B. Warning sign on top plate states: "When testing the camera without a film, it is important that the Transport Knob is transported NOT less than half a turn before the body release is depressed"!

Halina A1: R1* C
1957. TLR with two lenses linked by gear rings on edges for focusing. 80mm f3.5 Halina Anastigmat. Shutter 1/25-1/100s + B.

Halina Prefect: R? B
1957. TLR look-alike box camera for 12 exp on 120. f8 double meniscus lens. Everset shutter.

Pet: R1* B
1961. Modestly specified 35mm camera. Halina Achromat lens. Shutter for I & B. Aperture scale for dull, bright and sunny. Synch for flash.

Viceroy: R1* A
1959. 12 exp on 120. Similar to the Prefect but with addition of masking plates to take 24 24 x 36mm images on 120. TLR-style box camera. Non focusing f8 double meniscus lens. Shutter for I & T (not B).

Hanimex
(HANnes IMport and EXport)
Australia

Though not actually a manufacturer of cameras, Hanimex is a very large dealer in photographic equipment. Like so many other large photographic houses,

HANIMEX contracted with camera manufacturers for "house brands".

Electra II: R2* B–

c1961, 35mm VFR camera, Hanimar f2.8/45mm lens, automatic aperture and shutter control by means of a built-in Selenium light meter, focusing by use of four separate shutter release buttons, actually a Dacoramatic 4D.

Hanimar: R2* B–

c1953, 35mm VFR camera with interchangeable Finetar f2.8/45mm lens, shutter 1/25-1/200s, actually a Finetta 88.

Holiday 35: R2* B–

c1957, 35mm RFR camera, Kominar f3.5/4.5cm lens, leaf shutter 1-1/300s, CRF, looking like the Petrie 35.

Holiday 35, c1957.

Eaglet: R2* B–

c1951, metal box camera for 6 x 6cm or 6 x 4.5cm on 120 rollfilm, simple lens and shutter, made in Italy by Fototecnica.

Hanimex Box: R2* B–

c1955, metal box camera for 6 x 9cm frames on roll film, simple lens and shutter, built-in yellow filter, actually an Alka box camera made by Vredeborch in West Germany.

Hanimex RF35d: R4* C

c1970s. The first 35mm SLR with a built-in flashgun. Styled more like a compact of the day with the addition of a pentaprism.

E. Hanau
Paris, France

L'Omnigraphe: R5* G+

c1887-1906, guillotine shutter. 12 plates, 9 x 12cm.

Le Marsouin: R4* F−

c1900, 45 x 107mm stereo camera; Tessar 55mm f6.3 lenses; 3 speed guillotine shutter. 12 stereo exp on 45 x 107mm dry plates in push-pull magazine #1 used 45 x 107cm plates, #2 6 x 13cm plates about equal in value.

Le Handy: R4* F

c1900, Lemardley 135mm f7.7 lens; guillotine shutter 1/25-1/100s. 9 x 12cm exp; helical focusing. Manufactured in Paris, France.

George Hare
London, England

George Hare Stereoscopic Wet Plate:
R5* H

c1865-1870, brass bound mahogany camera; Petzval lenses; 2 sets of waterhouse stops in leather cases; flap shutter; rack focusing from rear.

Tourist Stereo Camera: R5* H−

c1860, 8 x 17cm stereo camera; Dallmeyer 110mm f11 lens; sliding lens panel; 8 x 17cm exp in Berry system magazine.

Tailboard Camera: R2* F

c1865; Brass and Mahogany construction; Rack focusing; Dallmeyer Landscape lens;Half-plate, quarter-plate and 12" x 10" sizes.

Victor Hasselblad
Sweden

Hasselblad 1600F: R3* F−

c1948-1954, 120 roll film SLR; Kodak Ektar 80mm f2.8 coated lens, interchangeable bayonet mount; CFPS 1-1/1600s. 12 exp, $2\frac{1}{4}$" x $2\frac{1}{4}$" on 120 roll film in special magazine.

Hasselblad 1000F: R3* F−

c1954-1960, 120 roll film SLR; Zeiss Tessar 80mm f2.8 coated lens, interchangeable bayonet mount; CFPS 1-1/1000s. 12 exp, $2\frac{1}{4}$" x $2\frac{1}{4}$" in special magazine.

Hasselblad Super Wide Camera:
R4* G

c1956-1960, 120 roll film SLR; Carl Zeiss Biogon 38mm f4.5 coated non-removable lens with 90 degree field of view; Synchro-Compur shutter 1-1/500s. 12 exp, 2¼" x 2¼" in special magazine.

Dr. Hans Hensold *see ISO*

Herbert George
USA

Donald Duck Camera: **R3* C**
1947. Plastic rollfilm camera for 8 exposures on 127. Fixed aperture, shutter and meniscus lens. Unique for having figures of Donald with Huey, Dewie and Louie in relief on the camera back, with the sun represented by the camera's red window. Early rare models in dark green, later models in back.

Roy Rogers Camera: **R4* E**
c1945. Variant of the Donald Duck camera but with Roy Rogers nameplate around lens in place of the Donald Duck name.

Happi-Time: **R2* B**
c1950. Another variant on the Donald Duck camera with different name plate.

J. Fleury Hermagis
Paris, France

Hermagis Field Camera: **R4* E–**
c1890. Hermagis Aplanastigmat 210mm f6.8 lens; Thornton Pickard roller blind shutter. 5" x 7" exp on plates. Rotating maroon bellows; polished walnut with brass fittings.

Instantaneous Stereoscopic Camera:
R5* H
c1888. Hermagis Aplanat f8 lens; 8 speed guillotine shutter. 12 stereo exp on 8 x 16cm dry plates.

Jumelle Hermagis: **R4* E–**
c1895, 6.5 x 9cm camera; Aplanastigmatic lens.

Velocigraphe: **R5* G–**
c1891, satchel type detective camera; Hermagis rapid rectilinear lens; central rotary shutter. 12 ¼ plates or 25 exp on film. Invented by Ricard et Lacroix.

A. Herzog
New York, USA

Herzog Camera: **R5* G+**
c1876, periscopic 100mm f8 lens; 3¼" x 4¼" plates.

Dr. Adolf Hesekiel & Co E
Berlin, Germany

Archimedes Stereoscop Camera:
R5* H–
c1904, 35mm stereo camera; Aplanat; Zeiss Anastigmat; Goerz Double Anastigmat lenses; B & I shutter, pneumatic release; 8¼" x 17cm exp.

Dr. A. Hesekiel's Quarter-Plate:
                                    R5* G+
c1895. Goerz 140mm f6.3 double anastigmat lens; FPS (no markings). Mahogany, nickel fittings.

Pompadour: R5* I+
c1907, pocket book-type detective camera; Certomat 105mm f8 lens; 3 speed shutter. 6.5 x 9cm exp on plates. Consists of folding Certo in crocodile skin covered pocketbook.

Hess-Ives Corp
Philadelphia, Pennsylvania, USA

Hicro Colour Camera: R3* D
c1915 Achromatic lens. Simple tri-colour camera using a film system designed by Dr. Ives. Manufactured by Eastman Kodak under contract to the Hess-Ives Corporation.

Hetherington & Hibben
Indianapolis, Indiana, USA

Hetherington Magazine Camera:
                                    R4* F–

c1890. 4" x 5" box-type detective camera. All operations such as: plate changing, aperture changing and shutter tensioning are accomplished by means of key inserted from outside the camera box.

Emil Hofert, Eho Kamera Fabrik
Dresden, Germany

See Altissa for post war camera production.

Baby Box Eho: R2* B+
c1930. Duplar f11 lens; 3 x 4cm frames on 127 roll film.

Eho: R2* C–
c1932, box camera, Duplar f11/50mm lens; single speed shutter; 3 x 4cm frames on 127 roll film.

Stereo Box Eho: R3* D
c1930, box camera, Duplar 80mm f11 lens; 5 stereo exp, 6 x 13cm or 10 single exp, 6 x 6cm frames on 120 film.

Eho Box 110:   R2* A
c1930, metal box camera, f11 lens, simple shutter, 6 x 9cm frames on roll film.

Altissa Box: R2* A
c1930, box camera for 6 x 6 frames on roll film, optical VFR on early cameras is a simple squared tube affair, later cameras used a large distinctive VFR, simple f10 lens, simple shutter. This same camera was continued after 1945 with little outward change and is not so rare. It was copied by the Chinese in the 1950s and called the "Xing Fu".

Super Altissa: **R2* B–**
c1930, with focusing f4.5 lens.

Altiflex: **R3* B+**
c1935, metal TLR for 6 x 6cm frames on roll film, lever focusing Victor f4.5/75mm lens among others, Automat, Prontor or Compur shutter.

Altiscope: **R3* D**
c1935, stereo camera for 6 x 13 frames on roll film, Victor f4.5 lenses, simple shutter, lever focusing.

Horne & Thornthwaite
England

Wet Plate Camera: **R5* G+**
c1850. Petzval lens.

E.I. Horsman & Co
New York, USA

No. 3 Eclipse Camera: **R4* E–**
c1896, folding view camera; meniscus lens – 3 insertable metal circular stops; $4\frac{1}{4}"$ x $6\frac{1}{2}"$ exp on dry plates.

George Houghton & Son Ltd
London, England

*Houghton-Butcher Ltd from 1926
Ensign Ltd from 1930*

George Houghton was in the photographic business from the beginning when he became the sole importer into Great Britain of Daguerreotype cameras, equipment and pictures. Great expansion took place under his son and the firm became a major manufacturer and wholesaler of cameras. In the first few years of the new century Houghton's absorbed a number of small firms that had made cameras for them. These included Holmes Bros, who made the famous Sanderson. Like Butcher, Houghton's also imported many of their cameras from Germany, a supply which abruptly ended in 1914 on the outbreak of war. Together with Butcher, the Houghton Butcher Manufacturing Company Ltd. was formed to make cameras for both companies. Houghton's were the senior partners because they already had a much stronger manufacturing base. Each company continued to sell its own models under its own name until complete amalgamation came in 1926 with the formation of Houghton-Butcher (Great Britain) Ltd. Ensign Limited (Ensign was an old Houghton brand name) was formed in 1930 as the selling company. A new series of modern cameras was introduced under Ensign, but many Houghton and Butcher models continued into the early years of the Ensign era. Name changes after WWII reflected further amalgamations: Barnet Ensign in 1945, Barnet Ensign Ross in 1948, and Ross Ensign Ltd, in 1954. A few years later the company disappeared into the Rank Organisation, which already owned Ensign's rivals, Kershaw (Soho) and Ross' rivals, Taylor, Taylor and Hobson, and camera production ceased.

**All-Distance Ensign Box: R1* Black A
Red blue or brown c1931;**   **R1* B–**
c1928; 6 x 9cm T.B.I. shutter

All-Distance Ensign Folding camera:
        R2* C+
c1928, 6 x 9cm; T.B.I. shutter.

Commando: R2* D–

c1946. Ensar 75mm f3.5 lens; Epsilon shutter 1-1/200s, crf; 6 x 6cm exp on roll film. 12 or 16 exp on 120 film-format selected by adjusting internal baffles prior to loading film. Camera is unusual in that rfr was coupled to the film plane; lens and mount were fixed. The pressure plate was spring loaded to adjust to film plane movement.

Cupid: R2* C

c1922. Meniscus 70mm f12 lens; guillotine shutter; 36 x 56mm exp on 120 roll film.

Ensign All-Distance "Twenty" box:
R1* A
c1934; 6 x 9cm Box camera; Black.

**Ensign All-Distance "Twenty"
No.2 box:** R1* A
c1936; As (HO136) with filter.

Ensign Autorange 820: R3* E+

c1953; 8/12 exp on 120 roll film; Coupled RFR; Ross Xpres f3.8 in Epsilon shutter.

Ensign Autorange 16/20: R2* E–

c1953; 16 exp on 120 roll film; Ross xpres f3.8 lens; 9 speed Epsilon shutter.

Ensign Autorange camera: R2* E–
                                   R2* E+

Ensign Double-8:   R1* D–

c1930; Folding camera; 3 x 4cm on 127 roll film; F4.5 Ensar lens; 1/25-1/100 shutter;

c1934; 9 x 6cm exp on 120 roll film; Ten models with various lens shutter combinations; coupled range-finder; Model prefix A7 changed in 1936 to AR.

Ensign Autorange Camera: R2* E+
c1936; With Focal Plain Shutter 1-1/500s; Various lenses.

Ensign Cameo: R2* C+
c1936. Camera takes plates or film; 9 x 6cm. Quarter plate and Postcard sizes; several lens shutter combinations.

Ensign Carbine folding camera: R1* C
c1932-1936. Eleven models.

Ensign Carbine No. 6 Tropical Model:
                                   R2* E
c1925. Zeiss Tessar 10.5cm f4.5 lens; Compur shutter 1/250s. Brass body; tan bellows.

Ensign Focal Plane Camera: R5* I

c.1920. Unusual design of folding camera for quarter plates, film packs or cut film. Lens cover doubles as fold-up lens hood. Direct vision wire viewfinder. Non-pleated bellows. Helical focusing. Self-capping focal plane shutter, 1/15-1/1000s. Choice of standard lenses – 5$\frac{1}{2}$-inch f4.5 Ross Xpres Anastigmat, 5$\frac{1}{4}$-inch Cooke Aviar Anastigmat, 5$\frac{1}{4}$-inch Zeiss Tessar Anastigmat,

Ensign Ful-Vue: R2* B+
c1939-1943. 12 exp on 120 roll film; All distance lens; T & I shutter.

Ensign Ful-Vue.

Ensign Ful-Vue: R1* A

c1946-1949. First post-war model. Classic curved shape.

Ensign Ful-Vue A La Monde: R2* B+
As previous model in red, blue or grey.

Ensign Ful-Vue Super: R2* B+

c1954; This model was a little more angular in shape; pull up hood on view-finder carrying the Ross-Ensign logo; removable back; die-cast aluminium body; flash sockets; T. & I. shutter; 12 exp 6 x 6cm on 620 roll film. Also found with ruby red body. Found in black and rarer in red.

Ensign Fulvueflex: R1* A
c1957-1959. All plastic box; 120 roll film.

Ensign Ideal: R3* E
1939. Wooden half-plate camera employing swing front and back, rise, fall and cross front. Quick-change lens panels. Made from mahogany with ebonised surface.

Ensign Midget: R1* C+

c1934. 3.5 x 4.5cm exp on E-10 roll film; models 22 and 33; three speed shutter T. I.

Ensign Midget Model 55:   R1* D–
f6.3 lens in three speed shutter.

**Ensign Midget Silver
Presentation model:**   R3* D+
1936.

Multex: **R4* F**

1936. Metal bodied camera made to take 14 exposures on 127 film, frames automatically counted after first is lined up in red window. Focal plane shutter speeded 1-1/1000s + 'T'. Telescopic lens mount locked with a bayonet catch, focusing down to 21 inches, with coupled coincident image rangefinder. Xpress f3.5 or f2.9 lenses.

Popular Pressman Reflex: **R3* E+**

c1920. Large quarter-plate reflex, made from mahogany and leather covered. Focal plane shutter speeded 1/15-1/1000s. Revolving back, infinity indicator, large lift-up lens cover.

Ensign Popular Tropical Reflex: R4* E

c1917. 3¼" x 4¼" tropical SLR; Ross Xpres 6" f4.5 lens; CFPS. Teak wood and brown leather bellows, brass fittings.

Ensign All Distance Pocket camera:

                       R1* B

c1920s. Successor to the same company's all -distance box cameras, now made in a 3¼" x 2¼" folding design with fixed focus lens. Special simple spool loading device to appeal to beginners.

Ensign Pocket E20:   **R1* A**

c1939. Self erecting camera; 6x9 cm.

Ensign Ranger: **R1* B+**

c1952, 8 exp on 120 roll film; Esnar f6.3 lens; Trikon 3 spd. shutter.

Ensign Ranger, c1952.

Rollfilm Reflex: **R2* D**

1925. Simple single lens reflex with fixed focus lens, set at f8 for focusing but automatically stopping down to f11 as the exposure is made to cover for small inaccuracies in focusing. Made to take 3¼" x 2¼" negatives on rollfilm. Also available with a Taylor Taylor Hobson f7.7 lens.

Ensign Roll Film Reflex
Tropical Model: **R4* F**

c1925, 6 x 9cm roll film SLR camera; Aldis 4¼" f7.7 lens; single speed shutter.

Ensign Selfix "20" folding camera:

                       R2* C−

c1926, 6 x 9cm; Several lens shutter combinations.

Ensign Selfix 220:   **R2* C−**
With Tessar or Schneider lens R3* C+

c1938, 12/16 on 120 roll film; Optical finder; film counter. Several lens shutter combinations.

Ensign Selfix 320:   R2* C
c1946, 8/16 on 120 roll film; Four
shutter/lens combinations; two with
body release; chrome trim;

Ensign Selfix 420:   R2* C
c1946, 8/12 on 120 roll film; Six
shutter/lens combinations.

Ensign Selfix 820:   R2* C+
c1950; 12 or 16 exp on 120 roll film;
various lens shutter combinations.

Ensign Selfix 820 Special: R3* D+
c1954; As model above with built-in uncoupled rangefinder.

Ensign Selfix 16/20:   R2* D

c1950; 16exp on 120 or 620 roll film;
Model I f4.5 Ensar lens; 4 speed Epsilon
shutter; optical finder; Model II f3.5
Ross Xpres in 8 speed Epsilon shutter;
Albada finder; Model IV f4.5 Rosstar
lens; Epsilon 8 speed shutter.

Ensign Selfix 12/20:   R2* C+
c1953; 12 exp on 120 or 620 roll film; 4
models with Rossitar or Ross Xpres lens
in 4 or 8 speed Epsilon shutters; with
Optical or Albada finders.

Ensign Selfix 12/20 Special: R2* D+
c1955; As model above with un-coupled
rangefinder.

Ensign Snapper: R1* A
c1955, plastic folding camera; f11 lens;
focusing; T & I shutter.

Ensign Special Reflex Camera: R2* E–
c1935; various models in 9 x 6cm,
9x12cm, quarter plate; FP shutter 1/15-
1/1000s; leather covered.

Ensign Speed Reflex: R2* C+
1929. New version of the Ensign
Rollfilm reflex, designed specifically for
$3^{1}/_{4}$" x $2^{1}/_{4}$" rollfilm and fitted with f3.4
or f4.5 lens. Focal plane shutter
speeded 1/25-1/500s.

Ensignette: R2* C+

c1910-1920s. Aluminium bodied folding
roll film camera; Zeiss Tessar 75mm f6.8
lens; single speed shutter. No. 1: $1^{1}/_{2}$" x
$2^{1}/_{4}$" exp, No. 2: 2" x 3" exp, No. 2 Junior:
$2^{1}/_{4}$" x $3^{1}/_{4}$".

Ensignette De-Luxe: R2* D+
c1914; same as the Ensignette No.1
and No.2 with Goerz f6.3 or Tessar
f5.6 lenses.

Ensignette Silver: R5 G

Very rare silver-plated version of the No. 1 Ensignette. It is thought that only four exist, probably having been made to special order and for presentation purposes. At least one of them has a Taylor Taylor and Hobson Cooke f5.8 anastigmat lens. Never listed in the Houghton catalogues.

Folding Klito: R2* B+

c1912, 6 x 9cm folding plate camera; Symmetrical 'Rectimat' f11 lens; Ensign-Simplex shutter 1/25-1/100s.

"Holborn" Postage Stamp Camera: R4* F+

c1900, 9 postage stamp size exp.

Klito Hand cameras: R1* B+

c1904-1919; a range of 13 models most having rise and cross fronts; compact well constructed; some with double extension; quarter-plate, half-plate and 5 x 4 sizes.

Klito No. 0: R2* C–

c1906. Rapid Rectilinear lens, adjustable focus with supplementary lenses; guillotine shutter. $3\frac{1}{4}$" x $4\frac{1}{4}$" dry plates; drop plate changing mechanism.

Klito No.1: R1* C

c1910. Folding plate camera with wood body and metal baseboard, rising and crossing front. Made for quarter plate and post card sizes.

Klito No.2: R1* C

c1910. Similar to No.1, but with double extension and focusing by rack and pinion.

Klito No.3: R1* D

c1910. Deluxe version of the No.2 with all metal body. Ensign sector shutter with speeds from 1-1/100s. Choice of Plutar Rapid Aplanat f8 or Aldis Anastigmat f6 lenses.

Ticka: R4* E+

c1907, pocket-watch camera (similar to Expo); Meniscus 30mm f16 lens; 25 exp, 22 x 16mm on roll film in special cassette. The Ticka and Expo were made under licence by separate manufacturers, from the Swedish inventor Magnus Niell.

Focal Plane Ticka: R4* H

1908. Improved version of the original Ticka, made in a limited edition. Cooke f6.5 lens. Focal plane shutter 1/75-1/400s + T.

Watchface Ticka: R4* H

1912. Rare version of the original Ticka, incorporating a fake watchface. The hands stand at 7 minutes past 11 and their angle indicates the field of view, to form a crude viewfinder.

Tropical Watch Pocket Carbine No. 4:
R3* D+

c1925. Aldis Butcher f4.5 lens; Compur 1-1/250s.

Tropical Watch Pocket Carbine No. 4.

The Mascot: R1* B+

c1909-1920; Magazine plate camera; several models; 3½" x 2½" and quarter plate; taking 6 or 12 plates; supplementary lenses for 3 and 6 ft focusing.

Vest Pocket Ensign: R1* B+

c1924; VP film giving 4 x 6.5cm exp on 127 roll film; f11 lens in a three speed shutter;

Sanderson Cameras
In connection with Houghton

F.H.Sanderson was a cabinet maker and keen photographer whose principal interest was architectural photography. He was granted a patent in 1895 for his design of a unique strut system, consisting of two pairs of slotted arms, for the support of the lens panel of a camera, giving a high degree of freedom in rise, tilt and swing. He licensed the design to Houghton's for manufacture and the basic design remained in production from 1896 until the beginning of the Second World War. Sandersons were produced both as field (view) cameras and hand-and-stand cameras. The original slotted arms had been straight, but in 1902 the forward pair were angled below the slot.

Sanderson Regular Model: R3* E–

c1900's. 5" x 8" view camera; Rapid Rectilinear 5" x 8" brass lens; behind-lens Thornton Pickard shutter. Black leather bellows; Sanderson patent movements; British Ensign trademark.

Sanderson Regular Model Hand Camera: R3* E–

c1900s, 3¼" x 4¼" hand camera; Beck Symmetrical lens; Unicum shutter.

Sanderson Tropical: R4* G

c1905. 3¼" x 4¼" tropical camera; Beck Convertible f7.7 lens; teak with brass fittings.

Sanderson Hand and Stand "Regular" Camera: R2* E–

c1896-1901; Quarter-plate, Half-plate, 5" x 4" and 5" x 7"; wide range of movements; Seven lenses available; Wood construction leather bound; c1902-1909; new angular front struts introduced.

Sanderson De-Luxe Hand and stand camera: R3* F–

c1902; As the Regular but superior finish; Rack and pinion focusing also lens panel movements and rear focusing when the baseboard is dropped for wide angle lens; same lens combinations as the Regular; detachable focusing chamber in place of a cloth.

Sanderson Junior: R2* E+

c1904; Folding plate camera; lower priced version of the Regular; Half-plate and 5" x 4" sizes; Beck Symmetrical lens in Unicum shutter.

Sanderson Tropical: **R3* G**

c1905; Folding plate camera; same sizes as the Regular; made of polished teak; brass bound; lenses were Beck Double Aplanat f7.7 or Bausch & Lomb RR.

Sanderson Tropical: **R4* D**
c1909; As previous model with rear rack and pinion focusing for w/a lens; rise & fall rack and pinion controlled; improved reversing back.

Sanderson Tropical: **R4* G+**
c1925, 4" x 5"; Homocentric f6.3 lens; Compur 1-1/200s. 4" x 5" exposure on cut film.

Sanderson View Camera: **R4* F–**
c1920. Suter B. No. 5 Aplanat lens; 8" x 10" plates. Mahogany wood, brass fittings.

R.F. Hunter Ltd
London, England

Purma Special: **R2* B**

c1938; Black plastic miniature camera. Beck anastigmat $2^1/_4$" f6.3 lens 16 exp, $1^1/_4$" x$1^1/_4$" inch on 127 roll film. Unusual shutter design, very likely unique. Position of camera (horizontal or vertical) determined shutter speed. Reintroduced briefly after WWII.

Purma Plus: **R2* B+**

1951. Metal version of the Purma Special. 55mm f6.3 Purma Anastigmat. Three speed shutter identified as 'slow', 'medium' and 'fast', engraved around viewfinder eyepiece. Shutter controlled by gravity. Takes 16 32 x 32 exp on 127.

Hurlbut Manufacturing Co
Belvidere, Illinois, USA

**Hurlbut Velox Magazine
Detective Camera:**   **R4* F**
c1890, magazine-type detective camera. Plates are gravity fed into position; then returned to storage by inverting the camera.

R. Huttig A.G.
Dresden, Germany

Atom: **R4* E–**
c1908. 90mm f8 lens; Compound shutter 1-1/250s; 4.5 x 6cm plates.

Cupido: R2* C
c1906. Helios Rapid Rectilinear lens;
Lloyd central shutter 1-1/100s; 9 x
12cm exp.

Fichter's Excelsior Detective: R4* F+
c1893, drop plate magazine camera;
rectilinear lens; rotating shutter; 12 exp,
9 x 12cm.

Aviso: R4* E
c1920, plate box camera; 4.5 x 6cm exp,
magazine load. Sold in England as the
Gnome camera.

Lloyd Stereo Camera: R4* E–
c1906. Busch Aplanatic 90mm f8
lenses; Stereo Compound shutter 1-
1/200s. 9 x 18cm exp on plates or roll
film. 2 sizes: 8 x 14cm, 9 x 18cm.

Monopol: R4* D+
c1895, rectilinear lens; variable speed
rotary sector shutter; 9 x 12cm dry
plates in magazine.

Stereo Ideal: R4* E–
c1906, 6 x 13cm stereo camera; Lloyd
Anastigmatic 90mm f6.8 lenses;
pneumatic central shutter 1-1/100s.

I

ICA A.G.
Dresden, Germany

Artist Reflex: R3* E–
c1910, Zeiss Tessar 15cm f4.5 lens; FPS 1/11-1/1000s; 3¼" x 4¼" exp. Sliding lens panel.

Aviso: R3* C–
c1920, box camera for 4.5cm x 6cm plates or sheet film with internal changing mechanism, meniscus lens, simple shutter, which is quite visible on the front of the camera.

Aviso Nr.4: R3* C–
c1920, box camera for 4.5cm x 6cm single plates, meniscus lens, simple shutter, which is quite visible on the front of the camera.

Atom Nr. 53: R3* E+
c1913, horizontal format, folding VFR camera, for 4.5cm x 6cm plates, several lens and shutter combinations including Tessar f6.3 or f4.5/65mm lens Compur shutter 1-1/300s.

Atom Nr. 51: R3* D+

c1913, vertical format folding VFR camera, for 4.5cm x 6cm plates, several lens and shutter combinations including Maximar f5.4/9cm lens, Automat or Compur shutter, VFR mounted below the lens.

Bébé Nr. 40: R3* E–

c1920, strut folding VFR camera for 4.5cm x 6cm film packs or plates, several lens and shutter combinations, including Tessar f6.3 or f4.5/7.5cm lens, Compur shutter.

Bébé Nr. 41: R3* D–
c1920, strut folding VFR camera for 6.5 x 9cm film packs or plates, several lens and shutter combinations, including Maximar f6.8/12cm lens, Compur shutter.

Corrida Nr. 156: R3* B+
c1920s, folding camera for 9cm x 12cm plates or film packs, lever focusing, several lens and shutter combinations offered including Icar f6.3/13.5cm lens, Automat shutter.

Cupido Nr. 75: R3* C
c1920s, self erecting folding VFR camera for 6cm x 9cm or 6.5cm x 9cm plates or film packs, several lens and shutter combinations including Tessar f4.5/12cm lens, Compur shutter.

Cupido Nr. 77:   **R3* C**

c1915, horizontal self-erecting folding VFR camera for 7.5cm x 10.8cm or roll film, several lens and shutter combinations offered including Hekla f6.8-10.5cm lens, Automat shutter.

Cupido Nr. 79:   **R3* B+**

c1918, vertical self-erecting folding VFR camera for 7.5cm x 10.8cm or roll film, several lens and shutter combinations offered including Tessar f6.3-13.5cm lens, Automat shutter.

Folding Reflex: **R4* E–**

compact folding SLR camera; Zeiss Tessar f4.5 lens; CFPS 1/15-1/1000s. c1925. Model A: 2¼" x 3¼" exp on film packs, $150. Model B: 9 x 12cm exp on plates or film packs.

Icarette 501:   **R2* C–**

Folding pocket camera; 6 exp 4½" X 2½"; Tessar f6.3 lens in compound shutter;

Icarette A: **R2* B+**

c1925, folding roll film camera; f6.3 lens; 12 exp, 2¼" x 2¼".

Icarette II: **R2* C–**

Folding pocket camera; 6 x 9cm exp on roll film, film pack or plates; Tessar f4.5 in Compur shutter.

Ideal Nr. 111: R2* C–
c1925, folding plate camera for 6cm x 9cm or 6.5 x 9cm, several lens and shutter combinations available including Protar f6.3/10.5cm lens, Compur shutter.

Ideal Nr. 205: R2* C–
c1925, folding plate camera for 9cm x12cm plates, several lens and shutter combinations available including Tessar f4.5/13.5cm lens, Compur shutter.

Ideal Nr. 246: R2* C–
c1925, folding plate camera for 9cm x12cm plates, double extension bellows, several lens and shutter combinations available including Tessar f6.3/15cm lens, Compur shutter.

Lloyd Stereo Nr. 675: R4* E–
c1910, folding stereo/panoramic camera for 8 x 14cm exp on plates or roll film, several lens and shutter combinations offered including Maximar Double Anastigmatic f6.8/90mm lens, Stereo Compur shutter 1-1/100s. Rising and sliding front, panoramic setting.

Minimum Palmos Nr. 453: R4* E
c1920s, strut type folding VFR camera for 4.5 x 6cm exp on plates, several lens and shutter combinations offered including Tessar f4.5/8cm lens, CFPS 1-1/1000s.

Minimum Palmos Nr. 454: R3* D+
c1920s, strut type folding VFR camera for 6 x 9cm or 6.5cm x 9cm plates, several lens and shutter combinations were available, including Tessar f6.3/12cm lens, CFPS 1-1/1000s.

Minimum Palmos Nr. 456: R3* D+
c1920s, strut type folding VFR camera for 9 x 12cm plates, several lens and shutter combinations offered including Tessar f4.5/15cm lens, CFPS 1-1/1000s.

Minimum Palmos Nr. 457: R3* D+
c1920s, strut type folding VFR camera for 10cm x 15cm plates, several lens and shutter combinations offered including Amatar f6.8/16.5cm lens, CFPS 1-1/1000s.

Niklas Nr. 109: R3* B+
c1920s, folding bed plate camera for 6 x 9cm exp on plates, Ica Doppel Anastigmat 12cm f6.8 lens, Dial-set Compur shutter.

Polyscop Nr. 603: R4* D–

c1920s, box type stereo camera for single 4.5cm x 10.7cm plates, fixed focus achromat lenses, simple single speed shutter.

Polyscope Nr, 605: R3* D+
c1920s, box type stereo camera for single 4.5 x 10.7cm plates, several lens and shutter combinations available including Hekla f6.8/6cm lenses, shutter to 1/250s.

Polyscope Nr, 605/1: R3* D+
c1920s, box type stereo camera for 4.5 x 10.7cm plates, delivered with magazine back for 12 plates, several

lens and shutter combinations available including Maximar f6.8/6cm lenses, simple shutter.

Polyscope Nr, 608, c1920s.

Polyscope Nr, 606:   **R3* D**
c1920s, close focusing box type stereo camera for single 4.5 x 10.7cm plates, several lens and shutter combinations available including Hekla f6.8/6cm lenses, shutter to 1/250s.

Polyscope Nr, 606/1:   **R3* D+**
c1920s, close focusing box type stereo camera for 4.5 x 10.7cm plates, delivered with magazine back for 12 plates, several lens and shutter combinations available including Maximar f6.8/6cm lenses, simple shutter.

Polyscope Nr, 607:   **R3* E–**
c1920s, box type stereo camera for single 4.5cm x 10.7cm plates, focusing and close focusing capability, several lens and shutter combinations available including Tessar f6.3/6.5cm lenses, shutter to 1/250s.

Polyscope Nr, 607/1:   **R3* E–**
c1920s, box type stereo camera for 4.5 x 10.7cm plates, focusing and close focusing capability, delivered with magazine back for 12 plates, several lens and shutter combinations available including Tessar f4.5/6.5cm lenses, shutter to 1/250s.

Polyscope Nr, 608:   **R3* D+**
c1920s, close focusing folding strut stereo camera for single 4.5cm x 10.7cm plates, several lens and shutter combinations available including Hekla f6.8/6cm lenses, shutter to 1/250s.

Polyscope Nr, 608/1:   **R3* D+**
c1920s, folding strut type stereo camera for single 4.5cm x 10.7cm plates, several fixed focus lens and shutter combinations available including Hekla f6.8/6cm lenses, shutter to 1/250s.

Polyscope Nr, 608/2:   **R3* F**
c1920s, close focusing folding strut type stereo camera for 4.5cm x 10.7cm plates, delivered with magazine back for 12 plates, several lens and shutter combinations available including Novar f6.8/6cm lenses, shutter to 1/250s.

Polyscope Nr, 608/3:   **R3* E–**
c1920s, folding strut type stereo camera for 4.5cm x 10.7cm plates, delivered with magazine back for 12 plates, several fixed focus lens and shutter combinations available including Tessar f4.5/6.5cm lenses, shutter to 1/250s.

Polyscope Nr, 609:   **R3* E–**
c1920s, box type stereo/panoramic camera for single 6 x 13cm plates, focusing lenses, several lens and shutter combinations available including Tessar f6.3/9cm lenses, Compur shutter to 1/150s.

Polyscope Nr, 609/1:   **R3* E–**
c1920s, box type stereo/panoramic camera for 6cm x 13cm plates, delivered with magazine back for 12 plates, focusing lenses, several lens and shutter combinations available including Tessar f4.5/10.5cm lenses, Compur shutter to 1/150s.

Stereofix Nr. 604:   **R4* D+**
c1920s, truncated box type stereo camera for 4.5 x 10.5cm plates or film packs, several lens and shutter combinations available including Tessar f6.3/6.5cm lenses, Compur shutter, with close up focusing.

Stereofix Nr. 604/1:   **R4* D+**
c1920s, truncated box type stereo camera for 4.5 x 10.5cm plates or film packs, several lens and shutter combinations available including Tessar f6.3/6.5cm lenses, Compur shutter, without close up focusing.

Stereo Ideal: **R4* E**
c1920s, 6 x 13cm stereo camera; Zeiss Tessar 9cm f6.5 lenses; Compur shutter 1-1/250s.

Stereolette: **R3* E–**
c1912, compact folding stereo camera for 4.5cm x 10.7cm plates, Anastigmatic 60mm f6.8 lenses; Stereo Compur shutter 1-1/250s.

Stereo Palmos: **R4* E**
c1920s, folding stereo camera for 6 x 13cm plates, Zeiss Tessar 80mm f4.5 lenses, CFPS 1/30-1/1000s.

Trilby Nr. 5:   **R3* C+**
c1919, metal box camera for 6 x 9cm plates with internal changing mechanism for 6 plates, meniscus lens, simple shutter, single waist level VFR.

Trilby Nr. 11:   **R3* C+**
c1919, metal box camera for 6 x 9cm plates with internal changing mechanism for 6 plates, achromat 12cm lens, simple shutter, double waist level VFR.

Trilby Nr. 12:   **R3* C+**
c1919, metal box camera for 6.5 x 9cm plates with internal changing mechanism for 6 plates, achromat 12cm lens, simple shutter, double waist level VFR.

Trilby Nr. 13:   **R3* C+**
c1919, metal box camera for 6 x 9cm plates with internal changing mechanism for 12 plates, achromat 12cm lens, simple shutter, double waist level VFR.

Trilby Nr. 14:   **R3* C+**
c1919, metal box camera for 6.5 x 9cm plates with internal changing mechanism for 12 plates, achromat 12cm lens, simple shutter, double waist level VFR.

Trilby Nr. 17:   **R3* C+**
c1919, metal box camera for 9 x 12cm plates with internal changing mechanism for 6 plates, meniscus lens, simple shutter, waist level VFR.

Trilby Nr. 18:   **R3* C**
c1919, metal box camera for 9 x 12cm

plates with internal changing mechanism for 12 plates, achromat 14cm lens, simple shutter, double waist level VFR.

Trilby Nr. 20:   **R3* C+**
c1919, metal box camera for 9cm x 12cm plates with internal changing mechanism for 12 plates or 24 sheet film holders, achromat 14cm lens, simple shutter, double waist level VFR.

Trilby Nr. 29:   **R3* D–**
c1919, leather covered wooden box camera for 9 x 12cm plates with internal changing mechanism for 12 plates or 24 sheet film holders, achromat 14cm lens and three built-in auxiliary lenses for focusing at 1, 3, and 5 meters, 1-1/100s shutter, double waist level VFR.

Trilby Nr. 31:   **R3* D–**
c1919, leather covered wooden box camera with polished mahogany interior for 9 x 12cm plates with internal changing mechanism for 12 plates or 24 sheet film holders, achromat 13.5cm lens and three built-in auxiliary lenses for focusing at 1, 3, and 5 meters, 1-1/100s shutter, double waist level VFR, opening front.

Trilby Nr. 33:   **R3* D–**
c1919, leather covered wooden box camera with polished mahogany interior for 9 x 12cm plates with internal changing mechanism for 24 plates or 24 sheet film holders, focusing Alpha f11/14.5cm or Helios f8/13cm lens, Ica Automat shutter 1-1/100s shutter, double waist level VFR, opening front.

Trona Nr. 210:   **R2* B+**
c1920s, folding camera for 9 x 12cm plates or film packs, double extension bellows, several lens and shutter

combinations available including Novar f6.8/13.5cm lens, Automat shutter.

Tropica: **R4* G+**
c1925, 5" x 7" tropical camera; Carl Zeiss f4.5 lens; Compur shutter 1-1/250s; 5" x 7" exp on plates, teak construction with enamelled or nickel plated fittings.

Universal Juwel: **R4* D–**
c1925, Tessar 165mm f4.5 lens; Compur shutter 1-1/250s; double extension, rotating back, wide-angle feature, rising and sliding panel.

Victrix Nr. 48:   **R3* D**

c1925, 4.5 x 6cm folding plate camera, several lens and shutter combination including Ica Dominar f4.5/75mm lens, Compur shutter.

Volta Nr. 105:   **R3* B+**
c1920, folding VFR camera for 6 x ?cm or 6.5 x 9cm plates or film packs, Alpha f11/12cm or Novar f6.8/10.5cm lens, Automat shutter.

Ideal Toy Corp
Hollis, New York, USA

Kookie Kamera: **R3* D+**
comic plastic novelty camera; plastic meniscus 80mm f11 lens; single speed shutter; 4.5 x 4.5cm exp on "in-camera" processed positive paper. c1968.

Ihagee Kamerawerk A.G.
Dresden, Germany

For further information on Exakta cameras see Exakta Cameras 1933-1976 by Clament Aguila and Michel Rouah, Hove Collectors Books, 1987.

Exakta A: **R3* E–**

c1933; 127 roll film SLR camera; CFPS 1/25 -1/1000s; 8 exp, $1\frac{5}{8}$" x $2\frac{1}{2}$" on 127 film. Lens fitted to model A had thread dia. 39.5mm pitch 0.5mm Ihagee Exaktar 75mm-F 3.5 Meyer Primotar 75mm-F 3.5; Schneider Xenar 75mm-F2.9; Zeiss Tessar 75mm-F 3.5; Zeiss Tessar 75mm-F2.8; all the lenses available in both mount sizes for the range of cameras; Lenses not inter-changeable on model "A"; Five versions available; No.2 c1933; Lens mount changed to 39.8mm pitch 0.75mm; No.3 c1934; Winder lever replaced knob; red window cover; Ihagee logo

added to hood cover; No.4 c1934; As No.3 with Vacublitz 2 or 3 pin flash socket; No.5 c1939; As No.4 with top plate & front logo plate in matt chrome;

Exakta B: **R2* E–**

c1937, 127 roll film SLR camera; Zeiss Tessar 75mm f3.5 lens, non-interchangeable mount; CFPS 12-1/1000s; second speed knob for slow speeds; delayed speeds 6s-1/10s; 8 exp, $1\frac{5}{8}$" x $2\frac{1}{2}$" on 127 roll film. c1933. Seven versions of the camera; No.2 c1934; as No. 1 with Ihagee logo on Vfr cover; No.3 c1934; red window cover; film advance lever;infinity lock; lens mount 0.75mm pitch; No.4 c1935; Vacublitz flash socket; No.5; threaded socket for flash gun; No.6 c1938; No.6 c1938; first chrome Exacta B; No.7 c1938; as model No.6 painted black.

Parvola: **R3* C+**
c1930s. Characterised by large helical focusing mount. First turn brings lens to infinity setting. Further turning allows closer focusing. Models for 8 and 16 exp. on 127 plus a third dual format model for both. 7cm f4.5 Ihagee Anastigmat. Pronto shutter 1/25-1/100s + B & T. Also known as Klein Ultrix.

Parvola, c1930s.

Night Exakta: R3* F+

1934-1937, 127 roll film SLR camera; Dallmeyer Super-Six 80mm f1.9 lens, interchangeable mount; CFPS 12-1/1000s. Similar to Exakta B except for modified large size outer diameter focusing ring. Contrary to popular belief, ordinary Exakta lenses and Night Exacta lenses were perfectly interchangeable!; Serial numbers on finder frame; Four versions of this camera; No.1 c1934; Black body; no flash contacts; No.2 c1934;no slow speeds;flash socket added; No.3. c1937; Chrome top plate and front; No.4 c1937; as Exakta model "A"; CFPS 1/25-1/1000s, B T; lever wind; flash sockets.

Exakta C: R2* D+

c1935. Similar to Model B with addition of plate back adapter for plates and cut film, with rear ground glass focusing. When plate back is used, reflex finder cannot be utilised. Lens spacing ring used with film; c1935. Three versions of the camera; No.1; black body: No.2 c1937; as No.1 chrome finish: No.3. c1939; as No.2 shutter speeds 1/25-1/1000s. T. B. full range of lenses;

Exakta Junior: R3* F–

c1936; Simple version of the model "B"; CFPS 1/25-1/500s. T. B.; non-interchangeable, telescopic tube, Ihagee anastigmat 75mm F 4,5 lens, front cell focusing; Three versions; No. 1 c1936; black leather covering;no flash socket; knob film advance; No. 2 c1937; as No. 2 with flash socket; lever wind; No. 3. c1938; as No. 3 chrome finish:

Zeiss lenses for VP Exakta

55mm f8.0 Tessar **C–**
120mm f6.3 Tele-Tessar **D+**
180mm f6.3 Tele-Tessar **E–**
250mm f5.5 Tele-Tessar **E–**

Kine Exakta: R4* E+

c1936; The first Ihagee 35mm SLR; a scaled down version of the VP model B.; CFPS 12s-1/1000s T B; delayed speeds

6s-1/10s; Ziess Tessar 50mm F 3.5 lens.; frame counter; lever wind; flash sockets;folding Vfr; film cutter; removable back; Five versions; No.2 c1937; as No.1 with larger screen magnifier; No.3 c1937; as No.2 with name "Exacta" spelt with a "C" in place of the "K"; No.4 c1938; threaded flash attachment; No.5 c1948; as No.4 strap lugs fixed; new slow speed dial; mirror chamber changed; some bodies marked "Made in Germany": price with round Vfr £500; with square Vfr as below.

Zeiss Lenses for the Kine Exakta

35mm f2.8 Flektogon **B**
40mm f4.5 Tessar **B**
75mm f1.5 Biotar **E–**
80mm f2.8 Tessar **D**
85mm f4.0 Triotar **C+**
105mm f3.5 Tessar **D–**
135mm f4.0 Triotar (uncoated) **C**
135mm f4.0 Triotar (coated) **D–**
165mm f3.5 Tessar **D–**
180mm f6.3 Tele-Tessar **D+**
180mm f2.8 Sonnar **E–**
250mm f6.3 Tele-Tessar **E–**
300mm f4.0 Sonnar **E**
Stereflex set for use on normal lenses **F+**

Kine Exakta II: **R2* E–**
c1948; 35mm SLR; As the Kine Exakta with; cover on Vfr; frame counter window; rewind knob; ribbed film pressure plate; Version No. 2. c1949; as No. 1; Two socket flash;

Exakta Varex: **R2* D–**
c1950; 35mm SLR camera; as Kine Exakta; with removable Vfr. & hood; Pentaprism right-way-round viewing with lock button on front plate;two sets of flash contacts for X and PF synch; takes full range of lenses.

Exakta V: **R3* D–**
c1950, 35mm SLR camera; Xenon 50mm f2 lens, interchangeable bayonet mount; CFPS 12-1/1000s. Snr 665,000-695,000(?). First 35mm SLR with interchangeable finder. Known as the Varex in the USA.

Exakta VX: **R2* D–**

c1950; 35mm SLR camera; as the Varex with hinged & removable back; curved wind lever; X & PF flash contacts; milled knob rewind; film speed reminder in Weston & ASA; Meyer Primoplan 58mm F 1.9 lens; Five versions; No. 2 c1954; Straight film tensioning lever; second lens bayonet for tele lens; full aperture focusing with auto closing, first of the Automatic lenses; No. 3 c1954; as No. 2 Called Exakta Automatic in the USA; No.4. c1965; as No. 4. Co-ax flash socket;shutter release cover; No. 5 c1956; as No.4 film speed in DIN.

Exakta VX: **R2* D–**
c1955; 35mm SLR camera; Tessar 50mm f2.8 lens, interchangeable bayonet mount; CFPS 12-1/1000s. Snr 695,000-(?). Similar to Exakta V except has preset lens. Known as the Varex VX in the USA.

Exakta Varex IIa: R2* D

c1957; 35mm SLR camera. Varex IIa engraved on front plate; CFPS; 12s-1/5s octagonal slow speed dial; 1/10-1/1000s fast speeds; three flash sockets "M" 1/50-1/1000, "F" to 1/25, "X" 1/50 or slower; full range of lenses; Eight versions; No. 2. c1957; no 1/150s, shutter speed; No. 3. c1958; as No. 2 name plate in relief; No.4. c1958; as No.3 engraved "VXII" some also USSR OCCUP Germany; No's. 6, 7 and 8; c1961-1962; as Varex IIa; wider front panel;Exakta in upper case letters in white on black; Ihagee Dresden in upper case engraving on front plate.

c1957. 35mm SLR camera; Zeiss Pancolar 50mm f2 lens, interchangeable bayonet mount; CFPS 12-1/1000s. Similar to Exakta VX, but has quieter slow speed shutter mechanism, and a third, "F" type flash socket was added.

Exakta VXIIa: R2* D+

Exakta Varex IIb: R2* D+

c1963; 35mm SLR camera; Same as the Varex IIa with slow speed knob round with milled edge; better slow speed regulation 1/8-10s; fast speeds 1/30-1/1000s T. B; PF & X flash sockets; simple Vfr removal; accepts all lenses in the Exakta range.

Exakta VX 1000:   R1* C+
c1967; 35mm SLR camera; same as Varex IIb with few changes except for

the instant return mirror; non interchangeable back.

Exakta VX 500:   R1* C

c1969; 35mm SLR camera; CFPS 1/30-1/500s, B; no slow speeds; no FP flash socket; accepts full range of lenses; low cost version of the VX1000.

Exakta RTL 1000:   R1* C+

c1970; 35mm SLR camera; Slightly modified version of the Praktika VLC; produced when Ihagee was absorbed by Pentacon; MFPS 8-1/1000s; instant return mirror; X flash 1/125s, PF 1/30; full range of auto lenses; interchangeable Vfr's; TTL meter;

Exakta Twin TL: R1* C
c1970. 35mm SLR camera; Made in Japan for IHagee; MFPS 1-1/1000s; two shutter releases; X & M flash 1/125s auto return mirror.

Exakta 66:   R4* G

c1938, 6 x 6cm SLR camera; Tessar 8cm f2.8 lens; CFPS 12-1/1000s. 12 exp on 120 roll film.

Exakta 66:   R4* G
c1954, 6 x 6cm SLR camera; CFPS 12-1/1000s. Tessar 80mm f2.8 lens. 12 exp on 120 roll film. Originally announced at the 1952 Leipzig Fair, this camera was finally delivered in 1954. About 2000 were made, and it seems that all of them were exported to the USA. Not at all like the Exakta 66, and should not be considered as just another body style, but as a rarity in its own right!

Ihagee

Exa: R2* C
c1952, 35mm SLR taking Exakta mount lenses, but with a very simple shutter, removable waist level finder, and limited range of shutter speeds.

Exa I: R1* C

c1963; 35mm SLR new body shape; sector shutter; single flash socket.

Exa Ia: R1* C
c1965. redesigned body with lever advance.

Exa II: R1* C
c1950; 35mm SLR camera;CFPS $\frac{1}{2}$-1/250s; two flash sockets PF 1/15s X 1/30s; split image rangefinder screen.

EXA IIa: R1* C
c1964: 35mm SLR camera; Same as Exa II; except for plain ground glass screen or split-image rangefinder.

Exa 500:   R1* C+
c1966; 35mm SLR camera; same as IIa; fastest shutter speed 1/500; Fresnal lens focusing screen.

Exa VX 100:   R1* C–
c1968, now with external automatic aperture.

Exa Ib: R1* C–
c1975, now with internal automatic aperture.

Exa IIb: R1* C–
c1965, with built-in, permanent pentaprism.

Roll-Paff: R4* D–

c1922, 6 x 6cm SLR box camera; f6,8 Trioplan lens; single speed mirror shutter; 12 exp on 120 roll film.

Patent Folding Reflex: R4* F
c1925. One of the smallest and lightest reflex cameras of its time. Fairly complicated unfolding procedure protects lens when folded and unfolds on lazy tongs. Focal plane shutter speeded 1/15-1/1000s. Used normally with hooded focusing screen, a wire frame sports finder was also available. Made for plates, cut film or film packs, taking 6.5 x 9 cm images. Choice of f4.5 Meyer Veraplan or f4.5 Tessar lenses.

Patent Klapp Reflex: **R4* E+**
c1925, compact folding SLR camera; Dogmar 125mm f4.5 lens; CFPS 1/15-1/1000s. 6.5 x 9cm exp.

Ultrix Auto: **R2* C–**
c1934, 4 x 6.5cm roll film folding camera for 127 film; Schneider Xenar 70mm f4.5 lens; Compur shutter 1-1/300s.

Ikko Sha Co Ltd
Japan

Start 35:   **R2* D**
c1948-1950. Simple Bakelite camera for Bolta size film, taking 24 x 24 negatives. Fixed focus, fixed aperture f8 lens. I & B shutter. Later models had hinged back. Later still, c1958, metal was added to the body and the camera was synchronised for flash. Original model similar in style to the Rich-Ray Junior and Ebony, probably made by the same manufacturer.

Ilford Ltd
London, England

Advocat: **R2* C**

1949. Made for Ilford by Kennedy Instruments. Unusual for its 35mm focal length on standard 35mm image size, and for its white body, made from pressure die casting of aluminium silicon alloy, finished in a hard-stoved ivory enamel. f4.5 Dallmeyer. Shutter 1/25-1/200s.

Advocat Series II: **R2* B+**
1952. Similar to original model but with f3.5 Dallmeyer. 35mm focal length retained. Focusing engravings changed to make easier reading, hinge and lock mechanism modified.

Ilfoflex: **R1* B**

Cheap plastic camera made to resemble a small format TLR. f8 Brytex lens. Fixed focus and aperture. I & B shutter. 12 exp on 127. Similar in style to the Bedfordflex.

P.I.M. Monorail Camera: **R3* NSR**
1953. 5x4-inch monorail camera. Monorail in aluminium alloy, rack in plated brass. Lens panel and back supported in U-shaped brackets. Full range of camera movements. Square leather bellows with extension and movements.

Prentice: **R2* A**

1951. Folding camera for 8 exp on 120. Three-point focusing scale. f11 and f16 apertures, I & B shutter.

Sporti 4:   **R1* B**

1960. Made for Ilford by Dacora Kamerawerk. Aimed at children. 12 exp on 127. Made for use with Selochrome Pan film, with apertures for 'sunny' or 'cloudy'. Body made of polystyrene. Sold in 1961 as part of a kit containing camera, flashgun, film and flashbulbs.

Sportsman: **R1* B**

1957. Made for Ilford by Dacora Kamerawerk. Inexpensive but well specified 35mm camera. 45mm f3.5 Dacora Dignar lens Vario shutter 1/25-1/200s + B. Shutter release on front of body. All metal construction.

Sportsman Rangefinder: **R1* B**

1960. Similar to other Sportsman cameras, with addition of coupled rangefinder. Symbol focusing also allows manual focus. 45mm f2.8 Dacora Dignar lens. Pronto shutter 1/30-1/250s + B.

Sportsmaster: **R2* B+**

1961. Unusual version of the Sportsman with four shutter releases, each linked to the focusing mechanism. Setting the appropriate shutter sets the focus in one of four zones. Prontor-lux shutter coupled with auto-exposure control, speeds governed by speed setting of film: 1/30s for 10ASA to 1/500s for 200ASA. 45mm f2.8 Dacora. Apertures set automatically or manually for flash photography.

Super Sporti: **R1+ B**

1960. Similar to original model, with film wind and shutter interlocked. Shutter and aperture interlocked for three settings; 'sunny,' 'cloudy' and 'cloudy-dull'. Two apertures, f11 & f9. Two shutter speeds.

Witness: **R5* G**

1951. High quality 35mm CRF camera, showing strong influences from both Leitz and Zeiss. Witness lenses can be fitted quickly on bayonet, but mount also incorporates 39mm screw to take Leica lenses. Dust cover on accessory shoe. 5cm f2.9 collapsible Daron or 2-in f1.9 Dallmeyer Super-Six. FP shutter 1-1/1000s.

Ingersoll & Bros
New York

Shur-Shot Camera: **R4* E−**

c1897. Small all-wood plate camera; meniscus lens; guillotine shutter. Single exp on 2½" square, glass plates.

International Metal & Ferrotype Co
Chicago, Illinois, USA

The Diamond Gun Ferrotype Camera:
R5* G+

c1910. Large nickel plated all metal ferrotype camera in shape of a cannon, constructed so as to attract attention to a street operator. Has internal masks for formats down to button tintypes. Camera is 18" in length and 8" in diameter.

I.O.R.
Bucharest, Romania

Orizont: **R4* C–**
c1960, metal 35mm VFR camera, Tricolar f3.2/50mm lens, simple shutter 1/30-1/125s.

Orizont Amator: **R4* A**
c1970. plastic and metal 35mm VFR camera, Fotoclar f2.8/40mm lens, combined aperture/shutter f2.8 at 1/30s – f16 at 1/300s.

ISO, Industria Scientifica Ottica S.R.L.
Milan, Italy

Duplex 120:   **R3* E**
c1950. Unusual stereo camera using 120 roll film. A pair of stereo images are made on each side of the film. The interocular separation of the lenses limits the depth sensation at any distance beyond about 8 feet. The camera is important for a stereo collector. A special viewer was available. Iperang 25mm f/6.3 fixed focus lenses.

Duplex 120, c1950.

Duplex Super 120:   **R3* E+**

c1965. Similar to IS100 but fitted with Iriar 35mm, f3.5 lenses.

Iso Standard: **R4* G–**
c1953, 35mm RFR camera, Leica copy, interchangeable Iriar f3.5 or 2.8/50mm lens, among others, CFPS shutter speeds 1/20-1/1000s, interchangeable eyepieces for use with different focal length lenses, no strap lugs.

Iso Meter Lux: R4* G+
c1947, 35mm RFR camera, Leica copy, interchangeable Trixar f3.5/50mm lens, CFPS 1-1/1000s, coupled vertical RFR, built-in light meter.

Iso Bilux: R4* G+
c1950, 35mm RFR camera, Leica copy, interchangeable Trixar f3.5/50mm lens, CFPS 1-1/1000s, bottom trigger wind.

Iso Reporter: R4* G+
c1954, with improvements.

Hensold Reporter: R4* G+
c1955. Made for Dr. Hans Hensold of Wetzlar, and engraved with the Hensold name. Arion f1.9/5cm lens among others.

Eugen Ising
Germany

Isis: R2* B+
Metal body with lens drawn out on tube. 120 film. Direct vision finder. f3.5 Westar, Prontor S shutter 1-1/300s.

Ives Corp
Philadelphia, Pennsylvania, USA

Ives' Kromscope Viewer: R4* F
The wooden bodies were made by an English firm. Name unknown. Filters etc, installed in Philadelphia.

Hensold Reporter, c1955.

J

M. Janovitch
England

Jano While You Wait Camera: R4* F
c1930s. Huge box camera with slightly tapered back, incorporating small trays to hold developer and fixer. Took pictures on small bromide cards, which were then developed inside the camera body by the operator by inserting an arm into a light-tight sleeve and viewing the result through a hooded red filter in the top of the body. Negative print was then mounted in front of the lens and rephotographed to make a positive.

Jano Postcard Camera: R4* F
c1930. Similar to While You Wait Camera, but more box-shaped. Vario shutter with f5.5 lens. Reversable camera back for horizontal or vertical pictures.

Japy & Cie
Paris, France

Le Pascal: R4* F–
c1898, Le Pascal was fitted with a clockwork mechanism which advanced the paper-backed roll film after each exposure. This was the first such camera on the market. There were two models identical in outside appearance. Model I was all wood with a leather hinged back. The second model had a removable metal back. A landmark first camera.

Jeanneret & Co
Paris, France

Monobloc: R3* E–

c1925, 6 x 16cm stereo camera; Boyer Saphir 75mm f4.5 lenses; Stereo Compur shutter 1-1/150s. Interchangeable (rising) lens panel. Converts to take single panoramic pictures, 6 x 13cm.

Johnson & Harrison
England

Pantascopic Camera: R5* J–
Unusual panoramic wet plate camera; Grubb 20cm lens. Clockwork mechanism moves a flat wet plate past a slit as the lens and camera body rotates. So rare as to be for all practical purposes unavailable.

F. Jonte
Paris, France

F. Jonte Field Camera: R4* E+
5" x 7" field camera; Rapid Rectilinear lens. Bellows rotate for format change. Polished mahogany finish, brass fittings. Mother-of-pearl label with mfr. name.

Joseph Peter
Hamburg, Germany

Jos-Pe: R5* H

c1925. Single shot, tri-colour camera; Steinheil Munchen Anastigmat Quinar 10.5cm f2.5 lens; Compound shutter ½-1/100s; 3¼" x 4¼" exp on plates.

L. Joux
Paris, France

Steno Jumelle: R3* E+
c1894. Goerz 130mm f8 Anastigmat lens; 5-speed guillotine shutter; 12 exp, 9 x 12cm on plates.

Stereo Jumelle de Joux: R4* E+
c1898. Zeiss Krauss 110mm, f8 Anastigmatic lens; guillotine shutter. Special rotating magazine for 12 plates, 8 x 17cm. Mfd in Paris, France.

Jumeau & Jannin
Paris, France

Le Cristallos: R4* E–
c1890. Meniscus lens; rotary shutter. 6 x 9cm exp on film.

Jumelle Bertoni: R4* E+
c1900. Stereo camera; Elio 7cm f5.5 lens; shutter 1-1/200s; leather covered wooden body; magazine; 45 x 107mm.

Max Jurnick

Tom Thumb Camera: R5* H–
c1889. Detective camera concealed in wooden box; Rapid Rectilinear lens; spherical shutter.

Steno Jumelle de Joux, c1898.

K

Kalos Kamerabau
Germany

Kalos: R3* E

c1950. 24 exp 9 x 12mm on 16mm rollfilm in a camera the size of a matchbox. 20mm f4.5 Mikro-Anastigmat. Shutter 1/30-1/100s + B.

Kalart Co
New York, New York, USA

Kalart: R3* E

Petitux IV: R3* E

c1960. Design based on the Kalos. Changes included a focusing 25mm f2.8 Röschlein Supronar and shutter speeds $1/2$-1/125s. Image size changed to 14 x 14mm.

c1948-1950, $3\frac{1}{4}$" x $4\frac{1}{2}$" press camera; Wollensak Raptor 127mm f4.5 coated lens; Rapax shutter 1-1/400s. Dual left and right RFR windows for left-eye or right-eye operation. Has die-cast aluminium body with all built-in parts. Rising and lateral lens movements. The "Electric Brain" controls dual shutter release triggers; safety interlock requires holder to be inserted and the slide withdrawn to release the shutter. Two plug-in flash reflectors for midget lamps can be mounted on top of camera; interlocks prevent lamps from firing unless shutter has been cocked, film holder inserted and slide pulled. Built-in "Focuspot"

Kamera

Kamera Werkstütten
see – Guthe & Thorsch

Kashiwa Seiko Co
Japan

Cooky 35:   **R3* F**
1949. One of the smallest 35mm cameras made. Two models, one with a 40mm f2.8 Runer Anastigmat, the other with a 40mm f3.5 Zephyr. Shutter on both 1/25-1/100s. Auto frame counter on top plate.

Alfred C. Kemper
Chicago, Illinois, USA

Kombi: **R3* F**

Miniature metal-bodied camera and graphoscope (viewer) combination; biconvex single element lens. Permanently fixed pinhole diaphragm; single speed shutter, 25 exposures $1\frac{1}{8}''$ round on special film made by Eastman Kodak. After exposure the film was processed to a positive transparency and reloaded into the camera. The back was removed and the image viewed through the lens which acted as a 3X magnifier. Very collectable and still found in the US without too much difficulty.

Keio Department Store
Tokyo, Japan

Tyre Camera (Potenza):   **R1 A**

c1981; 110 camera in the shape of an automobile tyre. Meniscus lens, f11, 26mm. Shutter 100s.

Kennedy Instruments
London, England

KI Monobar: **R3* G**

1954 35mm monorail view camera, using cut film holders, ground glass focusing, very unusual.

Kern
Aarau, Switzerland

Bijou: **R4* F**
1924. An unusually designed camera for
$3^1/_2$" x $2^1/_2$" plates in a revolving back.
Aluminium body, f4.5 anastigmat lens,
shutter speeds from 1-1/200s. Body
incorporated twin viewfinders.

Kern Folding Camera: **R4* F**
Kern Anastigmat 120mm f4.5 lens;
Compur shutter 1-1/200s. $3^1/_4$" x $4^1/_4$"
exp. Aluminium construction. c1920.

Stereo Kern: **R4* G**
c1920. 35mm stereo camera; Kernon
35mm f3.5 lenses; guillotine shutter
1/25-1/300s.

Super Stereo: **R4* G**
c1930. 35mm stereo camera; Kern f3.5
lens. 20 x 20mm format. Interlens
separation increased to 64mm.

Thomas Kerr
Walthamstow, England

Abraham's Detective Camera: **R4* F**
c1888, wooden box-type detective
camera; plate changing by lever.

Keys Stereo Products
USA

Trivision Camera: **R3* C**
c1946, fixed focus f8 lenses; single
speed shutter 1/50s. 6 stereo or 12
single exp on 828 film.

Odon Keyzlar
Slatinany, Czechoslovakia

Okam: **R3* NSR**

1925; Trioplan 75mm
f4.5 lens; 4.5 x 6cm
dry plates, shutter $^1/_5$
to 1/1000s. Unusual
focal plane shutter
design varied slit width
and transit speed to
reach high speeds.

Back view.

Kiko-do Co
Japan

Baby Superflex: **R5* F**
1938. Miniature single lens reflex, the
first Japanese SLR to use 4 x 4 cm
format. Behind lens shutter speeded
1/25-1/100s, 70mm f4.5 Super
Anastigmat lens. Made with two types
of shutter release – swing lever and
vertical plunger type

KGB
(Manufactured for former Russian Intelligence Services)

F21:   **R3* F**

c1980, metal 35mm VFR camera for 18x24mm frames with film loaded in special cassettes. Built-in spring motor, f2.0 28mm fixed focus lens. The first model of the F-21 appeared about 1950 and was available only to the KGB. Much later a civilian version was available on a limited basis. Focusing version, f2.8 fixed focus lens, f2.9 lens with automatic exposure control. These cameras started bringing very high prices, upwards of $3500. Now the market has calmed a bit, and recently one changed hands for $700. It is rumoured that a large stock of cameras exists. It will be interesting to see what happens to the price.

Kiddie Kamera
Taiwan

     R2* B

This company made a number of cameras during the 1980s based on the faces of clowns and animals. All were for 110 film, all had fixed focus, aperture and shutter speeds. Styles included a bear, panda, Father Christmas, man clown and girl clown. The latter was the last made in the early 1990s and is the most common of the various models.

Kiev
Ukraine

John Player Special: **R4* F**

c1970. Disguised version of the Kiev Vega 16mm camera. Outer body designed to look like a pack of cigarettes and actually held two real cigarettes. The false cigarettes poking out the top are the camera's controls. Might have been a true spy camera, but the more likely origin is as a fake, manufactured in Poland.

Kiev: **R2* C**
1947. Copy of Contax II. CRF camera made with Zeiss parts following the seizure of the Contax plant by the Russian Army at the end of WWII. Equipment taken from Jena made lenses and production was shifted to Kiev. More Contax copies followed.

Kiev 2:   **R2* C+**
1947. 50mm f2 Jupiter 8 Shutter 1/2-1/250s.

Kiev 2A: **R2* C+**
1956. Similar to Kiev 2 with flash synch added.

Kiev 3:   **R2* D**
1952. Similar to Kiev 2 with uncoupled Selenium meter

Kiev 3A: R2* D
1956. Similar to Kiev 3 with flash synch
added.

Kiev 4:   R2* D
1957. A Kiev 3A with minor body
changes.

Kiev 4A: R2* D
1958. Similar to Kiev 2A with small body
changes.

Kiev 5:   R2* D+

1970. Updated and restyled version of
the Kiev 4A with meter incorporated
into body.

*More details of Kiev cameras and their
association with Contax can be found in
The Zeiss Compendium by Charles M.
Barringer and Marc James Small,
published by Hove Books.*

Benjamin Kilburn

Kilburn Photographic Gun: R5* NSR
c1884, gun-type detective camera. 10.5
x 12.5cm exp on plates; trigger released
shutter.

Kin-Dar Corporation

Kindar Stereo Camera: R3* D+

c1953, 35mm stereo camera; Steinheil
Cassar f3.5 coated lenses; shutter 1/10-
1/200s. Designed by Seton Rochwhite.

K.K.W. Lighter Camera: R2* B

c1975, cigarette lighter and compass.
Pressing shutter release on this toy trips
a lighter. Mfd in Japan.

King KG
Germany

Mastra V35:   R1* A
1958. Inexpensive 35mm VFR camera in
a slim, die-cast body. 45mm f2.8 Cassar
lens in Verio shutter 1/25-1/200s + B.

Regula II: R1* A
1951. Basic 35mm VFR camera in
chrome and black plastic fabric finish.
50mm f3.5 Staeble-Werk Kataplast lens
in Prontor S shutter 1-1/300s + B.

Kilfit
Munich, Germany

Mecaflex: **R4* F+**

1953. Rare and unusual 35mm SLR for 24 x 24mm negatives. Waist-level finder covered by snap-up magnifier. 40mm f2.8 or f3.5 Kilar standard lenses in interchangeable bayonet mount. Shutter release, film, rewind and viewfinder found under hinged top plate. Matte chrome body with black leather covering. A few models made with brown covering. Rare 105mm f4 Teke-Kinar can sometimes be found. Even rarer accessory for converting viewfinder for eye-level use (mirror type, not pentaprism).

Kinn
France

Baby Kinax: **R2* B**
1951. Folding camera for 8 exp on 620. All metal body in black grained finish, chrome fittings. Three numbered stop on lens for f16, f22 and f32. I & B shutter. Flash synch.

Kinaflex: **R2* C**
1952. TLR for 12 exp on 120 or 620. Twin lenses geared together for focusing. 75mm Som Berthiot Flor lenses f3.5 for taking, f3 for focusing. Inter-lens shutter 1-1/300s + B. Flash synch at 1/25s or 1/50s.

Kinax-Cadet: **R2* C**
1950. Folding camera for 8 exp on 620. Self erecting. 10cm Kior Anastigmat. Shutter 1/25-1/100s + B. Synch for flash. Red spot on focusing and aperture scales give a snapshot setting and depth of field of 10ft to infinity.

Kinax I: **R2* B**
1948. All metal folding camera. 105mm f4.5 Angenieux. Shutter 1/10-1/50s + B.

Kinax II: **R2* B**
1948. Essentially the same as the Kinax I but with a smoother shutter and better pressure pad.

Kinax III: **R3* A**
1951. Similar to Kinax I and II, but with masking frames to take 8, 12 or 16 exp on 620. 105mm f4.5 Berthiot Special lens, nine speed shutter 1-1/300s + B. An aluminium frame pulls up from behind the lens and swings in front of the optical viewfinder, two horizontal bars dissecting the view to give the fields for the smaller formats. Three red windows for three different formats.

Franz Kochmann
Korellewerk, Dresden, Germany

After 1945 this factory was "nationalised" and became part of the

Werkestette für Feinmechanik und Optik (WEFO), VEB, Dresden, East Germany. Post-war cameras made by this firm are treated as a continuation of the pre-war line, and are found at the end of this listing.

Korelle: R2* C–

c1932, 4 x 6.5cm roll film camera, various lens and shutter combinations including Radionar 75mm f3.5 lens, Compur shutter 1-1/250s.

Korelle P: R3* E+
4.5 x 6cm folding plate camera, various lens and shutter combinations including Xenar f2.9 lens, Compur shutter 1-1/250s.

Reflex-Korelle: R3* D+

c1932, SLR camera for 6 x 6cm frames on 120 roll film, Ludwig-Dresden Victar

f2.9 or f3.5/75mm lens, interchangeable screw mount, CFPS, 1/25-1/500s, black painted name plate, external selftimer, double stroke lever advance.

Reflex-Korelle II: R3* D+
c1934, SLR camera for 6 x 6cm frames on 120 roll film, Ludwig-Dresden Victar f2.9 or f3.5/75mm lens, interchangeable screw mount,CFPS, 2-1/500s, chrome name plate, external selftimer, double stroke lever advance.

Reflex-Korelle Chrome III: R3* E
c1936, SLR camera for 6 x 6cm frames on 120 roll film, Radionar or Xenar f3.5 or Radionar f2.9/75mm lens, interchangeable bayonet mount, CFPS, 2-1/1000s, chrome name plate, VFR hood, and front plate, internal selftimer, single stroke lever advance.

Sport Korelle 66:   R4* E
c1939, folding VFR camera for 6 x 6cm frames on 120 roll film, Tessar f2.8/8cm lens, interchangeable mount, CFPS to 1/1000s.

Korelle K: R3* F
c1933, Bakelite 35mm half frame VFR camera 18 x 24mm frames on standard 35mm film, various lens were available including Tessar f3.5 or f2.8/35mm lens, Compur shutter (dark brown body brings 100% more, as does Leitz Elmar f3.5/3.5cm lens.)

Korelle 6x6:   R3* C
c1932, folding VFR camera for 6 x 6cm frames on 120 roll film, various lens and shutter combinations available including Radionar f2.9 or f3.5/75mm lens, Prontor or Compur shutter.

Korelle 6x9:   **R3* C**
c1932, folding VFR camera for 6 x 9cm frames on 120 roll film, various lens and shutter combinations available including Radionar f4.5/105mm lens, Prontor or Compur shutter.

Enolde A, I, Ia, II, III, IV, V, VI: **R3* B**
c1918, folding plate or sheet film cameras in 6.5 x 9 cm, 9 x 12cm, and 10 x 15cm sizes, leather covered wooden or metal bodies, rising and shifting fronts, more expensive models have double extension bellows, many lens and shutter combinations including Meyer, Steinheil, Rodenstock, and Schneider lenses and Vario, Ibsor and Compur shutters, models include I, Ia, A, II, III, IV, V and VI, all of which differ only slightly. (+30% for 6.5 x 9cm size and double extension bellows).

Enolde: **R4* E**
c1930, folding camera for 6 x 9cm frames on roll film, unusual focusing tube/viewfinder swings away from the camera body and attaches to the lens standard when the camera is opened in the working position, moving the lens thereby focuses the image in the VFR, Zeiss Tessar f4.5/105mm lens, Compur shutter.

Meister-Korelle: **R3* E**
c1950, SLR for 6 x 6cm frames on roll film, interchangeable Tessar f3.5/9cm Primotar f3.5/85mm lens, CFPS 1-1/1000s.

Eastman Kodak Co
Rochester, New York, USA

George Eastman began the manufacture of dry plates in 1880, supplying all the needed capital for the new enterprise out of his own pocket. Henry Strong, a Rochester businessman loaned him some money and then in 1881 they formally founded the Eastman Dry Plate Company, with Strong as President and Eastman Treasurer. Dry Plates which were the company's main source of income were distributed by the E. & H.T, Anthony Co, at that time the largest jobber of photographic supplies in the U.S. In 1884 when the firm added flexible stripping film to the product line, they changed the corporate name to the Eastman Dry Plate and Film Company. The film was for use in the recently introduced Eastman-Walker Roll Holder, a product designed primarily as an accessory for use with cameras made by a number of domestic U.S. and foreign manufacturers. The corporate name was shortened to the Eastman Company in 1889 and then lengthened to the Eastman Kodak Company early in the 1890s.

One of the most important cameras ever produced, called simply The Kodak had been introduced in 1888. At the same time, George Eastman created the photofinishing industry. The purchaser of the $25.00 camera mailed it back to the company where the 100 pictures were developed, printed, mounted and the camera reloaded for $10.00. The original sales slogan of "You Press the Button, We Do the Rest" was fully justified. By this division of labour, Eastman had revolutionised photography extending it to vast untouched markets.

By the mid 1920s, despite the postwar WWI economic boom we call the "roaring twenties" camera sales had become somewhat sluggish. Photographic technology hadn't changed much in the past two decades so there was little reason to replace a perfectly good camera. The company did not have a formal design department relying instead on the services of engineers who had some "flare" for product design. This policy had mixed success. In 1927 they hired the industrial designer Walter Dorwin Teague to upgrade the design of existing products and ultimately to create entirely new designs. Teague designed both the cameras and the packaging in which they were sold. Teague's packaging designs are of special interest to collectors because of their classic art-deco appearance adding considerably to its contents value.

Several of his designs include: the Gift Kodak for the 1930 Christmas market, an otherwise standard folding camera but fitted with a re-designed front and sold in a cedar box which could be used for cigarettes, and the Kodak Bantam Special which has been called the most beautiful small hand camera ever made. It is safe to say that all Kodak cameras made in the decade of the 1930s were either of his design or strongly influenced by him.

Note: Most of the more expensive Kodak cameras were supplied with a variety of lens and shutter combinations during their production spans. Usually we have listed the most readily available.

The Kodak: R5* H+

1888 Small simple box camera loaded with film for 100 round pictures each 2$^{1}/_{2}$" in diameter. Periscopic lens, barrel shutter. Camera was returned to factory in Rochester, NY where the film was processed, printed and the camera reloaded and returned. No viewfinder, lines embossed in the top of the camera served as a guide to give an approximate angle of view.

No. 1 Kodak: R4* G–

c1889-1895. Rapid Rectilinear lens; sector shutter; 100 exp, 2" diameter.

No 2 Kodak: R4* F

1889 Round pictures as original Kodak and #1 but for 3$^{1}/_{2}$" pictures, other technical features are identical to Kodak #1 but scaled up and, of course, the camera is larger. Only the first of the production run did not have a viewfinder. Later a round viewfinder was added. A number 2 without a viewfinder is somewhat more valuable.

No 2 Kodak, 1889.

No. 3 Kodak: R4* F–
c1890-1897, focusing box roll film camera; Bausch & Lomb Universal lens; sector shutter; 100 exp, $3^1/_4$" x $4^1/_4$".

No. 3 Kodak Junior: R4* F–
c1890-1897. Bausch & Lomb Universal lens; sector shutter; 60 exp $3^1/_4$" x $4^1/_4$".

No. 4 Kodak: R4* F–

c1890-1898. Bausch & Lomb Universal lens; sector shutter; 48 exp, 4" x 5".

No. 4 Kodak Junior: R4* E+
c1890-1897. Bausch & Lomb Universal lens; sector shutter; 48 exp, 4" x 5".

No. 4 Folding Kodak: R4* F–
Bausch & Lomb Universal lens; special Kodak sector shutter*; 48 exp, 4" x 5". C 1890-1892.

Eastman Interchangeable View 5" x 8":
R4* F–

c1885. Brass Rapid Rectilinear lens; waterhouse stops; behind-the-lens shutter. Tilting back; rising and falling front; ground glass back; side tripod holder attachment; ivory label.

No. 4 Folding Kodak Improved:
R4* F–
c1893-1897. Bausch & Lomb Universal lens; Bausch & Lomb Iris Diaphragm shutter; 48 exp, 4" x 5".

No. 5 Folding Kodak (first model):
R5* F–
c1890. Special Kodak sector shutter; film or plates; Eastman-Walker roll holder for 54 exp, 5" x 7" on roll film.

No. 5 Folding Kodak (first model), c1890.

No. 5 Folding Kodak (second model): R5* F

c1892. Barker shutter; Eastman-Walker roll holder for 54 exp, 5" x 7" on roll film.

No. 5 Folding Kodak Improved: R5* F–

c1893-97. Bausch & Lomb Universal lens; Bausch & Lomb Iris Diaphragm

shutter; double swing, sliding front. Eastman-Walker roll holder for 54 exp, 5" x 7" on roll film or plates. Provisions for stereo.

No. 6 Folding Kodak Improved: R5* G–
c1893-1895. Bausch & Lomb Universal lens; Bausch & Lomb Iris Diaphragm shutter; 48 exp, $6^{1}/_{2}$" x $8^{1}/_{2}$".

"A" Ordinary Kodak: R5* G–

c1891-1895. Single lens; Special sector shutter; 24 exp, $2^{3}/_{4}$" x $3^{1}/_{4}$".

"A" Daylight Kodak: R5* G–
c1891-1895. Single lens; fixed diaphragm; Special sector shutter; 24 exp, $2^{3}/_{4}$" x $3^{1}/_{4}$". c1891-1895.

"B" Ordinary Kodak: R5* F
c1891-1895. Single lens; revolving waterhouse diaphragm. Special sector shutter; 24 exp, $3^{1}/_{2}$" x 4".

Eastman Interchangeable View 8" x 10":
R3* F–
c1888. 8" x 10" view camera; Prosh triple model shutter and lens. Separate front extension; ivory label.

"B" Daylight Kodak: **R4* F–**
c1891-95. Double lens; revolving waterhouse diaphragm. Special sector shutter; 24 exp, 3½" x 4".

"C" Ordinary Kodak: **R4* F+**
c1891-1895. Single lens; revolving waterhouse diaphragm. Special sector shutter; 24 exp, 4" x 5".

"C" Daylight Kodak: **R4* F–**
c1891-1895. Double lens; revolving waterhouse diaphragm. Special sector shutter; 24 exp, 4" x 5".

No. 4 Kodak: **R4* F–**
c1894-1897. Leather covered box camera; Achromatic lens; rotating waterhouse stops; Kodet (built-in) shutter. 4" x 5" plate or roll holder.

No. 4 Folding Kodet: **R4* F–**
c1894. 4" x 5" folding camera; 6⅛" lens; finder for horizontal or vertical photos on 4" x 5" plates or film; leather covered mahogany construction.

No. 4 Folding Kodet Special: **R4* F–**

c1895-1897. Achromatic lens; Kodet (built-in) shutter*. 4" x 5" plate or roll holder.

No. 4 Folding Kodet Junior: **R4* F–**
c1894-1897. Achromatic lens; Kodet (built-in) shutter. 4" x 5" plate or roll holder.

No. 5 Folding Kodet: **R5* F–**
c1895-1897. Achromatic lens*; Kodak (built-in) shutter. 5" x 7" plate or roll holder.

No. 5 Folding Kodak Special: **R4* F–**
c1895-1897. Rapid Rectilinear lens; Kodet (built-in) shutter*. 5" x 7" plate or roll holder.

Pocket Kodak: **R3* D**

c1896-1900. Single lens; rotary shutter; 1½" x 2" exp on 102 roll film. First model had round vf. C 1895-1896, $80-$115. Second model has rectangular vf.

No. 3 Folding Pocket Kodak De Luxe:
                                   R4* E+
c1907.

No. 4 Folding Pocket Kodak: **R2* C–**
c1899. Suter Anastigmatic 150mm f6.3 lens; Ibsor shutter 1-1/100s; 4" x 5" exp.

No. 4 Folding Pocket Kodak, c1899.

No. 2 Bulls-Eye camera.

No. 1A Folding Hawk Eye: **R2* B+**
c1905. Bausch & Lomb Rapid Rectilinear lens; ball-bearing shutter; 6.5 x 11cm exp.

No. 2 Bullet: **R2* C–**
c1895-1896. Achromatic lens; rotary shutter; $3\frac{1}{2}$" x $3\frac{1}{2}$" exp on 101 roll film.

No. 2 Bullet Improved: **R2* C**
c1896-1900. Achromatic lens; rotary shutter $3\frac{1}{2}$" x $3\frac{1}{2}$" exp on 101 roll film or single plate holder.

No. 2 Bullet Special Kodak: **R3* D–**
c1899, covered box camera; Rapid Rectilinear lens; Triple-Action shutter; for plates or roll film; $3\frac{1}{2}$" x $3\frac{1}{2}$" exp.

No. 2 Bulls-Eye: **R2* D–**
c1896-1913, fixed focus achromatic lens; rotary shutter; 12 exp, $2\frac{1}{2}$" x $3\frac{1}{2}$" on 101 roll film.

No. 2 Bulls-Eye Improved: **R2* C–**
c1896-1913. Achromatic lens; Rotary shutter; $3\frac{1}{2}$" x $3\frac{1}{2}$" exp on 101 roll film.

No. 2 Bulls-Eye Special: **R2* C+**
c1898-1904. Rapid Rectilinear lens; Eastman Triple Action shutter; $3\frac{1}{2}$" x $3\frac{1}{2}$" exp on 101 roll film.

No. 4 Bullet: **R3* D–**
c1896, box camera for film or plates.

No. 4 Bulls-Eye: **R3* D–**
c1896, roll film camera; rotary shutter; focused by external sliding lever.

No. 4 Bulls-Eye Improved: **R2* C–**
c1896-1904. Achromatic lens; Rotary shutter; 4" x 5" exp on 103 roll film.

No. 4 Bulls-Eye Special: **R2* C+**
c1898-1904. Rapid Rectilinear lens; Eastman Triple Action shutter; 4" x 5" exp on 103 roll film.

No. 2 Folding Bulls-Eye: **R2* C+**
c1899-1901. Achromatic lens; Rotary shutter; $3\frac{1}{2}$" x $3\frac{1}{2}$" exp on 101 roll film.

No. 2 Falcon: R3* C+

c1897-1899. Box camera; $4\frac{1}{2}$" Achromatic lens; rotary 3 stop shutter; 12 exp, $3\frac{1}{2}$" x $3\frac{1}{2}$" on 101 roll film.

No. 2 Eureka: R3* D

c1898-1899. Leather covered box camera; Achromatic lens; Rotary shutter; $3\frac{1}{2}$" x $3\frac{1}{2}$" exp on 106 roll film.

No. 2 Eureka, Model B: R3* D
c1899, leather covered box camera; rotary shutter; $3\frac{1}{2}$" x $3\frac{1}{2}$" exp on plates or roll film.

No. 2 Eureka Junior: R3* D
c1899, leatherette covered box camera; $3\frac{1}{2}$" x $3\frac{1}{2}$" plates.

No. 4 Eureka: R3* D
c1899. Achromatic lens; Rotary shutter 4" x 5" exp on 109 roll film.

No. 1 Panoram Kodak: R3* E+
c1900-1901. Rapid Rectilinear lens; swinging lens and focal plane slit; $2\frac{1}{4}$" x 7" exp on 105 roll film.

No. 1 Panoram Kodak, Model B: R3* E+

c1901-1903. Meniscus lens; swinging lens and focal plane slit; $2\frac{1}{4}$" x 7" exp on 105 roll film.

No. 1 Panoram Kodak, Model C: R3* E+
c1903-1907. Meniscus lens; swinging lens and focal plane slit; $2\frac{1}{4}$" x 7" exp on 105 roll film.

No. 1 Panoram Kodak, Model D: R3* G+
c1907-1926. Meniscus lens; swinging lens and focal plane slit; $2\frac{1}{4}$" x 7" exp on 105 roll film.

No. 3A Panoram Kodak: R3* F–
c1926-1928. Meniscus lens; swinging lens and focal plane slit; $3\frac{1}{4}$" x $10\frac{3}{8}$" exp on 122 roll film.

No. 3A Panoram Kodak, c1926-1928.

No. 5 Cartridge Kodak, c1898-1901.

No. 4 Panoram Kodak: **R3* E+**
c1899-1900. Rapid Rectilinear lens; swinging lens and focal plane slit; $3\frac{1}{2}$" x 12" exp on 103 roll film.

No. 4 Panoram Kodak , Model D:
                   R3* E+
c1907-1924. Meniscus lens; swinging lens and focal plane slit; $3\frac{1}{2}$" x 12" on 103 roll film.

No. 2 Flexo Kodak: **R3* C+**
c1899-1913. Achromatic lens; Rotary shutter; $3\frac{1}{2}$" x $3\frac{1}{2}$" exp on 101 roll film.

No. 3 Cartridge Kodak: **R3* D**
c1900-1907. Rapid Rectilinear lens*; Eastman Triple Action shutter; $4\frac{1}{4}$" x $3\frac{1}{4}$" exp on 119 roll film.

No. 4 Cartridge Kodak: **R3* D**
c1897-1907. Rapid Rectilinear lens; Eastman Triple Action shutter; 4" x 5" exp on 104 roll film.

No. 5 Cartridge Kodak: **R3* D**
c1898-1901. Rapid Rectilinear lens; Eastman Triple Action shutter; 5" x 7" exp on 115 roll film or plates.

No. 0 Folding Pocket Kodak: **R3* D–**
c1902-1906. Meniscus lens; Automatic shutter; $2\frac{1}{2}$" x $1\frac{5}{8}$" exp on 121 roll film.

No. 0 Brownie: **R2* B–**
c1914. Meniscus lens; Rotary shutter; 4 x 6cm on roll film.

No. 1 Brownie: **R2* A**

1900. The camera that truly brought photography to everyone. It cost just $1.00 when introduced in 1900. The viewfinder was extra and not available immediately. It cost 25 cents. The box was covered with Brownies, little figures popularised by Palmer Cox in his children's stories. The boxes are very rare since they were used for only a few years and can easily double the price of the camera. Curiously the rollfilm, first made for this ultimate snapshot camera became #120, the only paper-backed film still made by Kodak and very nearly a professional only product. In Japan 120 film is still called "Brownie Film."

No. 2 Brownie: R2* A

1901. The image size was increased to $2\frac{1}{4}$" x $3\frac{1}{4}$" and it now had a built-in viewer for both vertical and horizontal pictures.

No. 2 Folding Brownie, Model A:
R2* A

c1904. Achromatic meniscus lens; Pocket Automatic shutter; 6 x 9cm exp.

No. 2 Stereo Brownie: R4* F–

c1905, folding roll film stereo camera; paired exp, $3\frac{1}{4}$" x $2\frac{1}{2}$" each; shutter adjustable for I, B & T; four lens openings.

No. 2 Brownie, Model C: R2* A

c1905, box roll film camera; $2\frac{1}{4}$" x $3\frac{1}{4}$" exp.

No. 2A Folding Autographic Brownie:
R2* A

c1915. Achromatic lens; ball-bearing shutter; $2\frac{1}{2}$" x $4\frac{1}{4}$" exp.

No. 3 Brownie: R2* A

c1908. Meniscus lens; Rotary shutter; Took $3\frac{1}{4}$" x $4\frac{1}{4}$" size exp.

Brownie Reflex: R1* A

1946. Elegant plastic camera for 12 exp on 127. Not a true reflex, but a TLR look-alike with fixed focus lens and viewfinder. I & B shutter. Synch for flash.

Duaflex II: R1* A

1955. Box camera specification in a TLR-like design. Mirror in viewfinder hood allows eye-level viewing. Kodet meniscus lens. I & B shutter.

OO Cartridge Premo (Kodak): R3* C–

1916; Meniscus lens, Kodak Rotary shutter. Smallest Kodak box camera it produced an image $1\frac{1}{4}$" x $1\frac{3}{4}$". Although this was the first Kodak camera to use 35mm wide film, it was unsprocketed and paper-backed. The film made for the OO Premo (Kodak) was nearly identical to Bantam film produced several decades later.

No. 1 Folding Pocket Kodak: R3* D

c1898-1915. Achromatic lens; Rotary shutter*; $2\frac{1}{4}$" x $3\frac{1}{4}$" exp on 105 roll film.

No. 1A Folding Pocket Kodak: R3* C–
c1899-1915. Achromatic lens; Pocket Automatic shutter; $2\frac{1}{2}$" x $4\frac{1}{2}$" exp on 116 roll film. Version no. 1 – 2 vfs. Version no. 2 – 1 vf.

No. 1A Folding Pocket Kodak Special: R3* C–

c1908-1912. Rapid Rectilinear lens; F.P.K. Automatic shutter; $2\frac{1}{2}$" x $4\frac{1}{4}$" exp on 116 roll film.

No. 1A Folding Pocket "RR" Kodak: R2* C–
c1912-1915. Similar to No. 1A Folding Pocket Kodak Special . Kodak Ball Bearing shutter.

No. 2 Folding Pocket Kodak: R2* B–
c1899-1903. Achromatic lens; Eastman Automatic shutter; $3\frac{1}{2}$" x $3\frac{1}{2}$" exp on 101 roll film.

No. 3 Folding Pocket Kodak: R2* B–
c1900-1915. Rapid Rectilinear* lens; Unicum shutter; $3\frac{1}{4}$" x $4\frac{1}{4}$" exp on 118 roll film.

Kodak

No. 3A Folding Pocket Kodak: R2* B–

c1903-1915. Rapid Rectilinear lens; F.P.K. Automatic shutter; $3\frac{1}{4}$" x $5\frac{1}{2}$" exp on 122 roll film.

No. 1A Special Kodak: R3* B+
c1912-1914. Zeiss Kodak Anastigmat f6.3 lens; Bausch & Lomb Compound* shutter; $2\frac{1}{2}$" x $4\frac{1}{4}$" exp on 116 roll film.

No. 3 Special Kodak: R3* C–
c1911-1914. Zeiss Kodak Anastigmat f6.3 lens; Bausch & Lomb Compound shutter; $3\frac{1}{4}$" x $4\frac{1}{4}$" exp on 118 roll film.

No. 3A Special Kodak: R3* C
c1910-1914. Zeiss Kodak Anastigmat f6.3 lens; Bausch & Lomb Compound shutter*; $3\frac{1}{4}$" x $5\frac{1}{2}$" exp on 122 roll film.

No. 4 Folding Kodak: R3* C
c1907-1912. Rapid Rectilinear lens; F.P.K. Automatic shutter; 4" x 5" exp on 123 roll film.

No. 4A Folding Kodak: R2* C
c1906-1912. Rapid Rectilinear lens; Bausch & Lomb Automatic shutter; $4\frac{1}{4}$" x $6\frac{1}{2}$" exp on 126 roll film.

No. 4 Screen Focus Kodak: R4* E
c1904-1909. Rapid Rectilinear lens; Kodak Automatic shutter; 4" x 5" exp on 123 roll film.

3B Quick Focus Kodak: R4* E–
c1906-1911. Meniscus Achromatic lens, Rotary shutter; $3\frac{1}{4}$" x $5\frac{1}{2}$" exp on 125 roll film.

Stereo Kodak Model 1: R4* E+
c1917-1925. Kodak Anastigmat f7.7 lenses; Stereo Automatic shutter; pair of $3\frac{1}{8}$" x $3\frac{3}{16}$" exp on 101 roll film.

No. 2 Stereo Kodak: R4* F–

c1901-1905. Box-type stereoscopic camera; periscopic 5" f14 lenses; wl finder; oscillating sector between-the-lens shutter. 2, 3 or 5 paired exp, $3\frac{3}{8}$" x $3\frac{3}{8}$" on roll film. The only box-type stereo camera for roll film produced in America.

No. 4A Speed Kodak: R4* F–

c1908-13. Bausch & Lomb Zeiss Tessar f6.3 lens; Kodak fps; 4$\frac{1}{4}$" x 6$\frac{1}{2}$" exp on 126 roll film.

No. 1A Speed Kodak: R4* E–
c1909-1913. Zeiss Kodak Anastigmat f6.3 lens; Graflex fps; 2$\frac{1}{2}$" x 4$\frac{1}{4}$" exp on 116 roll film.

Kodak Enlarging Outfit: R3* D
c1920, for 4" x 5" or smaller; ground glass back; accessory for lantern slide camera; monorail; polished oak finish. With original box.

No. 1 Autographic Kodak Junior:
    R1* B–
c1914-1926. Achromatic lens; Kodak Ball Bearing shutter; 2$\frac{1}{4}$" x 3$\frac{1}{4}$" exp on 120 roll film.

No. 1 Autographic Kodak Special:
    R3* B+
c1921. Zeiss Kodak Anastigmat f6.3 lens; Optimo shutter; 2$\frac{1}{4}$" x 3$\frac{1}{4}$" exp on

A120 roll film. c1915-1920. New model: Kodak Anastigmat f6.3 lens; Kodamatic shutter.

No. 1 Autographic Kodak Special, Model B: R2* C–
c1922-1926. Kodak Anastigmat f6.3 lens; Kodamatic shutter 2$\frac{1}{4}$" x 3$\frac{1}{4}$" exp on A120 film.

No. 1A Autographic Kodak: R1* A
c1917-1924. Rapid Rectilinear lens; Kodak Ball Bearing shutter; 2$\frac{1}{2}$" x 4$\frac{1}{4}$" exp on 116 roll film. New model: Kodak Anastigmat f7.7 lens; Kodak Ball Bearing shutter.

No. 1A Autographic Kodak Junior:
    R1* A
c1914-1926. Achromatic lens; Kodak Ball Bearing shutter; 2$\frac{1}{2}$" x 4$\frac{1}{4}$" exp on A116 roll film.

No. 1A Autographic Kodak Special:
    R2* B–
c1914-1916. Zeiss Kodak f6.3 lens; Bausch & Lomb Compound shutter; 2$\frac{1}{2}$" x 4$\frac{1}{4}$" exp on A116 roll film.

No. 1A Autographic Kodak Special with coupled range-finder: R3* D–
c1923-1926. Kodak Anastigmat f6.3 lens; Optimo shutter; 2$\frac{1}{2}$" x 4$\frac{1}{4}$" exp on A116 roll film. c1917-1923. New model: Kodak Anastigmat f6.3 lens; Kodamatic shutter.

No. 2C Autographic Kodak Junior:
    R1* A
c1916-1927. Achromatic lens; Kodak Ball Bearing shutter; 2$\frac{7}{8}$" x 4$\frac{7}{8}$" exp on A130 roll film.

No. 2C Autographic Kodak Special:
R2* E
c1923-1928. Kodak Anastigmat lens; Kodamatic shutter; $2\frac{7}{8}$" x $4\frac{7}{8}$" exp on A130 roll film.

No. 3 Autographic Kodak: R1* A
c1914-1926. Rapid Rectilinear lens; Kodak Ball Bearing* shutter; $3\frac{1}{4}$" x $4\frac{1}{4}$" exp on A118 roll film.

No. 3 Autographic Kodak Special:
R2* B+
c1914-1924. Zeiss Kodak Anastigmat f6.3 lens; Bausch & Lomb Compound shutter; $3\frac{1}{4}$" x $4\frac{1}{4}$" exp on A118 roll film.

No. 3A Autographic Kodak: R3* A

c1918-1927. Rapid Rectilinear lens; Kodak Ball Bearing shutter; $3\frac{1}{4}$" x $5\frac{1}{2}$" exp on A122 roll film.

No. 3A Autographic Kodak Junior:
R1* A
c1918-1927. Achromatic lens; Kodak Ball Bearing shutter; $3\frac{1}{4}$" x $5\frac{1}{2}$" exp on A122 roll film.

No. 3A Autographic Kodak Special:
R3* C
c1914. Zeiss Kodak Anastigmat f6.3lens; Bausch & Lomb Compound shutter; $3\frac{1}{4}$" x $5\frac{1}{2}$" exp on A122 roll film.

No. 3A Autographic Kodak Special with coupled range-finder: R3* D+
c1916-1924. Zeiss Kodak Anastigmat f6.3 lens; Optimo shutter; $3\frac{1}{4}$" x $5\frac{1}{2}$" exp on A122 roll film. First mfd camera with CRF.

Sterling II: R1* B
1954. Folding design for 8 exp on 620. Die-cast body finished in black grained plastic. Top plate in grey plastic. 105mm f4.5 Anaston lens. Pronto shutter 1/25-1/200s + B.

Vest Pocket Kodak Special: R2* B–
c1912-1914. Zeiss Kodak Anastigmat f6.3lens; Kodak Ball Bearing shutter; $1\frac{5}{8}$" x $\frac{1}{2}$" exp on 127 roll film.

Vest Pocket Autographic Kodak Special: R2* B+
c1915-1926. Zeiss Kodak Anastigmat f6.9 lens; Kodak Ball Bearing shutter.

Vest Pocket Kodak Model B: R2* B+
c1925-1934. Meniscus lens; Rotary shutter; $1\frac{5}{8}$" x $2\frac{1}{2}$" exp on 127 roll film.

Vest Pocket Kodak Series III: R2* B+
c1926-34. Kodak Anastigmat f6.3 lens;

Diomatic shutter; 1⅝" x 2½" exp on 127 film.

Vest Pocket Kodak Series III, c1926-34.

No 1A Gift Kodak: R4* E+

c1930. 116 roll film, folding camera. Achromatic lens, Kodex shutter, 2¼" x 4¼" on 116 roll film. Art Deco design. (Add 30% for complete set with instructions and box).

Beau Brownie: R4* C+
c1930, Box camera; Doublet lens; 116 roll film. c1930-1932. Black, Blue, Brown and Rose.

Beau Brownie, c1930.

Boy Scout Kodak: R3* E–
c1932. Meniscus lens; Rotary shutter; 1⅝" x 2½" exp on 127 roll film. With case add 25%

Girl Scout Kodak: R3* E–
c1929-1934. Meniscus lens; Rotary shutter 1⅝" x 2½" exp on roll film. Engraved with the official Girl Scout emblem. With case add 25%.

Camp Fire Girls' Kodak: R4* E
c1931-1934. Meniscus lens; Rotary shutter. With case add 25%.

Kodak Ensemble: R4* G–
c1929-1933. (Kodak Petite in suede leather case with mirror, compact and lipstick).

Kodak Petite: R3* D+
c1929-1933. Vest Pocket Kodak Model B Camera, in blue, brown, gray, green or red. Black bellows are not original, and sell for 50% less. Meniscus lens; Rotary shutter; 1⅝" x 2½" exp on 127 roll film.

Vanity Kodak: R4* E+

c1928-1931. Similar to Vest Pocket Kodak Series III Camera in blue, brown, gray, green or red. (see above) c1928-1933. Vanity Kodak Ensemble: Art-deco case includes lipstick, compact with face powder, mirror and change pocket, with Vest Pocket Kodak Series III, Model B.

Kodak Coquette: R4* F+
c1930-1931. (Kodak Petite with matching lipstick holder and compact.)

No. 1 Pocket Kodak Special: R2* B–
c1926-1929. Kodak Anastigmat f6.3 lens; Kodamatic shutter; $2^1/_4$" x $3^1/_4$" exp on 120 roll film.

No. 1A Pocket Kodak Series II: R2* B
c1928-1931. Achromatic lens; Kodex shutter $2^1/_2$" x $4^1/_4$" exp on 116 roll film. In blue, brown, gray, green or red.

No. 1A Pocket Kodak: R2* A
c1926-1931. Achromatic lens; Kodex shutter; $2^1/_2$" x $4^1/_4$" exp on 116 roll film.
No. 2C Pocket Kodak Series III: R2* A
c1924-1931. Kodak Anastigmat f7.7 lens; Diomatic shutter; $2^7/_8$" x $4^7/_8$" exp on 130 roll film.

No. 3 Pocket Kodak Series III: R2* B–
c1926-1933. Kodak f7.9 lens; Kodex shutter; $3^1/_4$" x $4^1/_4$" exp on 118 roll film.

No 2C Pocket Kodak Series III cameras.

Primoette Junior: R2* A+
1913. Unusual folding camera in which the baseboard rests at an angle to the body. Apertures numbered 1-4. Kodak Ball Bearing Shutter 1/25, 1/50, T & B. $2^1/_4$" x$3^1/_4$" format on film pack.

Kodak Bullet: R2* A
c1935. 127 roll film camera; meniscus lens; sector shutter.

Kodak 50th Anniversary Box Camera:
R2* C–

1930; Brown with silver seal. The camera was given free to any child turning 12 in 1930 to celebrate Kodak's corporate half-century (1880-1930).

Kodak Baby Brownie Special: R1* A

c1939. 127 roll film camera; meniscus lens; sector shutter; 8 exp on 127 roll film.

Kodak Regent: R3* D
c1935. Tessar 105mm f4.5 lens; Compur Rapid shutter 1-1/250 s; compact RFR; 6 x 9cm on 620 roll film.

Kodak Regent II: R4* F–
c1939. Schneider Xenar 105mm f3.5 lens; Compur Rapid shutter 1-1/400s, CRF; 6 x 9cm exp.

Suprema: R4* E+
c1939. Schneider Xenar 80mm f3.5 lens; Compur Rapid shutter 1-1/400s; 6 x 6cm exp on 620 roll film.

Kodak Six-16: R1* A
c1932-1936. Meniscus Achromatic lens; Kodak shutter; $2^1/_2$" x $4^1/_4$" exp on 616 roll film.

Kodak Six-20: R2* B

Kodak Six-20 (left) and Six-20 with Compur shutter (right).

c1934-1937, 620 roll film camera; Kodak Anastigmat 100mm f4.5 coated lens; No. 1 Diodak shutter 1/10-1/100s; $2^1/_4$" x $3^1/_4$" exp on 620 roll film.

Kodak Six-20: R2* C–
c1932-1937. 620 roll film camera; Kodak Anastigmat 105mm f4.5 lens; Compur shutter 1-1/250s; $2^1/_4$" x $3^1/_4$" exp on 620 roll film.

Kodak

Kodak Six-20, c1932-1937.

Kodak Junior II: **R2* A**
1954. Folding design for 8 exp on 620. Die-cast light alloy body, top plate in grey plastic moulding, the whole covered in black grained leathercloth. 105mm f6.3 Anaston lens, Dakon II shutter 1/25s & 1/50s.

Kodak Senior Six-20:   **R2* A**
c1937-1939. Kodak Anastigmat f6.3 lens; Kodex shutter; 2$\frac{1}{4}$" x 3$\frac{1}{4}$" exp on 620 roll film.

Jiffy Kodak Six-20:   **R1* A–**
c1933-1937. Twindar lens; Sector shutter; 2$\frac{1}{4}$" x 3$\frac{1}{4}$" exp on 620 film.

Kodak Vigilant 616 Special: **R1* A**
c1940, 616 roll film folding camera; Kodak Anastigmat 12mm f4.5 lens; No. 2 Supermatic shutter 1-1/400s; 8 exp on 616 roll film.

Kodak Vigilant Six-20:   **R1* A**
Kodak Anastigmat f6.3 lens; Diomatic shutter; 2$\frac{1}{4}$" x 3$\frac{1}{4}$" exp on 620 roll film. c1939-1948.

Kodak Monitor Six-20:   **R1* A**
c1939-1948. Kodak Anastigmat Special f4.5 lens; Supermatic shutter; 2$\frac{1}{4}$" x 3$\frac{1}{4}$" exp on 620 roll film.

Kodak Monitor Six-16:   **R1* A**
c1939-1946. Kodak Anastigmat Special f4.5 lens; Supermatic shutter; 2$\frac{1}{2}$" x 4$\frac{1}{4}$" exp on 616 roll film.

Super Kodak Six-20:   **R4* G**

c1938-1945. Kodak Anastigmat Special f3.5 lens; Kodak shutter controlled by Selenium photo-electric exp meter, CRF. 2$\frac{1}{4}$" x $\frac{1}{4}$" exp on 620 roll film. First camera with built-in photo-electric exp control

Kodak Duex: **R3* A**

c1940-1946. 620 roll film camera; 16 exp on 620 roll film.

Kodak Bantam: R1* A
c1938. 828 roll film camera; Kodak Anastigmat 53mm f6.3 lens; shutter, T, I.

Kodak Bantam Special: R3* E+

c1936-1940. Kodak Anastigmat Ektar f2 lens; Compur Rapid shutter 1-1/500s, CRF. 28 x 40mm exp on 828 roll film. After World War II the Bantam Special was sold with a Kodak Ektar f/2.0 in a Supermatic shutter.

Kodak Bantam f5.6: R2* A
c1938-1941. Kodak Anastigmat Special lens; Kodak shutter.

Kodak Bantam f8: R1* A
c1938-1946. Kodalinear f8 lens; sector shutter; 28 x 40mm exp on 828 roll film.

Kodak Bantam f4.5: R1* A
c1938-1948. Kodak Anastigmat Special f4.5 lens; Kodak shutter.

Kodak Flash Bantam: R1* A
c1947-1953. Kodak Anastigmat Special f4.5 lens; Kodak Flash Synch shutter.

Kodak Flash Bantam, c1947-1953.

Bantam Colorsnap: R1* A
1955. 8 exp on 828 film. Made to make colour photography easy for the beginner. Exposure control by light value numbers on aperture scale, recommended settings given by scale built into camera back. Exposure system sets the shutter at 1/50s or 1/25s according to subject.

Colorsnap 35: R1* A
1959. Update of the Bantam Colorsnap, made to take standard 35mm cassettes in place of 828 rollfilm. Single speed shutter at 1/40s. Exposure control by weather symbols on aperture scale. Synch for flash with Brownie Flasholder.

**Kodak Retina – Stuttgart type
No. 117:** R3* D+
c July 1934-July 1935. 35mm vf camera; Schneider-Kreuznach Xenar Anastigmat 5cm f3.5 lens; Compur 00 1-1/300s. Large nickel plated knobs for film wind and rewind; rewind clutch lever positioned in film wind knob. Single film sprocket on top of camera with short shaft. Black lacquer with nickel trim.

Kodak Retina – Stuttgart type No. 117, c July 1934-July 1935.

Kodak Retina – Stuttgart type
No. 118:   **R3* D**

c July 1935-April 1936. 35mm vf camera. Similar to Stuttgart type no. 117 except: the rewind clutch lever was moved from film wind knob to the back of top cover, the film sprocket shaft extends across camera body. Black lacquer, nickel trim.

Kodak Retina – Stuttgart type
No. 119:   **R2* D**

c April 1936-January 1938. 35mm RFR camera; Schneider Xenar 5cm f3.5 or Kodak Anastigmat Ektar 5cm f3.5 lens; Compur 00 1-1/300s. Wind and rewind knobs reduced in diameter; exp counter moved to raised housing on right side of camera. Black lacquer, nickel trim. C April 1936-January 1938.

Kodak Retina – Stuttgart type
No. 126:   **R2* C**

c March 1936-October 1937. 35mm vf camera; Kodak Ektar 5cm f3.5 lens (also Tessar, Alcor, Angenieux and Ysar lenses); Compur-Rapid shutter 1-1/500s. Chrome or black lacquer with polished aluminium trim. Some cameras provided with accessory shoe.

Kodak Retina I – Stuttgart type
No. 141:   **R2* D**

Retina 1 (black finish).

c October 1937-March 1939. 35mm vf camera; Kodak Ektar 5cm f3.5 lens (also Xenar); Compur or Compur-Rapid 1-1/500s. Body shutter release in front edge of enlarged exp counter. Wind and rewind knobs taller than previous model.

Kodak Retina I – Stuttgart type
No. 143:   **R2* D**

c January 1938-March 1939. 35mm vf camera; Schneider Xenar 5cm f3.5 lens; Compur shutter 1-1/300s. Similar to Stuttgart type no. 141 except: black lacquer finish, chrome wind and rewind knobs.

Kodak Retina I – Stuttgart type
No. 148:   **R2* D**

c March 1939-December 1940. 35mm vf camera; Kodak Ektar 5cm f3.5 lens; Compur-Rapid shutter 1-1/300s. Exp counter reduced in size and moved closer to vf. First Retina to have film transport coupled to shutter to prevent double exp. Chrome finish.

Kodak Retina I – Stuttgart type
No. 149:   **R2* D**

Retina 1.

c March 1939-December 1940. 35mm vf camera; Schneider Xenar 5cm f3.5 lens; Compur-Rapid shutter 1-1/300s. Similar to Stuttgart type no. 148 except, black lacquer finish and trim.

Kodak Retina 1 (Compur Rapid shutter).

Kodak Retina I – Stuttgart type
No. 010:   **R2* D**

c May 1946-April 1949. 35mm vf camera; Retina Xenar 50mm f3.5 coated lens (also Ektar, Xenar, Zenar, Rodenstock lenses); Compur-Rapid shutter 1-1/500s. Mfd from combination of prewar and postwar parts. Same body and interlock as Stuttgart type no. 011, otherwise similar to Stuttgart type no. 148. Chrome finish.

Kodak Retina I – Stuttgart type
No. 013:   **R2* D**

c April 1949-January 1951. 35mm vf camera; Retina Xenar 5cm f3.5 or f2.8 coated lens; Compur-Rapid shutter 1-1/500s (X synch was added to some cameras in 1949; after 1950 it was added to all production cameras.) One piece chrome top cover with integral vf.

Kodak Retina Ia – Stuttgart type
No. 015:   **R2* D**

c January 1951-July 1951. 35mm vf camera; Retina Xenar 50mm f3.5 or f2.8 coated lens (also Rodenstock, Heligon, Ektar lenses); Compur-Rapid shutter 1-1/500s, X flash synch. First Retina with top mounted rapid-wind film-advance coupled to shutter cocking.

Kodak Retina Ia – Stuttgart type
No. 015:   **R2* D**

c July 1951-April 1954. 35mm vf camera; Retina-Xenar 50mm f3.5 or f2.8 coated lens (also Kodak Ektar lens); Synchro-Compur shutter 1-1/500s, X-M flash synch. Similar to Stuttgart type no. 015 except for film indicator dial on top of rewind knob instead of under camera.

Kodak Retina Ib – Stuttgart type

No. 018:   **R2* D**

Kodak Retina II – Stuttgart type No. 122.

c1954-1958. 35mm vf camera; Xenar 50mm f2.8 coated lens, interchangeable front component; Synchro- Compur LVS 1-1/500s, VXM flash synch. New body design with rounded contours, concealed bellows, first bright frame vf in Retina camera.

Kodak Retina IB – Stuttgart type
No. 019:   **R2* D**

c1957-1960. 35mm vf camera; Xenar 50mm f2.8 coated lens, interchangeable front component; Synchro-Compur LVS 1-1/500s, VXM flash synch. Similar to Stuttgart type No. 018 except, top cover enlarged vertically to accept built-in, non-coupled selenium single-range exp meter. Enlarged vf with second window added in 1958 to permit projected frame line.

Kodak Retina II – Stuttgart type
No. 122:   **R2* D+**

c October 1936-June 1937. 35mm RFR camera;   Schneider-Kreuznach Anastigmat Ektar 5cm f3.5 lens (also 5cm f2 Xenon lens); Compur-Rapid shutter 1-1/500s. First Retina with separate optical vf and CRF. Retractable body release, rewind knob brake lever.

Kodak Retina II – Stuttgart type
No. 142:   **R2* D+**

c June 1937-May 1939. 35mm RFR camera; Schneider-Kreuznach Xenon 5cm f2.8 lens (also other lenses); Compur-Rapid shutter 1-1/500s, CRF. Similar to Stuttgart type no. 122, except film wind knob instead of slow wind lever; top cover redesigned.

Kodak Retina IIa – Stuttgart type
No. 150:   **R2* D+**

c May 1939-December 1940. 35mm RFR camera; Schneider Kreuznach Xenon 5cm f2.8 lens; Compur-Rapid shutter 1-1/500s. Redesigned top cover. First Retina with combined vf and CRF. Smaller (extensible) rewind knob.

Kodak Retina II – Stuttgart type
No. 011:   **R2* D+**

c Summer 1946-Spring 1949. 35mm RFR camera; Retina-Xenon 50mm f2.0 coated lens (also Heligon and 47mm Kodak Ektar lenses); Compur-Rapid shutter 1-1/500s, CRF. First RFR Retina with coated lenses (although variations exist with uncoated lenses). Serial no. inside back; Rochester imports prefixed with letters "EK".

Kodak Retina II – Stuttgart type
No. 014: R2* D+

c Summer 1949-January 1951. 35mm RFR camera; Retina-Xenon 50mm f2 or Retina-Heligon 50mm f2 coated lenses; Compur-Rapid shutter 1-1/500s, X synch, CRF. Similar to Stuttgart type no. 011 except has redesigned sloping front plate on front of shutter, also X flash synch.

Kodak Retina IIa – Stuttgart type
No. 016: R2* D+

c January 1951-July 1951. 35mm RFR camera; Retina-Xenon 50mm f2 coated lens; Compur-Rapid shutter 1-1/500s, X flash synch, CRF. Similar to Stuttgart type no. 014 except rapid-wind film-advance lever coupled to shutter cocking mechanism. Synchro-Compur with XM flash synch installed between July 1951-August 1954.

Kodak Retina IIc – Stuttgart type
No. 020: R2* D+

c1954-1958. 35mm RFR camera; Xenon-C 50mm f2.8 coated lens, interchangeable front component (also Heligon-C lens); Synchro-Compur LVS 1-1/500s, VXM flash synch, CRF. Redesigned body with rounded contours and concealed bellows. Accepts either 80mm f4 telephoto or 35mm f5.6 wide-angle lens components.

Kodak Retina IIC – Stuttgart type
No. 029: R2* E

c1958. 35mm RFR camera; Xenon-C 50mm f2.8 coated lens, interchangeable front component (also Heligon-C lens); Synchro-Compur LVS 1-1/500s, VXM flash synch, CRF. This camera is similar to Stuttgart type no. 020 except enlarged vf has bright frame lines for 50mm, 35, and 80mm lenses.

Kodak Retina IIIc – Stuttgart type
No. 021: R2* E

c1954. 35mm RFR camera; Xenon-C 50mm f2 coated lens, interchangeable front component; Synchro- Compur LVS 1-1/500s, VXM flash synch, CRF. Similar to Stuttgart type no. 020 except non-coupled selenium photo-electric exp meter with hinged cover, built into top cover.

Kodak Retina IIIC – Stuttgart type
No. 028: R3* F–

c1958-1961. 35mm RFR camera; Xenon-C 50mm f2 coated lens, interchangeable lens component (also Heligon-C lens); Synchro-Compur LVS 1-1/500s, VXM flash, synch, CRF. Similar to Stuttgart type no. 021 except selenium meter redesigned. Has plastic honeycomb with non-hinged cover; enlarged vf has bright frame lines for 50mm, 35mm and 80mm lenses.

Retina lenses and accessories

Kodak Retina IIc, IIIc and IIIC cameras with Retina-Xenon C lens are matched for use with the Retina-Longar-Xenon C 80mm f4 and Retina Curtar-Xenon C 35mm f5.6 lenses; Kodak Retina cameras with Retina-Heligon lenses are matched for use with the Retina-Heligon C 80mm f4 and the Retina-Heligon C 35mm f4.5 lenses. Cameras with Xenon lenses were originally distributed in the US market, while cameras with Heligon lenses were distributed in the overseas market, both lenses are optically equivalent.

35-80 Multi finder: **B+**
Xenon or Heligon f5.6/35mm lens: **B+**
Xenon or Heligon f4/80mm lens: **C**

Kodak Retina IIIs: **R2* D**
c1959-1961. Retina-Xenon 50mm f1.9 lens; Synchro-Compur shutter 1-1/500s. c1959-1961.

Kodak Instamatic Reflex: **R2* D**
35mm SLR,interchangeable Xenon 50mm f1.9 lens or Xenar 50mm f2.8 lens.

Kodak Retina Reflex: **R2* D**

c1958-1959, 35mm SLR, inter-changeable Retina-Xenon 50mm f2 lens; Synchro-Compur shutter 1-1/500s.

Kodak Retina Reflex S: **R2* D**
c1959-60, 35mm SLR, interchangeable Xenar f2.8/50mm lens, Synchro Compur shutter, coupled light meter.

Kodak Retina Reflex III: **R2* D**
c1961-1964, 35mm SLR, inter-changeable Xenon f1.9/50mm lens; Synchro-Compur shutter 1-1/500s.

Kodak Retina Reflex IV: **R2* D**

c1964-67, 35mm SLR, interchangeable Xenar or Ysarex f2.8/50mm lens, or Xenon or Heligon f1.9/50mm lens, Synchro Compur, shutter speed and lens opening visible in the VFR.

Kodak Retinette: **R2* B+**

c1952-1954. Recomar f4.5/45mm lens; Pronto SV shutter 1-1/300s.

Match-Box (-X):   **R5* H**
c1945, match-box detective camera; 25mm f5 lens; 1/50 s shutter; 10 x 10mm exp on 16mm film. About the size of a small wooden matchbox, hence its name. It was made by Eastman Kodak for the O.S.S. as an espionage camera.

Kodak Pony 828:   R1* A

c1949-1959. Kodak Anaston f4.5 lens; Kodak Flash 200 shutter; 28 x 40mm exp on 828 roll film. c1949-1959.

Kodak Pony 135:   R1* A

c1950-1954. Kodak Anaston f4.5 lens; Kodak Flash 200 shutter; 36 exp on 35mm film.

Kodak 35:   R2* B

1938-1948: 35mm VFR camera. Camera was available with three different lenses when first introduced, Kodak Anastigmat f/5.6, Kodak Anastigmat f/4.5, and Kodak Anastigmat Special f/3.5. In 1946, flash synchronisation was added.

Kodak 35 Kodamatic shutter.

Kodak 35 Flash Kodamatic shutter.

Kodak 35 Kodex shutter.

Kodak 35 (Military):   R3* E

c1938-1951, 35mm VFR camera, Kodak Anastigmat f4.5 lens/51mm Kodak No.1 Diomatic shutter 1/25-1/150s, B. T. C.

Kodak

Kodak 35 Rangefinder: R2* C

c1940-1951, Kodak Anastigmat Special f3.5 lens, Flash Kodamatic shutter, CRF.

Kodak Ektra: R4* G

c1941-1948. Kodak Ektar 50mm f1.9 lens; cfps 1-1/1000s; 36 exp on 35mm roll film. Features interchangeable magazine back, rapid film advance, CRF.

Interchangeable lenses for Ektra cameras

Ektar 50mm f3.5 lens **E–**
Ektar 50mm f1.9 lens **E–**
Ektar 35mm f3.3 lens **E–**
Ektar 90mm f3.5 lens **E–**
Ektar 135mm f3.8 lens **E–**
Ektar 153mm f4.5 lens **G**

Kodak Signet 35:   R2* B–

Kodak Ektar 50mm f3.5 lens; Kodak Synchro 300 shutter. c1951-1958.

Kodak Signet 40:   R2* B–
c1956-1959. Kodak Ektanon 50mm f3.5 lens; Kodak Synchro 400 shutter.

Kodak Signet 30:   R2* B–
c1957-1959. Kodak Ektanar 50mm f2.8 lens; Kodak Synchro 250 shutter.

Kodak Signet – "Signal Corps, U.S. Army Camera, Still picture KE-7(1)":   R3* E

c1955. 35mm RFR camera; Kodak Ektar 44mm f3.5 lens; Kodak Synchro 300 shutter. Black finish.

Kodak Signet 50: R2* C–

c1957-1960. Kodak Ektanar 50mm f2.8 lens; Kodak Synchro 250 shutter.

Kodak Signet 80: R3* C

c1958-1962, interchangeable Kodak Ektanar f2.8/50mm lens; behind the lens shutter, built-in light meter.

Signet Multi Frame Finder B–
Signet Wide Angle lens f3.5/35mm C
Signet Telephoto lens f4/90mm C

Kodak Automatic 35: R2* B+

c1959. Kodak Ektanar 50mm f2.8 lens; Kodak Synchro 80 shutter. Auto exp control.

Kodak Motormatic 35F: R3* C–

c1962. Kodak Ektanar 50mm f2.8 lens; Kodak Automatic Flash shutter. Spring-wound motor drive.

The Kodak Pupille, Ranca and Vollendas were Nagel cameras which continued in production after Eastman Kodak bought Dr. August Nagel Camerawerk, Stuttgart, in 1932. See Nagel.

Kodak Pupille: R4* E
With Elmar lens +100%

c1932. Schneider Xenon 50mm f2 lens; Compur shutter 1³⁄₁₆" x 1⁹⁄₁₆" exp on 127 roll film.

Kodak Ranca: R4* E
With Elmar lens +100%

c1932-1934. Nagel Anastigmat f4.5 lens; Pronto shutter; 1³⁄₁₆" x 1⁹⁄₁₆" exp on 127 roll film.

Kodak Vollenda: R4* F–
With Elmar lens +100%

c1932-1937. Radionar Anastigmat 50mm f3.5 lens; Compur shutter; 1³⁄₁₆" x 1⁹⁄₁₆" exp on 127 roll film.

Kodak Vollenda (6 x 9cm model):
R3* E–

c1939, Folding camera; Elmar 10.5cm f4.5 lens; Compur shutter 1-1⁄250s; 8 exp, 6 x 9cm on 120 roll film.

Kodak Vollenda (6 x 9cm model), c1939.

Kodak Duo Six-20:   R3* C–

c1934-1937. Kodak Anastigmat 75mm f3.5 lens; Compur shutter; $1\frac{5}{8}$" x $2\frac{1}{4}$" exp on 620 roll film.

**Kodak Duo Six-20
(rangefinder model):**   R3* E+
c1937. Schneider Kreuznach Xenar 75mm f3.5 lens; Compur Rapid shutter 1-1/500s, CRF; $1\frac{5}{8}$" x $2\frac{1}{4}$" exp on 620 roll film.

Kodak Duo Six-20 (rangefinder model), c1937.

Kodak Recomar 18:   R3* B+
c1932-1940. Kodak Anastigmat f4.5 lens; Compur shutter; $2\frac{1}{4}$" x $3\frac{1}{4}$" exp on film pack.

Kodak Recomar 33:   R3* C–
c1932-1940. Kodak Anast gmat f4.5 lens; Compur shutter; $3\frac{1}{4}$" x $4\frac{1}{4}$" exp on film pack.

Kodak Medalist I: R3* D+
c1941-1946. Kodak Ektar 100mm f3.5 lens; Supermatic shutter 1-1/400s, CRF; 8 exp, $2\frac{1}{4}$" x $3\frac{1}{4}$" on 620 roll film.

Kodak Medalist II: R3* E

Black version.

---

c1946-1952. Kodak Ektar 100mm f3.5 lens; Flash Supermatic 1-1/400s, CRF; 8 exp, 2¼" x 3¼" on 620 roll film.

Specialist Model 2:   R3* D+

1950. Half plate stand camera. Wood and chrome-plated brass. Recommended lens shutter assembly was 203mm f7.7 Kodak Ektar in 8-speed Epsilon shutter 1-1/150s.
Accessory gave double extension of bellows for close-ups.

Kodak Reflex: R2* B

c1946. TLR; Kodak Anastigmat 75mm f3.5 lens; Flash Kodamatic shutter; 12 exp, 2¼" x 2¼" on 620 roll film.

Kodak Tourist: R1* A

c1948-1951. Kodak Anaston f4.5 lens; Flash Kodamatic shutter; 8 exp, 2¼" x 3¼" on 620 roll film.

Kodak Stereo: R2* D+

c1954-1959. 35mm stereo camera; Kodak Anastigmat 35mm f3.5 lenses; Kodak Flash 200 shutter 1/25-1/200s. 29 stereo pairs, 23 x 24mm on 35mm film.

Kodak Chevron: R3* D+

c1953-1956. Kodak Ektar 78mm f3.5 lens; Synchro-Rapid shutter 1-1/800s; 12 exp, 2¼" x 2¼" on 620 roll film.

In 1963 Eastman Kodak brought out the #126 Instamatic System. The film was pre-loaded into a plastic cassette that in turn dropped easily into a camera eliminating the "nuisance" of spool-to-

Kodak Instamatic 50, 154 and 100.

Kodak

spool loading. The system was very successful, and a number of manufacturers purchased licenses from Kodak to make both the cameras and special cassettes.

Instamatic 44:   **R2* A–**
1969-73, Knob wind, uses flash cubes.

Instamatic 100:   **R1* A**
1963-66, Lever wind, uses AG1 flashbulbs, first Instamatic, the most collectable.

Instamatic 104:   **R1* A–**
1965-68, Lever wind, uses flash cubes.

Instamatic 124:   **R1* A–**
1968-71, Lever wind, uses flash cubes.

Instamatic 134:   **R3* B–**
1968-71, Spring motor drive, with light meter, uses flash cubes.

Instamatic 150:   **R2* A**
1964-66, Spring motor drive, uses AG1 bulbs.

Instamatic 154:   **R2* A**
1965-69, Spring motor drive, uses flash cubes.

Instamatic 174:   **R2* A**
1968-71, Spring motor drive, uses flash cubes.

Instamatic 250:   **R2* B+**
1965-67, Lever wind, uses AG1 bulbs, coated f2.8 lens focusing from 2.5' to infinity, shutter speeds 1/30-1/250s, made in Germany.

Instamatic 300:   **R2* A**
1963-66, Lever wind, light meter, uses AG1 bulbs.

Instamatic 300:   **R2* A–**
1965-69, Lever wind, light meter, uses AG1 bulbs.

Instamatic 304:   **R2* A–**
1965-69, Lever wind, light meter, uses Flash cubes.

Instamatic 314:   **R2* A–**
1968-71, Lever wind, light meter, uses Flash cubes.

Instamatic 324:   **R2* A–**
1966-68, Lever wind, light meter, uses Flash cubes, made in Germany.

Instamatic 400:   **R2* B+**
1963-66, Spring motor drive, light meter, uses AG1 bulbs.

Instamatic 404:   **R2* B+**
1965-69, Spring motor drive, light meter, uses Flash cubes.

Instamatic 414:   **R2* B+**
1968-71, Spring motor drive, light meter, uses Flash cubes.

Instamatic 500:   **R3* C–**

1963-66, Lever wind, PC connection and hot shoe, light meter, f2.8 lens, speeds 1/30-1/500s, made in Germany.

Instamatic 700:   R3* C–
1963-66, Spring motor drive, uses AG1 bulbs, light meter, f2.8 lens, shutter speeds 1/60-1/250s.

Instamatic 704:   R2* C–
1965-69, Spring motor drive, uses Flash cubes, light meter, f2.8 lens, shutter speeds 1/60-1/250s.

Instamatic 714:   R2* C–
1968-70, Spring motor drive, uses Flash cubes, light meter, f2.8 lens, shutter speeds 1/60-1/250s.

Instamatic 800:   R2* C
1964-66, Spring motor drive, AG1 bulbs, rangefinder, light meter, f2.8 lens, shutter speeds 1/60-1/250s.

Instamatic 804:   R1* C
1965-70, Spring motor drive, uses Flash cubes, built-in rangefinder, light meter, f2.8 lens, shutter speeds 1/60-1/250s.

Instamatic 814:   R2* C
1968-70, Spring motor drive, uses Flash cubes, built-in rangefinder, light meter, f2.8 lens, shutter speeds 1/60-1/250s.

Instamatic X-15:   R1* A–
1970-76, Lever wind, uses "X" cubes which require no battery to be fired.

Instamatic X-15F: R1* A–
1976-1986, Lever wind, uses Flip flash.

Instamatic X25:   R2* A
1970-74, Spring motor drive, uses "X" cubes.

Instamatic X30:   R2* A
1970-74, Lever wind, light meter, uses "X" cubes.

Instamatic X35:   R2* A
1970-76, Lever wind, light meter, uses "X" cubes.

Instamatic X35F: R2* A
1976-86, Lever wind, light meter, uses "Flip flash".

Instamatic X45:   R2* A
1970-74, Spring motor drive, light meter, uses "X" cubes.

Instamatic X90:   R2* F
1970-73, Spring motor drive, light meter, uses "X" cubes, f2.8 lens, coupled rangefinder, shutter speeds 1/60-1/250s.

Instamatic S-10:   R2* A–
1967-70, Knob wind on the end of the camera body, pop out lens, uses Flash cubes.

Instamatic S-20:   R2* A–
1967-71, Knob wind on the end of the camera body, pop out lens, light meter, uses Flash cubes.

Instamatic 50:   R2* A–
Lever wind, made in Rochester for the export market.

Mickeymatic: R2* A+
1988. Version of the Pocket Instamatic for 110 film with Mickey Mouse label. Found in blue and pink.

Hawkeye II: R2* A–
1969. Knob wind, uses flash cubes, grey and black, used as a give-away premium.

Hawkeye: R1* A–
1963. Lever wind, uses separate flash gun, Chrome and olive.

Hawkeye-F: R2* A–
1964. Lever wind, uses Flip flash.

Hawkeye-R4:   R2* A–
1965. Lever wind, uses Flash cubes.

Hawkeye-A1:   R2* B
1969. Spring motor drive, with light meter, uses Flash cubes.

Hawkeye-X: R2* A–
1971. Lever wind, uses "X" cubes, much like the Instamatic X15.

Six-20 Brownie Model F: R2* A
1954. One of the more attractive Brownie box cameras, finished in buff leather cloth with brown metal front plate and polished brass trim. 8 exp on 620. Fixed focus lens for 10ft to infinity, supplementary lens built in for 5-10ft. I & B shutter. Two tripod bushes for vertical or horizontal use.

Vest Pocket Kodak: R2* B
c1912. 127 roll film. Kodak Ball Bearing Shutter. A large variety of lenses were offered for the Kodak VP during it's very long life from a simple meniscus to a Zeiss Kodak Anastigmat. Later models fitted with an Autographic back.

Vest Pocket Kodak, c1912.

Jiffy Kodak 127:   R2* B

1935. This is an advanced version of the popular VP (vest-pocket) series of cameras. A molded bakelite body was fitted with a fixed focus doublet lens. The camera and packaging were designed by Walter Dorwin Teague. An original box greatly increases the value of the camera.

Kodak Bantam: R2* B

1935. First model of Bantam Camera introduced by Eastman Kodak to use new film format. Unsprocketed 35mm paperbacked film for images 28 x 40mm. Anastigmat f6.3 lens. First model fitted with rigid viewfinder. Camera and packaging designed by Walter Dorwin Teague.

Kodak Pinhole Camera: R3* D

1930. This was given as a kit to schools as part of science projects. All the material needed for assembly (cardboard, sticky tape, a pin, and careful instructions, were included. A piece of $3\frac{1}{4}$" x $4\frac{1}{4}$" sheet film was used. On occasion they turn up in the original unassembled package at twice the price

Kodak A.G.
Stuttgart, Germany

Mini Instamatic S-40:   R2* B

c1977. Very compact pocket Instamatic 110 camera for 13 x 17mm images. Kodak Reomar fixed-focus f5.6, 25mm lens. Two shutter speeds automatically selected 1/40 and 1/80s. Automatic exposure control.

Kogaku
Seiki, Japan

Nippon: R5* H–
1942 cfps, 1/20-1/500s, no RFR, vfr only, screw mount K.O.L. Xebec F2.0/5cm lens. This camera was also known as the "Nippon Standard".

Nippon: R5* H–
1943 cfps, 1-1/500s, separate RFR/vfr windows, screw mount Sun Xebec F2.0/5cm lens. A copy of the Leica III, without diopter adjustment, this camera was also known as the "Nippon III".

Kinrad Kohnlein
Nurnberg, Germany

Wiko: R3* D+
1939. Unusual for having a focal plane shutter in a Bakelite body. Models can be found with fixed focus and variable focus lenses, f4.5 and f2.8. Image size 14 x 18mm on paper-backed 16mm rollfilm. Shutter 1/20-1/200s.

Wiko, 1939.

Kolar
Prague, Czechoslovakia

Kola: R4* E+

Set of masks greatly increases value.

c1936, VFR camera for 4 x 4cm and 3 x 4cm images on 127 film or 24 x 36cm images on 35mm film. A variety of lens shutter combinations were available. Zeiss Tessar f/2.8 60mm most common. Early models have a folding VFR, later versions a tubular finder (reverse Galilean telescope). Camera sold with a complete set of three internal masks for different formats and fittings for 35mm film. Presence of all of these items greatly increases the value of the camera.

Konishiroku Photo Co Ltd
Tokyo, Japan

Konica C35AF: R2* B

1977; 35mm eye-level auto-focus camera. First auto focus production camera in the world based on a design by Honeywell Corp. in the U.S. Hexanon lens, f2.8, 38mm. Built-in electronic flash.

Sakura Pocket Camera: R4* F–
1907. Folding plate camera for 8.2cm x 10.8cm glass plates. Rapid Rectiliniar f8 lens T, I, B shutter. Quite rare.

Idea: R4* F–
1909 Folding 4 x 5 camera for glass plates or sheet film, front shifts and revolving back. Tessar f6.3/165mm lens, Compur shutter, both imported from Germany. Quite rare.

Idea "A":   R3* D
1909-24 Folding 8 x 10cm camera for glass plates. Many versions were made during its production, early cameras used imported lenses and shutters, either from the USA or Germany. All are quite rare.

Idea Hand Camera: R3* C+
1930-35 Folding, 8 x 10.5cm or 6.5 x 9cm camera for glass plates. Many versions were made during its production, most cameras used imported lenses and shutters, either from the USA or Germany. Less rare than the Idea "A" camera. An exception is the Idea Hand Camera of 1935, with one of the first Nikkor lenses, which is about 20 times more valuable.

The Pearl II: R3* D+
1909 Folding camera, 8 x 10.5cm on 118 roll film. The first Japanese roll film camera. Models III, and IV could also use glass plates. All are rare.

Special Pearl: R3* D+
1913 Folding roll film camera, 8 x 10.5cm on glass plates, or 8 x 13.7cm on 101 roll film. Quite rare.

Pearl No. 2:   R3* C+
1923-31 Folding roll film camera, 6 x 9cm or 6 x 4.5cm on 120 roll film. Several versions with various shutters, Wooden body. This is the first Japanese camera to use 120 roll film.

Baby Pearl: R2* D+

c1935; Folding camera; 3 x 4cm exp on 127 roll film; front cell focusing; 50mm f4.5 Hexor lens in Rox shutter B, 1/25-1/100s.

The Lily Camera: R3* C+
1909-38 Folding plate cameras of various sizes, most with German lenses and shutters. Early cameras are quite rare. A tropical Lily was said to have been made in the 1930s, and was the only tropical camera to come from Japan. Either the tropical model, or a camera equipped with an Anytar lens, made by Nippon Kogaku (Nikon), are valued at about 20 times the value of any other Lily camera.

Pearlette: R3* C+

1928-40 Folding roll film camera using lazy tong struts, and 127 film. Simple fixed focus lenses or various types. Some cameras had provision for 4 x 6.5cm and 3 x 4cm negative sizes on 127 film. Similar in looks to the Vest Pocket Kodak. The earliest camera lacked the unusual close-up lens attached to the wire frame finder. This line was started again after the Second World War, and the Pearl name found its way to quite a number of roll film cameras, both 127 and 120.

Semi-Pearl: R3* C−

c1938. Folding rollfilm camera for 16 exposures on 120 film Hexar 7.5cm/f4.5 lens, Durex shutter, 1-1/100s.

Pearl I: R2* C+

1949 Folding roll film camera, uncoupled RFR, leaf shutter,1-1/500s, Hexar F4.5/75mm lens. 6 x 4.5cm on 120 film. The Pearl RS used a Konirapid shutter.

Konica 35:   R3* D

1965. 35mm camera with CRF btl shutter, speeds 1-1/500s, Hexar 50mm/f3.5 lens. marked "Made in Occupied Japan".

Konica Autoreflex: R2* D

1968. The first automatic 35mm SLR. Shutter priority, TTL metering. 52mm f1.8 standard lens. Shutter 1-1/000s.

Konica FS-1:   R2* D

1978. The first 35mm SLR to feature a built-in electric motordrive, used also for auto film load. Totally electronic shutter using twin micro solenoids to activate the first and second curtains. Copal shutter that travels vertically. Shutter priority automation, TTL metering.

E. B. Koopman
New York, USA

The Presto Camera: R4* F+

c1899 meniscus lens with rotating stops; single speed shutter; 4 exp, 18 x 18cm on special roll film. Invented by H. Casler.

Korsten
Paris, France

La Litote: R4* D
c1902. 45 x 107mm stereo; Aplanatic lenses; 3 speed guillotine shutter. Leather covered box camera.

Kowa Co Ltd
Nagoya, Japan

Komaflex-S: R3* D
1960. 127 roll film SLR camera; Prominar 65mm f2.8 coated lens; Seikosha-SLV shutter 1-1/500s, MX synch.

Ramera: R3* D+

1959, combination portable AM radio and detective camera; Prominar 65mm f2.8 coated lens; 3 speed synch shutter; 20 exp, 10 x 14mm on 16mm film (Minolta 16 cassettes).

Kowa 35 N: R2* C–
1960: Leaf shutter, 1/25-1/300s, vfr only, fixed Prominar F.C. F3.5/45mm lens. interesting trigger wind mechanism.

Kowa SW: R2* D+
1964: Leaf shutter, 1-1/500s, vfr only, using a strange system, available in black or chrome. Fixed wide angle f3.2/28mm lens. Perhaps more valuable as a user camera than a collector's item.

Komaflex: R2* C–
1960-64. Leaf shutter, 1-1/500s, fixed Kowa F2.0/50mm, or f1.9/50mm lens. Inexpensive 35mm slr, with wide angle and telephoto conversion lenses available. Several models, some with built-in light meters including SE, SER, SET, SETR. Only the Kowa UW 190, sporting a fixed f4/19mm lens seems to be highly prized, bringing about 8 times the price of an ordinary Komaflex.

shutter adjustment on bottom in addition to the two levers on top. Later models had a two-winged tensioning lever.

Komaflex, 1960-64.

Kozy Camera Company
Boston, Massachusetts, USA

Pocket Kozy Camera: **R4* E–**
c1892. Meniscus lens; single speed shutter; 9 x 9cm exp on roll film

Krasnogorsk Mechanical Works
Krasnogorsk, USSR

(Same as KMZ)

FT-2 Panoramic Camera: **R4* E+**

1958-1965. Rotating Industar 50mm f5 lens; shutter 1/100, 1/200, 1/400s; 12 exp. 24 x 110mm on 35 mm film in special cassettes. Early models had

Hapyucc: **R3* A**

c1960. English corruption of the Cyrillic letters that make up the Russian name on the front of the camera. 16mm SLR. It was exported under the name Narciss (see below).

Horizont: **R3* A**

1968. Panoramic swing lens camera for 24 x 58mm images on 35mm giving 120° angle of view. 28mm f2.8 lens. Shutter 1/25-1/125s. Clip-on viewfinder (often missing) incorporates spirit level.

Narciss: R3* B+

1961-1965; 16mm subminiature camera SLR fitted with Industar f2.8/35mm lens. Originally designed as a specialised instrument for medical photography it was eventually offered to the general public. This was the first ever miniature SLR.

Zenit Photosniper: R2* E–

c1960, 35mm camera; Tair 300mm f4.5 coated lens, interchangeable screw mount; cfps 1/30-1/500s. Zenit camera mounted on gunstock with telephoto lens. Outfit including normal lens, filters for 300mm lens, screwdrivers, and empty film cassettes.

Zenit Photosniper 12: R2* E

c1970- today (written "Photosnaiper on the shoulder stock but referred in English translation Soviet literature without the "a"). Introduction of a modified Zenit 12 black camera body, which includes a built-in light meter, and integral connections to the gunstock and 300mm lens. The modified body is designated "12S". At least one European sale for £200 in 1990, but many others at less than half that price!

Zenit Photosniper: R3* E

Latest version of (KM100) now sporting a Zenit Automat 35mm SLR with aperture priority, a Telezenitar-K f4.5/300mm lens in "K" type bayonet mount, and a redesigned shoulder stock. Available new, but not found yet in great numbers in the "West".

Zenit: R2* C+

c1953, 35mm SLR, interchangeable (39mm screw mount) 50mm normal lens, CFPS 1/30-1/500s, non-instant return mirror.

Zenit S (C): R2* C

c1956, with flash synch.

Zenith C: R2* C

c1962. 35mm SLR. Screw-thread interchangeable lenses. 50mm f3.5 Industar-50 lens. FP shutter 1/25-1/500s + B & T. Adjustable flash synch 0-12 milliseconds.

Zorki-1: R2* D–

1948-56, Cfps, 1/20-1/500s, no slow speeds, no synch, CRF. Interchangeable Leica-type screw mount, f3.5/50mm Industar-22 lens in collapsible mount, though some rigid mount lenses were made. Lens serial numbers usually indicate year of production as the first two digits. The null series camera with both FED and Zorki markings and 5cm F2 collapsible lens is worth $500. Prices are 20% higher in the United States for ordinary Zorki-1 cameras. Australian and Japanese collectors are starting to buy at higher prices too.

FED Zorki-1: R4* F

Produced 1948-1949.

Zorki-2: R4* E–

1955, Cfps, 1/20 to 1/500s, no slow speeds, no synch, CRF. Interchangeable Leica-type screw mount, f3.5/50mm Industar-22 lens in collapsible mount, though some rigid mount lenses were made. Lens serial numbers usually indicate year of production as the first two digits. This camera differs from the Zorki-1 by the addition of a self timer. Though very few Zorki-2 cameras were made, their current price does not reflect their rarity.

Zorki-S (C):   **R2* D–**
1956-58, Cfps, 1/20 to 1/500s, no slow speeds, synch, CRF. Interchangeable Leica-type screw mount, f3.5/50mm Industar-22 lens in collapsible mount, or rigid mount f3.5/50mm Industar 50 lens. Camera serial numbers indicate year of production as the first two digits. Though not an exact copy of the Leica II(D); this camera keeps many of the features of the previous Zorki cameras. The rigid mount lens adds 15% to the value of the camera. Models in green and grey were made and add 100% or more to the price.

Zorki-2S (C):   **R2* D–**
1956-58 Cfps, 1/20 to 1/500s, no slow speeds, synch, CRF. Interchangeable Leica-type screw mount, rigid mount f3.5/50mm Industar-50 lens or F2.0/52mm Jupiter-8. Camera serial numbers indicate year of production as the first two digits. This camera differs from the Zorki-C by the addition of a self timer.

Zorki-3:   **R3* E–**

1954-55 Cfps, 1 to 1/1000s, slow speeds, no synch, CRF. Interchangeable Leica-type screw mount, rigid mount F2.0/50mm Jupiter-8 lens. Camera serial numbers indicate year of production as the first two digits. Very few Zorki-3 cameras were made, but the collectors' market price does not reflect this.

Zorki-3M: **R2* D+**
1955 Same as the Zorki-3, slow speeds moved to the top dial. Cfps, 1-1/1000s, slow speeds, no synch, CRF. Interchangeable Leica-type screw mount, rigid mount f2.0 Jupiter-8. Camera serial numbers indicate year of production as the first two digits. More common than the Zorki-3, but almost the same market value.

Zorki-3S (C):   **R2* D**
1956. This camera adds flash synch and a redesigned top cover to the features of the Zorki-3M. Cfps, 1-1/1000s, slow speeds, synch, CRF. Interchangeable Leica-type screw mount, rigid mount f2.0/50mm Jupiter-8 lens. Camera serial numbers indicate year of production as the first two digits.

Zorki-4:   **R2* C+**
1956-73 Cfps, 1-1/1000s, slow speeds, synch, CRF. Interchangeable Leica-type screw mount, rigid mount f3.5/50mm

Industar-50 lens or f2.0/52mm Jupiter-8 lens. Camera serial numbers indicate year of production as the first two digits. This camera differs from the Zorki-C by the addition of a self timer. Some cameras were marked celebrating the 50th anniversary of the Communist Party in Russia. These models more than double the price of the camera. Cameras marked "50th Anniversary" £150.

Zorki-4K: **R2* C+**
1973-77 Cfps, 1-1/1000s, slow speeds, synch, CRF. Interchangeable Leica-type screw mount, rigid mount F2.0 52mm Jupiter-8. Camera serial numbers indicate year of production as the first two digits. This camera is the same as the Zorki-4, with the addition of a rapid wind lever, and a fixed take-up spool. The Zorki-4K was made in large numbers, and was widely exported. Quite popular in Europe where it is commonly found, this camera fetches about 30% more in the United States.

Zorki-5:   **R2* D–**
c1958-59 Cfps, 1-1/1000s, slow speeds, synch, CRF. Interchangeable Leica-type screw mount, rigid mount f3.5/50mm Industar-50 lens or F2.0/52mm Jupiter-8 lens. Camera serial numbers indicate year of production as the first two digits. Incorporates a longer base rangefinder (67mm) than previous Zorki cameras, uses a combined RFR/vfr window.

Zorki-6:   **R2* D–**
1960-66 Cfps, 1-1/1000s, slow speeds, synch, CRF. Interchangeable Leica-type screw mount, rigid mount f3.5/50mm Industar-50 lens or f2.0/52mm Jupiter-8 lens. Camera serial numbers indicate year of production as the first two digits. This camera is the same as the Zorki-5, with the addition of a hinged back and a self timer. Less common in the US than in Europe.

Zorki-10:   **R3* C**
1964-78. Not a Leica copy, but based on Ricoh cameras of the 1960s. Fixed lens, automatic shutter, CRF.

Zorki-11:   **R3* C**
1964-66. Fixed lens, automatic shutter, the same as the Zorki-10, but without a coupled rangefinder.

Zorki-12:   **R4* E–**
(ZR114); 1967-1968. Fixed lens, automatic shutter, $1/2$ frame format.

Russian accessory lenses after 1945

20mm, f5.6, MR-2, w/o finder **E–** w/finder **F**
28mm, f6.0, Orion-15 **D**
35mm, f2.8, Jupiter-12 **D**
50mm, f1.5 Jupiter-3 **D**
85mm, f2.0, Jupiter-9 **D–**
135mm, f4.0, Jupiter-11 **D–**

Russian accessory finders

2cm optical finder **E+**
Universal finder for 28, 35, 50, 80, and 135mm views **B+**

Russian accessory lenses before 1945

FED F4.5/28mm **D**
FED F2.0/50mm **D+**

FED F3.5/50mm, Macro **D**

FED F3.5/50mm – close focusing **E+**

FED F6.3/100mm **D**

FED F6.3/100mm **G**

FED f4.5/28mm **D**

E. Krauss
Paris, France

Eka: **R4* F+**

c1924. Krauss Tessar 50mm f3.5 lens; Compur shutter 1-1/300s; 100 exp, 30 x 42mm on non-perforated 35mm film. c1924.

Nanos: **R3* E+**
1924. Strut camera for plates or film packs, $2^3/_8$" x $1^3/_4$". Dial-set Compur shutter.

Peggy I: **R4* G**
c1930. Folding strut camera for 35mm film. Compur shutter, f3.5 Tessar lens.

Peggy II: **R4* G**
1933. Similar to Peggy I, but with addition of rangefinder and facility for cutting film mid-way through roll.

Photo Revolver: **R5* H–**

c1921, revolver-type detective camera; Krauss Tessar 40mm f4.5 lens; shutter in helical mount 1/25, 1/50 and 1/100s. 48 exp on 2.2 x 3.6cm plates or roll film holder for 25, 50 or 100 exp, 20 x 30mm.

Rolette: **R3* D**
1925. Small folding camera for 2" x 3" pictures on 129 size film. Rollar f6.3 anastigmat lens.

Takyr: **R4* E+**
c1906. Zeiss Krauss 136mm f6.3 lens; fps. $3^1/_4$" x $4^1/_4$" exp on plates.

G.A. Krauss
Stuttgart, Germany

Krauss Peggy I: **R4* F–**

c1935. 35mm camera; often found with Zeiss Tessar 50mm f3.5 lens, though many lens options were available; Compur shutter 1-1/300s.

Krauss Peggy II: **R4* F**

c1935. 35mm RFR camera; often found with Schneider Xenon 45mm f2 lens, though many lens options were available; Compur shutter 1-1/300s, CRF. c1935.

Rollette: **R2* C**

c1922. Folding Rollfilm camera, 4 x 6.5cm format, front struts, Compur shutter, various lenses, simple models had Pronto shutter.

Rolette: **R22* C**
1928. New version of the original model, designed in the more traditional drop-bed folding camera design. New lever focusing reckoned to be the first

on this size of camera. Choice of Krauss Anastigmat lenses – f6.8, f6.3 or f5.5 in Pronto shutter, f4.5 in Ibsor shutter or f4.5 in Compur shutter.

Stereo Polyskop: **R3* E+**

c1906. Stereo camera making images on glass plates held in changing magazine. Twin 63mm f6.3 Tessar lenses.

Stereoplast: **R2* D+**

c1921. Stereo camera for 45x107mm held in push-pull changing magazine. Fitted with twin Schneider 55mm f4.5 Xenar lenses

Dr. Rudolph Krugener
Bockheim, Germany

Delta Camera: **R4* D+**
c1895, folding plate camera; meniscus lens; 3 speed rotary shutter; 9 x 12cm exp on plates.

Delta Klapp: **R4* D**
c1904, Rapid Aplanatic lens; pneumatic

shutter 1/15-1/100s; 3¼" x 4¼" exp on plates. Double ext bellows.

Delta Magazine Camera: R4* F+
c1892, Aplanat 145mm f13 lens; string cocked guillotine shutter; 12 exp, 9 x 12cm on dry plates.

Delta Patronen Flach Kamera: R4* D
c1903, Rapid Rectilinear lens; central shutter 1-1/100s; 3¼" x 4¼" exp on plates or roll film.

Delta Periskop: R4* D–
c1903, Periskop 150mm f12 lens; central shutter 1/25-1/100s; 3¼" x 4¼" exp on plates.

Dr. Krugener's Book Camera: R5* H+
c1889, book-type detective camera; Rectilinear 60mm f12 lens; guillotine shutter; 24 exp on 40 x 40mm plate.

Dr. Krugener's Million Camera:
R4* D+
c1903, 9 x 18cm stereo camera; Rapid Periskop lenses; guillotine shutter. 9 x 18cm exp on roll film.

Mini Detective: R4* F+
c1900, miniature box detective camera. Leather changing bag for 12 plates; polished mahogany wood; size: 4" x 3¼" x 7".

Normal Simplex: R4* G+
c1900, 9 x 12cm reflex camera; three diaphragm stops on sliding brass bar. Vf fitted to concealed bellows; mahogany finish.

Simplex Magazine Camera: R4* G

c1889, TLR detective camera; Achromatised Periscopic 100mm f10 lens; sector self-capping shutter; 24 exp, 6 x 8cm on dry plates.

Delta Stereo: R4* E–
c1900-1909, folding stereo camera for 9 x 18cm plates, Aplanat lenses and simple two speed shutter, some models allowed the use of roll film.

Vestpocket Kronos: R3* D+
c1920, strut folding VFR camera for 4.5 x 6cm plates, Anticomar f4.2/75mm lens, Compur shutter.

Stereo Kronos: R4* E+
c1920, strut folding stereo camera for 4.5 x 10.7cm plates, Anticomar f3.5/75mm lenses, Compur Stereo shutter.

Quer Kronos: R3* C–
c1920, metal bodied horizontal folding camera for 9 x 12cm glass plates, Anticomar f6.3/10.5cm lens, Compur shutter.

Nestor: R3* B+
c1920, horizontal folding VFR camera for 6 x 6cm frames on roll film, Anticomar f5.4/75mm lens, Compur shutter.

Pastoscope: R4* E–
c1900, strut folding stereo camera 4.5 x 10.7cm plates, Simplex f7.7/60mm lenses, simple four speed shutter.

Kromskop Manufactory
Philadelphia, Pennsylvania, USA

Ives Kromskop Triple Camera: R4* E+
c1897 single exposure tri-colour camera using internal prisms as beam-splitters. Mahogany and brass fittings. The wooden bodies were made for Ives in England. They were shipped to Philadelphia where the prisms, filters and other items were added.

Kunick, Walter KG
Frankfurt, Germany

Lighter Petie: R3* F–

cigarette lighter-type detective camera; built along lines of Petie Compact,

camera separable; meniscus 24mm f11 lens; single speed shutter; 16 exp, 16 x 16mm on 16mm roll film. c1957. Red, green, blue, deco or leather and chrome finish.

Petie: R3* C+

c1958, subminiature camera; meniscus 25mm f9 lens; single speed shutter; 16 exp, 14 x 14mm on 16mm.

Petie Vanity-Case: R4* F

c1958, ladies compact-type subminiature detective camera; 35mm f9 lens; single speed shutter. 16 exp, 14 x 14mm on 16mm roll film. Red, green, blue, deco or leather with chrome/gold finished case contains lipstick, compact and camera.

Petietux: **R5* F**
1957. Subminiature for 16mm rollfilm, 14 x 14 mm exposures. Improved version of other Petie cameras, with flash synch and built-in meter. Lens focuses down to 0.5 metre, adjustable apertures from f16 – f2.8.

Kürbi & Niggeloh, Bilora
Radevormwald, Germany

Radix 56:   **R2* B–**
c1950, metal 35mm VFR camera for 24 x 24mm frames on 35mm film, Biloxar f5.6/40mm lens, simple shutter, lever advance.

Radix 35B: **R2* B–**
c1950, with Biloxar f3.5 lens.

Radix 35S: **R2* B–**
c1950, with Schneider Radionar f3.5/38mm lens.

Radix 35BH: **R3* B**
c1951, with improved shutter, $^1/_2$-1/200s.

Radix 35SH: **R3* B**
c1951, with improved shutter, $^1/_2$-1/200s.

Boy: **R2* A**
c1950, bakelite box camera for 6 x 4.5 frames on 127 film, simple lens and shutter.

Luxus Boy: **R2* C**
c1954, red bakelite box camera for 6 x 4.5cm frames on 127 film, f11 lens, simple shutter.

Bilora Stahl-Box: **R2* A–**
c1950, metal box camera for 6 x 9cm frames on roll film, reflex VFRs, simple lens and shutter.

Bilora Blitz Box: **R2* A–**
c1950, with synchro contacts.

Bilora Blitz Box D: **R2* A–**
metal box camera for 6 x 9cm frames on roll film, simple lens and shutter, optical VFR allowing for better positioning of the flash.

Bilora Standard Box: **R2* A–**
c1950, metal box camera for 6 x 9cm frames on roll film, f11 lens and simple shutter.

Bilora Special Box: **R2* A–**
c1950, with built-in close-up lens.

Bilora Mikro Box: **R3* C–**
c1953, special purpose metal box camera, no VFR. (one offered for £50 in April, 1991).

Bilora Bonita 66:   **R2* A**
c1953, TLR type box camera for 6 x 6cm frames on roll film, simple lens and shutter.

Bilora Bella: **R3* A**
c1950, Metal VFR camera for 6 x 4.5cm frames on 127 film, all black with chrome trim, simple f9 lens and shutter.

Bilora Bella, c1950,

Bilora Bella 55:   R3* A
c1955. With chrome top plate and simple f8 lens.

Bilora Bella D: R2* A
c1957. In "Swiss-Air Blue" and "Fashion-Grey".

Bilora Bella 44:   R2* A–

c1959, metal VFR camera for 4 x 4cm frames on 127 film, simple f8 lens and shutter.

Bilora DC 4:   R2* A–
c1959-60, with Trinar f5.6/55mm lens in vario shutter, or Trinar f3.5/55mm lens in Prontor shutter.

Bilora Bella 46:   R2* A
c1957, metal VFR camera for 4 x 6cm frames on 120 roll film, simple lens and shutter, available in "Swiss-Air Blue" and "Fashion-Grey".

Bilora Bella 66:   R2* A
c1957, metal VFR camera for 6 x 6cm frames on 120 roll film, simple lens and shutter, available in "Swiss-Air Blue" and "Fashion-Grey".

Kyoto Seiki
Japan

Lovely: R5* H

c1948. Subminiature for 17.5mm rollfilm. One of the first horizontal style subminiature cameras that led the way for Minolta and Mamiya. 14 x 14mm images, despite box claiming 18 x 18mm. Shutter 1/25-1/100s. Very rare.

L

Lamperti & Garbagnati
Italy

Lamperti: R4* E+

c1890. 9 x 18cm stereo detective camera; 13cm lens; 3 speed guillotine shutter. Leather covered wooden body; rack focusing; 9 x 18cm exp on plates.

Lancart
Paris, France

XYZ: R4* F+

c1935. Subminiature camera; nickel plated finish.

J. Lancaster & Son
Birmingham, England

Camrex Deluxe: R3* E–

c1900. 3¼" x 4¼" folding hand camera; RR lens; pneumatic shutter. Red leather bellows. Mahogany finish with brass fittings.

Gem Apparatus: R5* H+

c1880. 12-lens tin-type camera. 12 Petzval-type 2" f4.5 lenses. Shutter: horizontally sliding panel on front of camera is operated manually. 12 exp, ¹¹⁄₁₆" x ¹³⁄₁₆" on ¼"x 4¼" ferrotype plates.

Instantograph B: R3* E+

c1883. Quarter plate view camera. Brass barrel Lancaster f8 or f10 lens with iris diaphragm; rotary shutter; tapered red bellows; wood body.

The 1888 Patent Instantograph:
R4* E+

c1888. 4" x 5" view camera. Lancaster & Son brass lens with adjustable diaphragm. Reversible back; red Russian leather bellows. Lancaster & Son made several models of this camera.

Ladies' Camera: R5* H–
c1897. Pocketbook-type detective camera. Achromatic lens; iris diaphragm; Lancaster see-saw single speed shutter. Quarter, half- or whole-plate pictures.

Lancaster's Patent Watch Camera:
R5* K–

c1886. Collapsible watch-type detective camera. Grubb-type achromatic 45mm f22 lens; variable speed rotary shutter. Single exp, 1" x ½" on dry plates. NSR.

Le Meritore: R2* E
c1880-1905. Wood and brass view camera. Blue or brown double extension bellows. A range of Lancaster lenses. Quarter plate to 10" x 12".

Le Merveilleux: R4* E–
c1888. 3¼" x 4¼" view camera. Aplanatic lens. 3¼" x 4¼" exp on plates.

Omnigraph Detective Camera:
R4* D+
(LN106). c1891-1907. Box-type detective camera.

The Rover Detective Camera: R4* F–
c1892. 3¼" x 4¼" box-type detective camera. Magazine load; mahogany finish.

E. Ludwig Lausa
Dresden, Germany

Leader: R3* C+
c1950. 35mm stereo camera. Leader Anastigmat 45mm f4.5 lenses; shutter TMBK 1/25-1/100s. Mfd in Japan.

R. Lechner
Vienna, Austria

Juwel: R4* E+
c1909. Folding stereo camera. Achromat lens; T and I shutter; central finder; side-flaps covered retracted lens panel; leather covered metal body. 45 x 107mm exp on plates.

Lechner's Schutzen-Camera (Marksman's Camera): R5* NSR

c1892. Rifle-type detective camera. 30 exp, 3cm diameter, on roll film. A camera that attached beneath the barrel of any gun.

Nanna IA: R4* E+

c1909. Folding bellows stereo camera. Nanna Aplanat 80mm f8 lens with sliding stops; guillotine shutter. Central frame finder; 6 x 13cm exp on plates. Size: 2.5 x 19 x 10.5cm.

Lecoultre & Cie
Le Sentier, Switzerland

Compass: R3* G+

c1938. 24 x 36mm miniature RFR camera; Kern CCL 3B Anastigmat 35mm f3.5 lens with variable stops to f16; rotary sector shutter – 22 speeds from 4½-1/500s. Pivoting mirror for right-angle viewing, CRF. Machined Duralumin body, stereoscopic head, panoramic head, built-in yellow, orange and green filters, ground glass back with focusing magnifier, collapsible lens shade, spirit level on top of camera, built-in extinction meter visible through VFR window, hinged lens cap with depth of field scale, collapsible lens mount. Single exp on 24 x 6mm dry plates (sold ready loaded in small heavy paper "Compass envelopes" complete with dark slide). A wide range of accessories was available for the Compass. A roll film back held six exp on special 1½" film, a pocket tripod the size of a fountain pen, and an enlarger-projector that fit into a 4" x 4" x 16" box and could be powered by a 12 volt car battery. Mfg. by Le Coultre & Cie, Le Sentier, Switzerland for Compass Cameras, Ltd, London, England.

Compass accessories

Tripod **F**
Roll film back **F**

Armand Le Docte
Brussels, Belgium

Photo Detective: R5* G–

c1889. Rectilinear 18cm f8 lens; flap shutter. Reflex viewer for either vertical or horizontal format. Changing mechanism for 18 plates, 8.3 x 10.8 cm.

Plastron: R5* NSR
c1886. Concealed vest-type detective camera. Rectilinear 45mm lens. Size: 2cm from front to rear; 14.9cm diameter. Similar to Gray, Stirn and Photo Eclair.

A. Lehmann
Berlin, Germany

Ben Akiba: R5* K–
c1903. Cane-type detective camera. Front meniscus 35mm f9 lens; oscillating sector, self-cocking shutter. 20 exp, 16 x 20mm on special daylight loading roll film. Handle contained extra rolls of film. Invented by Emil Kronke. Note: Extreme caution required as many replicas made. *(see below)*

Leidolf Kamerawerkes
Wetzlar, Germany

Leidox: R3* B+
c1950, metal VFR camera for 4 x 4cm frames on 127 roll film; Triplon f3.8, 50mm lens; Vario shutter.

Leidox IIS: R3* B+
c1952, metal VFR camera for 4 x 4cm frames on 127 film. Triplon f2.8, 50mm lens; Prontor-S shutter.

Lordox: R3* B+
c1952, 35mm VFR camera. Lordon f2.8, 50mm lens; Prontor-SV shutter, body release, knob wind.

Lordomat: R2* C–
c1955, 35mm RFR camera. Interchangeable Lordon f1.9 or Lordonar f2.8, 50mm lens; Prontor-SV or SVS shutter; double stroke lever advance operating from front to back; CRF; marked "Lordomat" on top.

Lordomat C35: R3* C+
c1956, 35mm RFR camera with built-in light meter. Lordon f1.9 or Lordonar f2.8, 50mm lens; Prontor-SVS shutter; CRF; VFR with fields of view for 35mm, 90mm, and 135mm.

Lordomat SLE: R3* C–
1959. Modified version of the Lordomat C35. CRF camera, top plate redesigned for a neater appearance with one window of the rangefinder incorporated into the meter window, the other in the viewfinder. Made for interchangeable lenses with frames for 35mm-135mm in viewfinder. Lenses fit into the Prontor SVS shutter speeded 1-1/300s + B. Two stroke lever wind.

Lordomat SE: R3* C–
c1960, 35mm RFR camera. Lordon f1.9 or Lordonar f2.8, 50mm lens; Prontor SVS shutter; new body and RFR style; CRF; interchangeable lens mounting system; marked Lordomat on the front.

Lordox II: R3* B+
c1955, 35mm VFR camera. Fixed Triplon f2.8, 50mm lens; Prontor-SV shutter; same body style and double stroke lever advance.

Ben Akiba.

Lordox 57:   R2* B+

1957. VFR 35mm camera. 5cm f2.8 Leidof Tripon. Prontor SVS shutter 1-1/300s. Double wind through 180° for film advance.

Lordox Junior: R2* A

c1960, 35mm VFR camera. Fixed Triplon f2.8, 50mm lens; Prontor-SVS shutter; same body style as (LY105).

Lordox Junior B: R2* A

c1950, 35mm VFR camera with built-in light meter.

Lordox Blitz: R2* A

c1960, 35mm VFR camera with built-in AG1 flash lamp holder.

Lordomatic: R2* A

c1960, 35mm VFR camera, fixed Lordonar f2.8, 50mm lens; Prontor-SLK shutter; coupled light meter.

Accessory lenses for Lordomat cameras

Lordonar f3.5/35mm lens **B+**
Travenar f3.5/35mm lens **B+**
Telordon f5.6/90mm lens **B+**
Travenar f4.0/90mm lens **B+**
Travenar f4.0/135mm lens **C**

Ernst Leitz GmbH
Wetzlar, Germany

For further information see Leica Collectors Guide by Dennis Laney, Hove Collectors Books, 1992, also other Leica books from Hove Collectors Books advertisement at the back of this book.

Note: Leica prices are for items in original condition, one grade higher than other makes.

UR Leica.

UR Leica Replica: R4* G

c1970. Non-operational display replica.

O-Series Leica: R5* L+

c1923. Leitz Anastigmat f3.5, 50mm lens; non-self-capping CFPS 1/20-1/500s.

Leica I (A) Anastigmat: R5* K–

c1925. Leitz Anastigmat f3.5, 50mm lens; CFPS 1/25-1/500s. Snr 126-300. Qty 175.The original Anastigmat design used five elements. A four element lens would indicate a later Leitz conversion or a counterfeit camera. When considering buying such a camera, it is suggested that a complete examination of the camera and lens be undertaken by an expert with the specialised tools and knowledge to determine the camera's authenticity. Any attempt by an inexperienced person to take apart Leitz Anastigmat lens to find out the number of elements used could drastically lower the cameras worth!

Leica I (A) Elmax: R5* J

c1926-1930. Leitz Elmax f3.5, 50mm lens; CFPS 1/20-1/500s. Snr 300-1,300. Qty 1000. The original Elmax design used five elements. A four element lens would indicate either a later Leitz conversion or a counterfeit camera.

Leica I (A) Elmar: R3* G+

c1926-1930. Leitz Elmar f3.5, 50mm lens; CFPS 1/20-1/500s. Snr 1,300-71,250. Qty 53,000(?). Four digit serial numbered Leica I (A):

Five digit serial numbered Leica I (A):   R3* G–

Close focus (18") model Leica I (A):   R3* G

Leica I (A) Luxus: R5* K–
c1928-1931. Leitz Elmar f3.5, 50mm lens; CFPS 1/20-1/500s. Snr 28,692-48,441. Qty 95. Gold plated Leica I(A) with red, blue, green or brown lizard skin.

Leica I (A) Luxus, c1928-1931.

Leica I (A) Luxus Replica: R4* G+
Collectors and others have remanufactured replica Luxus cameras from Leica I (A) cameras.

Leica Mifilmca: R4* I+
c1927, for use on microscope with fixed focus MIKAS attachment – using microscope optics. (One sold at auction in April, 1991 for more than £5000.)

Leica I (A) Hektor: R4* I–
c1930. Hektor f2.5, 50mm lens; CFPS 1/20-1/500s. Snr 38,662-71,230. Qty 1330. Counterfeit Hektor cameras have been offered on the market for $4000. To verify a Hektor camera, check the serial number against the factory list and inspect the rear lens bezel for alterations.

Leica I (B) Compur, Dial-set: R4* J–

c1926-1929. Leitz Elmar f3.5, 50mm lens; Compur shutter 1-1/300s. Snr 5,700-13,200(?). Qty 638.

Leica I (B) Compur, Rim-set: R4* I+

c1929-1930. Leitz Elmar f3.5, 50mm lens; Compur shutter 1-1/300s. Snr 13150-50710. Qty 969.

Leica I (C) with non-standardised lens mount: R4* H–

c1930-1931. Leitz Elmar f3.5, 50mm lens; CFPS 1/20-1/500s. Snr 37,280. When the swing-in vf mask is intact and matched 135mm and 35mm lenses are included, add $1000-$1500. First Leica with interchangeable lens mount (shown above). It is difficult to find this model in historically accurate condition (the lens flange must not have a "0" engraved at the 12 o'clock position. The rear lens bezel must be marked with the last three digits of the body serial no.)

because in most cases they were standardised by E. Leitz when returned for service. With Hektor add 20%. With matched 50mm lens **G+**; with mask **H–**; with Hektor **H–**; with three lenses **I+**.

Leica I (C) with standardised lens mount: R3* F

c1931. Leitz Elmar f3.5, 50mm lens; CFPS 1/20-1/500s. Snr 55404-99755. Qty 7231. First Leica to permit interchange-ability of standardised lenses with any standardised camera body. The lens flange has a "0" engraved at the 12 o'clock position.

Leica II (D):   R3* Chrome: F–
Black: F

c1932-1948. Leitz Elmar f3.5, 50mm lens; CFPS 1/20-1/500s. Snr 71,200-358,650. Qty 52509.

Leica E (Standard):   R3* F–

c1932-1946. CFPS 1/20-1/500s. Snr 101,101-355,670. Qty 27,255.

Leica E (Standard), c1932-1946.

Leica III (F), c1933-1939.

Leica E (Standard): R4* H
Postwar 1946 model with Wollensak
Velostigmat 50mm f3.5 lens. Snr
355,001-355,650. Qty 650.

Leica III (F): R3* Chrome: F–
Black: F
c1933-1939. CFPS 1-1/500s. Snr
107,601-343,100. Qty 69,300.

Leica 250 (FF) Reporter: R4* J+

c1933. CFPS 1-1/500s. Snr 114,051-
150,124. Qty 126(?).

Leica 250 (GG) Reporter: R4* J–
c1942. CFPS 1-1/1000s. Snr 150,125-
353,800. Qty 824(?).

Leica 250GG with Motor, c1942
Courtesy to 1996 Auction Team Breker, Köln.

Leica IIIa (G):   R2* Chrome: F+
c1935-1950. CFPS 1-1/1000s. Snr 156,201-357,200. Qty 92,687(?). Black body appears on factory list, but no genuine example has been verified.

Leica IIIb (G) – 1938:   R2* F–
c1935-1950. CFPS 1-1/1000s. Snr 240,001-368,563. Qty 32, 105.

Leica IIIc (1939-1945):
CFPS, 1-1/100s, Snr 360,175-367,600. Qty, 33,750. After 1945, Snr 4,000,01-525,000, Qty 100,876.

Civilian cameras:
In chrome below Nr.400,000: **F**
Above Nr.400,000: **F–**
In blue-grey, with blue/grey body covering: **H–**

With "K" after the body SNR, standing for "Kugellager", meaning ballbearing. This special shutter was designed to operate in extremes of climatic conditions.

                    Chrome, Qty 400 **H+**
                    Blue/grey **H**

Military cameras:
With "Luftwaffen Eigentum" and "FL No.38079" blue-grey body only: **H**

Complete with Summitar f2.0, 5cm lens, also engraved "Luftwaffen Eigentum" and "FLNo.38079" and "K" for Kugellager, in chrome and blue/grey: **H+**

Marked "HEER" (meaning "Army" with f3.5/5cm Elmar also marked "HEER": **H+**

(At auction these cameras can bring higher prices. It seems they get some collectors' blood boiling and the bidding goes sky high! One auction in autumn 1990 saw almost $4000 for this camera and lens combination, and again in April of 1991 the same price!)

Leica IIId: R4* I+

c1940-1942. CFPS 1-1/1000s. Snr 360,002-360,134; 367,000-367,325. Qty 427. Similar to the Leica IIIc (1940-1946) with self-timer. An internal inspection is necessary to confirm a genuine Leica IIId camera.

Leica IIc: R3* F–
c1948-1951. CFPS 1/30-1/500 s. Snr 440,000-451,000. Qty 11,000.

Leica Ic: R3* F–
c1949-1952. CFPS 1/30-1/500s. Snr 455,001-563,100. Qty 12,000.

Leica IIIa "Monte en Sarre":   R4* H+
c1950. Mfd in France on a Leica IIIa body. Late models had IIIf flash synch. Snr 359,xxx.

Leica IIIf: R3* E+
                                         Black J

c1950-1952. CFPS 1-1/1000s. Black dial version: Snr 525,001-611,000. Qty 71,000.

Red dial version: R3* F–
c1952-1954. Snr 615,000-685,000. Qty 54,000.

IIIf Canada version: R4* H–
Engraved: Midland, Ontario

IIIf black version with black Elmar 50mm f3.5 lens: R4* J

Leica IIf: R4* F–
c1951-1952. Black dial version: CFPS 1/30-1/500s. Snr 451,000-574,000. Qty 8400(?).

Red dial version: R4* E+
c1952-1957. CFPS 1/25-1/1000s. Snr 574,000-851,000. Qty 15,240.

Leica If: R4* G

c1952. Black dial version: CFPS 1/30-1/500s. Snr 562,293-564,200.

Red dial version: R4* F
c1956. CFPS 1/25-1/500s. Snr 564,201-851,000.

Leica 72:   R5* J

c1954. CFPS 1-1/1000s. Snr 357,301-357,500. Midland, Ontario version: qty 149. The Leica 72 was the only screw half-frame 35mm camera marketed by Ernst Leitz.

Wetzlar, Germany version: R5* J+
Qty 33.

Leica IIIg: R3* G

c1957-1960. CFPS 1-1/1000s. Snr 825,001-988,280. Qty, chrome version 41,589.

Leica IIIg Swedish military version:
R5* J

black body with chrome Elmar 50mm f2.9 lens-both marked with Swedish three-crown emblem. Qty 125.

Leica Ig:
R4* G

c1958-1960. CFPS 1-1/1000s. Qty 5,986. Snr 887,001-987,600.

Leica M3:

Intro-1954. CFPS 1-1/1000s. Null series Snr 00xx, Snr 700,000-700,500.
First 500: **H–**
Double stroke: **F**
Serial numbers over 1,000,000: **G**
Black: **H+**
Olive supplied to German army.
c1954-1966. **I+**

Leica MP:
R4* J+

CFPS 1-1/1000s. With Leicavit black enamel version. Snr 12-150. Qty 139.

Chrome version:
R4* J

Snr 1-11, and 151-450, qty 310, c1956-1957.

Leica MP Counterfeit:
R4* G+

CFPS 1-1/1000s. 5 counterfeit MP cameras were sold in the USA for $500-$1000 each (1972); one was resold for $2000 in Japan (it was later returned).

Leica M2:
R3* F+

c1957-1967. CFPS 1-1/1000s. Snr 926,001-970,261. Button rewind release (early version). Chrome, qty 24,800.

Lever rewind release (late version) with self-timer. Snr 970,261-1,165,000.
Chrome, qty 59,000(?) **R3* F+**
Black enamel, qty 1350(?) **R3* H**
Cut-away display model, qty 1000(?)

Leica M2 cut-away display model.

Leica M2-M: R4* I+
c1956. CFPS 1-1/1000s. Snr 1,163,771-
1,164,046. Qty 275. Complete with
motor.

*Ten different Leica 'M' cameras
viewed from above: Left, top to
bottom: MD-2, M4-2 (red dot), KE-7,
M4 enamel, MD, Right, top to bottom:
M1, M2, M2 chrome, M3, M3 chrome.*

Leica M1: R3* G
CFPS 1-1/1000s. Button rewind release (early version), Snr 950,001-966,729. Chrome, qty 1515(?)

Lever rewind release (late version), Snr966,730-1,102,900. Chrome, qty 7925(?): R3* G

Olive enamel, qty 325. c1959-1964. R3* I

Leica MD: R3* G
c1964-1966. CFPS 1-1/1000s. Snr 1,102,501-1,160,820. Qty 3200 plus.

Leica M4 (1967): R3* G

CFPS 1-1/1000s. Snr 1,175,001-1,286,700. Qty chrome 47,260 plus.

Black enamel 4,590 plus. R3* H+

Military olive, qty 30 plus. c1967-1972. R3* I–

Leica M4-M (motordrive): R4* I+
Snr 1,206,xxx-(?). Complete with motor:

Leica M4 (1974): R3* G+
c1974-1975. CFPS 1-1/1000s. Snr 1,380,000-(?). Qty black chrome, 5000 plus.

Fiftieth Anniversary Leica M4: R3* H
c1975. Wetzlar, Germany. Qty black chrome 1400.

Fiftieth Anniversary Leica M4: R3* H+
Midland, Canada. c1975. Qty black chrome, 350.

Leica M4-2: R3* G–

c1978. CFPS 1-1/1000s. "Red-dot" version: $2.25k. £1.5k DM3.6k Midland, Canada version and Wetzlar, Germany version.

Leica MDa: R3* G–
c1966-1975. CFPS 1-1/1000s. Snr 1,159,001-(?).

Leica MD-2: Body only R4* G
c1980. CFPS 1-1/1000s.
Hologon lens, finder, and filter: **R4* I+**

Leica M2-R: **R3* G+**
c1969-1970. CFPS 1-1/1000s. Snr
1,248,201-1,250,200. Qty 2000.

Leica M5:   **R3* G**

c1971-1975. Leitz Summicron f2,
50mm lens; CFPS 1/2-1/1000s. Snr
1,287,001-(?).

Fiftieth Anniversary Leica M5: R3* H
c1975. Qty 1750. Black chrome version:

Chrome version: **R3* H**

Leica KE-7A: **R4* I**

U.S. Army, Camera-Still Picture: c1972.
Leitz Elcan f2, 50mm lens; CFPS
1-1/1000s. Snr 1,294,xxx-(?). Qty
released for the civilian market, 50(?)
bodies; 70(?) Elcan lenses. Civilian
version, with lens.

KE-7A with 50mm F2 lens; military
version, with lens: **R4* I+**

*The following six Leicas are not true
classics in so far as they were manufactured during the past six years. But each
was manufactured as a special edition to
celebrate an event or anniversary and,
as such, immediately became collectors'
items. They are all based on the Leica
M6, first made in 1984.*

Leica M6J: **R3* I**
1994. Body, shutter and meter as M6,
but with a top plate copied from original
M3, made in 1954. Made to mark 40
years of Leica cameras. Limited edition
of 1,640.

RPS M6:   **R3* I**
1994. Made to mark the centenary of
the Royal Photographic Society. Top and
base plates finished in satin chrome with
matt black controls and top plate
engraved with the RPS coat of arms.
Limited edition of 100.

Danish Royal Wedding M6:   R3* I
1995. Engraved with the Danish Royal
Crest and the wedding date, 18th
November 1995. Limited edition of 200.

Anton Bruckner M6:   **R3* I**
1996. Made to commemorate the 100th
anniversary of the death of the Austrian
composer, the camera is covered in grey-
blue embossed iguana leather. Limited
edition of 200, representing 20 cameras
for each of Bruckner's 10 symphonies.

Ein Stuck M6:   **R4* I**
1996. Made to mark the listing of Leica
AG on the stock exchange. Covered in
calf skin embossed with the Leica logo.
Limited edition of 996.

Jaguar M6:   **R4* J**

1998. Commissioned by Jaguar to mark the 50th anniversary of the Jaguar XK120 sports car in 1948. Limited edition of 50 cameras, numbered XK1 to XK50.

Leica CL: **R2* F+**

c1973-1975. Leitz Summicron f2, 40mm lens; CFPS ½-1/1000s. Snr 1,300,001-(?).

Fiftieth Anniversary Leica CL: **R3* G+**
qty black chrome, 1750. c1975. with lens;

Leicaflex Standard: **R3* F–**

c1964-1968. Interchangeable bayonet mount; CFPS 1-1/2000s. Snr 1,173,001-1,174,700. First SLR by Leitz. Chrome version:

Black enamel version: **R3* H–**

Leicaflex SL: **R3* F+**
          Black: R4* G+

(EL152). c1968-1974. CFPS 1-1/12000s. Snr 1,173,001-(?). Chrome:

Leicaflex SL2:

        Black: R3* G
      Chrome: R3* G+
(EL153). Leitz Summicron f2, 50mm lens; CFPS 1-1/2000s.

Fiftieth Anniversary Leicaflex SL2:
        Chrome: H
        Black: H–
c1975. Qty black chrome, 1750.

Leica R3 Electronic: **R3* F–**

c1977. Mfps 4-1/1000s. Body only.

Leica Screw-mount Lenses

21mm f4 Super Angulon: G+
Qty 1400(?). c1958-1963

28mm f6.3 Hektor: F–
Qty 10,000(?). c1935-1953

28mm f5.6 Summaron: F+
Qty 6200(?) c1955-1963

33mm f3.5 Stemar: I+
Complete outfit c1954-1957

35mm f3.5 Elmar: E–
Qty 42,500(?) c1930-1950   **Nickel** E+

35mm f3.5 Summaron: E+
Qty 80,000(?) c1949-1958

35mm f2.8 Summaron: F+
Qty 52,000(?) c1958

35mm f2 Summicron: G+
Qty 500(?). c1958

50mm f3.5 Elmar: D+
       Red scale E+
Qty 360,000(?). c1926-1959

50mm f2.5 Hektor: F
Qty 10,300(?). c1930-1939

50mm f2 Summar: C+
Qty 123,000(?). c1933-1939

50mm f2 Rigid Summar:
c1933-1939   **Nickel** G+
       Chrome H–

50mm f1.5 Xenon: F–
Qty 6000(?). c1936-1949

50mm f2 Summitar: E–
Qty 170,000(?). c1939-1953

50mm f1.5 Summarit: E+
Qty 39,000(?). c1949-1960

50mm f3.5 Wollensak Velostigmat: G+
c1947-1949

50mm f2 Collapsible Summicron: F–
Qty 61,000 c1953-1961

50mm f2 Rigid Summicron: G+
Qty 100(?). c1958-1962

50mm f2 Compur Summicron: I
Shutter with lever

50mm f2.8 Elmar:
c1957-1962   E–

50mm f1.4 Summilux: H+
Qty 550(?). c1960-1963

65mm f3.5 Elmar: **Black** G–
c1960-1969.   **Chrome** F+

73mm f1.9 Hektor: G–
Qty 7000(?). c1932-1940

85mm f1.5 Summarex: **Black** H+
Chrome with lens hood and caps   G+
Qty 4000(?). c1949-1962.

90mm f2 Summicron: H–
Qty 600(?). c1957-1962

First version with removable shade **G+**
Second version with built-in lens shade.
(Original screw mount doesn't have red
dot at the base of the lens mount.) **G+**

90mm f4.5 Wollensak Velostigmat: E–
Made in USA: 1945-1950

90mm f4 Elmar: D+
Qty 114,000(?). c1931-1964

90mm f2.8 Elmarit: H
Qty 2000(?). c1959-1962

90mm f2.2 Thambar:	I–
Without filter	**H**

Qty 3000(?). Disk shade and caps. c1935-1939.

105mm f6.3 Mountain Elmar:	**G+**

Qty 4000(?).
With shade and caps. c1932-1937. **G**

125mm f2.5 Hektor:	**G**

Qty 3300(?). c1954-1963. With shade and caps.

127mm f4.5 Wollensak Velostigmat:	**E+**

Made in USA c1944-1951.

135mm f4.5 Elmar:	**F–**

Qty 5200(?). c1930-1936.

135mm f4.5 Hektor:	**E–**

Qty 70,000(?). c1933-1960

135mm f4 Elmar:	**F+**

Qty 5000(?). c1960.

180mm f2.8 Tele-Elmarit:	**F+**

(Bayonet mount for Visoflex II, IIa and III); c1965

200mm f4.5 Telyt:	**E+**

Qty 11,500(?). c1935-1960

280mm f4.8 Telyt:	
c1961-1970	**E+**

400mm f5 Telyt:	**F**

Qty 4000(?). c1937-1967.

With removable shade,	**G+**
with built-in shade	**G**

Leica M-mount Lenses

Hologon 15mm f8.0 lens with finder	**I+**
Super Angulon 21mm f4.0:	**G–**
Super Angulon 21mm f3.4:	**G+**
Elmarit 21mm f2.8:	**G+**
Elmarit 28mm f2.8 (old style):	**F+**
Elmarit 28mm f2.8 (new style):	**G+**
RF-Summicron 35mm f2.0:	
	Chrome F+

400mm f5 Telyt:	**G+**

Qty 4000(?). c1937-1967. black lacquer.

RF-Summaron 35mm f2.8:	**G**
Summicron Chrome 35mm f2.0:	**F+**
Summicron Black lacquer 35mm f2.0:	
	H–
Summaron 35mm f2.8:	**F–**
Summaron 35mm f3.5:	**E+**
Summilux 35mm f1.4:	**G–**
Summicron C 40mm f2.0:	**E+**
Elmar 50mm f2.8:	**E+**
Elmar 50mm f3.5:	**E+**
Summarit 50mm f1.5:	**F–**
Summicron Chrome Wetzlar 50mm f2.0 Rigid:	**F–**
Summicron Chrome Collapsible 50mm f2.0:	**F–**
Summicron Black lacquer Wetzlar 50mm f2.0:	**H–**
Dual Range Summicron 50mm f2.0 with finder	**F**
Summilux Black 50mm f1.4:	**G–**
Summilux Chrome 50mm f1.4:	**G–**
Noctilux 50mm f1.2:	**H+**
Noctilux 50mm f1.0:	**G+**
Summilux 75mm f1.4:	**Chrome G+**
Elmarit 90mm f2.8:	**G–**
Elmar C 90mm f4.0:	**F–**

Tele Elmarit 90mm f2.8:	G
Elmar Rigid 90mm f4.0:	E–
Elmar Collapsible 90mm f4.0:	F
Summicron 90mm f2.0: Black or Chrome	G–
Summicron 90mm f2.0: Black (new style)	G–
Hektor 135mm f4.5:	
Elmarit 135mm f2.8:	E
Tele Elmar 135mm f4.0:	F+
Summicron 50mm f2: Cutaway display model	G

Leica Reflex lenses

Leica 15mm f3.8 R:	H+
Leica 16mm f2.8 R:	G+
Leica 19mm f2.8 R:	G
Leica 21mm f4.0 R:	G+
Leica 24mm f2.8 R:	G+
Leica 28mm f2.8 R:	G–
Leica 35mm f2.0 R:	F+
Leica 35mm f2.8 R:	E+
Leica PA-Curtigon 35mm f4 R:	J
Leica 50mm f2 R: (Canadian)	E+
Leica 50mm f1.4 R:	F+
Leica 60mm f2.8 R:	G
Leica 80mm f1.4 R:	G+

Leica 90mm f2.8 R:	F+
Leica 90mm f2 R:	F+
Leica 100mm f4 R with mount:	F+
Leica 135mm f2.8 R:	F
Leica 180mm f3.4 APO:	G+
Leica 250mm f4 R:	F
Leica 180mm f2.8 R: (Compact)	G+
Leica 180mm f2.8 R: (Original)	F+
Leica 250mm f4 R: lightweight	G+
Leica 350mm f4.8 R:	H
Leica 400mm f6.8 R:	G
Leica 500mm f8 Mirror-R:	G
Leica 560mm f6.8 R:	G+
Leica Angenieux P 45-90mm f2.8:	G–
Leica 35-70mm f3.5 R:	G–
Leica 75-200mm f4.5 R:	G–
Leica 2X Extender R:	F+

Leica Reflex Accessories

Leica R4 Motor:	E–
Leica R4 Winder:	D+
Leica R4 Data Back:	D+
Leica R4 Bellows:	F–
Leicaflex Motor:	G–
Megoflex Viewer: (non-Leitz manufacture)	F–

Megoflex Viewer.

Viewfinders

Torpedo type: VISOR	E+
VISAX, VIUNA, VIZWO, VITRE	E
VIFUR	E

Other Universal Viewfinders

VIDOM, Black	D+
VIDOM, Early	E−
VIDOM, Chrome	D
VIOOH, round body	E−
VIOOH, earliest, unthreaded nose piece	E−
VIOOH, later, pinched or sloped body	D
TUVOO, (28mm adaptor)	E+

Waist-level Viewfinders

AUFSU E+ without shoe	F−
AYOOC, with swing lens 35mm	F
AHOOT, with swing lens 28mm	F+

Right-angle Viewfinders

WINKO	D+
WINTU (in chrome or black)	D+

Early Optical Viewfinders

WEISU, 35mm, chrome or black	E+
SUWOO, 50mm	F

Later Optical Viewfinders

SBLOO, 35mm	E
SBOOI, 50mm	D+
SGOOD, 85mm	F−
SGVOO, 90mm	D+
SHOOC, 135mm	D+
SBKOO, 21mm	E+
SLOOZ, 28mm	E+
OIDYO, for Stereo Stemar	F+

Folding Optical Sportsfinder

SUOOQ, 28mm	F−
SAIOO, 73mm, black or chrome	F
SEROO, 90mm, black	G
SYEOO, 135mm, black or chrome	E+

Non-Folding Optical Sportsfinder

SOODL, 50mm	G−
SOOAW, 73mm	G
SOOUT, SEVUE, 90mm	E+
SOOYV, 135mm	E+

Folding Frame Finders

RASUK, 50mm & 90mm	D
RASUK, 35mm & 73mm	D
RASAL, 35mm, 73mm, 90mm, & 135mm	D+
ROSOL, 50mm, 90mm, & 135mm	D

Non-Folding Frame Finders

SFTOO, 200mm	D+
TZOON/TZFOO, tube for 200mm	C+
SQTOO, 400mm	E+

Rangefinders

FODIS, FOFER, long, black only	E−
FOKOS, black or chrome	E
HFOOK, same as FOKOS with mounting foot	E+

Reflex Housing, complete units

PLOOT	D+
VISOFLEX I	D
VISIFLEX II	E–
VISOFLEX III	F–

Small Accessories

Single exposure camera:	
OLIGO/OLEYO with IBSOR shutter	H
Self-timer: APDOO	C–
Slow-speed device: HEBOO	E–
Close-up device: NOOKY,	
NOOKY-HESUM	C+
Close-up device, 9cm: OMIFO	F–
Three filter turret:	E+
Panorama head, 5cm (early) FIAMA	D+
Panorama head, interchangeable rings:	
FARUX	D+
De Mornay Budd Viewfinder	E
(non-Leitz manufacture)	

Motors and Winders

MOOLY motor, one-speed	G
MOOLY motor, two speed	D+
MOOLY motor IIIc: black or chrome	H+
MOOLY motor IIIc: grey	I–
Rapid winder: SCNOO, chrome	F+
Rapid winder: SCNOO, black/nickel	G–
Rapid winder: SCNOO, IIIc, chrome	G–
Leicavit: SYOOM	F
Leicavit, M: SMYOM	H–
Leicavit, MP, black enamel	H+
Remote winder: OOFRC	H–

Lennor Engineering Company
Chicago, Illinois, USA

Delta Stereo: R2* D
c1955. 35mm Stereo camera with optical VFR, fixed focus La Croix 50mm, f6.3 lenses, shutter speeds of 1/25-1/100s. plus B. Shutter marked for "shade" "normal" and "very bright". Blue or black plastic body with satin finished metal cover.

Leotax Camera Company
Japan (see SHOWA)

Leader: R3* C+
c1950. 35mm stereo camera. Leader Anastigmat 45mm f4.5 lenses; shutter TMBK 1/25-1/100s. Mfd in Japan.

Lucien Leroy
Paris, France

Stereo Panoramique Leroy: R3* F–
1906, Metal stereo camera. Krauss 82mm, f9 Protar or similar lenses 6 x 13cm exp. Stereoscopic or panoramic pictures by rotating lens in centre of camera.

L. Leullier
Paris, France

Stereochrome: R3* D
c1939. 35mm stereo camera. Boyer Saphir 40mm f3.5 fixed focus lens; guillotine shutter 1-1/300s.

Summum: R3* E–
c1925. 6 x 13cm stereo camera. Boyer Saphir 85mm f4.5 lenses; Stereo Compur shutter 1-1/150s. Rising lens panel.

Summum-Sterechrome: R4* F–
c1950. 35mm stereo camera. Berthiot Flor f3.5 lens.

S.J. Levi
London, England

The Pullman Detective Camera: R4* F+
c1896. Stereo detective camera in shape of carved leather carrying case. Roller blind shutter; bellows focusing; 5" x 7" exp on plates.

Levy-Roth
Berlin, Germany

Minigraph: R4* G–

c1915. 35mm camera. Minigraph Anastigmat 54mm f3.5 or Trioplan f3 lens; flap shutter 1/30s and T. 50 half-frame exp, 18 x 24mm on 35mm perforated film in special cassettes. First German 35mm camera; also used as contact printer or projector.

W. & W.H. Lewis
New York, USA

Daguerreotype Camera:
c1855; Harrison lens (Petzval design). Most common type although it is still very rare is for $^1/_4$ plate pictures. One of the first American cameras to use a bellows.

Daguerreotype Camera: R5* G+
c1855; Harrison or Holmes, Booth & Hayden Lenses. Overall physical appearance except for size is identical to the $^1/_4$ plate model.

Lewis Wet Plate Camera: R5* G+

c1862. Wet plate studio portrait camera. Exp up to 12" x 12" on wet plates.

Lexa Manufacturing Co
Melbourne, Australia

Lexa 20:   R3* B+

Announced October, 1948, metal box camera for 6 x 9cm frames on 120 roll film, simple lens and shutter, a number of these cameras appeared in the mid 1980's, none, however, was complete with internal metal film carrier, leading to the assumption that production or other problems may have prevented the Lexa 20 from ever having been sold!

L.F.O. & Co
Paris, France

Le Franceville: **R3* D+**

c1908. Cardboard plate camera Meniscus lens; drop shutter; 4 x 4cm glass plates.

V. Liebe
Paris, France

Monobloc: **R3* E–**
c1920. 6 x 13cm stereo camera. Berthiot Flor 85mm f5.7 lenses; 6 speed shutter. Panoramic setting, rising front panel.

Linex Corp
Division of Lionel Corp
New York, USA

Linex: **R3* D**

c1950. Subminiature 35mm stereo camera, f6 fixed focus lenses; shutter 1/65s. 8 pairs of stereo exp on 16mm film in special cassette. In the USA, prices are 50% lower. Outfit included camera, viewer and case.

Linhof Prazasions-Kamera-Werke GmbH
Munich, Germany

Linhof Technika IV: **R3* G–**

c1953. 4" x 5" folding press camera. Schneider Xenar f4.5 lens; Synchro Compur shutter 1-1/500s, CRF.

Linhof Technika III: **R3* F**
1946, black. 4" x 5" technical/press camera. Likely to be found with f4.5 Kenar lens.

Linhof Universal: **R4* F**
c1920s. A versatile plate camera that combined the movements available on older field cameras with the benefits of a compact hand camera. All metal construction, triple extension, extra high rising front, revolving back. Made in $3^1/_2$" x $2^1/_2$", quarter plate and half plate formats with f4.5 Tessar or f6.3 Double Protar lenses. Stereo accessory was also available.

Special Wideangle 65:   R3* F
1961. Equipped with 65mm f8 Super
Angulon. Two models: with Super Rolex
back for 10 exp on 120, or Cine Rolex
back for 50 exp on 70mm perforated
film. First camera in 2$^1/_4$" x 3$^3/_4$" format
to have this huge film capacity.

Lippische Kamerafabrik Barntrup
Germany

Flexora: R3* C+
1952. TLR with two lenses mounted on
common lens board for focus link. Both
are 75mm f3.5 Ennars. Prontor-S
shutter. Parallax correction marks in
viewfinder. Pull up wire frame finder for
eye-level use.

Rollop: R3* D

c1955. Rollei-type TLR; 6 x 6cm exp on
120 roll film; 75mm Ennagon f3.5 lens;
SVS shutter.

Lithoscope: R4* F
c1904. 8 x 17cm stereo camera. Aplanat
lens; 4-speed shutter; 8 x 17cm exp.

J. Lizars
Glasgow, Scotland

Challenge Dayspool Tropical Camera:
R4* F+

c1905. Beck Symlens lens; Bausch &
Lomb shutter. Teak and brass, red
leather bellows.

Challenge DeLuxe: R4* G–
c1910. 4" x 5" tropical camera. Dagor
150mm lens; 4" x 5" exp on plates.
Polished mahogany, brass fittings.

Challenge View Camera: R4* E+

c1898. Compact folding ½ plate view camera; Lizars Kram Triple Convertible lens and shutter; front and rear tilt and swing; built-in brass tripod base; plumb bob; double ext bellows to 17"; Spanish mahogany construction. C 1898.

Challenge Hand Camera, Model C:
R4* E–

c1902. Goerz Double Anastigmat Dagor Series III 150mm f6.8 lens; Bausch & Lomb shutter, up to 1/100s.

Challenge Stereo Camera, Model B:
R4* F

c1900. Aldis Anastigmat lenses; Bausch & Lomb Stereo shutter; 3¼" x 6¾" exp on plates.

Challenge Stereo Dayspool: R4* G–
Mahogany stereo camera. Aldis Anastigmat lenses; Bausch & Lomb shutter; pair of 3¼" x 3¼" exp on roll film or plates. Mahogany finish, brass hardware. c1905.

Lollier
Paris, France

Stereograph (Stereo Marine):   R5* H
c1903-1923. Binocular-type detective camera; revolving diaphragm 60mm f8 lens; guillotine shutter, T, I. 45 x 107mm exp. on plates.

London Stereoscopic Company
London, England

Artist Hand Camera: R4* H–
c1889. Black-band 4¼" x 3¼" lens. Mahogany finish.

Binocular: **R4* E+**

c1890s; Jumelle-style stereo camera. 12 exp 1½" x 2½" plate magazine; Krauss-Zeiss f6.3 lenses;

Carlton: **R4* F**
c1895. Ross Goerz Double Anastigmat 6" f7.7 lens; variable speed guillotine shutter 1-1/80s. 4" x 5" exp on plates – changed by gravity feed.

The Dispatch Detective Camera:
R4* NSR
c1888. Wooden box-type detective camera. Shutter to 1/100s. 8 x 10.5cm or 10.5 x 12.5cm exp on plates.

Improved Artist Reflex: **R5* H–**
c1910. Voigtlander 15cm f4.5 Heliar lens; CFPS. Rising front panel; tropical mahogany finish; green leather bellows.

Jumelle Capsa de Maria: **R3* E–**
c1910. Zeiss Protar 85mm f8 lenses.

The King's Own Tropical Camera:
R5* G+
c1907. Dagor lens; Volute shutter. Roll film or plates. Teak construction, brass fittings.

Lumiere & Cie
Lyons, France

Eljy: **R2* D–**

c1937. 35mm miniature camera. Folding VFR Lumiere Lypar 40mm f3.5 lens; Lumiere shutter 1/10-1/200s. 8 exp, 24 x 36mm on unperforated 35mm film in special cassettes; pull-out lens mount; scale focusing.

Eljy-Club: **R3* D**

c1951. 35mm miniature camera. Optical VFR mounted in top housing, early models with built-in extinction meter, while later models sport an accessory

shoe. Lumiere Lypar 40mm f3.5 lens; Lumiere shutter 1-1/00s. 8 exp, 24 x 36mm on unperforated 35mm film in special cassettes; pull-out lens mount; scale focusing. available in Grey, yellow, red, green, white and Blue. (worth 100% more) in addition to a "Luxus" model covered in crocodile skin! (worth 200% more).

Lumiclub: **R4* E**

c1950. Som Berthiot Flor 75mm f3.5 lens. Built-in extinction meter; telescoping lens mount; eye-level and waist-level finders; rapid wind lever. 6 x 6cm or 4.5 x 6cm format. Made from dies prepared by the Pontiac company before going bankrupt, this camera was originally intended to use perforated 70mm film, less than 1000 cameras are said to have been made.

Lumiére 6 x 6:   **R4* D+**

c1952. Folding camera for 6 x 6cm or 4.5 x 6cm format on roll film. 80mm f4.5 Spector lens. Built-in extinction meter; telescoping lens mount; eye-level and waist-level finders; rapid wind lever. Sharing some of the features of the more expensive Lumiclub, this camera also shared the same short life. About 1000 cameras are thought to have been made.

Le Periphot: **U I+**

c1910; panoramic camera of unusual design powered by a clockworks motor. The film is placed on the inside of a cylinder remaining stationary whilst the lens rotates around the cylinder. Pictures covering a full 360 degrees are possible. Very rare, really in the unavailable category.

Lumiere

Le Periphot, c1910.

Sterelux Lumiere: **R3* E+**
c1947, folding stereo camera. Nacor Boyer Anastigmat 80mm f6.3 lenses; shutter 1/25-1/200s; 6 x 13cm exp on 116 roll film. c1920.

Lumix: **R2* B–**
c1947. Post WWII folding roll film camera for 8 negatives 6 x 9 on 120 film, simple lens, and one speed shutter.

Ludax: **R2* A–**
c1950. Folding roll film camera for 8 negatives 6 x 9 on 620 film, 105mm, f6.3 Fidor lens, shutter speeds 1/10-1/200s, folding optical finder, body release. Made in large numbers.

Lumirex: **R2* B**
c1950. Folding roll film camera for 8 negatives 6 x 9 on 620 film. 105mm, f6.3 Fidor lens, or 105mm/f4.5 Spector lens; shutter speeds 1/10-1/200s; self-timer folding optical finder; body release. Along with the Ludax, made in large numbers.

Lumirex III: **R3* C–**
c1949. Folding roll film camera for 8 negatives 6 x 9 on 620 film. 100mm, f3.5 Angenieux type 11 lens; Prontor S shutter 1-1/300s; optical finder built-into the top housing along with an extinction meter; body release. (At the end of production, a cheaper version having 105mm, f4.5 Spector lens and Sido shutter 1/10-1/200s was offered for the budget minded.)

Lumiére 6.5 x 11:   **R4* C+**
c1950. Folding camera for 6.5 x 11 negs on 616 film. Folding optical finder; 125mm/f4.5 Berthiot or Topaz lens; shutter speeds 1-1/300s. Thought to be the last camera made for 616 film, and probably one of the few made for that film with a coated lens and flash synch.

Optax: **R4* D+**
October 1948-Spring 1949. 35mm black plastic camera with folding optical VFR. 50mm, f3.5 Lypar lens in collapsible mount; shutter speeds 1/10-1/200s. Marking Lumiére's entry into the standard 35mm market, this first model Optax lasted only a few months in production.

Optax 2nd model: **R2* C+**
c1948. 35mm black plastic camera with tubular optical VFR. 40mm, f3.5 Altar lens in fixed mount, shutter speeds 1/10-1/200s. A continuation of the Optax line, made in large quantities and much less rare than the original Optax.

Starter: **R2* B+**
c1955. 35mm black plastic camera with grey plastic top housing. 45mm, f3.5 Lypar lens; shutter speeds 1/25-1/150s; made to capture a share of the "low" end of the camera market.

Elax: R4* F

c1938. Pre WWII high quality precision folding camera for 3 x 4cm negatives on 127 film. 50mm, f3.5 Flor lens, lever wind mfps speeds 4-1/1000s, Optical finder said to have been made by Leitz.

Elax II: R4* F

c1948. Post WWII version of the Elax (LM108). Thought to have been made from stocks of pre-war parts. 50mm, f3.5 Flor lens, lever wind mfps 4-1/1000s. Has a satin chrome top plate. The high price of this camera on the French market killed it.

Lumiflex: R2* B+

c1951. Black plastic twin lens reflex camera for 6 x 6 format. The 80mm, f4.5Spector lens is not coupled to the viewing lens; shutter speeds 1-1/300s; built-in extinction meter.

Lumireflex: R4* C+

c1950. Black plastic twin lens reflex. 80mm, f3.4 Spector taking lens coupled to the 80mm, f3.5 viewing lens; Atos shutter, speeds 1-1/300s. Did not sell well and was quickly taken off the market.

Lutac: R2* A

c1949. Simple black plastic roll film camera, very similar to the Ultra-Fex.

M

H. Mackenstein Fabricant
Paris, France

La Francie: R3* E–

c1906. 45 x 107mm Press-type stereo camera. Max Balbreck Aplanatic lenses; variable speed guillotine shutter; Red leather bellows.

Mackenstein Tailboard Camera: R4* F
c1890. 13cm x 18cm Compact view camera. Grande Angle Gibauet brass lens; Mahogany finish; brass fittings.

Photo Livre: R5* H–

c1890. Book-type detective camera. Rectilinear 60mm f12 lens; guillotine shutter; 24 exp, 40 x 40mm on plates.

Stereo Jumelle: R3* E–
c1895. 6.5 x 9cm stereo camera. Goerz Dagor 110mm f6.3 lens; variable speed guillotine shutter; magazine for 12 plates.

Macris-Boucher
Paris, France

Nil Melior Stereo: R* D+
c1920. 6 x 13cm Stereo camera. Boyer Saphir or E. Krauss Tessar f4.5 lens; 7 speed spring shutter; Magazine holds 12 plates, 6 x 13cm.

Hacoflex: R3* D

c1950. 6 x 6cm TLR camera. Japanese Copy of Rolleicord. 80mm f3.5 Tri-Lansar lens in 1-1/300 shutter.

H. Mader
Isny, Germany

The Invicibel: R4* G
c1898. Aplanat 180mm f6 lens; double action rotary shutter; 13 x 18cm plates.

Magic Introduction Co
New York, USA

Photoret Camera: R4* F+

c1893. Watch-type detective camera. Meniscus lens; front-of-lens shutter; 6 exp, ½" x ½" on 1¾" diameter plates. Outfit, with box and film tin. Camera only.

Mamiya Camera Co Ltd
Tokyo, Japan

Mamiyaflex: R2* E–

1957. TLR camera. Mamiya-Sekor 105mm f3.5 coated lens, interchangeable lens mount; Seikosha-S 1-1/500s. 12 exp, 6 x 6cm on 120 roll film.

Mamiyaflex Junior: R4 C+

1948. 6 x 6cm TLR camera; Neocon 75mm f3.5 lens in Stamina shutter, B. 1-1/200s.

Mamiya Pistol Camera: R5* H+
c1954, pistol-type detective camera. 50mm lens; 6 square diaphragm stops; single speed shutter. 65 exp, 18 x 24mm on 35mm film. Made for Japanese police training.

Mamiya Six: R2* D–
c1958. 2¼" x 2¼" RFR camera. T.S.M. Anastigmat 75mm f3.5 lens; Copal shutter 1-1/200s. 12 exp, 6 x 6cm on 120 roll film. Rfr coupled to movable film plane; lens remains stationary. Many variations of lens/shutter combinations found. All are worth about the same.

Mamiya Six, c1958.

Mamiya 16 Automatic: R2* C

1959. Subminiature for 10x14mm images on 16mm film. 25mm f2.8 Sekor lens, focused by slide on body. Shutter 1/5-1/200s. Built-in yellow filter. Build-in meter with match needle automation.

Mamiya 16: R2* C

1949. The first of several 16mm cameras made by this company. 25mm f3.5 Cute fixed focus lens. Guillotine shutter 1/25-1/100s. 10x14mm images.

Mamiya 16 Police Camera: R4* D
1949. Made for Japanese Police Intelligence Division. As original model, but in black with detachable waist-level viewfinder. Rarest of all Mamiya 16 cameras.

Mamiya 16 Super (Model III): R2* C
c1953. 25mm f3.5 lens; shutter ½-1/200s. 32 x 14mm exp on 16mm film in special cassettes. Slide-in yellow filter.

Mamiya Family: R3* C+

c1962. 35mm SLR with leaf shutter. The first leaf-shutter SLR with instant-return mirror and instant re-opening shutter. 48mm f2.8 Sekor lens; shutter speeds 1/8-1/250s.

Mamiya Auto-Lux 35: R3* C+

c1963. 35mm SLR camera. Co-operative design with the Canon company, derived from Mamiya Family. Practically identical externally to the Canon Canonex, but with important internal differences. 48mm f2.8 Mamiya sekor lens; leaf shutter.

Mamiya/Sekor 1000 TL: R2* C+

c1960. 35mm SLR camera. FPS. B. 1-1/1000s. Interchangeable 55mm f1.4 Auto Mamiya Sekor. First Mamiya with TTL metering.

Mammy: R3* D
c1953. Black plastic body for a 35mm camera using unsprocketed paperbacked film. Anastigmat f3.5 44mm lens. Three zone focusing with zones indicated in the viewfinder, a first for this innovation. The least expensive camera made by the Mamiya Camera Company.

Mamiya Magazine 35:   R3* C+
c1957. 35mm camera with coupled rangefinder, Mamiya-Sekor f/2.8, 50mm. Shutter Seikosha 1-1/500s. Unusual feature was fully inter-changeable magazine backs. Several different films could be used. Very few production cameras have used this feature, the only earlier one being the Kodak Ektra of 1941.

Argus 260 Automatic: R2* B+
c1964. Camera for 126 Instamatic film (first of Japanese manufacture) for the Argus Camera Co. in the U.S. where it was exported. Cintar lens, fixed shutter speed 1/1000s. Exposure set automatically by coupled selenium cell. Built-in miniature flashbulb and pop-up reflector.

Mamiyaflex C: R2* D
1956. Mamiya's move into professional TLRs. 12 exp on 120. One of the few TLRs with interchangeable lenses. Standard lens was 105mm f3.5 Sekor. Seikosha-MX shutter 1-1/400s + B. Shutter interchangeable with the lens. Also available: 85mm and 135mm lenses.

Mamiyaflex C2:   R2* D
1957. TLR for 12 exp on 120. Interchangeable 10.5cm f3.5 Sekor with Seikosha-S shutter 1-1/500s +B.

Mamiyaflex C3:   R2* C+

1962. TLR for 12 exp on 120. Interchangeable 80mm f2.8 Sekor with Seikosha-S shutter 1-1/500s + B.

This is just a small selection of the earlier Mamiyaflex range of interchangeable lens TLRs. The company went on to offer various upgrades during the 1960s that included the C33 (1965), C22 (1966), C220 (1968) and C330 (1969).

MFAP Pontiac
(Manufacture Française d'Appareils Photographique)
Paris, France & Casablanca, Morocco

Pontiac: **R3* C–**
c1938; 6 x 9cm folding roll film camera with thermaplastic bodies offered in two models. With simple lens and single speed shutter, or front focusing 105mm, f4.5 Berthiot, in MFAP shutter with speeds of 1/25-1/100s, plus B. Closely resembles earlier Gallus and Ebner cameras of the same design.

Pontiac: **R4* C+**
c1938, 6 x 9cm folding roll film camera offered in brown bakelite as a "Luxus" model. Front focusing 105mm, f4.5 Berthiot, in MFAP shutter with speeds of 1/25-1/100s, plus B. Brown bellows.

Pontiac: **R3* E–**
16 exposures on 127 roll film. Polished aluminium body, CFPS with speeds 1/25-1/500s. SOM Berthiot Flor 50mm, f3.5 lens in collapsible mount. At first glance the lens and mount look very much like Leica. Don't be fooled into trying to unscrew the lens. You will only end up hurting your hand, and possibly damaging the lens!

Pontiac Bloc Metal 41:   **R2* C**
c1941-1946. 6 x 9 folding roll film camera of cast aluminium. Produced during the second World War in quite large numbers. Various 105mm, f4.5 lens and shutter combinations. The lack of quality construction material made necessary the rethinking of some design ideas, such as the use of textures body castings painted black instead of the more traditional leather covered bodies. These cameras often suffer from poor bellows and rusting nickel plated parts. The "41" indicates the year of introduction.

Bloc Metal 45:   **R3* C**
c1946. 6 x 9cm folding roll film camera with cast aluminium body. Early cameras have 105mm, f4.5 Flor Berthiot or Trylor Roussel lens in Prontor II shutter, speeds of 1-1/200s, textured bodies painted black while later cameras have "leather" covering, and a Gitzo shutter labelled "Zotic-I".

Bloc Metal 145:   **R4* D**
c1946. 6 x 9cm folding roll film camera with cast aluminium body. 105mm, f4.5 Flor Berthiot lens in a Compur Rapid shutter marked "licence française", speeds of 1-1/400s. Said to have been assembled in France from earlier Compur parts shipped from Germany.

Lynx-1:   **R4* D**
c1943, 3 x 4cm exp. on 127 film; between the lens shutter with speeds of 1/25-1/200s; front focusing 50mm, f3.5 Flor Berthiot lens; cast aluminium body, with textured finish, often painted black. Perhaps less than 100 made.

Lynx-1, c1943.

Lynx-II: R3* D

c1946. 3 x 4cm on 127 film, CFPS 1/25-1/500s; some cameras have self-timer; front focusing 50mm, f2.8 or f3.5 Flor Berthiot, or f2.9 Angénieux lens in collapsible mount; cast aluminium body with textured finish; often painted black. Perhaps more than 100,000 made.

Lynx de Nuit (Night Lynx):   R4* E+
c1946. 3 x 4cm on 127 film, CFPS 1/25-1/500s, coated 50mm, f1.5 Flor Berthiot lens; cast aluminium body with textured finish. Very few made.

Compur Lynx: R4* E+
c1946. 3 x 4cm on 127 film, fixed mount front focusing 50mm, f3.5Flor Berthiot lens; rim set Compur shutter speeds of 1-1/300s; cast aluminium body with textured finish. Very few were made.

Standard Lynx: R4* E+
c1948. 3 x 4cm on 127 film, CFPS 1/25-1/500s; fixed mount 40mm, f3.5 Flor Berthiot or Roussel lens; cast aluminium body with textured finish.

Super Lynx-I: R4* D+

c1948. 35mm VFR camera. With cast aluminium body; CFPS 1/25-1/500s coupled to film advance; 50mm, f3.5 or f2.8 Flor Berthiot lens in collapsible mount; polished or painted textured body. Unlike earlier 127 roll film Lynx's, these 35mm cameras were clearly marked on the camera body above the lens.

Super Lynx "Standard":   R4* E+

c1950. 35mm VFR camera. With cast aluminium body; CFPS 1/25-1/500s coupled to film advance; 35mm, f3.5 Flor Berthiot wide angle lens in fixed mount; painted textured body.

Super Lynx-II: R4* F–

c1953. 35mm VFR camera. With cast aluminium body; CFPS 1/25-1/500s coupled to film advance; self-timer; 50mm, f3.5 or f2.8 Flor Berthiot lens in collapsible interchangeable bayonet mount; painted textured body; 28mm, f3.3 Angulor, 35mm, f3.5 Flor, 75mm, f2.8 Flor, and 90mm, f3.5 Flor accessory lenses were made for this camera. Marked "made in French Morocco" or "made in Morocco". Along with a few Super Lynx-I and Super Lynx cameras, perhaps the only camera made in Africa. A complete outfit increases the price 200%.

Super Lynx: R4* E+

c1953. 35mm VFR camera. With cast aluminium body; CFPS 1/25-1/500s coupled to film advance, 50mm, f3.5 Flor Berthiot lens in fixed collapsible mount; painted textured body. Made at the same time as the Super Lynx-II, and post-dating the Super Lynx-I. This camera was a simplified version, without the self timer available on the Super Lynx-II.

Baby Lynx: R3* E–

c1951. 35mm VFR camera. With between the lens shutter, speeds of 1-1/300s; front focusing 50mm, f3.5 or 2.8 Flor Berthiot lens in collapsible mount; cast aluminium body with black covering. Made in Paris and then in Morocco, early cameras were not marked with the name. Brown body covering adds 100%.

Baby Standard: R4* D

c1953. 35mm camera. With between the lens shutter, speeds of 1/25-1/200s; front focusing 50mm, f3.9 Trylor Roussel lens in collapsible mount; cast aluminium body with black covering. Sold by Central-Photo in France, a cheaper version of the Baby Lynx with a simpler Pronto shutter.

MIOM

(Manufacture d'Isolents et d'Objects Moulés)
France

Photax: R3* B+

c1938. Bakelite VFR camera. For 6 x 9cm or 6 x 4.5cm on roll film; simple lens and shutter; metal focusing ring with handle; similar to the Rex camera made in Argentina.

Jacky: R3* B+

c1950, as PF100) but for the name.

Photax Blinde: R2* B+

c1950. Bakelite VFR camera. For 6 x 9cm frames on roll film; curved film plane; simple lens and shutter; redesigned body now without metal focusing ring. Called Blindé (armoured) because of the bakelite lens/shutter cover delivered with the camera. Also made in Spain under the Fotex name.

C. Marelli
Rosario, Argentina

Mecabox: **R4* C–**

c1950. "Rustic" metal box camera. For 6 x 9cm on roll film; simple lens and shutter.

Marion & Co Ltd
London, England

Marion's Metal Miniature Camera:
       R4* H
c1888. Petzval-type 55mm f5.6 lens; rack and pinion focusing; guillotine drop shutter; 30 x 30mm dry plates.

Marion's Radial Detective Camera:
       R4* F+
c1890. Quarter plate mahogany box camera. Plate changing mechanism.

No. 1 Academy Camera: **R5* H+**

c1885. TLR camera. Petzval-type 2" f5 lens; rotary shutter in front of lens; eye-level finder. 12 plates in magazine. One of the earliest TLR cameras.

Curlew I: **R1* C–**
c1948. Self erecting Folding Camera. 9 x 6cm exp on 120 roll film.

Curlew II: **R1* C**
c1948. As Curlew I above.

Curlew III: **R1* C+**
c1948. As Curlew II above.

King Penguin: **R1* B–**
c1953. Self erecting roll film camera. Eight exp on 120 roll film; B & I Shutter.

Penguin: **R1* A**
c1953. Self erecting roll film camera.

Peregrine I: **R1* D–**
(mid 1950's),6 x 6cm exp on 120 roll film. F3.5, 80mm lens; shutter 1-1/400s B.

Peregrine II: **R2* D+**
(Mid 1950's). As Peregrine I above with Taylor-Hobson f2.8 lens.

Peregine III: **R3* E+**
Mid 1950s. As Peregrine II above with Taylor-Hobson Adotal f2.8 lens and coupled rangefinder.

Raven: **R2* C+**
Mid 1950s. Folding Bakelite roll-film camera. Leather effect finish on body; folding finder; f4.5, 100mm Kershaw lens.

Le Parcel Detective Camera: R4* I
c1885. Wrapped-package type detective camera. Fixed focus double lens; simple shutter. 8 x 10.5cm plates in simple holder.

Rajar No.6:   R1* B+

c1929-? One of the earliest Bakelite folding body cameras.

Soho Reflex: R2* E+
c1905. All models were made by A. Kershaw and Sons, of Leeds, for Marion, incorporating Kershaw's mirror patent of 1904.

Soho Tropical Reflex: R4* H+
c1928-39. 3¼" x 4¼" tropical SLR. Dallmeyer 6½", f4.5 lens; CFPS 1/16-1/800s. Teak wood, brass fittings; red leather bellows.

Soho Tropical Reflex, c1928-39.

Marshall Optical Works
Tokyo, Japan

Marshall Press Camera: R3* G
1966. 120/220 roll film for 6x9cm images. Nikkor f3.5, 105mm lens coupled to rangefinder. Accessory lenses were available. Shutter 1-1/500s. A very sturdy camera which was designed by Mr Seiichi Mamiya, who founded the Mamiya Optical Company.

G. Mason & Co
Glasgow, Scotland

G. Mason & Co. Tailboard Camera:
**   R3* F–**
Brass-bound mahogany field camera. Ross lens; rotating disc stops; 4¾" x 6½" tilting ground glass back; vertical and horizontal adjustment on lens board.

Mast Development Co
Iowa, USA

Lucky Strike: R5* NSR

c1949-1950. Cigarette package type detective camera. 17.5mm, f2.7 lens; shutter 1/15, 1/125, 1/500s and B. Designed to fit inside a Lucky Strike cigarette package. Three false cigarettes controlled the diaphragm, focus and shutter trip. Manufactured for the U.S. Signal Corps.

Mattioli

La Belle Gamine: R4* E–
c1920. 45 x 107mm stereo camera. Balbreck Rapid Rectilinear lenses; 3-speed guillotine shutter. 45 x 107mm exposures.

Mawson
Newcastle, England

Mawson: R5* H+
c1865. Stereo wet plate camera. Achromat lens; cylindrical diaphragm; rectangular bellows; archimedian screw

focus adjustment; 3¼" x 6¾" exp on wet plates.

Mazo
Paris, France

Le Graphostereochrome: R5* H–
c1910. Colour stereo folding camera. Special slide-in filters for Autochrome and Tri-colour processes. Sliding plateholder for three plates. 10 x 15cm exp and 6 x 13cm stereo exp. Designed by Abbe Tauleigne.

Jumelle Mazo: R3* D
c1900. Double Triplet 135mm, f6.5 lens; 5 speed shutter; 12 quarter plates.

Meagher
London, England

Meagher Sliding Box Wet Plate Camera: R5* H–
c1858. Lens with brass barrel; rack and pinion focusing; 7" x 7" ground glass. Mahogany finish.

Meagher Stereo Camera: R5* I–
c1860. Collapsible box-type stereo camera. Ross landscape lens.

Meagher Wet Plate: R5* G
c1860. Dallmeyer Rectilinear lens with waterhouse stops. Ground glass focusing. Mahogany finish, maroon leather bellows.

Laboratorias MC
Argentina

Joya: R4* B+
c1950. Bakelite TLR box camera. For 6 x 6cm frames on 120 or 620 film, simple lens and shutter.

lens. Hinged back. Less than 2000 cameras were produced, with the first two digits of the serial number giving the year of production. Quite rare.

Joya, c1950.

Melcon original with non-original Canon lens.

Meikai: **R3* D–**

35mm TLR camera. M.K. Anastigmat 50mm, f3.8 lens. Mfd in Japan.

Meguro Kogaku Kogyo Co Ltd
Japan

Melcon Original: **R4* G–**
c1955. 35mm RFR camera. CFPS, 1-1/500s; interchangeable Leica-type screw mount f3.5, 50mm Hexar (Konika) lens or f2.0, 50mm Nikkor-H

Melcon-II: **R5* G+**
c1957. 35mm RFR camera. CFPS, 1-1/500s; interchangeable Leica-type screw mount f2.0, 50mm Nikkor-H lens. Hinged back. Very few cameras were produced. This camera looks more like a Contax or Nikon than the previous model. Extremely rare.

Mejori Optical Works
Japan

Honor S1 (first version):   **R2* G**
c1956. 35mm camera. CFPS, 1-1/500s; separate RFR/VFR windows; diopter adjustment. Screw mount Hexar f3.5, 50mm lens. This camera is quite similar to the Ichicon 35 camera from the Dai-ichi Optical Works.

Honor S1 (second version):   **R4* G**
c1957. 35mm camera. CFPS, 1-1/1000s; separate RFR/VFR windows; diopter adjustment. Screw mount Honor f1.9, 50mm lens. Quite rare, this camera is an improved version of the Honor S1, with the addition of 1/1000s to the shutter speeds.

Mentor Werke
Dresden, Germany

Mentor: R3* E+
c1914-1931. Press-type stereo camera. Tessar 90mm, f4.5 lenses with coupled diaphragms and coupled helicoid focusing. Rising front; panoramic exp. 6 x 13cm exp.

Mentor Folding Reflex: R4* F
c1913. Unusual SLR that folded into a long, flat shape. Focal plane shutter speeds to 1/1000s. Variety of models, each fitted with f4.5 Tessar lens in varying focal lengths according to the picture size, which included $3^1/_2$" x $2^1/_2$", $3^1/_4$" x $4^1/_4$", $3^1/_2$" x $5^1/_2$" and $4^3/_4$" x $6^1/_2$".

Mentor Studio Reflex: R4* F
c1927. Principally a waist-level SLR made specially for studio work. Tilt and swing movements to tilt lens up, down, right or left. Separate mirror and hood also allowed eye level focusing. Made only in 7 x 5 inch format.

Mentor Focal Plane Camera: R3* E
1932. Press camera with lens panel extending on struts. Made in five sizes from 6.5 x 9 cm to 13 x 18 cm.

Mentor Compur Reflex: R4* F
1932. Small reflex camera for $3^1/_2$" x $2^1/_2$" and $3^1/_2$" x $3^1/_2$" sizes. Traditional box shape but with Compur shutter and reversing back. Choice of f4.5 or f3.5 Tessar lenses.

Mentorett: R4* G
1936. Twin lens reflex with focal plane shutter up to 1/600s. Single lever to wind film, set shutter and release it. Aperture in taking lens linked to similar in viewing lens to preview depth of field.

Meopta
Prerov, Czechoslovakia

(There are now two countries, the Czech Republic & the Republic of Slovakia – Instruments made prior to the breakup of the country will continue to be to considered as having been "Made in Czechoslovakia."

Meopta was founded in 1946 as a united enterprise for the production of optics and precision mechanics. With the communist takeover in 1948, the firm was seized by the government becoming a state organisation. Meopta had been created by the unification of a number of Czech optical manufacturers including Optikotechna, Eta, Sonet, Srb & Sty, Loschner, Bradac Brothers Co., and J. Suchanek. It was a very large operation making products for both the military and civilian markets with factories in Prague, Brno, Prerov, Hynicice,and Bratislava. In the 1970's camera production ceased when the military equipment area was expanded. As expert glassmakers, the Czechs always had a good supply of optical glasses and were considered the main source of precision optics within the old Eastern bloc.

A long awaited master list of Meopta cameras with dates of manufacture will reportedly be produced in the near future. Hopefully this will end some ongoing disagreements about production dates. The most common Meopta cameras found in the West, are probably the Flexaret with the sub-miniature Mikroma running a close second.

It is a possibility that the rarity rating on some cameras will drop with the complete opening of the country.

Mikroma: R3* D

c1946. Subminiature camera. For 11 x 14mm size negatives on single perforated 16mm film. Four-speed shutter 1/25-1/200s. Designed before WWII, but only produced from 1946.

Mikroma II: R2* D

c1964. Subminiature camera. Mirar 20mm, f3.5 lens; shutter 1/5-1/400s; with brown or green body covering.

Stereo Mikroma: R2* E–

c1965. Subminiature stereo camera. Mirar 25mm, f3.5 lenses; shutter 1/5-1/100s. 12 to 14 stereo exp on single perforation 16mm film. Viewers are still available in Czechoslovakia.

Stereo Mikroma II: R2* E–

c1970. Subminiature stereo camera. Mirar 25mm, f3.5 lenses; shutter 1/5-1/100s. 12 to 14 stereo exp on single perforation 16mm film. As first model but with improved film transport and shutter cocking systems.

Mikronette: R5* H–

c1945 Subminiature camera. For 240 exposures 11mm x14mm size on single perforated 16mm film. Four speed shutter 1/25-1/200s. Designed before WWII, and made by Optikotechna in limited numbers for the military.

Stereo 35: R4* D+

c1970. Cream coloured stereo camera for 35mm film, but yielding about 80 Viewmaster size stereo pairs from a 36 exposure roll of film. Fixed focus Mirar f3.5, 25mm lenses in a simple shutter. These cameras were hard to sell, and eventually went to state owned discount shops where they were sold out. Rare.

Opema (II): R3* E–

c1955-60. 35mm CRF camera. CFPS, 1/25-1/500; combined RFR/VFR window; screw mount f3.5, f2.8, or f2.0, 45mm lenses. Removable back; cassette to cassette film transport. Considered by some to be a Leica copy, the Opema uses a smaller diameter screw thread than Leica. Do not try to force your Leitz lenses, you are only asking for trouble!

Meopta

Opema (I): R4* E–

c1954-59. 35mm CRF camera. CFPS,1/25-1/500s; as Opema II, but without RFR. Screw mount f3.5, f2.8, or f2.0, 45mm lenses. Removable back; cassette to cassette film transport.

Milona: R4* D+

c1946-50. Well made folding camera for 6 x 6 or 6 x 4.5 negatives on 120 roll film. Mirar f4.5, 80mm lens in Prontor II or Prontor S shutter. Scale focusing from 1M. Built-in slide for tilting lens to straighten converging lines when photographing buildings from a low angle. Quite rare.

Milona II: R4* D+

c1951-56. Folding camera for 6 x 6 or 6 x 4.5 negatives on 120 roll film. Mirar f3.5, 80mm lens in Prontor S shutter. Same lens tilting feature as Milona. Quite rare.

Iskra: R4* C+

c1951-56. Folding camera for 6 x 6 or 6 x 4.5 negatives on 120 roll film. Mirar f3.5, 80mm lens in Prontor S shutter. Without lens tilting feature. (Not to be confused with the Soviet "Iskra" which is a copy of Agfa.) Quite rare.

Magnola: R4* F

c1947-53. Ground glass focusing folding metal bodied view camera. For 13 x 18cm negatives; Compound type shutter with Belar f4.5, 210 lens, three built-in levels; lens tilts and shifts. According to a factory source, this camera was exported.

Flexaret: R4* D

(original) c1945. Twin lens reflex camera. For 6 x 6 negatives on 120 roll film. Uncoated Mirar f4.5, 80mm taking lens in Prontor II shutter Optikotechna Anastigmat f3, 80mm viewing lens. Knob advance not coupled to shutter cocking; no provisions for double exposure prevention. Made by Opitkotechna before merging with Meopta in 1946. Quite rare.

Flexaret II: R3* C+

c1946-47. TLR. camera for 6 x 6 negatives on 120 roll film. Mirar f4.5, 80mm taking lens in Prontor II shutter. Anastigmat f3, 80mm viewing lens.

Knob advance not coupled to shutter cocking; no provisions for double exposure prevention. Made after merger into Meopta. Transition models still have Optikotechna marked on the lenses, but not on the camera body.

Flexaret III: **R3* C+**
c1948-50. TLR camera for 6 x 6 negatives on 120 roll film. Coated Mirar f3.5, 80mm taking lens in Prontor S or Metax shutter. Anastigmat f3, 80mm viewing lens; crank advance coupled to shutter cocking; automatic frame counting double exposure prevention. The only crank advance model.

Flexaret IV: **R2* C+**
c1950-57. TLR camera for 6 x 6 negatives on 120 roll film. Coated Belar f3.5, 80mm taking lens in Prontor SVS or Metax shutter. Anastigmat f3, 80mm viewing lens. Knob advance coupled to shutter cocking; automatic frame counting double exposure prevention. First model with depth of field scale built-into the focusing handle. Easily recognised by its strange body mounted shutter release. Quite common.

Flexaret V: **R2* C+**

c1958-59 TLR camera for 6 x 6 negatives on 120 roll film. Coated Belar f3.5/80mm taking lens in Prontor SVS shutter. Anastigmat f3, 80mm viewing lens. Knob advance coupled to shutter cocking; automatic frame counting double exposure prevention. Redesigned front; focusing lever and shutter release.

Flexaret Va: **R2* C+**
c1959-61. TLR Camera for 6 x 6 negatives on 120 roll film. Coated Belar f3.5, 80mm taking lens in Prontor SVS shutter. Anastigmat f3, 80mm viewing lens. Knob advance coupled to shutter cocking; automatic frame counting; double exposure prevention. Provision for using 35mm film with the appropriate adaptor. This is the first model with this feature. (Price given is for the camera complete with 35mm adaptor set.)

Flexaret VI: **R3* D–**
c1961-67. Grey covered body twin lens reflex camera for 6 x 6 negatives on 120 roll film. Coated Belar f3.5, 80mm taking lens in Prontor SVS shutter. Belar f3.5, 80mm viewing lens. Knob advance coupled to shutter cocking; automatic frame counting double exposure prevention; provision for using 35mm film with the appropriate adaptor. (Price given is for the camera complete with 35mm adaptor set -30% without adaptor).

Flexaret VII: **R3* D**
c1966-71. Grey covered body twin lens reflex camera for 6 x 6 negatives on 120 roll film. Coated Belar f3.5, 80mm taking lens in Prontor SVS shutter. Belar f3.8, 80mm viewing lens. Knob advance coupled to shutter cocking; automatic frame counting double exposure

prevention; provision for using 35mm film with the appropriate adaptor. The last of the Flexarets. (Price given is for the camera complete with 35mm adaptor set (-30% without adaptor).

Optineta: **R3* B+**
c1959. 35mm VFR camera. Front element focusing, coated f3, 45mm Belar lens in Metax shutter.

Etareta: **R3* C–**

1947-48. 35mm VFR camera front-cell focusing coated f3.5, 5cm Etar II lens in collapsible mount; Etaxa shutter 1/10-1/200s; marked "Eta Praha" on the lens, and "made in Czechoslovakia" on the front of the camera body.

Spektareta: **R5* NSR**

c1939. "The smallest three-colour camera in the world" (according to the National Technical Museum in Prague). Three exposures made at the same time through red, green, and blue filters to produce three colour separation negatives. 12 sets of negatives 24 x 24mm per 36 exposure roll. f2.9, 70mm Spektar lens in Compur shutter, 1-1/250s CRF; parallax correcting VFR. Made by Optikotechna, very rare.

Coloureta: **R5* NSR**
c1939. Three-colour camera, without CRF. Helical focusing Spektar f2.9, 70mm lens in Compur shutter, 1-1/250s. 12 sets of negatives 24mm x 24mm per 36 exposure roll. Made by Optikotechna, very rare.

Meta: **R4* D**
c1956? Simple 35mm VFR camera. F3.5, 63mm Belar lens in focusing mount; Metax shutter, 1-1/400s; marked "Meta" on the front of the top plate. Not produced in large numbers, quite rare.

Meta II: **R4* E–**
c1957? With added coupled RFR. F3.5, 63mm Belar lens; Metax shutter, 1-1/400s. Marked "Meta" on the top plate, quite rare.

Meta III: **R5* G**
1959? 35mm camera. With coupled RFR and interchangeable lenses; f3.5, 35mm Meopta S.O. lens in breech mount; Metax behind-the-lens shutter, 1-1/400s; very Voightländer Prominant in appearance; was never made in large scale production and may exist only in prototype form. No information is available concerning accessory lenses.

Kamerad: R5* D+

c1936. Metal TLR for 6 x 6 exposures on 120 roll film. f3.9, 7.5cm Bellar from Ernst Ludwig Optical works, Dresden, are used for both lenses. Prontor II shutter, 1-1/175s; knob film transport with automatic frame counting. Made by the Bradéc Brothers, Hovorcovice (near Prague).

Kamerad MII: R5* E–

c1936. Metal TLR for 6 x 6 exposures on 120 roll film. f2.9, 7.5cm Trioplan lenses are used for both viewing and taking lenses. Compur shutter 1-1/250s; knob film transport with automatic frame counting. Made by the Bradéc Brothers, Hovorcovice (near Prague).

Autoflex: R4* D–

c1938. Metal TLR for 6 x 6 negatives on 120 roll film. f2.9, 7.5cm Trioplan lenses are used for both viewing and taking lenses. Compur shutter 1-1/250s; knob film transport with automatic frame counting. Made by Optikotechna. Rare.

Optiflex: R5* D–

c1938. Metal TLR for 6 x 6 negatives on 120 roll film. F2.9, 7.5cm Mirar lenses

are used for both viewing and taking lenses. Compur shutter 1-1/250s; knob film transport with automatic frame counting. Made by Optikotechna. Rare.

Vega: R3* C+

c1950's. Simple 35mm VFR camera with cassette to cassette film transport. Collapsible f3.5 or f4.5 50mm lens (Druoptar or Etar) in Etaxa, Chrontax, Metax, or "no-name" shutters; with or without accessory shoe. Made by Druopta, Prague.

Druoflex I: R3* B+

c1950's. Bakelite TLR in the style of Lubitel, which is itself a loose copy of Voightländer Brilliant, for 6 x 6 exposures on 120 roll film. Body by Atak. Non-focusing VFR; front cell focusing taking lens; f6.3, 75mm Druoptar in Chrontax shutter, 1/10-1/200s. Made by Druopta, Prague.

Fokaflex: R4* C–

c1950's. Bakelite TLR for 6 x 6 exposures on 120 roll film. Boxier than the Druoflex, with unusual two piece back. Fixed focus "special" lens; Fokar 2 shutter, 1/25-1/100s. Made by Foka.

Rix: R4* C–

c1950s. Bakelite TLR camera. Smoother body than the Druoflex; grey painted metal front and focusing hood; for 6 x 6 exposures on 120 roll film. Nonfocusing VFR, fixed focus f11 taking lens in Fokar shutter, 1/25-1/75s. Made by Foka. Rare.

Pionyr I: R3* C

c1950s. Bakelite VFR camera. For 6 x 6cm or 6 x 4.5cm frames on roll film, simple lens and shutter. Made by Dufa, near Prague.

Pionyr II: R3* C

c1950s. With focusing. Copied by the Chinese as the "Great Leap" camera.

Mephisto Camera: R5* G–

c1900. Meniscus lens, exp controlled by lens cap. 5 exp on plates. Mfd in Germany.

Stereo Mikroma II: R2* E

c1970. Subminiature 16mm stereo camera. Mirar lenses, 25mm f3.5; shutter 1/5-1/400s. Available in several colours, green being the most common. The stereo images were usually mounted in a disc very similar to a system still used in the U.S. called "Viewmaster."

Metropolitan Supply
Chicago, Illinois, USA

The King Camera: R3* D+

Miniature cardboard camera. 2" x 2" x 3½" exp on glass plates.

Micro Precision Products
Surrey, England

Microcord: R1* D–

c1952. TLR camera. 6 x 6cm, 12 exp on 120 roll film; Ross Xpres f3.5, 75mm lens; Prontor SVS 1-300s, shutter.

Microflex: R2* E

c1959; 6 x 6cm TLR camera. F3.5, 77mm lens in Prontor SVS shutter.

MPP Press Camera: R3* D

c1950. Intro-duced as a technical camera and improved to make a press camera. Front panel with a 2³/₄-inch diameter aperture to accommodate range of lenses. Wray self-capping FP shutter with 3 tensions and 6 slit widths, 1-1/1000s + B & T. Double extension Rise and cross movements. Rangefinder coupled.

D. Millard & Co
Cincinnati, Ohio, USA

Robinson's Patent Photograph Album: R4* E

c1865. Carte-de-visite photos mounted on a fabric belt; displayed by turning knobs.

*Robinson's Patent Photograph Album,
c1865.*

Mimosa I, c1947.

Robinson's Photographicon: R4* E+

c1865.   Carte-de-visite   photograph
viewer.   Early   hand-coloured   stencil
design. Patent April 11th. 1865.

Mimosa II: R3* D

c1948. Meritar 50mm f2.9 lens; Velax
shutter 1/10-1/200s.

T. Miller
Manchester, England

Adelphi Detective Camera: R3* E–
c1899. Box-type detective camera.

Mimosa Cameras
Germany

Mimosa I: R4* D
c1947. 35mm box-type camera. Meyer
Trioplan 50mm f2.9 lens; Compur-Rapid
1-1/500s.

**Minolta –
Chiyoda Kogaku Seiko Co Ltd**
Osaka, Japan

Konan 16 Automat: R3* D+

c1952. Rokkor 25mm f3.5 lens.

Best Model 1:   **R3* D**

1934. Unusual folding camera that used three telescopic boxes in place of bellows. 75mm f8 fixed focus Coronar Anastigmat. Marble shutter 1/25-1/100s + B & T. Also known as the Minolta Vest. (Camera sometimes gets incorrectly referred to as the Marble because of the prominence of the shutter name.) Early use of plastic in body. Dual format for 8 & 16 exposures on 127 film.

Best Model II: **R3* D**

Similar to Model I with 75mm f5.6 front focusing lens.

Best Model III: **R3* D**

Similar to Model II with 75mm f4.5 lens.

Minolta 16 Model I: **R2* B**

1957. Subminiature for 10x14mm images on 16mm. 25mm f3.5 Rokkor Shutter 1/25-1/200s. Push-pull Minox-style film advance. Common in chrome, rarer in gold, black, blue, red & green.

Minolta 16 Model II: **R2* B**

1960. Similar to first model, but with 22mm f2.8 lens and shutter 1/30-1/500s + B. Fixed focus, but with supplementary lenses for close-ups to 30 in.

Minolta 16 Model P: **R2* B**

1960. Simpler version with only 1/100s shutter. Symbols for aperture setting.

Minolta 16EE: **R2* B**

1962. Similar to Model II plus auto exposure via Selenium cell.

Minolta 16PS: **R2* B+**

1964. Similar to Model P, but with added shutter speed 1/30s for flash.

Minolta 16 MG: **R2* B**

1966. 20mm f2.8 Rokkor. Shutter 1/30-1/250s. Match-needle metering.

Minolta 16 MG-S: **R2* B**

1969. Image size changed to 12 x 17mm. 23mm f2.8 Rokkor. Shutter 1/30-1/500s. Match needle metering.

Minolta 16 QT: **R2* B+**

1972. Similar to MG-S, but shutter 1/30-1/250s. Auto metering.

Minolta Auto Press: **R3* F–**

c1935. 6 x 9cm Press camera. Promar Anastigmat Nippon 100mm f3.5 lens; Crown Rapid shutter 1-1/400s; CRF; 6 x 9cm exp on cut film and film pack.

Minolta Auto Press, c1935.

Minolta 35 I: **R4* F**
                                   Original F+
c1947. 35mm camera. CFPS, 1-1/500s;
combined Rfr/Vfr window; self-timer;
unusual 24mm x 32mm frame size
known as "Nippon" size, and also used
by Nikon, is found on both the "Original"
and type "B" cameras. Screw mount
Super Rokkor F2.8, 45mm lens. 24 x
33mm frame size was used on the type
"C" camera, and a 24 x 34mm frame on
the type "D" and "E" cameras. Types "C",
"D", and "E" though rare, bring roughly
50% of the price of the original and type
"B" cameras.

Minolta 35 Model II: **R2* E+**

c1953. 35mm camera. CFPS, 1-1/500s;
combined Rfr/Vfr window; self-timer;
24 x 34mm frame size. Screw mount
Super Rokkor f2.8, 45mm or Super
Rokkor f2.0, 5cm lens. This is the most

common of the Minolta Leica copies.
Minolta 35 Model IIB: **R3* F–**
c1958. CFPS, 1-1/500s; combined
RfR/VfR window; self-timer; 24 x 36mm
frame size. Screw mount Super Rokkor
f1.8, 5cm lens. This was the first
Minolta to use the standard 24 x 36mm
frame size, and the last Minolta Leica
copy. Though not particularly rare this
camera is still valuable as a Leica copy.

Minolta A: **R3* F**
1955. First Minolta to be exported.
35mm RFR camera. 45mm f3.5 Chiyoko
Rokkor. Unusual shutter speed control is
wheel protruding from top plate.
Speeds 1-1/300s + B. 45mm f3.5
Chiyoko Rokkor

Minolta A5:   **R3* B**

1961. 35mm CRF camera, more
conventionally styled than the original
Minolta A. 45mm f2.8 Rokkor. Optiper
shutter 1-1/1000s + B. X & M synch.

Minolta AL: **R3* B**
1961. CRF 35mm camera. Unusual
focusing system moves both lens and
between-lens shutter together in a
helical focusing mount. 45mm f2
Rokkor. Optiper Citizen MLT shutter
1-1/1000s. Shutter and aperture
controls linked for match needle
metering.

Minolta Uniomat: **R3* B**

1961. Fully auto 35mm CRF camera. 45mm f2.8 Rokkor. Optiper 'Brain' shutter, $1/8$-1/100s. Shutter speeds and apertures connected to built in meter for match needle metering. Manual override if needed.

Minoltaflex: **R3* E**

c1936. TLR Camera. For 6 x 6cm exp on roll film; the first Japanese TLR; marked only "Minolta" on the front, Promar f3.5, 75mm taking lens among others; Minolta viewing lens; shutter 1-1/300s.

Minoltaflex II: **R3* E**

c1950. First post-war Minoltaflex; similar to Rokkor 75mm f3.5 lens in S-Konan shutter B.1-1/500s. See page 326.

Minolta CLE: **R2* F**
Gold model G

1980. Cfps, 1-1/1000s, electronically controlled; combined Rfr/Vfr window; "M" type bayonet mount Minolta Rokkor f2.0, 40mm lens. The limited edition model available in gold, increases the price by a factor of three.

Accessory lenses for Minolta CLE

28mm/f2.8 lens:	F
90mm/f4.0 lens:	E

Minolta XM: **R2* E+**

(XK in USA)-(X-I in Japan). c1973. System 35mm SLR camera. Electronic MFPS 1-1/2000, titanium blades. Interchangeable view-finders; shutter coupled to SPD-TTL meter; Auto shutter speeds 16-1/2000s.

Minolta AC101 Courreges: R3* C

1983. "Designer" version of Minolta Disc Camera. f2.8, 12.5mm fixed focus lens. Strobe and exposure completely automatic. Shutter speed range 1/100-1/200s.

Minolta Autopak 500:   R1* A

1966. 126 camera with fixed 38mm Minolta Rokkor f2.8 lens. Zone-focusing. Fully programmed shutter coupled to selenium exposure meter. Shutter operates at 1/90s.

Minolta Hi-Matic F: R2 B+

1972. 35mm rf camera, Rokkor f2.7, 38mm lens. Seikosha shutter programmed to operate 4s to 1/720s. Available in chrome or black.

Minolta 110 Zoom: R2* C

1976. First SLR 110 format. Auto exposure via CdS meter. Rokkor Macro lens 25-50mm f4.5. Shutter 10-1/1000s.

Minolta Zoom SLR MkII: R2* D

1979. Complete restyle of the Model I to look more like a miniature 35mm SLR. 25-67mm f3.5 Zoom Rokkor incorporating macro focusing. Aperture priority automation with apertures set by dial on top plate.

Minolta Disc 7:   R1* A+

1983. Fitted with a f2.8, 12.5mm fixed focus lens. Strobe and exposure control completely automatic. An unusual feature was the small mirror in front of the camera. An individual could take their own picture by framing themselves in the mirror and using the camera's self timer.

Minolta SR-1:   R2* C

1959. Manual control 35mm SLR. Optional Selenium meter. FP shutter 1-/500s. Synch speed 1/50s.

Minolta SR-2:   R2* D
1958. Similar to SR-1 with 1-1/1000s and higher synch speed of 1/100s.

Minolta SR3:   R2* D
1961. Similar to SR-2 with detachable Selenium meter and split image rangefinder.

Minolta SR-7:   R2* D
Similar to SR-3 but with built-in CdS meter for manual non TTL metering. Synch speed reduced to 1/60s.

Minolta SRT-100:   R2* C
1971. Minolta's first 35mm SLR with TTL metering. Incorporated Minolta's contrast light metering system.

Minolta XD-7:   R2* Chrome E

1977. Come to be known as the world's first multi-mode 35mm SLR, offering shutter priority, aperture priority and manual modes, although the Savoyflex Automatique offered similar in the late 1950s. Viewfinder information via LEDs. Shutter 1-1/1000s. Synch at 1/100s. Multi-exposure capabilities.

Minolta 7000:   R2* D

1985. First 35mm SLR with body-integral autofocus. Exposure modes include shutter priority, aperture priority, manual, standard programme, wide programme and tele programme. Auto program selection takes data from autofocus lenses and translates date for most appropriate exposure mode.

Note: Minolta made many more SLRs in the 1970s and 1980s, some with only minor variations in specification. They included models such as the SRM, SRT101, SRT303, SRT100b, SRT101b, SRT303b, SR-T MC-II, SRT SC-II, X-7A, X-9, X-370, X-300, X-370s, X-500, X-700, XD-5, XE-5, XE-1, XG-1, XG-2, XG-S, XG-A, XG-M, XM and XK Motor. It is also worth noting that many of these names were subtly changed for American and Japanese markets. Full details and specifications of all these models can be found in the book Japanese 35mm SLR Cameras by Bill Hansen and Michael Dierdorff, published by Hove Books.

Minox
Geissen, West Germany

For further information see Spy Camera, The Minox Story by Morris Moses, Hove Collectors Books, 1990.

Minox I: R3* F+

c1938. Subminiature detective camera; Minostigmat 15mm f3.5 fixed aperture, 3 element lens; guillotine, front-of-lens shutter ½-1/1000s. 8 x 11mm exp on 9.5mm film in special cassettes. Snr 1-20,000. The original Minox was made from stainless steel; later models were made from aluminium. Valsts Electro-Techniska Fabrika, Riga, Latvia.

Minox I "Riga":   R4* G–
c1940-1941 and again 1944-1945. The two periods during which Riga was occupied by Russia during WWII. These "Russian Rigas" are engraved "Made in USSR" on the back of the camera.

Minox B: Chrome version: R2* D+
                Black version: R3* H+

c1958-1972; Subminiature detective camera; 15mm f3.5 lens; shutter ½-1/1000s; coupled light meter; two filters. Very few in Gold, at the abov price guide.

Minox BL: R2* E
c1976, subminiature camera; 15mm f3.5 lens; shutter ½-1/1000s. Coupled CdS exp meter. Chrome.

Minox C: R3* Chrome model E
                 R3* Black model E+

c1976, subminiature detective camera; 15mm f3.5 lens; electronic shutter 10-1/1000s; coupled to CdS exp meter for auto exp control with manual override.

Minox IIIS: Chrome model; R3* E+
                  Black model; F
                  Gold model; H–

Subminiature camera; 15mm f3.5 lens; shutter ½-1/1000s.

Minox LX: R1* F–

c1978; subminiature camera; new curved to fit the finger shutter release next to focusing dial; Three LED's next to shutter dial; both dials have milled edges;shutter to 1/2000s.; Black or chrome finish;

Minox EC: R1* D

c1981; Subminiature camera; f5.6 fixed focus lens; shutter release button coloured plastic; no parallax markings on Vfr.; plastic body normally black, very few white bodies. All prices are for cameras with chain and case or with Riga case.

Minox accessories	
Tripod	C
tripod clamp	B
Bulb flash	B
Binocular attachment	B+

Miranda Camera Company
Tokyo, Japan

In 1946, the Orion Camera Company, predecessor of the Miranda Camera Company, Ltd., was established in Tokyo. Although the company did manufacture a limited line of photographic related products, its main function was as a service centre for professional photographic equipment.

Among the products made by Orion were a special adaptor which allowed the use of Contax or Nikon mount lenses on Leica type screw mount bodies, and the "Focabell" close-up bellows.

In 1956, the Orion Company adopted the well known "Miranda" name.

In all, a total of 36 different basic camera models were produced before financial difficulties forced the company to close its doors in 1977. Though much maligned in the past as poor cousins to their more popular competitors, Miranda has seen recent growth in collector interest, to the point of the establishment of a Miranda Collectors Club.

Adam Geschwind, from Sydney, Australia,

has put together the information which appears here, along with the photographs. He welcomes correspondence concerning all models of Miranda cameras, especially serial number information on both cameras and lenses for use in compiling a computer data base.

He may be reached at: Adam Geschwind, PO Box 28, Waverly Post Office, Waverly, Sydney, Australia, 2024

Mirax: R4* E

1950 marked "Orion Camera Company" later version marked "Miranda Camera Company", mirror box with interchangeable reflex finder (after 1953), which allowed upright TTL viewing on Nikon, Contax, Leica, Canon, or similar 35mm camera bodies.

Orion T: R4* G+

c1954, 35mm SLR with interchangeable Zunow f1.9, 5cm lens in 44mm screw mount. CPFS 1-1/500s; removable pentaprism; knob wind; non-instant return mirror; top and front mounted shutter release; chrome body; serial numbers 554xxx to 556xxx. (black body adds at least 100%) Miranda Identification hint: Many models contain the model designation before the serial number, on the back of the camera.

Orion T, c1954.

Miranda T: R3* F

c1956. 35mm SLR with interchangeable Zunow f1.9, 5cm, Arco f2.4, 5cm, Soligar-Miranda f1.9, 5cm or Miranda f1.9, 5cm lens in 44mm screw mount. CPFS 1-1/500s; removable penta-prism; knob wind; non-instant return mirror; top and front mounted shutter release; chrome body; serial number 558xxx. (camera illustrated shows rare black trim on advance, rewind, shutter speed, and film counter dials.)

Miranda S: R3* E–

c1959. 35mm SLR with interchangeable Soligar-Miranda f2.8/5cm lens in 44mm screw mount, 1/30-1/500s. Removable WL finder, pentaprism sold as accessory; knob wind; non-instant return mirror;

only front mounted shutter release, chrome body, serial number 59xxxx.

Miranda ST: R3* E+

c1959. 35mm SLR with interchangeable Soligar-Miranda f2.8, 5cm lens in 44mm screw mount. 1-1/500s; removable WL finder; pentaprism accessory; knob wind; non-instant return mirror; top and front mounted shutter release; chrome body; serial number 55xxxx to 56xxxx.

Miranda A: R2* D+

c1957; 35mm SLR with interchangeable preset Soligar-Miranda f1.9, 5cm lens in either 44mm screw mount or external semi-automatic (similar to Exakta) bayonet mount. 1-1/1000s; removable finder; lever wind; non-instant return mirror; top and front mounted shutter release; chrome body; serial number 57xxxx.

Miranda AII: **R3* G+**
c1957. Small frame counter dial, and red triangles marked at 20 and 36 exposures.

Miranda B: **R2* D+**
c1957. 35mm SLR with interchangeable, black finished Prominar-Miranda f1.9, 5cm external semi-automatic lens in bayonet mount. CFPS 1-1/1000s; removable finder; lever wind; instant return mirror; top and front mounted shutter release; chrome body; serial number 58xxxx.

Miranda C: **R2* D+**
c1959. 35mm SLR with interchangeable black finished Prominar-Miranda f1.9, 5cm external semi-automatic lens in bayonet mount. CFPS 1-1/1000s; removable finder; lever wind; instant return mirror; self-timer; top and front mounted shutter release; chrome body; serial number 60xxxx.

Miranda D: **R1* D**

c1960. 35mm SLR with interchangeable preset Soligor-Miranda f2.8, 5cm lens in 44mm screw mount, or bayonet mount Soligor-Miranda or Prominar-Miranda f1.9, 5cm external semi-automatic lens. CFPS 1-1/500s; lever wind; instant return mirror; new rounded body shape; front shutter release only; serial number 63xxxx (sequence shared by Automex III (MI3xx)

Miranda DR: **R2* D**
c1962. 35mm SLR with interchangeable preset Soligor-Miranda f2.8, 5cm lens in 44mm screw mount, or bayonet mount Soligor-Miranda f1.9, 5cm external semi-automatic lens. CFPS 1-1/500s; lever wind; instant return mirror; new rounded body shape; front shutter release only; split image focusing screen standard; both "Miranda" and "MIRANDA" logos are found; no model designation on the camera back; red leatherette covering on the frame counter dial; serial number 65xxxx to 66xxxx.

Miranda F: **R1* D**

c1963. 35mm SLR with interchangeable Auto Miranda f1.9, 5cm len., CFPS 1-1/1000s, (a few cameras in this series had 1/500s top speed); depth of field preview button on the camera body; no model designation on the camera back; serial number 67xxxx to 70xxxx. (Black body add 100%).

Miranda FM: **R2* D**
(MI312): c1963. As model "F" (MI311), but for non-TTL CDS pentaprism. Any "F" body could be updated simply by adding this metered pentaprism. (Black body add 100%).

Miranda FM, c1963.

Miranda FT: R2* D
c1967. As model "F", but for uncoupled TTL CDS pentaprism. Any "F" body could be updated simply by adding this metered pentaprism. (Black body add 100%).

Miranda Fv: R2* D
c1966. As model "F" (MI311), but for no depth of field pre-view, and removable shutter speed dial, for use when using clip on meter. Model designation on the camera front; serial number 72xxxx. (Black body add 100%).

Miranda FvM: R2* D

c1966. As model "Fv", but for non-TTL CDS meter prism. Model designation

"Fv" on the camera front; any "Fv" camera body could be up-dated simply by adding this metered prism(Black body add 100%).

Miranda FvT: R2* D
c1967. As model "Fv" (MI314), but for uncoupled TTL CDS meter prism. Model designation "Fv" on the camera front; "T" on the prism; any "Fv" camera body could be updated simply by adding this metered prism (Black body add 100%).

Miranda G: R2* D

Miranda G with clip on meter.

c1965. 35mm SLR with interchangeable Auto Miranda f1.9, 5cm lens. CFPS 1-1/1000s; removable finder; interchangeable focusing screens; mirror lock-up; self-timer; top and front shutter release; removable shutter speed dial for use when using clip-on meter; model designation on the camera front. (Black Body adds 100%).

Miranda GM: R2* D
c1965-66. For non-TTL CDS prism finder. Any "G" camera body could be updated simply by adding this metered prism. (Black body adds 100%).

Miranda GT: R2* D

c1967. For uncoupled TTL CDS prism finder. Model designation "G" on the camera front; "T" on the prism. Any "G" camera body could be updated simply by adding this metered prism. (Black body adds 100%)

Miranda Sensomat: R2* D

c1969. 35mm SLR with interchangeable Auto Miranda f1.8, 5cm lens. CFPS 1-1/1000s; coupled TTL CDS meter for stopped down metering with two button operation; all metal lever advance; serial number 81xxxx to 83xxxx.

Miranda Sensomat RE: R2* D

c1970. As previous model but for single button meter operation, and black plastic tipped lever advance. Tops of lever advance, shutter speed dial, and rewind knob are chrome, not black, serial numbers 68xxxxx.

Miranda Sensomat RS: R2* D

c1970. Without meter, serial number 37xxxxx.

Miranda Sensomat RE II: R2* D

c1975. 35mm SLR with interchangeable Auto Miranda EC f1.4 or f1.8, 5cm lens. CFPS 1-1/1000s; single top mounted shutter release; "Q.I.S." "Quadrascopic Image System" circular multi image rangefinder focusing system; serial number 58xxxxx to 59xxxxx. (Black body adds 100%).

Miranda TM: R2* D

c1975. 35mm SLR with interchangeable Auto Miranda TM f1.8, 5cm lens in 42mm (Praktica/Pentax size), CFPS 1-1/1000s. Single top mounted shutter release; stopped down metering; serial number 46xxxxx (type I); slight variations seen over the production life serial number 56xxxxx (type II). (Also sold as the "Soligor TM".

Soligor TM: R2* D

c1975. Has Auto Soligor f1.8, 50mm lens.

Soligor TM, c1975.

Miranda Automex: **R2* D**

c1959. 35mm SLR camera with interchangeable Soligor-Miranda f1.9, 5cm lens. CFPS 1-1/1000s; coupled selenium light meter to 400 ASA; provision for motor wind on some cameras though no winder has yet been found; serial number 61xxxx.

Miranda Automex II: **R2* D**
c1963. Redesigned flash synch and 1600 ASA sensibility; serial number 61xxxx.

Miranda Automex III: **R2* D**

c1964. Side mounted flash synch and CDS light meter to 1600 ASA; serial number 63xxxx.

Miranda Sensorex: **R2* D**

c1967. 35mm SLR with interchangeable Auto Miranda f1.4 or f1.9, 5cm lens. CFPS 1-1/1000s; first Miranda with open aperture metering; maximum aperture of lens in use must be set on a special dial under the front of the camera, under the rewind knob marked -1.4, 1.9, 2.8, 3.5, 4, 5.6, and 8, serial numbers 7xxxxx.

Miranda Sensorex 1.8:   **R2* D**
c1968. For use with f1.8 lens instead of f1.9; serial number 9xxxxx. (Black body add 100%).

Miranda Sensorex II: R2* D

Miranda Sensorex II in chrome (above) and black (below)

c1971. 35mm SLR with interchangeable Auto Miranda f1.4 or f1.8, 5cm lens. CFPS 1-1/1000s; first Miranda with hot shoe; lens aperture selection dial moved to under rewind knob; serial number 83xxxxx. (Black body add 100%).

Miranda Sensorex EE: R2* D

AIC on the camera body means Allied Impex Corporation, the American owners of Miranda Company, and official importers and distributors.

c1971. 35mm SLR with interchangeable Auto Miranda E f1.4 or f1.8, 5cm lens. CFPS 1-1/1000s; shutter speed preferred automatic TTL exposure control; top shutter release only; serial number 91xxxxx. (Black body add 50%)

Miranda Sensorex EE-2: R1* D

c1974. 35mm SLR with interchangeable Auto Miranda EC f1.4 or f1.8, 5cm lens. CFPS 1-1/1000s; shutter speed preferred automatic TTL exposure control; top shutter release only; shutter speeds visible in finder; Q.I.S. focusing system, serial number 93xxxxx. (Black body add 100%).

Miranda dx-3: R1* D+

c1975. 35mm SLR with interchangeable Auto Miranda EC f1.4 or f1.8, 5cm lens. Electronically controlled CFPS 4-1/1000s; the only Miranda SLR with a fixed prism; motor drive capable; the last Model produced by MIranda; often found not working; serial number 39xxxxx. (Black body less 50%).

vertical VFR; type A has button VFR lock; type B uses a locking ring located under the rewind knob; X synch only; serial number type A 113xxx – 115xxx; serial number type B 116xxx – 119xxx; it is not known if a Laborec I was ever made.

Miranda Sensoret: R3* C

c1972. 35mm RFR camera with fixed Miranda Soligor f2.8, 38mm lens. Seiko ESF shutter; the only non-SLR Miranda; serial number 24xxxxx.

Mirax Laborec II: R3* E+

c1970. 35mm SLR for laboratory use. Suitable for mounting on a microscope or telescope; CFPS 1-1/125s; two bayonet mounts and one screw mount; oversized knob advance; cable release only top and front; removable VF-5

Mirax Laborec Electro-D: R4* F–

c1972. 35mm SLR for laboratory use. Black body and built-in motor winder capable of two frames/sec. 12V DC required to power the motor either from rectified/reduced AC, or from rechargeable battery unit, serial number 114xxx Mx.

Miranda Laborec: R3* E+

c1975. 35mm SLR for laboratory use. Miranda bayonet and 44mm screw mount, serial number 12xxxx.

Miranda

Miranda Laborec III: R3* E+

c1975. 35mm SLR for laboratory use. Additional 1/250 and 1/500s shutter speeds; the only Laborec with model designation indicated on the camera front; serial number 21xxxxx.

Accessories and lenses for Miranda SLRs:

Extension tube set, 8mm, 16mm, 32mm	A
Universal helicoid	A–
Lens adaptors, (39mm screw, 42mm screw, Exakta, etc.)	A–
VF-1 WL VFR	A
VF-3 critical focusing VFR	B–

VF-3 critical focusing VFR opened and closed

VF-4 critical focusing VFR	B–
"M" pentaprism w/CDS meter	B–
"T" pentaprism w/ TTL CDS meter	B+
Focabell twin rail bellows (Miranda "T")	B+
Focabell AII twin rail bellows (Sensomat)	B+
Focabell AIII twin rail bellows (Sensomat RE)	B+
Bellox JR single rail bellows (DR)	A
Focabell S single rail bellows (F)	A
Pistol grip with release	B
Microscope adaptor	B+
Double cable release	A–
Clip-on CDS light meter	B–
Flash bracket	A–
Slide copier	A–
Focusing screens for "G" and Laborec	A–
Miranda Panorama head	B+
Motor drive for Automex	D
Motor drive for dx-3	D
Bulk film back for dx-3	D

Radio remote release for dx-3	D
Scope meter for microscope use	C

Soligor Miranda lenses, preset or external automatic

28mm f2.8 automatic	C+
35mm f2.8 preset	C
35mm f3.5 preset	C
35mm f2.8 automatic	C
105mm f2.8 automatic	C+
135mm f2.8 preset	C
135mm f2.8 automatic	C
135mm f3.5 preset	C
135mm f3.5 automatic	C
135mm f3.5 bellows mount	D
180mm f4.5 preset	D+
250mm f4.5 preset	D+
400mm f5.5 preset	E

Soligor Miranda lenses for Automex cameras

28mm f2.8	C+
35mm f2.8	C+
105mm f2.8	C+
135mm f2.8	C
135mm f3.5	C

Auto Miranda lenses for Automex cameras

25mm f2.8	D+
28mm f2.8	C+
35mm f2.8	C+
105mm f2.8	C+
135mm f2.8	C+
135mm f3.5	C+
200mm f3.5	D+

Auto Miranda lenses for Sensorex cameras

25mm f2.8	D
28mm f2.8	D
35mm f2.8	C+
105mm f2.8	C+
135mm f2.8	C+
135mm f3.5	C+
180mm f3.5	D+

| 200mm f3.5 | D+ |
| 52mm f3.5 Macron | D+ |

Auto Miranda E lenses

25mm f2.8	D
28mm f2.8	C+
35mm f2.8	C+
105mm f2.8	D
135mm f2.8	C
135mm f3.5	C
180mm f3.5	D+
200mm f3.5	D+
52mm f3.5 Macron	D+

Auto Miranda EC lenses

28mm f2.8	D
35mm f2.8	D
105mm f2.8	D+
135mm f2.8	D
200mm f3.5	E–
80-200mm f3.5 zoom	E–
52mm f3.5 Macron	D+

Misuzu Kogaku Kogyo & Co Ltd
Japan

Alta: **R4* G+**
1957-59. CFPS, 1-1/500s; separate RFR/VFR windows; diopter adjustment. Screw mount Altanon f2.0, 50mm or Altanon f3.5/50mm lens. Similar to the Leica IIIA. Maybe only 600 made.

J.D. Moller
Hamburg, Germany

Cambinox-N: **R4* G**
c1956. Binocular with subminiature camera built-in. Interchangeable Idemar 90mm f3.5 lens, bayonet mount (for 35mm, 135mm and 180mm lenses). 6 speed rotary FPS 1/30-1/800s; 10 x 14mm exp on 16mm film; after focusing the binoculars, the distance reading is transferred to the camera lens.

Cambinox-S: **R4* NSR est G+**
c1960. Monocular form, originally available on special order.

Accessories for Cambinox

Jedmar f3.5/35mm lens	F
Jedmar f3.5/135mm lens	F
Jedmar f3.5/180mm lens	F

Mollier
Paris, France

Le "Cent Vues":   **R4* H–**

c1924. Metal 35mm VFR camera for 100 exp, 18 x 24mm on perforated 35mm film in special cassettes. Hermagis f3.5, 40mm lens; single speed guillotine shutter or Compur shutter; also used as a projector; horizontal and vertical styles exist. Invented by Etienne N. Mollier.

Molteni Detective Camera: R5* G+
Molteni Aplanat lens. Body unfolds to form vf; brass fittings. 9 x 12cm exp on plates. Mfg. in Paris, France. c1885.

MOM
Budapest, Hungary

Mometta: R3* E–

c1953. 35mm RFR camera. Fixed mount Ymmar f3.5, 50mm lens; CFPS 1/25-1/500s; CRF.

Mometta II: R3* E–
c1955. With interchangeable mount (42mm screw), interesting in that the lens flange to focal plane distance is the same as that used on SLR cameras having a "Universal" screw mount. This would allow the SLR lens to be used on the Mometta camera.

Mometta III: R3* E–
c1958. With flash synch.

Monroe Camera Co
Rochester, New York, USA

The Monroe Camera Co. was established in 1897 in Rochester, New York. In 1899 they merged with several other companies – the Rochester Optical Co., the Rochester Camera & Supply Co., the Ray Camera Co., and the Western Camera Mfg. Co. – to form the Rochester Optical & Camera Co.

Monroe No. 7 Folding Plate Camera:
R3 * D+
c1898. 4" x 5" folding plate camera; Rapid Rectilinear lens; Unicum shutter. Double extension red bellows; reversible and shifting back; polished mahogany body, brass fittings; ivory label; leather covered case.

Pocket Monroe: R3* D+
c1898. Folding plate camera; $3\frac{1}{2}$" x $3\frac{1}{2}$" exp on dry plates.

Vest Pocket Monroe: R3* E–
c1898, miniature camera; collapsible bellows; single exp, $3\frac{1}{2}$" x $3\frac{1}{2}$" on dry plates.

Montanus-Camerabau
Solingen, Germany

Plascaflex V45:   R3* C+
c1950. TLR for 6 x 6cm on 120 roll film, f4.5, 75mm lens, Vario shutter.

Plascaflex PS35:   R3* C+
c1950. TLR for 6 x 6cm on 120 roll film, f3, 75mm lens, Prontor-S shutter..

Rocca Automatic: R3* C+
c1953. TLR for 6 x 6cm on 120 roll film,
Trinar f2.9 or Cassar f2.8, 80mm lens,
Prontor-SVS shutter, interchangeable
focusing hood.

Delmonta: R3* C
c1955. TLR for 6 x 6cm frames on 120
roll film, Pluscanar f3.5, 75mm lens,
Vario shutter.

Montiflex: R3* C
c1955. TLR for 6 x 6cm frames on 120
roll film, Pluscanar f3.5, 75mm lens,
Prontor-SVS shutter.

Montana: R2* C
c1956. 35mm VFR camera, Deltamon
f3.5, 45mm lens, Vario shutter.

Charles Monti
Paris, France

Lumiere Magazine Camera: R4* F

c1892. Box-type magazine camera;
Rapid Rectilinear 135mm f11 lens; 2
leaf scissors behind-the-lens shutter.
Waist-level finder; 12 exp, 9 x 12cm on
dry plates. Invented by L. Lumiere,
Lyons, France.

Moore & Co
Liverpool, England

Aptus Ferrotype Camera: R3* E+
c1913-1956. Black leather covered
wooden ferrotype camera; meniscus
lens. Suction disk takes unexposed plate
and swings it into position to be
exposed; after exposure, the suction
disk dropped the plate into the
developing tank attached to the camera.
Very popular among "while you wait"
beach photographers. 4.5 x 6.3cm exp
on plates.

Morita Trading Company
Japan

Kiku 16:   R3* D

c1960. Subminiature made for 16mm
rollfilm. 25mm f8 lens. I & B shutter set
by tiny knob on front of body, giving it
the appearance of a miniature Leica.
Originally sold as part of a kit that
contained lens hood and filter. Also
known as the Gem 16 Model II.

H. Morse
London, England

Single Lens Stereoscopic Camera:

R5* H+

c1865. Ross Landscape lens. Stereo exp on 3½" x 7" wet plates; camera slides laterally on rails for second exp.

William Muller
Vienna, Austria

Delta-Stereo Flat Cartridge: R4* E+
c1900. Stereo folding camera;Extra Rapid Aplanat 120mm f6.5 lens (also Anastigmat 260mm f9, Triple Anastigmat 280mm f12, or Collinear III M 300). Reflecting finder; scale focusing. 9 x 18cm exp on roll or sheet film.

Neue Reflex Stereoskop Camera:

R4* F–

c1901, box-type reflex stereo camera; Suter Anastigmat 340K lens, (also Goerz Series III 120mm 510K, Voigtlander Collinear Series III 120mm 570K); FPS. 9 x 18cm exp on stereo plates.

Multicoloure: R4* F
c1905, tri-colour magazine box camera. Tri-colour filters were sequentially moved into position (behind the lens) by using external controls. Manufactured in Paris, France.

Le Multi Photo: R4* G+
c1924, all metal camera; two Boyer Saphir 40mm f4.5 lenses; FPS 1/70-1/500s. 9 exp, 27 x 27mm. Also takes stereo pictures using 10 x 15cm plate holder. Manufactured. in Lyon, France.

Multiscope & Film Co
Burlington, Wisconsin, USA

All Al-Vista panoramic cameras shared a common method of controlling the transit speed of the lens. A set of vanes ranging in size from about ¹/₂ to 1 inch were fitted to a small rotating post either on top or bottom of the cameras. The larger the vane, the greater the wind resistance and the slower the lens movement. They were usually stored inside the camera. If they all are missing, deduct at least 40% from the value of the camera and adjust the value for the number of wind vanes present.

**Al-Vista Panoramic Camera
(Model 4B):   R4* E+**

c1900. 4" x 12" exp on roll film.

**Al-Vista Panoramic Camera
(Model 5B):   R4* E+**
c1900. 5" x 12" exp on roll film.

Baby Al-Vista: R4* F–
c1900, panoramic camera; 2¼" x 6¾" exp on roll film.

Multi-Speed Shutter Co

Morris Park, Long Island, New York,
USA; later became
Simplex Photo Products Company

Simplex Camera: R5* I
c1914. 35mm camera; Bausch & Lomb
Tessar 50mm f3.5 lens; built-in shutter
1-1/300s. 800-35mm half-frame exp or
400-35mm full-frame exp. The Simplex
was the first commercially produced
camera designed to take full-frame
photographs on 35mm film. See picture
opposite.

Mundus

France

Camerette: R5* F
1948. First camera from this company
and very different to those that
followed. A vertically-styled
subminiature, similar to the Steky, made
to take 50 exposures, each 10 x 15mm
on16mm film. Cinor Berthiot lens,
shutter speeded to 1/200s,

Mundus 16: R5* F
1950. Made to resemble a small cine
camera and taking Standard-8 cine film
to produce approximately 375 images,
each one 8 x 14 mm across the full
16mm width. Mundar 25mm f2.5 lens,
Orec shutter, manufactured by SEM,
speeded to 1/400s.

Mundus Color: R3* E+
1958. Similar design and film format to
the Mundus 16, but finished in beige
crackle finish, as opposed to black, and
with Atos shutter speeded to 1/300s.

The Simplex Camera – the first
commercially produced camera
designed to take full-frame
photographs on 35mm film.

Interchangeable Som Berthiot lens. More common in Europe, especially France, than in the UK or US.

Mundus Color 60:   R3* E+
1960. An updated version of the 1958 camera, with the same film format, but now designed with a slightly smaller body with more rounded corners. Knob film wind on previous models now replaced by lever that also cocks shutter as film is advanced. Som Berthiot 20mm f2.8 lens, shutter speeded 1-1/300s. Accessory meter available as extra to fit beneath lens.

Mundus Color 65:   R3* E+
1974. Similar to previous model, but with 25mm f2.8 lens.

Murer & Duroni
Milan, Italy

Murer: R3* D–

c1920. 6 x 9cm camera; Murer Anastigmat 102mm f6.3 lens with helicoidal focusing; FPS. Sliding lens cap with built-in viewer.

Murer Express: R3* D
c1905, mirror reflex camera; Anastigmat 9cm f7 lens; FPS 1/30-1/1000s. Leather covered wood body. 6 x 13cm exp on plates.

Murer Express Stereo: R3* F–
c1896-1897. Mirror reflex stereo camera; anastigmat f6.3 lens. Aluminium body. 45 x 107mm and 6 x 13cm exp on plates.

Murer Folding Express: R4* E–
c1920. 45 x 107mm folding stereo camera; Anastigmatic 60mm f4.5 lens; FPS 1/15-1/1000s.

Murer Sprite: R3* C+

c1919. 4.5 x 6cm folding camera; Rapid Aplanat 70mm f8 lens; shutter 1/25-1/100s. Roll film version, $175. Plate:

Murray & Heath
London, England

Stereoscopic Camera: **R5* H+**
c1865. Ross lenses, sliding box focusing. Stereo exp on 9 x 17cm wet plates. Rising front; Mahogany construction.

Muse Optical Co
Japan

Museflex: **R4* D**
1948. Small format TLR-style camera for Bolta size film (similar to Kodak's 828 but with different spool configurations). Early models with fixed focus meniscus lenses and single-speed shutters. Later models synch for flash and with 2 apertures. Some models with focusing lens, though not coupled to viewfinder.

Museflex IIa: **R4* D**
1951. Similar to original Museflex, but with shutter 1/25-1/150s and coupled focusing to make it a true TLR.

Mutschler, Robertson & Co
Rochester, New York, USA

Mutschler, Robertson & Co. was founded in 1895 by Albert Mutschler and John A. Robertson. The company name was changed to the Ray Camera Co. in 1898; located at 204 Commercial Street in Rochester, New York. In 1899 they merged with several other companies the Rochester Optical Co., the Rochester

Camera & Supply Co., the Monroe Camera Co. and the Western Camera Mfg. Co. – to form the Rochester Optical & Camera Co.

Ray Folding Plate Model A: **R3* D–**

c1898. 4" x 5" folding plate camera; Rapid Rectilinear lens; Victor shutter. Red bellows; shifting, rising and falling front; side loading.

Ray No. 2:   **R3* D–**

c1895. 5" x 7" folding plate camera; Rapid Rectilinear lens; Unicum shutter. Shifting, rising and falling front. Leather covered exterior; mahogany interior, brass fittings; red bellows.

Ray No. 4:   **R3* D–**
c1895. 4" x 5" folding plate camera; Rapid Rectilinear lens; Unicum shutter. Leather covered exterior; mahogany

interior, brass fittings; red bellows. Mutschler, Robertson & Co. brass label above lens board.

The Ray Junior: **R3* C–**
c1898, small box-type dry plate camera; $2\frac{1}{2}$" x $2\frac{1}{2}$" exp on dry plates.

N

Dr. August Nagel Camerawerk
Stuttgart, Germany

Pupille: R4* E+

Pupille with Leitz rangefinder

c1930. Metal VFR camera for 16 exp, 3 x 4cm on roll film, Schneider Xenon 50mm, f2.0 or Xenar f2.9 or f3.5 lens; Compur shutter 1-1/300s. Leitz Elmar 50mm f3.5 lens doubles the price.

Ranca: R3* F–
c1931. Nagel Anastigmat 50mm f4.5 lens; Ibsor shutter 1-1/150s.

Recomar: R3* D
c1928-1932. Folding plate camera; 6 x 9cm & 9 x 12cm; Leitz Elmar 10.5cm f4.5 lens in Compur shutter.

Recomar:, c1928-1932.

Rolloroy: R4* F
1930. Small metal camera for 16 exposures on 127 film. Lens extends on tube from body in rimset Compur shutter. Unusual depth of field device built into top plate. Leitz f3.5 Elmar or Schneider f2 Zenon lenses.

Triumph: R2* C
c1930. Self-erecting folding camera, incorporating Nagel's patent book form back for easy film loading. Three speed shutter, f6.5 Anastigmat lens.

Vollenda 3x4, No. 48:   R4* F–

c1930. Elmar 50mm f3.5 lens; Compur shutter 1-1/300s.

Vollenda B: **R4* C+**

c1930. Folding roll film camera; 5 x 7.5cm exp; 9cm f6.3 Nagal Anastigmat lens; 3 speed shutter B T 1/25-1/100s.

National Photocolour Corp
New York, USA

One shot or single exposure colour cameras used two internal pellicle mirrors to divide the light into three portions which made simultaneous exposures through red, green, and blue filters on high-speed black & white film or plates. These "separation negatives" were then used to make a natural colour print by the dye transfer process. The National Photocolor Corp. made a number of sizes ranging from $3^{1}/_{4}$ x $4^{1}/_{2}$ inch to 5 x 7 inches.

National Color Camera: **R4* F+**
c1938; $3^{1}/_{4}$" x $4^{1}/_{4}$" format; Tessar 135mm f4.5 lens; Dial set Compur shutter. The Goertz Dagor & Dogmar lenses were also

very popular and found frequently on National Cameras. It is rare to find the pellicle mirrors intact. They are made of a very thin mirrored collodion membrane and were very fragile.

National Color Camera, c1938.

Neidig
Germany

Perlux: **R3* C**
1952. 35mm VFR camera. Die-cast light alloy body, matt chrome with black leatherette. 45mm f2.8 Kataplast with front cell focusing. Prontor-S shutter 1-1/300s + B. Depth of field indicator.

Perlux II: **R3* C+**
1953. Similar to first model with slightly changed body design to incorporate uncoupled rangefinder.

Perlux IIa: **R3* C+**
1953. Similar to Perlux II with coupled rangefinder.

Nettel Kamerawerk
Sontheim a/M, Germany

Argus Camera: R4* G
c1911. monocular-type detective camera; Tessar 50mm f4.5 lens; single speed cylindrical shutter. 4.5 x 6cm exp on plates.

New Ideas Mfg Co
New York, USA
Sold by Herbert & Huesgen
Company, New York, USA

Tourist Multiple: R4* H–

c1914. 35mm camera. Bausch & Lomb Zeiss Tessar 50mm f3.5 lens; 7 speed guillotine MFPS 1/40-1/200s; 750 exp, 18 x 24mm on 50' rolls of perforated 35mm cine film. Qty less than 1000. The camera originally sold for $175; the complete outfit (camera and matching projector) sold for $250. The Tourist Multiple was the first 35mm still camera produced commercially and sold in substantial quantity.

Newman & Guardia
London, England

Baby Sibyl: R3* F+
Rangefinder version H

c1914. Tessar 75mm f4.5 lens; Newman & Guardia shutter 1/2-1/200s. c1910. Roll film version, and plate version.

Folding reflex: R4* F
1922. SLR for 6 x 9.5 cm plates or sheet film that folded to a very compact box shape. Rollfilm holder for $3^1/_4$" x $2^1/_4$"

inch film available. Revolving back, rise and swing front, shutter speeds 1/10-1/800s.

New Ideal Sibyl: R3* E+
c1914. Ross Xpres f4.5 lens; Newman & Guardia shutter. $3\frac{1}{4}$" x $4\frac{1}{4}$" exp.

New Special Sibyl: R3* E
c1914. 6 x 9cm; Ross Xpres 112mm f4.5 lens; special Newman & Guardia shutter. Rising and sliding front; vf adjusted for use of rise and cross facility and had two sets of adjustment marks depending on which axis the vf was turned. Two spirit levels, to check for correct horizon. 6 x 9cm exp.

Pattern B Detective Camera: R3* E
c1895. $3\frac{1}{4}$" x $4\frac{1}{4}$" exp on plates.

N&G Reflex Camera: R3* E
c1906. Single lens reflex with twin shutters. Front shutter 1-1/64s, plus focal plane shutter with top speed of 1/800s. Double extension, revolving plate back, rising front. Made from mahogany covered in black Morocco leather.

Nydia: R3* F

c1890. Wray Rectilinear lens; double guillotine shutter; 12 exp, magazine

changed by manipulation of plates through soft leather pouch.

Nydia: R3* G–
c1901-1913. Quarter-plate pocket camera; weighing one pound; Wray – Ross or Aldis lens; Pneumatic shutter; reversible finder; DD. slide; focusing screen; Newman magazine changing bag for 12 cut films in sheaths; detachable tapered bellows & struts for folding.

Special: R3* E–
Magazine box camera; lens board moves vertically and horizontally; pneumatic shutter. Extended bellows for close-ups and copying. $3\frac{1}{4}$" x $4\frac{1}{4}$" exp, 12 plate magazine.

Stereo Detective Camera: R4* G–
c1895. Rectilinear 120mm f8 lens; guillotine shutter $\frac{1}{2}$-1/100s. Leather bag changing mechanism for plates. 10 x 16cm.

Sibyl De luxe: R2* E+
c1910-1917. Quarter-plate double ext.; folding reflector finder; fold away tripod screw; model 1 later known as model 83 with Zeiss VIIa f6.3-5" lens; model 1a with roll-film holder; model 83 had Ross F6.3 lens.

Sibyl Excelsior: R4* F
c1927. Rollfilm camera for $4\frac{1}{4}$" x $2\frac{1}{2}$" format. Following the traditional drop bed folding style, but incorporating the well-known Sibyl faceplate and lazy tongs. Rise and cross-front movements. First of the range to use a new type of shutter speeded from 2-1/150s. Fitted with f4.5 Dallmeyer Serrac lens.

Sibyl Trellis: R3* F
c1910-1938. Quarter-plate Hand and stand camera; N&G focal plane shutter on reversing back; Anastigmat f4.5 lens and other lens; rising & cross front.

Sibyl "Ordinary" Pocket camera:
          R2* D+

c1906-1913. 12 models, 3¼" X 2¼" to Quarter-plate; Optical DV. Vfr; Shutter ½-1/100s; lenses include Ross, Ziess, Cook.

Special: R4* F
1925. Compact folding reflex camera with f2.9 lens.

Nicca Camera Works
Japan

Nicca III (Type 3):   R3* F–
1949. Cfps, 1-1/500s; separate RFR/VFR windows; diopter adjustment; screw mount Nikkor HC f2.0/5cm lens. Now called the Nicca Camera Works Ltd. This camera is a copy of the Leica III.

Nicca IIIA: R2* F–
1951. Cfps, 1-1/500s; separate RFR/VFR windows; diopter adjustment; screw mount Nikkor HC f2.0/5cm or Nikkor SC f1.5/cm lens. The company name changed once again in November 1951 to the "Nicca Camera Company Ltd." IIIA cameras can be found with both company markings. It was also distributed by Sears Roebuck and Co. as the Tower Type-3, which is valued about 10% less than cameras marked "Nicca".

Nicca IIIB: R3* F–
1951. Cfps, 1-1/500s; FP flash synch; separate RFR/VFR windows; diopter adjustment; screw mount Nikkor HC f2.0, 5cm or Nikkor SC f1.5, 5cm lens. The same as the Nicca IIIA, with flash synch added It was also distributed by Sears Roebuck and Co. as the Tower Type-3B, which is valued about 10% less than cameras marked "Nicca".

Nicca IIIS: R2* F–

1952. Cfps, 1-1/500s; FP and X flash synch; separate RFR/VFR windows; diopter adjustment; screw mount Nikkor QC f3.5, 5cm lens. It was also distributed by Sears Roebuck and Co. as the Tower Type-3S, which is valued about 10% less than cameras marked "Nicca".

Nicca 4: R3* F

Tower camera with a Culminar 8cm/f2.8 lens – similar to Nicca 3F.

1953. Cfps, 1-1/1000s; FP and X flash synch; separate RFR/VFR windows; diopter adjustment; screw mount Nikkor SC f1.5, 5cm lens.

Nicca 3S: R2* F–

1954. Cfps, 1-1/500s; FP and X flash synch; separate RFR/VFR windows; diopter adjustment; screw mount Nikkor QC f3.5, 5cm lens. The same as the Nicca IIIs, with new shutter speed progression, and synch at 1/25 instead of 1/20. It was also distributed by Sears Roebuck and Co. as the Tower Camera valued about 10% less than cameras marked "Nicca".

Nicca 3F: R3* F–

1956. Cfps, 1-1/500s; FP and X flash synch; separate RFR/VFR windows; diopter adjustment; screw mount Nikkor H f2.0, 5cm or Nikkor S f1.4, 5cm lens. One piece top plate, hinged back. It was also distributed by Sears Roebuck and Co. as the Tower Camera valued about 10% less than cameras marked "Nicca". A 3F version with a quick wind lever was made, and is valued at about 15% less than the wind knob version.

Nicca 5: R2* F–

1955. Cfps, 1-1/1000s; FP and X flash synch; separate RFR/VFR windows; diopter adjustment; screw mount Nikkor S f1.4, 5cm or Nikkor S f2.0, 5cm lens. One piece top plate, hinged back. Leica IIIF copy, with synch contact under the accessory shoe. Also sold by Sears Roebuck and Co. with the f2/50mm lens as the Tower 45, and with the f1.4, 50mm lens as the Tower 46.

Nicca 33: R3* F–

1957. Cfps, 1/2-1/500s; FP and X flash synch; separate RFR/VFR windows; diopter adjustment; screw mount Nicca F2.8, 50mm lens. Continued after Nicca Camera Company Ltd. was taken over by Yashica, and then known as the Yashica YE.

Nicca IIIL: R3* F+

1958. Cfps, 1-1/1000s; FP and X flash synch; separate RFR/VFR windows; diopter adjustment; screw mount Nikkor H f2.0, 5cm lens. Completely redesigned top plate. Continued as the Yashica YF, after the company was taken over by Yashica.

Nicnon TF Binocular Camera: R4* F+

c1968. Half-frame 35mm binocular camera; Nicnon 165mm f3.5 lens; Copal square MFPS 1⁄60, 1⁄125 and 1⁄250s. The SLR camera uses right-hand optics of the binocular as an objective; springwound motor allows up to 20 exp per wind.

Nicnon S Binocular Camera: **R4* F+**
c1970; 7x50 monocular telescope, fitted to a half frame 35mm camera. The Nicnon was one of the highest quality binocular cameras. They were frequently used by law enforcement agencies.

Nichiryo Trading Co
Tokyo, Japan

Teflex Binocular Camera: **R4* F**
c1968. Binoculars with a half-frame 35mm camera attached. Tefnon lens f3.5, 165mm effective focal length. Focus through right half of binocular. Camera spring driven. Nearly identical cameras were the Ricoh Teleca and The Nicnon

Niell and Simons
Brussels, Belgium

Lopa: **R4* F–**
c1900, meniscus 120mm f11 lens; single speed guillotine shutter. 6.5 x 9cm exp.

Nikon Inc Nippon Kogaku K.K.
Tokyo, Japan

For further information see Nikon Rangefinder Cameras by Robert Rotoloni, Hove Collectors Books, 1983, and Nikon Compendium, Handbook of

the Nikon System by Rudolf Hillebrand and Hans-Joachim Hauschild, Hove Collectors Books, 1993, for SLR and underwater cameras.

Nikon I: **R5* Rare K**

c1948-49. 35mm RFR camera. Nikkor 50mm f2 coated lens, interchangeable bayonet mount; CFPS 1-1⁄500s; CFR. 40 exp, 24 x 32mm. Qty 758. No factory installed synch; removable take-up spool. One offered in 1989 for K Worth at least H if damaged, non-working, or modified in any way.

Nikon M: **R4* G+**
Without synch, 1643 cameras made
                                    R4* H

c1949-52. 35mm RFR camera. Nikkor 50mm f2 coated lens, interchangeable bayonet mount; CFPS 1-1⁄500s; CFR. 36 exp, 24 x 34mm. Qty 1643. No factory installed flash synch; M prefix on serial number.With synch, about 1700 cameras made.

Nikon S: R4* F+
Eight digit serial number: R3* F−
Others: R2* F−

Nikon S3: Chrome body: R3* G
Black body: R4* I−
Black Olympic: R4* I

c1950-54. 35mm RFR camera. Nikkor 50mm f2 coated lens, interchangeable bayonet mount; CFPS 1-1/500s; CFR; flash synch. 36 exp, 24 x 36mm. Qty 36,746. Double spring synchro socket. "Made in Occupied Japan"

c1958. 35mm RFR camera. Nikkor 50mm f2 coated lens, interchangeable bayonet mount; CFPS 1-1/1000s; CFR; flash synch. Combined range-vf for 3 lens fields. 36 exp, 24 x 36mm. Qty 14,310.

Nikon S2: Black body: R4* I−
Chrome body, chrome dial: R3* F
Chrome body, black dial: R3* F+

Nikon S4: Chrome body: R3* H−

c1954-55. 35mm RFR camera. Nikkor 50mm f2 coated lens, interchangeable bayonet mount; CFPS 1-1/1000s; CFR; flash synch. 36 exp, 24 x 36mm. Qty 56,715. Single stroke rapid wind lever, enlarged vf.

c1959. 35mm RFR camera. Nikkor 50mm f2 lens, interchangeable bayonet mount; CFPS 1-1/1000s; CFR; flash synch. 36 exp, 24 x 36mm. Qty 5698. No self-timer, manual reset frame counter.

Nikon SP:
> **Chrome body, normal lens: R3* G+**
> **Black body: R4* I–**

c1957. 35mm RFR camera. Nikkor 50mm f2 coated lens, interchangeable bayonet mount; CFPS 1-1/1000s; flash synch. Combined range-vf for 6 lens fields; 1:1 viewing, parallax correction for normal and telephoto lenses, adjacent eye-level optical finder for 28mm and 35mm lenses. Self-timer. Qty 21,534. Electric motor drive available automatically advances film and fires shutter at maximum rate of 3 exp per second. The motor is powered by 6 penlight or 6C size batteries.

Nikon SP with stereo Nikkor lenses.

Nikon S3M:
> **Chrome with motor: R5* K**
> **Black: R5* K**

c1960. Half-frame 35mm RFR camera. Nikkor 35mm f2 coated lens, interchangeable bayonet mount; CFPS

1-1/1000s; CFR; flash sync. 72 exp, 18 x 24mm, half-frame format. Qty 195. One offered in 1989 with matching S72 motor for $15,000. This same matched set today could easily command $20,000!

Nikon F: R4* G+

Introduced in 1959. 35mm SLR with interchangeable lenses, backs, viewing screens, prisms etc. CFPS speeds 1-1/1000s. This camera, considered by some to be the first 35mm SLR system camera has finally reached the ranks of the collectables! With Nikon RFR equipment becoming harder and harder to find, many Nikon enthusiasts have begun the search for early Nikon SLRs, particularly Nikon F Photomics. We expect to see a greater interest in the coming years in collecting these cameras. For now at least, the early Nikon "F" Photomic cameras with serial numbers from 640000 to 641000 are actively being looked for. Because of their popularity as "working" cameras, pristine examples are particularly hard to find. Competition from users is great. (price is for low numbered camera bodies only 640000-641000, black model is about 50% more, other serial numbers are about 70% cheaper)

Nikon F cutaway model: **R4* G+**
non-working Nikon F camera sliced in half for use as a display piece, showing some of the internal workings. Includes half a lens.

Nikon F made for the United States Space program: **R5* H**
with special markings, this camera is one of the rarest Nikon SLRs (for the moment at least!) including lens.

Nikon F made for the United States Navy: **R4* G+**
with special markings, hard to find in clean condition. Price includes motor drive and lens.

Nikkor F: **R4* F+**
Nikon F made for the European market. Harder to find in the USA than in Germany.

Nikon F Photomic: **R2* F–**
c1962-1966. 35mm SLR camera. MFPS; 1-1/1000s, T, B; Cds meter; needle display; 1/60s, X, M. Flash exp.

Nikon F Photomic T: **R2* F–**
c1965-1966. 35mm SLR camera. MFPS; 1-1/000s.T.B.;Cds meter; Needle display; 1/60s.X,M flash exp.

Nikon F Photomic TN: **R2* F–**
c1967-1968. 35mm SLR camera. MFPS; 1-1/000s, T, B; Cds meter; needle display; 1/60s, X, M flash exp.

Nikon F Photomic FTN: **R2* F–**
c1968-1972. 35mm SLR camera. MFPS; 1-1/000s. T, B; Cds meter; needle display; 1/60s, X, M flash exp.

Nikon F2: **R2* E–**
c1971-1980. 35mm SLR camera. MFPS; 10-1/2000s, T, B; Cds meter; 1/80s, X, M flash exp.

Nikon F2 Photomic: **R2* E**
c1971-1977. 35mm SLR camera. MFPS 10-1/2000s, T, B; Cds.meter; needle display; 1/80s X, M flash exp.

Nikon F2S Photomic: **R2* E+**
c1973-1976. 35mm SLR Camera. MFPS 10-1/2000s, T, B; Cds meter; LED display; 1/80s, X, M flash exp.

Nikon F2SB Photomic: **R2* F–**
c1976-1977. 35mm SLR Camera. MFPS 10-1/2000s, T, B; SPD Meter; LED display; 1/80s, X, M flash exp.

Nikon F2A Photomic: **R2* F**

c1977-1980. 35mm SLR Camera. MFPS 10-1/2000s T, B; Cds Meter; Needle display; 1/80s, X, M flash exp.

Nikon F2AS Photomic: **R2* F+**
(NK143) c1977-1980. 35mm SLR camera. MFPS 10-1/2000s, T, B; SPD meter; LED display; 1/80, X, M flash exp.

Nikon F2T: **R3* H–**
c1978-1980. 35mm SLR camera. Titanium version of the F2 camera. First series marked with gold coloured logo "Titan" on the front later versions only had "T" to the left of the serial number; The F2T is 5 grams lighter than the F2; recognised by the textured metal surface.

Nikon F3:   **R2* E+**
1980. The third generation of Nikon professional SLRs. Aperture priority and manual. Titanium electronic shutter 8-1/2000s + T & B. Interchangeable finders.

Nikon F3T: **R3* H–**
c1982. 35mm SLR camera. Titanium version of the F3 camera; First series have textured silver finish of the metal. later versions are black; Both models have HP-type finder only.

Nikon F3AF: **R3* F**
1983. First Nikon with autofocus capabilities. Similar to F3 but with relay contacts to link with special Nikon AF lenses. Forerunner of, but different to, the current Nikon autofocus system.

Nikon FA: **R3* F**
1983. Introduced Automatic Multi-Pattern Metering to measure and compare five segment areas for the most accurate reading. Aperture priority, shutter priority and manual modes. Electronic shutter 1-1/4000s.

Nikon EM: **R2* E**

1979. Nikon's first SLR aimed at amateur use. Aperture priority auto without manual option. Electronic shutter with 1/90s mechanical setting for flash. Audible signal when speed drops below 1/30s. Accepts Nikkor AI lenses, but launched with its own cheaper 'E' range of lenses.

Nikkormat FT: **R2* D**

c1965-1966. 35mm SLR camera. MFPS 1-1/1000s, B; 1/125s, X flash exp; TTL Cds exp meter with needle display; Accepts all Nikon Lenses; single stroke winder sets shutter, switches on meter, transports film.

Nikkomat FS: **R3* F+**
c1965-1971. 35mm SLR camera. Same as FT except No mirror lock-up; No Exp meter; (Rare model).

Nikkormat FTN: **R2* D+**
c1967-1975. 35mm SLR camera. MFPS 1-1/1000s, B; 1/125s X flash exp; Cds Meter Needle display.

Nikkormat EL: **R2* D+**
c1972-1977. 35mm SLR camera. Auto exp mode; MFPS 4-1/1000s; 1/125s, X, M flash exp.; Cds meter; exp lock; single stroke winder sets shutter, meter and film.

Nikkormat FT2:   **R2* D+**
c1975-1978. 35mm SLR camera. MFPS 1-1/1000s, B; 1/125s, X, M flash exp; plus & minus symbols in Vfr.

Nikkormat ELW: **R2* E**
c1967-1968. 35mm SLR camera. As the EL model modified to take winder.

Nikkormat FT3:   **R2* E**
c1977-1979. 35mm SLR camera. As the FT2 with AI auto aperture coupling; Accessory shoe.

Nikon FM: **R2* E**
c1977-1984. 35mm SLR camera. Bayonet mount for all Nikon lenses; FP Copal shutter 1-1/1000s B; 1/125s, X flash exp; 2Cds/SPD/Gas meter; LED display; Accepts AW1 motor.

Nikon FE: **R2* E**
c1978-1984. 35mm SLR camera. Auto/manual version of the FM model; Interchangeable screens; MFP Electronic shutter 8-1/1000s, B; 1/90s, M; 1/125s, X flash exp.

Nikon FM2:   **R1* F–**

c1982-1988. 35mm SLR camera. As FM with titanium shutter to 1/4000s and 1/200 X flash exp; Cds/SPD/Gas meter; LED display.

Nikon FG: **R1* D**
c1982-1987. 35mm SLR camera. MFPS 1-1/1000s, B; M 1/90, X 1/125 flash exp; SPD meter; LCD display; Manual & progamme exp; TTL flash metering.

Nikon FE2:   **R1* F–**
c1983-1989. 35mm SLR camera. As FE with shutter speeds to 1/4000s; TTL flash control 1/200s exp.

Nikon FM2n: **R1* F–**
c1983. 35mm SLR camera. As the FM2 with flash shutter speed of 1/250s.

Nikon F3/T: **R3* G+**
1983-86. Full system 35mm SLR with titanium finish; fps 1-1/1000s.

Note: Nikon continued to make professional SLRs throughout the 1980s that included the F3HP, F3T and F3P before introducing the F4 in 1988, which was followed by its own variations up to the F5 and on into the N series of cameras. Full details and specifications of all these models can be found in the book Japanese 35mm SLR Cameras by Bill Hansen and Michael Dierdorff, published by Hove Books.

Nikonos I: **R3* E–**
             Calypso F
35mm underwater camera; Nikkor 35mm f2.8 lens.

Nikon Super Zoom 8:   **R3* C+**
Super 8mm movie camera. Cine Nikkor Zoom 8.8mm-45mm f1.8 lens; Electric motor drive-12, 18 or 24 frames per sec.

Nikkorex Zoom 35:   **R2* D**
c1963. SLR fitted with non-interchangeable 43-86mm zoom lens, f3.5, 1-500s, auto-exposure. First camera with a non-interchangeable zoom lens.

Nikon Accessories
Nikon Rangefinder motor drives

Motordrive S36 for Nikon SP:
chrome	**H+**
black	**H+**

Motordrive S72 for Nikon S3M   **I+**

Nikon Rangefinder lenses

21mm/f4 lens w/finder	**H**
25mm/f4 lens chrome	**F+**
25mm/f4 lens black	**G–**
28mm/f3.5 lens chrome	**F**
28mm/f3.5 lens black	**F**
35mm/f3.5 lens "MIOJ"	**F**
35mm/f3.5 lens chrome	**E**
35mm/f3.5 lens black	**E+**
35mm/f2.5 lens chrome	**E+**
35mm.f2.5 lens black	**F–**
35mm/f2.5 lens black: type II	**F+**
35mm/f1.8 lens black	**F**
35mm/f1.8 lens, type II	**F**
50mm/f3.5 micro lens	**G+**
50mm/f3.5 collapsible lens	**G+**
50mm/f2 collapsible lens marked "Tokyo"	**G–**
50mm/f2 lens chrome	**D+**
50mm/f2 lens black with chrome	**E–**
50mm/f2 lens all black	**G**
50mm/f1.5 lens	**G+**
50mm/f1.4 lens marked "Tokyo"	**E**
50mm/f1.4 lens chrome	**E–**
50mm/f1.4 lens black and chrome	**E–**
50mm/f1.4 lens all black	**G+**
50mm/f1.4 lens aluminium	**H–**
50mm/f1.4 lens "Olympic"	**G+**
50mm/f1.1 lens internal mount	**G+**
50mm/f1.1 lens external mount	**H–**
85mm/f2 lens chrome	**E+**
85mm/f2 lens black	**F–**
85mm/f2 lens "MIOJ"	**F+**
85mm/f1.5 lens	**H–**
105mm/f4 lens	**G+**
105mm/f2.5 lens	**F**
135mm/f4 lens: short mount	**F**
135mm/f4 lens	**G–**
135mm/f3.5 lens chrome	**D+**
135mm/f3.5 lens black	**E–**
180mm/f2.5 lens	**G**
250mm/f4 lens manual aperture	**G–**
250mm/f4 lens pre-set aperture	**F+**
350mm/f4.5 lens	**H**
500mm/f5 lens	**I+**
1000mm/f6.3 lens black	**K–**
1000mm/f6.3 lens grey	**J**
Stereo outfit	**K–**

Nikon produced innumerable accessories for their rangefinder system. They produced chrome optical finders in 35, 85, 105, and 135mm lengths. Very early 35, 85 and 135mm finders are marked Nippon Kogaku Tokyo and cover 24 x 34. Later finders are marked Nippon Kogaku Japan and cover 24 x 36. Types marked with an L on the base were designed for Leica type cameras and covered 24 x 36. Those marked with a C were made for Contaxes and have a longer foot. The 21 and 25mm finders were produced in black finish. Nikon also produced a series of brightline finders. The 35, 85, 105 and 135 brightline finders are not uncommon. The 50mm brightline is quite rare. The stereo brightline finder is extremely desirable.

21mm finder black	F+
25mm finder black	E+
28mm finder chrome	E−
35mm finder chrome	D
35mm finder black	E
35mm "mini" finder	G
50mm finder black	G
85mm finder chrome	D
85mm finder black	E+
105mm finder chrome	D
105mm finder black	E+
135mm finder chrome	D
135mm finder black	E
Stereo Finder	H
Sportsfinder	G−

Nikon produced a variable finder called the Variframe similar to the Leitz Vidom. The original model is finished in dull chrome and marked 24 x 32 for use with the Model I . The black screw-in 28mm adaptor for the variframe is extremely desirable. Nikon also made a very common zoom finder covering focal lengths 35 to 135mm. Some of these have markings for the Leica type lenses as well. These are quite common. The 28mm adaptor for this finder is uncommon. Two types of sportsfinder exist with yellow and silver backs.

Variframe 24x32 dull	I−
Variframe 24x32 bright	H+
Variframe M "MIOJ"	F
Variframe chrome	E
Variframe black with shoe	F+
Variframe black without shoe	F+
28mm adaptor for variframe	F+
Varifocal Zoom "MIOJ"	G
Varifocal Zoom type I	E

Varifocal Zoom type II	E
28mm adaptor for Varifocal Zoom:	E+
RF Illuminator:	F
Reflex housing type I:	I−
Reflex housing type II 45 degree	H
90 degree prism only	i−
Bellows model I	H−
Exposure meter, grey top	F
Exposure meter, black top	E
Microflex type I	H−
Microflex type II	H−
"S" copy stand	G+
"SA" copy stand	G
"P" copy stand	H−
"PA" copy stand	G
21mm lens shade	F−
25mm lens shade	E−
50mm lens shade for f1.1lens	E+
Micro Collar	F+

Lenses for Nikon F

2.1cm/f4.0 with finder	F−
2.8cm/f3.5	H−
3.5cm/f2.8	E−
5.0cm/f2.0	C+
5.8cm/f1.4	E−
5.5cm/f3.5 preset macro	G
10.5cm/f2.5	E+
10.5cm/f4.0	F−
13.5cm/f3.5	E−
20.0cm/f4.0	E−
8.5 to 25cm zoom, two touch	F−
8.5 to 25cm zoom, one touch	F−
50cm mirror, with case and filters	G
100cm mirror	I−

Meters for Nikon F

Model 1 meter, round type	E+
Model 2 meter, long window	D+
Nikkorex type	D
Model 3 meter, square type	D+
Booster module for the above	C+

Motors for Nikon F

Type one, number on base plate	F+
Type two, Nippon Kogaku logo	

on front   **F–**
Type three, marked Nikon, numbered
on back   **E+**
Grey pack   **E–**
Brown battery pack   **D**
Black battery pack   **C+**
250 exposure back   **F–**
Misc. Accessories for Nikon   **F**
Waist level finder, type one,
with Nippon Kogaku logo   **D**
Waist level finder type two, with
Nikon F markings   **C+**
Copy stand for Nikon F   **E–**
Electronic flash, S.B. 1   **D+**
Flash BC 7, for flash bulbs   **B**

Nimslo
USA

Nimslo: **R2* C**
1980. First seen at photokina, then
again at the next photokina in 1982
before finally reaching the market in
1983. Four-lens stereo camera invented
by Jerry Nims and Allen Lo. Processing
by Nimslo labs cut the four images into
strips and overlaid them with screen
made up of minute prisms to give 3-D

effect without the need for viewer. Fixed
focus, fixed aperture lens. Auto shutter.
Film speeds adjustable for 100 &
400 ASA.

Nitto Shashin Yohin KK
Japan

Elega: **R4* F+**
                          With "Olympic" name: G
c1951, 35mm VFR camera, Leica copy,
Elega or Eleger f3.5/45mm lens in a
fixed mount, guillotine shutter 1-1/200s,
built-in film cutter.

Normura Optical Co
Japan

Tanzer: **R3* C**
c1950. Bakelite TLR-style box camera
for Bolta film. 4.2cm fixed focus lens. I
& B shutter.

Flash Tanzer: **R3* C**
c1950. Similar to first model but with
flash synch.

Nimslo, 1980.

O

Odeon Photo
Paris, France

Isographe: **R4* F**
6 x 13cm stereo camera, Boyer Saphir f4.5 or Berthiot Flor f5.7 lens; shutter 1-1/200s. Two models: 6 x 13cm exp on plates, fixed focus, or 6 x 13cm exp on 620 roll film, micrometer focusing.

Officiene Galileo
Milan, Italy

Gami 16:   **R3* C+**
1953. Superior CRF subminiature for 12 x 17mm images on 16mm film. Opening lens cover winds clockwork motor drive and advances film. 25mm f1.9 Esamitar lens behind metal shutter, 1/2-1/1000s. Built in extinction meter and yellow filter. Focusing my moving film plane. Accessories included close-up lenses, developing tank, underwater housing and auxiliary telephoto lenses.

Office General de La Photographie
Paris, France

The Express Detective Nadar: R4* G+
c1888. Mahogany (reinforced with brass) box-type detective camera; Anastigmat Zeiss 86mm f18 wide angle lens; for 13 x 18cm plates or roll film with Eastman Walker back. Distributed by Nadar. Nadar was George Eastman's French representative. He added exposure counter.

Okam: **R3* E+**
See Section K Odon KEYSLAR.

O.I.P.
(Society Belge d'Optique et d'Instruments de Precision Paris, France

Cinescopie: **R4* E**
c1929. Miniature made for 24 x 24mm images on paper-backed 35mm film. f3.5 O.I.P. Labor lens. Lens and shutter assembly removable for use with an enlarger. Approx 300 made.

Okada Optical Co Ltd
Japan

Gemmy: **R4* I**

c1950. Pistol-type detective camera; 35mm f4.5 lens; 3 speed shutter. 11 x 18mm exp on 16mm film; film advanced by trigger action.

Olympus Optical Co Ltd
Tokyo, Japan

Semi Olympus: **R3* E**
1936. The first Olympus camera. Vertical folding bellows type for 16 exp on 120. 75mm f4.5 Coroner lens. Shutter was imported rimset Compur on early models, Japanese Crown copy on later models $^{1}/_{5}$-1/200s + T & B. Folding viewfinder

Semi Olympus II: R3* E
1938. Style changed to horizontal type. 16 exp on 120. Rigid viewfinder. 75mm f4.5 Zuiko lens, Koho shutter.

Olympus Six: R3* E
1939. Bellows camera similar to Semi Olympus Model II, but format increased for 12 exp 6 x 6cm on 120. 75mm f3.5 Zuiko. Koho shutter. Postwar models used improved lens and, late models used Copal shutters.

Olympus Chrome Six: R2* D

1948. Original model based on Semi Olympus II with chrome top plate. 75mm f3.5 Zuiko. Copal shutter 1-1/200s + B.

Olympus Chrome Six II: R2* D
1948. Similar to first model with f2.8 lens.

Olympus Chrome Six II: R2* D
1950. Similar to Model II plus flash synch. Found with f2.8 and f3.5 lenses.

Olympus Pen F: R3* Black E
Chrome D+

1960. The first 35mm half-frame SLR camera made for production. Use of a porro prism does away with the familiar pentaprism hump on most other 35mm SLR cameras. FPS, to 1/500s; no metering system, but an accessory meter was available. With Zuiko 38mm, f1.8 lens. This camera, along with the Pen FT and Pen FV, is less rare in the USA, where prices for all Pen F cameras tend to be about 30% less than in Europe. Black version; double the prices.

Pen S2.8: R2* C+

c1960. Zuiko 30mm f2.8 lens; Copal X shutter.

Olympus

Pen EE: R2* C+
c1961; Fixed focus 28mm f3.5 lens large electric eye surrounds the lens.

Pen EES: R2* C+

c1962. As the EE model, but with zone focusing 30mm f2.8 lens.

Pen D: R2* C+
c1962. Zuiko f1.9 32mm lens; Copal X shutter; meter read out on top of camera.

Pen D2: R2* C+
c1964. As model D, but with Cds meter.

Pen W: R2* D+
c1964. As Pen S, but with 25mm f2.8 wide-angle lens; all black body.

Pen Rapid EE.S: R2* C–
c1965. As the EES model, but designed to take the Agfa-rapid cassette.

Pen Rapid EE.D: R2* C–
c1965. As the EED model, but with Agfa-rapid easy loading system.

Olympus Pen FT: R3* E+
Updated version of the Pen F, using a semi-silvered mirror to permit through-the-lens metering at full aperture; self-timer. Black version less common, and brings 50% more. With Zuiko 38mm, f1.8 lens.

Olympus Pen FV: R4* E
Simplified version of the Pen FT, using a fully silvered mirror in order to brighten the finder image. This results in the loss of through-the-lens metering. The last model made. With 38mm, f1.8 Zuiko lens.

Olympus Pen F Microscope camera: In Chrome only. R3* E

Olympus Pen FT Microscope camera: In Black only. R4* E

Lenses for Olympus Pen F SLR cameras

20mm/f3.5 G Zuiko Auto W E
25mm/f2.8 G Zuiko Auto W E
25mm/f4.0 E Zuiko Auto W E–
38mm/f1.8 F Zuiko Auto S C+

38mm/f2.8 D Zuiko Auto S: E
Made for Europe during a six month period, without the diaphragm ring used for the Pen FT metering system, rare.

38mm/f2.8 Compact E Zuilo Auto S D+
38mm/f3.5 E Zuiko Macro E
40mm/f1.4 G Zuiko Auto S F–
42mm/f1.2 M Zuiko Auto S E+
60mm/f1.5 G Zuiko Auto T F–
70mm/f2.0 F Zuiko Auto T F–
100mm/f3.5 E Zuiko Auto T D+
150mm/f4.0 E Zuiko Auto T D–
250mm/f5.0 E Zuiko Auto T F
400mm/f6.3 E Zuiko Auto T G
800mm/f8.0 Zuiko Mirror T G+
50-90mm/f3.5 Zuiko Auto Zoom E
100-200mm/f5.0 Zuiko Auto Zoom E+
100-200mm/f5.0 Zuiko Zoom E+

Accessories for Pen F SLR cameras

Bellows Pen F	D–
Slide copier Pen F	C
Bellows Pen F II	D
Slide copier Pen F II	C+
Light meter for Pen F and FV	C+
Microscope adaptor Pen F	C+

Olympus Ace: R3* D+

1958-60, The first Olympus 35mm RFR camera to be sold with interchangeable lenses. Four lenses including the E Zuiko 4.5cm, f2.8 normal lens were available for this camera, not three as is widely believed. with 4.5mm, f2.8 lens.

Olympus Ace E: R3* E–

1959-61. Same as the Olympus Ace (OY105), but with the addition of match needle metering. With normal 4.5cm, f2.8 lens.

Accessory lenses for Olympus Ace cameras

3.5cm/f2.8 E Zuiko W ACE	D+
8cm/f4.0 E Zuiko T ACE	E–
8cm/f5.6 E Zuiko T ACE	E–

Olympus 35 I: R3* D+

1948-49, 24 x 32mm format on 35mm film, coated 4cm, f3.5 Zuiko lens in Seikosha Rapid shutter.

Auto Eye: R2* C–

1961. Shutter priority 35mm VFR camera. Set aperture indicated in viewfinder. Click stop focusing with feet and symbols markings. 45mm f2.8 D-Zuiko lens. Copal SV shutter to 1/500s + B.

Olympus 35 III: R4* D+

1949-50. 24 x 36mm format on 35mm film, the first from Olympus in this format. coated 4cm, f3.5 Zuiko lens in Seikosha Rapid shutter. Made for only three months.

Olympus Trip 35:   R1* C

35mm VFR camera with built-in light meter, made in very large numbers.

Olympus Pen W: R4* E–

1964-65. Black version of the Pen S but with fixed 25mm, f2.8 lens.

Olympus M-1:   R3* F

c1972. 35mm SLR camera; FPS 1-1/1000s; full range of lenses; later to be called OM-1.

Olympus: OM-1:   R1* D

1972. Commercial version of the MI, made after Leica objected to the name. 35mm manual SLR. TTL metering. FP shutter 1-1/1000s.

Olympus OM-1N: R1* D
1979. Similar to OM-1 with redesigned film lever and rewind, plus flash ready signal in viewfinder.

Olympus OM-2:   R1* D
1976. Manual metering 35mm SLR. First with Off The Film metering for flash and long speeds above 1/15s. FP shutter 60-1/1000s.

Olympus OM-10:   R1* D+
1978. Aperture priority auto 35mm SLR. FP shutter 2-1/1000s. Needed manual adaptor for use as manual camera.

Olympus OM-2N: R1* D
1979. Similar to OM-2 plus aperture priority automation. FP shutter 120-1/1000s.

Olympus OM-3:   R2* D
1983. Similar to OM-2 with metering for centre weighting, average and 2% spot. FP shutter 1-1/2000s

Olympus OM-30:   R2* D
1983. 35mm SLR, made to offer autofocus capability when used with its Zuiko 35-70mm zoom AF lens with focusing mechanism built in. Otherwise used as manual focus camera. Follow focus with motor drive was claimed to be possible.

Note: This is only a selection of Olympus 35mm SLRs made during the 1970s and 1980s. Other models, with slight variations in specification, included the OM-25P, OM-3Ti, OM-4, OM4-T, OM10FC, OM10 Quartz, OM 77AF, OM101, OM20 and OM40. Some of these had name variants in the US. Full details and specifications of all these models can be found in the book Japanese 35mm SLR Cameras by Bill Hansen and Michael Dierdorff, published by Hove Books.

XA: R1* C

1979. Unusually styled 35mm CRF camera. Aperture priority automation. Manual focus with rangefinder. 35mm f2.8 Zuiko lens with sliding cover. Electronic shutter 10-1/500s. Backlight control.

XA1:   R1* C
Similar to XA with Selenium meter cell around lens. Fixed focus f4 Zuiko. Programmed automation 1/30-1/250s.

XA2:   R1* C

Similar to XA but with focusing lens at three symbol settings. f3.5 Zuiko.

XA3:   R? C

Similar to XA2 with DX film coding option.

XA4:   R1* C

Similar style to other XA cameras, but with 28mm wideangle lens. Programmed automation. Easy film load system. Focuses down to 0.3 metres.

Optik Primar Kamera Werke VEB
Görlitz, East Germany

Post-War successor to the Bentzin Factory

Primarflex II: R3* E–

c1950, SLR for 6 x 6cm frames on 120 roll film, interchangeable Trioplan f2.8/10cm lens, interchangeable VFR, same shutter problems as pre-war Primarflex.

Studio Primar: R4* E–

c1950, SLR camera for 9cm x 12cm plates, specially reinforced lens standard and focusing rails in order to maintain "even the heaviest lenses" parallel to the film plane! CFPS 1-1/300s.

OPL (Optique de Précision Levallois)
France

Foca PF1 (*) one star: R3* E

1946-53. CFPS, 1/20-1/500s; viewfinder only. Non-interchangeable f3.5, 35mm model made only in 1946 (5300 cameras made). From 1947 to 1953 the lens was interchangeable (11,900 cameras made). Vfr shows fields of view for the 35mm lens. With minor modifications this camera became the Foca Standard of 1953. (see ID and dating section in the front of the Blue Book for Foca serial number information).

Foca "Post":   R4* E+

1952-? CFPS 1/25s only; 24mm x 30mm frame size; VFR not modified; 50mm, f3.5 Oplar lens; focusing between 30 and 35cm; diaphragm blocked between f5.6 and f8. Easily recognised by four ball shaped protrusions located on the front of the camera. Used to photograph telephone registers, just as the Leica "Post" cameras.

Foca Standard: R3* E–
1953. Cfps, 1/20-1/500s; Viewfinder only with field of view for 35mm lens; interchangeable screw mount f3.5, 35mm or f2.8, 50mm lens. Early cameras are easily distinguished from later ones by their lack of rewind lever on the front of the top plate. At least six models were made, each with slight physical variations. Not the most common of Focas, as some might think!

The PF2b.

Foca PF2 (**) two star: R3* E–

1946. Cfps, 1/20-1/500s; combined RFR/VFR; 36mm interchangeable screw mount f3.5, 5cm or f2.8, 5cm Oplar lens. Only the 50mm lenses couple accurately with the rangefinder. Early cameras had brown body covering, worth about 75% more.

Foca PF2b: R3* E–
The PF2b (the "b" meaning "bis", continued in French) has 1/25-1/1000s shutter and factory installed X and M synch, otherwise the same as PF2. Same price for either camera. Military examples exist and are worth about 200% more.

Foca PF3 (***) three star: R3* E

1952. Cfps, 1-1/1000s; combined RFR/VFR; 36mm interchangeable screw mount f3.5, 5cm or f2.8, 5cm Oplar lens or with faster f1.9, 5cm Oplarex lens. Only the 50mm lenses couple accurately with the rangefinder. With and without synch. Military examples do exist and are worth about 200% more.

Foca PF3 L (***) three star: R3* E
1956. Cfps, 1-1/1000s; combined RFR/VFR; 36mm interchangeable screw mount f3.5, 5cm or f2.8, 5cm Oplar lens or with faster f1.9, 5cm Oplarex lens. Only the 50mm lenses couple accurately with the rangefinder. Military examples do exist and are worth about 200% more.

Foca Universel: R3* F+

1946. Cfps, 1-1/1000s; combined RFR/VFR; bayonet mount f1.9 or f2.8 50mm coated lenses coupled to the RFR; X and M synch indicated by letters.

Foca Universel "R": R3* F–

1955. Cfps, 1-1/1000s; combined RFR/VFR; bayonet mount f1.9 or f2.8 50mm coated lenses coupled to the RFR; X and M synch. An improved version of the Universel with lever wind, and a quieter shutter. Graphic symbols indicate flash synch sockets.

Foca Universel "RC": R3* F

1959. Cfps 1-1/1000s; combined RFR/VFR; bayonet mount f1.9, or 2.8 lens, coupled to RFR; bright line projected frame in VFR. An improved version of the Universel "R". Less than 2000 cameras are thought to have been made. Thought by some to be the best made French 35mm camera. Some outfits were made for the French Navy, and bear the markings "Marine Nationale" on the front, along with a contract number. These cameras are worth about 300% more than normal Universel "RC".

Focaflex: R3* E+

1960-68. SLR; BTL leaf shutter, 1-1/250s; fixed mount f2.8, 5cm

Neoplex lens. Since no pentaprism was used, the camera body is quite slim.

Focaflex, 1960-68.

Focaflex II: R3* E

1962-68. SLR; BTL leaf shutter, 1-1/250s; interchangeable bayonet mount lenses. Retroplex f4.0, 3.5cm wide-angle lens, f2.8, 5cm Neoplex normal lens, f4.0, 9cm Teleoplex telephoto lens and very rare f4.0, 15cm Super Teleoplex lenses were available.

Focaflex Automatic: R3* D+

1961-68. SLR; BTL leaf shutter, 1-1/250s; fixed mount f2.8, 5cm Neoplex lens. Since no pentaprism was used, the camera body is quite slim. This camera is the same as the Focaflex, with the addition of a built-in light meter.

Focaflex Automatic, 1961-68.

Foca Sport: R2* D–
1954. BTL leaf shutter, 1-1/300s; fixed f3.5, 4.5cm Neoplar lens with scale focusing, knob advance and removable back.

Foca Sport I: R2* D–
1956. BTL leaf shutter, 1-1/300s; fixed f3.5, 4.5cm Neoplar lens with scale focusing; removable back. Differs from Foca Sport by addition of lever advance.

Foca Sport C: R2* D–
1957. BTL leaf shutter, 1-1/300s; fixed f3.5, 4.5cm Neoplar lens with scale focusing; lever advance and removable back. Differs from Foca Sport I by the addition of a built-in light meter.

Foca Sport Ib: R2* D–
1958. BTL leaf shutter, 1-1/300s; fixed f2.8, 4.5cm Oplar-Colour lens with scale focusing; lever advance and removable back, differs from Focasport I by addition of faster lens, and projected frame in the VFR.

Foca Sport Id: R2* D–
1958. BTL leaf shutter, 1-1/300s; fixed

f2.8, 4.5cm Oplar-Colour lens with scale focusing; lever advance and removable back. Combines the projected frame and faster lens of the Foca Sport Ib with the light meter of the Foca Sport C.

Foca Sport II: R2* D–
1963. BTL leaf shutter, 1-1/300s; fixed f2.8, 4.5cm Oplar-Colour lens coupled to RFR; lever advance and removable back.

Lenses and accessories for Foca and Focaflex

Screw mount

28mm f4.5 Oplex	D
35mm f3.5 Oplex	C+
90mm f3.5 Oplex or Teleoplar	D
135mm f4.5 Teleoplar	D
200mm f6.3 Teleoplar, for use with "Micro Foca" mirror box	E–

Screw mount lenses for Foca cameras. Left to right, they are the 135mm f4.5 Teleoplar, 90mm f3.5 Oplex and 28mm f4.5 Oplex.

Bayonet mount

28mm f4.5 Oplex	E
35mm f3.5 Oplex	D+
90mm f3.5 Oplex or Teleoplar	E–
135mm f4.5 Teleoplar	E–
200mm f6.3 Teleoplar, for use with "Micro Foca" mirror box	E+

Accessories for rangefinder Focas

Foca Universel finder, fields of view for 28mm, 35mm,50mm,90mm, 135mm	**D**
35mm optical finder	**C+**
Sports finder	**D–**
Focanox, brightline finder for 50mm lenses	**D**
Micro Foca mirror box	**Rare F**
Focascaph underwater housing	**E+**

Lenses for Focaflex IIF

3.5cm f4 Retroplex	**D–**
9cm f4 Teleoplex	**D**
15cm f4 Super-Teleoplex	**Rare F**

*Foca screwmount lenses are not the
same thread size as Leica screw.*

Amourette, c1925.

Oshira Optical Works
Japan

Emi K: **R3* C–**
1956. Lens shutter, 1/25-1/300s; VFR
only; fixed Eminent Colour, or Fujiyama
F2.8, 50mm lens. Not often seen, but
not very valuable.

Emi 35 A: **R3* C+**
1956. Lens shutter, 1-1/300s; VFR only;
fixed Tri-Lausar Anistigmat f3.5, 45mm
lens. Not often seen.

Osterreichishe Telephon A.G.
Vienna, Austria

Amourette: **R4* F**
c1925. 35mm camera. Double
microscope 35mm f6.3 lens; shutter
1/25-1/100s. 50 exp on 35mm film in
special double cassette. First camera to
have form of interchangeable back.

Thomas Ottewill
England

Ottewill 8 x 10 Wet Plate Camera:
                                            FR5* H
c1856, sliding box and wet plate
camera; Andrew Ross lens.

Ottico Meccanica Italiana, OMI
Rome, Italy

Sunshine: **R5* H–**
c1947. Three-lens 35mm VFR camera
for three colour separation negatives,
each 9 x 12mm on standard 35mm film.
f3.5, 35mm lenses; simple shutter. The
negatives were contact printed into
positives, and then the camera was used
as a projector for viewing the resulting
full colour pictures! Rare and
interesting, this camera has a very
volatile price. (price indicated includes
all parts for using as projector.)

Owla

Owla
Japan

Owla Stereo: **R3* E**
c1958. 35mm VFR stereo camera.
Focusing Owla Anistigmat 35mm, f3.5
lenses; shutter speeds 1/10-1/200s; top
mounted accessory shoe. Two versions
seem to exist with different focusing
knobs.

Owla Stereo, c1958.

P

Panon Camera Co
Tokyo, Japan

Panon Camera: **R3* H–**

1952. Wide-angle panoramic VFR camera for 6 exp on 120 roll film. Panon 50mm, f2.8 coated lens; 140° coverage angle.

Widelux: **R3* H**

1959. Panoramic camera for 24 x 59mm images on 35mm film. 26mm f2.8 Lux lens rotates during exposure to give 140° angle of view. Speed of rotation determines shutter speeds 1/5s, 1/50s & 1/200. Apertures to f11.

Note: New models of the Widelux have been produced since this original version, right up until the present day. They include the Widelux FV, F6, F6B and F7. Later models tend to be bought for use rather than collecting.

Papigny

Jumelle Papigny: **R3* E+**
c1902. 8 x 16cm Box-type stereo camera. Chevalier 10cm, f6.5 lens; speed guillotine shutter. Bellows; rack focusing; central finder. 8 x 8cm exp on plates.

Parker Pen Company
Janesville, Wisconsin, USA

The Parker Camera: **R4* G+**
c1948-50. Subminiature camera. Black & white or colour daylight loading cartridge; film exposed on inner rim of cartridge through mirror.

H.V. Parsells et Fils
France

Parsell's Detective Camera: **R5* D–**
c1885. Wooden box-type detective camera. Rapid rectilinear lens; pneumatic front-of-lens shutter; 6 double holders, 6.5 x 6.5cm exp. Tripod in form of cane. With tripod.

Pax Golden View: **R3* D+**
c1954. 35mm RFR camera. Luminor Anastigmat 45mm, f3.5 lens; 1/10-1/300s. Mfd in Japan.

Pax Golden View, c1954.

Samuel Peck & Co
New Haven, Connecticut, USA

Peck Four-Tube Ferrotype Camera:
                                    R5* G–
c1868. Takes four ninth-plate tintypes.

VEB Pentacon
see Guthe & Thorsch

Perken Son & Rayment
London, England

Optimus Detective Camera: R5* F+
c1890. Leather money-pouch type
detective camera; rapid rectilinear lens;
Thornton Pickard FPS. 8 x 10.5cm
plates.

**Perken, Son & Rayment Detective
Camera: R5* F**
c1896. Thornton Pickard roller blind
shutter.

**Perken, Son & Co. Ltd. 4" x 5"
Folding Plate Camera: R3* E**
c1900s. 4" x 5" Folding plate camera;
brass lens and shutter, rotating
diaphragm stops. Removable ground
glass back; reversible back. Front
standard adjustable; leather covered,
brass fittings.

*Perken, Son & Co. Ltd. 4" x 5" Folding
Plate Camera, c1900s.*

**Perken, Son & Rayment
Tailboard Camera: R3* E+**

c1910. P.S. & R. brass barrel Rapid
Euryscope lens slotted for waterhouse
stops. Mahogany finish, brass fittings;
maroon leather bellows and lens cap.

Le Perreaux
France

Stereo Simda: R4* F
c1950. Roussel Microcolor 25mm, f3.5
lenses; shutter 1-1/250s, flash synch.
300 exp on 16mm movie film.

Perry Mason & Co
Boston, Massachusetts, USA

The Argus: **R5* G**
c1890. Leather handbag type detective camera. 12 exp, 8cm diameter; plate changed by turning lens mount.

Harvard Camera: **R4* D+**

c1880. Simple tin box camera finished in black with gold striping; meniscus lens; $2^1/_2$" x 4" pictures on individual glass plates. No shutter, exposure made by removing lens cap. A complete outfit with plates, tripod, and all developing and printing accessories cost $1.75. It was offered at a reduced price (50 cents) to subscribers of the magazine "The Youth's Companion." A variety of different models were produced over a period of about 10 years, all of them very simple. A complete intact outfit is rare indeed and worth easily 2 to 3 times the price of a stand-alone camera.

Le Petit Poucet: **R3* C+**
French magazine camera; 4 x 4cm plates. Mfd in France.

Petri Camera Co
Tokyo, Japan

Fotochrome: **R2* C+**

1965. Made by Petrie for the American importer Fotochrome Inc and used for promotional purposes. Special purpose film pre-loaded in its own cassette gave direct positive colour prints when processed by the Fotochrome company. 5.3 x 8cm. Film runs at right angles to lens. Auto exposure via Selenium cell surrounding lens. Focusing by distance settings and symbols. Built-in flashgun.

W. Phillips
Birmingham, England

Demon Detective Camera No. 1:
                            R5* G

c1889. Small metal detective camera. Achromatic doublet 30mm, f10 lens; rubber band activated flap type, front-of-lens shutter; single exp, 2¼" diameter on 2¼" square dry plates. Invented by Walter O'Reilly; mfd. for American Camera Co., London, England.

Phoenix: **R3* E**
H. Roussel Stylor 13.5cm, f4.5 lens; Compur shutter 1-1/200s. 6" x 9" exp on plates.

Photavit-Werk
Nurnberg, Germany

Photavit I: **R3* D**

c1930. Miniature camera for 14 exp, 24 x 24mm on 35mm film in special cassette. Schneider-Kreuznach Radionar f7, 40mm lens among others, Photavit or Prontor II shutter.

Photavit I Luxus: **R4* E**
c1930. Same as (PW100) but in "Luxus" edition.

Photavit II: **R2* D**
c1935. Miniature camera for 14 exp, 24 x 24mm on 35mm film in special cassette. Primotar f2.9, 40mm lens among others; Compur shutter.

Boltavit: **R4* D+**
c1935. Same camera as (PW102) but for name. Much more rare.

Photavit III: **R3* D**

c1949. Miniature camera for 25 exp, 24 x 24mm on 35mm film in special cassette. Radionar f3.5, 37.5mm lens; Compur shutter.

Photavit IV: **R3* D**
c1950. Miniature camera for 25 exp, 24 x 24mm on 35mm film in special cassette. Xenar f2.8, 40mm lens; Compur shutter.

Photavit V: **R3* D**
c1950. As (PW105) but with Luxar f2.9 lens.

Photina I: **R2* C+**
c1950. TLR for 6 x 6cm frames on 120 roll film. f4.5, 75mm lens; Vario shutter.

Photina II: **R2* C+**
c1950. TLR for 6 x 6cm frames on 120 roll film. f3.5, 75mm lens; Prontor shutter.

Photina Reflex: R2* C+

c1955. TLR for 6 x 6cm frames on 120 roll film. f3.7, 75mm lens geared to viewing lens for focusing much like the Ricohflex; Prontor shutter.

Photavit 36: R3* C+

c1956. 35mm RFR camera. The first 24 x 36mm "full frame" camera from Photavit. Interchangeable Ennit f2.8, 45mm lens; Prontor-SVS shutter; CRF.

Photavit 36B: R2* C+

c1956. Built-in light meter.

Photavit 36 Automatic: R3* C+

c1958. 35mm RFR camera. Interchangeable Ennalyt f1.9, 50mm lens; Prontor-SLK shutter; coupled built-in light meter.

Photo Cycle: R4* D+

c1895. Berthiot Eurigraphe 135mm, f8 lens; Thornton Pickard shutter, 1/15-1/90s; 10 x 12cm exp on roll film. Mfd in France.

Photo-Etui-Jumelle: R5* G+

c1892. Binocular case detective camera. Rapid rectilinear 120mm, f12 lens; central guillotine shutter; 9 x 12cm plates. Patented by Frank-Valery.

Photolet: R3* D

c1935. Meniscus 31mm, f8 lens; single speed rotary shutter; 20 x 20mm exp. Mfd in France.

Photo Developments Ltd
Birmingham, England

Envoy Wideangle: R3* E

1950. Wideangle camera for 8 exp 5.5x8cm on 120. 64mm Envoy fixed focus lens gives 82° angle of view and has apertures marked to f11, but opens wider, probably to f6.5. Shutter 1/25-1/150s + T & B. Could also be used with cut film back.

Photogrammetry Inc
USA

Underwater Panoramic Camera:
R5* E+

c1950s. Drum-shaped camera, takes 70mm film in cassettes to produce 6 x 19cm images. Convex glass side becomes part of the optical system under water. Exposure made by rotating lens. Very rare.

The Photo Materials Co
Rochester, New York, USA

The Trokonet Camera:　　R4* F–

c1895. 4" x 5" Magazine camera. 30 exp, 4" x 5" or 12 glass plates.

Photo-See Corp
New York, USA

Photo-See:　　　　R3* B+
c1939. Simple camera for direct positive paper photography. After exposing the paper, it was developed and fixed in a single solution tank fitted to the camera. Really a primitive form of a street photographers camera. Not exactly an "instant" camera but results were possible in several minutes. A number of these turned up in New York in their original boxes several years ago keeping the price down.

Picopoulos Camera Service
Greece

Picopoulos Camera Service was founded in 1936 by Dimitri Picopoulos for the repair of all types of photographic and optical equipment. The workshop is still running today, specialising in camera repairs from the earliest models up to the latest technology.

Picca:　　　　　　R5* F

1952. Probably the only real attempt at camera manufacture in Greece, designed and produced by Dimitri Picopoulos. All metal body with retractable German lens, made for rollfilm. The camera was withdrawn in 1953, due to lack of Government funding.

John Piggott
London, England

English Sliding Box Wet-Plate Camera:
R5* G+

c1858. Petzval type lens.

Pignons S.A.
Ballaigues, Switzerland

Bolca I: **R4* F+**
c1942-1946. 35mm SLR camera. S.O.M. Berthiot 50mm, f2.9 lens; interchangeable bayonet mount; CFPS 1-1/1000s. Waist level reflex finder; split image RFR. Some late models were marked "Bolsey Model A", rare.

Bolca (Standard):   **R4* G+**
c1942-1946. 35mm SLR camera. S.O.M. Berthiot 50mm, f2.9 lens, interchangeable bayonet mount; CFPS 1-1/1000s. Split image RFR.

Alpa (I Standard):   **R4* G**

c1947-1952. 35mm SLR camera. Angenieux 50mm, f2.9 lens; interchangeable bayonet mount; CFPS 1-1/1000s, some without slow speeds, only 1/25-1/1000s. Split image RFR. Snr begins at 11,000. Without slow speeds, prices 25% more.

Alpa (II) Reflex: **R3* F+**
35mm SLR camera. Angenieux 50mm, f2.9 lens, interchangeable bayonet mount; CFPS 1-1/1000s. Split image RFR; waist level reflex finder with flip-up magnifier. Also sold as Bolsey Reflex; called Alpax or Bolsey Reflex G with Angenieux 50mm f2.9 lens; Alitax or

Bolsey Reflex H with Angenieux 50mm, f1.8 lens. With f2.9 lens, or with f1.8.

Alpa (II) Reflex.

Alpa (III) Prisma Reflex: **R3* F+**
c1949-1952. 35mm SLR camera. Angenieux 50mm, f2.9 lens, interchangeable bayonet mount; CFPS 1-1/1000s. Split image RFR; 45 degree Kern prism finder. Called Primitax with f1.8 lens. With either lens, also with Xenon 50mm f2.0 lens.

Alpa 4:   **R3* F+**
c1952-1960. 35mm SLR camera. Spektros Alovar f3.5 lens, interchangeable bayonet mount; CFPS 1-1/1000s. on a single dial. Enclosed (fixed housing and magnifier) 90 degree reflex vf; redesigned body configuration.

Alpa 5:   **R3* F+**
c1952-1960. 35mm SLR camera. Old Delft Alfinon f2.8 or Kern Switar f1.8 lens, interchangeable bayonet mount; CFPS 1-1/1000s. on single dial. 45 degree Kern eye level prism finder.

Alpa 6:   **R3* F**
c1955-1959. 35mm SLR camera. Old Delft Alfinon f2.8 or Kern Switar f1.8 lens, interchangeable bayonet mount; CFPS 1-1/1000s on single dial. Self-timer; prism RFR on ground glass.

Alpa 7:   R3* F

c1952-1959. 35mm SLR camera. Kern Switar f1.8 lens, interchangeable bayonet mount; CFPS 1-1/1000s on single dial. Coupled RFR (vertical base) and multi-focal (50-90-135) combined vf.

Alpa 8:   R3* G

c1958-1959. 35mm SLR camera. Kern Switar f1.8 lens, interchangeable bayonet mount; CFPS 1-1/1000s on single dial. Added coupled RFR (vertical base) and multi-focal (50-90-135) combined vf; with prism RFR.

Alpa 7s: R4* G+

c1958-1959. Half-frame 35mm SLR camera. Kern Switar f1.8 lens, interchangeable bayonet mount; CFPS 1-1/1000s on single dial. Added coupled RFR (vertical base) and multi-focal (50-90-135) combined vf; single frame (18 x 24mm).

Alpa 4b: R3* F+

c1959-1965. 35mm SLR camera. Spektros Alovar f3.5 lens, interchangeable bayonet mount; CFPS 1-1/1000s on single dial. Enclosed (fixed housing and magnifier) 90 degree reflex vf; rapid return mirror; lever wind.

Alpa 5b: R3* F+

c1959-1965. 35mm SLR camera. Kern Macro Switar f1.8 lens; focus to 8"; interchangeable bayonet mount; CFPS 1-1/1000s on single dial. 45 degree Kern eye level prism finder; rapid return mirror; lever wind.

Alpa 6b: R3* F

c1959-74. 35mm SLR camera. Macro Switar f1.8 lens, interchangeable bayonet mount; CFPS 1-1/1000s on single dial. Self-timer, prism RFR on ground glass; rapid return mirror; lever wind.

Alpa 7b: R3* G

c1959-1970. 35mm SLR camera. Macro Switar f1.8 lens, interchangeable bayonet mount; CFPS 1-1/1000s on single dial. Coupled RFR (vertical base) and multi-focal (50-90-135) combined vf; rapid return mirror; lever wind.

Alpa 8b: R3* F+

c1956-1969. 35mm SLR camera. Macro Switar f1.8 lens, interchangeable bayonet mount; CFPS 1-1/1000s on single dial. Prism RFR on ground glass; rapid return mirror; lever wind.

Alpa 6c: **R3* F**
c1960-1969. 35mm SLR camera. Macro Switar f1.8 lens, interchangeable bayonet mount; CFPS 1-1/1000s on single dial. Redesigned prism, straight through viewing, and uncoupled selenium exp meter; rapid return mirror; lever wind.

Alpa 9d: **R4* F+**
c1964-1969. 35mm SLR camera. Macro Switar f1.8 lens, interchangeable bayonet mount; CFPS 1-1/1000s on single dial. Through-the-lens match needle Cds meter, uncoupled. Some models gold or black finish with red or green covering.

Alpa 9f: **R3* G+**
c1965-1967. 35mm SLR camera. Macro Switar f1.8 lens, interchangeable bayonet mount; CFPS 1-1/1000s on single dial.

Alpa 10d: **R3* F+**
                       Coloured models F+

c1968-1972. 35mm SLR camera. Reformulated Macro Switar f1.9 lens, interchangeable bayonet mount. Redesigned body configuration; through-the-lens match needle Cds meter; cross coupled zero centre meter. Some models gold or black finish with red or green covering.

Alpa 11e: **R3* G**
                       Coloured models F+
c1970-1972. 35mm SLR camera. Reformulated Micro Switar f1.9 lens, interchangeable bayonet mount; CFPS 1-1/1000s on single dial. Cross coupled zero centre meter with illuminated over-under exp arrows in finder. Some models gold or black finish with red or green covering.

Alpa 10s: **R3* G+**
c1972. Half-frame 35mm SLR camera. Reformulated Macro Switar f1.9 lens, interchangeable bayonet mount; CFPS 1-1/1000s on single dial. Redesigned body configuration; cross coupled zero centre meter; single frame (18 x 24mm).

Alpa 10f: **R3* F+**
c1968-1972. 35mm SLR camera. Reformulated Micro Switar f1.9 lens, interchangeable bayonet mount; CFPS 1-1/1000s on single dial. No meter.

Alpa 11el: **R3* G**
c1972-1974. 35mm SLR camera. Reformulated Micro Switar f1.9 lens, interchangeable bayonet mount; CFPS 1-1/1000s on single dial. Cross coupled zero centre meter with illuminated over-under exp arrows in finder.

Alpa 11si: **R3* G+**
                       Gold models H
35mm SLR camera. Reformulated Microc1976-1978. Switar f1.9 lens, interchangeable bayonet mount; CFPS 1-1/1000s on single dial. Cross coupled zero centre meter (red, green, yellow L.E.D.s). Most have black finish.

Alpa 11z: **R3* H–**
c1977. Half-frame 35mm SLR camera. Reformulated Micro Switar f1.9 lens, interchangeable bayonet mount; CFPS 1/60s. No meter; single frame (18 x 24mm). Very rare.

Alpa 11fs: **R3* G+**
c1977. Half-frame 35mm SLR camera. Reformulated Micro Switar f1.9 lens, interchangeable bayonet mount; CFPS 1-1/1000s on single dial. Cross coupled zero centre meter; single frame (18 x 24mm).

Pinnock Rty Ltd
Sydney, Australia

Gymea Minor: **R5* NSR**

c1948. Metal box camera for 6 x 6cm frames on roll film. Simple lens and shutter. Perhaps fifty prototype cameras were made for Pinnock which itself made photographic darkroom equipment and sewing machines. The Gymea was never sold to the public.

Pinnock 35:   **R5* NSR**
Announced January, 1947. 35mm camera. Copy of the Leica Standard, at least one prototype camera was made, and was seen by Australian lens designer and manufacturer Eric Waterhouse. No camera is known to exist today.

Plaubel & Co
Frankfurt, Germany

Plaubel Makina I: **R3* E**

c1924. 6.5 x 9cm Press camera. Anticomar 100mm, f2.9 lens, front elements removable; can be replaced with wide-angle and telephoto components; Compur dial-set shutter 1-1/300s. The Makina I was introduced in 1920 and discontinued in 1932. It came with non-removable 100mm, f4.5 Anticomar lens until 1924; after this it came with 100mm, f2.9 Anticomar lens with removable front elements. 6.5 x 9cm exp on sheet film.

Plaubel Makina II (1938):   **R3* E**
c1938. 6.5 x 9cm Press camera. Anticomar 100mm, f2.9 lens; Compur shutter 1-1/200s. 6.5 x 9cm exp on sheet film.

Plaubel Makina II, c1938.

Plaubel Makina IIS: R4* F
1938. Similar to Makina II, but with all lens elements now in front of the shutter. Choice of two new interchangeable lenses – 10cm f2.9 Anticomar or 7.3cm f6.8 Orthar wideangle. Tele-Makinar S 19mm f4.8 long focus lens also available.

Plaubel Makina III: R3* F
c1949. 6.5 x 9cm press camera; Anticomar 100mm f2.9 lens; Compur shutter 1-1/200s.

Plaubel Makinette: R4* F+

c1935. Miniature roll film camera. Supercomar 45mm, f2 lens; Compur shutter 1-1/300s. 1¼" x 1⅝" exp on 127 roll film.

Plaubel Rollop: R3* E

c1935. Folding roll film camera. Anticomar 75mm, f2.8 lens; Compur Rapid shutter 1-1/400s; CRF; 16 exp on 120 roll film.

Veriwide: R4* A
1960. Wideangle camera giving a 100° angle of view on 120 film. 47mm f8 Super Angulon lens. Similar in style to Contarex Hologon, but made for rollfilm rather than 35mm.

Plucker's Pocket Stereograph:
R5* G+
c1871. Darlot 21cm, f8 Planigraph lens; built-in circular shutter; 13 x 18cm exp on plates. Mfg. by various opticians, including Dubroni.

Polaroid Inc
Cambridge, Massachusetts, USA

Model 95: R3* F

1948. The first instant picture camera. Folding design. Apertures f11-f45, speeds 1/8-1/60s, linked and controlled by single dial, numbered 1-8. Took Polaroid's first instant rollfilm to make sepia pictures in around a minute. Early models had rigid viewfinder mast, later models had folding mast.

Polaroid 95A:	R2* B+
Polaroid 95B:	R2* B+
Polaroid 80:	R2* A
Polaroid 80A:	R2* A
Polaroid 80B:	R2* A

Polaroid J33: R2* A
1961. Programmed automation 1/15s at f19 to 1/1000s at f64. Built in flashgun for AG1 bulbs.

Polaroid J66: R2* A

Automatic 100: R2* A
1963. World's first camera with fully automated electronic shutter. First Polaroid camera for flat pack film in place of previous rollfilm.

Polaroid 101:	R2* A
Polaroid 110:	R2* B
Polaroid 110A:	R2* C
Polaroid 110B:	R2* C
Polaroid 150:	R2* A
Polaroid 160:	R2* B+

Polaroid 180: R3* E+

Polaroid 195:	R3* F–
Polaroid 210:	R2* B–

Polaroid 420: R1* B–

Polaroid 450:	R1* B–
Polaroid 800:	R1* B–
Polaroid 900:	R1* B–

Highlander: R2* B

1954. First Model 80 uses similar exposure system to Model 95. Model 80S changes numbers to exposure values. Model 80B with parallax correction marks in viewfinder.

Electric Eye: R2* B

1960. First Polaroid camera to offer auto exposure with programmed automation from $1/_2$s at f8.8 to 1/600s at f82. Lighten darken control for manual adjustment.

Polaroid SX70: R2* D–

Polaroid SX70, Model II: R2* D

Polaroid SX70 Sonar: R2* C+

Big Shot: R2* B+

1971. Made specifically for portraiture. Lens fixed focus at 1 metre with built-in rangefinder set for same distance. Flashcube slots behind diffuser panel on top.

Polaroid

Polaroid Cool-Cam: **R2* B+**
c1980. Simple to use inexpensive point and shoot auto focus, auto exposure, instant imaging camera for images 3" x 3$\frac{1}{2}$". Originally sold with sunglasses. Pink for the ladies.

Popular Photograph Co
New York

Nodark Ferrotype Camera: **R4* F+**
c1899. Wooden box camera. Magazine loading; 26 exp, 2$\frac{1}{2}$" x 3$\frac{1}{2}$" on ferrotype plates.

Nodark Ferrotype Camera, c1899.

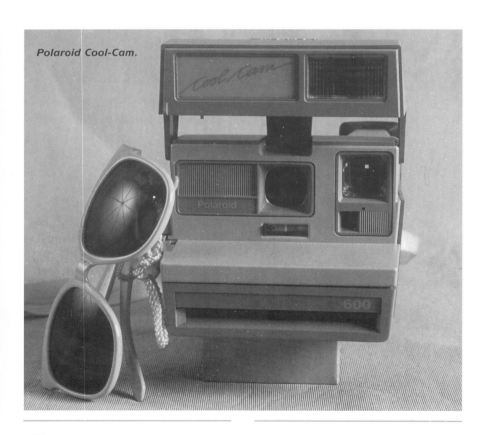

Polaroid Cool-Cam.

Xavier Portafax
France

Photo Volume: R5* G

c1894. Book-type detective camera. Rapid rectilinear or Zeiss lens; direct vf. 9 x 12cm plates.

Premier Instrument Corp
New York, USA

Kardon: R3* F

1945. Leica copy. Cfps, 1-1/1000s; diopter adjustment; screw mount f2, 47mm Kodak Ektar. (The exact year of manufacture can be determined using the code described in the ID section of this book.) The military model has enlarged shutter winding and release controls, allowing use of the camera while wearing gloves. The military model now sells for about 20% less than the civilian model. Price given is for a civilian model with lens.

Kardon, Leica facsimile.

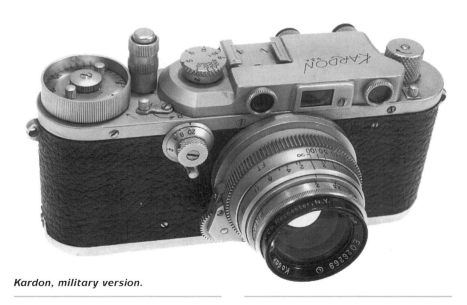

Kardon, military version.

R

Ray Camera Co
refer to Mutschler, Robertson & Co

The Record Camera: **R5* G**
TLR box camera. All wooden body;
single exp, 3¼" x 4". Mfr unknown –
English construction.

Rectaflex Starea
Rome, Italy

Rectaflex 1000:   **R3* F**

c1949. 35mm SLR with interchangeable
Xenon f2, 50mm lens among others.
CFPS 1-1/1000s. Historically important,
along with the Contax S, as being the
first 35mm SLR with fixed pentaprism
sold on the marketplace.

Rectaflex 1300:   **R3* F**
c1950. 35mm SLR camera with
interchangeable Angenieux f1.8, 50mm
lens, among others. CFPS 1-1/1300s.

Rectaflex Rotor with gunstock: R4* H
c1950. With special rotating mount for
three different lenses, including
Angenieux f1.8, 90mm, f1.8, 50mm and
f2.8, 35mm.

Rectaflex Rotor with gunstock, c1950.

Rectaflex Junior: **R3* E+**
c1950. 35mm SLR with interchangeable
Xenon f2.8, 50mm lens among others.
CFPS 1/25-1/500s. The cheaper version
of the Rectaflex.

Recta: **R5* NSR**
c1953. 35mm RFR camera with
interchangeable Westar f3.5, 50mm
lens. CFPS 1-1/1000s. Made in only
small numbers, (some say 6!) this
camera never made it to the market
place.

Director 35:   **R5* NSR**
c1954. 35mm VFR camera. 39mm
screw mount; FPS; made only in
prototype units, never delivered to
the public.

Reflex Camera Co
Newark, New Jersey, USA

Focal Plane Postcard Camera: R4* E–
c1912. Postcard size camera; FPS. Ground glass focusing back; 3¼" x 4¼" exposure.

Junior Reflex Camera: R3* D
c1903. 3¼" x 4¼" box-type SLR; fixed focus lens; 4-speed shutter.

Reflex Camera: R3* E+
c1898. Anastigmat 210mm f16 lens; variable speed FPS; 5" x 7" plates, space for 3 double holders.

Reid & Sigrist Ltd
Leicester, England

Reid III: R3* F+

1951-55. Cfps, 1-1/1000s. Type I had no flash synch, while type II used synch contacts marked "E" for electronic flash, and "B" for bulbs. Screw mount Taylor-Hobson f2, 2" lens. This camera is a high quality copy of the Leica III B. In 1958 Reid announced Models II and IA. Type II cameras are valued 25% less than type I cameras. Price given is for type I camera with normal lens.

Reid II: R4* H

1953. Similar to the original Reid III but with flash synch added. Flash is connected via two sockets beside the slow speed dial. Sockets marked 'E' for electronic flash or F class bulbs, or 'B' for normal expendable bulbs.

Reid I: R3* R
1958-62. Cfps, 1/20-1/1000s; no Rfr; Vfr only. Screw mount Taylor-Hobson f2, 2" lens. Originally offered at £20 less than the Reid III camera, the Reid I is found mostly in the ex-military version. This military version can easily be identified by the code impressed into the leather on the back of the camera body, consisting of the letters A.P., A.P.F., or F. followed by the numbers 8810, or marked entirely in numbers, such as 0553/8810. These markings are known, though others may exist. It is thought about 1500 of these cameras were made.

Revere Camera Co
Chicago, Illinois, USA

Revere Stereo 33:   R3* E–

c1952. 35mm stereo camera. Wollensak Revere Amaton 35mm f3.5 lenses; Synchromatic or Rapax shutter ½-1/2000s; MFX synch; crf.

Rex Magazine Camera Co.
Chicago, Illinois, USA

Rex Magazine Camera: R3* E–
c1899, meniscus lens; single speed shutter. Magazine load: 4" x 5" dry plates changed by wooden sheath.

Rex Photographic Outfit: R3* C–
cardboard box camera, covered with black paper; 2" x 2" exp on dry plates.

Jules Richard
Paris, France

Glyphoscope (first type):   R2* D
1904. Stereo camera, made as a simplified version of the same company's more sophisticated Veroscope. Fixed focus and instantaneous shutter. With the shutter assembly removed from the front and the plate holder removed from the back, the camera became a stereoscope for viewing stereo pictures.

Glyphoscope (second type):   R2* D

1905. Similar to first model, but with ebonite body in more angular design.

Filmpack Glyphoscope: R3* D
1925. New version of the original camera, introduced for film packs. Takes 45 x 107 mm pack.

Homeos: R5* H–

c1914-1920. 35mm stereo camera. Zeiss Tessar 30mm, f4.5 lens; horizontal guillotine shutter ⅙-1/142s; 2 finders, one on top for horizontal exp, one on left side for vertical exp. 27 stereo exp, 2.5 x 1.9cm or 54 single exp on 35mm film. Qty 1500(?). The Homeos was the first 35mm stereo camera.

Homeoscope: R3* E
1897. Early Richard stereo available for two formats. Fitted with Anastigmat Zeiss Krauss lenses, f/6.3 124mm focal length. Guillotine shutter.

Verascope: R3* D

c1905. Goerz Double Anastigmatic 85mm f6.8 lens; 6 speed guillotine shutter. Plate and roll film magazine.

Verascope F40:   R4* F
c1938. 35mm stereo camera. Optis f4.5 or Berthiot 40mm, f3.5 lens; shutter 1-1/250s; 40 stereo pairs on 35mm film, also single-frame.

Ricoh Co Ltd
Tokyo, Japan

Golden Ricoh "16":   R2* E–

c1956. Subminiature camera. Ricoh 25mm, f3.5 lens; sector shutter 1/50-1/200s; 20 exp on 16mm film on special cassettes.

Ricoh "16":   R2* E
c1956. Subminiature camera. Ricoh 25mm, f2.8 interchangeable lens; shutter 1/50-1/200s; 24 exp, 10 x 14mm on 16mm film in special cassettes.

Ricolet: R2* B+

c1950. 35mm Camera. Ricoh Anastigmat 45mm, f3.5 coated lens; Riken 1/25-1/50s.

Ricoh 35:   R3* D

1955. Similar in shape to the Richolet, but with crf. Riken shutter, speeds 1-1/200s; 4.5cm, f3.5 Riken Ricomat lens.

Ricohflex Model III: R3 C
c1950. Twin lens reflex, fitted with Ricoh anastigmat f3.5 80mm lens. Riken shutter 1/25-100s. 120 rollfilm yielded 12 6 x 6cm images. There were a total of 20 Ricohflex models through about 1959.

Super 44:   R3* D
1959. TLR for 12 exp on 127. 6cm f3.5 Riken lens. Shutter 1-1/400s. Depth of field sale linked to focusing knob.

Super 44, 1959.

company's contemporaries (Chinon, Cosina), early models adopted the M42 Universal screw lens mount made popular by Pentax, then switched to the K-mount bayonet when Pentax introduced that in the 1970s. In this way, Ricoh cameras could be used with the vast variety of independent lenses made for these two popular mounts. Few of these cameras are of real interest to the collector, but full details of Ricoh SLRs can be found in the book Japanese 35mm SLR Cameras by Bill Hansen and Michael Dierdorff, published by Hove Books.

Rietzschel GmbH Optische Fabrik
Munich, Germany

Ricoh XRS: **R3* D**

c1980s. 35mm SLR that used solar panels to charge internal battery. Otherwise conventional aperture priority SLR.

Note: From the mid-1960s, through to the 1990s, Ricoh produced a significant range of quality SLRs, of which the XRS is probably the only one worth collecting due to its solar panels. Like the

Heli-Klack: **R4* F+**

c1920. Folding stereo camera. 3 Interchangeable lenses; Compound shutter; rising front; rack focusing; double extension bellows. 9 x 18cm exp.

Kosmo Klack: **R4* E+**

c1914-1925. 45 x 107mm Stereo camera. Combinable Rietzschel 65mm, f4.5 lens; Stereo Compur 1-1/250s. Panoramic setting; rising lens panel.

Riken Optical Industry
Tokyo, Japan

Steky II: R4* E+
Marked "Made in TOKYO"   R4* E+

1950; 16mm subminiature camera. Stekinar Anastigmat 25mm f3.5 coated lens; 1/25-1/100s; 24 exp, 10 x 14mm on 16mm film in cassettes.

Riley Research
Santa Monica, California, USA

Rilex: R4* D–
1946-47. 2¼" x 3¼" View camera. Kodak Anastigmat Spec. 127mm lens.

John Roberts
Boston, Massachusetts, USA

John Roberts Daguerreotype Camera (1850):   R5* J–
c1850. 8" x 10" daguerreotype camera; Jamin Darlot Sr. Landscape 350mm, f11 lens, sliding box focusing. 8" x 10" or 6½" x 8½" plates. Largest known American daguerreotype camera.

John Roberts Daguerreotype Camera (1850).

John Roberts Daguerreotype Camera (1854):   R5* I
c1854. Holmes, Booth & Hayden, New York lens with reversing prism; ¼ plate daguerreotypes. Boston Box style daguerreotype camera.

C.N. Robinson
Philadelphia, Pennsylvania, USA

Camera Obscura: R5* H+
c1820-1830. 32.5 x 18.5 x 19.5cm; mahogany with dovetail construction; sliding box focusing; 15 x 16cm image.

J. Robinson & Sons
England

Luzo Detective Camera: R4* G
c1890, first British-made box camera; Aplanat 2½", f11 lens; variable speed sector shutter. Used Eastman-type roll film, 100 exp, 6 cm diameter.

Luzo Detective Camera, c1890.

Robot II, c1938-1950.

Robot-Berning & Co
Dusseldorf, Germany

Robot I: R3* D+

c1934-1938. 35mm Motor drive camera. Zeiss Tessar 32.5mm, f2.8 lens; interchangeable screw mount; rotary metal shutter 1-1/500s; 24 x 24mm exp on 35mm film in special cassettes. "Detective-type" swivelling vf. Spring motor: 24 exp on one winding.

Robot II: R3* D+
c1938-1950. 35mm Motor drive camera. Zeiss Biotar 40mm, f2 lens, interchangeable screw mount; rotary metal shutter 1-1/500s; 24 x 24mm exp on 35mm film in special daylight loading cassettes. Spring motor: 24 exp on one winding; optional motor was available for 48 exp on one winding.

Luftwaffe Robot: R3* F

c1940. 35mm Motor drive camera. Schneider Tele-Zenar 75mm, f3.5 lens, interchangeable screw mount; rotary metal shutter ½-1/500s; 24 x 24mm exp on 35mm film in special cassettes. Manufactured for the German Air Force during WWII. One variation has the double spring for 48 exp on a single wind. The finish is black enamel; internal film channel is made from black plastic material. "Luftwaffen Eigentum" always marked on rear of top cover; the Tele-Zenar 75mm f35 is marked "Luftwaffen Eigentum" on rear of lens mount or on side of barrel. Shutter speeds below 1/100s have been ground off the shutter speed dial in some examples.

camera. Schneider Xenar 45mm, f2.8 coated lens; rotary metal shutter ½-1/500s; crf. 24 x 24mm exp. Has auto "burst" operation.

Robot Ila: R3* D+

c1951-1953. 35mm Motor drive camera. Schneider Xenon 40mm, f1.9 lens, interchangeable screw mount; rotary metal shutter ½-1/500s; 24 x 24mm exp on 35mm film in special cassettes. Spring motor for 24 exp on one winding; optional motor was available for 48 exp on one winding.

Robot Royal 36: R3* F+

c1956-1959. 35mm Motor drive camera. Schneider Xenar 45mm, f2.8 coated lens, interchangeable bayonet mount; rotary shutter ½-1/500s, crf. 24 x 36mm exp. No auto "burst" operation.

Robot Junior: R2* D+

c1951-1953. Similar to Robot IIa except does not have adjustment for right angle viewing.

Robot Star I: R3* E–

Robot Royal 24: R2* F

c1956-1959. 35mm Motor drive

c1952-1959. 35mm Motor drive camera. Schneider Xenon 40mm, f1.9 coated lens, interchangeable screw mount; rotary metal shutter ½-1/500s. 24 x 24mm exp on 35mm film in standard cartridge. Spring motor for 24 exp on one winding; optional motor was available for 48 exp on one winding.

Robot Star II: R3* E+

c1958-63. 35mm Motor drive camera. Schneider Xenar f2.8, 38mm or Xenon f1.9, 40mm coated lens, interchangeable screw mount; rotary metal shutter $^1/_2$-1/500s. 24 x 24mm exp on 35mm film in standard cartridge. Spring motor for 18 exp on one winding; optional motor was available for 50 exp on one winding, electromagnetic shutter release, field of view for 40mm and 75mm in VFR.

Robot Star 25: R3* E–

c1960. 35mm Motor drive camera for 25 – 24 x 24mm frames on standard 35mm film with one winding of the built-in spring motor, Xenar f2.8, 38mm lens, burst operation up to 6 frames per second, all metal rotary shutter, $^1/_4$-1/500s, electromagnetic release.

Robot Star 50: R3* H

c1960. With 50 shot spring motor.

Robot 400: R3* F+

c1955. Royal Robot 24 with built-in long film holder for 400 frames 24 x 24 on standard 35mm film, electric motor drive was available in addition to built-in spring motor.

Robot Royal II: R3* F–

c1955. As Royal Robot 24 but without RFR, and without burst operation.

Robot Recorder 24: R3* F

c1958. As Robot Royal 24, but without any finder at all, or burst operation.

Robot Recorder 36: R3* F

c1958. As Robot Royal 36, but without any finder at all.

Accessories for Robot cameras

Ennalyt f4/24mm lens	E–
Primotar f3.5/30mm lens	D
Xenogon f2.8/35mm lens	E–
Tele-Xenar f3.8/75mm lens	E–
Tele-Arton f4/90mm lens	E–
Sonnar f2/90mm lens	F–
Tele-Xenar f4/135mm lens	E
Tele-Xenar f4/150mm lens	E
Tele-Xenar f5.5/200mm lens	E+
universal finder 30mm-150mm	D
30mm optical finder	D
folding finder for 40mm and 75mm	C+
90mm optical finder	D
135mm optical finder	D
200 optical finder	E–
accessory coupled RFR for Robot II	E–
under-water housing	F
beam-splitter microscope adaptor	E
series flash lamp holder (4 lamps)	D+

Rochester Optical and Camera Company
Rochester, New York, USA

The Rochester Optical Company was producing "Premo" cameras in 1893; it merged with several other companies in 1900 to form the Rochester Optical and Camera Company. In 1907 the firm was acquired by the Eastman Kodak Company. From 1907 to 1917 the designation was Rochester Optical Division, Eastman Kodak Company; from 1918 to 1922 – Rochester Optical Department, Eastman Kodak Company.

The Carlton Twin Lens Camera: R5* NSR

c1895. 4" x 5" plate TLR camera.

Carlton View Camera: R4*
4 x 5 size E+
11 x 14 size F–

Folding Gem Poco, c1890s.

c1890s. $6^{1}/_{2}$" x $8^{1}/_{2}$" View camera. Brass tripod base built into lens bed; reversible double swing back; polished wood body with brass fittings. 8 sizes from 4" x 5" to 11" x 14".

The Folding Premier: **R2* D**
c1895. Folding plate camera. Bausch & Lomb pneumatic shutter with built-in rotating waterhouse stops.

The Empire State Camera: **R3***
5 x 7 size E
8 x 10 size E+
11 x 14 size F–

The Handy: **R2* C**
c1895. Box-type camera. 4" x 5" exp on plates.

The Ideal Camera: **R3* D+**
c1895. View camera. Made in 4" x 5", 5" x 7", 8" x 10" sizes.

The Kenwood Camera: **R3* E–**
c1895. Compact view camera. Wide front for stereo lenses. 5" x 7", 8" x 10".

King Poco: **R3* D+**
c1890s. $6^{1}/_{2}$" x $8^{1}/_{2}$" Folding plate camera. Rochester Symmetrical Convertible lens; Unicum shutter. Double extension red leather bellows; horizontal or vertical format swing back; mahogany. Sizes: 4" x 5" to 8" x 10".

c1895. View camera.

Folding Gem Poco: **R3* D+**
c1890s. $3^{1}/_{4}$" x $4^{1}/_{4}$" Folding plate camera. Built-in shutter. Polished wood finish, red bellows. Folded size 6" x $5^{1}/_{4}$" x $1^{1}/_{2}$" ; weight 1 lb.

King View Camera: **R3* E**
c1890s. 8" x 10" View camera. Rising and falling front; front and rear swings; double extension red leather bellows;

polished mahogany, lacquered brass fittings. Sizes: 5" x 7" to 11" x 14". Top of the line view camera, original price $36.

The Long Focus Premo: R3* D+
c1895. 5" x 7" Folding plate camera.

Midget Pocket Camera: R2* D
c1895. Compact view camera. c1895. 4" x 5" exp on plates.

The Monitor Camera: R3* E
c1895. Compact view camera. 4" x 5", 8" x 10".

New Model Camera: R3* E–

c1895. View camera. 4" x 5"; 5" x 7"; 8" x 10".

New Model Improved Camera: R3* E
c1895. View camera. Polished wood finish, nickel plated fittings. 4" x 5"; 5" x 7"; 10" x 8".

New Model Stereo Camera: R4* F

c1895. Stereo view camera.

The Premo: R2* C+
c1895. 4" x 5" folding plate camera.

Poco, Series A: R3* D
c1890s, 4" x 5" Folding plate camera. Symmetrical brass lens. Shifting, rising and falling front; wood interior, red bellows.

Poco, Series B: R3* D–

c1890s. 4" x 5" Folding plate camera. Rapid Rectilinear Symmetrical lens; Unicum shutter. Single swing back; rising front; Poco reversible finder; red bellows.

Poco, Series E: **R3* D**

c1890s. 4" x 5" Folding plate camera; built-in lens and shutter. Polished wood finish, red bellows and leather covered bed; reversible finder. Original price $8. Also in 5" x 7" size.

Pony Premo No. 6:   **R3* D**

c1890s. 4" x 5" Folding plate camera. Goerz Double Anastigmat 5" lens; Eastman Kodak Bausch & Lomb shutter. Reversible back with swings; shifting, rising and falling front; double extension red bellows.

The Premaret: **R3* C+**
c1895. Box-type camera. 4" x 5" exp on plates.

The Premier: **R3* D–**
c1895. Box-type detective camera. Brass lens; built-in shutter in front

swing down face; 4" x 5" exp on plates. Leather exterior, cherrywood interior.

The Premo B: **R2* C+**

c1895. Folding plate camera. 4" x 5" exp on plates.

The Premo C: **R2* C+**
c1895. 4" x 5" Folding plate camera.

The Premo D: **R2* C+**
c1895. 4" x 5" Folding plate camera.

The Premo Sr: **R2* C+**
c1895. 4" x 5" Folding plate camera.

Reversible Back Premo: **R3* D**
c1900. Folding plate camera. Goerz Double Anastigmat $10\frac{3}{4}$", f11 lens; Bausch & Lomb "Iris Diaphragm" shutter. Whole plate size, $6\frac{1}{2}$" x $8\frac{1}{2}$"

Rochester Optical Co. 8" x 10"
View Camera: **R3* E**
c1900s. 8" x 10" view camera; rear Folmer & Schwing FPS; rising and falling front. Polished wood finish, brass fittings; red leather bellows.

Standard View Camera: R3* D+
c1890s. 8" x 10" view camera; rear focus; reversible back; mahogany finish, brass fittings. 7 sizes: 3¼" x 4¼" to 8" x 10" (single or double swing back).

The Stereoscopic Premo: R4* F–
c1895. 5" x 7" Folding plate camera.

Telephoto Poco A: R3* D+
c1902. Rapid Rectilinear lens; Bausch & Lomb shutter. 5" x 7" exp on plates. Polished wood interior, red leather bellows.

Telephoto Cycle B: R3* E
c1900. 5" x 7" Folding. Telephoto Triple Convertible lens or Zeiss, Goerz, Wide Angle or Voigtlander; double extension; reversible back; rising and falling front; back swings horizontally or vertically; mahogany, brass fittings; covered in Moroccan leather. 4 sizes: 4" x 5" to 8" x 10".

Universal Camera: R3* E+
c1890s. Compact folding 5" x 7" view camera. Wide-angle brass lens; rack and pinion focusing; swinging, rising and falling front; polished wood finish with brass fittings. 11 sizes from 3¼" x 4¼" to 17" x 20" in single and double swing models.

New Model View Camera: R3* D
c1895. Wood bellows view camera with a modest number of tilts and swings. The instrument pictured is for 5 x 8" glass plates but they were available in many sizes ranging from 4" x 5" to 8" x 10". They are occasionally found with a simple front mounted shutter, just a slide of wood pulled by gravity past the lens.

New Model View Camera, c1895.

Dr. Rodehuser Kamera Mechanik
Heessen, Germany

Panta: R2* B+

c1948. Metal VFR camera for 6 x 4.5cm frames on 120 roll film. Ennar f4.5, 74mm lens in collapsible tube mount among others, Vario or other shutter.

Rokuwa
Tokyo, Japan

Stereo Rocca: R3* D+
c1955. Stereo camera. Single meniscus 42mm lens; shutter 1/30s, B, flash. Direct vision optical finder; 24 pairs, 24 x 3mm on 120 roll film.

Roland: R4* G

c1931. 1^5/$_8$" x 2^1/$_4$" RFR camera. Kleinbild Plasmat 70mm, f2.7 lens; Compur Rapid shutter 1-1/400 s, crf. 16 exp, 1^5/$_8$" x 2^1/$_4$" on 120 roll film. Probably the first combined range-viewfinder in a commercially produced camera. See picture overleaf.

Andrew Ross
London, England

Andrew Ross Stereo Wet Plate: R5* H–

Sliding box stereo camera. Dovetailed mahogany; brass lenses; rack and pinion focusing.

Thomas Ross & Co
London, England

Panros: R3* E

c1920. Folding camera with focal plane shutter. Designed for high speed, hand-held photography. Made for 3^1/$_2$" x 2^1/$_2$", quarter plate, post card and 5 x 4 inches sizes. Ross Xpress f4.5 plus Ross Homocentric f6.3 and f6.8 lenses.

Photoscope: R5* NSR

c1889. Binocular-type detective camera. Special cassette from roll film allowing 3.5 x 4cm exp. Patented by William Sanders.

Ross Divided: R4* F

c1895. 3^1/$_4$" x 4^1/$_4$" TLR camera. Goerz Doppel Anastigmat f7.7 lenses.

Ross 13" x 18" Tailboard Camera: R3* F–

c1880s. 13" x 18" tailboard camera. Voigtlander & Son, Brauschweig lens; shifting front for stereo; rear tilts and swings; double extension.

Ross Twin Lens Reflex: R4* F+

c1891. Ross Homocentric 7" f6.3 lens; Bausch & Lomb pneumatic shutter 1-1/1000s. 4" x 5" plates; rotating back.

Standard Reflex: R3* E

c1920. Focal plane shutter with fixed tension, exposures adjusted by width of slit. Reversing back, rising and crossing front. Optional swing front could be fitted. Made for 3$\frac{1}{2}$" x 2$\frac{1}{2}$", quarter plate, post card, 5" x 4" and half plate sizes. Ross Xpress f4.5 and Ross Homocentric f6.3 and f6.8 lenses.

Rouch
London, England

Eureka Detective Camera: R4* F

c1888. Mahogany box-form camera. 150mm f6 Doublet lens; behind-the-lens roller blind shutter; flexible leather plate changing bag.

Rouch Excelsior Hand Camera: R4* F

c1890. Two mahogany boxes joined by leather bellows; rack and pinion focusing.

Roussel
Paris, France

Stella Jumelle: R3* E

c1900. 9 x 12cm Stereo camera; Anti Spectroscopique 130mm f7.7 lens; 7 speed guillotine shutter.

Rubix: R4* E–

c1950. Subminiature camera. Hope 5mm f3.5 lens; shutter 1/25-1/100s; 50 exp, 10 x 14mm on 16mm film. Mfg. in Japan.

Royer
France

Savoyflex Automatique: R4* D

c.1958. 35mm SLR with Selenium cell to offer automation. Shutter and aperture priorities. 50mm f2.8 Som Berthiot lens. Prontor Reflex shutter 1-1/300s + B.

Teleroy: R3* D+

1951. Folding camera for 8 or 16 exposures on 120 or 620. Coupled split image rangefinder. 100mm f3.5 Angenieux lens. Shutter 1-1/300s + B. Synch at 1/25s.

Rubix, c1950.

S

Saint-Etienne
France

Universal: R4* F

c1908. Folding plate camera that could be adapted for rollfilm with the addition of a special back. f6.8 Beckers lens stopping down to f64. Unicum shutter $^1/_2$-1/100s.

Sakura
Japan

Petal: R3* F
Hexagonal style   F
Round style   E

c1950. Watch-type detective camera. 6 Circular exp, on 25mm diameter disc of film. Round style, Hexagonal style, Petal Outfit: film cutter, developing holder and two tins of film discs, in wooden boxes with directions.

Samei Sangyo
Japan

Samoca 35II: R2* B+

c1957. 35mm Camera. C. Ezumar 50mm, 3.5 lens; shutter 1/25-1/100s.

Samoca 35III: R2* B+
c1958. 35mm Camera. Ezumar Anastigmat 50mm, 3.5 lens; very similar to the Samoca II, except for the name and faster shutter!

Samoca Super: R3* C

c1956. 35mm Camera. C. Ezumar 50mm, 2.8 lens; CRF and (sometimes) built-in lightmeter; btl shutter speeds 1-1/200s. Its value lies in its strange looks!

Samocaflex: R4* E+

1955. 35mm TLR. Waist-level finder with split image rangefinder, plus direct vision viewfinder. First model with Seikosha Rapid shutter, following year with Seikosha MX shutter. 50mm f2.8 lenses. 1-1/500s + B.

San Georgio
Italy

Parva: R5* J

1947. Very rare 16mm subminiature. 2cm f3.5 San Georgio Essegi interchangeable lens (though no evidence of other lenses). FP shutter 1/40s, 1/100s & 1/150s. Eye-level finder.

Sawyers Inc
Portland, Oregon, USA

Mark IV: R2* C+
c1959. 127 Roll film TLR camera. Topcor 6cm, f2.8 coated lens; shutter 1-1/500s; 12 exp on 127 roll film.

View-Master Personal Stereo Camera:
R3* E

c1952-1960. 35mm Stereo camera. Anastigmat 25mm, f3.5 coated lenses; guillotine shutter 1/10-1/1000s; flash. Double run 5mm film produces 37 pairs on 20 exp film, or 69 pairs on 36 exp film. View master format.

View-Master accessories

Close-up attachment – 24" with case   **D**

Close-up attachment – 36" with case   **D**

Viewmaster film cutter   **D+**

View-Master Stereo Colour Camera:
                                    R3* F

c1950. German made for the European market. 35mm stereo vfr camera for viewmaster format stereo pairs. Rodenstock Trinar 20mm, f2.8 fixed focus lenses shutter coupled to lens opening using EV scale; slanting film travel allows all the frames to be made without rewinding the film, as on the Viewmaster Personal Stereo Camera. More often seen in Europe than the USA, where the price is often 25% lower.

View-Master Stereo Europe: **R E–**
Manufactured in Germany.

A. Schaeffner
Paris, France

Photo Album: **R5* H**
c1890. Book detective camera. Achromat 120mm, f12 lens; guillotine shutter. 9 x 12cm plates in metal double plate holders. Also available with rapid rectilinear lens and central guillotine shutter. Invented by Cadot.

Schlesicky & Strohlein of Leipzig
Leipzig, Germany

The Comfort: **R4* F–**
c1890. Leather covered detective camera. Achromatic 80mm, f7.5 lens; vertical guillotine shutter; 6 x 7.3cm exp on 8 dry plates. A turn of a spool brings the new plate into position. Invented by C. F. Schlesicky.

Field Camera: **R3* E–**
c1880s. 24 x 30mm Field camera. Brass convertible lens. Blue bellows; mahogany finish; brass fittings; black striped edges.

Schmitz & Theinemann
Dresden, Germany

Uniflex: **R3* D–**
c1933. Unar 75mm, f4.5 lens; self-cocking Pronto shutter coupled to the mirror

Uniflex Reflex Meteor: **R3* D**
c1931. Trioplan 105mm, f4.5 lens; Pronto shutter; front element focusing. Box camera for 6 x 9cm exp.

Scovill Mfg Co
proprietors of American Optical Co
New York, USA

American Optical Revolving Back Camera: **R3* E–**
c1888. 5" x 8" Revolving back camera. Front focus; revolving back (Flaming's patent); Daisy dry plate holder. Sizes: 4" x 5" to 8" x 10".

American Optical Revolving Back Camera, c1888.

Book Camera, c1892.

American Optical View Camera:

                                R3* D+

c1883. Brass fittings and lens; lens slotted for waterhouse stops; 5½" x 8½" exp on plates.

Antique Oak Detective Camera: R4* F

c1892. Wooden box-type detective camera. 4" x 5" exp on plates.

Book Camera: R5* I+

c1892. Book-type detective camera. Achromatised periscopic 75mm, f12 lens; variable speed horizontal guillotine shutter. Single exp on 4" x 5" dry plates.

Centennial Stereo Outfit: R4* F+

c1876. 5" x 8" Stereo outfit. Matched pair of stereo lenses, single achromatic Scovill lens; swing back; polished mahogany, brass fittings. Nickel plated label: American Optical Co., New York. Scovill Mfg. Co. proprietors.

Klondike: R3* C+

c1898. Meniscus lens; rotary shutter, T and I. 4" x 5" dry plates.

Knack Detective Camera: R4* E

c1891. Box-type detective camera. 4" x 5" exp on plates.

Scovill 4" x 5" Vertical View Camera:
R3* D+

c1881. R. Morrison N.Y. lens, rotating stops. No rising front. With holder and case.

Scovill 5" x 8" View Camera: R3* D+

c1888. Waterbury lens; rotating stops; original box in brass and light mahogany.

The Triad Camera: R4* E
c1892. Leather covered box-type detective camera. 4" x 5" Exp on plates or roll film – using an Eastman Walker roll holder.

Scovill Detective Camera: R4* F+
c1886. Leather covered box-type detective camera. 4 x 5 Size; Instantaneous lens; variable speed rotary shutter. 4" x 5" exp on plates. 4 sizes: 8 x 10.5cm; 10.5 x 12.5cm; 11.5 x 16.5cm; 13 x 18cm. In 1888 a pivoting vf was adapted to the camera.

Scovill Detective Camera, c1886.

Waterbury Detective Camera
(Original Model): R4* E+
c1888. Black painted box type detective camera. String cocking shutter; 4" x 5" exp on plates. Storage for extra plate holder in recessed base of camera; "T" bar extends through base of camera for focusing.

Waterbury Detective Camera
(Second Model): R4* E+
c1890. Leather covered box-type detective camera. 4" x 5" Exp on plates. "T" bar extend through base of camera for focusing.

Improved Waterbury Detective
Camera: R4* E+
c1892. Leather covered box-type detective camera. 4" x 5" Exp on dry plates. The focusing knob has been positioned on the top front of the camera body.

Scovill

Waterbury 5" x 8" Field Camera:
R4* F–

c1885. Rubber-band shutter. Original price, $17.

Sears, Roebuck & Co
Chicago, Illinois, USA

Kewpie Kamera: R1* A
c1921. Leatherette covered box roll film camera.; 2¼" x 3¼" Exp on 120 roll film.

Seroco 8" x 10" View Camera: R3* E–
c1920. 8" x 10" View camera. Conley lens; Auto shutter. Front and rear focusing; rising and falling front; mahogany; nickel-plated.

Seroco Stereo Camera: R4* E+
c1920. Seroco 4" x 5" Rapid Symmetrical lenses; Wollensak shutter; 5" x 7" exp on plates. Brown leather covered wood, red bellows.

Tower Type 3: R3* F–
c1950, 35mm RFR camera, Nikkor 50mm f2 coated lens, interchangeable screw mount; CFPS 1-1/500 s, Copy of Leica IIIa, made in Japan by Nicca Camera Company, (Nicca III or IIIA) sold by Sears, Roebuck & Co.

Tower Type 3S: R3* F–
c1951. Added flash synch, (Nicca IIIB).

Tower 35: R3* F–
c1956. 35mm RFR camera with interchangeable Nikkor f2.8, 50mm lens; CFPS 1-1/1000s, (Nicca 3F) with lever or knob wind.

Tower 45: R3* F–
c1957. 35mm RFR camera with interchangeable f2, 50mm Nikkor screw mount len; CFPS 1-1/1000s; flash calculator on the hinged back, (Nicca 5L).

Tower 46: R3* F
c1957. Delivered with Nikkor f1.4, 50mm lens.

Tower Stereo: R3* D+
c1954. 35mm Stereo camera. Vfr; Isconar 35mm, f3.5 lenses; Prontor S shutter 1-1/300s. Made by Wilhelm Witt of Hamburg, West Germany for Sears. similar to the Iloca Stereo II.

Secam
Paris, France

Stereophot: R4* E–
c1955. Stereo version of pen camera. Consists of two Stylophot cameras mounted on a bracket, with tripod attachment. Leather carrying case.

Stylophot Standard: R4* E–

1955. Pen-type detective camera. f6.3 Coated lens; fixed shutter speed of 1/50s. 10 x 10mm on 16mm film in a special cassette. Camera is in shape of large pen. Auto film transport advances film and cocks shutter.

Stylophot Deluxe: R4* E

c1956. Pen-type detective camera. Roussel Anastigmat 27mm, f3.5 lens; fixed shutter speed of 1/50s. 18 exp, 10 x 10mm on 16mm film in a special cassette.

H. Seemann Stereo Camera: R4* F–

c1910. Wooden stereo camera. Pair of Goerz Dagor 120mm lenses, original cap; sliding front focus; ground glass screen; black ebonised wood, nickel plated fittings.

Seitz Phototechnic
Switzerland

Roundshot: R4* NSR

Subminiature panoramic camera for 10 images on Minox 9.5mm film. 10mm f16 fixed focus lens. Camera rotates on its handle to give pictures from 100° to full 360°.

SEM, Sociéte des Etablissements Modernes
SA Aurec, France

Established after the second world war, by Paul Royet, the company produced cameras affordable to every household in France. From the first Sem Kim in 1946, to the last Semflex of 1978, these cameras left their mark with the camera enthusiasts of France. Though they didn't find their way out of France in any great numbers, they are still seen at fairs and fleamarkets in France, and sometimes hanging around the necks of provincial visitors to Paris! A total of more than 350,000 Semflex cameras are estimated to have been made.

Semflex I: R2* C
1948-49, TLR for 6cm x 6cm frames on roll film. Angénieux or Berthoit f4.5, 75mm taking lens; f3.3 viewing lens; knob advance; shutter 1-1/300s; framing counting by ruby window

Semflex T950:   R2* C
1950-54. TLR for 6cm x 6cm frames on roll film. Angénieux or Berthoit f4.5, 75mm taking lens; f3.3 viewing lens; knob advance; shutter 1/10-1/250s; grey body

Semflex Standard 4.5:   R2* C
1955. TLR for 6 x 6cm frames on roll film. Angénieux or Berthoit f4.5, 75mm taking lens; f3.3 viewing lens; knob advance; shutter 1/10-1/250s; grey body; sports finder.

Semflex Standard 4.5:   R2* C
1956-60, as previous model but for cast "Semflex" logo inside a raised frame.

Semflex Standard 61:   R2* C
1961-67. Cast "Semflex" logo inside a raised frame with grey relief

Semflex SI: R2* C
1950-54. TLR for 6 x 6cm frames on roll film. Angénieux or Berthoit f3.8, 75mm taking lens; f3.3 viewing lens; knob advance; shutter 1/10-1/250s; grey body; sports finder. (Angénieux lens adds 25%)

Semflex Standard 3.5:   R2* C
1953-55. TLR for 6 x 6cm frames on roll film. Angénieux or Berthoit f3.5, 75mm taking lens; f3.3 viewing lens; knob advance; Synchro Sem shutter 1-1/400s; grey body; sports finder; large lens bezels. (Angénieux lens adds 25%).

Semflex Standard 3.5:   R2* C
1956-63. Cast "Semflex" logo inside a raised frame.

Semflex II: R2* C
1948-49. TLR for 6 x 6cm frames on roll film. Angénieux or Berthoit f3.5, 75mm taking lens; f3.3 viewing lens; knob advance; black body.
(Angénieux lens adds 25%).

Semflex S II: R2* C
1950-53. Sports finder.

Semflex Standard 3.5:   R2* C+
1954. Sports finder; larger focusing knob which incorporates a film reminder; second ruby window for 28mm x 40mm framing.

Semflex Standard 3.5 B: R2* C+
1960-64. As previous model but for lack

of film reminder; totally grey; possibility of 24mm x 36mm or 4cm x 4cm on 120 film; cast "Semflex" logo inside raised frame with grey relief

Semflex Standard 3.5 B: R2* D–
1965-69. As previous model but for bayonet filter mount.

Semflex Studio Reflex: R? A
1954. TLR for 12 exp on 120 film. Longer than usual 150mm short tele lens made it ideal for portraiture. Taking lens at f5.4, finder lens at f3.9. Two move together for focusing. Shutter 1-1/400s + B. Flash synch. Film wind by two strokes of lever.

Semflex Otomatic I: R2* C
1949. TLR for 6 x 6cm frames on roll film. Angénieux or Berthoit f4.5, 75mm taking lens; f3.3 viewing lens; double throw crank advance; 1-1/300s.

Semflex Oto SI: R2* C+
1950-52. TLR for 6 x 6cm frames on roll film. Angénieux or Berthoit f3.8, 75mm taking lens; f3.3 viewing lens; double throw crank advance; 1-1/300s; sports finder; grey body

Semflex Semi Otomatic 3.5 B: R2* D–
1956-64. TLR for 6 x 6cm frames on roll film. Angénieux or Berthoit f3.5, 75mm taking lens; f2.8 viewing lens; crank advance with double exposure protection; 1-1/400s; sports finder; film reminder; bayonet filter mount; leather body covering.

Semflex III: R5* NSR
1948. TLR for 6 x 6cm frames on roll

film. Angénieux or Berthoit f3.5, 75mm taking lens; f3.3 viewing lens; shutter speed and aperture visible from above.

Semflex Oto II: R2* C+
1949. TLR for 6 x 6cm frames on roll film. Angénieux or Berthoit f3.5, 75mm taking lens; f3.3 viewing lens; crank advance; shutter 1-1/400s; condensing lens on VFR ground glass. Angénieux lens adds 25%.

Semflex Oto S II: R2* C+
1950-53. as (SX218) but for addition of sportfinder and large magnifier in the VFR. Angénieux lens adds 25%.

Semflex Oto 154:   R2* C+
1954. Decorative lens bezels; film reminder; side mounted shutter release and second ruby window for 28mm x 40mm. Angénieux lens adds 25%.

Semflex Oto 3.5 B: R2* C
1955-62. Berthoit f3.5, 75mm taking lens. Angénieux or Berthoit f3.3 viewing lens; shutter cocking coupled to crank film advance; black body

Semflex Oto 3.5 B: R2* D–
1959-71. As previous model, but grey body, possible 24 x 36mm or 4 x 4cm on 120 film; Compur shutter available on special order. Compur shutter lens adds 100%.

Semflex 72:   R4* E–
1972-74. TLR for 6 x 6cm frames on 120 roll film. Berthiot or Tourret-Narrat f3.5, 75mm lens (four elements); Orec or Compur shutter; reinforced advance mechanism; film loading possible while

mounted on a tripod; 36mm or 4 x 4cm on 120 film; black body; about 1000 cameras made. Compur shutter lens adds 100%.

Note: Semflex Studio cameras are usually found in well used condition, as they were the workhorse studio camera for many French portrait photographers.

Semflex Studio Oto: **R3* E–**
1953-54. TLR for 6 x 6cm frames on 120 roll film. Shutter 1-1/400s; ground glass with condensing lens; sport finder; crank advance; lens panel black enamel.

Semflex Studio Oto: **R3* E–**
1955-58. Lens panel black crinkle finish.

Semflex Studio Standard: **R3* E–**
1955-59. Knob advance.

Semflex Studio Oto model 2:   R3* E–
1959-71. Logo cast in relief; black or grey available.

Semflex Studio Standard 2:   R3* E–
1959-71. Logo cast in relief; black or grey available.

Semflex Studio 72:   **R3* E–**
1972-78. Compur shutter.

Semflex Studio: **R4* E+**
"Atelier" c1976. New film loading permitting changing rolls while attached to a tripod; a protective heavy wire frame around taking and viewing lenses served as a prudent precaution while doing this manoeuvre.

Semflex "Joie de Vivre" 3.5:   R3* D+
1956-64. TLR for 6 x 6cm frames on roll film. Berthiot f3.5, 75mm taking lens (four elements); f2.8 viewing lens; simple shutter 1/50s; side mounted release. Complete outfit comprising hard case, flash, ever-ready case, and camera adds 50%.

Semflex "Joie de Vivre" 4.5:   R3* D+
1959-64. TLR for 6 x 6cm frames on roll film. Berthiot f4.5, 75mm taking lens (three elements); f2.8 viewing lens; simple shutter 1/50s, front mounted shutter release; decorative front plate; large "S" on the VFR hood, possible 24 frames on 120 roll film.

Semflash Standard: **R4* E–**
1951-56. TLR for 6 x 6cm frames on roll film. Berthiot f4.5/75mm taking lens (three elements); simple shutter 1/50s; focusing scale has seven numbers which allow distance/diaphragm flash control; delivered in a hard carrying case.

Semflash Couple: **R4* D+**
1951-59. With diaphragm coupled directly to the focusing mechanism. Sometimes marked "Semflash Location".

Semflash Couple: **R4* E–**
1960. With fixed "chimney" type VFR.

Grenaflex: **R3* C+**
1955-57. sold under the "Grenaflex" name.

Photo Hall: **R3* C+**
1955-57. Sold under the "Photo Hall" name.

No Name Semflex: R4* D–
1955-57. Sold without name brand by Manufrance.

A. Semmendinger
Fort Lee, New Jersey, USA

Excelsior Wet Plate Camera: R5* G–
c1872. Wet plate camera. 5" x 5" ground glass.

Seneca Camera Co
Rochester, New York, USA

Busy Bee: R3* C+
c1903. 4" x 5" Box-type detective camera. 4" x 5" exp on plates.

Chautauqua: R3* C
c1912. 3½" x 4½" Folding plate camera.

New Improved Seneca View Camera:
    R3* 5 x 7 size E
    17 x 20 size F–

c1900s. 5" x 7" View camera. Seneca Triple convertible lens and shutter. Horizontal and vertical swings; double extension reversible back; double tongued bed; plumb bob; black ebonite wood. 7 sizes from 5" x 7" to 17" x 20".

Seneca Folding Roll Camera: R3* C+

c1915. Ground glass focusing on special Vidax film.

Seneca No. 8:   R3* C+
Folding plate camera. Seneca Sym-Convertible lens; Seneca Auto shutter. Reversible back; black double extension bellows.

Seneca Stereo View Camera: R3* E
c1910. Wollensak Optical Co. stereo shutter. 5" x 7" exp on plates.

Septon Camera: R4* F
c1953. Pen-type detective camera. 20mm, f2.8 lens; 14 x 14mm exp on 16mm roll film. Mfd in Japan.

Sfomax: R4* F–

c1950. fomax 30mm, f3.5 lens; shutter 1/30-1/400s, CRF; 20 exp on 16mm film in special cassettes; slide-in yellow filter.

Shanghai Camera Factory
Shanghai, China

Shanghai 58-I: R5* H–

1958. Cfps, 1-1/1000s; separate Rfr/Vfr windows; diopter adjustment. Screw mount Shanghai f3.5, 50mm lens. A copy of the Leica IIIB, this camera was in production for less than one year. Fewer than 2000 cameras were made, and few survived the violence of China in the 60s. Serial numbers always begin 58XXXXX. Quite rare.

Shanghai 58-II: R3* F–

1958-63. Cfps, 1-1/1000s; combined Rfr/Vfr windows; flash synch. Screw mount Shanghai f3.5, 50mm lens. A continuation of the camera line started by the Shanghai 58-I. Several types exist, the earliest ones having strap lugs, five screws in the accessory shoe, and diopter adjustment, while later cameras have no strap lugs, no diopter adjustment, and only three screws in the accessory shoe. Serial numbers always begin 58XXX.

Shanghai 203:   R3* D+

1963. Folding 120 roll film camera with between the lens leaf shutter, 1-1/300s. Coupled RFR; flash synch; self-timer; built-in mask for 6 x 6 or 6 x 4.5 frame size. Coated f3.5, 75mm lens. This camera was produced in small numbers just before the brand name changed to "Seagull". Rare even in China.

Seagull 203:   R3* C+

1964-1986. Folding 120 roll film camera with between the lens leaf shutter, 1-1/300s. Coupled RFR; flash synch; self-timer; built-in mask for 6 x 6 or 6 x 4.5 frame size. Coated f3.5, 75mm lens. Somewhat Zeiss Ikon like in its styling, the Seagull 203 exists in several models, the earliest having no accessory shoe, and the latest having a black plastic top plate, and hot shoe. Common in China, though not often seen in the West.

Shanghai TLR: R3* D–

1958-63. TLR camera with between the lens leaf shutter, 1-1/300s. Flash synch; self-timer; automatic frame counting; knob advance; manual shutter cocking. Coated F3.5, 75mm lens. This well made TLR survived after 1963 as the Seagull 4 TLR. Serial numbers always begin 63XXX.

Seagull 4:   R3* D+

1964. TLR camera with between the lens leaf shutter, 1-1/300s. Flash synch; self-timer; automatic frame counting; knob advance; manual shutter cocking. Coated f3.5, 75mm lens. A continuation of the Shanghai TLR. The serial numbers always begin 4-63XXX. Not to be confused with the Seagull 4A, exported in the 1970s, the Seagull 4 has Knob film advance, while the 4A uses a crank, not unlike Rollei TLRs.

Seagull 4A: R3* C

1970s. TLR camera with between the lens leaf shutter, 1-1/300s. Flash synch, self-timer; automatic frame counting; crank advance; manual shutter cocking. Coated f3.5, 75mm lens. A continuation of the Shanghai TLR. The serial numbers always begin 4A-XXX. the Seagull 4A has automatic frame counting, and no provision for 6 x 4.5 framing.

Seagull 4B: R3* C

1965. TLR camera with between the lens leaf shutter, 1-1/300s. Flash synch; self-timer; ruby window frame counting; removable metal mask for 6 x 4.5 frame size.

Seagull 4C: R3* D

1968. TLR camera with manually set between the lens leaf shutter, 1-1/300s. Flash synch; self-timer; ruby window frame counting; removable metal mask for 6 x 4.5 frame size. Special adaptor for using 35mm film, with built-in exposure counter. Not often seen in China.

Seagull DFAB: R4* E+

Seagull DFAB with f1.4/50mm lens
1970s. Cfps, 1-1/60s, no viewing system. Sometimes equipped with f2, 58mm lens or f1.4, 50mm lens (the

same as used on the Red Flag 20 camera) in 42mm screw mount for use as a CRT camera. Available without a lens for use on microscopes. Made at the same time as the Red Flag 20 camera, and using some of the same parts. Not very popular, and quickly replaced on the marketplace by specialty Japanese cameras. Rare, even in China.

East Wind: R4* I–

1970s. Lens shutter, 1-1/1000s on the normal lens, 1-1/500 on all others, waist level Vrf, interchangeable magazine backs. Bayonet mount F2.8/80mm normal lens, with f4/50mm wide angle and f4/150mm telephoto lenses available. This Hasselblad copy was made in very small numbers at the order of Jiang Ching, the wife of Chairman Mao. Very rare even in China, usually seen in quite used condition. A complete set including filters, backs, and all three lenses adds 100% to the price. Prices are higher in Japan.

Red Flag 20:   R4* H+
                                          Lenses G each

1971-77. Cfps, 1-1/1000s, combined Rfr/Vfr windows, field of view for 35mm, 50mm, and 90mm lens automatically selected upon mounting lens. "M" type bayonet Red Flag f1.4, 50mm lens, with f1.4, 35mm and f2, 90mm lenses available. A copy of the Leica M4 camera, the Red Flag 20 was made in very small numbers, surely less than 200. The first two digits of the serial number indicate the year of manufacture. Prices have gone down from a high of £6,000 for a complete set in the early 1980s. Camera and all three lenses add 100% to the price. Prices are higher in Japan. Quite rare.

Sharp & Hitchmough
Liverpool, England

Aptus Pic-Nic-Basket: **R5* H**
c1889. Picnic basket-type detective camera. 8 x 10.5cm or 10 x 12.5cm plates.

Le Sherlock Holmes: **R5* G–**
c1912. Valise-type detective camera. Fixed focus meniscus lens; close-up lens swings into position; single speed shutter; 6.5 x 9cm plates.

J.F. Shew & Co
London, England

Aluminium Xit: **R2* E–**

c1905. Goerz Dagor Series III f6.8 lens; mahogany and aluminium construction.

Eclipse: **R3* E–**
c1888. Denlot rapid rectilinear lens; Rotary shutter.

Focal Plane Eclipse: **R3* F–**
c1895. Same as Eclipse with FPS.

Stereoscopic Eclipse: **R3* G**
c1891-1900. 6¾" x 3¼" plates; with two lenses; removable partition for non-stereoscopic use.

Shew Tailboard 4" x 5" Camera: R3* F
c1870s. Shew lens; Waterhouse stops; rubberband powered shutter. Glass plates; finder; book-type holders; original box.

Showa Optical Works
Japan

Gemflex: **R3* F**

c1954. Subminiature TLR camera. Gem 25mm, f3.5 lens; Swallow 1/25-1/100s; 10 exp, 14 x 14mm on 16mm roll film.

Showa Optical Co
Japan

(Marked Showa Kogaku, this section also contains cameras marked Leotax Camera Co. Ltd.)

Leotax (original):   **R5* G+**
1940. Cfps, 1/20-1/500; uncoupled RFR; screw mount Letana Anastigmat f3.5, 50mm lens. Viewed from the front, the vfr window is to the left of both the RFR windows, unlike most other Leica copies, and just the opposite of the later Leotax Special A and Special B cameras. Reportedly about 50 cameras made.

Leotax Special A: **R4* G+**
1942. Cfps, 1/20-1/500; coupled RFR; separate RFR/vfr windows; screw mount Letana Anastigmat f3.5, 50mm lens. Viewed from the front, the vfr window is to the right of both the RFR windows, unlike most other Leica copies, and just the opposite of the earlier Leotax (original).

Leotax Special B: **R4* G+**
1942. Cfps, 1-1/500; coupled RFR; separate RFR/vfr windows; screw mount Letana Anastigmat f3.5, 50mm lens. The same as the Leotax Special A, except with slow speeds.

Leotax Special: **R4* G**
1946. Cfps, 1/20-1/500; coupled RFR; separate RFR/vfr windows; screw mount Letana Anastigmat f3.5, 50mm or State f3.5, 50mm lens. The same as the Leotax Special A, but produced after the end of the Second World War.

Leotax Special DII: **R4* G**
1947. Cfps, 1/20-1/500; coupled RFR; separate RFR/vfr windows; screw mount C. Similar f3.5, 50mm lens. This camera is the first Leotax to have the front vfr window between the two RFR windows.

Leotax Special DIII: **R4* G**

Leotax Special DIII NR III variation for the US Army.
1947. Cfps, 1-1/500; coupled RFR; separate RFR/vfr windows; screw mount C. Similar f3.5, 50mm lens. The same as the Leotax Special DII, except with slow speeds. (Also produced as the NR III, and marked "made in occupied Japan". Only about 50 such examples were made.)

Leotax DIV: **R3* F**

1950. Cfps, 1-1/500, coupled RFR; separate RFR/VFR windows; screw mount Similar f1.5, 50mm lens. Body strap lugs. Not so rare as earlier Leotax's.

Leotax S: R3* F+

1952. Cfps, 1-1/500; coupled RFR; F and FP synch; separate RFR/VFR windows; screw mount Similar f1.5, 50mm lens. Body strap lugs. The same as Leotax DIV, with addition of synch.

Leotax F: R2* F–

1954. Cfps, 1-1/1000; coupled RFR; F and FP synch; separate RFR/vfr windows; screw mount Topcor f1.5, 50mm lens. Single piece top plate, body strap lugs. The first Leotax camera with 1/1000s shutter. In 1956, the company name changed to Leotax Camera Company, and Leotax F cameras made after that time were so marked, and are considered second version F cameras.

Leotax K: R2* F–

1955. Cfps, 1/25-1/500; coupled RFR; flash synch; separate RFR/vfr windows; screw mount Topcor f3.5, 50mm lens. Single piece top plate, body strap lugs.

Leotax T: R2* F–

1955. Cfps, 1-1/500; coupled RFR; flash synch; separate RFR/vfr windows; screw mount Topcor f3.5, 50mm lens. Single piece top plate, body strap lugs. Similar to Leotax F, but lacking 1/1000s shutter speed.

The following cameras are marked Leotax Camera Co. Ltd, not Showa.

Leotax TV: R2* F

Leotax TV with Topcor f3.5/ 50mm lens.

1957. CFPS, 1-1/500; coupled RFR; self-timer; separate RFR/VFR windows; screw mount Topcor f2.0, 50mm lens. Single piece top plate, body strap lugs.

Leotax FV: R3* F

1958. CFPS, 1-1/1000; coupled RFR; self-timer; separate RFR/VFR windows; screw mount Topcor f2.0, 5cm or Leonon f2.0, 50mm lens. Single piece top plate, body strap lugs. First Leotax using lever instead of knob advance.

Leotax K3:   R3* F

1958. CFPS, $1/8$-1/500; coupled RFR; separate RFR/VFR windows; screw mount Fujinon f2.8, 5cm lens. Single piece top plate, body strap lugs.

Leotax T2:   R2* F

1958. CFPS, 1-1/500; coupled RFR; separate RFR/VFR windows; screw mount Fujinon f2.0, 50mm lens. Single piece top plate, body strap lugs.

Leotax TV2 (Merit):   R2* F

1958. CFPS, 1-1/500; coupled RFR; self-timer; separate RFR/VFR windows; screw mount Topcor f2.0, 5cm or Leonon f2.0, 5cm lens. Single piece top plate, body strap lugs. Lever advance.

Leotax TV2 (Merit) with f2/50mm Topcor.

Leotax T2L (Elite):   R2* F
1959. CFPS, 1-1/500; coupled RFR; separate RFR/VFR windows; screw mount Topcor f2.0, 5cm or Leonon f2.0, 5cm lens. Single piece top plate, body strap lugs. Lever advance.

Leotax G: R4* G+
1961. CFPS, 1-1/1000; coupled RFR; self-timer; separate RFR/VFR windows; screw mount Topcor f1.8, 5cm or Leonon f2.0, 5cm lens. Single piece top plate, body strap lugs. Lever advance. More a Leica M copy in body style, the last Leotax.

Baby Leotax:
1941. Small folding camera for 16 exposures on 127 film. Reitz 5cm f3.5 lens, rapid shutter speed 1-1/500s.

Semi-Leotax: R3* E
1941. Folding camera for 16 exposures on 120 film. Folding optical viewfinder, Reitz 75mm f3.5 lens and Orient shutter speeded 1-1/200s. Postwar version made in 1949 but with Reginon 75mm f3.5 lens and Wester shutter.

Semi-Leotax DL: R3* D
1951. Similar to 1949 model, but with rigid optical viewfinder.

Semi-Leotax R: R3* E
1952. Similar to previous model, but with viewfinder built into housing on top plate and addition of uncoupled rangefinder. Toko 75mm f3.5 lens with Copal shutter.

Shock & Co KG
Feinmechanik-Optik-Geratebau
Bergkamen, Germany

Panta: R2* B+
c1954. Metal VFR camera for 6 x 4.5cm frames on 120 roll film. Steiner f3.5, 75mm lens; Vario shutter. A continuation of the Panta camera made by Dr. Rodehuser.

Sida GmbH
Germany

Note: Although manufacture of Sida camera began in Germany, production moved around Europe post-war and cameras with the name Sida were also manufactured in France, England and even Poland.

                                       R2* C
1936. Small Bakelite camera with optical viewfinder. Snapshot and Time shutter. Fixed focus, fixed aperture, f8 meniscus lens. Took ten exposures on own size film. Found in black, red, green and brown.

Sida Standard: R2* C
1938. Similar to original Sida, but made in cast metal.

Sidax: R2* C
1948. Similar to original model, made
again in Bakelite, but manufactured in
France.

J. Guido Sigrist
Paris, France

Jumelle Sigrist Stereo: R4* J–
c1900. Tessar 100mm, f3.5 and tele-
Quatryl 150mm, f4.5 lenses; special
FPS 1/60-1/4000s. 6 x 13cm plates.

Sigrist: R4* I
c1898. Krauss-Zeiss Planar 110mm,
f3.6-f32 lens; iris diaphragm; variable
speed MFPS 1/40-1/1000s. 18 exp, 6.5 x
9cm on dry plates. Shutter cocked
automatically when plate changed. First
camera with 1/1000s shutter speed.

Simmon Bros Inc
New York, USA

Omega 120:   R3* E

c1954-55. 2¼" x 2¾" RFR camera.
Omicron 90mm, f3.5 lens; Wollensak-
Rapax 1-1/400s. 9 exp, 2¼" x 2¾" on
120 roll film. Eye level optical vf with

parallax compensation – coupled RFR.
Push-pull film advance coupled to
shutter cocking; large focusing heel with
depth of field scale. Omega flash
attachment automatically coupled to
film advance permitting 6 flash bulb exp
in rapid sequence. The Omega 120 was
the prototype for the Koni-Omega
Rapid cameras.

James Sinclair & Co Ltd
London, England

Nanos: R3* E+
1924. Strut camera for plates or film
packs, 2³/₈" x 1³/₄". Dial-set Compur
shutter.

Sinclair Traveller Una: R4* I

c1930. Ross Combinable lens; "NS"
Perfect shutter. Duralumin construction.
2½" x 3½" exp on plates.

Sinclair Tropical Una: R4* G+
c1907-1929. Ross Convertible lens;
Optimo shutter. Teak, brass fittings.

Sinclair Tropical Una, c1907-1929.

Sinclair Una: R3* F+
c1920. ½ plate camera. N & S Perfect
shutter ½-1/100s. Double extension
bellows; rising front; revolving back;
double spirit levels.

Una Cameo: R3* D+
c1925. 9 x 12cm folding plate camera.
Aldis Uno Anastigmat f7.7 lens.

Thomas Skaife
London, England

Pistolgraph: U* NSR
c1859. Dallmeyer Petzval-type 50mm,
f2.2 lens; double flap shutter. 28mm
circular exp on 30 x 40mm wet collodion
plates.

Smart Stereo: R4* E+
c1910. Meniscus 110mm f11 lenses;
guillotine shutter 1/10-1/100s. Stereo
exp on 8 x 10cm dry plates.

F. W. Smith & Co
New York, USA

Monocular Duplex: R5* H–
c1884. F.W. Smith & Co. Rapid
Rectilinear 180mm f5.6 lens; guillotine
shutter (operates in conjunction with
mirror); variable speed by tension
adjustment. 4" x 5" exp on plates.

Jas J. Smith
Chicago, Illinois, USA

The Sunflower Multiplying Camera:
R4* G–
c1885. Portrait lens; pneumatic flap
shutter. Multiple exp: 2 to 32 exp on a
4¾" x 6½" plate. Mahogany finish.

Sanders & Crowhurst
Brighton, England

Birdland Reflex: R4* F–
c1908. ¼ plate SLR camera. Aldis
Anastigmat f8 lens. Ebonised pear wood
finish.

Snappy: R3* D
c1950. Meniscus lens; shutter 1/25-
1/1000s; 14 x 14mm exp on 16mm roll
film. Mfd in Japan.

Sola: R5* G+

c1939. Schneider Xenar 25mm, f2 lens;
rotary shutter 1-1/500s; reflex and

frame vf; 13 x 18mm exp on 16mm roll film.

Sirius

Action Tracker: R1* C

c1980. Unusual 35mm compact camera for four images from four lenses on standard 35mm frame. Images are exposed sequentially to capture sporting sequences. Fixed aperture, speed and focus. Fold up frame viewfinder. Black and red versions. Made in China.

Societa Construzioni Articoli Technici
Rome, Italy

Scat: R4* E–

c1950. Subminiature camera. 7 x 9mm exp on Minox cassettes. Mfd in Italy.

Soligor
Japan

Soligor Semi-Auto: R2* B+

c1950. 2¼" x 2¼" TLR camera. Soligor 80mm, f3.5 lens; Rektor shutter 1-1/300s; 12 exp, 2¼" x 2¼" on 120 roll film.

Sony
Japan

Mavica: R4* NSR

1982. Announced as the first digital camera to record images on magnetic disc, rather than film. The name was a corruption of Magnetic Video Camera. SLR with interchangeable lens. 50 exp to a disc. Prototypes exist, but the camera never went into commercial production.

Spartacus Corp
Chicago, USA

Spartus 35: R1* A
35mm Camera. Brown and gray plastic.

Star-Kist Food Inc
USA

Charlie Tuna: R3* C
1971, toy plastic camera in shape of a tuna fish. 8 exp, 126 cartridge. c1967.

Star Mfg Co
Brooklyn, New York, USA

Star 8" x 10" View Camera: R4* E

c1930s. Century Planograph Convertible lens. Roller blind shutter, lens board moves horizontally and vertically.

Double ext bellows; polished wood finish, brass fittings.

Star Watch Camera: R5* NSR J+
c1912. Watch-style detective camera, resembles Lancaster. Mfd in Japan.

Steineck Kamerawerk
Germany

Steineck A.B.C: R3* F+

c1948. Subminiature watch-style detective camera. Steinheil 12.5mm, f2.5 lens; rotary MFPS 1/125s; 8 exp, 6mm diameter on 25mm diameter film in metal cassette.

G.A. Steinheil Sons
Munich, Germany

Steinheil Casca I: R3* E–
Range-finder version. E+
c1948. Culminar 50mm f2.8 lens; FPS 1/25-1/1000s.

Detective Camera: R4* F+
c1888. Magazine loading box-type wooden detective camera. Achromatic lens; 9 x 12cm on plates.

Detective Camera, c1888.

Stereo Corporation
Milwaukee, Wisconsin, USA

Contura 35mm Stereo Camera:
                                    R4* G+

c1950. 35mm stereo camera. Volar f2.7 lens; flash. Combined range-vf window at base of camera. Double exp prevention device with override. Aluminium body finished in tan leather. Designed by Seton Rochwhite. Only 150 manufactured.

Stereo Crafters Inc
Milwaukee, Wisconsin, USA

Videon: **R3* C+**
c1953. Black plastic and aluminium bodied 35mm stereo vfr camera. Front focusing Ilex Stereon Anastigmat 35mm, f3.5 lenses; shutter speeds 1/10-1/100s. Also sold as the "Videon Challenger".

Videon II: **R3* C+**
c1954. Black plastic and aluminium bodied 35mm stereo vfr camera. Front focusing Ilex Stereon Anastigmat 35mm, f3.5 lenses; shutter speeds 1/10-1/100s. Quite similar to the Videon, with only a few minor changes.

H. Steward
England

J.H. Steward Magazine Camera:
R4* D+
c1890. Detective drop plate magazine camera. Rising, falling and sliding front.

C.P. Stirn, Stirn & Lyon
New York, USA

Stirn's America Detective Camera:
R5* NSR H+
c1887. Wooden box-type detective camera. Periscopic 105mm, f17 lens; 25 exp, 7.5 x 10cm on Eastman 85mm film. Probably the first camera especially made for flexible film. Invented by R. Gray, New York; mfd by Rudolph Stirn, Germany.

Stirn's Concealed Vest Camera, No. 1:
R5* G+
c1886. 6" Diameter detective camera. 6 circular 1¾" exp on glass plate. Nickel, or brass. With wooden case.

Stirn's Concealed Vest Camera, No. 2:
R5* H–

c1886. 7" Diameter detective camera; 4 circular 2½" exp on glass plate.

Stirn's Detective Camera: **R5* G**
c1891. Mahogany magazine camera. Aplanatic lens; variable speed rotating shutter; 2 vf. 12 exp on 6 x 8cm plates; leather changing bag back. It's rare to find these cameras with the wooden case intact. Without wooden box, R4 and value reduced.

Stirn's Stereo Detective Camera:
R5* NSR G+
c1893. Aplanatic 90mm f11 lens; variable speed rotating shutter; 9 x 18cm plates – changing mechanism with leather bag.

Suffize & Molitor
Paris, France

Sumo Stereo Camera: **R2* E**

c1912. 6 x 13cm stereo pairs were made on glass plates carried in changing magazines. Compur shutters, Krauss Tessar f4.5 lenses. These cameras were most commonly used for making Lumiere Autochromes and are frequently found with changing magazines for use with Autochrome plates. They could, however, be used with any standard glass plates.

Sugaya Optical Co Ltd
Japan

Minimax 110EE: R3* C+
1978. Resembles a small-scale 35mm camera, but made for 110 film. Detachable flashgun out of proportion to camera. 32mm f2 Minimax lens, auto shutter, CdS meter.

Minimax-Lite: R3* C+
Combination camera and lighter, made for 8 x 11mm images on Minox film. Fixed focus f8 lens.

Mycro III A: R3* C+

c1950. Mycro 20mm, f4.5 lens; shutter 1/25-1/100s; 10 exp, 10 x 14mm on 16mm roll film.

Myracle: R3* D
c1949. Subminiature camera. 10 x 14mm exp on roll film.

Sunart Photo Co
Rochester, New York, USA

Sunart Vidi No. 2:   R4* D–
c1898. Leather covered folding plate camera. Red bellows, mahogany interior.

Sunpak Corporation
Tokyo, Japan

Nimslo-3D: R2* or R1* D
c1982. Stereo using the lenticular principle. The camera has four lenses about 2cms apart. The four images require special processing and result in an image with significant apparent depth. No special glasses are required for viewing. The first version of the Nimslo-3D was manufactured in Scotland c1978-9 before production was moved to Japan. Depending on location R2 for first model, R1 for second

E. Suter Basle
Switzerland

Suter's Detective Magazine Camera:
R4* E+
c1890. Suter Detective lens; rotating shutter. Leather covered mahogany box camera, brass fittings.

Suter's Stereo Detective Camera:
R3* F+
c1897. Rectilinear lenses; rotating shutter. Changing mechanism for 9 x 18cm plates.

Suzuiki Optical Co
Japan

Echo 8:   R4* F+
c1951. Cigarette lighter-type detective camera. Echor 15mm, f3.5 lens; shutter 1/50s. 8 exp, 6 x 6mm on 8mm film.

Echo 8, c1951.

Swank Mfg Co
USA

Schnapps-O-Flex: R2* C
c1965. Liquor container in shape of a
camera. Flash reflector uncorks from
flashgun revealing clay container with
one pint capacity.

T

Takahashi Kogaku
Japan

Arsen: **R3* C+**
c1938. Small camera for 12 exp on 127. Similar style to the Gelto D III.

Romain Talbot Berlin
Germany

Errtee Button Tintype Camera:
R5* NSR

c1910. Cannon shaped street camera. Laak 50mm, f4.5 lens; single speed shutter; 100 exp, 1" diameter tintype plates.

Walter Talbot
Berlin, Germany

Talbot Invisible Camera: **R5* NSR**
c1914-1930. Belt-type detective camera; Anastigmat f5.5 lens; shutter 1/125s; 15 to 30 exp on 35mm film. Rapid trigger release to cock shutter and advance film. Long, thin rectangular (7 x 34cm) shape. Camera was worn on a belt under coat, with lens protruding through button hole.

Tanaka Optical Co Ltd
Japan

Tanack II C: **R4* F–**
1953. Cfps, 1/20-1/500; FP flash synch; hinged back separate Rfr/Vfr windows. First produced with a screw mount Tanar f3.5, 50mm lens. Later cameras used screw mount Tanar f2.8/50mm lens. Similar to the Leica IIIB, but without slow speeds.

Tanack IIIF: **R4* F–**
1954. Cfps, 1-1/500; FP flash synch; separate Rfr/Vfr windows. First produced with a screw mount Tanar f3.5, 50mm lens or Tanar F2.8, 50mm lens. Same as the Tanak IIC, but with slow speeds.

Tanack IIIS: **R3* F–**
1954-55. Cfps, 1-1/500s; FP and X flash synch; separate Rfr/Vfr windows. With screw mount Tanar f3.5, 50mm lens or Tanar f2.8, 50mm lens. Similar to the Tanak IIIF but with additional X synch contact, and one piece top plate.

Tanack IV-S: **R3* F–**

1955-58. Cfps, 1-1/500s; FP and X flash synch; separate Rfr/Vfr windows. With screw mount Tanar f3.5, 50mm lens, Tanar f2.8, 50mm lens or Tanar f2.0, 50mm lens. Late cameras had a film type reminder dial added to the wind knob.

Tanack SD: R4* F

1957. Cfps, 1-1/1000s; flash synch; self-timer; combined Rfr/Vfr windows; bright line parallax corrected finder. Screw mount Tanar f2.0, 50mm or Tanar f1.5, 50mm lens. Very few of these cameras were made. More like the Contax II or Nikon S2, but using screw mount lenses.

Tanack V3: R3* F

1958. Cfps, 1-1/500s; flash synch on the right side next to the rewind crank; combined Rfr/Vfr window; film type reminder in the back of the camera; no self-timer. Bayonet mount Tanar f2.8, 50mm or Tanar f1.9, 50mm or Tanar F1.5, 50mm lens. Though similar to the Leica M type bayonet mount, the Tanack V3 camera used three lugs instead of four. Screw mount lenses could be used by means of a bayonet to screw mount adaptor.

Tanack VP: R4* F

1959. Cfps, 1-1/500s; flash synch; combined Rfr/Vfr window; film type reminder in back of camera; no self-timer. Screw mount Tanar F1.8, 50mm lens. Development of the V3 camera, the VP used only screw mount lenses.

Tasco Binocular Camera: R3* E+

c1978. Subminiature 4 x 20mm binocular camera. Tele-Tasco 112mm, f5.6 coated lens; 12 exp on 110 cartridge. Mfd in Japan.

Tasco Binocular Camera, c1978.

A. & G. Taylor
London, England

A & G Taylor Tailboard Camera: R4* E

c1890s. 13" x 18" Tailboard camera. Brass Clement Gilmer lens. Mahogany finish, brass fittings; leather bellows.

Tek Serra & Co
Torino, Italy

Teleca: R4* G

c1950. Subminiature binocular-type detective camera. Telesigmar 35mm, f4.5 coated lens; shutter 1/25, 1/50, 1/100s; binoculars function as vf. 10 x 14mm exp on 16mm film in special cassette. Mfd in Japan.

THE HOVE INTERNATIONAL BLUE BOOK 509

Teleca, c1950.

A. Themsteyr

Photo Sport: R4* E+
c1926. Laako Dyalitar 45mm, f4.5 lens;
Compur shutter 1-1/300s. 24 x 30mm
exp on 35mm film.

Thomas of Pall Mall Wet Plate:
R5* H–
c1860. Mahogany sliding box camera.
Ross portrait lens, Waterhouse stops.
Multiplying back takes 2 exp on
horizontal plate.

W.J. Thompson Co Inc
New York, USA

Thompson Tintype Camera: R4* E–
c1910. Suitcase-type street camera.

Thornton Pickard Mfg Co
Altrincham, England

Aerial Camera Type A: R4* I–
c1915-?. Mahogany and brass camera. 4
x 5" plates in special magazines; FPS;
Type C as A except Long body accom-
modates Ross Xpres f4.5-10" lens.

Amber: R3* F–
c1899-1906. Compact folding field
camera. Quarter to whole-plate sizes;
tripod turntable; lens and shutter
protrude through base when closed;
cheaper version of the Ruby.

College: R3* F–
c1912-1926. Compact double extension
folding field camera. Mahogany with
brass fittings; 9 x 12 to 18 x 24cm; TP
roller-blind shutter; Rectoplant lens.

Duplex Ruby Reflex Tropical: R4* H+
c1920. Teak and brass camera, for the
overseas market; 6.5 x 9cm or quarter-
plate; double extension orange bellows;
FPS 1/1000; Cook Anastigmat f6.3 lens.

Hythe Gun Camera: R4* G
c1915. Lewis gun style camera for
training British RAF machine gunners
during WWI. Copied by Japanese in
WWII. 300mm, f8 lens; central shutter;

Hythe Gun Camera.

16 exp, 4.5 x 6cm or 11 exp, 6 x 6cm on 120 roll film.

Imperial Triple Extension: R3* F
(TP108) c1904-1926. Field camera. Triple ext. tapered bellows; mahogany with brass fittings; Beck Symmetrical or TP Rectoplant lenses.

Imperial Pocket: R2* C
c1915. Square bellows camera with lens panel that pulls out on plated stretchers. Rapid loading hinged spool chambers, T & I shutter, direct vision viewfinder

Junior Special Ruby Reflex: R3* F
1924. Budget price single lens reflex with Thornton Pickard focal plane shutter, with quick wind speed setting, rising front and reversing back for horizontal or vertical pictures on $3^1/_4$" x $4^1/_4$" plates. Cooke f4.5 anastigmat lens.

Ruby: R3* F
c1899-1905. Compact folding field camera. Ruby RR lens; TP roller blind shutter.

Royal Ruby: R3* F+
c1904-1930. Triple extension version of the Ruby.

Ruby Duplex Tropical Reflex: R4* H+
c1916. Tropical SLR camera. Cooke Series IIa $6^1/_2$" f3.5 lens; CFPS 1-1/1000s; $2^1/_4$" x $3^1/_4$" exp on film pack.

Ruby Press Camera: R3* E
c1920. Folding camera, introduced primarily for press photographers, specially made to withstand all-weather, rough usage.

Rubyette: R3* D+
c1934. One of the smaller SLRs from this company, made for 6 x 9cm plates and cut film, or 120 rollfilm if used with a rollfilm back. 4-inch f4.5 Dallmeyer Anastigmat. FP shutter 1-1/100s. Shutter release linked to mirror movement to give return after exposure.

Ruby Speed Camera: R5* I
1925. Small metal camera with f2 Taylor Hobson Cooke Supper Speed f2 lens. Design is similar to the Ermanox. Made for use in artificial light. Takes 6 x 4.5 cm plates or cut film.

Stereo Puck: R2* D

c1926. Roll film stereo box camera.

Thornton Pickard Stereo Camera:
**   R4* F+**

Roll blind shutter. Mahogany finish, brass fittings.

J. Thorpe
New York, USA

Thorpe Four-Tube Camera: **R5* G+**
c1862. Four lens camera for Carte-de-visite or wet plate. 5" x 7" exp.

Thury & Amey Stereo Folding Camera:
R4* E–
c1890. Zeiss Protar 120mm, f9 lenses;
Thury & Amey 4-speed guillotine
shutter. Mfd in Geneva, Switzerland.

Tiranti
Rome, Italy

Summa Report: **R5* NSR**

c1950s. Unusual and rare camera for 6 x
9 plates, cut film or rollfilm. Four lenses
mounted on revolving turret, two for
taking and two or viewing. Standard pair
105mm f4 Xenar coupled with f4 Galileo
Reflar, wideangle pair 65mm f6.8
Schneider Angulon coupled with f3.5
Galileo Reflar. As well as optical finder,
extra frame finder on top of body.

Aristographe: **R3* E**
c1921. Stereo camera for 6 x 13 cm film
and plates in special changing box.
Tiranti Transpar anastigmat f4.5 or
Tessar f4.5 lenses, shutter speeds to
1/500s. Focusing mechanism with
automatic depth of field indicator.

Ph. Tiranty
Paris, France

Gnome: **R3* D**
c1920. Folding pocket camera for $2^{1}/_{4}$"
x $3^{1}/_{4}$" film packs. Unusual feature that
allowed focusing to be adjusted when
the camera was folded – when opened it
was automatically adjusted as previously
set. Gnome Transpar f4.5, Olor Berthiot
f5.7 lenses, in Acmé, Compur or Ilex
shutters.

Polygraph: **R3* E**
c1920. Stereo camera, advertised as
'the simplest, cheapest stereo camera in
the world'. Made to take single plates or
a changing box containing 12 plates.
Fixed focus f5 lenses, shutter speeds
from 1/25-1/100s.

Simda: **R4* F+**

c1957. 16mm Camera for either single
exposure or stereo pairs using either

single or double perforated cine film. Fixed focus Angénieux 25mm, f3.5 of Roussel Special 25mm, f3.5 lenses, shutter speeds 1-1/250s, holds enough film for 100 shots. Available in either black or grey. Also known as the "Panoramascope 3D".

Verographe: **R4* E+**
c1920. Stereo camera made in two sizes for 45 x 107mm or 6 x 13 cm plates. Transpar f4.5 and f6.3 lenses as standard, plus option for Tessar f6.3 or Stylor f4.5 lenses. Shutter speeds 1/10-1/180s.

A. Tischlere Heinemann & Dressler
Munich, Germany

Monachia: **R4* F–**
c1889. Meniscus lens; front of lens rotary shutter. 35 x 40mm exp.

Tisdell & Whittelsey
New York, USA

Tisdell & Whittelsey Detective Camera:
Leather covered model R4* G–
Wooden model   H–

c1887. Box-type detective camera. Achromatic meniscus lens; variable speed shutter; $3\frac{1}{4}$" x $4\frac{1}{4}$" exposures on dry plates.

Tisdell Camera and Mfg Co
Scranton, Pennsylvania, USA

Tisdell Hand Camera: **R4* F–**

c1893. Leather covered box-type detective camera. 4" x 5" exposures on dry plates.

Tizer Company
Tokyo, Japan

Coca Cola camera: **R1* A**

c1978. The original can camera later copied by Taiwan. Fixed focus, aperture and shutter speed. Takes 110 film. Some models have hot shoes synch for flash.

Snoopy Can Camera: R3* D+

1979. 110 camera in the form of a soft drink can decorated with cartoon character Snoopy. Fixed-focus meniscus lens, shutter works at about 1/75s. Also made as a Coca-Cola can.

TKC
Japan

Kalimar A: R3* B–

c1956. 35mm Camera. Terionon 45mm, f3.5 coated lens; shutter 1/25-1/200s.

Toakoki Seisakusho
Japan

Gelto D III (pre-war model):   R2* C+
1938. Small, neatly designed camera for 16 ex on 127. 5cm f4.5 Grimmel lens extends on collapsible tube. Shutter 1/5-1/250s. Eye-level viewfinder. Black body.

Gelto D III (post-war model):   R3* D

1950. Similar to pre-war version, but with f3.5 lens and made in silver or gold. Very attractive camera.

Tokiwa Seiki Co
Tokyo, Japan

Pentaflex: R3* F–
1955. SLR for eye-level viewing, the first Japanese camera with this feature. A penta mirror worked like a pentaprism. Tokinon Anastigmat f3.4, 50mm lens which was interchangeable. Behind the lens shutter 1-1/400s.

Tokyo Optical Co
Tokyo, Japan

Topcon RE Super: R2* D
1963. SLR fitted with Auto-Topcor f1.8, 5.8cm interchangeable lens. Focal plane shutter 1-1000s. First SLR to be fitted with a TTL exposure meter.

Topcon RE Super, 1963.

Tokyo Koki
Japan

Rubina 16 Model II: **R3* E**

c1950. Better than average quality 16mm subminiature for 10 x 14 mm images. Styled like a small 35mm camera. 25mm f3.5 Ruby Anastigmat lens, focusing down to 1 metre. Shutter 1/25-1/100s. Miniature accessory shoe on top plate, though no evidence of accessories. Model I unknown.

Tokyo Shashin
Japan

Mighty: **R3* D**
1947. Japanese subminiature. Meniscus lens; single speed shutter; 13 x 13mm exp on 16mm roll film; Double vf; adjustable diaphragm. A 2x telephoto was an available accessory. Unusual for a very simple sub-miniature.

Tone: **R3* C+**

1949. Subminiature camera. Tone Anastigmat 25mm, f3.5 lens. Direct optical vf and waist level reflex finders. Mfd in Japan.

Topper Toy Division
De Luxe Reading Corporation
New Jersey, USA

Secret Sam Attache Case Camera:
                              R4* E–
c1965. Toy spy attache case, pistol assembly and camera. Takes 127 roll film. Includes a toy pistol, plastic bullets.

Secret Sam's Spy Dictionary: R4* D+
c1965. Plastic book-type detective camera; 16 exp on 127 film

Tougo-Do Mfg Co
Tokyo, Japan

Hit: **R2* B**
c1948. Sub-miniature camera for 14 x 14mm images on paper-backed rollfilm. Lens meniscus f11, 30mm. Single speed shutter works at about 1/30s. It was made in very large quantities under a variety of names.

Tougo-Do

Hit, c1948.

Stereo Hit: R3* D+

Roll film stereo camera. S-Owla 4.5cm coated lenses; guillotine shutter, I, B. 8 stereo exp on 127 film (single frame capacity). Mfd in Japan.

Toys Clan
Hong Kong

Donald Duck Camera: R5* E+
c1970s. Simple plastic camera to give 16 exposures on 127, incorporated into Donald's head. One eye is the lens, the other is the viewfinder, the tongue is the shutter release.

Triad Corporation
Encino, California, USA

Fotron III: R3* B+
c1960. Automatic camera. 10 exp, 1" x

1" on cartridge film, 35mm wide. Built-in electronic flash with rechargeable batteries; electric film advance.

Turf folding camera: R4* F–
c1935. Folding camera with thermoplastic body for 16 exp 6 x 4.5cm on 120 film. Front cell focusing Turf Extra Anastigmat 7cm, f3.8 lens; btl shutter, speeds 1/25-1/100s. Made in Germany.

W. Tylar
Birmingham, England

Gnu Stereoscopic Magazine Hand Camera: R4* F
c1904. Box form magazine camera. Single achromat lens; rotating Water-house stops; shutter, T, I. Single exp option; reflecting finder. 2 sets of 12 plates, $4\frac{3}{4}$" x $3\frac{1}{4}$".

Tylar Detective Camera: R4* E
c1890. Guillotine shutter; $\frac{1}{4}$ plate exp on dry plates.

Tynar Corporation
Los Angeles, California, USA

Tynar: R3* C
c1950. Subminiature camera. 45mm, f6.3 lens; single speed guillotine shutter. 10 x 14mm exp on 16mm cassettes.

Donald Duck Camera, c1970s.

U

Ulca Camera Corp
Pennsylvania, USA

Ulca: **R3* C**

c1930s. Subminiature for 20 x 20mm images on special rollfilm. Although generally known as an American camera, models were also made in Germany (where it was designed and patented) and Britain. Fixed focus, aperture and speed. Varying models include the Ulca TSL, STI, STM and TMS.

United Feature Syndicate Inc
USA

Snoopy-Matic Camera: **R3* D–**

c1966. Meniscus lens; sector shutter. 12 exp on 126 roll film.

Four of the several different styles of Ulca.

United Optical Instruments
Essex, England

Merlin: **R4* D**

1936. Simple subminiature for 20 x 20mm images on special rollfilm. Fixed focus, aperture and speed. Fold-up viewfinder. No markings on body. Uncommon in black, rare in red and green. (This camera was later incorporated into a Bakelite shell shaped vaguely liked a pistol and called the Erac.)

Unitek Mfg Co
Monrova, California, USA

Unitek Precision Intra-oral Dental Camera: **R4* E–**

c1965. Geared belt-driven moving prism with internal light source is used for oral photographs on 3¼" x 4¼" Polaroid film. A separate power unit charges the camera's nicad batteries and warms the optical assembly.

Universal Camera Corporation
New York, USA

Buccaneer: **R2* B+**
c1945. 35mm Camera with CRF. Built-in extinction meter; Bakelite construction; collapsible Tricor 50mm f3.5 lens; Chrono-matic shutter 1/10-1/300s, flash synch.

Corsair I: **R2* B+**
c1938. 35mm VFR camera with built-in extinction meter for special perforated film. Bakelite construction, similar to Vitar. Collapsible Univex Anastigmat f4.5, 50mm lens; shutter 1/25-1/200s.

Corsair II: **R2* B+**
c1946. 35mm VFR camera. With built-in extinction meter. As previous model except uses standard 35mm film. Bakelite construction. Similar to Vitar. Collapsible Univex Anastigmat f4.5, 50mm lens, shutter 1/25-1/200s.

Iris: **R2* B+**

c1939. Dark painted metal bodied VFR camera. Collapsible Ilex Vitar 50mm, f7.9 lens. T. B. I. shutter, 8 exp 1x1.5" on 00 universal roll film.

Iris Delux: **R2* B+**
c1939. Metal bodied VFR camera. Collapsible Ilex Vitar 50mm, f7.9 lens; T. B. I. Shutter. 8 exp 1 x 1.5" on 00 universal roll film, polished metalwork synchronised version add 50% .

Mercury I: **R2* C+**
c1947. Metal bodied half-frame 35mm VFR camera. Interchangeable Tricor 35mm, f3.5 lens, rotary sector MFPS 1/20-1/1000s. Using 35mm film in special rolls.

Mercury I, model CC1500:   **R4* D**
c1947. Metal bodied half-frame 35mm VFR. Interchangeable Tricor f3.5 or f2.7, 35mm lens; rotary sector MFPS 1/20-1/1500s. Using 35mm film in special rolls; as (UC103) but for 1/1500s shutter speed.

Mercury II: **R2* C+**

c1948. Metal bodied half-frame 35mm VFR camera. Interchangeable Universal Tricor 35mm, f2.8 lens; rotary sector MFPS 1/20-1/1000s. Using standard 35mm film.

Meteor: **R2* A**
c1949. metal bodied VFR camera. For 6cm x 6cm frames on 620 roll film; f11 lens in collapsible tube; simple shutter; built-in extinction meter.

Minicam: **R3* B+**
c1938. Brown metal bodied strut folding camera for 00 film. Ilex-Achromar 50mm lens; simple shutter.

Minute 16:   **R3* C+**

c1950. Subminiature camera. Meniscus lens; guillotine shutter. 10 x 14mm exp on 16mm film in special cartridge.

Norton: **R2* B+**
c1935-1936. Black plastic camera. 6 Exp, 1⅛" x 1½" on No. 00 universal roll film.

Roamer I: **R2* B–**
c1949. Metal bodied folding VFR camera. For 6 x 9cm frames on either 120 or 620 film. Universal Anastigmat f6.3, 100mm lens; synchromatic shutter; as (UC122) but for lens.

Roamer II: R2* B–
c1949. Metal bodied folding VFR camera. For 6 x 9cm frames on either 120 or 620 film. Universal Anastigmat f4.5, 100mm lens; synchromatic shutter.

Roamer 63: R2* B–
c1949. Metal bodied folding VFR camera For 6 x 9cm frames on either 120 or 620 film. Universal Anastigmat Synchromatic 100mm, f6.3 lens; 6cm x 9cm frames on 120 roll film.

Ster-all: R3* D
c1957. 35mm stereo VFR camera. Tricor f3.5 fixed focus lens; shutter 1/50s.

Stereo Univex Model A: R4* E

c1938. Paired Univex cameras attached by bracket.

Twinflex: R3* B+
c1938. Meniscus lens; sector shutter; reflex viewing. 6 exp on No. 00 roll film.

Twinflex, c1938.

Univex AF: R2* B+
c1937. Compact metal bodied strut folding camera for 00 roll film.

Univex AF-2: R2* B+
c1938. Compact metal bodied strut folding camera for 00 roll film.

Univex AF-3: R2* B+

c1938. Compact metal bodied strut folding camera for 00 roll film.

Univex Model A Camera: R2* B–

c1940. VFR camera. For 6 exp on Univex 00 roll film. Bakelite construction.

Uniflash: R2* A

c1940. Simple VFR camera. For 00 film. Bakelite construction. Vitar 60mm lens. Sold with flash.

Vitar: R2* B+

c1950. 35mm VFR camera. Bakelite construction. Universal Tricor Anastigmat 50mm f3.5 lens; Flash Chronomatic shutter 1/25-1/100s; built-in extinction meter. (prices higher in Europe).

Univex Zenith: R4* D+

1939. Similar style to Univex Iris Delux, but with f4.5 lens, shutter 1/25-1/200s + T & B. Rigid lens mount. Flashgun hot shoe and body release via add-on accessory screwed to top plate. Rare.

Univex: R4* C–

c1950?. Bakelite VFR camera. For 6x4.5 frames on roll film; simple lens and shutter; marked "Univex", but the shutter is marked "P and I" like a French camera would be.

Usines Gallus
Courbevoie, France

Gallus 00:   R4* D+

c1924. 6 x 13cm plate magazine camera. Detachable shutter unit.

Gallus 0:   R4* E

c1924. 6 x 13cm plate magazine camera. For use as a stereoscope.

Gallus 100:   R4* D+

c1924. 6 x 13cm plate magazine camera. Fixed focus Gallus 75mm, f6.3 lens; guillotine shutter $\frac{1}{5}$-1/200s. T. B. Rising front.

Gallus 110:   R4* D+
c1924. 6 x 13cm plate magazine camera. Leather covered Gallus 100.

Gallus 120:   R4* D+
c1924. 6 x 13cm plate magazine camera. Fixed focus Gallus 75mm, f6.3 lens; Ibsor shutter 1-1/100s. Ring front; leather covered.

Gallus 130:   R4* D+
c1924. 6 x 13cm plate magazine camera. Helicoidal focusing; Compur shutter.

Gallus 140:   R4* D+
c1924. 6 x 13cm plate magazine camera. Helicoidal focusing; shutter 2-1/300s.

Gallus 150:   R4* D+
c1924. 6 x 13cm plate magazine camera. optical finder.

Gallus: R4* C+
c1938. 6 x 9cm Bakelite roll film camera. With various lens and shutter combinations. Looks the same as the Pontiac and Ebner cameras of that era. Though not as often seen.

Cady-Lux: R3* C
c1940. Metal bodied folding camera. Making 6 x 9cm or 6 x 6cm negatives on roll film through the use of two ruby windows and internal masks. Fixed optical finder and adjustable depth of field gauge on the camera top plate. Front focusing 105mm, f4.5 Berthiot Special lens in a Gallus shutter, speeds of 1/25-1/100s.

Derby-Gallus: R3* D
c1939. 3 x 4cm on roll film camera. CFPS speeds of 1/25-1/500s. Optical VFR; front focusing 50mm, f3.5 Saphir lens. This camera is the continuation of the famous "Foth" Derby, originally made in Berlin, Germany. Because of the beginning of WWII, not many cameras were made.

Derlux: R3* D+
c1947, 3 x 4cm on roll film camera. CFPS speeds of 1/25-1/500s. Optical VFR, front focusing 50mm, f3.5 or f2.8 Saphir lens or the more often found 50mm, f3.5 Gallix lens. Early cameras use the old style "Foth" body, with a new polished aluminium lens board, later cameras were entirely polished aluminium.

Lenses for Gallus 1924 models:
Hermagis Aplanastigmatic 75mm, f6.8; Dogmar 75mm, f6.3; Stylor 75mm, f4.5 or f6.3; Berthiot Perigraphe 75mm, f6.8; Olor 75mm, f6.8 or f5.7; Tessar 75mm, f6.3.

Utility Mfg Co
Chicago, USA

Note: to make life simple, cameras made by the "Falcon Camera Company" (Chicago and New York) and the "Spartus Camera Company" are also included in this listing. Someday, it may be made clear when and how these three companies went their separate ways, here is a sample from each. Most of these cameras are much less expensive in the USA.

Spartus Full-Vue: R2* A
c1950. Bakelite TLR box camera. For 6 x 6cm on roll film, simple lens and shutter.

Spartus Press Flash: R2* B–
c1946. Bakelite box camera for roll film. Built-in flash reflector.

Spartus 35:   R2* B+
c1950, Bakelite 35mm VFR. Simple lens and shutter.

Spartus 35F: R2* B+
c1950. With flash synch. (price includes flash).

Spartus: R3* B+
c1939. Bakelite strut folding camera. For 3 x 4cm on 127 roll film; simple lens and shutter.

Falcon Junior Model: R2* B+
c1947. Made by Falcon.

Falcon Miniature: R2* B+
c1947. Bakelite VFR camera. For 3 x 4cm on 127 roll film; simple lens and shutter. Several variations.

Falcon Miniature Deluxe: R3* B+
c1947. In brown.

Falcon Rocket: R3* B+
c1947. Streamlined Bakelite VFR camera. For 3 x 4cm on 127 roll film; simple lens and shutter.

Falcon G: R3* B+
c1937. Bakelite VFR camera. For 3 x 4cm on 127 roll film; f3.5 lens in collapsible tube focusing mount in Deltax shutter 1/25-1/100s.

Falcon F: R3* B+
c1937. With f4.5 lens.

Falcon Special: R3* B+
Built-in extinction meter.

Falcon Press Flash: R3* B+
c1939.

Uyeda Camera
Japan

Vero Four: R3* E
1938. Small metal bodied camera for 12 exposures on 127 film. Verona 60mm f3.5 lens extends on telescopic tube. Shutter speeded 1-1/500s.

Falcon Miniature Deluxe, c1947.

V

Van Neck
England

VN Press Camera: **R3* E**
1932. Made in one size only for 9 x 12 cm. Lens panel extends on struts, with choice of 6" f3.5 or f 4.5 lenses. Small amount of rise and fall, plus cross movement. Focal plane shutter. Wire frame viewfinder.

Kapsa, c1950.

D.F. Vasconcellos
Sao Paulo, Brazil

Bieka: **R3* B–**

c1950. Metal box camera. For 6 x 9cm frames on roll film; simple lens and shutter.

Kapsa: **R3* C**
c1950. Well made Bakelite box camera. For 6 x 9cm or 6 x 4.5 cm on roll film; simple lens and shutter.

Vega Co
Geneva, Switzerland

Telephote Vega: **R5* H+**
c1901. 13 x 18cm; Achromatic 120mm, f20 lens; FPS up to 1/500s. Compact structure – long focal length achieved by reflecting light beam with two mirrors.

Vega: **R5* G–**

c1900. Book-style detective camera. Aplanatic 180mm f7.8 lens; guillotine shutter 1/2-1/100s; closing and opening this book-style camera operates the plate changing mechanism.

Le Verographe: **R3* D+**
c1920. Krauss Tessar 90mm, f6.3 lenses; 5-speed guillotine shutter; 2 plate magazine. Mfd in Paris, France.

Vestkam: R3* D
c1947, subminiature camera. TKK shutter. Mfd in Japan.

Vidmar Camera Co
USA

Vidax: R5* G

c1951. Press camera. Using 120 roll film and 2¼" x 3¼" sheet film; Schneider Xenotar 80mm, f2.8 coated lens in interchangeable mount; Synchro-Compur 1-1/500s, X, M flash synch. Variable crf; interchangeable backs; 8, 12 or 16 exp on 120 roll film. Rare.

Viscawide 16:   R3* E+

c1961, subminiature panoramic camera. Ross 25mm f3.5 coated lens; shutter 1/60-1/300s. 10 x 52mm exp on 16mm film in special cassette. Mfd in Japan. Only 16mm panoramic camera ever made.

Vive Camera Co
Chicago, Illinois, USA

Vive Souvenir Camera: R3* D
c1897. Premium box camera.

Vive No.1:   R3* D–
c1898. Simple lens; single speed shutter; 12 exp, 11 x 11cm on dry plates, manipulated through light tight sleeve. First American camera to use the dark sleeve to change plates.

Vive No. 2, Improved Model: R3* C+
c1897. Box magazine camera. Self-capping shutter; 12 exp, 4¼" x 4¼" on dry plates.

Vive No. 4:   R3* C+
c1895. 4" x 5" plate camera.

Vive Stereo Camera: R4* F–
c1899. Stereo box camera. 6" x 3½" exp on dry plates in magazine.

Josef Vojta
*Prague, Bohemia
(Austro-Hungarian Empire)*

Stereo Dry Plate Camera: R5* E
c1910. 9 x 18cm images on glass plates in holders. Matched anastigmat lenses f7. Many of Vojta's cameras were fitted with a front mounted curtain shutter of his design.

Voigtlander A.G.
Braunschweig, Germany

Voigtlander Daguerreotype Camera (Replica):   R4* H+
c1956. Replica of the first portrait

Josef Vojta Stereo Dry Plate Camera.

camera produced in 1841. Brass construction. Petzval 159mm, f3.7 lens was 20 times faster than lens used by Daguerre in 1859. Exposure time was reduced to 1½ minutes or less on sunny days, 80mm diameter sensitized daguerreotype plate was contained in circular brass holder. Those made by others, 20% less.

Alpin: **R3* E**
Stereo version F+

c1912. Folding plate camera. Voigtlander Collinear 120mm, f6.8 lens; Kolios shutter 1-1/300s; 9 x 12cm plates.

Avus: **R2* B+**
c1920. 9 x 12cm Folding camera. Skopar 105mm, f4.5 lens; Compur shutter 1-1/250s. 9 x 12cm exp on sheet film.

Bergheil: **R2* C**

c1930. Folding plate camera. Heliar 12cm f4.5 lens; Compur shutter 1-1/200s. 6.5 x 9cm exp on plates..

Bergheil De Luxe: **R3* F**
c1930. Folding plate camera. Heliar 105mm, f4.5 lens; Compur shutter 1-1/200s; rising and cross front; 6.5 x 9cm exp on plates. Covered with green leather.

Bessa 6 x 6 (Baby Bessa): R3* C
c1930. Folding roll film camera. Heliar 75mm, f3.5 lens; Compur-Rapid shutter 1-1/300s; 6 x 6cm exp on roll film.

Bessa I: R3* C+
1952. Folding camera for 8 or 16 exp on 120. Fitting the accessory mask for the smaller format automatically removes cover from second red window. Four masks in viewfinder give views at close distances and infinity for the two formats. 105mm f4.5 Vaskar, Prontor-S shutter 1-1/250s. Flash synch.

Bessa II, c1960.

Bessa II: R3* F
With Skopar lens F+
APO Lanthar lens H
c1960. Roll film folding camera. Colour-Heliar 105mm, f3.5 coated lens; Synchro-Compur shutter 1-1/500s. crf; 8 exp, 6 x 9cm on 120 roll film.

Brilliant: R2* B+
c1932. Roll film TLR camera. Voigtar 75mm, f7.7 lens. Not a true TLR, effectively a box camera with a large reflecting vfr., much like the Kodak Duoflex. In 1938, a focusing Brilliant appeared, bakelite body and a very

Brilliant, c1932.

different appearance. It had gears to couple the focusing mounts of the two lenses, a system used by the Kodak Reflex. Until recently, a Russian-made copy of the focusing Brilliant was sold in Britain as the Lubitel.

c1932. Roll film folding camera. Voigtlander Heliar 10.5cm, f4.5 lens; Compur shutter 1-1/250s; crf.; 8 exp, 2¼" x 3¼" on 120 roll film. Built-in extinction meter; cast metal body.

Prominent: **R3* E**

Perkeo I: **R2* C**

c1960. 6 x 6cm roll film camera. Colour Skopar 75mm, f3.5 lens.

c1958. 35mm RFR camera. Ultron 50mm, f2 coated lens, interchangeable mount; Synchro-Compur shutter 1-1/500s, crf. Version 1, c1953-1954. detachable accessory shoe; knob-wind film advance. Version 2, integral accessory shoe, knob-wind film advance. Version 3, rapid wind film advance lever (two stroke). Prices for version 3, versions 1 and 2 25% less.

Perkeo II: **R2* C+**

c1960. 6 x 6cm roll film camera. Colour Skopar 75mm, f3.5 lens; Synchro-Compur shutter.

Prominent (1932):   **R4* G**

Prominent II: **R3* F+**

c1959. With bright frame lines for 35mm, 50mm and 100mm lenses in a redesigned VFR.

Accessories for Prominent

Scoparon f3.5, 35mm lens	**D**
Dynaron f4.5, 100mm lens	**D+**
Super-Dynaron f4.5, 150mm lens	**E+**
Reflex viewer with Telomar f5.5, 100mm lens	**F−**

Stereflektoscop: **R4* E+**

c1914. Stereo plate camera. Heliar 65mm, f4.5 lenses; Compur shutter 1-1/250s; 45 x 107mm exp on plates.

Superb: **R4* E+**

c1938. 6 x 6cm TLR camera. Heliar 75cm, f3.5 lens; Compur shutter 1-1/250s; 12 exp. 6 x 6cm on 120 roll film.

Vag: **R1* C+**

c1925. Plate cameras made in two sizes for quarter plate and 3$\frac{1}{2}$" x 2$\frac{1}{2}$". Focusing by lever moving through a wide arc. Rise and cross movements incorporated. Choice of lens/shutter combinations include f6.3 Voigtar in Embezet or Ibsor shutter; or f4.5 Skopar in Ibsor shutter.

Virtus: **R4* F−**

c1935. Folding roll film camera. Heliar 75mm, f3.5 lens; Compur shutter 1-1/250s; 16 exp on 120 roll film.

Vitessa: **R3* F−**

c1956. 35mm RFR camera. Fixed mount Colour Skopar f3.5 or f2.8 or Ultron f2, 50mm coated lens. Synchro-Compur shutter, LVS 1-1/500s; CRF. Camera has unique rapid film advance plunger that advances the film and cocks the shutter. With and without built-in light meter.

Vito III: **R4* E**

c1951. Folding 35mm RFR camera. Untron f2, 50mm lens; Compur shutter; CRF.

Vitessa T: **R3* E–**
c1956. 35mm RFR camera. As previous model but now with rigid interchangeable mount lenses; built-in light meter.

Accessories for Vitessa T	
Skoparet f3.4, 35mm lens	**D**
Dynaret f4.8, 100mm lens	**D**
Turnit VFR for 35mm, 50mm,	
and 100mm	**D**

Vito: **R2* B+**
c1950. Folding 35mm VFR camera. Skopar f3.5, 5cm coated lens; Prontor II shutter.

Vito II: **R2* C–**
c1951. With redesigned top plate and Colour Skopar lens.

Vito IIa: **R2* C**
c1953. With lever advance.

Vito B: **R2* B+**
c1954. 35mm VFR camera. Solid mount Skopar f3.5 or f2.8, 50mm lens; Pronto or Prontor shutter.

Vito BL: **R2* C–**
c1956. With built-in light meter.

Vito CLR: **R3* C+**
c1961. 35mm camera. With CRF Colour-Skopar 50mm, f2.8 lens; Prontor 500 LK shutter speeds 1/15-1/500s.; coupled light meter, needle visible in finder and also on the top plate. One of the last photographic products in a 120 year history of continuous camera manufacturing.

Bessamatic: **R2* D**
c1959. 35mm SLR camera. With interchangeable Skopar f2.8, 50mm lens in Synchro Compur shutter. Coupled built-in light meter.

Bessamatic, c1959.

Accessory lenses for Bessamatic and Ultramatic cameras	
Skoparex f3.4, 35mm lens	D
Skopagon f2, 40mm lens	E+
Dynarex f3.4, 90mm lens	E+
Super-Dynarex f4, 135mm lens	D
Super-Dynarex f4, 200mm lens	E+
Super-Dynarex F4, 350mm lens	F+
Zoomar f2.8, 36-82 zoom lens	F

Bessamatic m: R3* E–
c1962. No light meter.

Bessamatic CS: R2* E–
c1965. With TTL metering.

Tourist: R2* C
c1927. Small plate camera made in $3^1/_2$"
x $2^1/_2$" and quarter plate sizes. Double
extension with infinity catch, rise, fall
and cross lens movements, brilliant and
direct vision viewfinders. Heliar f4.5 lens
in dial-set Compur shutter.

Ultramatic: R2* E
c1961. 35mm SLR camera. With
interchangeable Septon f2 or Skopar
f2.8, 50mm lens; Synchro Compur
shutter. Built-in light meter, shutter
priority full automatic exposure.

Ultramatic CS: R3* E
c1965. With TTL metering.

Vokar Corporation
USA

Vokar I: R2* C–
c1946. 35mm RFR camera. Vokar
Anastigmat 50mm, f2.8 lens; leaf
shutter 1/200s.

VOOMP, Experimental Factory
Leningrad, USSR,
(now St. Petersburg, Russia)

Pioneer: R4* H–
c1934. 35mm RFR camera. Leica copy.
Screw mount VOOMP f3.5, 50mm lens;
CFPS 1/20-1/500s. No accessory shoe.
200-300 made.

Vredeborch GmbH
Nordenham, West Germany

Nordetta 3-D: R3* C+
c1950. Strut type folding stereo camera
for 127 roll film. Fixed focus 8cm, f11
lenses; single speed shutter; PC flash
synch; and top mounted accessory shoe.

Nordina I: R2* B

1953. 12 exp on 620. Lens on telescopic extension. 75mm f4.5 lens. Vario shutter.

Nordina II: R2* B

1953. Similar to Model I but with f/3.5 Steinar.

Nordina III: R2* B+

c1956. New redesigned top plate. Retractable lens in square housing. 75mm f2.9 Steinar. Prontor SVS shutter 1-1/300s + B.

Pioneer, c1934.

W

Bernard Wachtl

Stock Apparat: **R5* NSR I+**
c1893. Cane handle detective camera.
Round exp, 42mm diameter.

Walker Mfg Co
Palmyra, New York, USA

The TAKIV Camera: **R5* F+**
c1892. Cardboard and leatherette
multiple exp camera. Rotary shutter.
4 exp, $2\frac{1}{2}$" x $2\frac{1}{2}$" on dry plates.

Warzawskie Zaklady Foto-Optyczne, (WZFO)
Warsaw, Poland

Alfa-2:   **R4* D**
c1950. Grey and white vertically styled
metal 35mm VFR camera. Emitar f4.5,
45mm lens.

Druh: **R3* B–**
c1950s. Bakelite VFR camera. For 6 x
6cm on roll film. Simple lens and
shutter.

Watlz
Japan

Automat: **R3* C**
1960. TLR for 12 exp on 127. 60mm
f2.8 Zunow lenses. Copal shutter
1-1/500s + B.

Automat, 1960.

Envoy 35:   **R3* C**
c1959. 35mm CRF camera. 48mm f1.9
Kominar. Copal SLV shutter 1-1/500s.

W. Watson & Sons
London, England

Acme: **R3* F**
c1890s. Wood and brass field camera,
made in sizes from half-plate to 15" x
12".

Alpha: **R5* G**
c1890s. A versatile camera, made in
quarter plate and 5" x 4" sizes, whose
life went on well into the 1920s and
1930s. Could be used in the hand, but
on a tripod was capable of offering a full
range of movements, including rise, fall
and swing. Reversing back for portrait
or landscape shots and capable of
working with extreme wideangle lenses.

Vanneck: R4* F–
c1890. Taylor and Hobson Cooke lens; shutter mechanism works by means of the mirror's upward and downward action   1/25-1/100s.   Changing mechanism for 12 plates $3\frac{1}{4}$" x $4\frac{1}{4}$".

Watson Alpha: R5* G
c1900s. Hand camera but with features more usually associated with tripod-mounted field cameras, including reversing back, swing front and back and double extension. Also adaptable for wideangle work. Found in quarter plate and 5" x 4" sizes.

Watson's Detective Camera: R4* F+
c1886. Wooden box-type detective camera. Rectilinear lens; front-of-lens guillotine shutter. 8 x 11.5cm exp on plates (adaptor for roll film).

Premiere: R3* F
c1900s. Solidly-made wooden field camera designed for maximum strength. Could be used at home or in the tropics.

Watson Tailboard Camera: R3* E+

c1880s. Rising and falling front. Red Russian leather bellows.

Watson Twin Lens Reflex: R4* F–
c1890. Wray Anastigmat f8 lenses.

Watson View Camera: R3* E+

c1890s. 13" x 18" View camera. Bush Rapid Symmetrical lens; Thornton Pickard behind-lens shutter. Reversible and tilting back. Mahogany finish with brass fittings.

Webster Industries Inc
Webster, New York, USA

Winpro 35:   R4* F–

c1948. Simple sturdy fixed focus 35mm camera, fitted with a Crystar 40mm lens. The camera was made with Tenite, a tough Kodak plastic. The Winpro enjoyed a brief period of popularity at the end of WWII.

Welta Kamera Werke
Waurich & Weber, Freital,
Germany. (after 1946, VEB Welta)

Welti (pre-war):   R2* C–
c1936. Folding 35mm VFR camera.
Xenar f3.5 or f2.8 or Tessar f2.8, 50mm
lens in Compur shutter 1-1/300s or
Compur Rapid.shutter to 1/500s.

Weltix: R2* C–
c1938. Folding 35mm VFR camera.
Xenar f3.5 or Cassar f2.9, 50mm f2.9
lens in Compur shutter 1-1/300s.

Welti (post-war):   R2* B+
c1946. Folding 35mm VFR camera.
Meritar f3.5, 50mm lens in Compur
shutter.

Welti I: R2* B+
c1954. Folding 35mm VFR camera.
Tessar f3.5, 50mm lens in Cludor or
Ovus shutter.

Welti Ic: R2* B+
c1955. Folding 35mm VFR camera.
Tessar f2.8, 50mm lens; Vebur shutter.
New designed top plate.

Weltini: R2* D
c1935. Folding 35mm camera. With
coupled RFR; Xenar f2.8, Xenon f2,
Elmar f3.5, or Tessar f2.8, 50mm lens;
Compur-Rapid shutter. (add 200% or
more for Elmar lens!).

Weltur: R3* B+
c1934. 6 x 6 or 6 x 9 folding roll film
camera. (6 x 4.5 possible with adaptor)
coupled RFR, Tessar f2.8 or f4.5, Xenar
f2.8 or 3.8, or Trinar f3.8 lens. Compur
or Compur Rapid shutter.

Weltax (pre-war):   R3* B+
c1937. Folding VFR camera. For 6 x
9cm frames on roll film(6 x 4.5 with
adaptor). Trioplan f4.5, Xenar f2.8,
Tessar f2.8 or Cassar f2.9, 105mm
lens. Prontor II, Compur or Compur
Rapid shutter.

Weltax (post-war):   R2* B+
c1946. Folding VFR camera. For 6 x
9cm frames on roll film (6 x 4.5 with
adaptor). Meritar f3.5, 75mm lens,
Junior shutter.

Trio: R2* B+
c1935-1937. Folding VFR camera. For 6
x 9cm frames on roll film (6 x 4.5 with
adaptor). Trioplan f4.5, Tessar f4.5 or
Trinar f3.8, 105mm lens. Prontor
II,Compur or Compur Rapid shutter.

Symbol: R2* B
c1935-1937. Folding VFR camera. For 6
x 9cm frames on roll film (6 x 4.5 with
adaptor); Weltar f6.3, 105mm lens,
Prontor II or Vario shutter.

Solida: R3* B+
c1935. Folding camera. For 6 x 9 frames
on roll film; coupled RFR; Xenar f3.9.
Radionar f4.5 or Tessar f4.5 lens.
Compur shutter.

Welta: R3* C+
c1930. Horizontal folding plate camera.
For either 9 x 12cm or 10 x 15cm exp.
FPS 1/10-1/1000s. Trinar, Eurynar or
Xenar lenses in 135mm or 150mm were
available, with or without Compur
shutter.

Dubla: R3* C+

c1933. Horizontal folding plate camera. As previous model, but only in 10 x 15cm, FPS 1/10-1/1000s. Trinar, Eurynar or Xenar 165mm lens, with or without Compur shutter.

Welta: R2* B+

c1932. Folding VFR camera. For 6 x 9 frames on roll film, Weltar f9, 105mm lens, single speed shutter.

Welta: R2* B+

c1931. Folding VFR camera. For 6 x 4.5mm frames on roll film, Weltar f6.3, 90mm lens, Prontor shutter.

Perle: R3* C+

c1936. Folding VFR camera. For 6 x 4.5mm frames on roll film, Weltar f4.5, Xenar f4.5, Trioplan f2.9 or Xenar f2.9, 75mm lens, Prontor or Compur shutter.

Perle: R3* C+

c1937. Folding VFR camera. For 6 x 6 frames on roll film, Cassar f2.9, 50mm lens in Compur shutter; parallax correcting VFR.

Garant: R2* B+

c1938. 6 x 9cm folding rollfilm camera. Trioplan f4.5 or Trinar f3.8, 105mm lens; Compur shutter.

Gucki: R3* C–

c1937, strut type folding VFR roll film camera for 3 x 4cm on 127 roll film. Trinar 5cm, f2.9 lens; Compur shutter.

Gucki: R3* C

c1935. Bed type folding VFR roll film camera. For 4 x 6.5cm frames, Xenar f2.9, 50mm lens; Compur shutter.

Welta Perfekta: R4* E+

c1934. Folding TLR camera. Meyer f3.5, 75mm lens; Compur shutter 1-1/300s. 12 exp, 6 x 6cm on 120 roll film.

Reflekta (pre-war): R3* B+

c1938. TLR camera. Pololyt f3.5 or f4.5, 75mm lens; Blitz shutter. 6 x 6cm exp on 120 roll film.

Reflekta II (post-war): R2* B+

c1952. TLR camera. Pololyt f3.5, 75mm lens; Prontor shutter. 6 x 6cm exp on 120 roll film. Often marked "Made in USSR Occupied Germany" Quite common in the USA.

Weltaflex: R3* D

c1954. TLR camera. Trioplan f3.5 or Rectan f3.5, 75mm lens; Vebur or Prontor SVS shutter.

Welta Superfekta: R4* G Perfekta F

c1934. 6 x 9cm TLR camera. Trioplan 10cm f3.8 lens; Compur shutter 1-1/250s. Horizontal and vertical format; 6 x 9cm exp on 120 roll film.

Sica: R3* A

c1950. Plastic 6 x 6 box camera. Wefo-Sicar lens.

Orix: R3* C+

c1958. Metal half-frame (18 x 24mm) VFR camera. Film transport and shutter arming by rod extending from the side of the camera. Gold coloured front and back with Blue, Red, Green or Brown coloured body. Trioplan f3.5, 30mm lens. Three speed shutter.

Penti: R2* C

c1959. Metal half-frame (18 x 24mm) VFR camera. Film transport and shutter arming by rod extending from the side of the camera. Gold coloured front and back with Blue, Red, Green or Brown coloured body. Trioplan f3.5, 30mm lens, three speed shutter. Some people feel that this camera was made by VEB Pentacon. Probably VEB Welta assumed some manufacturing role in the grander VEB Pentacon complex, since both factories were located relatively close in Freital and nearby Dresden, respectively. Now with the unification of Germany, in the near future a clearer picture may come to light concerning the relationships of East German camera manufacturers, and the relationship of VEB Pentacon with its "socialist" partners.

Penti I: R2* C

c1959. Metal half-frame (18 x 24mm) VFR camera. Film transport and shutter arming by rod extending from the side of the camera. Gold coloured front and back with Blue, Red, Green or Brown coloured body. Dimoplan f3.5, 30mm lens; three speed shutter.

Penti II: **R2* C**
c1959. Metal half-frame (18 x 24mm) VFR camera. Film transport and shutter arming by rod extending from the side of the camera. Gold coloured body, Dimoplan f3.5, 30mm lens, three speed shutter. Almost the same body as (WL128).

Weiner Kamera Werkstatte
Vienna, Austria

Wica: **R4* G+**
c1948-50. 35mm camera with coupled RFR. Leica copy. CFPS 1-1/1000s; flash synch; interchangeable Angénieux f2.9 or f1.8, Berthiot f2.8 or Heligon f2, 50mm lens; focusing mount to lenses of different focal lengths. Early model has wide separation between the RFR/VFR eyepieces, two synch contacts and strap lugs, while later ones use close together eyepieces, one flash synch and no strap lugs. Quite rare.

Gebr. Wenke
Nurnberg, Germany

Wenka: **R4* F+**

c1955 35mm camera. With CRF 24 x 30mm frame size, interchangeable

Xenar f2.8, 50mm lens in 40mm screw mount; odd "FPS" located just behind the lens 1/25-1/800s; CRF. Early models marked "24 x 30" on the top plate. Considered by some to be a Leica copy. About 1000 camera produced

Wenka I: **R4* F+**
c1951-52. Top shutter speed shutter marked 1/500s.

Wenka II: **R4* F+**
c1951-52. Green flash selector indicator.

Wescon Camera Company
Milwaukee, WI, USA

Wescon: **R4* NSR**
c1955. 35mm RFR camera. Collapsible f3.5, 50mm Wollensak lens, Alphax shutter 1/10-1/200s, CRF.

Western Electric Co.
New York, USA

Gray's Vest Camera: **R5* H–**

1886; Thin round detective camera worn under a man's vest. The upper "button" was the lens and the middle changed the plate and cocked the shutter. Six

exposures each $1^5/_8$" diameter were made on a $5^1/_2$" round plate. Its possible that Gray the inventor made the first cameras himself. In less than a year Western Electric a prominent maker of telegraph equipment briefly became the manufacturer. CP Stirn purchased the rights and began to make the camera in the US, Great Britain, France, and Germany.

Western Mfg Co
Chicago, Illinois, USA

Magazine Cyclone No. 2:   R3* C+
c1897. Drop plate box camera. 12-Plate magazine; after each exposure a key releases one plate to the storage chamber, a spring slides the next plate into film plane.

Magazine Cyclone No. 3:   R3* B+

Magazine Cyclone No. 4:   R3* B+

Magazine Cyclone No. 5:   R3* B+

David White Co
USA

Realist 45:   R2* E–
c1956. 35mm stereo camera. VFR; Steinheil Munchen Cassar S 35mm, f3.5 lenses; Vero shutter 1/25-1/200s. Made by Wilhelm Witt Iloca, Hamburg, West Germany for Realist Inc.

Realist Macro Stereo (model 1060):
                                      R4* G+

c1971. 35mm macro stereo camera. Realist Stereo Anastigmat 35mm, f3.5 coated lens, permanently set at f25. Self-cocking, behind-lens shutter 1-1/125s. Close up focus from $3^1/_2$" to $4^1/_2$".

Stereo Realist (model 1041):   R2* E

Realist 45, c1956.

c1951. 35mm stereo camera. David White Co. Anastigmat 35mm, f3.5 coated lenses. Shutter 1-1/150s; CRF. Focus adjustment moves film plane.

Stereo Realist (model 1042):   R4* F
c1951. 35mm stereo camera. Kodak Ektar 35mm, f2.8 coated lenses or David White Anastigmat 35mm, f2.8 coated lenses. Shutter 1-1/200s. CRF.

Stereo Realist Custom (model 1050):   R4* F+
c1960. 35mm stereo camera. Realist 35mm, f2.8 coated lenses; made in Germany; Shutter 1-1/200s; CRF. Larger wind and rewind knobs and different frame counter than the Realist 2.8.

Whitehouse Products Inc
Brooklyn, USA

Beacon: R2* A
c1954-55. Metal and plastic VFR camera. For 3 x 4cm frames on 127 film. Simple lens and shutter. available in black, white, red, brown, green and blue. (European prices higher, colour other than black add 50% or more).

Beacon 225:   R2* A
c1954-55. Metal and plastic VFR camera. For 6 x 6cm frames on roll film. Doublet 70mm coated lens and simple shutter mounted in a collapsible square tube. (European prices higher).

Beacon Reflex: R2* B

1947. TLR-style camera with non coupled lenses. Two-tone grey plastic. Fixed focus and shutter. Apertures marked for B&W and col.

Wilca Kamerabau
Germany

Wilca Automatic: R4* F

c1960. Subminiature for 24 exp on 16mm film in special cassettes. Built-in meter with film speed set by coding on film cartridge. 16mm f2 fixed focus Wilcalux lens. Shutter 1/25-1/250s. Auto programmed exposure.

Wm. R. Whittaker Co Ltd
Los Angeles, California, USA

Micro 16:   **R3* C+**

c1950. 16mm Subminiature camera. Doublet lens with three Waterhouse stops marked "bright", "dull" and "colour". Sector shutter with fixed speed of 1/60s. 20 exp on 16mm film in special cassettes.

Pixie: **R3* C+**

c1950. Microtar f6.3 lens; sector shutter; 16mm film in special cassettes.

Flash Pixie: **R4* D**

c1950. Version of the Pixie with detachable flashgun, twice the size of the camera! Otherwise as original model.

Williamson Manufacturing Company
England

Pistol Aircraft Camera: **R3* F**
1930. Designed for owners of private aircraft to take pictures from the air. The camera is contained within a metal cone with an eye-level viewfinder on top and a pistol grip release below. Could be used with rollfilm, darkslides or filmpacks.

Eagle Aircraft Camera No.3:   **R5* F**
c1931. Designed for aerial survey work when a hand-held camera is appropriate. Magazine for 5" x 5" roll film, 125 exposures to a roll. Could be operated manually or mechanically, giving a sequence of exposures at regular intervals. Data could also be recorded on the film between frames. Venetian blind-style shutter comprising eight thin steel strips.

Windsor Camera Co
USA

Windsor: R4* D+
c1957. 35mm stereo camera. Windsor
f3.5 lens; shutter 1/25-1/50s. Focusing
scale; direct vision optical finder.

Simon Wing Charleston
Massachusetts, USA

New Gem Camera: R5* G

*Simon Wing/A.S. Southworth
Multiplying Camera.*

**Simon Wing Nine Lens Multiplying
View Camera:**   R5* H+
c1895.

Wing 4" x 5" Multiplying View Camera:
                                                      R4* F+
c1900. Lens standard has vertical and
horizontal adjustments, to photograph
multiple images on a single plate.

c1901. Multiple exposure camera.
Darlot achromatised periscopic 120mm,
f6 lens; 2 blade scissor-type shutter. 15
separate exp, 1" x 1¼" on a single 5" x 7"
ferrotype plate, dry plate or sheet film.

**Simon Wing/A.S. Southworth
Multiplying Camera:**   R5* I–
Patent April 10th 1858. Wet plate
camera for multiple images on 4" x 5"
wet collodion plates.

Wirgin Brothers
Wiesbaden, Germany

Gewirette: R3* B+
c1936. Metal VFR camera. For 3 x 4cm
on 127 roll film; Collapsible Trioplan
f2.9, 50mm lens; Compur shutter;
tubular optical finder.

Klein Edinex: R2* B+
c1937. Metal VFR camera. For 3 x 4cm
exp on 127 roll film, collapsible Cassar
f2.8, 50mm lens. Prontor shutter;
accessory shoe; tubular optical finder.

Edinex (24 x 36):   **R3* C+**
c1927. Metal 35mm VFR camera. Radionar f3.5,50mm lens; Compur Rapid shutter; tubular optical finder; accessory shoe for "Fokas" RFR. Black body indicates early cameras, chrome bodies are mostly post-war. (deduct 50% for chrome body).

Edinex I (pre-war):   **R2* B+**
c1938. Metal 35mm VFR camera. Collapsible Cassar f2.8, 50mm lens; Prontor-S shutter; accessory shoe and optical finder in one piece top plate.

Edinex I (post-war):   **R2* B+**
c1949. Metal 35mm VFR camera. Collapsible Radionar f2.9 or Xenon f2,50mm lens; Prontor-S or Compur Rapid shutter. Accessory shoe and optical finder in one piece top plate.

Edinex III (pre-war):   **R4* C+**
c1939. Metal 35mm camera. Coupled RFR; Heligon f2, 50mm lens; Compur Rapid shutter.

Edinex III (post-war):   **R4* C+**
c1949. Metal 35mm camera. Coupled RFR; Radionar f2.9 or Xenon f2 50mm lens; Prontor-S or Compur Rapid shutter.

Wirgin: **R3* C–**
c1938. TLR camera for 6 x 6 on roll film. Trioplan f3.5, 73mm lens; Compur shutter. Identical to Welta Reflecta but for the name plate. The same style camera was exported to the USA and sold by Peerless camera of New York as the Peerflekta.

Edina: **R3* B+**
c1952-54. Metal 35mm camera with CRF. Cassar f3.5 or Isconar f2.8, 43mm lens; Pronto or Prontor-S shutter. Lever wind.

Edixa: **R2* B+**
c1954. Metal 35mm camera with CRF. Cassar f3.5 or Isconar f2.8, 43mm lens; Prontor-SVS shutter; Lever wind.

Edixa I: **R2* B+**
c1954. Metal 35mm camera. Cassar f3.5 lens; Vario shutter; lever wind.

Edixa IIL: **R2* C–**
c1955. Metal 35mm camera with CRF. Cassar f3.5 or Isconar f2.8, 43mm lens; Pronto or Prontor-SVS shutter. EV system on shutter.

Edixa Reflex: **R3* C+**
c1953. 35mm SLR. Interchangeable Cassar f2.8, 50mm lens (among others, some with automatic aperture); CFPS 1/25-1/1000s; interchangeable finder. Originally advertised as the "Komet", this camera model never made it big in the USA. Australia seems to be the one place where a collector has no problem finding a good example.

Edixa Reflex II-B: **R3* C+**
c1957. 35mm SLR. Interchangeable Travenar f2.8, 50mm lens (among others); CFPS 1-1/1000s; interchange-able finder.

Edixa Reflex II-C: **R3* C+**
c1957. 35mm SLR. Interchangeable Travenar f2.8, 50mm lens (among others); CFPS 1-1/1000s; interchange-

able finder; built-in uncoupled light meter.

Edixa Reflex II-D: **R3* C+**
c1957. 35mm SLR. Interchangeable Westromat f1.9, 50mm lens (among others); CFPS 1/1000s; interchangeable finder; self-timer.

Edixamat Reflex-B: **R3* C+**
c1960. 35mm SLR. Interchangeable Xenon f1.9, 50mm lens (among others); CFPS; 1-1/1000s; interchangeable finder, also model BL.

Edixamat Reflex-C: **R3* D–**

c1960. 35mm SLR. Interchangeable Iscolar f2.8, 50mm lens (among others); CFPS 1-1/1000s; built-in uncoupled light meter.

Edixamat Reflex-D: **R3* D**
c1960. 35mm SLR. Interchangeable Westromat f1.9, 50mm lens (among others); CFPS 1-1/1000s; interchangeable finder; self-timer; slow speed and self-timer, also model DL.

Edixa Standard: **R3* C+**
c1961. 35mm SLR. Interchangeable

Xenon f1.9, 50mm lens (among others); CFPS 1/2-1/500s; interchangeable finder. A cheap version of the then current Edixamat Reflex-B.

Edixa Kadett: **R3* C+**
c1961. 35mm SLR. Interchangeable Auto-Casseron f2.8, 50mm lens (among others). CFPS 1/30-1/500s; interchangeable finder. A cheap version of the then current Edixa Standard with simplified shutter.

Edixa Prismaflex: **R3* C+**
c1967. 35mm SLR. Interchangeable Iscotar f2.8, 50mm lens (among others). CFPS 1/4-1/1000s. Stopped down TTL metering, finder.

Edixa Prismat: **R3* C+**
c1970. 35mm SLR. Interchangeable Xenon f1.9, 50mm lens (among others). CFPS 1-1/1000s. Open TTL metering.

Edixa Stereo IA: **R3* D**

c1950. 35mm stereo camera. Steinheil Cassar f3.5, 35mm lenses; Vario or Prontor shutter 1/25-1/200s.

Edixa Stereo IB: **R3* D**
c1954. 35mm stereo camera. Edinar f3.5, 35mm lenses; Velio shutter, speeds 1/10-1/200s.

Edixa Stereo IIA: **R3* D+**
c1958 35mm stereo camera. Coupled RFR; Steinheil Cassar f3.5, 35mm lenses; Pronto SVS shutter 1-1/300s.

Edixa Stereo IIIA: **R3* D+**
c1958. 35mm stereo camera. Coupled RFR; Steinheil Cassar f3.5, 35mm lenses; Prontor SVS shutter 1-1/300s. Built-in meter.

Edixa 16:   **R3* C+**
c1960. Subminiature VFR camera. Travear or Trinar f2.8, 25mm lens. 12 x 16mm exp on 16mm film. Coupled meter available as accessory.

Edixa 16MB: **R3* C+**
c1969. Subminiature VFR camera. Travear or Trinar f2.8, 25mm lens. 12 x 16mm exp on 16mm film. Coupled meter available as accessory. Redesigned camera back, and film transport.

Witt Iloca
Hamburg, Germany

Citascope: **R4* E+**
c1951. Reflex stereo camera. Tessar lens; 45 x 107mm exp. Lenticular viewing screen.

Iloca: **R3* B+**
c1950. 35mm VFR camera. Iling??? Hamburg f3.5, 45mm lens; Pronto II shutter 1-1/250s.

Iloca I: **R2* B+**
c1950. Metal 35mm VFR camera. Ilitar f3.5, 45mm lens; Vario or Prontor-S shutter; knob wind.

Iloca Ia: **R2* B+**
c1951. Metal 35mm VFR camera. Ilitar f2.9, 45mm lens; Prontor-S shutter; knob wind; body mounted shutter release.

Iloca II: **R3* C**
c1950. Metal 35mm camera. Coupled RFR; Ilitar f3.5, 45mm lens; Prontor-S shutter; knob wind; no accessory shoe.

Iloca IIa: **R3* C**
c1952. Metal 35mm camera. Coupled RFR; Ilitar f3.5, 45mm lens; Prontor-S shutter; knob wind; no accessory shoe. Body mounted shutter release, and redesigned top.

Iloca Quick A: **R2* B−**
c1954. Metal 35mm VFR camera. Ilitar f3.5, 45mm lens; Vero shutter; no accessory shoe; knob wind.

Iloca Quick B: **R2* B+**
c1954. Metal 35mm camera. Coupled RFR, Ilitar f2.9 or Ilitar f3.5, 45mm lens; Prontor-S shutter; accessory shoe; knob wind; body mounted shutter release.

Iloca Quick S: **R3* B**
c1954. Metal 35mm VFR camera. Ilitar f3.5, 45mm lens; Prontor-S shutter; accessory shoe; knob wind; body mounted shutter release.

Iloca Quick R: **R3* B+**
c1956. Metal 35mm VFR camera. Cassar f2.8, 45mm lens, Vero shutter, lever advance, accessory shoe.

Iloca Rapid: **R2* B+**
c1956. Metal 35mm VFR camera. Ilitar

f2.8 or Cassar f2.8/45mm lens, Prontor SV shutter, folding lever advance, accessory shoe.

Iloca Rapid B: R2* C

c1956. Metal 35mm camera. Coupled RFR, Ilitar-Super f2.8, Cassar-S or Cassarit f2.8, 45mm lens; Prontor SV shutter; folding lever advance; accessory shoe.

Iloca Rapid I: R3* B+

c1956. Metal 35mm VFR camera. Cassarit f2.8, 45mm lens; Compur shutter; lever advance; accessory shoe.

Iloca Rapid IL: R3* B+

c1956. Metal 35mm VFR camera. Ilitar or Cassar f2.8, 45mm lens; Prontor SV shutter; lever advance; accessory shoe. Built-in light meter.

Iloca Rapid IIL: R3* C

c1956. Metal 35mm camera. With coupled RFR; Cassar-S or Cassarit f2.8 or Heligon f2, 50mm lens; lever advance; accessory shoe; Gauthier shutter or Compur Rapid shutter with EV settings.

Reporter: R3* B+

c1953. Metal 35mm VFR camera. Reporter 3.5, 45mm lens; Prontor-S shutter; accessory shoe; knob wind; body mounted shutter release. Made by Iloca for sale by other retailers.

Iloca Stereo: R2* E–

c1951. 35mm VFR stereo camera. Ilitar f3.5, 45mm individually focused lenses. Prontor S shutter 1-1/300s.

Iloca Stereo II: R3* E–

c1954. 35mm VFR stereo camera. Ilitar f3.5, 35mm lenses; Prontor S shutter 1-1/300s.

Iloca Stereo Rapid: R3* E–

c1955. 35mm stereo camera. CRF; lever wind; Steinheil Cassarit f2.8, 35mm lenses; Prontor S shutter 1-1/300s. Also available as the Iloca Stereo Rapid 3.8, a modified version of which was made for Realist Inc, and sold in the USA as the Realist 45.

Wohler
Saaland

Favor II: R3* D

c1950. 35mm VFR camera in satin chrome and black plastic imitation leather. 45mm f2.8 Docar lens, Prontor Shutter 1-1/300s.

Wolfgang Simons & Co
Bern, Switzerland

Sico: **R5* I–**

c1923. 35mm miniature camera. Rudersdorf Anastigmat 60mm, f3.5 lens; Dial-set Compur shutter 1-1/300s. 25 exp, 30 x 40mm on unperforated 35mm paperbacked roll film. Dark brown wooden body with brass trim. Only pre-Leica 35mm with wooden body.

Wollensak Optical Co
Rochester, New York, USA

Wollensak Stereo: **R3* E**
c1950. 35mm stereo camera. Wollensak Amaton f2.7 lens; Rapax shutter 1/2-1/300s, CRF. Similar to Revere design.

Wratten & Wainwright
London, England

Wratten and Wainwright Tailboard Camera: **R4* E+**

c1890. 13" x 18" Tailboard camera. Excelsior 3 Rochester Optical Company brass lens. Shifting stereo lens panel. Dark red Russian leather bellows.

Wray Optical Works
London, England

Farvu: **R5* F+**
c1930. Unusual box-shaped camera fitted with f10 20" telephoto lens as standard, focusing only from 20 ft to infinity. Shutter speeded 1-1/200s. Designed for $3^{1}/_{2}$" x $2^{1}/_{2}$" plates or film packs. Lens could be detached and carried inside camera.

Peckham-Wray: **R3* E**
1955. 5 x 4 SLR designed by Cyril Peckham, Chief Photographer at Hawker Siddeley. Originally designed for air-to-air photography. Designed to be hand-held. 135mm f4.5 Wray Lustrar. FP shutter 1/15-1/800s + B & T. Folding frame finder.

Wrayflex II: **R4* E+**

Peckham-Wray, 1955.

Wrayflex I: **R3* E**

1959. 35mm SLR. Basically the same spec as the first two models, but with a taller top plate to incorporate a pentaprism in place of the mirror system previously used. Only around 300 made.

Wray Stereo Graphic: **R2* D**

1950. Originally known simply as the Wrayflex. The 'I' was added when subsequent models were launched. Early eye-level 35mm SLR that uses mirrors in place of a pentaprism. Satin chrome and black grained leather. 50mm f2 Unilite lens. FP shutter $^1/_2$-1/500s + B. Film wind by key on base. Takes 40 exp 24x32mm. Around 700 made.

c1950s. Simple 1/50s shutter; coated Wray F4.0, 35mm lenses. Made under license from Graflex Corp. Basically the same camera as the Stereo Graphic.

Wrayflex Ia: **R3* E**
1954. 35mm SLR. Not a replacement for the first model, but made to sell as an alternative. Similar specification, but film format changed to standard 36 exp 24 x 36mm and flash synch socket changed to 3mm co-ax type. 50mm f2.8 Unilux launched with this model. This model was originally referred to by Wray as the Wrayflex Mark III. Around 1,700 made.

Emil Wunsche, Reick
Dresden, Germany

Emil Wunsche's Postage Stamp Camera: **R5* H–**
c1900. 12 exp, 25 x 30mm on a 13 x 18cm plate.

Mars Detective Camera: R5* F–
c1893. Mahogany box form camera.
Aplanat 130mm, f8 lens; rotary shutter.
9 x 12cm exp.

Mars Box camera: R4* NSR est E+
c1900. Leather covered box camera. For
8 x 10cm plates, internal plate changing
mechanism for 12 plates, external
shutter.

Mars 99: R4* NSR est E+
c1900. Leather covered box camera. For
9 x 12cm plates; external shutter.

Bosco: R4* D+
c1900. Leather covered box camera.
Exp. 9 x 9cm on rollfilm; external
shutter.

Elite stereo: R4* F–
c1900. Leather covered box camera.
Exp. 9 x 18cm stereo frames on glass
plates; internal plate changing
mechanism for 12 plates. Two speed
shutter.

Sport Stereo: R4* F
c1908. Leather covered box camera.
Taking 8.5 x 17cm stereo frames on
glass plates. Two speed shutter.

Victrix Stereo: R4* NSR est F
c1908. Leather covered folding camera.
Taking 6 x 13cm stereo frames on glass
plates. CFPS 1/25-1/200. Rapid-
Aplanate lenses.

Victrix: R3* D+
c1908. Strut type folding camera. For 9
x 12cm plates. Tessar f6.3, 135mm lens;
CFPS, 1/25-1/200s.

Kobold: R3* C+
c1904. Leather covered box camera.
Taking 9 x 12cm plates; internal
changing mechanism for 6 glass plates.
Two speed shutter; meniscus lens.

Nova: R4* NSR est D
c1908. Leather covered box camera.
Taking 9 x 12cm plates; internal
changing mechanism for 12 glass plates.
Dagor lens. Internal pneumatic shutter.
Automatic frame counting.

Legion: R4* NSR est D
Leather covered box camera. With nickel
plated fittings. Taking 9 x 12cm plates.
Offered as a "tropical" model in
catalogues of the day.

Nixe (roll film): R3* C
c1900. Leather covered folding camera.
For roll film only, 8.3 x 10.8cm and 6 x
9cm sizes. Many different lens shutter
combinations, typically Mars-
Anastigmat f6.8 lens, Univers shutter.
50% Less for simpler less decorative
models.

Nixe (roll film & plates): R3* C+
c1900. Leather covered folding camera.
Taking roll film or glass plates, 8.3 x
10.8cm on roll film. 9 x 12cm on glass
plates. Many different lens shutter
combinations, typically Dynar lens,
Compound shutter. 50% Less for simpler
less decorative models.

Afpi 6 x 9: R3* G–
c1900. Leather covered folding
camera.Taking 9 x 12cm plates. Many
lens and shutter combinations; typically
Extra-Rapid-Aplanat f8 lens; Automat
shutter. Camera interior polished
Mahogany or Walnut.

Afpi "querformat":   R3* C+

c1904. Leather covered folding camera. Two models: 9 x 12cm or 13 x 18. Square design allows the making of horizontal and vertical photos by simply turning the removable camera back 90 degrees. Many lens and shutter combinations, typically Imagonal f6 lens; S.V Automat shutter. Double extension bellows. Camera interior polished Mahogany or Walnut.

Minimum: R3* C+

Leather covered folding camera for 9 x 12cm glass plates or film packs. Double extension bellows. Many lens and shutter combinations; typically Rapid Aplanat f8 lens; Compound shutter.

Nymphe: R4* D

c1904. Leather covered scissors type folding camera. Taking 9 x 9cm exposures on roll film. Anastigmat lens. Two speed shutter.

Y

Yashica Co Ltd
Tokyo, Japan

Yashica Atoron Electro: **R2* C+**

c1970. Subminiature detective camera. Yashinon 18mm, f2.8 coated lens. Camera flash and right-angle finder.

Yashica 44:   **R2* D–**

c1962. TLR camera for 4 x 4cm exp on 127 Roll film. Yashinon f3.5, 60mm lens. Copal SV shutter 1-1/500s. Knob advance, built-in light meter. Usually found in grey.

Yashica YF: **R3* F**

c1956. TLR camera for 4 x 4cm exp on 127 roll film. Yashicor f3.5, 60mm lens. Copal SV shutter 1-1/500s. Crank advance. Usually found in grey.

c1959. RFR camera. CFPS, 1-1/1000s. FP and X flash synch. Separate Rfr/Vfr windows. Diopter adjustment. Screw mount Nikkor H. f2.0, 5cm lens. Completely redesigned top plate. The same as the Nicca IIIL. Produced by the Nicca Camera Company Ltd.

Yashica 44A: **R3* D–**
c1959. TLR camera for 4 x 4cm exp on 127 roll film. Yashicor F3.5, 60mm lens. Copal shutter 1/25-1/300s. Knob advance. Usually found in grey.

Yashica YE: R2* E+

c1959. RFR Camera. CFPS. $\frac{1}{2}$-1/500s. PF And X flash synch. Separate Rfr/Vfr windows. Diopter adjustment. Screw mount Niccor f2.8, 50mm lens. The same as the Nicca 33. Produced by the Nicca Camera Company Ltd.

Yashicamat: R2* C+

c1959. TLR camera. Taking 6 x 6cm exp on 120 roll film; Yashicor f3.5, 80mm lens. Copal shutter 1-1/500s.

Yashicamat 635:   R2* C+

c1959. TLR Camera. For 6 x 6cm exp on 120 roll film or 24 x 36mm on 35mm film with adaptor. Yashicor f3.5, 80mm lens. Copal shutter 1-1/500s. (Price includes 35mm adaptor)

Yashica A: R2* C+

c1959 TLR Camera. Taking 6 x 6cm exp on 120 roll film. Yashikor f3.5, 80mm lens. Copal shutter 1/25-1/300s. Knob advance not coupled to shutter. Screw mount filters.

Yashica C: R2* C

c1960. TLR Camera. For 6 x 6cm exp on 120 roll film.Yashikor f3.5, 80mm lens. Copal shutter 1-1/300s. Knob advance, coupled to shutter. Bayonet mount filters.

Yashica D: R2* C+

c1960. TLR Camera. Taking 6 x 6cm exp on 120 roll film. Yashikor f3.5, 80mm lens. Copal shutter 1-1/500s. Knob advance coupled to shutter. Bayonet mount filters.Users pay more than collectors.

Yashica LM: R2* C+

c1960. TLR Camera. For 12 exp. 6 x 6cm on 120 roll film. Yashikor f3.5, 80mm lens. Copal shutter 1-1/300s. Built-in light meter. Knob advance coupled to shutter. Bayonet mount filters.

Pentamatic: R2* C

1961. 35mm SLR. Probably one of the first cameras to utilise the rewind knob for opening the back. Interchangeable, bayonet-fit 55mm f1.8 Auto-Yashinon lens. FP shutter 1-1/1000s.

Rapide: R3* C+

c1962. Vertically styled 35mm half-frame (18 x 24mm) camera. Yashion f2.8, 28mm lens. Copal shutter 1-1/500s. Built-in light meter.

Yashica

Rapide, c1962.

Sequelle: R3* C+

c1962. 35mm Half-frame (18 x 24mm) camera. Yashinon f2.8, 28mm lens. Seikosha shutter, 1/30-1/250s. Built-in light meter.

Yamato Optical Co
Tokyo, Japan

Pax I: R4* C+

1952. According to the Collector's Guide to Japanese Cameras this is the smallest of the Leica type of 35mm camera. Fitted with a Luminor Anastigmat f3.5, 45mm lens and coupled to a rangefinder. Shutter 1/25-1/150s. It was just slightly over $4^1/_4$" (11cms) wide.

Pal 4: R* C

1960. Pocket size 35mm CRF camera. 45mm f2.8 Luminor lens. Shutter 1/10-1/300s.

Z

Paul Zeh Kamerawerk
Dresden, Germany

Zecaflex: R4* G+

c1938. Folding TLR camera. For 12 exp. 2¼" x 2¼" on roll film. Xenar or Tessar f3.5. or f4.5, 75mm lens in Compur Rapid shutter 1-1/400s.

Goldi: R3* C+
c1938. Folding camera for 3 x 4cm frames on roll film. Zecanar f2.9, 50mm lens in Compur shutter.

Beltax: R3* C–
c1938. Folding camera for 6 x 9cm or 6 x 4.5cm on roll film. Trinar f4.5, 105mm lens. Pronto or Compur shutter.

Zeiss Ikon A.G.
Dresden, Germany

For further information see Zeiss Compendium and Zeiss Ikon Cameras 1926-39, reissued 1993. Hove Collectors Books.

Zeiss Ikon A.G. was founded at Dresden, Germany in 1926 by the merger of a number of leading German camera manufacturers, among them: Contessa-Nettel A.G., Stuttgart; Ernemann Werke A.G., Dresden; Optisch-Anstalt C.P. Goerz, Berlin; and Ica A.G., Dresden. Camera production ceased in 1971, although assembly continued into 1972 at Stuttgart.

In a single year (1927) Zeiss offered 104 different models with an average of three formats each with more than three lens and shutter combinations – 936 choices of "stock" models in one catalogue! The camera model with the most variations was the Deckrullo later called "Nettel" press camera.

It could be ordered in five formats (4.5 x 6cm, 6.5 x 9cm, 9 x 12cm, 10 x 15cm and 13 x 18cm). All except the smallest size were available in Tropical models with varnished teak wood construction and brown leather bellows. A selection of 30 different lenses was available for the nine models – 39 possible variations for this single model. This was in the

1927 catalogue, before any of the really famous Zeiss Ikon cameras such as the Contax, Contarex, Kolibri, and Super Ikonta cameras had been introduced.

From the above you can get some idea of the complexity of identifying and pricing all Zeiss Ikon cameras, so please regard this list as covering only the more usual types and those of special interest. Where the Zeiss Ikon model number is likely to be found on the camera it is included in the description. The number is usually expressed as a fraction – 250/7 for a 9 x 2cm Ideal and 250/3 for a 6.5 x 9cm Ideal. The second part of the fraction gives the film size according to the following table. (1) These film size numbers were used from 1927-1960; decimal numbers were used after 1960. The focal length of the most usual lens for the format is also shown.

Number	Size	Usual lens
none	4.5 x 6cm	75mm
none	22 x 31mm	45 or 50mm
1	4.5 x 10.7cm	twin 65mm
2	6 x 9cm	105mm
3	6.5 x 9cm	105mm
4	6 x 13cm	twin 75mm
5	8.5 x 11.5cm	135mm
6	8 x 14cm	150mm
7	9 x 12cm	135mm
8	9 x 14cm (ICA)	Stereo
9	10 x 15cm	165mm
10	9 x 18cm (ICA)	Stereo
11	13 x 18cm (5" x 7")	210mm
12	4 x 6.5cm	75mm
13	13 x 18cm (ICA)	210mm
14	5 x 7.5cm	90mm
15	6.5 x 11cm	120mm
16	6 x 6cm	80mm
17	8 x 10.5cm	120mm
18	3 x 4cm	50mm
19		
24	24 x 36mm	50mm
27	24 x 24mm	40mm

Baby Box Tengor: R C

c1931. Small box camera marked "Baby Box" on front or rear. 3 x 4cm. Frontar f11 lens. Plain leather front.

Baby Box Tengor: R3* D

c1931-1934. 3 x 4cm. Novar f6.3 focusing lens. Black metal front plate.

Baby Deckrullo: R4* F

c1929. 4.5 x 6cm Plate camera. 80mm, f4.5 or f2.7 lens; FPS. Chrome struts, door closes. Focus knob on top.

Baby Ikonta: R2*   C– to D–

c1931. 3 x 4cm roll film camera. c1936. Novar 50mm, f3.5 lens. price 20% less. Tessar 50mm, f3.5 lens. Novar f6.3 and Tessar f4.5 lens.

Baldur Box: R3*   C+

c1938. Metal box camera. Taking 6 x 4.5cm. frames on roll film. Named for the leader of the Hitler Youth, and sold to its members!

Baldur Box: R3*   D–

c1938. 6 x 9cm. frames.

Baldur Box: R5*   E

c1938. Metal box camera for 6 x 4.5cm. frames on roll film. Named after the Facist Youth organisation in Italy the "Balilla" for children 11 to 13 years old. Only one camera has been recently discovered, where one might expect there to have been many thousands produced. The story of its production still waits to be told.

Bebe: R3*   E

c1928. 4.5 x 6cm camera. With struts and unpleated bellows. Tessar 75mm, f4.5 or Triotar f3.5 lens (front cell focus). Dial-set Compur. C.1930. Rim-set Compur (Z342/3), 6.5 x 9cm; Tessar 105mm, f4.5 lens, Tessar 105mm, f3.5 lens, Rim-set shutter, adds 20% to the price.

Bob: R2*   B+

c1931-1941. 4.5 x 6cm or 6 x 9cm Folding camera. Nettar lenses. Inexpensive black camera.

Bob IV and V: R2*   C–
                 Larger sizes C+

c1927. Clean up of Ernemann 4 x 6.5cm, 6 x 6cm, 6 x 9cm, 6.5 x 11cm and 7.25 x 12.5cm cameras. 33 different lens/shutter combinations. Smaller sizes.

Bobette I: R3*   D

c1929. Folding roll film camera. With struts 2.2 x 3.1cm format. Frontar 50mm, f9 lens. Ernoplast 50mm f4.5 or Erid f8 lens add 50% to the price.

Bobette I, c1929.

Bobette II: R4* F+

c1929. Folding roll film camera taking 2.2 x 3.1cm format. Ernon 40mm,f3.5 or Ernostar 42mm,f2 lens. Earliest f2 lens on a miniature roll film camera. Used the so-called "N" size film for 5 x 7.5cm film size

Box Tengor (127 roll film size – 5 x 7.5cm):   R3* D–

c1928-1934. Two models, both with Frontar f11 lens. First model had plain leather covered front with the two finder lenses located vertically – upper left. Winding knob on left side at bottom. Second model c1928-1934. Similar, except the two finder lenses are located horizontally across top of front, priced 25% less.

Box Tengor (half of 120 roll film size – 4.5 x 6cm):   R3* D–

c1934-1939. All models had the Frontar f11 lens. Rotating Waterhouse stops and close-up lens (controlled from front of camera). Diamond shaped winding knob. 2 ruby windows.

Box Tengor (full 120 roll film size – 6 x 9cm):   R3* B+

Six models. c1926-1928. Frontar f11 lens. Plain leatherette front. Vfr. objectives located vertically – one above the other – on the upper left of front. Winding knob on left side at bottom.

c1928-1934:   C–

Similar to above, except Vfr. objectives located horizontally across top of front. Winding knob on left side at top. Frontar f11 lens with waterhouse stops and close-up lens. Varieties include the following:

c1934-1938:   C–

Frontar f11 lens with Waterhouse stops and close-up lens in centre of hexagonal shaped front plate. Black enamel trim around front edge of camera. Diamond shaped winding knob located on left side at top.

c1938:   C+

Similar to above, except release button moved to top left of camera.

c1939:   C+

Similar to above, except serrated round winding knob with leatherette centre. Black enamel front trim. Double exp interlock coupled to winding knob.

Box Tengor Cameras.

c1948-1956:   **C–**
Chrome trim. Lever-type shutter release on lower front. Frontar f9 lens.

**Box Tengor (116 roll film size –
6.5 x 11cm):**   **C+**
c1926-1928. Three models. Vfr. windows of ground glass the objectives located one above the other on the left front. Winding knob on left side at bottom. Variations include the following:

c1928-1933:   **C–**
Mirror on front of shutter. Vfr. objectives located horizontally across top of front. Winding knob on left side at top. Controls for diaphragm and close-up lens located on top of camera.

c1933-1939:   **R3* C**
Similar to above, except has elongated hexagonal design on front around lens. Brilliant vfr with rectangular lenses. Control for diaphragm and close-up lens located on front metal plate. This size was discontinued after 1938-1939.

Cocarette: R2* C+

1926-1932. Roll film folding camera. Frontar, Periskop, Novar, Dominar or Tessar lenses. Derval, Klio or Compur shutters – 64 possible combinations. To load film, the finder and film track are removed from the side of the camera, the back does not open. (similar to loading film in a Leica camera). All models were finished in black. Five sizes, single extension. Variations include the following:

Three sizes, single extension no vertical lens adjustment, lever focus.

Two sizes, single extension, vertical lens adjustment, lever focus.

Two sizes, same as above. A plate model also exists. c1928. All variations.

Cocarette Luxus: R3* E+
with Dominar lens E–

Covered in brown leather with polished metal fittings. Dial-set Compur shutter. Double ext bellows. Two sizes. 6 x 9cm. with Dominar 105mm, f4.5 lens or Tessar 105mm, f4.5 lens. 8 x 10.5cm. Dominar f4.5 or Tessar f4.5 lens. with Tessar lens.

Cocarette (1930):   R3* C+

Black models were manufactured with Compur rim-set shutters. They are worth £5 to £10 more than models with dial-set shutters. No Cocarettes were offered after 1930.

Coloura: R3* B+

c1963-1965. Inexpensive 35mm camera. Novicar 50mm, f2.8 lens in Prontar 125 shutter, X synch. Camera is marked "Coloura" on right side of top. The Novicar is an unusual lens.

Coloura "F":   R3* B+

Similar to above, except accessory shoe (on top) tips back to become reflector for AG-1 flash bulbs, the flash socket is uncovered as the shoe tips back. Flash calculator built into rewind knob. c1963-1965.

Contaflex TLR: R3* G+

1935; This was one of the most advanced cameras of its time. Seven interchangeable lenses were available ranging from 35 to 135mm. (see following listing). The 80mm viewing lens was fixed and provided an unusually bright focusing surface. An albada type eye-level viewfinder was used for most of the lenses. It was the first camera to be fitted with a built-in but non-coupled electric exposure meter. Even cameras in mint cosmetic condition rarely have a fully functional shutter and exposure meter, unless it has been serviced recently. Since the camera is rarely actually used by collectors, overall cosmetic condition is of extreme importance when determining price.

Contaflex TLR Lenses

Biogon 35mm lens, with viewfinder	**G**
Sonnar 50mm f/2 lens	**F**
Sonnar 50mm f/1.5 lens	**F+**
Sonnar 50mm f2.8 lens	**F+**
Sonnar 80mm f/2 lens	**F+**
Triotar 85mm f/4 lens	**F+**
Sonnar 135mm f/4 lens	**F+**

All interchangeable lenses are rare and difficult to find.

Contaflex I: **R2* C+**

c1953-1958. 35mm SLR camera. Tessar 45mm, f2.8 lens. Synchro-Compur shutter. No exp meter.

Contaflex II: **R2* C+**
c1954-58. Similar to above except, has built-in exp meter.

Contaflex III: **R3* C+**
c1956-1958. 35mm SLR camera. Tessar 50mm lens, interchangeable front element. Last model with knob wind for film advance. No built-in meter. Stereo attachment £200. "O" stereo viewer, £180. "OO" stereo viewer, £100 c1957-1959. Camera alone.

Contaflex III, c1956-1958.

Contaflex IV: **R2* C+**
c1957-1959. Similar to above, except has LVS settings on shutter. Built-in exp meter with hinged door.

Contaflex "Alpha":   **R2* C+**
c1958-1959. Inexpensive version of Contaflex III. Pantar 45mm, f2.8 lens, interchangeable front element for Pantar series lenses.

Contaflex "Beta":   **R2* D–**
(Z10.1251). c1957-58. Similar to "Alpha" model, except has exp meter.

Contaflex "Rapid":   **R2* D**
1958-60. Tessar 50mm, f2.8 lens, interchangeable front element. Three special features first appeared on this camera and succeeding models: rapid film advance lever, accessory shoe on prism housing, interchangeable magazine backs.

Contaflex "Prima":   **R2* D**
c1959-1965. Similar to "Rapid" except has Pantar 45mm, f2.8 lens. Uncovered match needle exp meter (right side).

Contaflex "Super":   **R1* D+**
c1959-1962. Similar to "Rapid" except
has coupled exp meter. The uncovered
meter window is in the front of the
prism housing. Meter adjustment wheel,
is on the right front of the camera (the
only Contaflex with external wheel).

Contaflex "Super" (new style): R1* E–
c1962-1967. Tessar 50mm, f2.8 lens.
Shutter marked "Synchro-Compur Z".
Larger exp meter window marked "Zeiss
Ikon". Top mount exp meter window
shows two red arrows – no numbers.
Internal RFR images shows small "2x"
(visible at top of exp meter slot – right
side). No auto exp control.

Contaflex "Super B":   **R1* E–**
c1963-1968. Similar to above, except
shows numbers in top mounted exp
meter and in vfr. Shutter marked
"Synchro-Compur" under lens. Auto exp
control.

Contaflex "Super BC":
                Black model R3* E+
                Chrome model E–
c1967-1970. Similar to above, except
has no external exp meter window. Has
through-the-lens CdS photo-electric
meter. Marked "Zeiss Ikon" in rectangle
above lens. Battery compartment with
door located at 9 o'clock from lens. Was
produced in chrome or black finish.

Contaflex "S" Automatic:
                Black model R3* D–
                Chrome model E–
c1970-72. Similar to above, except has
no external exp meter window. Has
through-the-lens CdS photo-electric
meter. Marked "Zeiss Ikon" in rectangle
above lens. Battery compartment with

door located at 9 o'clock from lens.
Produced in chrome or black finish.

*Lenses for Contaflex SLR
(35mm: 24 x 36mm)*

Teleskop 1.7x (fits models I and II only).
Complete with bracket   **D+**

Steritar A (stereo prism for Teleskop
1.7x)   **E+**

Pro-Tessar 35mm f4-takes filters with
49mm external thread   **D+**

Pro-Tessar 35mm, f3.2-takes filters with
60mm external thread   **D+**

Pro-Tessar 85mm, f4-takes filters with
60mm external thread   **D+**

Pro-Tessar 85mm, f3.2-takes filters with 60mm external thread **D+**

Pro-Tessar 115mm, f4-takes filters with 67mm external thread **E–**

Pro-Tessar M-1:1 Macro lens **D+**

Lenses for Contaflex Alpha, Beta, Primar and Contina III

Pantar 30mm f4 lens **C+**

Pantar 75mm f4 lens **D–**

Steritar "D" **E–**

Lenses for Contaflex III to "S"

Steritar "B" **E+**

Contaflex 126: **R3* E–**

1966-71. Tessar 45mm, f2.8 or Colour Pantar 45mm, f2.8 lens. FPS. Automatic exp control. Marked Contaflex "126" on front of camera. 28 x 28mm exp on 26 Instamatic cartridge. Seven interchangeable lenses were available, 25 to 200mm.

Lenses for Contaflex 126 (28 x 28mm)

Distagon 25mm, f4. Rare	**E**
Distagon 32mm, f2.8	**D**
Colour Pantar 45mm, f2.8	**C**
Tessar 45mm, f2.8	**C**
Sonnar 85mm, f2.8	**D+**
Tele-Tessar, 135mm f4	**D+**
Tele-Tessar, 200mm f4	**E+**

Contarex cameras are marked "Contarex"; the microscope version is not marked.

Contarex "Bullseye": **R2* F**

1959-66. Planar 50mm, f2 (chrome) lens, interchangeable mount. Coupled exp meter has large round window on front of pentaprism. Early models lacked data strip slot at rear of camera

Contarex "Special": **R4* G**

c1960-66. Script style logo "Contarex". Interchangeable vfr – reflex or prism. No meter.

Contarex "Professional": **R4* G+**

1966-67. Fixed prism finder. No meter. Logo "Professional" on front at 11 o'clock position from lens.

Contarex "Super":   R3* G

Logo "Super" marked on front. c1968-75. First model had through-the-lens exp meter on front at 2 o'clock. (Black add 30%). Second model had switch under winding lever.

Contarex "Electronic":   R3* G+

c1968-75. Marked "Electronic" at 11 o'clock from lens. Chrome or black (rare) finish. Seldom offered.

Contarex "Hologon":   R4* H+

(outfit). c1969-75. Hologon 15mm, f8 fixed focus (fixed opening) lens. (linear type, not a fisheye). Outfit: camera, grip, cable release, special neutral density graduated filter and combination case.

Contarex Microscope Camera: R4* F+

Marked "Zeiss Ikon" on top. No lens, vfr. or exp meter. Takes interchangeable backs.

Contarex Lenses:

Manufactured between 1959 and 1973 by Carl Zeiss, Oberkochen. These lenses have seldom been equalled and never surpassed, even with modern technology. Prior to 1965, lenses with

focal length of 135mm and shorter were finished in chrome; those of 180mm focal length and longer were finished in black; after 1965 all lenses were finished in black.

Distagon Fisheye 16mm, f2.8. c1973.
Rare **G**

Distagon 18mm, f4, with adaptor ring for B96 filters. c1967-1973   **G+**

Biogon 21mm, f4.5, won't work on Contarexes after Bullseye model.
c1960-1963 **G**

Distagon 25mm, f2.8. c1963-1973.
Chrome **G–**
Black **G**

Distagon 35mm, f4. c1960-1963   **E+**

Blitz Distagon 35mm, f4, built-in flash automation. c1966-1973   **F–**

Distagon 35mm, f2. c1965-1973   **G–**

Tessar 50mm, f2.8. Chrome or black   **E+**

Planar 50mm, f2. c1960-1973.
Chrome **E+**

Blitz-Planar 50mm, f2. c1966-1973.
Chrome **F–**

S-Planar 50mm, f4, for critical closeups to 3". c1963-1968   **G+**

Planar 55mm, f1.4 c1965-1973.
Chrome, **F–**
Black, **F+**

Sonnar 85mm, f2. c1960-1973.
Chrome, **F–**
Black, **F+**

Planar 85mm, f1.4. C 1974. Rare   **H**

Tessar 115mm, f3.5, for use with bellows. c1960-1973   **G**

Sonnar 135mm, f4. c1960-1973.
Chrome **E**
Black **F–**

Olympia-Sonnar 135mm, f2.8.   c1965-1973   **F+**

Olympia-Sonnar 180mm, f2.8. c1967-1973   **H**

Sonnar 250mm, f4, manual preset ring focus. c1960-1963   **G–**

Olympia-Sonnar 250mm, f4, knob focus auto stop down. c1963-1973   **G**

Mirotar 500mm, f4.5,Catadioptric. c1963-1973   **I**

Mirotar 1000mm, f5.6, Catadioptric. c1964-1970. Rare, only four known to have been offered in last fourteen years, negotiated price,   around **J**

Tele-Tessar 400mm, f5.6. c1970-1973.   Rare **H+**

Vario-Sonnar 40-120mm, f2.8. c1970-1973.   Rare **H**

Vario-Sonnar 85-250mm, f4. c1970-1973.   Rare **H**

Monocular 8 x 30B: **E**
Third model   **F–**
c1969. With 27mm thread at eyepiece to fit Contaflex SLR or Contarex with an adaptor. First model had eyepiece focus and line for 140 feet. c1960. Second model had front end focusing and a distance scale. This was the most common type.

c1963. Third model had a porroprism and front end focus. The shape is straight, it looks like a small refracting telescope.

Curtagon 35PA f4:   **R5* H–**
c1973. Automatic stop-down with perspective control by lateral movement of up to 7mm in any of four directions. Mfd by Schneider, mounted and sold by Zeiss Ikon. Stuttgart. Rare.

Contax Series

Introduced in 1932, the Contax I was the most advanced 35mm system camera of its time. Early Zeiss literature stresses many competitive advantages: the long base RFR with pivoting gold-plated prism; the MFPS with 1/1000s top speed; the interchangeable bayonet lens mount; availability of a wide range of lenses and accessories; and the removable back for convenient film loading and cleaning. Production of subsequent models continued (except for the period from 1944 to 1952) until 1961.

Many design changes occurred during the production span of the Contax I (1932-1936). These variations have been grouped into six models, designated: I(a); I(b); I(c); I(d); I(e) and I(f). Dissimilar and yet similar, they shared many features: the rectangular body with removable back finished in black enamel; the logo "CONTAX" was marked on the front, above the lens mount in white letters; the bayonet lens mount; and the combination film wind knob and shutter setting dial located on the front of the body, to the left of the lens mount.

Price codes shown below include the value of the correct (period) lens.

Contax I(a):   **R4* G**

1932-36. No slow (below 1/25s) shutter speeds. No "foot" on tripod socket. Some models had one or more raised "dimples" on the front of the camera (covering ends of shafts). The Vfr. window eyepiece is to the right of the RFR window (looking at the rear). The distance scale around the base of the lens mount is finished in black enamel with white numerals. Serial numbers start with "AU" or "AV".

Contax I(b):   R4* F+
Similar to I(a) except front bezel extends across front of camera to Vfr and RFR window.

Contax I(c):   R4* F+
Slow shutter speeds added. Pivoting "foot" added to tripod socket. Lens bezel has guard attached which surrounds slow speed setting ring.

Note: the preceding models did not have a button to unlock the infinity stop when lenses with an external bayonet were in use.

Contax I(d):   R3* F+
Similar to I(c), except has button to release infinity lock located at 1 o'clock from lens. Distance scale around base of lens mount finished in chrome with black numerals.

Contax I(e):   R3* F+
Similar to I(d), except the Vfr window (viewing body from rear). A shallow vertical groove in the front bezel separates the area containing the logo "CONTAX" and the focus wheel.

Contax I(f):   R3* F+
Similar to I(e), except accessory shoe has four screws. The marker for setting the shutter speeds was changed from a slotted screw head to a small pointer.

Contax II: R3* E+

c1936-1942. Sonnar 50mm, f2 lens. MFPS to 1/1250s. No synch. Combined range and Vfr. Narrow frame around left RFR window. Chrome finish. Winding knob with shutter speed dial on top left.

Contax III: R3* E+

c1936-1942. Similar to Contax II. Except had uncoupled selenium photoelectric exp meter on top, and higher rewind knob.

"No Name" Contax, Contax S, D and Contax F: R2* F
Several variations of the Contax were

produced in East Germany after WWII. The Contax S was the first 35mm camera to use a pentaprism.

Contax IIIa.

Collectors prefer the early Contax lenses with black enamel finish and chrome trim (to the later chrome finished versions); early lenses, therefore, usually bring a higher price. The snr range is approximately 1,350,000 to 2,700,000.

Contax IIa: R3* F

1950-61. A superb 35mm camera produced at Stuttgart. Chrome finish; "CONTAX" logo marked on front. Wide frame around left RFR window. Film speed and type indicator on rewind knob. First model had black numerals on shutter speed dial. The synch connection looks like a flat plunger in socket – a special attachment is required to convert mechanical motion to electrical contact. £200. Second model similar, except the numbers on the shutter speed dial were in colour – 1-1/25s. Black. 1/50s. Yellow. 1/100-1/1250s. Red. Regular P.C. flash connector on rear.

Lens	Grade
Tessar 28mm, f8 non-coupled lens	E
Biogon 35mm, f2.8 lens, will not fit post-war Contaxes	E–
Orthometer 35mm, f4.5 lens, rare	F
Biotar 40mm and 42.5mm, f2 lenses, Chrome	H
Black	H
Tessar 50mm, f3.5 lens	D
Tessar 50mm, f2.8 lens	D
Sonnar 50mm, f2 lens	D+
Sonnar 50mm, f1.5 lens	D+
Triotar 85mm, f4 lens	D+
Sonnar 85mm, f2 lens	E–
Sonnar 135mm, f4 lens	D+
Tele-Tessar K 180mm, f6.3 lens, direct mount	G+

Contax IIIa: Black dial R3* F+
Coloured dial F+

Similar to Contax IIa, except has uncoupled selenium photo-electric exp meter on top. First model: Black dial. Second model: Coloured dial.

mount   **H–**

Sonnar 180mm, f2.8 lens, in Flektoskop
(inverted image) with case   **G+**

Tele-Tessar K 300mm, f8 lens, direct or
Flektoskop mount   **I–**

Fern 500mm, f8 lens (distance), in
direct or Flektoskop mount.   Rare **I**

Postwar Contax Lenses

Chrome finish, except the Fern 180mm
and 500mm, f2 lenses, and the Tessar
115mm, f3.5 lens, were offered in
black.

Biogon 21mm, f4 lens with finder   **G**

Topogon 25mm, f4 lens.   Rare **NSI**
                          Estimate **G+**

Biometer 35mm, f2.8 lens   **F–**

Planar 35mm, f3.5 lens   **F–**

(Z563/09), Biogon 35mm, f2.8 lens **F–**

Tessar 50mm, f3.5 lens   **E–**

Sonnar 50mm, f2 lens   **E–**

Sonnar 50mm, f1.5 lens   **E–**

Biotar 75mm, f1.5 lens, rare.
                          Estimate **G+**

Sonnar 85mm, f2 lens   **F–**

Triotar 85mm, f4 lens   **E–**

Panflex Tessar 115mm, f3.5 lens, for
bellows,   Rare **G+**

Sonnar 135mm, f4 lens   **E–**

Sonnar 180mm, f2.8 lens, direct or
Flektoskop mount.   Rare **H–**

Sonnar 300mm, f4 lens, Flektoskop
mount.   Rare **H+**

Direct mount.   Rare **I–**

Tele-lens 500mm, f8 lens, with
Flektoskop or Panflex mount, and case.
This lens sold for $835 in October
1952.   Rare, Estimate **I–**

**Stereotar "C" outfit, stereo lens
outfit:**   **Rare, estimate H+**
prism, special vf, closeup lenses and
leather case.

Contessa 35:   **R3* D+**

Tessar 45mm, f2.8 lens. Compur-Rapid
shutter, X synch only. Dual-range
uncoupled selenium photo-electric exp
meter. Logo "Contessa" marked in gold-
leaf letters on leather covered lens bed.
Round RFR window above lens. Film
advance coupled to shutter cocking.
First version. c1950-1953.
Second version. c1953-1955. Similar
except had Synchro-Compur shutter,
MX synch.
Third version. c1960-1961. Redesigned
body with built-in exp meter. Tessar
50mm, f2.8 lens in rigid mount. Pronto
1/30-1/250s. shutter. Logo "Contessa"
on top cover.
All three versions have lately been
selling around the same price.

Contessa LK: **R2* C+**
c1963-1965. Tessar 50mm, f2.8 lens. Prontor 500 LK shutter. coupled match needle exp meter. No RFR. Marked "Contessa LK" on top cover.

Contessa LKE: **R2* C+**
c1963-1965. Similar to LK except had coupled RFR. Marked with logo "Contessa LKE" on top cover.

Contessa S-310:   **R3* C+**

c1971. Tessar 40mm, f2.8 lens, rigid mount. Pronto S500 Electronic shutter coupled to photo-electric exp meter (max exp-8s). Logo "S-310" marked on front.

Contessa S-312:   **R3* D+**
Similar to S-310. Except has coupled RFR and marked with logo "S-312" on front.

Contessamatic "E":   **R2* B+**
c1960-1963. Tessar 50mm, f2.8 lens. Prontor SLK "Special" 1-1/500s, MX synch. Coupled RFR. Coupled photo-electric exp meter. Marked with logo "Contessa" on front above lens mount. top cover is not marked.

Contessamatic: **R1* C**
c1960-1961. Similar to "E" except has Prontor SLK shutter. No RFR.

Contessamat: **R2* C+**
c1964-1965. Colour Pantar 45mm, f2.8 lens. Prontormatic 1/30-1/125s. shutter. Coupled photo-electric exp meter. No RFR. Logo "Contessamat" on top cover.

Contessamat "SE":   **R2* C+**
c1964-1965. Similar to Contessamat (above), except has Prontormatic 1-1/500s. shutter. CRF. Logo "Contessamat SE" marked on top cover.

Contessamat "STE":   **R2* D–**
c1965. Similar to SE except has Tessar 50mm, f2.8 lens. Prontormatic 500 SL 1-1/500s. shutter. Logo "Contessamat STE" marked on top cover.

Contessamat "SBE":   **R2* C+**
c1963-1967. Similar to STE, except top cover has a cover over the flash contacts. Marked "flashmatic" in red letters and "Contessamat SBE" in black letters. Linkage between distance and diaphragm setting provided auto flash exp control.

Contina I: **R2* B+**
c1956-1957. 35mm folding camera. Novar 45mm, f3.5 lens. Prontor SV shutter, X synch. Also came with Tessar 45mm, f2.8 lens in Synchro-Compur shutter X synch. Model number impressed in leather on rear of body near latch.

Contina I: **R2* B+**

c1956-1957. Novicar 45mm, f2.8 lens, rigid mount. Prontor SVS 1-1/300s. MX synch. Came with Pantar 45mm, f2.8 lens in 1958. Marked "Contina" under lens and on bezel at 1 o'clock from lens. Model number impressed in leather on rear of body near latch.

Contina II: **R2* C+**

c1952-1953. Opton-Tessar 45mm, f2.8 lens. Synchro-Compur 1-1/500s. MX synch. Also with Novar 45mm, f3.5 lens and Prontor SV shutter. Uncoupled RFR. Marked "Contina" on leather of lens bed. Model number impressed in leather on rear of body near latch.

Contina IIa: **R2* C–**

c1956-1958. Novar 45mm, f35 lens, rigid mount or Novicar 45mm, f2.8 lens. Prontor 1-1/300s. MX synch. Rapid wind film advance. Top mounted uncoupled match-needle exp meter. Marked "Contina" on front under lens. Model number on back.

Contina III: **R2* D–**

c1956-1958. Similar to IIa, except has Pantar 45mm, f2.8 convertible lens – uses all lenses of Contaflex "Alpha" series. Marked "Contina" on front bezel at upper left (not under the lens as in IIa); model number on back.

Contina III lenses and finders

Pantar 30mm, f4 lens	**D–**
Pantar 75mm, f4 lens	**D**
Steritar "D", for 3D pictures	**E+**
Wide-angle (30mm) finder	**C+**
Telephoto finder	**C+**
Telephoto rangefinder,(correct field of view for 75mm Pantar)	**D–**
Universal finder for all above items	**E–**

Contina II Microscope Camera: R4* E
Modified III body used with standard Zeiss Microscope Connecting funnel. No lens. Has Ibsor B self-cocking 1-1/125s. X synch. No exp meter. No RFR. No vfr. Marked "Zeiss Ikon" in middle of rear. No other markings. Usual shutter release button does not release shutter but must be depressed to advance film.

Contina: **R2* C–**
c1962-1965. 35mm camera. Colour Pantar 45mm, f2.8 lens, rigid mount. Pronto 1-1/250s. X synch. Self-timer. Marked "Contina" on top cover.

Contina "L":   **R1* C–**
c1964-1965. Similar to Contina. Except has built-in uncoupled exp meter. Prontor 1/30-1/250s. Marked "Contina L" on top cover.

Contina "LK":   **R1* C–**
c1963-1965. Similar to "L" except has coupled exp meter. Marked "Contina LK" on top cover.

Continette: **R1* C–**
c1960-1961. Lucinar 45mm, f2.8 lens, rigid mount. Pronto 1/30-1/250s. Self-timer. The Continette was the only camera by Zeiss Ikon to use the Lucinar lens. Marked "Continette" on front next to vfr.

Citoskop: **R4* E+**
c1929. 45 x 107mm stereo camera. Tessar 65mm, f4.5 lenses. Dial-set Stereo Compur shutter. Reflex vfr.

Donata: **R3* C+**
c1927-1931. Inexpensive folding plate camera. Tessar f4.5 or Dominar f4.5 lens. Compur shutter. Marked "Donata" on or under handle. 6.5 x 9cm or 9 x 12cm exp on cut film.

Elegante: **R4* F–**
c1927-1934. Field camera with square bellows and rigid front. Polished wood finish. Brass fittings.

Era-Box: **R2* C–**
c1934-1938. Inexpensive version of Box Tengor. Marked "ERA-BOX" around lens. Two formats: 16 exp, 4.5 x 6cm or 8 exp, 6 x 9cm exp on 120 film.

Ergo: **R4* G+**
c1927-1931. Monocular-style detective camera. Tessar 55mm f4.5 lens. Self-cocking shutter. Rare.

Ergo, c1927-1931.

Ermanox: **R4* G+**
c1927-1931. 4.5 x 6cm plate camera. Ernostar 85mm, f1.8 lens, rigid mount with helical focus. FPS 1/20-1/200s. Shutter speed to 1/1000s

Ermanox: **G+**
c1927. Ernostar f1.8 lens. FPS to 1/1000s. Bellows with struts. 6.5 x 9cm on plates. Rare.

Ernostar 165mm, f1.8 lens: R5*   NSR
9 x 12cm exp on plates. Two other sizes – 10 x 15cm and 5" x 7" are listed in period catalogues.

Ermanox-Reflex: **R4* H+**
c1927-1929. 4.5 x 6cm SLR camera. Ernostar 105mm, f1.8 lens, rigid mount with helical focus. FPS 1/20-1/1200s.

Erni: **R3* E**
c1927-1930. Box camera with celluloid "ground glass". Rare.

Favorit: **R4* NSR**
c1927-1935. Plate camera. Tessar f4.5 or Dominar f3.5 lens. Usually marked with number or "Favorit" on handle. Number usually marked on rear door near hinge. 9 x 12cm or 10 x 15cm (rotating back). £120. 5" x 7". Rare.

Favorit: **R4* F+**
c1917-1931. Tropical plate camera. Tessar or Dominar f4.5 lens in Compur shutter. Polished teak construction. Brown leather handle marked with name "Favorit" and model number.

Hochtourist, Kosmopolit, Perfekt:
                    R4* E+
c1930. View cameras of polished wood with brass fittings; square bellows. Sizes: 5" x 7", 8" x 10", and 10" x 12" exp on plates. Although these cameras are not marked with a model name, they usually have a round metal plate with logo "Zeiss Ikon". These are rare and are seldom offered on the market. Estimate

Hologon:
Refer to Contarex.

Icarette: **R2* C−**
c1927-1936. Sizes. 4 x 6.5cm, 6 x 6cm, 6 x 9cm, 6.5 x 11cm, 8 x 10.5cm and a combination model which used 6 x 9cm

Icarex 35S with Super Dynarex 200mm f/4.

roll film or 6.5 x 9cm plates. There were more than 60 different lens and shutter combinations and four different bodies. Usually marked "Icarette" on handle or impressed in leather of body.

Icarex 35 (BM):   **R2* D+**
c1967-1973. Colour Pantar 50mm, f2.8 lens in interchangeable bayonet mount. CFPS ½-1/1000s. x synch. Interchangeable viewing screens and vfr. With Colour Pantar 50mm, f2.8 lens £80. With Tessar 50mm, f2.8 lens.

Icarex 35 (TM):   **R2* E–**
c1967-1973. Marked TM at 1 o'clock position from lens. With Tessar 50mm, f2.8 lens or Ultron 50mm, f1.8 lens.

Icarex CS   **R2* C+**
Either of the above cameras became an "Icarex CS" with the addition of a pentaprism D. Vfr containing a through-the-lens CdS meter the finder is marked "Icarex 35-CS". With the vfr.

Icarex 35S:
35S (TM) or 35S (BM), with
     Pantar D+
35S (TM) or 35S (BM) with Tessar
     f2.8 lens E–
35S (TM) or 35S (BM) with Ultron
     f1.8 lens D+
Black models are worth additional
     C+ R2*
Available in both "TM" and "BM" models, the "35S" differed from the previous two models Due to the vfr and viewing screens were not interchangeable. The CdS meter is built-in and coupled to the diaphragm by stop-down metering. Four Zeiss lenses were available for the "TM" model. With nine lenses for the "BM" model. Some of the

early black models were marked "PRO". ("TM" designates 42mm thread mount, "BM" designates bayonet mount).

Icarex SL-706:   **R3* E**
c1972-1973. Front of body marked "SL-706" at 11 o'clock from lens mount. Open aperture metering with Zeiss lenses. With Ultron 50m f1.8 lens:

Icarex Lenses
All accept 50mm bayonet or 56mm threaded filters and sunshades.

Skoparex 35mm, f3.4 lens	**C**
Colour Pantar 50mm, f2.8 lens	**C**
Tessar 50mm, f2.8 lens	**C+**
Dynarex 90mm, f3.4 lens	**E–**
Super Dynarex 135mm, f4 lens	**E–**
Super Dynarex 200mm, f4 lens	**E+**
Telomar 400mm, f5 lens, rare	**F–**
Zooman 36-82mm, f2.8 lens	**F–**
Ultron 50mm, f1.8 lens	**D–**
Distagon 25mm, f2.8 lens, rare	**E+**
Skoparex 35mm, f3.4 lens	**D+**
Tessar 50mm, f2.8 lens	**C**
Ultron 50mm, f1.8 lens	**D**
Super Dynarex 135mm, f4 lens	**D+**

Ideal: **6.5 x 9cm; 9 x 12cm B+**
     10 x 15cm C+
     13 x 18cm D
c1927-1938. Folding plate camera. Dominar, Tessar or Double Protar lenses. Usually marked with name "Ideal" and model number on leather under the

handle. Double ext bellows. Removable "pop-off" holders.

Ikoflex (Original):   **R3* E–**

c1935-1960. Novar 80mm, f6.3 or Novar f4.5 lens in Derval, Klio or Compur-Rapid shutter. Marked "Ikoflex" on shutter above lens. Called the "coffee can" model by collectors. All black enamel finish on body. Has 2 film counters; one for 120 film, and one for 620 film. Lever focus beside lens.

Ikoflex I: **R3* C+**

c1936-1950. Tessar 70mm, f3.5 or Novar 75mm, f3.5 lens in Compur shutter to 1/300s. until 1939. Klio shutter to 1/250s. after 1939. Chrome plate inscribed with "Ikoflex" at top front of camera. Models from first production year had lever focus on right side; later models had a knob.

Ikoflex I(a):   **R2* C+**

c1952-1956. Novar 75mm, f3.5 or Tessar 75mm, f3.5 lens in Prontor SV shutter to 1/300s. No folding shutter release. Marked "Ikoflex" in chrome on black background on front of Vfr.

Ikoflex I(b):   **R2* C+**

c1956-1958. Similar to I(a). But improved model. Tessar or Novar 75mm, f3.5 lens. Only Novar was available in 1957-1958. Prontor SVS shutter with folding shutter release. Focusing hood opens and closes with simple action. Magnifiers over diaphragm and shutter speed dials. No exp meter. Price for Novar lens. Tessar lens 20% more.

Ikoflex I(c):   R2* D–

c1956-1958. Similar to I(b). Except has built-in exp meter needle visible on ground glass inside hood.

Ikoflex II: R2* D–
c1937-1939. Tessar 75mm, f3.5 lens in Compur Rapid shutter to 1/300s. Auto film counter; double exp prevention. Viewing lens in extended chrome tube (as compared to other models). Marked "Ikoflex" on chrome plate on front. 1937 models had focus lever, 1938 and later had focusing knob.

Ikoflex II(a):   R2* D
c1950-1952. Similar to II. Except has flash synch. Magnifiers on peep windows over shutter speed and aperture setting dials (these are set by levers below the shutter housing).

Ikoflex II(a):   R3* D
c1953-1956. Similar to previous model, except the viewing lens bezel is black. The peep windows are directly over the lens. Shutter and aperture settings are adjusted with wheels. Does not have LVS settings as does the Favorit.

Ikoflex III: R3* E+

c1939-1940. Tessar 80mm, f2.8 lens. Only Ikoflex with huge Albada finder on front of viewing hood (similar to Albada finder on Contaflex TLR). Crank-type film advance coupled to shutter cocking mechanism.

Ikoflex Favorit: R3* E+
c1956-1960. Last model of the Ikoflex line. Tessar 75mm, f3.5 lens in Synchro-Compur shutter. Built-in LVS cross-coupled exp meter. Shutter and aperture adjustment set by wheels.

Ikoflex Favorit, c1956-1960.

Ikomatic "A":   **R2* B+**
c1964-1965. Inexpensive instamatic camera for 126 cartridge film. Colour Citar 45mm, f6.3 lens in two speed shutter 1/90s. for daylight 1/30s. for flash. Built-in photo-electric exp control. Hot shoe. Marked "Ikomatic A" on lower right front of camera.

Ikomatic "F":   **R2* B+**
c1964-1965. Similar to above except Frontar fixed focus lens. No exp control. Built-in pop-up reflector for AG-1 flash bulb (top right of camera). Marked "Ikomatic F" on lower right front of camera.

Ikonette: **R3* C–**
c1929-1931. Small 127 roll film camera. Frontar 80mm, f9 lens in self-cocking shutter. Removable back for film loading. There were at least two variations of the body latch mechanism.

Ikonette 35:   **R2* C–**

c1958-1960. 35mm camera of gray plastic. Novar 45mm, f3.5 lens in Pronto shutter, X synch. Unusual combination film advance lever and shutter release. Close fitting blue plastic case. Red signal appears in Vfr. when film advance lever is not cocked.

Ikonta Series
c1929-1956. Early model was called "Ikomat". All had lenses with front cell focus.

Ikonta: **R2* C–**

c1931. 5 x 7.5cm folding roll film camera. Novar 80mm, f6.3 lens and Derval shutter. 40% less. Price with Tessar 80mm, f4.5 lens and Compur shutter.

Ikonta A: **R2* C+**

c1933-1940. Half 120 film size. Compur shutter. Novar 80mm, f4.5 lens. 40% less than price with Tessar 80mm, f3.5 lens.

Ikonta A: **R2* C+**

Postwar version. Tessar 75mm, f3.5 lens and Synchro-Compur shutter. Novar 75mm, f4.5 or f3.5 and Prontar shutter. 40% less.

Ikonta C: **R2* C**

6 x 9cm folding roll film camera. c1930-1940. Tessar 105mm, f4.5 lens £25. Novar 105mm, f8.3 lens £20. c1936-1937 Tessar 105mm F3.8 lens £30. After 1937 Tessar 105mm, f3.5 lens.

Ikonta II: **R2* D+**

c1950-1956. 6 x 9cm folding roll film camera. Heavy chrome trim on top cover. Novar 105mm, f3.5 or f4.5, or Tessar 105mm, f3.5 lens.

Ikonta D: **R2* C–**

c1931-1939. Early version used 126 film; later version used 616 film. Most Ikomats are of this size. Novar 120mm, f6.3 lens and Derval shutter. Tessar 120mm, f4.5 lens and Compur shutter.

Ikonta B: **R2* C+**

c1937-1939. 12 exp. 6 x 6cm on 120 film. Novar 75mm, f3.5 or f4.5 in Compur or Klio shutter. Tessar 75mm, f3.5 lens and Compur-Rapid shutter.

Ikonta B: **R2* C**

c1948-1953. Similar to above, except had more chrome trim and chrome lens mount. with Tessar lens.

Ikonta B: **R2* C+**

c1954-1956. Similar to above, except had chrome top plate. Prontor SV or Synchro-Compur shutter.

Ikonta B: **R2* D+**

c1954-1956. 6 x 6cm roll film camera. With built-in uncoupled RFR. Novar 105mm, f3.5 or f4.5 lens and Prontor SV shutter. Tessar 105mm, f3.5 lens and Synchro-Compur shutter.

Ikonta 35:   R2* C+

c1949-1953. 35mm folding camera. Novar 45mm, f3.5 or Tessar 45mm, f2.8 lens. The Xenar 45mm, f2.8 lens was supplied during the first two years. Rigid front lens bed – centre of camera. Marked "Ikonta" on leather on rear of camera.

Juwel: R4* F

c1927-1938. 9 x 12cm leather covered metal case, plate camera. Revolving back; rising, falling, shifting and tilting front. Removable backs. Triple ext bellows. Double rack and pinion knobs on folding bed, one moves back and front, other moves lens stand. Bayonet mount interchangeable lenses. Marked "Juwel" or "Universal Juwel" on or under handle. Price depends on condition and lens.

Juwel: R3* F

c1927-1938. 13 x 18cm plate camera. Lens interchanges with aluminium board. Otherwise similar to above. Tessar or Triple convertible Protar. This was the most expensive camera mfg by Zeiss throughout the pre-war years. Camera used extensively by Ansel Adams. Rare and still usable. With Tessar 210mm f4.5 lens or Protar lens.

Kolibri: R3* to F+

Novar 50mm, f3.5 or f4.5 lens and Telma shutter   **R? E**

Tessar 50mm, f3.5 lens and rimset Compur shutter   **E+**

Tessar 50mm, f2.8 lens and Rimset Compur shutter   **F+**

Microscope version no lens or shutter, rare   **F**

Biotar 45mm, f2 lens and Rim-set Compur shutter   **F+**

Kolibri, Dial-Set Compur.

c1930-1935. Compact 127 roll film camera. Lens extends for picture taking on brightly polished chrome tube. Unique shaped brown or black case. "Kolibri" in leather below lens. Hinge on right side of open case has screw in "foot" to be inserted in lens mount for horizontal still pictures. 16 exp, 4 x 6.5cm on 12 roll film.

Kolibri f/3.5 Tessar, Rim-set Compur.

Kosmopolit: **R4* E**
c1927-1934. 5 x 7. 7 x 9.5. Field camera. Tapered bellows; reversing back, rising and sliding front, (no swing). Wood finish with brass fittings.

Lilliput: **R2* D+**
c1927-1928. 4.5 x 6cm. 6.5 x 9cm. Tiny strut-type folding plate camera. f12.5 lens. Celluloid "ground glass". Struts inside bellows.

Lloyd: **R2* B+**
c1928-1931. Black leather covered folding roll film camera. Tessar 120mm, f4.5 lens in Compur shutter. Ability to use cut film with ground glass focusing by sliding out back cover plate. Marked "Lloyd" in leather on front of camera.

Maximar A: **R2* C+**
c1927-1939. 6.5 x 9cm. Folding plate camera. Tessar 105mm, f4.5 lens in Compur shutter. Slide in holders. Marked "Maximar" in leather on rear of camera.

Maximar B: **R2* C+**
c1927-1939. 9 x 12cm. Folding plate camera. Similar to above. Tessar 135mm, f4.5 lens in Compur shutter.

Maximar: **R* D**
c1927-1937. 10 x 15cm. Folding plate camera. Similar to above. Tessar 165mm, f4.5 lens in Compur shutter. Rare.

Miroflex A: **R4* F–**
c1927-1936. 6.5 x 9cm. Folding SLR plate camera. FPS $^1/_3$-1/200s. Reflex viewing and sportsfinder. Marked

"Miroflex" in leather on front of camera. Tessar 120mm, f4.5 lens. With Tessar 135mm, f3.5 or Bio Tessar 135mm, f2.8 lens.

Miroflex B: **R4* E+**
c1934-1938. Takes 9 x 12cm film or plates. Similar to above. Tessar 165mm, f4.5 lens. £175. Tessar 165mm, f3.5 or Bio Tessar 165mm, f2.8 lens, more common.

Nettar: **R2* B+**
c1934-1941. 4.5 x 6cm, 6 x 9cm. The Bob camera. Was known as Nettar 510 in England. Inexpensive folding roll film camera with Nettar or Novar lens. "Nettar" impressed on leather. Postwar version. c1949-1957. Fancier style with body release and chrome top. Sixteen possible lens/shutter combinations. Novar models. Tessar models.

Nettar II: **R2* A**
c1950. Self erecting folding VFR camera for 12 exp on 120. 3in f4.5 Novar, Pronto shutter 1/25-1/200s + B.

Nettax: R4* Code

Tessar 50mm, f2.8 lens, rare   **F+**

Tessar 50mm, f3.5 lens, rare   **G–**

Extra for telephoto (rare),

Triotar 105mm, f5.6 lens   **F–**

Stereo Nettel, Tropical Model: **R3* F**

c1927. Makes 6 x 13cm images on glass dry plates. Focal plane shutter and matched Tessar lenses f4.5. The tropical model made from teakwood is at least twice the value of the regular leather covered instrument.

c1936-1938. 35mm camera looks somewhat like Contax II, except has rotating RFR window attached to interchangeable lens. FPS to 1/1000s.

Nettax: **R4* C+**

c1955-1957. 6 x 6cm. Folding roll film camera. Novar 75mm, f4.5 lens. Pronto shutter. Built-in uncoupled exp meter. Chrome top cover. Rare.

Nettel: **R2* C+**

c1929-1937. 4.5 x 6cm, 6.5 x 9cm, 9 x 12cm. Most common. 10 x 15cm, 5" x 7". "Nettel" marked on right side of camera below FPS winding and setting knob. Black leather covered. 12 lens/shutter/format combinations.

Nettel, Tropen: **R3* F**

c1930-37. Tropical model. Made in four larger sizes shown above. Focal plane press camera. Polished teak. brown leather bellows.

Nixe: **R2* B+**

c1927-1934. Folding camera. Dominar, Tessar or Double Protar lens. Double ext bellows. 8 x 10.5cm. Roll film or 9 x 12cm cut film. Marked "Nixe" on handle or impressed in leather of body.

Nixe: **R2* C–**

Similar to above, except 8 x 14cm roll film or 9 x 14cm cut film.

Onito: **R2* B+**

c1927-1929. 6.5 x 9cm, 9 x 12cm. Inexpensive folding plate camera. Novar f6.3 lens. Single ext bellows. Lever focus.

Orix: **R2* C**

c1928-1934. 10 x 15cm. Folding plate camera. Tessar 150mm, f4.5 lens. Double ext bellows. Rack and pinion focusing. Was used as press camera. Special model with spring back was available.

Palmos-O: R3* F–

c1927-1928. 4.5 x 6cm. Plate camera. Tessar 80mm, f2.7 (high-speed) lens. FPS 1/50-1/1000s. Struts. Folding door. Sold in Europe (1927) as Minimum Palmos.

Piccolette: R3* C+

c1927-1930. Inexpensive all metal strut-type camera; Achromat 75mm, f11, Novar 75mm, f6.3 or Tessar 75mm, f4.5 lens. Marked "Piccolette" below lens; "Zeiss Ikon" at 11 o'clock from lens; 3 x 4cm exp on 127 roll film. In Germany; available until 1932 in U.S.

Piccolette-Luxus: R3* E+

c1927-1930. 4 x 6.5cm. Top-of-the-line model, with folding bed. Dominar 50mm, f4.5 or Tessar 75mm, f4.5 lens. Dial-set Compur shutter. Lazy tong struts. Brown leather covering. Brown bellows.

Plaskop: R3* D+

c1927-1930. Inexpensive Stereo box camera. Marked "Plaskop" on front under left lens. 4.5 x 10.5cm exp.

Plaskop: R3* D+

c1927-1930. Stereo box camera. Novar 60mm, f6.8 lenses. Marked "Plaskop" on oval label – left front. 4.5 x 10.5cm exposures.

Plaskop: R3* E

c1927-1930. Stereo box camera. Similar to above, except has brilliant finder – top centre. 6 x 13cm. exp.

Polyskop: R3* E

c1927-1930. Precision Stereo box camera. Tessar 65mm, f4.5 lenses. Compur Dial-set stereo shutter. Brilliant finder – top centre. Covered with black leather. 12 exp, 4.5 x 10.5cm. on plates in septum magazine.

Polyskop: R3* E

c1927-1930. Similar to above except it has Tessar 75mm, f4.5 lenses. 6 x 13cm. exp on plates.

Simplex: R2* B+

c1928-1930. Inexpensive folding plate camera. For 9 x 12cm plates. Frontar 140mm, f9 lens or Novar 135mm, f6.3 lens. Marked "Simplex" on leather under handle. "Zeiss Ikon" under lens on front of lens standard.

Simplex: R3* C–

Brown plastic bodied 6 x 9cm. roll film camera. Nettar 105mm, f6.5 lens. Telma or Derval shutter. Marked "Simplex". The hardware and struts vary on this model.

Simplex-Ernoflex:

      4.5 x 6cm, R3* NSR G+
      6.5 x 9cm and 9 x 12cm F–

c1929-30. 4.5 x 6cm, 6.5 x 9cm, 9 x

12cm. SLR focal plane camera. Ernoplast f4.5 or f3.5. Ernon f3.5 or Tessar f4.5 lens. CFPS 1/20-1/1000s. The early model was marked "Ernemann" On right side and back. "Zeiss Ikon" on round metal plate. In 1930 it was marked "Simplex Ernoflex" over lens. "Zeiss Ikon." On right side and door of focusing hood.

Sirene: R2* B+
c1927. Inexpensive folding plate camera (9 x 12cm or 6.5 x 9cm). Marked "Sirene" under handle. The same model number used later on Volta cameras.

Sirene: R4* C
c1930-1931. Similar to above, 3¼" x 4¼" size for American market. Dominar 135mm, f4.5 lens. Compur shutter. Rare.

Sonnet: R3* G
c1927-1930. 4.5 x 6cm. Tropical folding plate camera. Novar 80mm or 75mm, f6.3. Dominar or Tessar 75mm, f4.5 lens. Teak wood construction. Brown leather door covering and brown bellows.

Sonnet: R4* F+
c1927-1930. Tropical 6.5 x 9cm folding plate camera. Similar to above, except 6.5 x 9cm size. Novar 105mm, f6.3 or Dominar or Tessar 120mm f4.5 lens.

Stereolette-Cupido: R3* E
c1927-1928. 4.5 x 10.7cm. Folding Stereo plate camera. Black leather covered. Marked "Stereolette-Cupido" on handle. "Stereolette" on outside of door.

Stereoco: R3* E
c1927-1930. 4.5 x 10.7cm. Leather covered Stereo box plate camera. Tapered shape. Tessar 55mm, f6.3 lenses. Derval or Dial-set Compur shutters. Marked "Stereoco" on upper front between lenses. "Zeiss Ikon" below lenses.

Stereo-Ernoflex: R4* H–
c1927-1929. Folding stereo camera. Ernotar 75mm, f4.5. Ernon 75mm, f3.5 or Tessar 75mm, f3.5 lenses. CFPS 1/20-1/1000s. Full length viewing hood cover.

Stereo-Simplex-Ernoflex: R3* F+
c1927-1930. Non-folding Stereo box camera. Ernon 75mm, f3.5 or Tessar 75mm or 80mm, f4.5 lenses. CFPS. Marked "Ernemann" on front between lenses. Viewing hood cover is on half of camera top. Pop-up frame finder on other half.

Stereo Ideal: R4* E
c1927-1928. 6 x 13cm. Folding stereo camera. Tessar 90mm, f4.5 lenses. Dial-set Compur shutter on 1927 version. Compound shutter on 1928 versions. Marked"Stereo-Ideal-651" on handle. "Zeiss Ikon" inside door. Covered with black leather.

Stereo Nettel: Black leather E+
Tropical model. Teak wood.
Brown bellows   R4* G–
c1927-1930. 6 x 13cm. Scissors strut Stereo camera. Tessar 90mm, f4 lenses. FPS. Wire finder. Focusing knob on right side (over shutter winding knob). Internal roller blind separates two images (removable for full frame use).

Stereo Nettel: **Black leather E+**
Tropical model. Teak wood.
Brown bellows **R4* G–**
c1927-1930. Similar to above, except
10 x 15cm model. Tessar 120mm, f4.5
lenses.

Super Ikonta Series

Folding roll film camera: lenses had
front cell focusing, coupled to a
coincidence type built-in RFR. Postwar
models had factory installed flash synch.

Super Ikonta "A": **R2* E**
(Z530). 1934-1937.

Super Ikonta "B": **R2* E+**
1937-1951.

Super Ikonta "B": **R2* F–**
1951-1956.

Super Ikonta "BX": **R2* E+**
1937-1952.

Super Ikonta "A": **R2* E+**
1937-1950.

Super Ikonta "A": **R2* E+**
Synchro Compur **G**
1950-1956.

Super Ikonta "B": **R2* E+**
1935-1937.

Super Ikonta "BX":   R2* F–
1952-1957.

Super Ikonta III: R2* F–
1954-1958.

Super Ikonta IV: R2* F
1956-1960.

Super Ikonta "C":   R2* E
1934-1936.

Super Ikonta "C":   R2* E+
1936-1950.

Super Ikonta "C":   R2* F–
1950-1955.

Super Ikonta "D":   R3* E
1934-1936.

Super Ikonta "D":   R4* E+
1936-1939.

Super Nettel: R3* F+

c1934-1937. 35mm folding bellows camera. Tessar 50mm, f3.5 or f2.8 lens. 1935 – Triotar 50mm, f3.5 lens offered. The Tessar lens was discontinued in 1936. FPS $^1/_5$-1/1000s. Black enamel finish with leather covering. Marked "Super Nettel" in leather on door.

Super Nettel II: R4* G
c1936-1938. Similar to above, except had polished chrome door. Top cover was finished with matte chrome. Tessar 50mm, f2.8 lens.

Symbolica: R2* B
c1959-1962. 35mm camera. Tessar 50mm, f2.8 lens. Coupled match-needle exp meter. No RFR; Lens had front cell focus. Marked "Symbolica" on top.

Taxo: **R2* B**
c1927-1931. 6.5 x 9cm, 9 x 12cm. Inexpensive folding plate camera. Periskop 105mm, f11. Novar 105mm or 135mm, f6.3 lens (Frontar or Dominar lens later). Derval shutter. Single ext bellows. Marked "Taxo" on body under handle. Lens had slide on track for focusing.

Taxo: **R2* B**
6.5 x 9cm, 9 x 12cm. Similar to above, except had radial focusing lever. c1927-1930.

Taxona: **R2* C**
Post WWII 35mm camera. 24 x 24mm. Made from captured Tenax I parts. Tessar 37.5mm, f3.5 lens. Marked "TAXONA" around lens. See Tenax below. 24 x 24mm exp on 35mm film.

Tenax: **R3* D**
c1927. Popular strut folding plate camera. 16 different lenses offered. Compound shutter. 4.5 x 6cm, 6.5 x 9cm, 4.5 x 10.7cm. (stereo). Clean-up items which were never actually mfd by or marked "Zeiss Ikon". Marked "TENAX" or "Taschen Tenax" on front or top.

Tenax I: **R2* D**

c1930-1941. Novar 35mm, f3.5 lens. Compur shutter. Lever on right side advanced film and cocked shutter. No RFR. 35mm film. 50 exp. 24 x 24mm on 36 exp roll. Marked "TENAX" under lens.

Tenax I: **R2* D+**
c1948. Similar to above, except Tessar 37.5mm, f3.5 coated lens. Flash synch contact on top of shutter. Marked "Zeiss Ikon"above lens. "TENAX" below lens. Possibly East German.

Tenax II: **R4***
    Tessar 40mm f2.4 lens F–
    Sonnar 40mm f2 lens F–

c1938-1941. 24 x 24mm format. Interchangeable lenses. Coupled rangefinder. Shoe for Vfr. and Contameter. A rare microscope (or X-ray) version exists with dark slide and without lens.

Accessory lenses for Tenax II	
Sonnar 75mm, f4 (telephoto) with vf	**F**
Orthometer 27mm, f4.5 W/A with vf	**F**

Tenax Automatic: **R2* B–**
c1960-1963. Full frame 35mm camera. Tessar 50mm, f2.8 lens. Prontormat shutter. No RFR. Front cell focus. Auto Exp control with selenium photo-electric cell. Marked "Tenax" at 11 o'clock from lens on Exp meter window.

Tengoflex: **R4* F–**

c1941-1942. Box camera. 6 X 6cm. exp on 120 roll film. Large brilliant finder on top gives appearance of TLR. Marked "Tengoflex" on front. Rare.

Tessco: **R4* C**

c1927-1928. 9 x 12cm. Folding plate camera. 5 different lenses range from, Periskop f11 to Tessar f4.5. Double ext bellows. Marked "Tessco" on leather handle.

Trona: **R2* C–**

c1929-1938. 6.5 x 9cm, 9 x 12cm. Tessar f3.5 lens. Compur shutter (Rimset after 1930). The original ground glass back was of aluminium and it is rare today. The camera is usually found with standard back. "TRONA" and model number marked under handle.

Tropen Adoro: **R4* F+**

c1927-1936. Tropical folding plate camera. Tessar 105mm or 120mm, 135mm or 150mm. 9 x 12cm. Tessar 165mm or 180mm, f4.5 lens 10 x 15cm. Compur shutter in all models. Double ext bellows. Brown leather covering on door and back. Brown bellows. "TROPEN ADORO" and model number marked on leather of door.

Trona Cameras.

Tropica: R5* G+
                              5" x 7" H–

c1927-1931 (1935 in foreign catalogues). 9 x 12cm, 10 x 15cm, 5" x 7". Folding plate camera. Polished teak wood construction (even the door to the ground glass back is of teak wood) with hardware of German silver. Rotating back. Marked "Zeiss Ikon" between knobs on front standard. 14 different lenses, all in Compur shutters. All sizes are rare today, especially the 5" x 7" size. NSR. Estimate.

Unette: R5* est E

c1927-1930. Leatherette covered wooden box camera. 40mm, f12.5 lens. Metal frame finder on top (rear). 22 x 31mm exp on roll film. Marked "UNETTE" on front over lens in the leatherette. "Zeiss Ikon" over lens. "Ernemann" on right side. Rare, only one sale known.

Victrix: R4* D–

c1927-1931. Small folding plate camera. Novar 75mm, f6.3. Dominar 75mm, f4.5 and Tessar lens. Compur shutter. 4.5 x 6cm exp. Marked "Victrix 101" in leather on top of camera. "Zeiss Ikon" marked on lens, between knobs and on door. Rare.

Volta: R4* B+

c1927-1931. Inexpensive folding plate camera. Novar, Dominar or Tessar lenses. Compur or Klio shutters. Single ext bellows. Radial arm focusing.

Volta: R4* B+

Similar to above but without radial arm focusing. c1926-1927.

Zorki

see Kraznogorsk Mechanical Works

Zuiho Precision Optical Co
Japan

Honor SL: R4* G

c1959. 35mm RFR camera. CFPS. 1-1/1000s. Combined RFR/VFR window. Lever advance and folding crank rewind. Honor 50mm f1.9 lens. This camera has a redesigned top plate and has lost some of its "Leica copy" looks. Now, more like a Canon VT or Tanack V3. Quite rare.

Honor: R4* F+

c1956. 35mm RFR camera. CFPS. 1-1/500s; separate RFR/VFR windows. Honor or Hexanon 50mm, f1.9 or Hexar 50mm, f3.5 lens. Quite "Leica" like!

Unknown

Inevitably with the passage of time, manufacturers' information may be lost or destroyed. We have included these cameras in this section. If any of our readers can supply us with more data, it will be incorporated in subsequent editions.

Probably Czechoslovakia

Nova: R3 C

c1938-39. Unusual simple camera. Two boxes extend the lens from a cast metal body. Shutter operated between 1/25-1/100s. Paper-backed rollfilm made images 30 x 40cm. These unusual cameras are difficult to locate in really good condition.

Made in France

Wet Plate Stereo Camera: R3* D
c1865. This is typical of a camera type much in use during the wet-plate era. Focus by sliding a box-in-box. This particular camera is fitted with American made lenses by Harrison & Harrison but many other makes both European and American were used.

Le Reve: R3* D
c1908. 3¼" x 4¼" camera; Anastigmatic Roussel 135mm f6.3 or Beck 135mm f6.3 lens; Unicum or pneumatic shutter. 3¼" x 4¼" plates or roll film with special roll film back. Mfd in Paris, France.

Photo Omnia: R3* D
c1925; 45 x 107mm stereo camera. Anastigmat 60mm f/6 lenses. Variable speed shutter.

Europe & USA

Wet Plate Camera Outfit: R5* G+
c1865. Wet Plate Camera Outfits were made by a number of makers in Europe and the United States. They came in a variety of sizes from what we now call "medium format" to very large indeed, up to 16" x 20" and larger. A complete outfit would have consisted of a camera, tripod, plate holders, sensitizing and developing tanks, and the paraphernalia used to manipulate the glass plates. If you are uncertain whether a camera was designed for wet plate or early dry-plate photography, check the holders and camera body. Wet plate cameras invariably have black stains from the silver halide salts.

Wonder Trick Camera: R3* B+

c1970. toy "camera" with squeaking mouse. Toy mouse squeaks and jumps out of the camera when shutter is tripped. Mfd in Japan.

Hong Kong

Micro 110 Key Chain Camera: **R1* D**

c1988. The camera itself consists of a very simple shutter and lens, a 110 film cassette actually makes the back of the camera. When not in use, a coin holder takes the place of a film cartridge.

Donkey Book Camera: **R3* D**

c1980. 110 camera in the form of a small book. Back of book rotates revealing meniscus lens. Shutter works at about 1/75s.

Japan

Baby Flex: **R4* G**
c1950. Sanko 20mm f3.5 lens; Peace Model 2 shutter 1/50-1/250; 10 exp, 13 x 14mm on special roll film. The Japanese maker of this simple camera is unknown. It is considered very rare in Japan.

Japanese Photographic Rifle: **R4* H–**
c1930, anti-aircraft training rifle; copy of Thornton Pickard rifle. Mfd in Japan.

England

Wembley Sports: **R2* E–**

c1950. Ugly Bakelite camera made in England for 8 exp. on 120. Lens extends on large diameter helical screw and click-stops at five positions for focusing. 8.5cm f11 London Sportar lens. Shutter 1/25-1/100s.

Manufacturer Index
&
Camera Index

Manufacturers Index

A

B

C

D

Index

Camera Index

A

Index

Index

CAMERA DIRECTORY

Index

M

Index

C A M E R A   D I R E C T O R Y

Index

X

Y

Z

A SELECTION OF OUR

COLLECTOR BOOKS...

...MORE OF OUR

COLLECTOR BOOKS

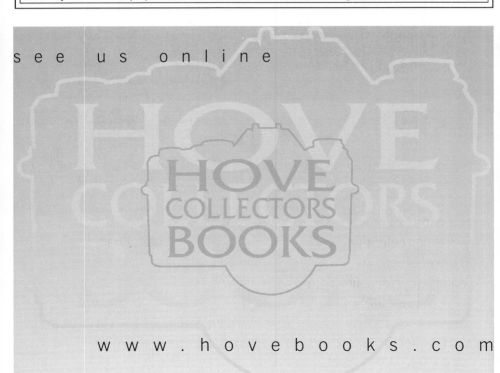